The UNITED STATES Department of Homeland Security

AN OVERVIEW

Second Edition

by CW Productions Ltd.
Edited by:
Richard White, Tina Markowski, and Kevin Collins

Learning Solutions

New York Boston San Francisco
London Toronto Sydney Tokyo Singapore Madrid
Mexico City Munich Paris Cape Town Hong Kong Montreal

Cover photograph courtesy of Terry Prekas Photography/Alamy.

Pearson Learning Solutions, 501 Boylston Street, Suite 900, Boston, MA 02116
A Pearson Education Company
www.pearsoned.com

Printed in the United States of America

72 2022

000200010270579553

RG/CM

ISBN 10: 0558-83488-4
ISBN 13: 978-0-558-83488-3

Preface

On November 25th, 2002, President George W. Bush signed into law the Homeland Security Act undertaking the largest government re-organization since the creation of the Department of Defense (DoD) in 1947. The first edition of this book was devoted to answering two pressing questions: "what is homeland security?" and "how is it different from national defense?" In the five years since this book was first published, the Department of Homeland Security (DHS) has undergone many changes, but one thing has become clear: homeland security is a unique mission, separate but related to national defense, to secure the safety of American citizens from the effects of disaster, whether natural or manmade. As the first edition went to press, Hurricane Katrina had just driven through the Gulf, wreaking unprecedented damage on Alabama, Mississippi, and Louisiana. The resulting affects on DHS and the country consequently occupy a great percentage of this second edition. Also, because we now have the perspective of time, this book now includes assessments of DHS' performance. Throughout, we have remained faithful to our original approach by drawing on the collective works of authoritative sources, and using judicial edits to create a concise, meaningful, and informative compendium addressing the fundamental issue: "What is the Department of Homeland Security and how does it protect America?"

About the Authors

Richard White

(BS History, MS Computer Science, PhD Candidate – Homeland Security). Rick is a Homeland Security/Defense Training & Exercise Planner at United States Northern Command where he facilitates tabletop exercises enhancing military readiness for defense support of civil authorities. As Associate Director to the UCCS Center for Homeland Security, Rick led curriculum development and technology application research for both national and international audiences. He taught national security policy and military strategy at the United States Air Force Academy and continues to teach HS/HD policy and strategy for various colleges and universities. A retired Air Force officer, Rick designed and taught "DOD-101" to government agencies including the National Geospatial-intelligence Agency, Defense Intelligence Agency, and National Security Agency. Other textbooks include *Homeland Defense: An Overview* (Pearson 2007), *Introduction to Joint and Coalition Warfare* (FastPlanet 2005), and *United States Military Power* (FastPlanet 2004).

Tina Markowski

(BA Psychology, Master of Public Administration). Tina is the Operations and Academic Programs Manager at the University of Colorado at Colorado Springs Center for Homeland Security. A former firefighter and emergency medical technician, Tina currently manages graduate programs in homeland security and homeland defense, and supports planning and execution of regional emergency response exercises. Tina also teaches courses in emergency and fire management services, public safety administration, and homeland security. While serving as the Associate Director for the CU-Trauma, Health and Hazards Center, she developed a peer support program to build resilience and assist recovery from high-risk occupational traumatic experiences that was implemented both in the UCCS Police and Colorado Springs Fire Departments.

Kevin Collins

(BS Management Studies, Master of Business Administration). Kevin manages operation and maintenance of unmanned aerial vehicle data networks supporting military operations in Afghanistan and Iraq. Since retiring from the Air Force, Kevin has been an industry leader developing national security programs and providing information assurance to the Department of Defense. His companies have provided strategic policy planning, risk and vulnerability assessment, disaster recovery planning, computer security incident response handling, intrusion detection, and security engineering for both government and commercial clients. Kevin teaches homeland security courses for various college and university programs.

Contents

Contents

Part I: Mission Requirement

Chapter 1

9-11 Survivors

Objectives

- Describe the ordeal of victims caught in the Twin Towers on September 11th.
- Identify successful survival tactics.
- Propose improved methods for surviving a similar disaster.
- Consider your chances of surviving such a catastrophe.

Introduction

The World Trade Center in New York City was a complex of seven buildings built around a central plaza, near the south end of Manhattan in the downtown financial district. The World Trade Center was best known for its iconic 110-story Twin Towers. When the towers were completed in 1972 and 1973, respectively, they were the tallest buildings on Earth. Their stature and symbolism made them the target of a failed terrorist attack in February 1993. On the morning of Tuesday, September 11, 2001, the World Trade Center was again targeted by terrorists.

North Tower, World Trade Center

Greg Trevor worked in the Public Affairs department for the New York Port Authority. His offices were on the 68th floor of the World Trade Center. He had just finished a phone call to a colleague and stood to stretch his legs. Greg was looking out the window at the Statue of Liberty when he was nearly knocked to the floor by the force of a sudden impact. American Airlines Flight 11 had just slammed into the north side of the North Tower of the World Trade Center between the 94th and 98th floors.[1] *"I heard a loud thud, followed by an explosion. The building felt like it swayed ten feet to the south. It shuddered back to the north, and shimmied back and forth. Out the window I saw a parabola of flame fall toward the street, followed by a blizzard of paper and glass. Then I heard two sounds: emergency sirens on the street, and phones ringing across the 68th floor—calls from reporters wondering what had happened."*[2]

Adam Mayblum's offices were on the 87th floor of the World Trade Center. Adam had arrived shortly before 8:00 a.m., and was just getting set for the day when Flight 11 crashed into the building. *"The building lurched violently and shook as if it were an earthquake. People screamed. I watched out my window as the building seemed to move 10 to 20 feet in each direction."* Adam grabbed a co-worker and ran for cover. *"Light fixtures and parts of the ceiling collapsed. The kitchen was destroyed. We were certain it was a bomb. We looked out the windows. Reams of paper were flying everywhere, like a ticker tape parade. I looked down at the street. I could see people in Battery Park City looking up. Smoke started billowing in through the holes in the ceiling."*[3]

Carmen and Arturo Griffith were elevator operators in the North Tower of the World Trade Center. Arturo was running 50A, a big freight elevator, and was going from the second-level basement to the 49th floor when American Airlines Flight 11 struck at 8:46 a.m... Arturo heard a sudden whistling sound and the impact. Cables were severed and Arturo's car plunged into free fall. *"The only thing I remember was saying 'Oh God, Oh, God, I'm going to die'."* The emergency brakes caught after 15 or 16 floors, but the elevator door imploded, crushing Arturo's right knee and breaking his tibia. All that morning, Carmen had been carrying hundreds of passengers from the 78th–floor sky lobby to the bond-trading offices of Cantor Fitzgerald on the 101st and 105th floors and the Windows on the World restaurant above that. A full elevator had just left the 78th floor, and Carmen was about to carry up six or seven stragglers. The plane struck as the doors of her elevator closed. They could hear debris smash into the top of the car; then the elevator cracked open, and flames poured in. Carmen jammed her fingers between the closed doors, pulled them partly open and held them as passengers clambered over and under her 5-foot-6 frame to escape.[4]

South Tower, World Trade Center

Cara LaTorre worked in the South Tower of the World Trade Center. She had just arrived at her 100th floor office and was walking over to wish her friends good morning. *"Oh my god, the building shakes, the lights flicker, and then I hear an explosion. I look out the window behind my best friend and I see fire, paper and bodies flying out the window. My best friend yells out, 'Cara, Paulie works there! Paulie works there!"*[5]

Jaede Barg worked in the same office with Cara LaTorre. He was preparing for a visit from a potential business partner when he heard a co-worker scream. *"As we quickly looked toward the windows, we all saw what was clearly a fireball hitting the [North Tower] head-on, the force and heat clearly felt upon my face. The force was so powerful that the wind from the strike picked up papers from the cubicle desks in between my office and the outer offices, and I felt the heat, along with an undeniable smell of fuel. The force of the fireball slamming into our tower made the building shake violently at first, and then sway. Amazingly, the windows did not break, as I ran to them in disbelief that they were still intact, and also to ascertain if the explosion was within our building or elsewhere."*[6]

Phyllis Borgo was checking meeting arrangements at the Millennium Hilton across the street from the World Trade Center. She was on her way back to her 102nd floor office in the South Tower, stepping from the hotel elevator when she noticed large pieces of debris flying in the air outside, and a gray cloud. Several people were standing at the lobby windows on their cell phones. When she asked what happened, they told her there was a "blast" at the World Trade Center across the street. *"I ran to the window, looked up and saw the most horrifying scene of my life. The North Tower was in ablaze from about floor 90! I immediately got on the phone to call home and let [my husband] know I was not in the building and was currently okay."*[7]

Ladder Company 6

Billy Butler and Sal D'Agostino were members of the Fire Department of New York Ladder Company 6. *"I was still asleep at 8:48 when the first plane hit,"* said D'Agostino. *"I had been up late working the night before and was getting every moment of sleep I could before the roll call at 9. When I heard that a plane had hit the North Tower, I thought it was a joke,"* he continued, explaining that false alarms are sometimes sounded to wake up the rookies in the department and get them to suit up. *"I also thought it was a bad joke until I saw our captain [John Jonas] suiting up, and he never was in on the rookie jokes,"* said Butler. *"Once we got outside we knew that this was really bad."*[8]

* * *

Back in the North Tower, Greg Trevor ran to alert his director who was already on the phone to the Port Authority's Chief Operating Officer, Ernesto Butcher. Greg picked up another line and contacted the Port Authority Police Department in Jersey City. He and his boss then forwarded the phones and prepared to evacuate when a staff member said two media calls were holding. Gregg picked up and answered one of them. *"Hi, I'm with NBC national news. If you could hold on for about 5 minutes, we're going to put you on a live phone interview."* Gregg answered that they were evacuating the building. *"But this will only take a minute."* Gregg repeated that they were leaving the building immediately. The caller seemed stunned. *"But, but this is NBC NATIONAL news".* Gregg said he was sorry and hung up.[9]

On the 87th floor, Adam Mayblum and his colleagues thought the worst was over. The building was standing, and though they were shaken, they were alive. They checked the halls. *"The smoke was thick and white and did not smell like I imagined smoke should smell. Not like your BBQ or your fireplace or even a bonfire."* Adam called home and left a message for his wife that he was okay and on his way out. He grabbed his laptop from his office. Then he removed his tee shirt, tore it into three pieces, gave two to his friends, soaked it in water, and tied it around his face to act as an air filter. Everybody started moving to the staircase.[10]

Shortly after starting down the stairwell, Adam Mayblum and an associate returned to their office to drag out a partner who stayed behind. There was no air, only white smoke. They called his name as they searched. No response. They figured he succumbed to the smoke and made their way back to the stairwell. They proceeded to the 78th floor where they had to change over to a different stairwell. *"I expected to see more people. There were some 50 to 60 more. Not enough. Wires and fires all over the place. Smoke too. A brave man was fighting a fire with the emergency hose. I stopped with two friends to make sure that everyone from our office was accounted for. We ushered them and confused people into the stairwell."*[11]

For more than an hour, Greg Trevor joined the thousands of fellow World Trade Center workers who patiently descended the emergency stairwells. *"I wasn't scared at first. My initial feelings were disorientation and disbelief."*[12]

Before finally throwing herself onto the lobby floor, Carmen Griffith glanced back to be sure her elevator was empty. That was when fire scorched her face with second- and third-degree burns, and literally welded her hooped right earring to her neck. Her hands were badly burned. Carmen was helped down the 78 floors to an ambulance just as her husband was carried out of the basement on a piece of plywood, each certain that the other was dead.[13]

At the Millennium Hilton, Phyllis Borgo's husband called back telling her to return home immediately. As Phyllis started to lose the call, she stepped outside to gain better reception. Standing on Church Street, Phyllis stared up and looked in disbelief at the burning North Tower. As she looked, she saw a man in a business suit jump from about the 60th floor. *"Oh my God, Oh my God, Oh my God!"* Phyllis became hysterical. She was rushed back inside the hotel and told to sit down and not look outside.[14]

* * *

Across the street, on the 100th floor of the South Tower, Cara LaTorre started screaming, *"We have to get out of here, we have to get the f*** out of here!"* Jaede Barg began to evacuate his office. Recalling his training as a fire marshal assistant, he told people not to use the elevators. Cara quickly grabbed her purse and started running down the stairs. *"After around 10 stories my shoes start to hurt so I take them off and start running barefoot."* Jaede held the stairwell door open for others to escape. Then he went back and checked the floor for stragglers before entering the stairwell himself.[15]

At the 87th floor of the South Tower, Jaede Barg paused to take a rest. He had just retrieved a Diet Coke from a vending machine when he heard several men scream. He ran over to the window and found himself staring almost eye level at the fire-engulfed hole in the North Tower. *"I saw the unthinkable: people jumping out of the building to escape the flames all around them. I painfully remember the same panic-stricken guy crying out '...they're holding hands' as a man and woman jumped out together toward their end. I did not view their leap, as I had to look away after the first two jumps I witnessed—there were so many people jumping."*[16]

On the way to the towers, the men of Ladder Company 6 could see the gaping hole in the upper floors of the North Tower. The streets were lined with thousands of people just staring at the tower, many with camcorders and cameras in their hands, said Butler. Debris was falling from the tower and large sections of the airplane were strewn across the ground directly beneath. *"We parked and immediately began to grab our gear, but we had to constantly watch out for falling debris. Computers were falling from 100 stories high and we had to make sure that no one in our unit got hit,"* said D'Agostino. When the men entered the building, they were met by the sight of buckled floors, smashed elevators, and a frenzy of people not knowing exactly where to go. *"We saved lives that day not by carrying people out on our backs, but by giving them direction,"* said Butler.[17]

* * *

High in the emergency stairwell, Greg Trevor and Adam Mayblum continued to make an orderly escape from the North Tower. *"We checked our cell phones. Surprisingly, there was a very good signal"*, said Mayblum. Greg Trevor called a colleague to let his wife know he was safe. *"I knew I could not reach my wife"* said Mayblum, *"so I called my parents. I told them what happened and that we were all okay and on the way down. Soon, my sister-in-law reached me. I told her we were fine and moving down. I believe that was about the 65th floor. We were bored and nervous. I called my friend Angel in San Francisco. I knew he would be watching. He was amazed I was on the phone. He told me to get out, that there was another plane on its way."*[18]

* * *

Jaede Barg had resumed his descent down the emergency stairwell in the South Tower when the fire department made an announcement over the public address system. They said the South Tower was secure, that a plane hit the North Tower. They offered that people could evacuate if they wished, but again asserted that the South Tower was secure. Jaede continued down the stairwell without hesitation. He did not go too far before he heard a roaring noise. *"The five of us were launched off our feet by the strike, into the wall, and back on our feet in an instant—remarkably, no one hurt. I remember my briefcase flying through the air up the stairs, and me automatically going after it. The incredible noise of the crash seemed like an explosion very close."*[19]

As the firemen from Ladder Company 6 raced toward the North Tower, they were stopped by the roar of jet engines. They saw the shadow of a plane on the ground, and finally a fireball resulting from the second plane hitting the South Tower.[20]

At 9:02 a.m., United Airlines Flight 175 impacted the south side of the South Tower of the World Trade Center between the 78th and 84th floors at a speed of over 500 miles per hour. Parts of the plane including an engine exited the building from its north side, and were found on the ground up to six blocks away.[21]

Cara LaTorre was descending the stairwell somewhere in the high 60's of the South Tower when she heard an explosion. *"The building shakes, the walls begin to crumble and a piece of metal comes flying between us. Oh my god, they bombed our building now! We don't know what to do. The only thing in my mind is that I have to call my husband, Frank, who works nearby to tell him that I am okay. The heat, we could feel the heat. We haven't started to cry yet because we are in shock."*[22]

Phyllis Borgo recalled, *"It all seemed to happen so fast, but there was more to come: the South Tower was hit—my building—my friends—everyone from the street began to run into the lobby of the Millennium and at that point I became panicky—we were being pushed to the back of a wall and elevator banks, and I thought we might be crushed. Luckily, the hotel personnel took charge and proceeded to lead all of us out the side door and out onto Fulton Street, telling us to get as far away from the Towers as possible."*[23]

Jaede Barg remembered the lights going out. *"There were cracks in the stairwell walls with exposed pipes breaking through the plaster. The building was forcefully swaying, enough to require significant balancing. I recall the incredible sound of twisting metal with each sway of the building. Smoke almost immediately started rising up from the lower floors, yet we all moved down the stairwell knowing this was the only way out."*[24]

Cara LaTorre also continued down the stairs with her companions. *"My legs are getting weaker and weaker I can hardly walk. Joanie wants to quit but Marci and I pump her up, then at times I feel like I can not run any more but they pump me up. Marci keeps us strong. I am having trouble breathing. A man hands me an energy water pack. My shirt become unbuttoned and I actually stop to button it up again."*[25]

* * *

Over at the North Tower, Ladder Company 6 started making their way up the stairwell. As they did, they continued to tell people where to go once they reached the lobby, and, in return, people kept giving them positive reinforcement. *"People were giving us water and saying 'God bless you' as we passed them in the stairwell,"* said Butler, explaining that the firefighters gave most of that water back to exhausted civilians walking down from their offices high atop the trade center.[26] Above them, Greg Trevor and Adam Mayblum continued to work their way downstairs.

Greg recalled, *"Every few floors, we would stop, move to the right of the stairwell and make room for injured people walking down—and firefighters and Port Authority Police officers running up".*[27]

On the 53rd floor, Adam came across a heavyset man sitting on the stairs. The man needed help. Adam knew he couldn't carry him, so he offered to tell the rescue workers his location. The man said okay. On the 44th floor Adam's cell phone rang. It was his parents. They were hysterical. They said a third plane was coming. Adam tried to calm his parents as he noticed rescue workers coming up the stairs. He stopped a number of them and told them about the man on the 53rd floor, and his partner he couldn't find back in the office on the 87th. "I later felt terrible about this. They headed up to find those people and met death instead."[28]

Outside, Phyllis Borgo ran up Fulton St. toward Broadway. She noticed many people injured and bleeding from the debris. One man was down on the pavement, blood pouring from his head as if a bucket had emptied. Two people were watching over him and paramedics were nearby. *"I prayed for him as I passed and looked away as to not get more upset."* Phyllis continued to walk uptown, trying to make her way home with the rest of the city. At Lafayette Street she noticed people milling about outside a Holiday Inn talking about the latest news. *"They told us the Pentagon had just been hit by another plane."*[29]

* * *

At 9:37 a.m., American Airlines Flight 77 was lost from radar screens and impacted the western side of the Pentagon.[30] Terry Morin, a Marine Corps aviator, witnessed the event.

"I can't remember exactly what I was thinking about at that moment, but I started to hear an increasingly loud rumbling behind me and to my left. As I turned to my left, I immediately realized the noise was bouncing off the 4-story structure that was Wing 5 [of Federal Office Building #2 across from the Pentagon]. One or two seconds later the airliner came into my field of view. By that time the noise was absolutely deafening. I instantly had a very bad feeling about this but things were happening very quickly. The aircraft was essentially right over the top of me and the outer portion of the FOB. Everything was shaking and vibrating, including the ground. I estimate that the aircraft was no more than 100 feet above me in a slight nose down attitude. The plane had a silver body with red and blue stripes down the fuselage. I believed at the time that it belonged to American Airlines, but I couldn't be sure."

Terry watched as the aircraft headed towards the Pentagon. *"I estimated the aircraft speed at between 350 and 400 knots. The flight path appeared to be deliberate, smooth, and controlled. As the aircraft approached the Pentagon, I saw a minor flash (later found out that the aircraft had sheared off a portion of a highway light pole down on Hwy 110). As the aircraft flew ever lower I started to lose sight of the actual airframe as a row of trees to the Northeast of the FOB blocked my view. I could now only see the tail of the aircraft. I believe I saw the tail dip slightly to the right indicating a minor turn in that direction. The tail was barely visible when I saw the flash and subsequent fireball rise approximately 200 feet above the Pentagon. There was a large explosion noise and the low frequency sound echo that comes with this type of sound. Associated with that was the increase in air pressure, momentarily, like a small gust of wind. For those formerly in the military, it sounded like a 2000 lb. bomb going off roughly ½ mile in front of you. At once there was a huge cloud of black smoke that rose several hundred feet up."*[31]

* * *

Back at the South Tower, Cara LaTorre managed to make it down from her 100th floor office. "*We finally get to the first floor and the lights are all out. There are guards directing us through the mall level, which leads us to an escalator near the Borders bookstore. I did not want to walk up the escalator but Marci pumped me up and Joanie said we are almost on the street. We finally get out of the building and I still don't have any shoes on. We slow down in the middle of the street to use our cell phones when a female cop starts to yell in our faces. She is telling us to run, it is not safe here. I will always remember the woman's face."*[32]

Still trying to manage his own escape from the South Tower, Jaede Barg ran into an impasse on the 77th floor. *"The stairwell was no longer passable and ended. The floor was filled with smoke, plaster, dust, and fire was all along the outside of the floor. There was destruction all over, with beams caved in from the above floor and rubble everywhere. It was very difficult to see, and as I wear glasses (thankfully so), but I could hear murmurs emanating from the perimeter of the floor. We were in the interior of the floor, and here we found two women who were apparently on the floor when the plane hit. I met the first lady, who was a very scared 30-year-old woman named Florence. We were together for the rest of our escape."*[33]

Jaede and Florence began frantically looking for an exit. They were breathing smoke and gasping for air. Everybody was coughing. They couldn't see each other. It was clear the fire was moving closer. *"We could not go back the way we came, as that was certain death. Three of us found another stairwell entrance door, but it would not open, no matter how hard we pushed and pulled."* Jaede despaired. *"This was the one point that day I began to lose faith in our escape."*[34]

"As if in a dream, the three of us banging on the stairway door, [we] heard a voice calling out to us from a place we thought was rubble. I do not really remember the guy, but he was the reason we made it off the burning floor." Jaede, along with a small group of people—including Florence—followed the man's voice until it brought them to an open stairwell. From there, the people slowly descended out of the South Tower. They escaped the building about 12 to 15 minutes before it collapsed.[35]

* * *

At 9:59 a.m., the South Tower of the World Trade Center suddenly collapsed, plummeting into the streets below. A massive cloud of dust and debris quickly filled lower Manhattan.[36]

When the men of Ladder Company 6 hit the 27th floor of the North Tower, they stopped to regroup and stood motionless as they heard the roar of the South Tower collapsing. Knowing that the fire was now the least of their concerns, the men turned and gave the order to evacuate. "*We were now walking briskly down the stairs hoping to make it out of the building before it collapsed*", said D'Agostino.[37]

Up on Lafayette Street at the Holiday Inn, Phyllis Borgo paused to watch the news unfolding on TV. "*As we watched in horror, the South Tower began to collapse to the ground in a matter of seconds. I put my hands in my face and began to cry... all I could think about were the firemen, EMS workers and police that were probably in the building trying to save lives and my fellow co-workers and friends that didn't make it out in time.*"[38]

* * *

Greg Trevor had reached the 5th floor of the North Tower when he heard a loud rumble. *"The building shook violently. I was thrown from one side of the stairwell to the other. We didn't know it at the time, but the South Tower had just collapsed. Our stairwell filled with smoke and concrete dust. Breathing became difficult. The lights died. A steady stream of water, about 4 inches deep, began running down the stairs. It felt like we were wading through a dark, dirty, rapid river—at night in the middle of a forest fire. The smartest decision I made that day was to wear a knit tie to work. I put the blue tie over my nose and mouth to block the smoke and dust. To keep from hyperventilating, I remembered the breathing exercises my wife and I learned in our Lamaze classes. Someone yelled that we should put our right hand on the shoulder of the person in front of us and keep walking down. We descended one more flight, to the fourth floor, when I heard someone say: 'Oh shit, the door's blocked.' The force from the collapse of the South Tower had apparently jammed the emergency exit. We were ordered to turn around and head back up the stairs, to see if we could transfer to another stairwell."*[39]

Minutes later, emergency workers cleared the fourth floor exit. Greg Trevor and the other survivors turned and darted down the stairs when they heard Port Authority Police Officer David Lim shout *"Down is good! Down is good!"* The emergency exit led to the mezzanine level of the North Tower. *"The mezzanine was filled with dull-beige concrete dust—on the floor, in the air, caked against the floor-to-ceiling windows. It felt like we were walking through a huge, dirty snow globe that had just been shaken. It was even worse when we walked outside, near Six World Trade Center. The plaza was a minefield of twisted metal, covered by a layer of concrete dust several inches thick. I am grateful for that dust, because it means I didn't see any bodies."* Greg exited the plaza and turned up Church Street and headed north. *"I looked back at the Trade Center. The upper third of the North Tower was on fire. There was so much smoke and dust, I couldn't tell that the South Tower had collapsed."*[40]

Adam Mayblum was on the 3rd floor when he heard the South Tower collapse next door. The lights went out. Adam recommended that everyone place a hand on the shoulder of the person in front of them and call out if they hit an obstacle so others would know to avoid it. As they reached another stairwell a female officer emerged soaking wet and covered in soot. She said they couldn't go that way, it was blocked. She told them to go up and use the 4th floor exit. Just as they turned she called back that it was okay to go down instead. Adam and his party emerged into an enormous room. *"It was light but filled with smoke. I commented to a friend that it must be under construction. Then we realized where we were. It was the second floor. The one that overlooks the lobby. We were ushered out into the courtyard, the one where the fountain used to be. My first thought was of a TV movie I saw once about nuclear winter and fallout. I could not understand where all this debris came from. There was at least five inches of this gray pasty dusty drywall soot on the ground as well as a thickness of it in the air."* Adam made it out and began walking towards Houston Street.[41]

* * *

Adam and his friend Kern walked several blocks until they came to a post office. Both stopped and looked up. *"Our building, exactly where our office is (was), was engulfed in flame and smoke. A postal worker said that the South Tower had fallen down. I looked again and sure enough it was gone."* Adam tried calling his wife, but couldn't get through. He called his parents to let them know he was fine, and they relayed the message to his wife. Adam and Kern sat down to rest. *"A girl on a bike offered us some water. Just as she took the cap off her bottle we heard a rumble. We looked up and our building, the North Tower collapsed."* Adam had escaped by less than 15 minutes.[42]

The crew of Ladder Company 6 was not so lucky. "*On the 18th floor we ran into Josephine Harris who was slowly walking down the stairs. We immediately helped her but the going was slow—one step at a time—and she kept insisting that we go on without her,*" said Butler. When the company reached the fourth floor, Harris stopped and said that she was going no further. As soon as she finished speaking, the men heard the dreaded and unmistakable rumble of the building above them. *"We could hear the floors above smashing together one by one and it became faster and louder,"* said D'Agostino. *"I was thrown down to the next landing and immediately the dust blacked out my vision. When the noise subsided, I thanked God I was alive and then started to move some of the debris out of my way. As I did so, Josephine popped out unhurt,"* said Butler.[43]

As the dust settled, the company took roll and found that all its members had survived and none were seriously injured. For the next four hours and 40 minutes, the men attempted to survive using their oxygen sparingly and trying to get through to the firefighters outside the building via a radio. *"The place was a mess,"* said D'Agostino. *"We knew where we were in the building, but the collapse of the two towers had made it hard for the firefighters on the outside to see anything or even recognize the former World Trade Center."*[44]

"A Port Authority officer who was trapped with us had two cell phones... I was able to get a hold of my wife... I told her to call the fire department and tell them that we are alive but trapped in the North Tower," said Butler.[45]

Eventually the men were found, and after walking across narrow I-beams and avoiding numerous fires, the entire company walked out of the North Tower after leaving Mrs. Harris with members of Ladder Company 43.[46]

Conclusion

Greg Trevor, Adam Mayblum, Jaede Barg, Phyllis Borgo, Cara LaTorre, Carmen Griffith, Arturo Griffith, and the men of Ladder Company Six survived the attacks of September 11th. Carmen and Arturo Griffith were taken to separate New York hospitals and later reunited.[47] An estimated 3,000 people were killed in the attacks, including 184 at the Pentagon, and 40 aboard United Airlines Flight 93 which crashed near Shanksville Pennsylvania.[48] Altogether is was the single worst loss of life on American soil since the Civil War, and the first attack against American territory since World War Two.

Questions

1. How do you escape a burning high rise?
2. What decisions proved fateful to survivors who escaped the Twin Towers on September 11th?
3. How could they have prepared better for this disaster?
4. Are you prepared to survive a similar catastrophe?

Chapter 2

9-11 Attacks

Objectives

- Understand the events of September 11th.
- Explain how the terrorists were able to conduct a successful attack.
- Identify weaknesses with the security measures of the day.
- Analyze the method and timing of the attacks.

Introduction

Tuesday, September 11, 2001, dawned temperate and nearly cloudless in the eastern United States. Millions of men and women readied themselves for work. Some made their way to the Twin Towers, the signature structures of the World Trade Center complex in New York City. Others went to Arlington, Virginia, to the Pentagon. Across the Potomac River, the United States Congress was back in session. At the other end of Pennsylvania Avenue, people began to line up for a White House tour. In Sarasota, Florida, President George W. Bush went for an early morning run.

For those heading to an airport, weather conditions could not have been better for a safe and pleasant journey. Among the travelers were Mohamed Atta and Abdul Aziz al Omari, who arrived at the airport in Portland Maine.

Boston: American 11 and United 175

On Tuesday, September 11, 2001, Mohammed Atta and Abul Aziz al Omari arrived at the airport in Portland Maine to catch a 6:00 a.m. flight to Boston's Logan International Airport.

When he checked in for his flight to Boston, Atta was selected by a computerized prescreening system known as CAPPS (Computer Assisted Passenger Prescreening System), created to identify passengers who should be subject to special security measures. Under security rules in place at the time, the only consequence of Atta's selection by CAPPS was that his checked bags were held off the plane until it was confirmed that he had boarded the aircraft.

At 6:45 a.m., Atta and Omari arrived in Boston. Between 6:45 and 7:40, Atta and Omari, along with Satam al Suqami, Wail al Shehri, and Waleed al Shehri, checked in and boarded American Airlines Flight 11, bound for Los Angeles. The flight was scheduled to depart at 7:45.

Elsewhere at Logan Airport, Marwan al Shehhi, Fayez Banihammad, Mohand al Shehri, Ahmed al Ghamdi, and Hamza al Ghamdi checked in for United Airlines Flight 175, also bound for Los Angeles. Their flight was scheduled to depart at 08:00.

As Atta's team passed through passenger screening, three members—Suqami, Wail al Shehri, and Waleed al Shehri—were selected by CAPPS. Their selection affected only the handling of their checked bags, not their screening at the checkpoint. All five men cleared the checkpoint and made their way to the gate for American 11. Atta, Omari, and Suqami took their seats in business class. The Shehri brothers had adjacent seats in row 2 in the first-class cabin. They boarded American 11 between 7:31 and 7:40. The aircraft pushed back from the gate at 7:40.

Shehhi and his team, none of whom had been selected by CAPPS, boarded United 175 between 7:23 and 7:28. Their aircraft pushed back from the gate just before 8:00.

Washington Dulles: American 77

At 7:15 a.m., Khalid al Mihdhar and Majed Moqed checked in with the American Airlines ticket counter at Dulles International Airport in Virginia. Both were ticketed for Flight 77 bound for Los Angeles. Within 20 minutes, three other members of the team checked in including Hani Hanjour, Nawaf al Hazmi, and Salem al Hazmi. Hani Hanjour, Khalid al Mihdhar, and Majed Moqed were flagged by CAPPS. The Hazmi brothers were also selected for extra security by the airline's customer service representative at the check-in counter. He did so because one of the brothers did not have photo identification nor could he understand English, and because the agent found both passengers to be suspicious. The only consequence of their selection was that their checked bags were held off the plane until it was confirmed that they had boarded the aircraft.

The five hijackers proceeded to the Main Terminal's west security screening point. The checkpoint featured closed-circuit television that recorded all passengers, including the hijackers as they were screened. Both Mihdhar and Moqed set off the metal detector and were directed to a second metal detector. Mihdhar did not trigger the alarm and was permitted through the checkpoint. Moqed set it off, a screener wanded him with a hand-held magnetic detector. He passed this inspection. About 20 minutes later, Hani Hanjour, Nawaf al Hazmi, and Salem al Hazmi entered the screening area. Nawaf al Hazmi set off both the first and second metal detectors and was then hand-wanded before being passed. In addition, his over-the-shoulder carry-on bag was swiped by an explosive trace detector and then passed.

At 7:50 a.m., Majed Moqed and Khalid al Mihdhar boarded American 77 and were seated in 12A and 12B in coach. Hani Hanjour, assigned to seat 1B in first class, soon followed. The Hazmi brothers, sitting in 5E and 5F, joined Hanjour in the first-class cabin.

Newark: United 93

At Newark Airport in New Jersey, another hijacking team assembled. Between 7:03 and 7:39, Saeed al Ghamdi, Ahmed al Nami, Ahad al Haznawi, and Ziad Jarrah checked in at the United Airlines Ticket counter for Flight 93, going to Los Angeles. Haznawi was selected by CAPPS. His checked bag was screened for explosives and then loaded on the plane.

The four men passed though the security checkpoint and boarded their plane between 7:39 and 7:48. All four had seats in the first-class cabin. Jarrah was in seat 1B, closest to the cockpit; Nami was in 3C, Ghamdi in 3D, and Haznawi in 6B.

The 19 men were aboard four transcontinental flights. They were planning to hijack these planes and turn them into large guided missiles, loaded with up to 11,400 gallons of jet fuel. By 8:00 a.m. on the morning of Tuesday, September 11, 2001, they had defeated all the security layers that America's civil aviation security system then had in place to prevent hijacking.

The 19 men were aboard four transcontinental flights. They were planning to hijack these planes and turn them into large guided missiles, loaded with up to 11,400 gallons of jet fuel. By 8:00 a.m. on the morning of Tuesday, September 11, 2001, [the terrorists] had defeated all the security layers that America's civil aviation security system then had in place to prevent hijacking.

The Hijacking of American 11

American Airlines Flight 11 provided nonstop service from Boston to Los Angeles. On September 11, Captain John Ogonowski and First Officer Thomas McGuinness piloted the Boeing 767. It carried its full capacity of nine flight attendants. Eighty-one passengers boarded the flight with them, including the five terrorists.

American Flight 11 took off at 7:59. Just before 8:14, it had climbed to 26,000 feet, not quite its initial assigned cruising altitude of 29,000 feet. All communications and flight profile data were normal. About this time, the "Fasten Seatbelt" sign would usually have been turned off and the flight attendants would have begun preparing for cabin service.

At this time, American 11 had its last routine communication with the ground when it acknowledged navigational instructions from the FAA's air traffic control (ATC) center in Boston. Sixteen seconds after that transmission, ATC instructed the aircraft's pilots to climb to 35,000 feet. That message and all subsequent attempts to contact the flight were not acknowledged. From this and other evidence, it is believed the hijacking began at 8:14 or shortly thereafter.

Reports from two flight attendants in the coach cabin, Betty Ong and Madeline "Amy" Sweeney, tell us most of what we know about how the hijacking happened. As it began, some of the hijackers—most likely Wail al Shehri and Waleed al Shehri, who were seated in row 2 in first class—stabbed the two unarmed flight attendants who would have been preparing for cabin service.

It's not known exactly how the hijackers gained access to the cockpit; FAA rules required that the doors remain closed and locked during flight. Ong speculated that they had "jammed their way" in. Perhaps the terrorists stabbed the flight attendants to get a cockpit key, to force one of them to open the cockpit door, or to lure the captain or first officer out of the cockpit.

At the same time or shortly thereafter, Atta—the only terrorist on board trained to fly a jet—would have moved to the cockpit from his business-class seat, possibly accompanied by Omari. As this was happening, passenger Daniel Lewin, who was seated in the row just behind Atta and Omari, was stabbed by one of the hijackers—probably Satam al Suqami, who was seated directly behind Lewin. Lewin had served four years as an officer in the Israeli military. He may have made an attempt to stop the hijackers in front of him, not realizing that another was sitting behind him.

The hijackers quickly gained control and sprayed Mace, pepper spray, or some other irritant in the first-class cabin, in order to force the passengers and flight attendants toward the rear of the plane. They claimed they had a bomb.

About five minutes after the hijacking began, Betty Ong contacted the American Airlines Southeastern Reservations Office in Cary, North Carolina, via an AT&T airphone to report an emergency aboard the flight. The emergency call lasted approximately 25 minutes, as Ong calmly and professionally relayed information about events taking place aboard the airplane to authorities on the ground.

At 8:19, Ong reported: *"The cockpit is not answering, somebody's stabbed in business class—and I think there's Mace—that we can't breathe—I don't know, I think we're getting hijacked."* She then told of the stabbings of the two flight attendants.

American's Southeastern Reservations Office quickly contacted the American Airlines operations center in Fort Worth, Texas, who soon contacted the FAA's Boston Air Traffic Control Center. Boston Center knew of a problem on the flight in part because just before 8:25 the hijackers had attempted to communicate with the passengers. The microphone was keyed, and immediately one of the hijackers said, "*Nobody move. Everything will be okay. If you try to make any moves, you'll endanger yourself and the airplane. Just stay quiet."* Air traffic controllers heard the transmission; Ong did not. The hijackers probably did not know how to operate the cockpit radio communication system correctly, and thus inadvertently broadcast their message over the air traffic control channel instead of the cabin public-address channel. Also at 8:25, and again at 8:29, Amy Sweeney got through to the American Flight Services Office in Boston but was cut off after she reported someone was hurt aboard the flight. Three minutes later, Sweeney was reconnected to the office and began relaying updates to her manager.

At 8:26, Ong reported that the plane was "flying erratically." A minute later, Flight 11 turned south. American also began getting identifications of the hijackers, as Ong and then Sweeney passed on some of the seat numbers of those who had gained unauthorized access to the cockpit.

At 8:41 Sweeney reported that passengers in coach were under the impression there was a routine medical emergency in first class. Other flight attendants were busy at duties such as getting medical supplies while Ong and Sweeney were reporting events.

At 8:41, American's operations center learned that air traffic controllers had declared Flight 11 a hijacking, and thought it was headed toward Kennedy airport in New York City. Air traffic control was busy moving other flights out of the way as they tracked Flight 11 on primary radar, which seemed to show the aircraft descending.

At 8:44 contact was lost with Betty Ong. About this time Sweeney reported *"Something is wrong. We are in a rapid descent... we are all over the place."* When asked to look out the window, Sweeney reported "*We are flying low. We are flying very, very low. We are flying way too low."* Seconds later she said, *"Oh my God we are way too low."* The phone call ended.

At 8:46:40, American 11 crashed into the North Tower of the World Trade Center in New York City. All on board, along with an unknown number of people in the tower, were killed instantly.

The Hijacking of United 175

United Airlines Flight 175 was scheduled to depart for Los Angeles at 8:00. Captain Victor Saracini and First Officer Michael Horrocks piloted the Boeing 767, which had seven flight attendants. Fifty-six passengers boarded the flight.

United 175 pushed back from its gate at 7:58 and departed Logan Airport at 8:14. By 8:33, it had reached its assigned cruising altitude of 31,000 feet. The flight attendants would have begun their cabin service.

The hijackers attacked sometime between 8:42 and 8:46. They used knives, Mace, and the threat of a bomb. They stabbed members of the flight crew. Both pilots had been killed. The eyewitness accounts came from calls made from the rear of the plane, from passengers originally seated further forward in the cabin, a sign that passengers and perhaps crew had been moved to the back of the aircraft.

The first operational evidence that something was abnormal on United 175 came at 8:47 when the aircraft changed beacon codes twice within a minute. At 8:51, the flight deviated from its assigned altitude, and a minute later New York air traffic controllers began repeatedly and unsuccessfully trying to contact it.

At 8:52, in Easton, Connecticut, a man named Lee Hanson received a phone call from his son Peter, a passenger on United 175. His son told him: "*I think they've taken over the cockpit—an attendant has been stabbed—and someone else up front may have been killed. The plane is making strange moves. Call United Airlines—Tell them it's Flight 175, Boston to LA.*" Lee Hansen then called the Easton Police Department and relayed what he had heard.

Also at 8:52, a male flight attendant called a United office in San Francisco. The flight attendant reported that the flight had been hijacked, both pilots killed, a flight attendant stabbed, and the hijackers were probably flying the plane. The call lasted about two minutes.

At 8:58, the flight took a heading toward New York City. At 8:59, Flight 175 passenger Brian David Sweeney tried to call his wife, Julie. He left a message on their home answering machine that the plane had been hijacked. He then called his mother, Luise Sweeney, told her the flight had been hijacked, and added that the passengers were thinking about storming the cockpit to take control of the plane away from the hijackers.

At 9:00, Lee Hanson received a second call from his son Peter: "*It's getting bad, Dad—A stewardess was stabbed—They seem to have knives and Mace—They said they have a bomb—It's getting very bad on the plane—Passengers are throwing up and getting sick—The plane is making jerky movements—I don't think the pilot is flying the plane—I think we are going down—I think they intend to go to Chicago or someplace and fly into a building—Don't worry Dad—If it happens, it'll be very fast—My God, my God.*"

The call ended abruptly. Lee Hanson had heard a woman scream just before it cut off. He turned on a television, and in her home so did Luise Sweeney. Both then saw the second aircraft hit the World Trade Center.

At 9:03:11, United Airlines Flight 175 struck the South Tower of the World Trade Center. All on board, along with an unknown number of people in the tower, were killed instantly.

The Hijacking of American 77

American Airlines Flight 77 was scheduled to depart from Washington Dulles for Los Angeles at 8:10. The aircraft was a Boeing 757 piloted by Captain Charles F. Burlingame and First Officer David Charlebois. There were four flight attendants. On September 11, the flight carried 58 passengers.

American 77 pushed back from its gate at 8:09 and took off at 8:20. At 8:46, the flight reached its assigned cruising altitude of 35,000 feet. Cabin service would have begun. At 8:51, American 77 transmitted its last routine radio communication. The hijacking began between 8:51 and 8:54. As on American 11 and United 175, the hijackers used knives and moved all the passengers to the rear of the aircraft. Unlike the earlier flights, the Flight 77 hijackers were reported by a passenger to have box cutters. Finally, a passenger reported that an announcement had been made by the "pilot" that the plane had been hijacked. Neither of the firsthand accounts mentioned any stabbings or the threat or use of either a bomb or Mace, though both witnesses began the flight in the first-class cabin.

At 8:54, the aircraft deviated from its assigned course, turning south. Two minutes later the transponder was turned off and even primary radar contact with the aircraft was lost. The Indianapolis Air Traffic Control Center repeatedly tried and failed to contact the aircraft. American Airlines dispatchers also tried, without success.

At 9:00, American Airlines Executive Vice President Gerard Arpey learned that communications had been lost with American 77. This was now the second American aircraft in trouble. He ordered all American Airlines flights in the Northeast that had not taken off to remain on the ground. After learning that United Airlines was missing a plane, American Airlines headquarters extended the ground stop nationwide.

At 9:12, Renee May called her mother, Nancy May, in Las Vegas. She said her flight was being hijacked by six individuals who had moved them to the rear of the plane. She asked her mother to alert American Airlines. Nancy May and her husband promptly did so.

At some point between 9:16 and 9:26, Barbara Olson called her husband, Ted Olson, the solicitor general of the United States. She reported that the flight had been hijacked, and the hijackers had knives and box cutters. She further indicated that the hijackers were not aware of her phone call, and that they had put all the passengers in the back of the plane. About a minute into the conversation the call was cut off.

Shortly after the first call, Barbara Olson reached her husband again. She reported that the pilot had announced that the flight had been hijacked, and she asked her husband what she should tell the captain to do. Ted Olson asked for her location and she replied that the aircraft was then flying over houses. Another passenger told her they were traveling northeast. The Solicitor General then informed his wife of the two previous hijackings and crashes. She did not display signs of panic and did not indicate any awareness of an impending crash. At that point the second call was cut off.

At 9:20, the autopilot on American 77 was disengaged; the aircraft was at 7,000 feet and approximately 38 miles west of the Pentagon. At 9:32, controllers at the Dulles Terminal Radar Approach Control *"observed a primary radar target tracking eastbound at a high rate of speed."* This was later determined to have been Flight 77.

At 9:34, Ronald Reagan Washington National Airport advised the Secret Service of an unknown aircraft heading in the direction of the White House. American 77 was then 5 miles west-southwest of the Pentagon and began a 330 degree turn. At the end of the turn, it was descending through 2,200 feet, pointed toward the Pentagon and downtown Washington. The hijacker pilot then advanced the throttles to maximum power an dove toward the Pentagon.

At 9:37:46, American Airlines Flight 77 crashed into the Pentagon, traveling at approximately 530 miles per hour. All on board, as well as many civilian and military personnel in the building, were killed.

The Battle for United 93

Crisis managers at the FAA and the airlines did not yet act to warn other aircraft. At the same time, Boston Center realized that a message transmitted just before 8:25 by the hijacker pilot of American 11 included the phrase, "We have some planes."

At 8:42, United Airlines Flight 93 took off from Newark (New Jersey) Liberty International Airport bound for San Francisco. The aircraft was piloted by Captain Jason Dahl and First Officer Leroy Homer, and there were five flight attendants. Thirty-seven passengers, including the hijackers, boarded the plane. Scheduled to depart the gate at 8:00, the Boeing 757's takeoff was delayed because of the airport's typically heavy morning traffic.

As United 93 left Newark, the flight's crew members were unaware of the hijacking of American 11. Around 9:00, the FAA, American, and United were facing the staggering realization of apparent multiple hijackings. At 9:03, they would see another aircraft strike the World Trade Center. Crisis managers at the FAA and the airlines did not yet act to warn other aircraft. At the same time, Boston Center realized that a message transmitted just before 8:25 by the hijacker pilot of American 11 included the phrase, *"We have some planes."*

The hijackers attacked at 9:28. While traveling 35,000 feet above eastern Ohio, United 93 suddenly dropped 700 feet. Eleven seconds into the descent, the FAA's air traffic control center in Cleveland received the first of two radio transmissions from the aircraft. During the first broadcast, the captain or first officer could be heard declaring *"Mayday"* amid the sounds of a physical struggle in the cockpit. The second radio transmission, 35 seconds later, indicated that the fight was continuing. The captain or first officer could be heard shouting: *"Hey get out of here—get out of here—get out of here."*

At 9:32, a hijacker, probably Jarrah, made or attempted to make the following announcement to the passengers of Flight 93: *"Ladies and Gentlemen: Here the captain, please sit down keep remaining sitting. We have a bomb on board. So, sit."* The flight data recorder (also recovered) indicates that Jarrah then instructed the plane's autopilot to turn the aircraft around and head east.

The cockpit voice recorder data indicate that a woman, most likely a flight attendant, was being held captive in the cockpit. She struggled with one of the hijackers who killed or otherwise silenced her.

Shortly thereafter, the passengers and flight crew began a series of calls from GTE airphones and cellular phones. The calls between family, friends, and colleagues took place until the end of the flight and provided those on the ground with firsthand accounts. They enabled the passengers to gain critical information, including the news that two aircraft had slammed into the World Trade Center.

Five calls described the intent of passengers and surviving crew members to revolt against the hijackers. According to one call, they voted on whether to rush the terrorists in an attempt to retake the plane. They decided, and acted.

At 9:57, the passenger assault began. Several passengers had terminated phone calls with loved ones in order to join the revolt. One of the callers ended her message as follows: *"Everyone's running up to first class. I've got to go. Bye."*

The cockpit voice recorder captured the sounds of the passenger assault muffled by the intervening cockpit door. Some family members who listened to the recording report that they can hear the voice of a loved one among the din. We cannot identify whose voices can be heard. But the assault was sustained.

In response, Jarrah immediately began to roll the airplane to the left and right, attempting to knock the passengers off balance. At 9:58:57, Jarrah told another hijacker in the cockpit to block the door. Jarrah continued to roll the airplane sharply left and right, but the assault continued. At 9:59:52, Jarrah changed tactics and pitched the nose of the airplane up and down to disrupt the assault. The recorder captured the sounds of loud thumps, crashes, shouts, and breaking glasses and plates. At 10:00:03, Jarrah stabilized the airplane.

Five seconds later, Jarrah asked, *"Is that it? Shall we finish it off?"* A hijacker responded, *"No. Not yet. When they all come, we finish it off."* The sounds of fighting continued outside the cockpit. Again, Jarrah pitched the nose of the aircraft up and down. At 10:00:26, a passenger in the background said, *"In the cockpit. If we don't we'll die!"* Sixteen seconds later, a passenger yelled, *"Roll it!"* Jarrah stopped the violent maneuvers about 10:01:00 and said, *"Allah is the greatest! Allah is the greatest!"* He then asked another hijacker in the cockpit. *"Is that it? I mean, shall we put it down?"* To which the other replied, *"Yes, put it in it, and pull it down."*

The passengers continued their assault and at 10:02:23, a hijacker said, *"Pull it down! Pull it down!"* The hijackers remained at the controls but must have judged that the passengers were only seconds from overcoming them. The airplane headed down; the control wheel was turned hard to the right. The airplane rolled onto its back, and one of the hijackers began shouting *"Allah is the greatest. Allah is the greatest."* With the sounds of the passenger counterattack continuing, the aircraft plowed into an empty field in Shanksville, Pennsylvania, at 580 miles per hour, about 20 minutes flying time from Washington, D.C.

Jarrah's objective was to crash his airliner into symbols of the American Republic, the Capitol or the White House. He was defeated by the alerted, unarmed passengers of United 93.[1]

Conclusion

More than 2,600 people died at the World Trade Center; 125 died at the Pentagon; 256 died on the four planes. The death toll surpassed that at Pearl Harbor in December 1941. This immeasurable pain was inflicted by 19 young Arabs acting at the behest of Islamist extremists headquartered in distant Afghanistan. Some had been in the United States for more than a year, mixing with the rest of the population. Though four had training as pilots, most were not well-educated. Most spoke English poorly, some hardly at all. In groups of four or five, carrying with them only small knives, box cutters, and cans of Mace or pepper spray, they had hijacked the four planes and turned them into deadly guided missiles.[2]

Questions

1. How were the highjackers able to overcome security measures?
2. What was the purpose of highjacking trans-continental flights?
3. How did the FAA respond to the highjackings?
4. Would similar highjackings succeed today?

Chapter 3

9-11 Analysis

Objectives

- Explain how the events of 9-11 should have been anticipated.
- Understand the roles and responsibilities of the different agencies protecting America on 9-11.
- Describe how the various agencies failed to prevent the attacks of 9-11.
- Identify policies that unwittingly supported the terrorist efforts.
- Discuss the difficulties encountered by emergency personnel responding to 9-11.

Introduction

On November 27, 2002, Congress and the President created the National Commission on Terrorist Attacks Upon the United States (Public Law 107-306) to investigate the "facts and circumstances relating to the terrorist attacks of September 11, 2001." Later known as the "9-11 Commission", the bi-partisan panel released its 585-page report July 22, 2004. The following analysis is excerpted from the "9/11 Report".

A Nation Transformed

At 8:46 on the morning of September 11, 2001, the United States became a nation transformed.

An airliner traveling at hundreds of miles per hour and carrying some 10,000 gallons of jet fuel plowed into the North Tower of the World Trade Center in Lower Manhattan. At 9:03, a second airliner hit the South Tower. Fire and smoke billowed upward. Steel, glass, ash, and bodies fell below. The Twin Towers, where up to 50,000 people worked each day, both collapsed less than 90 minutes later.

The 9/11 attacks were a shock, but they should not have come as a surprise. Islamist extremists had given plenty of warning that they meant to kill Americans indiscriminately and in large numbers.

At 9:37 that same morning, a third airliner slammed into the western face of the Pentagon. At 10:03, a fourth airliner crashed in a field in southern Pennsylvania.

More than 2,600 people died at the World Trade Center; 125 died at the Pentagon; 256 died on the four planes.

This immeasurable pain was inflicted by 19 young Arabs acting at the behest of Islamist extremists headquartered in distant Afghanistan. Some had been in the United States for more than a year, mixing with the rest of the population. Though four had training as pilots, most were not well-educated. Most spoke English poorly, some hardly at all. In groups of four or five, carrying with them only small knives, box cutters, and cans of Mace or pepper spray, they had hijacked the four planes and turned them into deadly guided missiles.

A Shock, Not a Surprise

The 9/11 attacks were a shock, but they should not have come as a surprise. Islamist extremists had given plenty of warning that they meant to kill Americans indiscriminately and in large numbers. Although Usama Bin Ladin himself would not emerge as a signal threat until the late 1990s, the threat of Islamist terrorism grew over the decade.

In February 1993, a group led by Ramzi Yousef tried to bring down the World Trade Center with a truck bomb. They killed six and wounded a thousand. Plans by Omar Abdel Rahman and others to blow up the Holland and Lincoln tunnels and other New York City landmarks were frustrated when the plotters were arrested. In October 1993, Somali tribesmen shot down U.S. helicopters, killing 18 and wounding 73 in an incident that came to be known as

"Black Hawk down." Years later it would be learned that those Somali tribesmen had received help from al Qaeda.

In early 1995, police in Manila uncovered a plot by Ramzi Yousef to blow up a dozen U.S. airliners while they were flying over the Pacific. In November 1995, a car bomb exploded outside the office of the U.S. program manager for the Saudi National Guard in Riyadh, killing five Americans and two others. In June 1996, a truck bomb demolished the Khobar Towers apartment complex in Dhahran, Saudi Arabia, killing 19 U.S. servicemen and wounding hundreds. The attack was carried out primarily by Saudi Hezbollah, an organization that had received help from the government of Iran.

Until 1997, the U.S. intelligence community viewed Bin Ladin as a financier of terrorism, not as a terrorist leader. In February 1998, Usama Bin Ladin and four others issued a self-styled fatwa, publicly declaring that it was God's decree that every Muslim should try his utmost to kill any American, military or civilian, anywhere in the world, because of American "occupation" of Islam's holy places and aggression against Muslims.

In August 1998, Bin Ladin's group, al Qaeda, carried out near-simultaneous truck bomb attacks on the U.S. embassies in Nairobi, Kenya, and Dar es Salaam, Tanzania. The attacks killed 224 people, including 12 Americans, and wounded thousands more.

The August 1998 bombings of U.S. embassies in Kenya and Tanzania established al Qaeda as a potent adversary of the United States.

In December 1999, Jordanian police foiled a plot to bomb hotels and other sites frequented by American tourists, and a U.S. Customs agent arrested Ahmed Ressam at the U.S. Canadian border as he was smuggling in explosives intended for an attack on Los Angeles International Airport.

In October 2000, an al Qaeda team in Aden, Yemen, used a motorboat filled with explosives to blow a hole in the side of a destroyer, the USS Cole, almost sinking the vessel and killing 17 American sailors.

The 9/11 attacks on the World Trade Center and the Pentagon were far more elaborate, precise, and destructive than any of these earlier assaults. But by September 2001, the executive branch of the U.S. government, the Congress, the news media, and the American public had received clear warning that Islamist terrorists meant to kill Americans in high numbers.

1998 to September 11, 2001

The August 1998 bombings of U.S. embassies in Kenya and Tanzania established al Qaeda as a potent adversary of the United States.

After launching cruise missile strikes against al Qaeda targets in Afghanistan and Sudan in retaliation for the embassy bombings, the Clinton administration applied diplomatic pressure to try to persuade the Taliban regime in Afghanistan to expel Bin Ladin. The administration also devised covert operations to use CIA-paid foreign agents to capture or kill Bin Ladin and his chief lieutenants. These actions did not stop Bin Ladin or dislodge al Qaeda from its sanctuary.

By late 1998 or early 1999, Bin Ladin and his advisers had agreed on an idea brought to them by Khalid Sheikh Mohammed (KSM) called the "planes operation." It would eventually culminate in the 9/11 attacks. Bin Ladin and his chief of operations, Mohammed Atef, occupied undisputed leadership positions atop al Qaeda. Within al Qaeda, they relied heavily on the ideas and enterprise of strong-willed field commanders, such as KSM, to carry out worldwide terrorist operations.

KSM claims that his original plot was even grander than those carried out on 9/11—ten planes would attack targets on both the East and West coasts of the United States. This plan was modified by Bin Ladin, KSM said, owing to its scale and complexity. Bin Ladin provided KSM with four initial operatives for suicide plane attacks within the United States, and in the fall of 1999 training for the attacks began. New recruits included four from a cell of expatriate Muslim extremists who had clustered together in Hamburg, Germany. One became the tactical commander of the operation in the United States: Mohamed Atta.

U.S. intelligence frequently picked up reports of attacks planned by al Qaeda. Working with foreign security services, the CIA broke up some al Qaeda cells. The core of Bin Ladin's organization nevertheless remained intact. In December 1999, news about the arrests of the terrorist cell in Jordan and the arrest of a terrorist at the U.S.-Canadian border became part of a "millennium alert." The government was galvanized, and the public was on alert for any possible attack.

U.S. intelligence frequently picked up reports of attacks planned by al Qaeda. Working with foreign security services, the CIA broke up some al Qaeda cells. The core of Bin Ladin's organization nevertheless remained intact.

In January 2000, the intense intelligence effort glimpsed and then lost sight of two operatives destined for the "planes operation." Spotted in Kuala Lumpur, the pair were lost passing through Bangkok. On January 15, 2000, they arrived in Los Angeles.

After arriving in California, the two al Qaeda operatives sought out and found a group of ideologically like-minded Muslims with roots in Yemen and Saudi Arabia, individuals mainly associated with a young Yemeni and others who attended a mosque in San Diego. After a brief stay in Los Angeles, the al Qaeda operatives lived openly in San Diego under their true names. They managed to avoid attracting much attention.

By the summer of 2000, three of the four Hamburg cell members had arrived on the East Coast of the United States and had begun pilot training. In early 2001, a fourth future hijacker pilot, Hani Hanjour, journeyed to Arizona with another operative, Nawaf al Hazmi, and conducted his refresher pilot training there. A number of al Qaeda operatives had spent time in Arizona during the 1980s and early 1990s.

During 2000, President Bill Clinton and his advisers renewed diplomatic efforts to get Bin Ladin expelled from Afghanistan. They also renewed secret efforts with some of the Taliban's opponents—the Northern Alliance—to get enough intelligence to attack Bin Ladin directly. Diplomatic efforts centered on the new military government in Pakistan, and they did not succeed. The efforts with the Northern Alliance revived an inconclusive and secret debate about whether the United States should take sides in Afghanistan's civil war and support the Taliban's enemies. The CIA also produced a plan to improve intelligence collection on al Qaeda, including the use of a small, unmanned airplane with a video camera, known as the Predator.

After the October 2000 attack on the USS Cole, evidence accumulated that it had been launched by al Qaeda operatives, but without confirmation that Bin Ladin had given the order. The Taliban had earlier been warned that it would be held responsible for another Bin Ladin attack on the United States. The CIA described its findings as a "preliminary judgment"; President Clinton and his chief advisers were waiting for a conclusion before deciding whether to take military action. The military alternatives remained unappealing to them.

The transition to the new Bush administration in late 2000 and early 2001 took place with the Cole issue still pending. President George W. Bush and his chief advisers accepted that al Qaeda was responsible for the attack on the Cole, but did not like the options available for a response.

The Bush administration began developing a new strategy with the stated goal of eliminating the al Qaeda threat within three to five years. During the spring and summer of 2001, U.S. intelligence agencies received a stream of warnings that al Qaeda planned, as one report put it, "something very, very, very big." Director of Central Intelligence George Tenet stated, " The system was blinking red."

Although Bin Ladin was determined to strike in the United States, as President Clinton had been told and President Bush was reminded in a Presidential Daily Brief article briefed to him in August 2001, the specific threat information pointed overseas. Numerous precautions were taken overseas. Domestic agencies were not effectively mobilized. The threat did not receive national media attention comparable to the millennium alert.

While the United States continued disruption efforts around the world, its emerging strategy to eliminate the al Qaeda threat was to include an enlarged covert action program in Afghanistan, as well as diplomatic strategies for Afghanistan and Pakistan. The process culminated during the summer of 2001 in a draft presidential directive and arguments about the Predator aircraft, which was soon to be deployed with a missile of its own, so that it might be used to attempt to kill Bin Ladin or his chief lieutenants. At a September 4 meeting, President Bush's chief advisers approved the draft directive of the strategy and endorsed the concept of arming the Predator. This directive on the al Qaeda strategy was awaiting President Bush's signature on September 11, 2001.

Though the "planes operation" was progressing, the plotters had problems of their own in 2001. Several possible participants dropped out; others could not gain entry into the United States (including one denial at a port of entry and visa denials not related to terrorism). One of the eventual pilots may have considered abandoning the planes operation. Zacarias Moussaoui, who showed up at a flight training school in Minnesota, may have been a candidate to replace him.

Some of the vulnerabilities of the plotters become clear in retrospect. Moussaoui aroused suspicion for seeking fast-track training on how to pilot large jet airliners. He was arrested on August 16, 2001, for violations of immigration

Some of the vulnerabilities of the plotters become clear in retrospect. Moussaoui aroused suspicion for seeking fast-track training on how to pilot large jet airliners.

regulations. In late August, officials in the intelligence community realized that the terrorists spotted in Southeast Asia in January 2000 had arrived in the United States.

These cases did not prompt urgent action. No one working on these late leads in the summer of 2001 connected them to the high level of threat reporting. In the words of one official, no analytic work foresaw the lightning that could connect the thundercloud to the ground.

As final preparations were under way during the summer of 2001, dissent emerged among al Qaeda leaders in Afghanistan over whether to proceed. The Taliban's chief, Mullah Omar, opposed attacking the United States. Although facing opposition from many of his senior lieutenants, Bin Ladin effectively overruled their objections, and the attacks went forward.

September 11, 2001

The day began with the 19 hijackers getting through a security checkpoint system that they had evidently analyzed and knew how to defeat. They took over the four flights, taking advantage of air crews and cockpits that were not prepared for the contingency of a suicide hijacking.

On 9/11, the defense of the U.S. airspace depended on close interaction between two federal agencies: the Federal Aviation Administration (FAA) and North American Aerospace Defense Command (NORAD).

On 9/11, the defense of the U.S. airspace depended on close interaction between two federal agencies: the Federal Aviation Administration (FAA) and North American Aerospace Defense Command (NORAD). Existing protocols on 9/11 were unsuited in every respect for an attack in which hijacked planes were used as weapons.

What ensued, was a hurried attempt to improvise a defense by civilians who had never handled a hijacked aircraft that attempted to disappear, and by a military unprepared for the transformation of commercial aircraft into weapons of mass destruction.

A shootdown authorization was not communicated to the NORAD air defense sector until 28 minutes after United 93 had crashed in Pennsylvania. Planes were scrambled, but ineffectively, as they did not know where to go or what target they were to intercept. And once the shootdown order was given, it was not communicated to the pilots. In short, while leaders in Washington believed that the fighters circling above them had been instructed to "take out" hostile aircraft, the only orders actually conveyed to the pilots were to "ID type and tail."

Like the national defense, the emergency response on 9/11 was necessarily improvised.

In New York City, the Fire Department of New York, the New York Police Department, and the Port Authority of New York and New Jersey, the building employees, and the occupants of the buildings did their best to cope with the effects of almost unimaginable events—unfolding furiously over 102 minutes. Casualties were nearly 100 percent at and above the impact zones and were very high among first responders who stayed in danger as they tried to save lives. Despite weaknesses in preparations for disaster, failure to achieve unified incident command, and inadequate communications among responding agencies, all but approximately one hundred of the thousands of civilians who worked below the impact zone escaped, often with help from the emergency responders.

At the Pentagon, while there were also problems of command and control, the emergency response was generally effective. The Incident Command System, a formalized management structure for emergency response in place in the National Capital Region, overcame the inherent complications of a response across local, state, and federal jurisdictions.

General Findings

Since the plotters were flexible and resourceful, it cannot be known whether any single step or series of steps would have defeated them. What can be said with confidence is that none of the measures adopted by the U.S. government from 1998 to 2001 disturbed or even delayed the progress of the al Qaeda plot. Across the government, there were failures of imagination, policy, capabilities, and management.

Imagination

Across the government, there were failures of imagination, policy, capabilities, and management.

The most important failure was one of imagination. We do not believe leaders understood the gravity of the threat. The terrorist danger from Bin Ladin and al Qaeda was not a major topic for policy debate among the public, the media, or in the Congress. Indeed, it barely came up during the 2000 presidential campaign.

Al Qaeda's new brand of terrorism presented challenges to U.S. governmental institutions that they were not well-designed to meet. Though top officials all said that they understood the danger, there was uncertainty among them as to whether this was just a new and especially venomous version of the ordinary terrorist threat the United States had lived with for decades, or it was indeed radically new, posing a threat beyond any yet experienced.

As late as September 4, 2001, Richard Clarke, the White House staffer long responsible for counterterrorism policy coordination, asserted that the government had not yet made up its mind how to answer the question: "Is al Qida [sic] a big deal?" A week later came the answer.

Policy

Terrorism was not the overriding national security concern for the U.S. government under either the Clinton or the pre-9/11 Bush administration.

The policy challenges were linked to this failure of imagination. Officials in both the Clinton and Bush administrations regarded a full U.S. invasion of Afghanistan as practically inconceivable before 9/11.

Capabilities

Before 9/11, the United States tried to solve the al Qaeda problem with the capabilities it had used in the last stages of the Cold War and its immediate aftermath. The capabilities were insufficient. Little was done to expand or reform them.

The CIA had minimal capacity to conduct paramilitary operations with its own personnel, and it did not seek a large-scale expansion of these capabilities before 9/11. The CIA also needed to improve its capability to collect intelligence from human agents.

At no point before 9/11 was the Department of Defense fully engaged in the mission of countering al Qaeda, even though this was perhaps the most dangerous foreign enemy threatening the United States.

America's homeland defenders faced outward. NORAD itself was barely able to retain any alert bases at all. Its planning scenarios occasionally considered the danger of hijacked aircraft being guided to American targets, but only aircraft that were coming from overseas.

The most serious weakness in agency capabilities were in the domestic arena. The FBI did not have the capability to link the collective knowledge of agents in the field to national priorities. Other domestic agencies deferred to the FBI.

The CIA had minimal capacity to conduct paramilitary operations with its own personnel, and it did not seek a large-scale expansion of these capabilities before 9/11. The CIA also needed to improve its capability to collect intelligence from human agents.

FAA capabilities were weak. Any serious examination of the possibility of a suicide hijacking could have suggested changes to fix glaring vulnerabilities—expanding no-fly lists, searching passengers identified by the CAPPS screening system, deploying federal air marshals domestically, hardening cockpit doors, alerting air crews to a different kind of hijacking possibility than they had been trained to expect. Yet the FAA did not adjust either its own training or training with NORAD to take account of threats other than those experienced in the past.

Management

The missed opportunities to thwart the 9/11 plot were also symptoms of a broader inability to adapt the way government manages problems to the new challenges of the twenty-first century. Action officers should have been able to draw on all available knowledge about al Qaeda in the government. Management should have ensured that information was shared and duties were clearly assigned across agencies, and across the foreign-domestic divide.

There were also broader management issues with respect to how top leaders set priorities and allocated resources. For instance, on December 4, 1998, DCI Tenet issued a directive to several CIA officials and the Deputy Director of Central Intelligence (DDCI) for Community Management, stating: "*We are at war. I want no resources or people spared in this effort, either inside CIA or the Community.*" The memorandum had little overall effect on mobilizing the CIA or the intelligence community. This episode indicates the limitations of the DCI's authority over the direction of the intelligence community, including agencies within the Department of Defense.

The U.S. government did not find a way of pooling intelligence and using it to guide the planning and assignment of responsibilities for joint operations involving entities as disparate as the CIA, the FBI, the State Department, the military, and the agencies involved in homeland security.

Specific Findings

Unsuccessful Diplomacy

Beginning in February 1997, and through September 11, 2001, the U.S. government tried to use diplomatic pressure to persuade the Taliban regime in Afghanistan to stop being a sanctuary for al Qaeda, and to expel Bin Ladin to a country where he could face justice. These efforts included warnings and sanctions, but they all failed.

The U.S. government also pressed two successive Pakistani governments to demand that the Taliban cease providing a sanctuary for Bin Ladin and his organization and, failing that, to cut off their support for the Taliban. Before 9/11, the United States could not find a mix of incentives and pressure that would persuade Pakistan to reconsider its fundamental relationship with the Taliban.

From 1999 through early 2001, the United States pressed the United Arab Emirates, one of the Taliban's only travel and financial outlets to the outside world, to break off ties and enforce sanctions, especially those related to air travel to Afghanistan. These efforts achieved little before 9/11.

Saudi Arabia has been a problematic ally in combating Islamic extremism. Before 9/11, the Saudi and U.S. governments did not fully share intelligence information or develop an adequate joint effort to track and disrupt the finances of the al Qaeda organization. On the other hand, government officials of Saudi Arabia at the highest levels worked closely with top U.S. officials in major initiatives to solve the Bin Ladin problem with diplomacy.

[Senior military officials] did not want to risk significant collateral damage, and they did not want to miss Bin Ladin and thus make the United States look weak while making Bin Ladin look strong.

Lack of Military Options

In response to the request of policymakers, the military prepared an array of limited strike options for attacking Bin Ladin and his organization from May 1998 onward. When they briefed policymakers, the military presented both the pros and cons of those strike options and the associated risks. Policymakers expressed frustration with the range of options presented.

Following the August 20, 1998, missile strikes on al Qaeda targets in Afghanistan and Sudan, both senior military officials and policymakers placed great emphasis on actionable intelligence as the key factor in recommending or deciding to launch military action against Bin Ladin and his organization. They did not want to risk significant collateral damage, and they did not want to miss Bin Ladin and thus make the United States look weak while making Bin Ladin look strong. On three specific occasions in 1998–1999, intelligence was deemed credible enough to warrant planning for possible strikes to kill Bin

Ladin. But in each case the strikes did not go forward, because senior policymakers did not regard the intelligence as sufficiently actionable to offset their assessment of the risks.

The Director of Central Intelligence, policymakers, and military officials expressed frustration with the lack of actionable intelligence. Some officials inside the Pentagon, including those in the special forces and the counterterrorism policy office, also expressed frustration with the lack of military action. The Bush administration began to develop new policies toward al Qaeda in 2001, but military plans did not change until after 9/11.

Problems with the Intelligence Community

The intelligence community struggled throughout the 1990s and up to 9/11 to collect intelligence on and analyze the phenomenon of transnational terrorism. The combination of an overwhelming number of priorities, flat budgets, an outmoded structure, and bureaucratic rivalries resulted in an insufficient response to this new challenge.

The FBI's approach to investigations was case specific, decentralized, and geared towards prosecution.

Many dedicated officers worked day and night for years to piece together the growing body of evidence on al Qaeda and to understand the threats. Yet while there were many reports on Bin Laden and his growing al Qaeda organization, there was no comprehensive review of what the intelligence community knew and what it did not know, and what that meant. There was no National Intelligence Estimate on terrorism between 1995 and 9/11.

Before 9/11, no agency did more to attack al Qaeda than the CIA. But there were limits to what the CIA was able to achieve by disrupting terrorist activities abroad and by using proxies to try to capture Bin Ladin and his lieutenants in Afghanistan. CIA officers were aware of those limitations.

Problems with the FBI

From the time of the first World Trade Center attack in 1993, FBI and Department of Justice leadership in Washington and New York became increasingly concerned about the terrorist threat from Islamist extremists to U.S. interests, both at home and abroad. Throughout the 1990s, the FBI's counterterrorism efforts against international terrorist organizations included both intelligence and criminal investigations. The FBI's approach to investigations was case specific, decentralized, and geared towards prosecution. Significant FBI resources were devoted to after-the-fact investigations of major terrorist attacks, resulting in several prosecutions.

The FBI attempted several reform efforts aimed at strengthening its ability to prevent such attacks, but these reform efforts failed to implement organization-wide institutional change. On September 11, 2001, the FBI was limited in several areas critical to an effective preventive counterterrorism strategy. Those working counterterrorism matters did so despite limited intelligence collection and strategic analysis capabilities, limited capacity to share information both internally and externally, insufficient training, perceived legal barriers to sharing information, and inadequate resources.

Permeable Borders and Immigration Controls

There were opportunities for intelligence and law enforcement to exploit al Qaeda's travel vulnerabilities. Considered collectively, the 9/11 hijackers:

- included known al Qaeda operatives who could have been watchlisted;
- presented passports manipulated in a fraudulent manner;
- presented passports with suspicious indicators of extremism;
- made detectable false statements on visa applications;
- made false statements to border officials to gain entry into the United States; and
- violated immigration laws while in the United States.

Neither the State Department's consular officers nor the Immigration and Naturalization Service's inspectors and agents were ever considered full partners in a national counterterrorism effort. Protecting borders was not a national security issue before 9/11.

Permeable Aviation Security

Protecting borders was not a national security issue before 9/11.

Hijackers studied publicly available materials on the aviation security system and used items that had less metal content than a handgun and were most likely permissible. Though two of the hijackers were on the U.S. TIPOFF terrorist watchlist, the FAA did not use TIPOFF data. The hijackers had to beat only one layer of security—the security checkpoint process. Even though several hijackers were selected for extra screening by the CAPPS system, this led only to greater scrutiny of their checked baggage. Once on board, the hijackers were faced with aircraft personnel who were trained to be nonconfrontational in the event of a hijacking.

Financing

The 9/11 attacks cost somewhere between $400,000 and $500,000 to execute. The operatives spent more than $270,000 in the United States. Additional expenses included travel to obtain passports and visas, travel to the United States, expenses incurred by the plot leader and facilitators outside the United States, and expenses incurred by the people selected to be hijackers who ultimately did not participate.

The conspiracy made extensive use of banks in the United States. The hijackers opened accounts in their own names, using passports and other identification documents. Their transactions were unremarkable and essentially invisible amid the billions of dollars flowing around the world every day.

To date, the origin of the money used for the 9/11 attacks has not been determined. Al Qaeda had many sources of funding and a pre-9/11 annual budget estimated at $30 million. If a particular source of funds had dried up, al Qaeda could easily have found enough money elsewhere to fund the attack.

An Improvised Homeland Defense

The civilian and military defenders of the nation's airspace—FAA and NORAD—were unprepared for the attacks launched against them. Given that lack of preparedness, they attempted and failed to improvise an effective homeland defense against an unprecedented challenge.

The events of that morning do not reflect discredit on operational personnel. NORAD's Northeast Air Defense Sector personnel reached out for information and made the best judgments they could based on information they received. Individual FAA controllers, facility managers, and command center managers were creative and agile in recommending a nationwide alert, ground-stopping local traffic, ordering all aircraft nationwide to land, and executing that unprecedented order flawlessly.

At more senior levels, communication was poor. Senior military and FAA leaders had no effective communication with each other. The chain of command did not function well. The President could not reach some senior officials. The Secretary of Defense did not enter the chain of command until the morning's key events were over. Air National Guard units with different rules of engagement were scrambled without the knowledge of the President, NORAD, or the National Military Command Center.

Effective decision making in New York was hampered by problems in command and control and in internal communications.

Emergency Response

The civilians, firefighters, police officers, emergency medical technicians, and emergency management professionals exhibited steady determination and resolve under horrifying, overwhelming conditions on 9/11. Their actions saved lives and inspired a nation.

Effective decision making in New York was hampered by problems in command and control and in internal communications. Within the Fire Department of New York, this was true for several reasons: the magnitude of the incident was unforeseen; commanders had difficulty communicating with their units; more units were actually dispatched than were ordered by the chiefs; some units self-dispatched; and once units arrived at the World Trade Center, they were neither comprehensively accounted for nor coordinated. The Port Authority's response was hampered by the lack both of standard operating procedures and of radios capable of enabling multiple commands to respond to an incident in unified fashion. The New York Police Department, because of its history of mobilizing thousands of officers for major events requiring crowd control, had a technical capability and protocols more easily adapted to an incident of the magnitude of 9/11.

Congress

The Congress, like the executive branch, responded slowly to the rise of transnational terrorism as a threat to national security. The legislative branch adjusted little and did not restructure itself to address changing threats. Its attention to terrorism was episodic and splintered across several committees. The Congress gave little guidance to executive branch agencies on terrorism, did not reform them in any significant way to meet the threat, and did not systematically perform robust oversight to identify, address, and attempt to resolve the many problems in national security and domestic agencies that became apparent in the aftermath of 9/11.[1]

Conclusion

In pursuing its mandate, the 9/11 Commission reviewed more than 2.5 million pages of documents and interviewed more than 1,200 individuals in ten countries, including nearly every senior official from the Bush and Clinton administrations. Their aim was not to assign individual blame, but to provide the fullest possible account of the events surrounding 9/11 and to identify lessons learned.

The Commission learned about an enemy who is sophisticated, patient, disciplined, and lethal. The enemy rallies broad support in the Arab and Muslim world demanding redress of political grievances, but its hostility toward the United States and American values is limitless. Its purpose is to rid the world of religious and political pluralism, the plebiscite, and equal rights for women. It makes no distinction between military and civilian targets. Collateral damage is not in its lexicon.

The Commission learned that the institutions charged with protecting the nation's borders, civil aviation, and national security did not understand how grave this threat could be, and did not adjust their policies, plans, and practices to deter or defeat it. The Commission learned about fault lines within our government – between foreign and domestic intelligence, and between and within agencies. It learned of the pervasive problems of managing and sharing information across a large and unwieldy government that had been built in a different era to confront different dangers.

In chronicling the terrible losses in its report, the Commission strove to create something positive – an America that is safer, stronger, and wiser.[2]

Questions

1. Why should the events of 9-11 have been anticipated?
2. Why didn't the DoD and CIA stop Bin Ladin in Afghanistan?
3. How was al Qaeda able to elude the FBI, NORAD, and CIA?
4. List some of the failures of the FAA on 9-11.
5. How were fire and rescue operations hindered on 9-11?

Chapter 4

Terrorist Threat

Objectives

- Describe the history of terrorism.
- Know the definition of terrorism according to the National Strategy for Homeland Security.
- Discuss changing terrorist tactics that made terrorism a significant threat.
- Understand the motives and objectives of terrorists.
- Summarize the al Qaeda threat.
- Explain the ultimate threat posed by terrorism today.

Introduction

September 11th 2001 was a wakeup call to the American public that the United States isn't immune to the effects of international terrorism. The American government, aware of the threat, was nonetheless unprepared for what happened. To prevent it from happening again, the president signed the Homeland Security Act establishing the Department of Homeland Security, November 25th 2002.[1]

Historical Perspective

Terrorism has been practiced throughout history and throughout the world. The ancient Greek historian Xenophon (c. 431 - c. 350 BC) wrote of the effectiveness of psychological warfare against enemy populations. Roman emperors such as Tiberius (reigned AD 14 - 37) and Caligula (reigned AD 37 - 41) used banishment, expropriation of property, and execution as means to discourage opposition to their rule.[2]

"Terrorism: Any premeditated, unlawful act dangerous to human life or public welfare that is intended to intimidate or coerce civilian populations or governments."

– National Strategy for Homeland Security, July 2002

The word 'terrorism' entered into European languages in the wake of the French revolution of 1789. In the early revolutionary years, it was largely by violence that governments in Paris tried to impose their radical new order on reluctant citizenry. As a result, the first meaning of the word 'terrorism', as recorded by the Academie Francaise in 1798, was 'system or rule of terror'.[3]

Today, there's no single, universally accepted, definition of terrorism.[4] The National Strategy for Homeland Security characterizes terrorism as:

> *"Any premeditated, unlawful act dangerous to human life or public welfare that is intended to intimidate or coerce civilian populations or governments."*
>
> *– National Strategy for Homeland Security, July 2002*

During the 19th century, terrorism underwent a fateful transformation, coming to be associated, as it still is today, with non-governmental groups. One such group—the small band of Russian revolutionaries of 'Narodnaya Volya' (the people's will) in 1878-81—developed certain ideas that were to become the hallmark of subsequent terrorism in many countries. They believed in the targeted killing of the 'leaders of oppression'; they were convinced that the developing technologies of the age—symbolized by bombs and bullets—enabled them to strike directly and discriminately. Above all, they believed that the Tsarist system against which they were fighting was fundamentally rotten. They propagated what has remained the common terrorist delusion that violent acts would spark off revolution. Their efforts led to the assassination of Tsar Alexander II on 13 March 1881—but that event failed completely to have the revolutionary effects of which the terrorists had dreamed.

Terrorism continued for many decades to be associated primarily with the assassination of political leaders and heads of state. In general, the extensive practice of assassination in the 20th century seldom had the particular effects for which the terrorists hoped.

In the half-century after World War Two, terrorism broadened well beyond assassination of political leaders and heads of state. In certain European colonies, terrorist movements developed, often with two distinct purposes. The first was obvious: to put pressure on the colonial powers (such as Britain, France, and the Netherlands) to hasten their withdrawal. The second was more subtle: to intimidate the indigenous population into supporting a particular group's claims to leadership of the emerging post-colonial state. Sometimes these strategies had some success, but not always. India's achievement of independence in 1947 was mainly the result, not of terrorism, but of the movement of non-violent civil disobedience led by Gandhi. In Malaya, communist terrorists launched a major campaign in 1948 but they failed due to a mixture of determined British military opposition and a program of political reform leading to independence.

Terrorism did not disappear as European nations relinquished their colonial holdings in the 1950s and 1960s. It continued in many regions in response to many circumstances. In South-East Asia, the Middle East and Latin America there were killings of policemen and local officials, hostage-takings, hijackings of aircraft, and bombings of buildings. In many actions, civilians became targets. In some cases governments became involved in supporting terrorism, almost invariably at arm's length so as to be deniable. The causes espoused by terrorists encompassed not just revolutionary socialism and nationalism, but also in a few cases religious doctrines. Law, even the modest body of rules setting some limits in armed conflict between states, could be ignored in a higher cause.

Change in Tactics

How did certain terrorist movements come to be associated with indiscriminate killings? When in September 1970 Palestinian terrorists hijacked several large aircraft and blew them up on the ground in Jordan but let the passengers free, these acts were viewed by many with as much fascination as horror. Then in September 1972, eleven Israelis were murdered in a Palestinian attack on Israeli athletes at the Olympic Games at Munich. This event showed a determination to kill: the revulsion felt in many countries was stronger than two years earlier.[5]

The terrorist attacks of the 1970s and 1980s had clear political objectives. These attacks resulted in just enough bloodshed and loss of life to gain attention to the terrorists' cause yet not enough to alienate them from the public support they sought. Bombings, kidnappings, and aircraft hijacking were accomplished by declared, identifiable groups with specific political goals in mind.

In contrast, the decade of the 1990s produced a different type of terrorism—terrorism designed to produce massive casualties with little regard for distinct political goals and often no claims of responsibility.[6] The change in tactics was noted with great concern by William Studeman, acting director of the Central Intelligence Agency, in 1995 testimony before Congress:

In contrast, the decade of the 1990s produced a different type of terrorism—terrorism designed to produce massive casualties with little regard for distinct political goals and often no claims of responsibility.

"Mr. Chairman, we have seen a most disturbing change in the nature of the terrorist threat over the recent past, and this change will make the world an increasingly dangerous place for Americans. In general, international terrorists today are focusing less on hostage-taking and hijackings and more on the indiscriminate slaughter of innocent men, women, and children. Although the number of international terrorist incidents has decreased over the past 10 years, the trend is toward a higher number of civilian casualties, more extensive property damage, and increasingly devastating effects on economies."

—Testimony of Acting DCI William O. Studeman, Omnibus Counter-terrorism Act of 1995, April 6, 1995

As evidence of the new trend, Mr. Studeman cited the 1993 bombing of the World Trade center that resulted in six deaths and over 1,000 injuries, the 1994 bombing of a Jewish cultural center in Buenos Aires that left nearly 100 dead and over 250 wounded, and the 1995 gassing in the Tokyo subway that killed 10 people and injured 5,500 more.[7]

In 1996, Saudi dissidents killed 19 U.S. airmen and wounded 240 others in attacks against the Khobar Towers barracks in Dahran Saudi Arabia. In 1998, simultaneous attacks against U.S. embassies in Nairobi, Kenya, and Dar es Salaam, Tanzania, killed 224 and wounded 4,500 more.[8]

Mass Casualties

Alarmed by the growing ferocity of terrorist attacks, Congress in 1998 established the National Commission on Terrorism. In a report issued June 5th 2000, the NTC attributed the trend toward higher casualties, in part on the changing motivation of terrorists:

"Religiously motivated terrorist groups, such as Usama bin Ladin's group, al-Qaida, which is believed to have bombed the U.S. Embassies in Africa, represent a growing trend toward hatred of the United States. Other terrorists groups are driven by visions of a post apocalyptic future or by ethnic hatred. Such groups may lack a concrete political goal other than to punish enemies by killing as many of them as possible, seemingly without concern about alienating sympathizers. Increasingly, attacks are less likely to be followed by claims of responsibility or lists of political demands."

—Countering the Changing Threat of International Terrorism, Report of the National Commission on Terrorism, June 5, 2000

While the NTC highlighted the growing threat represented by extremist Islamic groups, it also noted not all terrorist acts are religiously motivated nor perpetrated by foreign nationals. In April 1995 the Alfred P. Murrah Federal Building in Oklahoma City was destroyed by a car bomb killing 168 innocent civilians. Timothy McVeigh, a Gulf War veteran, was arrested by an Oklahoma Highway Patrolman within an hour of the explosion. At his trial, the United States Government asserted that the motivation for the attack was to avenge the deaths of Branch Davidians at Waco, Texas, whom McVeigh believed had been murdered by agents of the federal government.[9]

Classifying Terrorism

The Federal Bureau of Investigation distinguishes between domestic and international terrorism, depending on the origin, base, and objectives of the terrorist organization:

> *"Domestic terrorism is the unlawful use, or threatened use, of force or violence by a group or individual based and operating entirely within the United States or Puerto Rico without foreign direction, committed against persons or property to intimidate or coerce a government, the civilian population, or any segment thereof in furtherance of political or social objectives.*
>
> *International terrorism involves violent acts or acts dangerous to human life that are a violation of the criminal laws of the United States or any state, or that would be a criminal violation if committed within the jurisdiction of the United States or any state. These acts appear to be intended to intimidate or coerce a civilian population, influence the policy of a government by intimidation or coercion, or affect the conduct of a government by assassination or kidnapping. International terrorist acts occur outside the United States, or transcend national boundaries in terms of the means by which they are accomplished, the persons they appear intended to coerce, or the locale in which their perpetrators operate or seek asylum."*
>
> *—Federal Bureau of Investigation, Terrorism in the United States, 1998*

Although terrorism is defined in different ways by various U.S. government agencies, it is generally accepted that terrorism is a crime designed to coerce others into actions they would not otherwise take or into refraining from actions that they desire to take. Today's terrorists, like their predecessors, seek to instill fear, undermine government authority, and possibly goad the government into overreacting to the incident or threat. What has changed in the past decade is the willingness of the terrorist to inflict indiscriminate casualties. The possible inclusion of weapons of mass destruction in the terrorists' arsenal now makes this an even more dangerous proposition.[10]

Although terrorism is defined in different ways by various U.S. government agencies, it is generally accepted that terrorism is a crime designed to coerce others into actions they would not otherwise take or into refraining from actions that they desire to take.

al Qaeda

The attacks of September 11th 2001 were perpetrated by international terrorists and members of an extreme Islamic group known as al Qaeda founded by Saudi dissident Osama bin Laden.

In the 1980s, young Muslims from around the world went to Afghanistan to join as volunteers in a jihad (or holy struggle) against the Soviet Union. A wealthy Saudi, Osama bin Laden, was one of them. Following the defeat of the Soviets in the late 1980s, bin Laden and others formed al Qaeda ("the base") to mobilize jihads elsewhere.

The history, culture, and body of beliefs from which bin Laden shapes and spreads his message are largely unknown to many Americans. Seizing on symbols of Islam's past greatness, he promises to restore pride to people who consider themselves the victims of successive foreign masters. He uses cultural and religious allusions to the holy Qur'an and some of its interpreters. He appeals to people disoriented by cyclonic changes as they confront modernity and globalization. His rhetoric selectively draws from multiple sources—Islam, history, and the region's political and economic malaise.

Bin Laden also stresses grievances against the United States widely shared in the Muslim world. He inveighed against the presence of U.S. troops in Saudi Arabia, which is the home of Islam's holiest sites, and against other U.S. policies in the Middle East.

Upon this political and ideological foundation, Bin Laden built over the course of a decade a dynamic and lethal organization. He built an infrastructure and organization in Afghanistan that could attract, train, and use recruits against ever more ambitious targets. He rallied new zealots and new money with each demonstration of al Qaeda's capability. He forged a close alliance with the Taliban, a regime providing sanctuary for al Qaeda.

Since 9/11, the United States and its allies have killed or captured a majority of al Qaeda's leadership, toppled the Taliban, which gave al Qaeda sanctuary in Afghanistan; and severely damaged the organization. Yet terrorist attacks continue. Even as we have thwarted attacks, nearly everyone expects they will come. How can this be?

Killing or capturing [Bin Laden], while extremely important, would not end terror. His message of inspiration to a new generation of terrorists would continue.

The problem is that al Qaeda represents an ideological movement, not a finite group of people. It initiates and inspires, even if it no longer directs. In this way it has transformed itself into a decentralized force. Bin Laden may be limited in his ability to organize major attacks from his hideouts. Yet killing or capturing him, while extremely important, would not end terror. His message of inspiration to a new generation of terrorists would continue.[11]

The Terrorist Threat

Although many analysts agree that terrorists are most likely to use conventional explosives, their use of a WMD in the U.S. is now seen as a possibility.[12]

Writing before September 11th, 2001, the United States Commission on National Security/21st Century stated:

> *"The combination of unconventional weapons proliferation with the persistence of international terrorism will end the relative invulnerability of the U.S. homeland to catastrophic attack. A direct attack against American citizens on American soil is likely over the next quarter century."*
>
> *—U.S. Commission on National Security/21st Century, February 15, 2001*

Until recently, terrorism to many Americans was a remote, if frightening possibility that affected only individuals or groups outside the territorial boundaries of the United States. Events of the past decade indicate that the terrorist threat has changed significantly in ways that make it more dangerous and more difficult to counter. Although terrorists have long intended to harm the public, now they may posses much greater capabilities to do so.[13]

In December 2000, the Central Intelligence Agency and the National Intelligence Council forecast the following trends that may affect the future of the United States:

> *"Asymmetric threats in which state and non-state adversaries avoid direct engagements with the US military but devise strategies, tactics, and weapons—some improved by "sidewise" technology—to minimize US strengths and exploit perceived weaknesses.*
>
> *Internal conflicts stemming from religious, ethnic or political disputes will remain at current numbers or even increase in number.*
>
> *Prospects will grow that more sophisticated weaponry, including weapons of mass destruction—indigenously produced or externally acquired—will get into the hands of state and non-state belligerents, some hostile to the United States. The likelihood will increase over this period that WMD will be used either against the United States or its forces, facilities, and interests overseas.*
>
> *Chemical and biological threats to the United States will become more widespread; such capabilities are easier to develop, hide, and deploy than nuclear weapons. Some terrorists or insurgents will attempt to use such weapons against US interests—against the United States itself, its forces or facilities overseas, or its allies."*
>
> *—Central Intelligence Agency, Global Trends 2015, December 2000*

Post-9/11 Radicalization

While terrorism has been with us for centuries, the destructive power and global reach of modern terrorism is unprecedented. If the post-September 11th world has taught us anything, it is that the tools for conducting serious terrorist attacks are becoming easier to acquire. Therefore intention becomes an increasingly important factor in the formation of terrorist cells.[14]

In the immediate aftermath of September 11, the United States military and law enforcement captured, killed, or scattered much of al Qaeda's core leadership— eliminating its sanctuary and training camps in Afghanistan. As a result, the threat from the central core of al Qaeda was significantly diminished.

However, as al Qaeda's central core of leaders, operatives, and foot soldiers shrunk, its philosophy of global jihad spread worldwide at an exponential rate via radical Internet websites and chat rooms, extremist videotapes and literature, radical speeches by extremist imams—often creating a radical subculture within the more vulnerable Muslim diaspora communities.

In the years since 2001, the attacks of September 11 stand out as both the hallmark al Qaeda attack as well as the singular exception. Bali [2002], Casablanca [2003], Madrid [2004], and London [2005] all fit a different paradigm. The individuals who conducted the attacks were for the most part all citizens or residents of the states in which the attacks occurred. Although a few may have received training in al Qaeda camps, the great majority did not. While al Qaeda claimed responsibility for each attack after the fact, these attacks were not under the command and control of al Qaeda central, nor were they specifically funded by al Qaeda central. Rather, they were conducted by local al Qaeda inspired affiliate organizations or by local residents/citizens, who utilized al Qaeda as their ideological inspiration.[15]

While the threat from overseas remains, many of the terrorist attacks or thwarted plots against cities in Europe, Canada, Australia and the United States have been conceptualized and planned by local residents/citizens who sought to attack their country of residence. The majority of these individuals began as "unremarkable" - they had "unremarkable" jobs, had lived "unremarkable" lives and had little, if any criminal history.[16]

Where once we would have defined the initial indicator of the threat at the point where a terrorist or group of terrorists would actually plan an attack, we have now shifted our focus to a much earlier point—a point where we believe the potential terrorist or group of terrorists begin and progress through a process of radicalization. The culmination of this process is a terrorist attack.

Understanding this trend and the radicalization process in the West that drives "unremarkable"people to become terrorists is vital for developing effective counterstrategies. [17]

Conclusion

The consequences of failing to deter, detect, or preempt terrorist attacks, some possibly with WMD, would be devastating. In addition to the tragedy of hundreds of thousands of dead and injured citizens, the long and lasting serious economic and psychological damage to American society could well prove to be the terrorists' greatest victory.[18]

Questions

1. How long has terrorism existed?
2. How was the term "terrorism" originally applied?
3. How did terrorism evolve over time?
4. List some of the motives of modern terrorists.
5. How have terrorist objectives changed since 1995?
6. Would terrorism end if Bin Laden was captured?
7. What is the ultimate threat posed by terrorism today?

Chapter 5

Islamic Extremism

Objectives

- Discuss the history of Islam.
- Know the two major sects of Islam.
- Describe the political evolution of Islamic states.
- Understand the minority views of fundamental Islamists.
- Discuss the appeal of al Qaeda in the Muslim world.
- Explain Bin Ladin's objective.

Introduction

Islam is not the enemy. It is not synonymous with terror. Nor does Islam teach terror. Lives guided by religious faith, including literal beliefs in holy scriptures, are common to every religion, and represent no threat. The following dissertation excerpted from the "9/11 Report" examines Islamic extremism representing a minority of "violent zealots" following what the 9/11 Commission calls a "perversion of Islam".

A Declaration of War

In February 1998, the 40-year-old Saudi exile Usama Bin Ladin and a fugitive Egyptian physician, Ayman al Zawahiri, arranged from their Afghan headquarters for an Arabic newspaper in London to publish what they termed a fatwa issued in the name of a "World Islamic Front." A fatwa is normally an interpretation of Islamic law by a respected Islamic authority, but neither Bin Ladin, Zawahiri, nor the three others who signed this statement were scholars of Islamic law. Claiming that America had declared war against God and his messenger, they called for the murder of any American, anywhere on earth, as the "individual duty for every Muslim who can do it in any country in which it is possible to do it."

Islam is not the enemy. It is not synonymous with terror. Nor does Islam teach terror.

Three months later, when interviewed in Afghanistan by ABC-TV, Bin Ladin enlarged on these themes. He claimed it was more important for Muslims to kill Americans than to kill other infidels. *"It is far better for anyone to kill a single American soldier than to squander his efforts on other activities,"* he said. Asked whether he approved of terrorism and of attacks on civilians, he replied: *"We believe that the worst thieves in the world today and the worst terrorists are the Americans. Nothing can stop you except perhaps retaliation in kind. We do not have to differentiate between military or civilians. As far as we are concerned, they are all targets."*

Though novel for its open endorsement of indiscriminate killing, Bin Ladin's 1998 declaration was only the latest in the long series of his public and private calls since 1992 that singled out the United States for attack.

In August 1996, Bin Ladin had issued his own self-styled fatwa calling on Muslims to drive American soldiers out of Saudi Arabia. The long, disjointed document condemned the Saudi monarchy for allowing the presence of an army of infidels in a land with the sites most sacred to Islam, and celebrated recent suicide bombings of American military facilities in the Kingdom. It praised the 1983 suicide bombing in Beirut that killed 241 U.S. Marines, the 1992 bombing in Aden, and especially the 1993 firefight in Somalia after which the United States "left the area carrying disappointment, humiliation, defeat and your dead with you."

Bin Ladin said in his ABC interview that he and his followers had been preparing in Somalia for another long struggle, like that against the Soviets in Afghanistan, but *"the United States rushed out of Somalia in shame and disgrace."* Citing the Soviet army's withdrawal from Afghanistan as proof that a ragged army of dedicated Muslims could overcome a superpower, he told the interviewer: "*We are certain that we shall—with the grace of Allah—prevail over the Americans.*" He went on to warn that "*If the present injustice continues..., it will inevitably move the battle to American soil.*"

Plans to attack the United States were developed with unwavering singlemindedness throughout the 1990s. Bin Ladin saw himself as called "to follow in the footsteps of the Messenger and to communicate his message to all nations," and to serve as the rallying point and organizer of a new kind of war to destroy America and bring the world to Islam.

Bin Ladin's Appeal in the Islamic World

It is the story of eccentric and violent ideas sprouting in the fertile ground of political and social turmoil. It is the story of an organization poised to seize its historical moment. How did Bin Ladin—with his call for the indiscriminate killing of Americans—win thousands of followers and some degree of approval from millions more?

The history, culture, and body of beliefs from which Bin Ladin has shaped and spread his message are largely unknown to many Americans. Seizing on symbols of Islam's past greatness, he promises to restore pride to people who consider themselves the victims of successive foreign masters. He uses cultural and religious allusions to the holy Qur'an and some of its interpreters. He appeals to people disoriented by cyclonic change as they confront modernity and globalization. His rhetoric selectively draws from multiple sources—Islam, history, and the region's political and economic malaise. He also stresses grievances against the Untied States widely shared in the Muslim world. He inveighed against the presence of U.S. troops in Saudi Arabia, the home of Islam's holiest sites. He spoke of the suffering of the Iraqi people as a result of sanctions imposed after the Gulf War, and he protested U.S. support for Israel.

Islam is divided into two main branches, Sunni and Shia. Shia hold that any leader of the Ummah must be a direct descendant of the Prophet; Sunni argue that lineal descent is not required if the candidate meets other standards of faith and knowledge.

Islam

Islam (a word that literally means "surrender to the will of God") arose in Arabia with what Muslims believe are a series of revelations to the Prophet Mohammed from the one and only God, the God of Abraham and of Jesus. These revelations, conveyed by the angel Gabriel, are recorded in the Qur'an. Muslims believe that these revelations, given to the greatest and last of a chain of prophets stretching from Abraham through Jesus, complete God's message to humanity. The Hadith, which recount Mohammed's sayings and deeds as recorded by his contemporaries, are another fundamental source. A third key element is the Sharia, the code of law derived from the Qur'an and the Hadith.

Islam is divided into two main branches, Sunni and Shia. Soon after the Prophet's death, the question of choosing a new leader, or caliph, for the Muslim community, or "Ummah", arose. Initially, his successors could be drawn from the Prophet's contemporaries, but with time, this was no longer possible. Those who became the Shia held that any leader of the Ummah must be a direct descendant of the Prophet; those who became the Sunni argued that lineal descent was not required if the candidate met other standards of faith and knowledge. After bloody struggles, the Sunni became (and remain) the majority sect. (The Shia are dominant in Iran.) The Caliphate—the institutionalized leadership of the Ummah—thus was a Sunni institution that continued until 1924, first under Arab and eventually under Ottoman Turkish control.

Many Muslims look back at the century after the revelations to the Prophet Mohammed as a golden age. Its memory is strongest among the Arabs. What happened then—the spread of Islam from the Arabian Peninsula throughout the Middle East, North Africa, and even into Europe within less than a century—seemed, and seems, miraculous. Nostalgia for Islam's past glory remains a powerful force.

Islam is both a faith and a code of conduct for all aspects of life. For many Muslims, a good government would be one guided by the moral principles of their faith. This does not necessarily translate into a desire for clerical rule and the abolition of a secular state. It does mean that some Muslims tend to be uncomfortable with distinctions between religion and state, though Muslim rulers throughout history have readily separated the two.

To extremists, however, such divisions, as well as the existence of parliaments and legislation, only prove these rulers to be false Muslims usurping God's authority over all aspects of life. Periodically, the Islamic world has seen surges of what, for want of a better term, is often labeled "fundamentalism." Denouncing waywardness among the faithful, some clerics have appealed for a return to observance of the literal teachings of the Qur'an and Hadith. One scholar from the fourteenth century from who Bin Ladin selectively quotes, Ibn Taimiyyah, condemned both corrupt rulers and clerics who failed to criticize them. He urged Muslims to read the Qur'an and the Hadith for themselves, not to depend solely on learned interpreters like himself but to hold one another to account for the quality of their observance.

The extreme Islamist version of history blames the decline from Islam's golden age on the rulers and people who turned away from the true path of their religion, thereby leaving Islam vulnerable to encroaching foreign powers eager to steal their land, wealth, and even their souls.

Despite his claims to universal leadership, Bin Ladin offers an extreme view of Islamic history designed to appeal mainly to Arabs and Sunnis. He draws on fundamentalists who blame the eventual destruction of the Caliphate on leaders who abandoned the pure path of religious devotion.

Bin Ladin's Worldview

Despite his claims to universal leadership, Bin Ladin offers an extreme view of Islamic history designed to appeal mainly to Arabs and Sunnis. He draws on fundamentalists who blame the eventual destruction of the Caliphate on leaders who abandoned the pure path of religious devotion. He repeatedly calls on his followers to embrace martyrdom since "the walls of oppression and humiliation cannot be demolished except in a rain of bullets." For those yearning for a lost sense of order in an older, more tranquil world, he offers his "Caliphate" as an imagined alternative to today's uncertainty. For others, he offers simplistic conspiracies to explain their world.

Bin Ladin also relies heavily on the Egyptian writer Sayyid Qutb. A member of the Muslim Brotherhood executed in 1966, Qutb mixed Islamic scholarship with a very superficial acquaintance with Western history and thought. Sent by the Egyptian government to study in the United States in the late 1940s, Qutb returned with an enormous loathing of Western society and history. He dismissed Western achievements as entirely material, arguing that Western society possesses "nothing that will satisfy its own conscience and justify its existence."

Three basic themes emerge from Qutb's writings. First, he claimed that the world was beset with barbarism, licentiousness, and unbelief (a condition he called "jahiliyya", the religious term for the period of ignorance prior to the revelations given to the Prophet Mohammed). Qutb argued that humans can choose only between Islam and jahiliyya. Second, he warned that more people, including Muslims, were attracted to jahilyya and its material comforts that to his view of Islam; jahiliyya could therefore triumph over Islam. Third, no middle ground exists in what Qutb conceived as a struggle between God and Satan. All Muslims—as he defined them—therefore must take up arms in this fight. Any Muslim who rejects his ideas is just one more nonbeliever worthy of destruction.

Bin Ladin shares Qutb's view, permitting him and his followers to rationalize even unprovoked mass murder as righteous defense of an embattled faith. Many Americans have wondered, "Why do 'they' hate us?" Some also ask, "What can we do to stop these attacks?"

Some ask "What can we do to stop these attacks?" Al Qaeda answers that America should abandon the Middle East, convert to Islam, and end the immorality and godlessness of its society and culture

Bin Ladin and al Qaeda have given answers to both these questions. To the first, they say that America had attacked Islam; America is responsible for all conflicts involving Muslims. Thus Americans are blamed when Israelis fight with Palestinians, when Russians fight with Chechens, when Indians fight with Kashmiri Muslims, and when the Philippine government fights ethnic Muslims in its southern islands. America is also held responsible for the governments of Muslim countries, derided by al Qaeda as "your agents." Bin Ladin has stated flatly, *"Our fight against these governments is not separate from our fight against you."* These charges found a ready audience among millions of Arabs and Muslims angry at the United States because of issues ranging from Iraq to Palestine to America's support for their countries' repressive rulers.

Bin Ladin's grievance with the United States may have started in reaction to specific U.S. policies but it quickly became far deeper. To the second question, what America could do, al Qaeda's answer was that America should abandon the Middle East, convert to Islam, and end the immorality and godlessness of its society and culture: *"It is saddening to tell you that you are the worst civilization witnessed by the history of mankind." If the United States did not comply, it would be at war with the Islamic nation, a nation that al Qaeda's leaders said "desires death more than you desire life."*

History and Political Context

Few fundamentalist movements in the Islamic world gained lasting political power. In the nineteenth and twentieth centuries, fundamentalists helped articulate anticolonial grievances but played little role in the overwhelmingly secular struggles for independence after World War I. Western-educated lawyers, soldiers, and officials led most independence movements, and clerical influence and traditional culture were seen as obstacles to national progress.

After gaining independence from Western powers following World War II, the Arab Middle East followed an arc from initial pride and optimism to today's mix of indifference, cynicism, and despair. In several countries, a dynastic state already existed or was quickly established under a paramount tribal family. Monarchies in countries such as Saudi Arabia, Morocco, and Jordan still survive today. Those in Egypt, Libya, Iraq, and Yemen were eventually overthrown by secular nationalist revolutionaries.

The secular regimes promised a glowing future, often tied to sweeping ideologies (such as those promoted by Egyptian President Gamal Abdel Nasser's Arab Socialism or the Ba'ath Party of Syria and Iraq) that called for a single, secular Arab state. However, what emerged were almost invariably autocratic regimes that were usually unwilling to tolerate any opposition—even in countries, such as Egypt, that had a parliamentary tradition. Over time, their policies—repression, rewards, emigration, and the displacement of popular anger onto scapegoats (generally foreign—were shaped by the desire to cling to power.

The bankruptcy of secular, autocratic nationalism was evident across the Muslim world by the late 1970s. At the same time, these regimes had closed off nearly all paths for peaceful opposition, forcing their critics to choose silence, exile, or violent opposition. Iran's 1979 revolution swept a Shia theocracy into power. Its success encouraged Sunni fundamentalists elsewhere.

In the 1980s, awash in sudden oil wealth, Saudi Arabia competed with Shia Iran to promote its Sunni fundamentalist interpretation of Islam, Wahhabism. The Saudi government, always conscious of its duties as the custodian of Islam's holiest places, joined with wealthy Arabs from the Kingdom and other states bordering the Persian Gulf in donating money to build mosques and religious schools that could preach and teach their interpretation of Islamic doctrine.

In this competition for legitimacy, secular regimes had no alternative to offer. Instead, in a number of cases their rulers sought to buy off local Islamist movements by ceding control of many social and educational issues. Emboldened rather than satisfied, the Islamists continued to push for power—a trend especially clear in Egypt. Confronted with a violent Islamist movement that killed President Anwar Sadat in 1981, the Egyptian government combined harsh repression of Islamic militants with harassment of moderate Islamic scholars and authors, driving many into exile. In Pakistan, a military regime sought to justify its seizure of power by a pious public stance and an embrace of unprecedented Islamist influence on education and society.

These experiments in political Islam faltered during the 1990s: the Iranian revolution lost momentum, prestige, and public support, and Pakistan's rulers found that most of its population had little enthusiasm for fundamentalist Islam. Islamist revival movements gained followers across the Muslim world, but failed to secure political power except in Iran and Sudan. In Algeria, where in 1991 Islamists seemed almost certain to win power through the ballot box, the military preempted their victory, triggering a brutal civil war that continues today. Opponents of today's rulers have few, if any, ways to participate in the existing political system. They are thus a ready audience for calls to Muslims to purify their society, reject unwelcome modernization, and adhere strictly to Sharia.

Social and Economic Malaise

In the 1970s and 1980s, an unprecedented flood of wealth led the then largely unmodernized oil states to attempt to shortcut decades of development. They funded huge infrastructure projects, vastly expanded education, and created subsidized social welfare programs. These programs established a widespread feeling of entitlement without a corresponding sense of social obligations. By the late 1980s, diminishing oil revenues, the economic drain from many unprofitable development projects, and population growth made these entitlement programs unsustainable. The resulting cutbacks created enormous resentment among recipients who had come to see government largesse as their right. This resentment was further stoked by public understanding of how much oil income had gone straight into the pockets of the rulers, their friends, and their helpers.

Unlike the oil states (or Afghanistan, where real economic development has barely begun), the other Arab nations and Pakistan once had seemed headed toward balanced modernization. The established commercial, financial, and industrial sectors in these states, supported by entrepreneurial spirit and widespread understanding of free enterprise, augured well. But unprofitable heavy industry, state monopolies, and opaque bureaucracies slowly stifled growth. More importantly, these state-centered regimes placed their highest priority on preserving the elite's grip on national wealth. Unwilling to foster dynamic economies that could create jobs attractive to educated young men, the countries became economically stagnant and reliant on the safety valve of worker emigration either to the Arab oil states or to the West. Furthermore, the repression and isolation of women in many Muslim countries has not only seriously limited individual opportunity but also crippled overall economic productivity.

By the 1990s, high birthrates and declining rates of infant mortality had produced a common problem throughout the Muslim world: a large, steadily increasing population of young men without any reasonable expectation of suitable or steady employment—a sure prescription for social turbulence.

By the 1990s, high birthrates and declining rates of infant mortality had produced a common problem throughout the Muslim world: a large, steadily increasing population of young men without any reasonable expectation of suitable or steady employment—a sure prescription for social turbulence. Many of these young men, such as the enormous number trained only in religious schools, lacked the skills needed by their societies. Far more acquired valuable skills but lived in stagnant economies that could not generate satisfying jobs.

Millions, pursuing secular as well as religious studies, were products of educational systems that generally devoted little if any attention to the rest of the world's thought, history, and culture. The secular education reflected a strong cultural preference for technical fields over the humanities and social sciences. Many of these young men, even if able to study abroad, lacked the perspective and skills needed to understand a different culture.

Frustrated in their search for a decent living, unable to benefit from an education often obtained at the cost of great family sacrifice, and blocked from starting families of their own, some of these young men were easy targets for radicalization.

Bin Ladin's Historical Opportunity

Most Muslims prefer a peaceful and inclusive vision of their faith, not the violent sectarianism of Bin Ladin. Among Arabs, Bin Ladin's followers are commonly nicknamed *takfiri, or* "those who define other Muslims as unbelievers," because of their readiness to demonize and murder those with whom they disagree. Beyond the theology lies the simple human fact that most Muslims, like most other human beings, are repelled by mass murder and barbarism whatever their justification.

"All Americans must recognize that the face of terror is not the true face of Islam," President Bush observed. *"Islam is a faith that brings comfort to a billion people around the world. It's a faith that has made brothers and sisters of every race. It's a faith based upon love, not hate."* Yet as political, social, and economic problems created flammable societies, Bin Ladin used Islam's most extreme, fundamentalist traditions as his match. All these elements—including religion—combined in an explosive compound.[1]

Conclusion

Other extremists had, and have, followings of their own. But in appealing to societies full of discontent, Bin Ladin remained credible as other leaders and symbols faded. He could stand as a symbol of resistance—above all, resistance to the West and to America. He could present himself and his allies as victorious warriors in the one great successful experience for Islamic militancy in the 1980s: the Afghan jihad against the Soviet occupation. By 1998, Bin Ladin had a distinctive appeal, as he focused on attacking America. He argued that other extremists, who aimed at local rulers or Israel, did not go far enough. They had not taken on what he called "the head of the snake."

Finally, Bin Ladin had another advantage: a substantial, worldwide organization. By the time he issued his February 1998 declaration of war, Bin Ladin had nurtured that organization for nearly ten years. He could attract, train, and use recruits for ever more ambitious attacks, rallying new adherents with each demonstration that his was the movement of the future.

Questions

1. What is the birthplace of Islam?
2. Identify the two major sects of Islam and explain how they differ.
3. How did political failures of the 20th century give rise to fundamentalist views in the 21st century?
4. How is al Qaeda able to attract fundamentalist support?
5. What is Bin Ladin's goal?

Chapter 6

Catastrophic Terrorism

Objectives

- Understand the definition of WMD according to Title 50, US Code.
- Describe the different classes of WMD.
- Discuss why terrorists might resort to using WMD.
- Compare and contrast the various capabilities of different classes of WMD.

Introduction

The growing proclivity toward violence appears to be evidence of a portentous shift in terrorism, away from its traditional emphasis on discrete, selective attacks toward a mode of violence that is now aimed at inflicting indiscriminate and wanton slaughter. The implication, therefore, is that terrorism is now on an escalation spiral of lethality that may well culminate in the indiscriminate use of CBRN weapons.[1]

Weapons of Mass Destruction

"CBRN" refers to Chemical, Biological, Radiological, and Nuclear weapons which are generally classed as weapons of mass destruction. Just as there is no single definition for "terrorism", there are multiple interpretations of WMD. Title 50 of the U.S. Code, "War and National Defense", defines WMD:

> *"Any weapon or device that is intended, or has the capability, to cause death or serious bodily injury to a significant number of people through the release, dissemination, or impact of—(A) toxic or poisonous chemicals or their precursors; (B) a disease organism; or (C) radiation or radioactivity."*
>
> *—Title 50, United States Code, Chapter 40, Section 2302*

WMD: "Any weapon or device that is intended, or has the capability, to cause death or serious bodily injury to a significant number of people through the release, dissemination, or impact of—(A) toxic or poisonous chemicals or their precursors; (B) a disease organism; or (C) radiation or radioactivity."
—Title 50, US Code

The term "WMD" was first applied in 1937 to describe the effects of aerial bombardment on civilian populations. Most definitions agree that WMD are "weapons designed to kill large numbers of people."[2] Consequently, more recent U.S. laws, official statements, and documents define WMD as including additional types of weapons.[3] Both the terrorist attacks of September 11th 2001, and the Oklahoma City bombing, April 19th 1995 used conventional explosives to inflict mass casualties. As a result, the definition of WMD has been expanded to include any form of high explosives, thus CBRNE.

Motives and Rationales

If, in fact, we are approaching a new era of "super" CBRNE terrorism, why would groups seek to escalate to this level? One can identify five possible motivating rationales.

First, and at the most basic level, may be simply the desire to kill as many people as possible. CBRNE weapons could give a terrorist group the potential ability to wipe out thousands, possibly even hundreds of thousands, in a single strike. The following statement of a former FEMA director gives an indication of the potential killing power of these agents compared to conventional high explosives (HE): "To produce about the same number of deaths within a square mile, it would take 32 million grams of fragmentation cluster bomb material; 3.2 million grams of mustard gas; 800,000 grams of nerve gas; 5,000 grams of material in a crude fission weapon; 80 grams of botulinal toxin type A; or only 8 grams of anthrax spores." Such weapons would provide terrorist with the perfect means to seek revenge against, even to annihilate, their enemies, however defined, categorized, or otherwise determined.

A second reason for groups to seek to escalate to the CBRNE level could be to exploit the classic weapon of the terrorist—fear. Terrorism, in essence, is a form of psychological warfare. The ultimate objective is to destroy the structural supports that give society its strength by showing that the government is unable to fulfill its primary security function and, thereby, eliminating the solidarity, cooperation, and interdependence on which social cohesion and functioning depend. Viewed in this context, even a "limited" terrorist attack involving CBRNE agents would have disproportionately large psychological consequences, generating unprecedented fear and alarm throughout society. The 1995 Aum sarin nerve gas attack, for instance, which resulted in 12 deaths, not only galvanized mass panic in Tokyo, it also shattered the popular perception among the Japanese people, who, hitherto, had considered their country to be among the safest in the world. Moreover, it served to galvanize American attention to CBRNE terrorism, despite taking place overseas.

A third possible rationale for resorting to CBRNE weapons could be the desire to negotiate from a position of unsurpassed strength. A credible threat to use a chemical, biological, or nuclear weapon would be unlikely to go unanswered by a government and could therefore, provide an organization with a tool of political blackmail of the highest order.

A fourth reason, with specific reference to biological agents, could derive from certain logistical and psychological advantages that such weapons might offer terrorists. A biological attack, unlike a conventional bombing, would not likely attract immediate attention, and could initially go unnoticed, only manifesting itself days or even weeks after the event. This would be well suited to groups that wish to remain anonymous, either to minimize the prospect of personal retribution or to foment greater insecurity in their target audience by appearing as enigmatic, unseen, and unknown assailants.

Among weapons of mass destruction, biological weapons are more destructive than chemical weapons, including nerve gas. In certain circumstances, biological weapons can be as devastating as nuclear ones—a few kilograms of anthrax can kill as many people as a Hiroshima-size nuclear weapon.

Fifth, a group may wish to use CBRNE weapons, and more specifically biological agents, to cause economic and social damage by targeting a state's or region's agricultural sector. On several previous occasions in other parts of the world, terrorists have contaminated agricultural produce or threatened to do so. Between 1977 and 1979, more than 40 percent of the Israeli European citrus market was curtailed by a Palestinian plot to inject Jaffa oranges with mercury. In 1989, a Chilean left-wing group that was part of an anti-Pinochet movement claimed that it had lanced grapes bound for U.S. markets with sodium cyanide, causing suspensions of Chilean fruit imports by the Untied States, Canada, Denmark, Germany, and Hong Kong. In the early 1980s, Tamil separatists in Sri Lanka threatened to infect Sri Lankan rubber and tea plantations with nonindigenous diseases as part of a total biological war strategy designed to cripple the Sinhalese-dominated government.[4]

Biological Attack

Among weapons of mass destruction, biological weapons are more destructive than chemical weapons, including nerve gas. In certain circumstances, biological weapons can be as devastating as nuclear ones—a few kilograms of anthrax can kill as many people as a Hiroshima-size nuclear weapon.[5]

Terrorism involving biological weapons—referred to along with chemical weapons as "the poor man's nuclear weapon"—can range from putting deadly substances in the nation's food supply to the aerosolized release of a contagious virus over a city the size of New York or San Francisco.

The Biological Weapons Convention, signed in 1972, prohibits the manufacture, stockpiling and use of biological weapons. But there are several countries that continue to make and study them. Former President Nixon banned the production and use of biological warfare agents in 1969, ending the U.S. biowarfare program. The Soviet Union's biowarfare program, Biopreparat, lasted until the 1990s.

Anthrax, botulinum toxin, plague, ricin, smallpox, tularemia and viral hemorrhagic fevers are on the top of the Centers for Disease Control and Prevention's list of biological weapons, considered "Category A" weapons most likely to be used in an attack.

"Category B" weapons are second-highest priority to the CDC, because they are fairly easy to disseminate, cause moderate amounts of disease and low fatality rates. But these weapons require specific public-health action such as improved diagnostic and detection systems. These agents include: Q fever, brucellosis, glanders, ricin, Enterotoxin B, viral encephalitis, food safety threats, water safety threats, meliodosis, psittacosis and typhus fever.

"Category C" weapons, described by the CDC as "emerging infectious disease threats," are fairly easy to obtain, produce and disseminate and can produce high rates of disease and mortality. These include the Nipah virus and Hantavirus.

Other agents some nations may use as weapons include: aflatoxin, trichothecene mycotoxins, multi-drug tuberculosis, bacteria such as trench fever and scrub typhus, viruses such as influenza and various forms of hemorrhagic fever, fungi and protozoa.

Agricultural bioterrorism could produce famine or widespread malnutrition. These include foot-and-mouth disease, mad cow disease, swine fever and karnal bunt of wheat.[6]

The United States is unprepared to deal with a biological attack. Over the past several years, preparedness strides have been made, especially in the largest cities. However, much of the needed equipment is not available. Pathogen sensors are not in place to detect that a biological attack has taken place. New medicines are needed. In combating terrorist attacks, treatment is a more practical approach than prevention, yet many biological agents are extremely difficult to treat with existing medicines once the symptoms appear. In addition, many of the most important prophylactic drugs have limited shelf lives and cannot be stockpiled. Moreover, their effectiveness could be compromised by a sophisticated attacker.

Biological weapons can range in lethality from salmonella used to temporarily incapacitate to super bubonic plague engineered for mass casualties. Biological weapons include ricin, which an extremist may use to assassinate a single local official, as well as pathogens with high transmissibility and broad potential impact. Biological agents may be used to kill or disable humans or to attack plants or animals to harm a nation's economy Given that broad scope, biological attacks have already taken place and continue to be a distinct probability for the foreseeable future. However, of greatest concern is the capability to deliver a sizable lethal attack against a population center.

Making biological weapons requires art as well as science. Such weapons are not readily adaptable to "cookbook" type recipes that can be implemented by novices. Nevertheless, technical expertise and sophistication about biological processes have become much more widespread. Moreover, even though technical expertise is required to produce high-quality, military-grade biological weapons and reliable means of dissemination, terrorist applications are less demanding.

Making biological weapons requires sample cultures; the means to grow, purify, and stabilize them; and the means to reliably disseminate them. All these tasks pose substantial but not insurmountable challenges. More than 1,500 biological culture libraries worldwide, as well as numerous research institutions and natural sources, maintain cultures. Growth media and fermenters to multiply the sample cultures are widely available. Purifying, concentrating, and stabilizing agents is demanding and dangerous but not a great technical challenge. Freeze-drying the product and milling it into particles of uniform desirable size requires even more technical capabilities. A state sponsor may be needed to do it, although companies and institutes regularly spray dry and mill commercial microbes. Moreover, a respirable aerosol of germs can be achieved through other high-pressure devices.

Biological production and weapon-producing facilities can be small, inexpensive, and inconspicuous. Equipment to develop biological arms may have legitimate commercial and research purposes, as well as nefarious ones. Unlike nuclear weapons, biological weapons do not require unique ingredients that are ready objects of arms control.[7]

Chemical Attack

Chemical warfare is the use of non-explosive chemical agents (that are not themselves living organisms) to cause injury or death.[8]

The first major use of chemical weapons in modern times came when Germany launched a large-scale poison gas attack against French troops on the battlefield of Ypres in 1915. Allies responded with their own chemical weapons. By the end of the war, chemical warfare had inflicted over 1 million casualties, of which around 90,000 were fatal.

The 1925 Geneva Protocol prohibits "the use in war of asphyxiating, poisonous or other gases, and of bacteriological methods of warfare." But it didn't prohibit the manufacturing and stockpiling of these weapons.

A UN working group began work on chemical disarmament in 1980. On April 4, 1984, U.S. President Ronald Reagan called for an international ban on chemical weapons. U.S. President George H. W. Bush and Soviet Union leader Mikhail Gorbachev signed a bilateral treaty on June 1, 1990 to end chemical weapon production and start destroying each of their nation's stockpiles. The multilateral Chemical Weapons Convention (CWC) was signed in 1993 and came into effect in 1997. The Organization for the Prohibition of Chemical Weapons declared that at the end of 2003, 8000 metric tons of chemical agent had been destroyed worldwide from a declared stockpile of 70,000 metric tons. For its part, by 2003, the United States had destroyed 23% of its total chemical arsenal, although doubts existed whether it could reach total elimination by the treaty deadline of 2012 due to technical difficulties and environmental regulations.

Chemical agents are classified according to the symptoms they cause, such as blistering and nerve agents. Mustard gas, sarin (GB), VX, soman (GD) and tabun are blistering and nerve agents that were weaponized for military purposes. Other forms of chemical agents include: blood agents, including cyanide, arsine, cyanogens chloride and hydrogen chloride; choking agents, including chlorine, phosphane and phosgene; other nerve agents; and vesicants such as distilled mustard, ethyldichlorarsine, mustard-lewsite mixture and forms of nitrogen mustard.[9]

Chemical weapons are made from readily available material used in various industrial operations. The most common types of hazardous materials used in toxic weapons are irritants, choking agents, flammable industrial gas, water supply contaminants, oxidizers, chemical asphyxiates, incendiary gases and liquids, industrial compounds and organophosphate pesticides.[10]

Chemical weapons are made from readily available material used in various industrial operations. The most common types of hazardous materials used in toxic weapons are irritants, choking agents, flammable industrial gas, water supply contaminants, oxidizers, chemical asphyxiates, incendiary gases and liquids, industrial compounds and organophosphate pesticides.

On March 20, 1995, members of Aum Shinkrikyo released sarin gas on several lines of the Tokyo Subway, killing 12 people and injuring some 6000 more. The attack was initiated at the peak of Monday morning rush hour on one of the world's busiest commuter transport systems. Five teams of two-men were issued plastic bags containing approximately one liter of liquid sarin each. A single drop of sarin the size of the head of a pin can kill an adult.

Sarin is classified as a nerve agent. It was discovered in 1938 by two German scientists while attempting to create stronger pesticides. At room temperature, sarin is both odorless and colorless. Its relatively high vapor pressure means that it evaporates quickly. Its vapor is also odorless and colorless. Sarin attacks the nervous system of the human body. Initial symptoms following exposure are a runny nose, tightness in the chest and dilation of the pupils. The victim will begin to lose control of bodily functions and eventually become comatose and suffocate as a consequence of convulsive spasms.

Carrying their packets of sarin and umbrellas with sharpened tips, the perpetrators boarded their appointed trains; at prearranged stations, each perpetrator dropped his package and punctured it several times with the sharpened tip of his umbrella before escaping to his accomplice's waiting get-away car.

Passengers began to be affected immediately. Those nearest the release were overcome by symptoms and began to drop causing others to panic and press the emergency stop buttons. Witnesses have said that subway entrances resembled battlefields. In many cases, the injured simply lay on the ground, many unable to breathe. Incredibly, several of those affected by sarin went to work in spite of their symptoms. Most of these left and sought medical treatment as the symptoms worsened. Several of those affected were exposed to sarin only by helping passengers from the trains (these include passengers on other trains, subway workers and health care workers).

The sarin gas attack was the most serious terrorist attack in Japan's modern history. It caused massive disruption and widespread fear in a society that had been considered virtually free of crime.

Shortly after the attack, Aum lost its status as a religious organization, and many of its assets were seized. However, the Diet of Japan rejected a request from government officials to outlaw the sect altogether because the officials could not prove that the Aum posed a 'threat to society'.

About twenty of Aum's followers, including its leader, Shoko Asahara, are either standing trial or have already been convicted for crimes related to the attack. As of July 2004, eight Aum members have received death sentences for their roles in the attack.[11]

Nuclear Attack

Nuclear weapons produce devastating and long-term effects on human and animal life, as well as the environments in which they live. These are the hardest of all types of weapons to make because the critical nuclear elements—plutonium and/or highly enriched uranium—are hard to come by, and are very expensive.

Limited access to fissile materials—the essential ingredients of nuclear weapons—is the principal technical barrier to nuclear proliferation in the world today.

The United States dropped one atomic bomb on Hiroshima and Nagasaki in 1945, bringing an end to World War II. The Soviet Union became the next country to develop atomic weapons, igniting an arms race and a global interest in nuclear fission devices.

Decades of arms control have greatly reduced the number of nuclear weapons around the world. Since 1991, the U.S. Nunn-Lugar Cooperative Threat Reduction program has deactivated 6,032 nuclear warheads and has destroyed 491 ballistic missiles, 438 ballistic missile silos, 101 bombers, 365 submarine-launched missiles, 408 submarine missile launchers, and 25 strategic missile submarines. It has sealed 194 nuclear test tunnels.[12]

The key question is whether or not terrorists could build a nuclear explosive device. Weapons experts at the Nuclear Control Institute say the answer is "yes." They conjecture that a crude nuclear device could be constructed by a group not previously engaged in designing or building nuclear weapons. Successful execution would require efforts of a team having knowledge and skills additional to those usually associated with terrorist groups, but could be accomplished relatively quick with careful preparations and the right materials. The completed device would probably weigh more than a ton, but still be small enough to fit within the back of a truck. According to the experts, an implosion device could be constructed with reactor-grade plutonium or highly enriched uranium providing a nominal yield of 10 kilotons, equivalent to the atomic bombs used over Hiroshima and Nagasaki in World War II.[13]

Limited access to fissile materials—the essential ingredients of nuclear weapons—is the principal technical barrier to nuclear proliferation in the world today. Global stockpiles of such material are large and widespread. A decade after the end of the Cold War, there are still some 30,000 nuclear weapons in the world (more than 95% of them in the U.S. and Russian arsenals). The world's stockpiles of separated plutonium and highly enriched uranium (HEU), the essential ingredients of nuclear weapons, are estimated to include some 450 tons of military and civilian separated plutonium, and over 1700 tons of HEU. These stockpiles, both military and civilian, are overwhelmingly concentrated in the five nuclear weapon states acknowledged by the Nonproliferation Treaty, but enough plutonium for many nuclear weapons also exists in India, Israel, Belgium, Germany, Japan, and Switzerland. In addition, as of estimates made in 2000, a total of more than 2,772 kilograms of civilian HEU existed in research reactors in 43 countries, sometimes in quantities large enough to make a bomb.

Most of these weapons and materials are reasonably well secured and accounted for. But this is by no means universally the case. Levels of security and accounting for both the military and civilian material vary widely, with no binding international standards in place. Some weapons-usable material is dangerously insecure and so poorly accounted for that if it were stolen, no one might ever know.

Today, the problem is most acute in the former Soviet Union, where the collapse of the Soviet state left a security system designed for a closed society with closed borders, well-paid nuclear workers, and everyone under close surveillance by the KGB facing a new world it was never designed to address. Nuclear weapons, which are large and readily accountable objects, remain under high levels of security—though even there, scarce resources for maintaining security systems and paying nuclear guards raise grounds for concern. For nuclear material, the problem is more urgent. Many nuclear facilities in Russia have no detector at the door that would set off an alarm if someone were carrying plutonium in a briefcase, and no security cameras where the plutonium is stored. Nuclear workers and guards protecting material worth millions of dollars are paid $200 a month. As a result, there have been a number of confirmed cases of theft of kilogram quantities of weapons-usable material in the former Soviet Union. Russian officials have confirmed as recently as 1998, there was an insider conspiracy at one of Russia's largest nuclear weapons facilities to steal 18.5 kilograms of HEU—one that was stopped before the material actually left the gates. These are conditions that led a distinguished U.S. bipartisan panel to warn in 2001, that "the most urgent unmet national security threat to the United States today is the danger that weapons of mass destruction or weapons-usable material in Russia could be stolen and sold to terrorists or hostile nation states."

The problem of insecure nuclear material, however, is by no means limited to the former Soviet Union. Many analysts have expressed concern that the current anti-terrorist campaign could create instabilities in South Asia that could put nuclear stockpiles and facilities at risk. In the United States itself, which has among the toughest physical protection regulations in the world, there have been repeated scandals going back decades over inadequate security for weapons-usable nuclear material. In countries around the world, there are research facilities with fresh HEU fuel that simply do not have the resources to sustain effective security for this material over the long haul. The problem was highlighted by the 19.9% enriched uranium seized in 1998 from criminals trying to sell it in Italy, which appears to have been stolen from a research reactor in the Congo. Theft of insecure HEU and plutonium, in short, is not a hypothetical worry: it is an ongoing reality, not only from the former Soviet Union but from other states as well.

At the same time, tens of thousands of people worldwide have critical knowledge related to the manufacture of nuclear weapons and their essential ingredients, which must be controlled, and many thousands of these are seriously underemployed and underpaid, creating some serious proliferation risks. In 1998, for example, a weapons expert from one of Russia's premier nuclear weapons laboratories was arrested on charges for spying for Iraq and Afghanistan—in this case on advanced conventional weapons. In October 2000, an official of Russia's Security Council confirmed that Russia had blocked Taliban efforts to recruit a former Soviet nuclear expert from a Central Asian state. A knowledgeable expert from a major state weapons of mass destruction program could substantially accelerate a proliferator's weapons of mass destruction program, or make it possible for a terrorist group to achieve a nuclear capability that would otherwise be beyond their reach.[14]

Radiological Attack

Radiological weapons are thought by many to be the likely choices for terrorists. Unlike nuclear weapons, they spread radioactive material, which contaminates equipment, facilities, land and acts as a toxic chemical, which can be harmful, and in some cases fatal.

Radiological weapons are thought by many to be the likely choices for terrorists. Unlike nuclear weapons, they spread radioactive material, which contaminates equipment, facilities, land and acts as a toxic chemical, which can be harmful, and in some cases fatal.

A "dirty bomb" is the likely choice for terrorists and can kill or injure people by exposing them to radioactive materials, such as cesium-137, iridium-192 or cobalt-60.[15]

According to Dr. Henry Kelly, President of the Federation of American Scientists, "Radiological attacks constitute a credible threat." Radioactive materials that could be used for such attacks are stored in thousands of facilities around the US, many of which may not be adequately protected against theft by determined terrorists. Some of this material could be easily dispersed in urban areas by using conventional explosives or by other methods.

While radiological attacks would result in some deaths, they would not result in the hundreds of thousands of fatalities that could be caused by a crude nuclear weapon. Attacks could contaminate large urban areas with radiation levels that exceed the Environmental Protection Agency's health and toxic material guidelines.

Materials that could easily be lost or stolen from US research institutions and commercial sites could contaminate tens of city blocks at a level that would require prompt evacuation and create terror in large communities even if radiation casualties were low. Areas as large as tens of square miles could be contaminated at levels that exceed recommended civilian exposure limits. Since there are often no effective ways to decontaminate buildings that have been exposed at these levels, demolition may be the only practical solution. If such an event were to take place in a city like New York, it would result in losses of potentially trillions of dollars.

Because of the resultant high economic impact compared with the expected low loss of life, a "dirty bomb" is sometimes referred to as a "weapon of mass disruption." Radiological weapons have the advantage over nuclear weapons in as much as they don't require large quantities of restricted materials or specialized expertise for their fabrication. In fact, the required materials are readily available and used extensively throughout government and industry.

The radiation produced by radioactive materials provides a low-cost way to disinfect food, sterilize medical equipment, treat certain kinds of cancer, find oil, build sensitive smoke detectors, and provide other critical services to our economy. Radioactive materials are also widely used in university, corporate, and government research laboratories. As a result, significant amounts of radioactive materials are stored in laboratories, food irradiation plants, oil drilling facilities, medical centers, and many other sites.

Radioactive sources that emit intense gamma-rays, such as cobalt-60 and cesium-137, are useful in killing bacteria and cancer cells. Gamma-rays, like X-rays, can penetrate clothing, skin, and other materials, but they are more energetic and destructive. When these rays reach targeted cells, they cause lethal chemical changes inside the cell.

Significant quantities of radioactive material have been lost or stolen from US facilities during the past few years and thefts of foreign sources have led to fatalities. In the US, sources have been found abandoned in scrap yards, vehicles, and residential buildings.

Plutonium and americium also serve commercial and research purposes. When plutonium or americium decay, they throw off a very large particle called an alpha particle. Hence, they are referred to as alpha emitters. Plutonium, which is used in nuclear weapons, also has non-military functions. During the 1960s and 1970s the federal government encouraged the use of plutonium in university facilities studying nuclear engineering and nuclear physics. Americium is used in smoke detectors and in devices that find oil sources. These devices are lowered deep into oil wells and are used to detect fossil fuel deposits by measuring hydrogen content as they descend.

With the exception of nuclear reactors, commercial facilities do not have the types or volumes of materials usable for making nuclear weapons. Security concerns have focused on preventing thefts or accidents that could expose employees and the general public to harmful levels of radiation. A thief might, for example, take the material for its commercial value as a radioactive source, or it may be discarded as scrap by accident or as a result of neglect. This system works reasonably well when the owners have a vested interest in protecting commercially valuable material. However, once the materials are no longer needed and costs of appropriate disposal are high, security measures become lax, and the likelihood of abandonment or theft increases.

Significant quantities of radioactive material have been lost or stolen from US facilities during the past few years and thefts of foreign sources have led to fatalities. In the US, sources have been found abandoned in scrap yards, vehicles, and residential buildings. In September 1987, scavengers broke into an abandoned cancer clinic in Goiania, Brazil and stole a medical device containing large amounts of radioactive cesium. An estimated 250 people were exposed to the source, eight developed radiation sickness, and four died.

In almost all cases, the loss of radioactive materials has resulted from an accident or from a thief interested only in economic gain. In 1995, however, Chechen rebels placed a shielded container holding the cesium-137 core of a cancer treatment device in a Moscow park, and then tipped off Russian reporters of its location.

Gamma rays pose two types of health risks. Intense sources of gamma rays can cause immediate tissue damage, and lead to acute radiation poisoning. Fatalities can result from very high doses. Long-term exposure to low levels of gamma rays can also be harmful because it can cause genetic mutations leading to cancer. Triggering cancer is largely a matter of chance: the more radiation you're exposed to, the more often the dice are rolled. The risk is never zero since we are all constantly being bombarded by large amounts of gamma radiation produced by cosmic rays, which reach us from distant stars. We are also exposed to trace amounts of radioactivity in the soil, in building materials, and other parts of our environment. Any increase in exposure increases the risk of cancer.

Alpha particles emitted by plutonium, americium and other elements also pose health risks. Although these particles cannot penetrate clothing or skin, they are harmful if emitted by inhaled materials. If plutonium is in the environment in particles small enough to be inhaled, contaminated particles can lodge in the lung for extended periods. Inside the lung, the alpha particles produced by plutonium can damage lung tissue and lead to long-term cancers.

Impact of the release of radioactive material in a populated area will vary depending on a number of factors, many of which are not predictable. Consequences depend on the amount of material released, the nature of the material, the details of the device that distributes the material, the direction and speed of the wind, other weather conditions, the size of the particles released (which affects their ability to be carried by the wind and to be inhaled), and the location and size of buildings near the release site. Assuming the material is released on a calm day, and the material is distributed by an explosion creating a mist of fine particles to spread downwind in a cloud, then people will be exposed to radiation in several ways.

Long-term exposure to low levels of gamma rays can also be harmful because it can cause genetic mutations leading to cancer. Triggering cancer is largely a matter of chance: the more radiation you're exposed to, the more often the dice are rolled. The risk is never zero.

First, they will be exposed to material in the dust inhaled during the initial passage of the radiation cloud, if they have not been able to escape the area before the dust cloud arrives. If this material is plutonium or americium (or other alpha emitters), the material will stay in the body and lead to long term exposure.

Second, anyone living in the affected area will be exposed to material deposited from the dust that settles from the cloud. If the material contains cesium (or other gamma emitters) they will be continuously exposed to radiation from this dust, since the gamma rays penetrate clothing and skin. If the material contains plutonium (or other alpha emitters), dust that is pulled off the ground and into the air by wind, automobile movement, or other actions will continue to be inhaled, adding to exposure.

In a rural area, people would also be exposed to radiation from contaminated food and water sources.

The EPA has a series of recommendations for addressing radioactive contamination that would likely guide official response to a radiological attack. Immediately after the attack, authorities would evacuate people from areas contaminated to levels exceeding these guidelines. People who received more than twenty-five times the threshold dose for evacuation would have to be taken in for medical supervision.

In the long term, the cancer hazard from the remaining radioactive contamination would have to be addressed. Typically, if decontamination could not reduce the danger of cancer death to about one-in-ten-thousand, the EPA would recommend the contaminated area be eventually abandoned. Decontaminating an urban area presents a variety of challenges. Several materials that might be used in radiological attack can chemically bind to concrete and asphalt, while other materials would become physically lodged in crevices on the surface of buildings, sidewalks and streets. Options for decontamination would range from sandblasting to demolition, with the latter likely being the only feasible option. Some radiological materials will also become firmly attached to soil in city parks, with the only disposal method being large scale removal of contaminated dirt. In short, there is a high risk that the area contaminated by a radiological attack would have to be deserted.

Consider if a medical gauge containing cesium was exploded in Washington, DC in a bomb using ten pounds of TNT. The initial passing of the radioactive cloud would be relatively harmless, and no one would have to evacuate immediately. But what area would be contaminated? Residents of an area about five city blocks, if they remained, would have a one-in-thousand chance of getting cancer. A swath about one mile long covering an area of forty city blocks would exceed EPA contamination limits, with remaining residents having a one-in-ten thousand chance of getting cancer. If decontamination were not possible, these areas would have to be abandoned for decades. If the device was detonated at the National Gallery of Art, the contaminated area might include the Capitol, Supreme Court, and Library of Congress.

Options for decontamination would range from sandblasting to demolition, with the latter likely being the only feasible option. Some radiological materials will also become firmly attached to soil in city parks, with the only disposal method being large scale removal of contaminated dirt. In short, there is a high risk that the area contaminated by a radiological attack would have to be deserted.

Now imagine if a single piece of radioactive cobalt from a food irradiation plant was dispersed by an explosion at the lower tip of Manhattan. Typically, each of these cobalt "pencils" is about one inch in diameter and one foot long, with hundreds of such pieces often being found in the same facility. Again, no immediate evacuation would be necessary, but in this case, an area of approximately one-thousand square kilometers, extending over three states, would be contaminated. Over an area of about three hundred typical city blocks, there would be a one-in-ten risk of death from cancer for residents living in the contaminated area for forty years. The entire borough of Manhattan would be so contaminated that anyone living there would have a one-in-a-hundred chance of dying from cancer caused by the residual radiation. It would be decades before the city was inhabitable again, and demolition might be necessary.

A device that spreads materials like americium and plutonium would present an entirely different set of risks. Consider a typical americium source used in oil well surveying. If this were blown up with one pound of TNT, people in a region roughly ten times the area of the initial bomb blast would require medical supervision and monitoring. An area 30 times the size of the first area (a swath one kilometer long and covering twenty city blocks) would have to be evacuated within half an hour. After the initial passage of the cloud, most of the radioactive materials would settle to the ground. Of these materials, some would be forced back up into the air and inhaled, thus posing a long-term health hazard. A ten-block area contaminated in this way would have a cancer death probability of one-in-a-thousand. A region two kilometers long and covering sixty city blocks would be contaminated in excess of EPA safety guidelines. If the buildings in this area had to be demolished and rebuilt, the cost would exceed fifty billion dollars.[16]

Explosives Attack

An explosive is any material that, when ignited by heat or shock, undergoes rapid decomposition or oxidation. This process releases energy that is stored in the material in the form of heat and light, or by breaking down into gaseous compounds that occupy a much larger volume than the original piece of material. Because this expansion is very rapid, large volumes of air are displaced by the expanding gasses. This expansion occurs at a speed greater than the speed of sound, and so a sonic boom occurs. This explains the mechanics behind an explosion. Explosives occur in several forms: high-order explosives which detonate, low order explosives, which burn, and primers, which may do both.

High order explosives detonate. A detonation occurs only in a high order explosive. Detonations are usually incurred by a shockwave that passes through a block of the high explosive material. The shockwave breaks apart the molecular bonds between the atoms of the substance, at a rate approximately equal to the speed of sound traveling through that material. In a high explosive, the fuel and oxidizer are chemically bonded, and the shockwave breaks apart these bonds, and re-combines the two materials to produce mostly gasses. T.N.T., ammonium nitrate, and R.D.X. are examples of high order explosives.

Low order explosives do not detonate; they burn, or undergo oxidation when heated, the fuel(s) and oxidizer(s) combine to produce heat, light, and gaseous products. Some low order materials burn at about the same speed under pressure as they do in the open, such as black powder. Others, such as gunpowder, which is correctly called nitrocellulose, burn much faster and hotter when they are in a confined space, such as the barrel of a firearm; they usually burn much slower than black powder when they are ignited in unpressurized conditions. Black powder, nitrocellulose, and flash powder are good examples of low order explosives.

Primers are peculiarities to the explosive field. Some of them, such as mercury fulminate, will function as a low or high order explosive. They are usually more sensitive to friction, heat, or shock, than the high or low order explosives. Most primers perform like a high order explosive, except that they are much more sensitive. Still others merely burn, but when they are confined, they burn at a great rate and with a large expansion of gasses and a shockwave. Primers are usually used in a small amount to initiate, or cause to decompose, a high order explosive, as in an artillery shell. But they are also frequently used to ignite a low order explosive; the gunpowder in a bullet is ignited by the detonation of its primer.[17]

The production, storage, and distribution of explosive materials is regulated under Title 15 of US Code. Various regulatory organizations are responsible for enforcing the law. The Occupational Safety & Health Administration (OSHA) assures the safe and healthful working conditions for workers handling explosives in construction and manufacturing work. The Mine Safety & Health Administration (MSHA) protects the safety and health of miners while handling explosives, and enforces storage and record keeping rules at mining operations (surface and underground). The Department of Transportation (DOT) protects life and property against inherent risks of transporting hazardous materials in commerce. The Bureau of Alcohol Tobacco Firearms and Explosives (ATF) protects commerce and the public from the misuses and unsafe or insecure storage of explosives. The ATF investigates thefts, losses, and unexpected explosions to determine whether it was an accidental or criminal act. State and local fire and police authorities may also regulate explosive storage, transportation, and use.[18]

Despite intense government regulation, it's a matter of practical impossibility to prevent the proliferation of explosive materials since they may be easily manufactured from common materials using information that's widely available on the internet.

Despite intense government regulation, it's a matter of practical impossibility to prevent the proliferation of explosive materials since they may be easily manufactured from common materials using information that's widely available on the internet.

"The Terrorist's Handbook", available on the internet, includes recipes for twenty-three different types of explosives including impact, low order, high order, and other types of explosives. The handbook details methods for acquiring and fabricating materials, both legally and illegally.

For example, the handbook describes ammonium nitrate as a high explosive material that is often used as a commercial "safety explosive" because it's very stable, and difficult to ignite with a match. It explains how ammonium nitrate is used in "Cold-Paks" or "Instant Cold", available in most drug stores. To get the ammonium nitrate, simply cut off the top of the outside bag, remove the plastic bag of water, and save the ammonium nitrate in a well sealed, airtight container. The handbook also notes ammonium nitrate is the main ingredient in many fertilizers.[19] Indeed, Timothy McVeigh used ammonium nitrate found in fertilizer to build a truck bomb killing 168 people in the Alfred P. Murrah Federal Building, in Oklahoma City, Oklahoma, April 19, 1995.[20]

The handbook also describes methods for acquiring explosive materials illegally. Colleges, according to the handbook, are the best places to steal chemicals.

> *"Many state schools have all of their chemicals out on the shelves in the labs, and more in their chemical stockrooms. Evening is the best time to enter lab buildings, as there are the least number of people in the buildings, and most of the labs will be unlocked. One simply takes a book bag, wears a dress shirt and jeans, and tries to resemble a college freshman. If anyone asks what such a person is doing, the thief can simply say he is looking for the polymer chemistry lab, or some other chemistry-related department other than the one they are in. One can usually find out where the various labs and departments in a building are by calling the university... as a rule, college campus security is pretty poor, and nobody suspects another person in the building of doing anything wrong, even if they are there at an odd hour."*
>
> — *The Terrorist's Handbook*

The First Amendment of the Constitution protects the existence of sources such as "The Terrorist's Handbook." Even if they could be eliminated, it wouldn't eliminate the threat from high explosives. The fact of the matter is that many common items can be made into high explosive devices. Consider that the terrorist attacks of September 11th 2001 used commercial aircraft as weapons of mass destruction by hijacking heavily fueled aircraft and ramming them into large buildings. Any other aircraft, train, ship, or truck could serve a similar purpose.

Conclusion

The knowledge, technology, and materials needed to build weapons of mass destruction are spreading. These capabilities have never been more accessible and the trends are not in our favor. If terrorist enemies acquire these weapons and the means to deliver them, they are likely to try to use them, with potential consequences far more devastating than those suffered on September 11.

Biological weapons, which release large quantities of living, disease-causing microorganisms, have extraordinary lethal potential. Biological weapons are relatively easy to manufacture, requiring straightforward technical skills, basic equipment, and a seed stock of pathogenic microorganisms. Biological weapons are especially dangerous because we may not know immediately that we have been attacked, allowing an infectious agent time to spread. Moreover, biological agents can serve as a means of attack against humans as well as livestock and crops, inflicting casualties as well as economic damage.

Chemical weapons are extremely lethal and capable of producing tens of thousands of casualties. They are also relatively easy to manufacture, using basic equipment, trained personnel, and precursor materials that often have legitimate dual uses. As the 1995 Tokyo subway attack revealed, even sophisticated nerve agents are within the reach of terrorist groups.

Nuclear weapons have enormous destructive potential. Terrorists who seek to develop a nuclear weapon must overcome two formidable challenges. First, acquiring or refining a sufficient quantity of fissile material is very difficult—though not impossible. Second, manufacturing a workable weapon requires a very high degree of technical capability—though terrorists could feasibly assemble the simplest type of nuclear device. To get around these significant though not insurmountable challenges, terrorists could seek to steal or purchase a nuclear weapon.

Radiological weapons, or "dirty bombs," combine radioactive material with conventional explosives. They can cause widespread disruption and fear, particularly in heavily populated areas.

Terrorists, both domestic and international, continue to use traditional methods of violence and destruction to inflict harm and spread fear. They have used knives, guns, and bombs to kill the innocent. They have taken hostages and spread propaganda. Given the low expense, ready availability of materials, and relatively high chance for successful execution, terrorists will continue to make use of conventional attacks.[21]

Questions

1. What is the definition of WMD according to Title 50, US Code?
2. What are the different classes of WMD?
3. Describe three different motives or rationales for terrorists to use WMD.
4. Of the various forms of WMD, which do you think is most destructive, and why?
5. Of the various forms of WMD, which do you think is most likely to be used, and why?

Chapter 7

Natural Disasters

Objectives

- Understand events attendant to Hurricane Katrina in 2005.
- Summarize the resulting disaster.
- Explain the failure of government at all levels to adequately prepare and respond.

Introduction

Hurricane Katrina was an extraordinary act of nature that spawned a human tragedy. It was the most destructive natural disaster in American history, laying waste to 90,000 square miles of land, an area the size of the United Kingdom. In Mississippi, the storm surge obliterated coastal communities and left thousands destitute. New Orleans was overwhelmed by flooding. All told, more than 1500 people died. Along the Gulf Coast, tens of thousands suffered without basic essentials for almost a week.

But the suffering that continued in the days and weeks after the storm passed did not happen in a vacuum; instead, it continued longer than it should have because of – and was in some cases exacerbated by – the failure of government at all levels to plan, prepare for and respond aggressively to the storm. These failures were not just conspicuous; they were pervasive. Among the many factors that contributed to these failures, the Committee found that there were four overarching ones: 1) long-term warnings went unheeded and government officials neglected their duties to prepare for a forewarned catastrophe; 2) government officials took insufficient actions or made poor decisions in the days immediately before and after landfall; 3) systems on which officials relied on to support their response efforts failed, and 4) government officials at all levels failed to provide effective leadership. These individual failures, moreover, occurred against a backdrop of failure, over time, to develop the capacity for a coordinated, national response to a truly catastrophic event, whether caused by nature or man-made.

At every level of government, the chief executive has the ultimate responsibility to manage an emergency response.

The results were tragic loss of life and human suffering on a massive scale, and an undermining of confidence in our governments' ability to plan, prepare for, and respond to national catastrophes.

Roles of Government

Every level of government, and many components within each level, play important roles. At every level of government, the chief executive has the ultimate responsibility to manage an emergency response.

It has long been standard practice that emergency response begins at the lowest possible jurisdictional level – typically the local government, with state government becoming involved at the local government's request when the resources of local government are (or are expected to be) overwhelmed. Similarly, while the federal government provides ongoing financial support to state and local governments for emergency preparedness, ordinarily it becomes involved in responding to a disaster at a state's request when resources of state and local governments are (or are expected to be) overwhelmed. Louisiana's Emergency Operations Plan explicitly lays out this hierarchy of response.

During a catastrophe, which by definition almost immediately exceeds state and local resources and significantly disrupts governmental operations and emergency services, the role of the federal government is particularly vital, and it would reasonably be expected to play a more substantial role in response than in an "ordinary situation."

Unheeded Warnings

The potentially devastating threat of a catastrophic hurricane to the Gulf region has been known for forty years: New Orleans experienced flooding in some areas of remarkably similar proportions from Hurricane Betsy in 1965, and Hurricane Camille devastated the Gulf Coast in 1969. More recently, numerous experts and governmental officials had been anticipating an increase in violent hurricanes, and New Orleans' special and growing vulnerability to catastrophic flooding due to changing geological and other conditions was widely described in both technical and popular media.

Hurricane Georges hit the Gulf in 1998, spurring the state of Louisiana to ask FEMA for assistance with catastrophic hurricane planning. Little was accomplished for the next six years. Between 2000 and 2003, state authorities, an emergency-preparedness contractor, and FEMA's own regional staff repeatedly advised FEMA headquarters in Washington that planning for evacuation and shelter for the "New Orleans scenario" was incomplete and inadequate, but FEMA failed to approach other federal agencies for help with transportation and shelter or to ensure that the City and State had the matters in hand.

Then, in 2004, after a White House aide received a briefing on the catastrophic consequences of a Category 3 hurricane hitting New Orleans, the federal government sponsored a planning exercise, with participation from federal, state, and local officials, based on a scenario whose characteristics foreshadowed most of Katrina's impacts. While this hypothetical "Hurricane Pam" exercise resulted in draft plans beginning in early 2005, they were incomplete when Katrina hit. Nonetheless, some officials took the initiative to use concepts developed in the drafts, with mixed success in the critical aspects of the Katrina response. However, many of its admonitory lessons were either ignored or inadequately applied.

During the Pam exercise, officials determined that massive flooding from a catastrophic storm in New Orleans could threaten the lives of 60,000 people and trap hundreds of thousands more, while incapacitating local resources for weeks to months. The Pam exercise gave all levels of government a reminder that the "New Orleans scenario" required more forethought, preparation, and investment than a "typical" storm. Also, it reinforced the importance of coordination both within and among federal, state, and local governments for an effective response.

The specific danger that Katrina posed to the Gulf Coast became clear on the afternoon of Friday, August 26, when forecasters at the National Hurricane Center and the National Weather Service saw that the storm was turning west. First in phone calls to Louisiana emergency management officials and then in their 5 p.m. EDT Katrina forecast and accompanying briefings, they alerted both Louisiana and Mississippi that the track of the storm was now expected to shift significantly to the west of its original track to the Florida panhandle. The National Hurricane Center warned that Katrina could be a Category 4 or even a 5 by landfall. By the next morning, Weather Service Officials directly confirmed to the Governor of Louisiana and other state and local officials that New Orleans was squarely at risk.

Over the weekend, there was a drumbeat of warnings: FEMA held videoteleconferences on both days, where the danger of Katrina and the particular risks to New Orleans were discussed; Max Mayfield of the Hurricane Center called the governors of the affected states, something he had only done once before in his 33 year career; President Bush took the unusual step of declaring in advance an emergency for the states in the impact zone; numerous media reports noted that New Orleans was a "bowl" and could be left submerged by the storm; the Department of Homeland Security's Simulation and Analysis group generated a report stating that the levees protecting New Orleans were at risk of breaching and overtopping; internal FEMA slides stated that the projected impacts of Katrina could be worse than those in the Hurricane Pam exercise. The warnings were as widespread as they were dire.

Insufficient Preparation

Katrina was not a "typical" hurricane as it approached landfall; it was much larger, more powerful, and was capable of producing catastrophic damage.

In some respects, officials did prepare for Katrina with the understanding that it could be a catastrophe. Some coastal towns in Mississippi went to extraordinary lengths to get citizens to evacuate, including sending people door-to-door to convince and cajole people to move out of harm's way. The State of Louisiana activated more than twice the number of National Guard troops called to duty in any prior hurricane, and achieved the largest evacuation of a threatened population ever to occur. The City of New Orleans issued its first ever mandatory evacuation order. The Coast Guard readied its personnel, prepositioned its equipment, and stood by to begin search and rescue operations as quickly as humanly possible. Departing from usual practice, the Governors of the three affected states requested, and President Bush issued, emergency declarations before the storm made landfall.

But however vigorous these preparations, ineffective leadership, poor advance planning and an unwillingness to devote sufficient resources to emergency management over the long term doomed them to fail when Katrina struck. Despite the understanding of the Gulf Coast's particular vulnerability to hurricane devastation, officials braced for Katrina with full awareness of critical deficiencies in their plans and gaping holes in their resources. While Katrina's destructive force could not be denied, state and local officials did not marshal enough of the resources at their disposal.

In addition, years of short-changing federal, state and local emergency functions left them incapable of fully carrying out their missions to protect the public and care for victims.. For example, the lack of survivable, interoperable communications, which Governor Haley Barbour said was the most critical problem in his state, occurred because of an accumulation of decisions by federal, state, and local officials that left this long standing problem unsolved.

The Senate Report attributed leadership failures for needlessly compounding these losses. Mayor Nagin and Governor Blanco –who knew the limitations of their resources to address a catastrophe—did not specify those needs adequately to the federal government before landfall. For example, while Governor Blanco stated in a letter to President Bush two days before landfall that she anticipated the resources of the state would be overwhelmed, she made no specific request for assistance in evacuating the known tens of thousands of people without means of transportation, and a senior state official identified no unmet needs in response to a federal offer of assistance the following day. The state's transportation secretary also ignored his responsibilities under the state's emergency operations plan, leaving no arm of the state government prepared to obtain and deliver additional transportation to those in New Orleans who lacked it, when Katrina struck. In view of the long-standing role of requests as a trigger for action by higher levels of government, the state bears responsibility for not signaling its needs to the federal government more clearly.

Compounded by leadership failures of its own, the federal government bears responsibility for not preparing effectively for its role in the post storm response.

FEMA was unprepared for a catastrophic event of the scale of Katrina. Well before Katrina, FEMA's relationships with state and local officials, once a strength, had been eroded in part because certain preparedness grant programs were transferred elsewhere in the Department of Homeland Security; not as important to state and local preparedness activities, FEMA's effectiveness was diminished. In addition, at no time in its history, including in the years before it became part of DHS, had FEMA developed – nor had it been designed to develop – response capabilities sufficient for a catastrophe nor had it developed the capacity to mobilize sufficient resources from other federal agencies, and the private and nonprofit sectors.

Compounded by leadership failures of its own, the federal government bears responsibility for not preparing effectively for its role in the post storm response.

Moreover, FEMA's Director, Michael Brown, lacked the leadership skills that were needed. Before landfall, Brown did not direct the adequate pre-positioning of critical personnel and equipment, and willfully failed to communicate with Secretary Chertoff, to whom he was supposed to report. Earlier in the hurricane season, FEMA had pre-positioned an unprecedented amount of relief supplies in the region. But the supplies were not enough. Similarly, while both FEMA and the Department of Health and Human Services made efforts to activate the federal emergency health capabilities of the National Disaster Medical System (NDMS) and the U.S. Public Health Service, only a limited number of federal medical teams were actually in position prior to landfall to deploy into the affected area. Only one such team was in a position to provide immediate medical care in the aftermath of the storm.

More broadly, DHS— as the department charged with preparing for and responding to domestic incidents, whether terrorist attacks or natural disasters – failed to effectively lead the federal response to Hurricane Katrina. DHS leadership failed to bring a sense of urgency to the federal government's preparation for Hurricane Katrina, and Secretary Chertoff himself should have been more engaged in preparations over the weekend before landfall. Secretary Chertoff made only top-level inquiries into the state of preparations, and accepted uncritically the reassurances he received. He did not appear to reach out to the other Cabinet Secretaries to make sure that they were readying their departments to provide whatever assistance DHS – and the people of the Gulf – might need.

Similarly, had he invoked the Catastrophic Incident Annex (CIA) of the NRP, Secretary Chertoff could have helped remove uncertainty about the federal government's need and authority to take initiative before landfall and signaled that all federal government agencies were expected to think – and act – proactively in preparing for and responding to Katrina. The Secretary's activation of the NRP CIA could have increased the urgency of the federal response and led the federal government to respond more proactively rather than waiting for formal requests from overwhelmed state and local officials. Understanding that delay may preclude meaningful assistance and that state and local resources could be quickly overwhelmed and incapacitated, the NRP CIA directs federal agencies to pre-position resources without awaiting requests from the state and local governments. Even then, the NRP CIA holds these resources at mobilization sites until requested by state and local officials, except in certain prescribed circumstances.

The military also had a role to play, and ultimately, the National Guard and active duty military troops and assets deployed during Katrina constituted the largest domestic deployment of military forces since the Civil War. And while the Department of Defense (DOD) took additional steps to prepare for Katrina beyond those it had taken for prior civil support missions, its preparations were not sufficient for a storm of Katrina's magnitude. Individual commanders took actions that later helped improve the response, but these actions were not coordinated by the Department. The Department's preparations were consistent with how DOD interpreted its role under the National Response Plan, which was to provide support in response to requests for assistance from FEMA.

The National Guard and active duty military troops and assets deployed during Katrina constituted the largest domestic deployment of military forces since the Civil War.

However, additional preparations in advance of specific requests for support could have enabled a more rapid response.

In addition, the White House shares responsibility for the inadequate pre-landfall preparations. To be sure, President Bush, at the request of FEMA Director Michael Brown, did take the initiative to personally call Governor Blanco to urge a mandatory evacuation. As noted earlier, he also took the unusual step of declaring an emergency in the Gulf States prior to Katrina making landfall. On the other hand, the President did not leave his Texas ranch to return to Washington until two days after landfall, and only then convened his Cabinet as well as a White House task force to oversee federal response efforts.

Unacceptable Government Response

The effect of the long-term failures at every level of government to plan and prepare adequately for a catastrophic hurricane in the Gulf was evident in the inadequate preparations before Katrina's landfall and then again in the initial response to the storm.

Search and Rescue

Flooding in New Orleans drove thousands of survivors to attics and rooftops to await rescue. Some people were trapped in attics and nursing homes and drowned as the dirty waters rose around them. Others escaped only by chopping their way through roofs. Infrastructure damage complicated the organization and conduct of search-and-rescue missions in New Orleans and elsewhere. Destruction of communications towers and equipment in particular limited the ability of crews to communicate with one another, undermining coordination and efficiency. Rescuers also had to contend with weapons fire, debris, and polluted water. The skill and dedication of Louisiana Department of Wildlife and Fisheries officials and others working in these adverse conditions stand out as a singular success story of the hurricane response.

Applying a model developed in the Hurricane Pam exercise, rescue teams in Louisiana brought hurricane victims to high ground, where they were supposed to receive food, water, medical attention, and transport to shelters. Here, too, there were problems. Poor communications delayed state and federal officials learning about where rescuees had been dropped, in turn slowing shipments of food and water to those areas. The City of New Orleans was unprepared to help people evacuate, as many buses from the city's own fleet were submerged, while at the same time officials had not arranged in advance for drivers for those buses that were available.

Flooding in New Orleans drove thousands of survivors to attics and rooftops to await rescue. Some people were trapped in attics and nursing homes and drowned as the dirty waters rose around them.

The storm also laid waste to much of the city's police, whose headquarters and several district offices, along with hundreds of vehicles, rounds of ammunition, and uniforms were all destroyed within the first two days of landfall.

Planning for search and rescue was also insufficient. FEMA, for instance, failed to provide boats for its search and rescue teams even though flooding had been confirmed by Tuesday. Moreover, interagency coordination was inadequate at both the state and federal levels. While the Louisiana Department of Fisheries and Wildlife and FEMA are responsible for interagency search and rescue coordination at the state and federal levels respectively, neither developed adequate plans for this mission. Staggeringly, the City of New Orleans Fire Department owned no boats, and the New Orleans Police Department owned five. Meanwhile, widespread communications failures in Louisiana and Mississippi were so bad that many officers reverted to either physically running messages from one person to another, or passing messages along a daisy chain of officers using radios with limited range.

Situational Awareness

While authorities recognized the need to begin search-and-rescue missions even before the hurricane winds fully subsided, other aspects of the response were hindered by a failure to quickly recognize the dimensions of the disaster. These problems were particularly acute at the federal level. The Homeland Security Operations Center (HSOC) – charged with providing reliable information to decision-makers including the Secretary and the President – failed to create a system to identify and acquire all available, relevant information, and as a result situational awareness was deeply flawed. With local and state resources immediately overwhelmed, rapid federal mobilization of resources was critical. Yet reliable information on such vital developments as the levee failures, the extent of flooding, and the presence of thousands of people in need of life-sustaining assistance at the New Orleans Convention Center did not reach the White House, Secretary Chertoff or other key officials for hours, and in some cases more than a day. FEMA Director Michael Brown, then in Louisiana, contributed to the problem by refusing to communicate with Secretary Chertoff opting instead to pass information directly to White House staff. Moreover, even though senior DHS officials did receive on the day of landfall numerous reports that should have led to an understanding of the increasingly dire situation in New Orleans, many indicated they were not aware of the crisis until sometime Tuesday morning.

DHS was slow to recognize the scope of the disaster or that FEMA had become overwhelmed. On the day after landfall, DHS officials were still struggling to determine the "ground truth" about the extent of the flooding despite the many reports it had received about the catastrophe; key officials did not grasp the need to act on the less-than-complete information that is to be expected in a disaster. DHS leaders did not become fully engaged in recovery efforts until Thursday, when in Deputy Secretary Michael Jackson's words, they "tried to kick it up a notch"; after that, they did provide significant leadership within DHS (and FEMA) as well as coordination across the federal government. But this effort should have begun sooner.

The Department of Defense also was slow to acquire information regarding the extent of the storm's devastation. DOD officials relied primarily on media reports for their information. Many senior DOD officials did not learn that the levees had breached information about the scope of the damage, it also waited for the lead federal agency, FEMA, to identify the support needed from DOD. The lack of situational awareness during this phase appears to have been a major reason for DOD's belated adoption of the forward-looking posture necessary in a catastrophic incident.

Post-Storm Evacuation

Overwhelmed by Katrina, the city and state turned to FEMA for help. On Monday, Governor Blanco asked FEMA Director Michael Brown for buses, and Brown assured the state the same day that 500 buses were en route to assist in the evacuation of New Orleans and would arrive within hours. In spite of Brown's assurances and the state's continued requests over the course of the next two days, FEMA did not direct the U.S. Department of Transportation to send buses until very early on Wednesday, two days after landfall, and the buses did not begin to arrive at all until Wednesday evening and not in significant numbers until Thursday. Concerned over FEMA's delay in providing buses – and handicapped by the Louisiana Department of Transportation and Development's utter failure to make any preparation to carry out its lead role for evacuation under the state's emergency plan – Governor Blanco directed members of her office to begin locating buses on Tuesday and approved an effort to commandeer school buses for evacuation on Wednesday. But these efforts were too little, too late. Tens of thousands of people were forced to wait in unspeakably horrible conditions until as late as Saturday to be evacuated.

Logistics and Military Support

Problems with obtaining, communicating and managing information plagued many other aspects of the response as well. FEMA lacked the tools to track the status of shipments, interfering with the management of supplying food, water, ice and other vital commodities to those in need across the Gulf Coast. So too did the incompatibility of the electronic systems used by federal and state authorities to manage requests for assistance, which made it necessary to transfer requests from the state system to the federal system manually.

Supplies of commodities were especially problematic. Federal shipments to Mississippi did not reach adequate levels until 10 days after landfall. The reasons for this are unclear, but FEMA's inadequate 'surge capacity' – the ability to quickly ramp up the volume of shipments – is a likely cause. In both Mississippi and Louisiana, there were additional problems in getting the supplies the "last mile" to individuals in need. Both states planned to make supplies available for pickup at designated distribution points, but neither anticipated the problems people would face in reaching those points, due to impassable roads or other issues. And in Louisiana, the National Guard was not equipped to assume this task. One of Louisiana's greatest shortages was portable toilets, which were requested for the Superdome but never arrived there, as more than 20,000 people were forced to reside inside the Dome without working plumbing for nearly a week.

Supplies of commodities were especially problematic. Federal shipments to Mississippi did not reach adequate levels until 10 days after landfall.

For their part, Louisiana and Mississippi relied heavily on support from other states to supplement their own emergency resources. Both states were parties to an interstate agreement known as the Emergency Management Assistance Compact (EMAC), which provides a system for sharing National Guard troops and other resources in natural disasters. As in many other areas of Katrina response, however, the magnitude of the demands strained the EMAC process and revealed limitations in the system. Paperwork burdens proved overwhelming. Louisiana experienced difficulties processing the volume of incoming resources. On Wednesday, August 31, the federal National Guard Bureau, which ordinarily serves a coordinating function within the Department of Defense, relieved Louisiana and Mississippi of many of the bureaucratic responsibilities by making direct requests for available troops to state Adjutants General.

This process quickly resulted in the largest National Guard deployment in U.S. history, with 50,000 troops and supporting equipment arriving from 49 states and four territories within two weeks. These forces participated in every aspect of emergency response, from medical care to law enforcement and debris removal, and were considered invaluable by Louisiana and Mississippi officials.

Although this process successfully deployed a large number of National Guard troops, it did not proceed efficiently, or according to any pre-existing plan or process. There is, in fact, no established process for the large-scale, nationwide deployment of National Guard troops for civil support. In addition, the deployments of National Guard troops were not coordinated with the federal Northern Command, which was overseeing the large-scale deployments and operations of the active-duty military.

While the National Response Plan has specific procedures for active-duty involvement in natural disasters, their deployment raised unforeseen issues and was initially a source of frustration to Governor Blanco. The Governor directed her Adjutant General to secure additional troops on the day after landfall, but federal and state officials did not coordinate her requests well, and ground troops didn't arrive in significant numbers for several days. The Defense Department chose to rely primarily on the deployment of National Guard troops (versus federal active duty troops) pursuant to its declared strategy and because it believed they were best suited to the required tasks, including performing law enforcement. In addition, the need to resolve command issues between National Guard and active duty forces – an issue taken up (but not resolved) in a face-to-face meeting between President Bush and the Governor on Air Force One on the Friday after landfall, may have played a role in the timing of active duty troop deployments. The issue became moot as the two forces stayed under their separate commands, an arrangement that turned out to work well in this case thanks to the cooperation of the respective commanders.

While the large numbers of active-duty troops did not arrive until the end of the first week following landfall, National Guard troops did, and the Department of Defense contributed in other important ways during that period. Early in the week, DOD ordered its military commanders to push available assets to the Gulf Coast. They also streamlined their ordinarily bureaucratic processes for handling FEMA requests for assistance and emphasized movement based on vocal commands with the paperwork to follow, though some FEMA officials believe that DOD's approval process continued to take too long. They provided significant support to search-and-rescue missions, evacuee airlifts, logistics management of buses arriving in the State for evacuation, and other matters.

By Tuesday afternoon, the New Orleans Superdome had become overcrowded, leading officials to turn additional refugees away.

Toward the end of the week, with its own resources stretched thin, FEMA turned to DOD to take over logistics for all commodity movements. The Department of Defense acceded to the request, and provided some logistics assistance to FEMA. However, it did not undertake the complete logistical takeover initially requested by FEMA because that was not needed.

By Tuesday afternoon, the New Orleans Superdome had become overcrowded, leading officials to turn additional refugees away. Mayor Nagin then decided to open the Morial Convention Center as a second refuge of last resort inside the city, but did not supply it with food or water. Moreover, he communicated his decision to open the Convention Center to state and federal officials poorly, if at all. That failure, in addition to the delay of shipments due to security concerns and DHS's own independent lack of awareness of the situation, contributed to the paucity of food, water, security or medical care at the Convention Center, as a population of approximately 19,000 gathered there. Those vital commodities and services did not arrive until Friday, when the Louisiana National Guard, assisted by Guard units from five other states, brought in relief supplies provided by FEMA, established law and order, and then evacuated the Convention Center on Saturday within eight hours.

Law Enforcement

Law enforcement outside the Superdome and the Convention Center was a problem, and was fueled by several contributing factors, including erroneous statements by top city officials inflaming the public's perception of the lawlessness in New Orleans.

Without effective law enforcement, real or imagined safety threats interrupted virtually every aspect of the response. Fearing for their personal safety, medical and search and rescue teams withdrew from their missions. FEMA and commercial vendors of critical supplies often refused to make deliveries until military escorts could be arranged. In fact, there was some lawlessness, yet for every actual act there were rumors of dozens more, leading to widespread and inaccurate reporting that severely complicated a desperate situation. Unfortunately, local, state, and federal officials did little to stanch this rumor flow. Police presence on the streets was inadequate, in part because in a matter of hours Katrina turned the New Orleans police department from protectors of the public to victims of the storm. Nonetheless, most New Orleans police officers appear to have reported for duty, many setting aside fears about the safety of their families or the status of their homes.

Without effective law enforcement, real or imagined safety threats interrupted virtually every aspect of the response.

Even so, the ability of the officers who remained to perform their duties was significantly hampered by the lack of basic supplies. While supplies such as weapons and ammunition were lost to flooding, the NOPD leadership did not provide its officers with basic necessities such food; nor did the department have logistics in place to handle supplies. Members of the NOPD also identified the lack of a unified command for this incident as a major problem; eight members of the Command Staff were extremely critical of the lack of leadership from the city's Office of Emergency Preparedness (OEP). The department's rank and file were unfamiliar with both the department's and the city's emergency-operations manuals and other hurricane emergency procedures. Deficiencies in the NOPD's manual, lack of training on this manual, lack of familiarity with it, or a combination of the three resulted in inadequate protection of department resources.

Federal law-enforcement assistance was too slow in coming, in large part because the two federal departments charged under the NRP with providing such assistance – DHS and the Department of Justice (DOJ) – had done almost no pre-storm planning. In fact, they failed to determine even well into the post-landfall period which of the two departments would assume the lead for federal law enforcement under the NRP. As a result, later in the week, as federal law-enforcement officers did arrive, some were distracted by a pointless "turf war" between DHS and DOJ over which agency was in the lead. In the end, federal assistance was crucial, but should have arrived much sooner.

Health Care

Safety concerns were only one of numerous challenges faced by health-care providers. There were numerous other challenges, including the following.

Medical teams had to triage more than 70,000 rescuees and evacuees and provide acute care to the sick and wounded. While officials used plans developed in Hurricane Pam as a helpful framework for managing this process, existing emergency-room facilities were overwhelmed by the volume of patients. Local and state officials quickly set up temporary field hospitals at a sports arena and a K-mart in Baton Rouge to supplement hospital capacity.

New Orleans had a large population of "special needs patients," individuals living at home who required ongoing medical assistance. Before Katrina struck, the City Health Department activated a plan to establish a care facility for this population within the Superdome and provided transportation to evacuate several hundred patients and their caregivers to Baton Rouge. While Superdome facilities proved useful in treating special needs patients who remained behind, they had to contend with shortages of supplies, physical damage to the facility necessitating a post-landfall relocation of patients and equipment to an area adjacent to the Dome, and a population of more than 20,000 people using the Superdome as a refuge of last resort. Also, FEMA's Disaster Medical Assistance Teams which provide the invaluable resources of pharmacies and hospital equipment, arrived at the Superdome on the night following landfall, but left temporarily on Thursday, before the evacuation of the Superdome's special needs population was completed, because of security concerns.

While hospitals had evacuated some of their patients before landfall, they had retained others thought to be too frail for transport, and believed by staying open they would be available to serve hurricane victims. Their strategy became untenable after landfall when power was lost, and their backup generators were rendered inoperable by flooding and fuel shortages.

In Louisiana, hospitals had to evacuate after landfall on short notice principally due to loss of electrical power. While hospitals had evacuated some of their patients before landfall, they had retained others thought to be too frail for transport, and believed by staying open they would be available to serve hurricane victims. Their strategy became untenable after landfall when power was lost, and their backup generators were rendered inoperable by flooding and fuel shortages. The Louisiana Department of Health and Hospitals stepped in to arrange for their evacuation; while successful, it had to compete with search and rescue teams for helicopters and other needed resources.

Many nursing homes in and around New Orleans lacked adequate evacuation plans. While they were required to have plans on file with local government, there was no process to ensure that there were sufficient resources to evacuate all the nursing homes at once, and dozens of patients who were not evacuated died. When evacuation became necessary, some sent their patients to the Superdome, where officials struggling to handle the volume of patients already there were obliged to accept still more.

Long Term Factors

Actions taken – and failures to act – well before Katrina struck compounded the problems resulting from the ineffective leadership that characterized the immediate preparations for the hurricane and the post-landfall response. A common theme of these earlier actions is underfunding emergency preparedness. While the Committee did not examine the conflicting political or budget priorities that may have played a role, in many cases the shortsightedness associated with the underfunding is glaring. Among notable examples are the following:

The Louisiana Office of Homeland Security and Emergency Preparedness, the state counterpart to FEMA, suffered chronic staffing problems and employee turnover due to underfunding. LOHSEP's Planning Chief also testified that lack of resources prevented the agency from meeting its schedule for periodic review and updates of state emergency plans.

The Office of Emergency Preparedness for New Orleans, long known to be among the nation's cities most vulnerable to a catastrophic hurricane, had a staff of only three. Its police and fire departments, responsible for search and rescue activities, had five and no boats, respectively. In 2004, the city turned down a request by the New Orleans Fire Department to fund the purchase of six additional boats.

The Hurricane Pam exercise faced repeated delays due to funding constraints. It took nearly five years for the federal government to approve the state's initial funding request, and the limited funding finally granted necessitated last-minute cutbacks in the scope of the exercise. Follow-up workshops were delayed by funding shortfalls – some as small as the $15,000 needed for participants' travel expenses – shortfalls that either the state or federal government should have remedied.

Numerous witnesses testified that FEMA's budget was far short of what was needed to accomplish its mission, and that this contributed to FEMA's failure to be prepared for a catastrophe. FEMA witnesses also universally pointed out that the agency has suffered for the last few years from a vacancy rate of 15 to 20 percent (i.e., between 375 to 500 vacant positions in a 2,500-person agency), including several at key supervisory levels. FEMA sought additional funding but did not receive it. The Committee found that FEMA's budget shortages hindered its preparedness.

New Orleans failed to plan for the 100,000 people believed to lack the means to evacuate themselves.

Inadequate training in the details of the recently promulgated National Response Plan was a contributing factor in shortcomings in government's performance. Louisiana emergency management officials and National Guardsmen were receiving basic NRP and incident command system (ICS) training two days after the storm hit. Certain FEMA officials, also, were inadequately trained on the NRP and ICS. Only one large-scale federal exercise of the NRP took place before Katrina, the DHS Top Officials 3 exercise in April 2005, approximately three months after the NRP was issued. TOPOFF 3, sponsored by DHS, involved responders from all levels of government. A November 2005 report by the DHS Inspector General, echoing the findings of an earlier report by DHS itself in May 2005, found that the exercise, which involved federal, state and local responders, "highlighted – at all levels of government – a fundamental lack of understanding for the principles and protocols set forth in the NRP and [National Incident Management System]." The lack of familiarity with emergency- management principles and plans hampered the Katrina response.

New Orleans failed to plan for the 100,000 people believed to lack the means to evacuate themselves. Dating back to at least 1994, local and state officials have known about the need to address this problem. For its part, the federal government, which knew about this problem for some time, neither monitored their planning nor offered assistance. This evacuation problem was not included in the Pam exercise and, during follow up meetings in the summer of 2005, New Orleans officials informed counterparts from FEMA, other federal agencies, and the state preparedness agency that the City was not able to provide for the necessary pre-storm evacuation, but nothing was done to resolve the issue.

The City of New Orleans, with primary responsibility for evacuation of its citizens, had language in its plan stating the city's intent to assist those who needed transportation for pre-storm evacuation, but had no actual plan provisions to implement that intent. In late 2004 and 2005, city officials negotiated contracts with Amtrak, riverboat owners and others to pre-arrange transportation alternatives, but received inadequate support from the city's Director of Homeland Security and Emergency Preparedness, and contracts were not in place when Katrina struck. As Katrina approached, notwithstanding the city's evacuation plans on paper, the best solution New Orleans had for people without transportation was a private-citizen volunteer carpool initiative called Operation Brothers' Keepers and transit buses taking people – not out of the city, but to the Superdome. While the Superdome provided shelter from the devastating winds and water, conditions there deteriorated quickly. Katrina's "near miss" ripped the covering off the roof, caused leaking, and knocked out the power, rendering the plumbing, air conditioning, and public announcement system totally useless.

The Louisiana Department of Transportation and Development, whose Secretary had personally accepted departmental responsibility under the state's emergency operations plan to arrange for transportation for evacuation in emergencies, had done nothing to prepare for that responsibility prior to Katrina. While the Secretary attempted to defend his inaction in a personal appearance before the Committee, the Committee found his explanations rang hollow, and his account of uncommunicated doubts and objections to state policy disturbing. Had his department identified available buses or other means of transport for evacuation within the state in the months before the hurricane, at a minimum the State would have been prepared to evacuate people stranded in New Orleans after landfall more quickly than it did.

FEMA and the U.S. Department of Transportation, charged under the National Response Plan with supporting state and local government transportation needs (including evacuation) in emergencies, did little to plan for the possibility that they would be called on to assist with post-landfall evacuation needs, despite being on notice for over a month before Katrina hit that the state and local governments needed more buses and drivers – and being on notice for years that tens of thousands of people would have no means to evacuate.

Though much attention had been paid to addressing communications shortfalls, efforts to address interoperability – as well as simply operability – were inadequate. There was little advance preparation regarding how responders would operate in an area with no power and where virtually all forms of pre-existing communications were destroyed. And while satellite phones were available to some, they either did not function properly or officials were not trained on how to use these relatively complex devices. Moreover, the National Communications System, the agency within DHS that is primarily responsible under the National Response Plan for providing communications support to first responders during disasters, had no plans to do so.

These planning failures would have been of far less consequence had the system of levees built to protect New Orleans from flooding stayed intact, as they had in most prior hurricanes. But they did not, and the resulting inundation was catastrophic. The levee failures themselves turned out to have roots long pre-dating Katrina as well. While several engineering analyses continue, the Committee found deeply disturbing evidence of flaws in the design and construction of the levees. For instance, two major drainage canals – the 17th Street and London Avenue Canals – failed at their foundations, prior to their flood walls being met with the water heights for which they were designed to protect central New Orleans. Moreover, the greater metropolitan New Orleans area was literally riddled with levee breaches caused by massive overtopping and scouring of levees that were not "armored," or properly designed, to guard against the inevitable cascading waters that were sure to accompany a storm of the magnitude of Hurricane Katrina. The Committee also discovered that the inspection and maintenance regime in place to ensure that the levees, flood walls and other structures existing to protect the residents of the greater New Orleans area was in no way commensurate with the risk posed to these persons and their property.

Planning failures would have been of far less consequence had the system of levees built to protect New Orleans from flooding stayed intact, as they had in most prior hurricanes. But they did not, and the resulting inundation was catastrophic.

Equally troubling was the revelation of serious disagreement – still unresolved months after Katrina – among officials of several government entities over who had responsibility, and when, for key levee issues including emergency response and levee repair. Such conflicts prevented any meaningful emergency plans from being put in place and, at the time of Katrina, none of the relevant government agencies had a plan for responding to a levee breach. While the deadly waters continued to pour into the heart of the city after the hurricane had passed, the very government agencies that were supposed to work together to protect the city from such a catastrophe not only initially disagreed about whose responsibility it was to repair the levee breaches, but disagreed as to how the repairs should be conducted. Sadly, due to the lack of foresight and overall coordination prior to the storm, such conflicts existed as the waters of Lake Pontchartrain continued to fill central New Orleans.

Waste, Fraud and Abuse

Besides overwhelming many government emergency-response capabilities, Katrina severely affected the government's ability to properly track and verify its costs when it contracted for disaster relief goods and services.

It takes money to prepare, respond and recover from a disaster, and typically the bigger the disaster, the more money it takes. As of March 8, 2006, the federal government had committed $88 billion to the response, recovery and rebuilding efforts.

Unfortunately, not all of this money has been wisely spent. Precious taxpayer dollars have been lost due to waste, fraud and abuse.

Among other problems were FEMA's lack of financial controls, failures to ensure eligibility of individuals receiving disaster-related assistance, and poor contracting practices, including use of no bid contracts. A notable example of the resulting wastefulness was FEMA's purchase of 25,000 manufactured homes that are virtually useless because FEMA's own regulations prohibit them being installed in a flood plain. In a similar vein, FEMA's lack of controls in dealing with hotels providing temporary housing for evacuees resulted in instances where hotels charged for empty rooms; individuals held multiple rooms; hotel rooms were used as storage units for personal goods; individuals stayed at resorts; and hotels charged rates as high as $400 per night.

Conclusion

Effective response to mass emergencies is a critical role of every level of government. It is a role that requires an unusual level of planning, coordination and dispatch among governments' diverse units. Following the terrorist attacks of 9/11, this country went through one of the most sweeping reorganizations of federal government in history. While driven primarily by concerns of terrorism, the reorganization was designed to strengthen our nation's ability to address the consequences of both natural and man-made disasters. In its first major test, this reorganized system failed.

A notable example of the resulting wastefulness was FEMA's purchase of 25,000 manufactured homes that are virtually useless because FEMA's own regulations prohibit them being installed in a flood plain.

Questions

1. How was Hurricane Katrina different from previous hurricanes?
2. How, in some ways, was Hurricane Katrina anticipated?
3. Identify the failure of state and local government in planning and preparing for Hurricane Katrina.
4. Identify the failure of federal government in responding to Hurricane Katrina.

Part II: Organization Development

Chapter 8

U.S. National Security

Objectives

- Know that national security is a shared government responsibility under the Constitution.
- Identify the Instruments of National Power.
- Explain how the executive branch coordinates national security.
- Argue whether 9/11 was a criminal act or act of war.

If men were angels, no government would be necessary. If angels were to govern men, neither external nor internal controls on government would be necessary. In framing a government which is to be administered by men over men, the great difficulty lies in this: you must first enable the government to control the governed; and in the next place, oblige it to control itself.

—James Madison, *Federalist No. 51*, 1788

Introduction

National security is among the fundamental national purposes that the American people embedded in the Constitution. The United States relies on the complementary application of the basic instruments of national power (diplomatic, economic, informational, and military) for its security. Under the framework of shared responsibilities set out by the Constitution, the United States establishes specific policies and strategies in order to preserve its values, to identify its interests, and to assure the best use of its resources in advancing its interests and defending the security of the Republic and its citizens.[1]

National security is among the fundamental national purposes that the American people embedded in the Constitution.

American National Government

Power in American national government is decentralized, divided, dispersed, and limited. This distribution of power derives in part from the Constitution, through limitations imposed on the government, the system of checks and balances among the three branches, and independent bases of support and authority for each branch.

In his passage from the *Federalist No. 51*, James Madison, sometimes referred to as the "Father of the Constitution," offers a rationale for the form of national government operating here since 1789. Power in the national government is limited directly and indirectly by the Constitution. To protect certain individual rights and political liberties, this charter places explicit restrictions on the national government, principally through the Bill of Rights and the 14th Amendment. The First Amendment, for instance, mandates that "Congress shall make no law respecting an establishment of religion, or prohibiting the free exercise thereof; or abridging the freedom of speech, or of the press; or the right of the people peaceably to assemble, and to petition the Government for a redress of grievances." The Constitution also establishes checks and balances among the three branches of government—the executive, judiciary, and legislature—each of which has its own independent institutional base and its own enumerated and implied powers. The branches, moreover, share responsibility for policymaking at the national level. As a consequence of these characteristics, the Constitution issues an "invitation to struggle" over the direction of American public policy, as one of its foremost students, Edward S. Corwin, has observed.[2]

U.S. Constitution

The Constitution, replacing the Articles of Confederation in 1789, strengthened the national government. Article III declares that "This Constitution, and the Laws of the United States which shall be made in Pursuance thereof; and all Treaties made, or which shall be made, under the Authority of the United States, shall be the supreme Law of the Land." Despite this enhancement, the Constitution limited the power of the national government, recognizing the independence and powers of the states. It also established a new government regime that divided authorities among three branches, rather than consolidating these powers in a single entity, as existed under its short-lived predecessor.

The Constitution is a brief document, compared to many other national and state constitutions. It is not an elaborate blueprint, detailing the organization of government. Instead, it is a broad framework—sometimes referred to as a living constitution—that has allowed the national government to adapt its organizational arrangements and structures to the changing characteristics, needs, and demands of the American people over more than two centuries. The Constitution, moreover, is difficult to amend. An amendment requires a favorable two-thirds vote in the House and in the Senate, along with ratification by three-fourths of the individual states. The document can be amended in one other way: the legislatures of two-thirds of the states may call for a convention to propose amendments, which would then require ratification by three-fourths of the states. However, no national convention has been established under this approach; consequently, no constitutional amendment has been approved through this process.

Partly because of this structure, the constitutional system has achieved a high degree of stability. The U.S. Constitution is today the oldest written democratic charter for a national government. Since the Bill of Rights—the first 10 amendments—was ratified in 1791, the Constitution has been amended only 17 times, most recently in 1992. And one of these amendments canceled another (the 21st Amendment, in 1933, repealed the 18th Amendment, which in 1919 had established the prohibition of alcohol).[3]

Checks and Balances and Shared Responsibilities

Congress, the President, and the Supreme Court have separate and distinct political bases under the Constitution, to foster each branch's independence and integrity. The ultimate purpose behind this separation, James Madison argued in the *Federalist Papers*, is to prevent a "faction"—that is, a group "adverse to the rights of other citizens, or to the permanent and aggregate interest of the community"—from gaining control over the entire government.[4]

Under the Constitution, the three branches have both enumerated and implied powers that reinforce their institutional independence and political power. Accompanying these, however, is shared responsibility for public policy and a system of checks and balances. These "auxiliary precautions," as Madison called them in the Federalist Papers, are designed so that the "several constituent parts may, by their mutual relations, be the means of keeping each other in their proper places ... [and] may be a check on the other." [4]

Pursuant to the constitutional requirement of the Federal Government to "provide for the common defense," the executive and legislative branches share responsibility and authority for ensuring national security. Based on the constitutional foundation of checks and balances and civilian control of the military, Congress legislates an overall framework for national security and allocates resources to meet changing defense requirements as identified by the executive branch. Within the executive branch, Federal agencies operate within this overall framework and the resources allocated to provide for the Nation's present and future security.[5]

National Security Strategy

National security strategy (NSS) is the art and science of developing, applying, and coordinating the instruments of national power (diplomatic, economic, military, informational) to achieve objectives that contribute to national security. It encompasses national defense, foreign relations, and economic relations and assistance; and aims, among other objectives, at providing a favorable foreign relations position and a defense posture capable of defeating hostile action.[6]

The executive and legislative branches share responsibility and authority for ensuring national security.

The Goldwater-Nichols Act of 1986 requires the President to present to Congress on an annual basis his plan for the national security of the United States. This document identifies the President's objectives for maintaining the safety and security of United States citizens, and addresses how all the instruments of national power will be directed to achieve these goals.[7]

- The **diplomatic instrument** of national power is the principal instrument for accomplishing engagement with other states and foreign groups in order to advance US values, interests, and objectives.[8] United States foreign policy is formulated and advocated within the executive branch by the State Department under the direction of the Secretary of State working in coordination with a global network of ambassadors and embassies.
- The **military instrument** of national power is invested in the United States Armed Forces within the executive branch of government acting under the direction and control of the Secretary of Defense within the Department of Defense (DoD). The Department of Defense includes the Office of the Secretary of Defense, the Joint Chiefs of Staff, the Joint Staff, Defense agencies, DoD field activities, Military Departments and Military Services within those departments, combatant commands, and other organizations and activities that may be established or designated by law, the President, or the Secretary of Defense.[9]
- The **economic instrument** of national power is only partially controlled by governmental agencies. In keeping with US values and constitutional imperatives, American individuals and entities have broad freedom of action abroad. The responsibility of the US government lies with facilitating economic and trade relationships worldwide that promote US fundamental objectives, such as promoting general welfare and supporting security in-

terests and objectives. A strong domestic US economy with free access to global markets and resources is a fundamental engine of the general welfare, the guarantor of a strong national defense, and an influence for economic expansion by US trade partners worldwide.[10]

- The **informational instrument** of national power has a diffuse and complex set of components with no single center of control. In American culture, information is freely exchanged with minimal government controls. Constraints on public access to US government information normally may be imposed only for national security and individual privacy reasons.[11]

National Security Strategy is an unclassified document intended for Congress, the American public, foreign allies, and potential adversaries. The document is addressed to both friend and foe alike to reassure allies, and deter potential enemies.[12]

The NSS of the United States is based on American interests and values and its aim is to ensure the security of the nation while making the world a safer and better place. Its goals are political and economic freedom, peaceful relations with other states, and respect for human dignity. The NSS includes strengthening alliances and working with others to defeat global terrorism and defuse regional conflicts; preventing our enemies from threatening the United States, its allies, and friends with WMD; and transforming America's national security institutions.[13]

The National Security Strategy of the United States is based on American interests and values and its aim is to ensure the security of the nation while making the world a safer and better place.

The National Security Council

Since the end of World War II, each presidential administration has sought to develop and perfect a reliable set of executive institutions to manage national security policy. Each President has tried to avoid the problems and deficiencies of his predecessors' efforts and install a policy-making and coordination system that reflected his personal management style. The National Security Council (NSC) has been at the center of this foreign policy coordination system, but it has changed many times to conform with the needs and inclinations of each succeeding chief executive.

The National Security Act of July 26, 1947, created the National Security Council under the chairmanship of the President, with the Secretaries of State and Defense as its key members, to coordinate foreign policy and defense policy, and to reconcile diplomatic and military commitments and requirements. This major legislation also provided for a Secretary of Defense, a National Military Establishment, Central Intelligence Agency, and National Security Resources Board. The view that the NSC had been created to coordinate political and military questions quickly gave way to the understanding that the NSC existed to serve the President alone. The view that the Council's role was to foster collegiality among departments also gave way to the need by successive Presidents to use the Council as a means of controlling and managing competing departments.

For 60 years, 11 Presidents have sought to use the National Security Council system to integrate foreign and defense policies in order to preserve the nation's security and advance its interests abroad. Recurrent structural modifications over the years have reflected Presidential management style, changing requirements, and personal relationships.[14]

Declarations of War & Authorizations of Force

Article I, § 8, of the Constitution vests in Congress the power "to declare War." Pursuant to that power, Congress has enacted eleven declarations of war during the course of American history relating to five different wars, the most recent being those that were adopted during World War II. In addition, Congress has adopted a number of authorizations for the use of military force, the most recent being the joint resolution enacted on October 16, 2002, authorizing the use of military force against Iraq. To buttress the nation's ability to prosecute a war or armed conflict, Congress has also enacted numerous statutes which confer standby authority on the President or the executive branch and are activated by the enactment of a declaration of war, the existence of a state of war, or the promulgation of a declaration of national emergency.[15]

Previous Declarations of War

From the Washington Administration to the present, there have been eleven separate formal declarations of war against foreign nations enacted by Congress and the President, encompassing five different wars—the War of 1812 with Great Britain, the War with Mexico in 1846, the War with Spain in 1898, the First World War, and the Second World War. In each case the enactment of a formal declaration of war has been preceded by a presidential request to Congress for such an action, either in writing or in person before a joint session of Congress. In each such message requesting a war declaration, the President has cited what he deemed compelling reasons for doing so. These reasons have included armed attacks on United States territory or its citizens, and attacks on or direct threats to United States rights or interests as a sovereign nation. In the nineteenth century all declarations of war were passed by the Congress in the form of a bill. In the twentieth century all declarations of war were passed by the Congress in the form of a joint resolution. In every instance the measures were adopted by majority vote in both the House and the Senate and were signed into law by the President. The last formal declaration of war was enacted on June 5, 1942, against Rumania during World War II.

In the twentieth century, without exception, presidential requests for formal declarations of war by Congress were based on findings by the President that U.S. territory or sovereign rights had been attacked or threatened by a foreign nation. Although President Wilson had tried to maintain U.S. neutrality after the outbreak of the First World War, he regarded the German decision on February 1, 1917, to engage in unrestricted submarine warfare against all naval vessels in the war zone, including those of neutral states, to be an unacceptable assault on U.S. sovereign rights which the German Government had previously pledged to respect.

President Franklin D. Roosevelt requested a declaration of war against Japan on December 8, 1941, because of direct military attacks by that nation against U.S. territory, military personnel and citizens in Hawaii and other outposts in the Pacific area. The House and the Senate passed the requested declaration and the President signed it into law that same day. After Germany and Italy each declared war on the United States on December 11, 1941, President Roosevelt asked Congress to respond in kind by recognizing that a state of war existed between the United States and those two nations. Congress passed separate joint resolutions declaring war on both nations which the President signed on December 11, 1941. On June 2, 1942, President Roosevelt asked that Congress declare war on Bulgaria, Hungary and Rumania, nations that were under the domination of Germany, were engaged in active military actions against the United States, and had themselves declared war on the United States. Congress passed separate joint resolutions declaring war on each of these nations. The President signed these resolutions on June 5, 1942.

There is a striking similarity of language in the eight declarations of war passed by the Congress in the twentieth century. They all declare that a "state of war" exists between the United States and the other nation. With the one exception of the declaration of war against Austria-Hungary on December 7, 1917, the other seven declarations characterize the state of war as having been "thrust upon the United States" by the other nation. All eight of these twentieth century declarations of war state in identical language that the President is

> *"...authorized and directed to employ the entire naval and military forces of the United States and the resources of the Government to carry on war against [the 'Government' of the particular nation]; and to bring the conflict to a successful termination all of the resources of the country are hereby pledged by the Congress of the United States."*[16]

Statutory Authorizations for the Use of Military Force

From the Administration of President John Adams to the present, there have been various instances when legislation has been enacted authorizing the use of military force by the President instead of formally declaring war. In most cases such legislation has been preceded by a specific request by the President for such authority.

From the Administration of President John Adams to the present, there have been various instances when legislation has been enacted authorizing the use of military force by the President instead of formally declaring war. In most cases such legislation has been preceded by a specific request by the President for such authority. During the Presidencies of John Adams and Thomas Jefferson, these Chief Executives noted in messages to Congress that Congressional authorizations for use of force would be appropriate to enable the United States to protect its interests from predatory actions by foreign powers, in particular attacks on U.S. commercial vessels and persons on the high seas by France and by Tripoli. Congress responded with specific authorizations for the use of force under the President's direction in 1798 against France and in 1802 against Tripoli. In 1815 President James Madison formally requested that Congress declare war against the Regency of Algiers in response to its attacks on U.S. citizens and commerce in the Mediterranean. Congress responded with an Act authorizing the President to utilize U.S. armed vessels against Algerian naval attacks but did not declare war.

In the period following World War II, Presidential requests for authority to use military force, when made, have usually been for broad authority to use U.S. military force in a specific region of the world in order to defend U.S. interests or friendly states as the President deems appropriate. More recently, due to an expansive interpretation of the President's constitutional authority as Commander-in-Chief of the Armed Forces and of his inherent powers to use force without Congressional authorization, the President has welcomed support from the Congress in the form of legislation authorizing him to utilize U.S. military forces in a foreign conflict or engagement in support of U.S. interests, but has not taken the view that he is required to obtain such authorization.[17]

Implications Under International Law

Traditionally, peace and war have been deemed under international law to be distinctive forms of relations between states. Thus, peace has been defined as

> *A condition in which States maintain order and justice, solve their problems by cooperation, and eliminate violence. It is a condition in which States respect each other's sovereignty and equality, refrain from intervention and the threat or use of force and cooperate with one another in accordance with the treaties which they have concluded.*

War, in contrast, has been described as

> *A condition of armed hostility between States. A contention, through the use of armed force, between states, undertaken for the purpose of overpowering another.*

War has been said to terminate or suspend the laws and customs that prevail in peacetime and to substitute for them the laws of war. Under the traditional laws of war enemy combatants can be killed, prisoners of war taken, the enemy's property seized or destroyed, enemy aliens interned, and other measures necessary to subdue the enemy and impose the will of the warring state taken. Moreover, the existence of a state of war traditionally has been deemed to terminate diplomatic and commercial relations and most of the treaty obligations existing between the warring States. A state of war also has brought into play the law of neutrality with respect to relations between the belligerent and nonbelligerent States.

In this traditional understanding a declaration of war has been deemed, in and of itself, to have the effect of creating a state of war and changing the relationship between the states involved from one of peace to one of war. That has been the case even if no hostilities actually occur. Some question exists as to whether international law traditionally deemed a declaration of war to be a necessary prerequisite to the existence of a state of war; but it is clear that under international law a declaration of war has been viewed as "creating the legal status of war ... [and giving] evidence that peace has been transmuted into war, and that the law of war has replaced the law of peace."

Whether this traditional understanding of war and of the effect of a declaration of war continues to be viable is a matter of considerable dispute among scholars. The right of a state to initiate war, many contend, has been outlawed by such international agreements as the Kellogg-Briand Peace Pact and the Charter of the United Nations.

In the Kellogg-Briand Peace Pact, for instance, the Parties stated that they "condemn recourse to war for the solution of international controversies, and renounce it as an instrument of national policy in their relations with one another." After World War II the Nuremberg Tribunal gave teeth to this commitment by ruling that the Pact rendered aggressive war illegal under international law and makes those who plan and wage such a war guilty of a crime.

The Charter of the United Nations, in turn, states one of its purposes is "to save succeeding generations from the scourge of war," and it requires its Members "to refrain from the threat or use of force against the territorial integrity or political independence of any State, or in any other manner inconsistent with the Purposes of the United Nations." Moreover, it provides for a system of collective security through the Security Council as the primary means of maintaining or restoring international peace and security. Both instruments, it is contended, recognize that the concept of war as a legal right of states, except in self-defense, has been superseded. (The United States, of course, is a Party not only to the Charter but also to the Pact, and it still regards the latter as continuing to be in force.) Whether the traditional concept of war remains valid has been further complicated by the increasing participation in armed conflict of non-State actors such as insurgents, freedom fighters, and terrorists.

The right of a state to initiate war, many contend, has been outlawed by such international agreements as the Kellogg-Briand Peace Pact and the Charter of the United Nations.

Moreover, the clarity of the consequences of a state of war in traditional international law has become muddied in the modern era. Most States since 1945, even when engaged in armed conflict, have resisted describing the conflict as a war. States so engaged have not always automatically terminated diplomatic and commercial relationships, and the discontinuance of treaty obligations has increasingly been deemed to require a treaty-by-treaty examination.

Consequently, conventions that attempt to regulate the means used to wage war, such as the Hague Conventions and other more recent agreements, and those that attempt to ameliorate the consequences of war for certain categories of persons, such as the Geneva Conventions, are deemed to apply to armed conflicts regardless of what label the Parties attach to them. A state of war still triggers application of the various conventions regulating the means of waging war as well as of the general principles of necessity and proportionality. But the legal consequences of declared war have seemingly become less determinate.

Perhaps as a consequence of these developments, declarations of war have fallen into disuse and are virtually never issued in modern conflicts. One commentator asserts that since 1945 "[t]here are no cases of a formal declaration of war having been delivered by one state to another through diplomatic channels ...." As noted above, the United States last declared war in 1942 against Rumania and has since adopted only authorizations for the use of force.

Thus, declarations of war may have become anachronistic in contemporary international law. The legal right of States to engage in war has seemingly become constrained (for other than defensive purposes), and the most salient international laws regarding the means of waging war and the protection of certain categories of persons apply to the circumstance of armed conflict regardless of whether war has been declared. That circumstance can arise in the wake of an authorization to use force as well. States likely still retain a right to issue declarations of war, at least in exercising the right of self-defense; and such a declaration seemingly would still automatically create a state of war. But it is not clear that the legal consequences under international law that would flow from a declaration differ dramatically from those that occur if an armed conflict comes into being pursuant to an authorization for the use of force.[18]

U.S. Policy Response to 9/11

In the days immediately after the September 11 attacks, President Bush consulted with the leaders of Congress on appropriate steps to take to deal with the situation confronting the United States. One of the things that emerged from discussions was the concept of a joint resolution of the Congress authorizing the President to take military steps to deal with the parties responsible for the attacks on the United States. Between September 13 and 14, draft language of such a resolution was discussed and negotiated by the President's representatives and the House and Senate leadership of both parties. Other members of both Houses suggested language for consideration. On Friday, September 14, 2001, the text of a joint resolution was introduced. It was first considered and passed by the Senate in the morning of September 14, as Senate Joint Resolution 23, by a vote of 98-0. The House of Representatives passed it later that evening, by a vote of 420-1. President Bush signed the measure into law on September 18, 2001. The joint resolution authorizes the President

> *"To use all necessary and appropriate force against those nations, organizations, or persons he determines planned, authorized, committed, or aided the terrorist attacks that occurred on September 11, 2001, or harbored such organizations or persons, in order to prevent any future acts of international terrorism against the United States by such nations, organizations or persons."*[19]

9/11: Criminal Act or Act of War?

Past administrations have employed a range of measures to combat international terrorism, from diplomacy, international cooperation, and constructive engagement to economic sanctions, covert action, protective security measures, and military force. The application of sanctions is one of the most frequently used anti-terrorist tools of U.S. policymakers. Governments supporting international terrorism are prohibited from receiving U.S. economic and military assistance. Export of munitions to such countries is foreclosed, and restrictions are imposed on exports of "dual use" equipment. Presence of a country on the "terrorism list," though, may reflect considerations—such as its pursuit of WMD or its human rights record or U.S. domestic political considerations—that are largely unrelated to support for international terrorism.

Generally, U.S. anti-terrorism policy from the late 1970s to the mid-1990s focused on deterring and punishing state sponsors as opposed to terrorist groups themselves. The passage of the Anti-Terrorism and Effective Death Penalty Act of 1996 (P.L. 104-132) signaled an important shift in policy. The act, largely initiated by the executive branch, created a legal category of Foreign Terrorist Organizations (FTO) and banned funding, granting of visas and other material support to such organizations. The USA PATRIOT Act of 2001 (P.L. 107-56) extended and strengthened the provisions of that legislation.[20]

The law of war may be applied only to acts that are part of an "armed conflict." A terrorist act is not seen to be an act of war unless it is part of a broader campaign of violence directed against the state. Where terrorist acts amount to no more than *"situations of internal disturbances and tensions such as riots and isolated and sporadic acts of violence,"* the Hague and Geneva Conventions do not apply. Instead, peacetime domestic criminal laws and international conventions aimed at the repression of terrorism would come into play, obligating states parties to the agreements to try or extradite those believed responsible.[21]

The September 11 attacks clearly violated numerous laws and may be prosecuted as criminal acts, as past terrorist acts have been prosecuted in the United States. The unprecedented nature of the September 11 attacks and the magnitude of damage and loss of life they caused have led a number of officials and commentators to assert that the acts are not just criminal acts, they are "acts of war."[22]

The unprecedented nature of the September 11 attacks and the magnitude of damage and loss of life they caused have led a number of officials and commentators to assert that the acts are not just criminal acts, they are "acts of war."

On November 13, 2001, President Bush signed a Military Order pertaining to the detention, treatment, and trial of certain non-citizens as part of the war against terrorism. The order makes clear that the President views the crisis that began on the morning of September 11 as an attack "on a scale that has created a state of armed conflict that requires the use of the United States Armed Forces." The order finds that the effective conduct of military operations and prevention of military attacks make it necessary to detain certain non-citizens and if necessary, to try them "for violations of the laws of war and other applicable laws by military tribunals."

The President's Order of November 13, 2001 made it apparent that he planned to treat the 9/11 attacks as acts of war rather than criminal acts. The distinction may have more than rhetorical significance. Treating the attacks as violations of the international law of war could allow the United States to prosecute those responsible as war criminals, trying them by special military commission rather than in federal court.

Conclusion

The present conflict does not fit squarely within the definitions of internal or international armed conflicts. The attacks on New York, Pennsylvania, and the Pentagon do not appear to have been part of an effort to take control of territory or install a new government, nor is it certain that they were carried out under the direction of another state. However, the sophisticated planning and execution believed necessary to have accomplished the attacks suggest that they were carried out by organized members of a quasi-military force. The political and ideological purpose ostensibly motivating the terrorist attacks arguably distinguishes them from "ordinary" criminal acts of violence. The magnitude of harm combined with the threat of more attacks appear to be considered sufficient to give rise to a right of self-defense, not only in the viewpoint of the United States, but by many other states and the United Nations. If the attacks are viewed as the opening volley to the United States' military response in Afghanistan, and the reactions of other nations are taken into account, an armed conflict in the "factual sense" could be said to exist.[23]

Questions

1. List and describe four Instruments of National Power.
2. What is the purpose of National Security Strategy?
3. What agency within the executive branch coordinates national security?
4. Who has Constitutional authority to declare war?
5. Who has Constitutional authority to direct the use of military force?
6. When was the last time the United States declared war?
7. Why is a formal declaration of war considered out-of-date by many?
8. Explain why 9/11 may be considered an act of war.

Chapter 9

Combating Terrorism

Objectives

- Know the definitions of antiterrorism, counterterrorism, and combating terrorism.
- Discuss the basic dilemma in combating terrorism.
- Explain some of the policy tools available for combating terrorism.
- Describe the U.S. organization for combating terrorism.
- Describe the U.S. strategy for combating terrorism.

Introduction

> ***Antiterrorism (AT):*** *Defensive measures used to reduce the vulnerability of individuals and property to terrorist acts, to include limited response and containment by local military forces.*
>
> ***Counterterrorism (CT):*** *Offensive measures taken to prevent, deter, and respond to terrorism.*
>
> ***Combating Terrorism:*** *Actions, including AT and CT, taken to oppose terrorism throughout the entire threat spectrum.*
>
> *— DoD Instruction 2000.14*

Reporting in July 2004, the National Commission on Terrorist Attacks Upon the United States, otherwise known as the 9/11 Commission, identified Islamist terrorism as the single most serious threat to the nation. The 9/11 Commission made it clear that the enemy is not Islam, the great world faith, but a perversion of Islam that draws on a long tradition of extreme intolerance within a minority strain and does not distinguish politics from religion, and distorts both. The 9/11 Commission recognized that the enemy goes beyond al Qaeda to include the radical ideological movement, inspired in part by al Qaeda, that has spawned other terrorist groups and violence. Thus, the 9/11 Commission proposed the following objectives and end states for the global war on terrorism:

"Combating Terrorism: Actions, including AT and CT, taken to oppose terrorism throughout the entire threat spectrum."

— DoD Instruction 2000.14

1. Dismantle al Qaeda.
2. Prevail over the ideology that contributes to Islamist terrorism.

The 9/11 Commission acknowledged the first phase of post-9/11 efforts rightly included military action to topple the Taliban and pursue al Qaeda. But long-term success, according to the commission, demands the use of all elements of national power: diplomacy, intelligence, covert action, law enforcement, economic policy, foreign aid, public diplomacy, and homeland defense. The 9/11 Commission proposed using all these means to effect the desired ends in a strategy with three dimensions:

1. Attack terrorists and their organizations.
2. Prevent the continued growth of Islamist terrorism.
3. Protect against and prepare for terrorist attacks.

Attacking terrorists and their organizations means rooting out terrorist sanctuaries. According to the 9/11 Commission, the U.S. government should identify and prioritize actual or potential terrorist sanctuaries and have realistic country or regional strategies for each, utilizing every element of national power and reaching out to countries that can help.[1]

Unfortunately, the simplicity of these statements belie the difficulty entailed in actually going after the terrorists.

U.S. Policy Response

The application of sanctions is one of the most frequently used anti-terrorist tools of U.S. policymakers. Governments supporting international terrorism (as identified by the Department of State) are prohibited from receiving U.S. economic and military assistance. Export of munitions to such countries is foreclosed, restrictions are imposed on exports of "dual use" equipment such as aircraft and trucks.

In the wake of the September 2001 World Trade Center and Pentagon attacks, President Bush, in addressing the nation, stressed that the United States in responding to the attacks will make no distinction between the terrorists who committed these acts and those who harbor them. The President characterized the incidents as "acts of war." Secretary of State Colin Powell called for a "full scale assault against terrorism" and announced plans to launch a world wide coalition against terrorism. A military response option, once perpetrators and/or supporters have been identified, became a strong probability.

Most experts agree that the most effective way to fight terrorism is to gather as much intelligence as possible; disrupt terrorist plans and organizations before they act; and organize multinational cooperation against terrorists and countries that support them. The U.N.'s role in mandating sanctions against Libya for its responsibility in the 1988 Pan Am 103 bombing was significant as the first instance when the world community imposed sanctions against a country in response to its complicity in an act of terrorism. Several factors made the action possible. First, terrorism has touched many more countries in recent years, forcing governments to put aside parochial interests. (Citizens from over 30 countries have reportedly died in Libyan-sponsored bombings.) Second, the end of the Cold War has contributed to increased international cooperation against terrorism. And third, U.S. determination to punish terrorist countries, by military force in some instances, once their complicity was established, was a major factor in spurring other countries to join U.S.-sponsored action.

Most experts agree that the most effective way to fight terrorism is to gather as much intelligence as possible; disrupt terrorist plans and organizations before they act; and organize multinational cooperation against terrorists and countries that support them.

In the past, governments have often preferred to handle terrorism as a national problem without outside interference. Some governments were also wary of getting involved in others battles and possibly attracting terrorism in the form of reprisals. Others were reluctant to join in sanctions if their own trade interests might be damaged or they sympathized with the perpetrator's cause. Finally, there is the persistent problem of extraditing terrorists without abandoning the long-held principle of asylum for persons fleeing persecution for legitimate political or other activity.

Dilemmas

In their desire to combat terrorism in a modern political context, nations often face conflicting goals and courses of action: (1) providing security from terrorist acts, i.e., limiting the freedom of individual terrorists, terrorist groups, and support networks to operate unimpeded in a relatively unregulated environment versus (2) maximizing individual freedoms, democracy, and human rights. Efforts to combat terrorism are complicated by a global trend toward deregulation, open borders, and expanded commerce. Particularly in democracies such as the United States, the constitutional limits within which policy must operate are often seen by some to conflict directly with the desire to secure the lives of citizens against terrorist activity more effectively.

Another dilemma for policymakers is the need to identify the perpetrators of particular terrorist acts and those who train, fund, or otherwise support or sponsor them. Moreover, as the international community increasingly demonstrates its ability to unite and apply sanctions against rogue states, states will become less likely to overtly support terrorist groups or engage in state sponsored terrorism.

Today a non-standard brand of terrorist may be emerging: individuals who do not work for any established terrorist organization and who are apparently not agents of any state sponsor. The worldwide threat of such individual or "boutique" terrorism, or that of "spontaneous" terrorist activity such as the bombing of bookstores in the United States after Ayatollah Khomeini's death edict against British author Salman Rushdie, appears to be on the increase. Thus, one likely profile of the terrorist of the 21st century may well be a private individual not affiliated with any established group. Another profile might be a group-affiliated individual acting independent of the group, but drawing on other similarly minded individuals for support. The difficulty in countering the non-standard brand of terrorist is that they are immune to the traditional methods of imposing state sanctions and dealing with state sponsors of terrorism.

Nations often face conflicting goals and courses of action: (1) providing security from terrorist acts, i.e., limiting the freedom of individual terrorists, terrorist groups, and support networks to operate unimpeded in a relatively unregulated environment versus (2) maximizing individual freedoms, democracy, and human rights.

Another problem surfacing in the wake of the number of incidents associated with Islamic fundamentalist groups is how to condemn and combat such terrorist activity, and the extreme and violent ideology of specific radical groups, without appearing to be anti-Islamic in general. A desire to punish a state for supporting international terrorism may also be subject to conflicting foreign policy objectives.

Policy Tools

The U.S. government has employed a wide array of policy tools to combat international terrorism, from diplomacy and international cooperation and constructive engagement to economic sanctions, covert action, protective security measures, and military force.

Diplomacy/Constructive Engagement

Most responses to international terrorism involve use of diplomacy in some form as governments seek cooperation to apply pressure on terrorists. One such initiative was the active U.S. role taken in the March 1996 Sharm al-Sheikh peacemaker/anti-terrorism summit. Another is the ongoing U.S. effort to get Japan and major European nations to join in U.S. trade and economic sanctions against Iran. Some argue that diplomacy holds little hope of success against determined terrorists or countries that support them. However, in most cases, diplomatic measures are considered least likely to widen the conflict and therefore are usually tried first.

In incidents of international terrorism by subnational groups, implementing a policy response of constructive engagement is complicated by the lack of existing channels and mutually accepted rules of conduct between government entities and the group in question. In some instances, as was the case with the Palestinian Liberation Organization (PLO), legislation may specifically prohibit official contact with a terrorist organization or its members. Increasingly, however, governments appear to be pursuing policies which involve verbal contact with terrorist groups or their representatives.

The media remain powerful forces in confrontations between terrorists and governments. Appealing to, and influencing, public opinion may impact not only the actions of governments but also those of groups engaged in terrorist acts. From the terrorist perspective, media coverage is an important measure of the success of a terrorist act or campaign. And in hostage type incidents, where the media may provide the only independent means a terrorist has of knowing the chain of events set in motion, coverage can complicate rescue efforts. Governments can use the media in an effort to arouse world opinion against the country or group using terrorist tactics. Public diplomacy and the media can be used to mobilize public opinion in other countries to pressure governments to take action against terrorism. An example would be to mobilize the tourist industry to pressure governments into participating in sanctions against a terrorist state.

Diplomatic measures are considered least likely to widen the conflict and therefore are usually tried first.

Economic Sanctions

In the past, use of economic sanctions was usually predicated upon identification of a nation as an active supporter or sponsor of international terrorism. On August 20, 1998, President Clinton signed an executive order freezing assets owned by Saudi-born Islamic terrorist leader Usama bin Laden, specific associates and their self-proclaimed Islamic Army Organization, prohibits U.S. individuals and firms from doing business with them. Previously, the Clinton Administration had frozen the assets of 12 alleged Middle East terrorist organizations and 18 individuals associated with those organizations. On October 8, 1997, the State Department released a list of 30 foreign terrorist organizations. The 1996 Antiterrorism and Effective Death Penalty Act makes it a crime to provide support to these organizations, and their members shall be denied entry visas into the United States.

Economic sanctions fall into six categories: restrictions on trading, technology transfer, foreign assistance, export credits and guarantees, foreign exchange and capital transactions, and economic access. Sanctions may include a total or partial trade embargo, embargo on financial transactions, suspension of foreign aid, restrictions on aircraft or ship traffic, or abrogation of a friendship, commerce, and navigation treaty. Sanctions usually require the cooperation of other countries to make them effective, and such cooperation is not always forthcoming.

The President has a variety of laws at his disposal, but the broadest in its potential scope is the International Emergency Economic Powers Act. The Act permits imposition of restrictions on economic relations once the President has declared a national emergency because of a threat to the U.S. national security, foreign policy, or economy. While the sanctions authorized must deal directly with the threat responsible for the emergency, the President can regulate imports, exports, and all types of financial transactions, such as the transfer of funds, foreign exchange, credit, and securities between the United States and the country in question. Specific authority for the Libyan trade embargo is Section 503 of the International Trade and Security Act of 1985, while Section 505 of the Act authorizes the banning of imports of goods and services from any country supporting terrorism. Other major laws that can be used against countries supporting terrorism are the Export Administration Act, the Arms Export Control Act, and the specific items or provisions of foreign assistance legislation.

Public Law 104-132 prohibits the sale of arms to any country the President certifies is not cooperating fully with the U.S. anti-terrorism efforts. The law also requires that aid be withheld to any nation providing lethal military aid to a country on the terrorism list.

[Economic] sanctions usually require the cooperation of other countries to make them effective, and such cooperation is not always forthcoming.

Covert Action

Intelligence gathering, infiltration of terrorist groups and military operations involve a variety of clandestine or so called "covert" activities. Much of this activity is of a passive monitoring nature. A more active form of covert activity occurs during events such as a hostage crisis or hijacking when a foreign country may quietly request advice, equipment or technical support during the conduct of operations, with no public credit to be given the providing country.

Some nations have periodically gone beyond monitoring or covert support activities and resorted to unconventional methods beyond their territory for the express purpose of neutralizing individual terrorists and/or thwarting preplanned attacks. Examples of activities might run the gamut from intercepting or sabotaging delivery of funding or weapons to a terrorist group to seizing and transporting a wanted terrorist to stand trial for assassination or murder. Arguably, such activity might be justified as preemptive self defense under Article 51 of the U.N. charter. On the other hand, it could be argued that such actions violate customary international law. Nevertheless, a July 1989 memorandum by the Department of Justice's Office of Legal Counsel advises that the President has the authority to violate customary international law and can delegate such authority to the Attorney General level, should the national interest so require.

Assassination is specifically prohibited by U.S. Executive Order (most recently, E.O. 12333), but bringing of wanted criminals to the United States for trial is not. There exists an established U.S. legal doctrine that allows an individual's trial to proceed regardless whether he is forcefully abducted from another country, or from international waters or airspace. For example, Fawaz Yunis, a Lebanese who participated in the 1985 hijacking of a Jordanian airliner with two Americans among its 70 passengers, was lured aboard a yacht in international waters off the coast of Cyprus in 1987 by federal agents, flown to the United States for trial, and convicted.

Experts warn that bringing persons residing abroad to U.S. justice by means other than extradition or mutual agreement with the host country, i.e., by abduction and their surreptitious transportation, can vastly complicate U.S. foreign relations, sometimes jeopardizing interests far more important than "justice," deterrence, and the prosecution of a single individual. For example, the abduction of a Mexican national in 1990 to stand trial in Los Angeles on charges relating to torture and death of a DEA agent led to vehement protests from the government of Mexico, a government subsequently plagued with evidence of high level drug related corruption. Subsequently, in November 1994, the two countries signed a Treaty to Prohibit Transborder Abductions. Notwithstanding the unpopularity of such abductions in nations that fail to apprehend and prosecute those accused, the "rendering" of such wanted criminals to U.S. courts is permitted under limited circumstances by a January 1993 Presidential Decision Directive issued under the first Bush Administration, and reaffirmed by former President Clinton. Such conduct, however, raises prospects of other nations using similar tactics against U.S. citizens.

Although conventional explosives—specifically car bombs—appear to be terrorism weapons of choice, the world is increasingly moving into an era in which terrorists may gain access to nuclear, chemical or biological weaponry. Faced with the potential of more frequent incidents and higher conventional casualty levels, or a nuclear or biological attack, nations may be more prone to consider covert operations designed to neutralize such threats.

Assassination is specifically prohibited by U.S. Executive Order.

Rewards for Information Program

Money is a powerful motivator. Rewards for information have been instrumental in Italy in destroying the Red Brigades and in Columbia in apprehending drug cartel leaders. A State Department program is in place, supplemented by the aviation industry, offering rewards of up to $5 million to anyone providing information that would prevent or resolve an act of international terrorism against U.S. citizens or U.S. property, or that leads to the arrest or conviction of terrorist criminals involved in such acts. This program was at least partly responsible for the arrest of Ramzi Yousef, the man accused of masterminding the World Trade Center bombing, and of the CIA personnel shooter, Mir Amal Kansi. The program was established by the 1984 Act to Combat International Terrorism (Public Law 98-533), and is administered by State's Diplomatic Security Service. Rewards over $250,000 must be approved by the Secretary of State. The program can pay to relocate informants and immediate family who fear for their safety. The 1994 "crime bill" (Public Law 103-322) helps relocate aliens and immediate family members in the U.S. who are reward recipients. Expanded participation by the private sector in funding and publicizing such reward programs has been suggested by some observers.

Extradition/Law Enforcement Cooperation

International cooperation in such areas as law enforcement, customs control, and intelligence activities is an important tool in combating international terrorism. One critical law enforcement tool in combating international terrorism is extradition of terrorists. International extradition traditionally has been subject to several limitations, including the refusal to extradite for political or extraterritorial offenses and the refusal of some countries to extradite their nationals. The United States has been encouraging the negotiation of treaties with fewer limitations, in part as a means of facilitating the transfer of wanted terrorists. Because much terrorism involves politically motivated violence, the State Department has sought to curtail the availability of the political offense exception, found in many extradition treaties, to avoid extradition. Increasingly, extradition is being employed by the U.S. as a vehicle for gaining physical custody over terrorist suspects.

Military Force

Although not without difficulties, military force, particularly when wielded by a superpower such as the United States, can carry substantial clout. Proponents of selective use of military force usually emphasize the military's unique skills and specialized equipment. The April 1986 decision to bomb Libya for its alleged role in the bombing of a German discotheque exemplifies the use of military force. Other examples are: (1) the 1993 bombing of Iraq's military intelligence headquarters by U.S. forces in response to Iraqi efforts to assassinate former President George Bush during a visit to Kuwait and (2) the August 1998 missile attacks against bases in Afghanistan and an alleged chemical production facility in Sudan.

One critical law enforcement tool in combating international terrorism is extradition of terrorists.

Concerns about the terrorist threat prompted an extensive buildup of the military's counter-terrorist organization. A special unit known as "Delta Force" at Fort Bragg, NC, has been organized to perform anti-terrorist operations when needed. Details about the unit are secret, but estimates are that it has about 800 assigned personnel.

Use of military force presupposes the ability to identify a terrorist group or sponsor and its location, knowledge often unavailable to law enforcement officials. Risks of military force include (1) military casualties or captives, (2) foreign civilian casualties, (3) retaliation and escalation by terrorist groups, (4) holding the wrong parties responsible, (5) sympathy for the "bullied" victim, and (6) perception that the U.S. ignores rules of international law.

Public Law 104-264 includes a sense of the Senate statement that if evidence suggests "beyond a clear and reasonable doubt" that an act of hostility against any U.S. citizen was a terrorist act sponsored, organized, condoned or directed by any nation, then a state of war should be considered to exist between the United States and that nation.

International Conventions

To date, the United States has joined with the world community in developing all of the major anti-terrorism conventions. These conventions impose on their signatories an obligation either to prosecute offenders or extradite them to permit prosecution for a host of terrorism-related crimes including hijacking vessels and aircraft, taking hostages, and harming diplomats. An important convention is the Convention for the Marking of Plastic Explosives. Implementing legislation is in Public Law 104-132. On September 8, 1999 the U.S. signed the U.N. Convention on the Suppression of Terrorist Bombings; and on January 12, 2000, the U.N. Anti-Terrorism Financing Convention was signed as well.[2]

U.S. Organization and Program Response

Presidential Decision Directive 39 (PDD 39), signed in June 1995, is the foundation for current U.S. policy for combating terrorism. The document spells out three objectives for confronting terrorism:

1. Reduce the nation's international and domestic vulnerabilities to terrorism.
2. Deter terrorism.
3. Respond to terrorism rapidly and decisively.

PDD 39 designates Lead Federal Agencies (LFA's) for international and domestic terrorism policy. The Lead Federal Agency for combating terrorism overseas is the Department of State (DoS), and the agency designated to respond to terrorist attacks on U.S. soil is the Department of Justice (DoJ) through the Federal Bureau of Investigation (FBI). The Federal Emergency Management Agency (FEMA) has the primary responsibility to lead federal efforts to deal with the consequences and collateral second and third order effects of terrorist WMD attacks on American soil.[3]

The Lead Federal Agency for combating terrorism overseas is the Department of State (DoS), and the agency designated to respond to terrorist attacks on U.S. soil is the Department of Justice (DoJ) through the Federal Bureau of Investigation (FBI). The Federal Emergency Management Agency (FEMA) has the primary responsibility to lead federal efforts to deal with the consequences and collateral second and third order effects of terrorist WMD attacks on American soil.

In the wake of 9-11, The Homeland Security Act of November 25, 2002, established the Department of Homeland Security to (1) prevent terrorist attacks within the United States, (2) reduce the vulnerability of the United States to terrorism, and (3) minimize the damage, and assist in the recovery, from terrorist attacks that do occur within the United States. The Homeland Security Act preserved the roles for combating terrorism assigned to Lead Federal Agencies in PDD 39 by explicitly stating "primary responsibility for investigating and prosecuting acts of terrorism shall be vested not in the Department [of Homeland Security], but rather in Federal, State, and local law enforcement agencies with jurisdiction over the acts in question."[4]

Prior to 9-11, the job of coordinating the actions of the Lead Federal Agencies rested with the National Security Council. The chain of command on anti-terrorism planning ran from the President through the National Security Council's (NSC's) Principals Committee, through the NSC's Deputies Committee, a representative of which chaired a senior interagency Counterterrorism & National Preparedness Policy Coordinating Committee (PCC). The PCC oversaw four working groups charged with overseeing policy in four generic areas: (1) continuity of federal operations; (2) preventing and responding to foreign terrorism; (3) preventing and responding to weapons of mass destruction (WMD) attacks; and (4) preventing and responding to cyber threats.[5]

Following the attacks of 9-11, President George W. Bush issued Executive Order 13228, October 8, 2001, establishing the Whitehouse Office of Homeland Security (OHS) and Homeland Security Council (HSC) to assume the anti-terrorism roles previously assigned to the National Security Council.[6] OHS responsibilities were subsequently transferred to the Department of Homeland Security (DHS) and OHS closed in October 2005. Unlike the NSC, the HSC and DHS must deal with a far broader spectrum of U.S. agencies and organizations. The strategy acknowledges that there is a vital need for cooperation between the federal government and state and local governments on a scale never before seen in the United States. Cooperation must occur both horizontally (within each level of government) and vertically (among various levels of government). While the President has only one jurisdiction on the international side in the NSC, he has over 180 jurisdictions on the homeland side through federal, state, and local levels, while the DHS consolidates over 22 organizations with critical homeland security missions.[7] The Department of Homeland Security, develops and coordinates the implementation of a comprehensive national strategy to secure the United States from terrorist threats or attacks by coordinating the executive branch's efforts to detect, prepare for, prevent, protect against, respond to, and recover from terrorist attacks within the United States. The purpose of the Homeland Security Council is to advise the President with respect to all aspects of homeland security, and serve as the mechanism for ensuring coordination of homeland security-related activities of executive departments and agencies in the implementation of homeland security policies.

Today, the chain of command on anti-terrorism planning runs from the President through the Homeland Security Council's (HSC's) Principals Committee, through the HSC's Deputies Committee, to the HSC's Policy Coordination Committees.

The Homeland Security Council (HSC) was modeled on the structure of the National Security Council, and the two organizations share overlapping areas of responsibility. Today, the chain of command on anti-terrorism planning runs from the President through the HSC's Principals Committee, through the HSC's Deputies Committee, to the HSC's Policy Coordination Committees.

The HSC Principals Committee (HSC/PC) is the senior interagency forum under the HSC for homeland security issues. The HSC/PC is composed of the following members: the Secretary of the Treasury; the Secretary of Defense; the Attorney General; the Secretary of Health and Human Services; the Secretary of Transportation; the Director of the Office of Management and Budget; the Assistant to the President for Homeland Security (who serves as Chairman); the Assistant to the President and Chief of Staff; the Director of Central Intelligence; the Director of the Federal Bureau of Investigation; the Director of the Federal Emergency Management Agency; and the Assistant to the President and Chief of Staff to the Vice President.

The HSC Deputies Committee (HSC/DC) serves as the senior sub-Cabinet interagency forum for consideration of policy issues affecting homeland security. The HSC/DC can task and review the work of the HSC interagency groups. The HSC/DC ensures that issues brought before the HSC Principals Committee have been properly analyzed and prepared for action. The HSC/DC is comprised of representatives from the same federal agencies who are members of the HSC Principals Committee.

HSC Policy Coordination Committees (HSC/PCCs) coordinate the development and implementation of homeland security policies by multiple departments and agencies throughout the federal government, and coordinate those policies with state and local government. The HSC/PCCs are the main day-to-day forum for interagency coordination of homeland security policy. The HSC/PCCs provide policy analysis for consideration by the more senior committees of the HSC system and ensure timely responses to decision by the President. There are eleven assigned HSC Policy Coordination Committees:

1. Detection, Surveillance, and Intelligence
2. Plans, Training, Exercises, and Evaluation
3. Law Enforcement and Investigation
4. Weapons of Mass Destruction
5. Key Asset, Border, Territorial Water, and Airspace Security
6. Domestic Transportation Security
7. Research and Development
8. Medical and Public Health
9. Domestic Threat Response and Incident Management
10. Economic Consequences
11. Public Affairs[8]

National Strategy for Combating Terrorism

The National Strategy for Combating Terrorism:

- *Defeat*
- *Deny*
- *Diminish*
- *Defend*

In February 2003, the Whitehouse released the National Strategy for Combating Terrorism, defining the U.S. war plan against international terrorism. The intent of the national strategy is to stop terrorist attacks against the United States, its citizens, its interests, and our friends and allies around the world and ultimately, to create an international environment inhospitable to terrorists and all those who support them. To accomplish these tasks the nation will simultaneously act on four fronts.

The United States and its partners will *defeat* terrorist organizations of global reach by attacking their sanctuaries; leadership; command, control, and communications; material support; and finances. This approach will have a cascading effect across the larger terrorist landscape, disrupting the terrorists' ability to plan and operate. As a result, it will force these organizations to disperse and then attempt to reconsolidate along regional lines to improve their communications and cooperation.

As this dispersion and organizational degradation occurs, The U.S. will work with regional partners to implement a coordinated effort to squeeze, tighten, and isolate the terrorists. Once the regional campaign has localized the threat, America will help states develop the military, law enforcement, political, and financial tools necessary to finish the task. However, this campaign need not be sequential to be effective; the cumulative effect across all geographic regions will help achieve the desired results.

The U.S. will *deny* further sponsorship, support, and sanctuary to terrorists by ensuring other states accept their responsibilities to take action against these international threats within their sovereign territory. UNSCR 1373 and the 12 UN counterterrorism conventions and protocols establish high standards that the U.S. and our international partners expect others to meet in deed as well as word.

Where states are willing and able, the U.S. will reinvigorate old partnerships and forge new ones to combat terrorism and coordinate actions to ensure that they are mutually reinforcing and cumulative.

Where states are weak but willing, America will support them vigorously in their efforts to build the institutions and capabilities needed to exercise authority over all their territory and fight terrorism where it exists.

Where states are reluctant, the U.S. will work with our partners to convince them to change course and meet their international obligations.

Where states are unwilling, the U.S. will act decisively to counter the threat they pose and, ultimately, to compel them to cease supporting terrorism.

The U.S. will *diminish* the underlying conditions that terrorists seek to exploit by enlisting the international community to focus its efforts and resources on the areas most at risk. The nation will maintain the momentum generated in response to the September 11 attacks by working with our partners abroad and various international forums to keep combating terrorism at the forefront of the international agenda.

Most importantly, the government will *defend* the United States, its citizens, and its interests at home and abroad by both proactively protecting our homeland and extending our defenses to ensure we identify and neutralize the threat as early as possible.[9]

In response to our efforts, the terrorists have adjusted. Today, we face a global terrorist movement and must confront the radical ideology that justifies the use of violence against innocents in the name of religion.

Strategy Adjustment

The National Strategy for Combating Terrorism recognizes that the War on Terror is a different kind of war. From the beginning, it has been both a battle of arms and a battle of ideas. Combating terrorism involves the application of all elements of national power and influence. Not only do we employ military power, we use diplomatic, financial, intelligence, and law enforcement activities to protect the Homeland and extend our defenses, disrupt terrorist operations, and deprive our enemies of what they need to operate and survive.

Since 9/11, the United States and its partners have made substantial progress in degrading the al Qaeda network, killing or capturing key lieutenants, eliminating safehavens, and disrupting existing lines of support. From the beginning, however, the War on Terror involved more than simply finding and bringing to justice those who had planned and executed the terrorist attacks on September 11, 2001. US strategy involved destroying the larger al Qaida network and also confronting the radical ideology that inspired others to join or support the terrorist movement.

In response to our efforts, the terrorists have adjusted. Today, we face a global terrorist movement and must confront the radical ideology that justifies the use of violence against innocents in the name of religion. In September 2006, the National Strategy for Combating Terrorism was also adjusted. The new strategy identifies both near- and long-term objectives to ultimately win the War on Terror:

- Advance effective democracies as the long-term antidote to the ideology of terrorism;
- Prevent attacks by terrorist networks;
- Deny weapons of mass destruction to rogue states and terrorist allies who seek to use them;
- Deny terrorists the support and sanctuary of rogue states;
- Deny terrorists control of any nation they would use as a base and launching pad for terror; and
- Lay the foundations and build the institutions and structures we need to carry the fight forward against terror and help ensure our ultimate success.[10]

Since the September 11 attacks, America is safer, but we are not yet safe. We have done much to degrade al-Qaida and its affiliates and to undercut the perceived legitimacy of terrorism. Our Muslim partners are speaking out against those who seek to use their religion to justify violence and a totalitarian vision of the world. We have significantly expanded our counterterrorism coalition, transforming old adversaries into new and vital partners in the War on Terror. We have liberated more than 50 million Afghans and Iraqis from despotism, terrorism, and oppression, permitting the first free elections in recorded history for either nation. In addition, we have transformed our governmental institutions and framework to wage a generational struggle. There will continue to be challenges ahead, but along with our partners, we will attack terrorism and its ideology, and bring hope and freedom to the people of the world. This is how we will win the War on Terror.[11]

America is safer, but we are not yet safe.

Conclusion

Victory against terrorism will not occur as a single, defining moment. It will not be marked by the likes of the surrender ceremony on the deck of the USS Missouri that ended World War II. However, through the sustained effort to compress the scope and capability of terrorist organizations, isolate them regionally, and destroy them within state borders, the United States and its friends and allies will secure a world in which our children can live free from fear and where the threat of terrorist attacks does not define our daily lives.

Victory, therefore, will be secured only as long as the United States and the international community maintain their vigilance and work tirelessly to prevent terrorists from inflicting horrors like those of September 11, 2001.[12]

Questions

1. What is the definition of "combating terrorism" according to DoD Instruction 2000.14?
2. What is the basic dilemma in combating terrorism.
3. List and describe two different policy tools for combating terrorism.
4. Who are the lead federal agencies responsible for combating terrorism?
5. What is the U.S. strategy for combating terrorism?

Chapter 10

DHS Origins

Objectives

- Know the difference between crisis management and consequence management.
- Understand the organization for homeland security before 9-11.
- Describe some of the security shortcomings prior to 9-11.
- Explain the sequence of events leading to the establishment of the Department of Homeland Security.

"A direct attack against American citizens on American Soil is likely over the next quarter century. The risk is not only death and destruction but also demoralization that could undermine U.S. global leadership. In the face of this threat, our nation has no coherent or integrated governmental structures. We therefore recommend the creation of an independent National Homeland Security Agency (NHSA) with responsibility for planning, coordinating, and integrating various U.S. government activities involved in homeland security."

— Phase III Report of the U.S. Commission on National Security/21st Century, February 15, 2001

Introduction

The United Stated Department of Homeland Security (DHS) is a Cabinet department of the federal government of the United States that is concerned with protecting the American homeland and the safety of American citizens. The department was created primarily from a conglomeration of existing federal agencies in response to the terrorist attacks of September 11th, 2001.

The department was established on November 25th, 2002, by the Homeland Security Act and officially began operation January 24th, 2003. After months of discussion about employee rights and benefits and "rider" portions of the bill, Congress passed it shortly after the midterm elections, and it was signed into law by U.S. President George W. Bush. It was intended to consolidate U.S. executive branch organizations related to "homeland security" into a single cabinet agency.

It was the largest government reorganization in 50 years (since the United States Department of Defense was created). The department assumed a number of government functions previously in other departments.[1]

Evolution

The concept of operations for a federal response to a terrorist threat or incident provides for an overall lead federal agency to ensure multi-agency coordination and a tailored, time-phased deployment of specialized federal assets. Prior to 9-11, the U.S. strategy for combating terrorism consisted of crisis management and consequence management:

- Crisis management involved efforts to prevent and deter a terrorist attack, protect public health and safety, arrest terrorists, and gather evidence for criminal prosecution.
- Consequence management included efforts to provide medical treatment and emergency services, evacuate people from dangerous areas, and restore government services.

The government strategy for combating terrorism had evolved into a complex framework of programs and activities across more than 40 federal agencies, bureaus, and offices. The evolution of theses programs came from a variety of presidential decision directives, implementing guidance, executive orders, interagency agreements and legislation.[2]

National Security Decision Directive (NSDD) 30 signed by President Ronald Reagan, April 10th 1982, established a Special Security Group inside the National Security Council to advise the President with respect to decision options in the event of a terrorist incident or situation. NSDD 30 designated lead federal agencies to coordinate federal responses to federal agencies with the most direct operational role in dealing with the incident at hand. NSDD 30 appointed the Department of State (DoS) as the lead federal agency for international terrorist incidents taking place outside U.S. territory. NSDD 30 appointed the Federal Bureau of Investigation (FBI) under the Department of Justice (DoJ) as the lead federal agency for domestic terrorist incidents taking place within U.S. territory. The Federal Aviation Administration was appointed the lead federal agency for hijackings within the jurisdiction of the United States, and the Federal Emergency Management Agency (FEMA) assigned responsibility for planning and managing the public health aspects of a terrorist incident and recovery from the consequences of such incidents.

U.S. policy for combating terrorism for terrorist incidents overseas was formalized in 1986 under National Security Decision 207. The Department of State was reaffirmed as the lead federal agency for international terrorism policy, procedures, and programs. The FBI, through the Department of Justice, was reaffirmed as the lead federal agency for handling domestic terrorist threats.

NSDD 30 signed by President Reagan designated lead federal agencies to coordinate federal responses to federal agencies with the most direct operational role in dealing with the incident at hand.

Presidential Decision Directive 39 (PDD 39), issued in June 1995 in the aftermath of the bombing of the federal building in Oklahoma City, reaffirmed the Department of Justice, through the FBI, as the lead federal agency responsible for crisis management of domestic terrorist incidents. Although state and local governments have the primary responsibility for managing the consequence of a domestic terrorist incident, the 1995 directive designated the Federal Emergency Management Agency (FEMA) as the lead agency responsible for coordinating federal agencies' responses and activities when state and local authorities requested assistance.[3]

The federal response to a terrorist incident was seen as a highly coordinated interagency operation that included federal, state, and local participation. Primary federal agencies besides the DoJ, FBI, and FEMA included the Department of Defense (DoD), Department of Energy (DoE), the Environmental Protection Agency (EPA), and the Department of Health and Human Services (DHHS).

The National Security Council was the center of U.S. government efforts to coordinate the national response to threats or acts of domestic terrorism. The NSC Principals Committee, the Deputies Committee, and the Counterterrorism and National Preparedness Policy Coordination Committee (PCC) constituted the major policy and decision making bodies involved in the federal response to terrorism.

The PCC had four standing subordinate groups to coordinate policy in specific areas. The Counterterrorism and Security Group (CSG) coordinated policy for preventing and responding to foreign terrorism, either internationally or domestically. The Preparedness and Weapons of Mass Destruction Group provided policy coordination for preventing WMD attacks in the United States and developing response and consequence management capabilities to deal with domestic WMD incidents. The Information Infrastructure Protection and Assurance Group handled policy for preventing and responding to major threats to America's cyberspace, and the Continuity of Federal Operations Group was charged with policy coordination for assuring the continued operation of Constitutional offices and federal departments and agencies.

When the NSC was advised of the threat of a terrorist incident or actual event, the appropriate subordinate group would convene to formulate recommendations for the Counterterrorism and Preparedness PCC who in turn would provide policy analysis for the Deputies Committee. The Deputies Committee would ensure that the issues being brought before the Principals Committee and NSC were properly analyzed and prepared for a decision by the President.[4]

In May 1998, President Clinton issues PDD 62 establishing the position of a National Coordinator for Security, Infrastructure Protection, and Counterterrorism within the NSC. Part of the rationale for creating this National Coordinator was to improve leadership and coordination among the various federal agencies. The directive enumerated responsibilities for the coordinator that included general coordination of federal efforts, chairing certain meetings, sponsoring interagency working groups, and providing budget advice.

When the NSC was advised of the threat of a terrorist incident or actual event, the appropriate subordinate group would convene to formulate recommendations for the Counterterrorism and Preparedness PCC who in turn would provide policy analysis for the Deputies Committee.

Shortcomings

Other than the general responsibilities identified in PDD 62, the functions of the National Coordinator were never detailed in either an executive order or legislation. Many critical leadership functions were not given to the National Coordinator:

- Overall Accountability. In some cases, the President and Congress held different officials accountable for interagency functions. For example, while the President appointed a national coordinator, Congress directed a different official, the Attorney General, to develop an interagency strategy.
- Threat and Risk Assessment. The FBI made only limited progress to perform an assessment while agencies expended resources on less likely threats and scenarios.
- National Strategy. There was no unified effort. Agencies developed competing "national strategies".
- Monitoring Budgets. While the OMB attempted to track and analyze agency funding to combat terrorism, there was no effort to eliminate duplication and no linkage to national strategy.
- Tracking and Implementing Lessons Learned. There was no standard for tracking lessons learned from state and local exercises.
- Coordinating Agency Implementation. Different agencies developed programs to provide assistance to state and local governments that were similar and potentially duplicative. These multiple programs created confusion and frustration among state and local officials.

Concerned about the overall leadership and coordination of programs to combat terrorism, Congress established three separate commissions to include the Advisory Panel to Assess Domestic Response Capabilities for Terrorism Involving Weapons of Mass Destruction (also known as the Gilmore Panel because it was chaired by Governor James Gilmore III of Virginia); the United States Commission on National Security in the 21st Century (also known as the Hart-Rudman Commission because it was chaired by former Senators Gary Hart and Warren Rudman); and the National Commission on Terrorism (also known as the Bremer Commission because it Chairman was former Ambassador Paul Bremer).[5]

The Bremer Commission raised the issue that the National Coordinator, the senior official responsible for coordinating all U.S. counterterrorism efforts, didn't have sufficient authority to ensure the President's priorities were reflected in agencies' budgets. The United States didn't have a single counterterrorism budget. Instead, counterterrorism programs existed in the individual budgets of 45 departments and agencies of the federal government.[6]

In December 2000, the second report of the Gilmore Commission issued a finding that the organization of the federal government's programs for combating terrorism was fragmented, uncoordinated, and politically unaccountable. It linked the lack of a national strategy to the fact that no entity had the authority to direct all of the agencies that may be engaged. At the federal level, no entity had the authority even to direct the coordination of relevant federal efforts. As a consequence, the Gilmore Commission recommended that the next President should establish a National Office for Combating Terrorism in the Executive Office of the President, and should seek a statutory basis for this office.

The United States didn't have a single counterterrorism budget. Instead, counterterrorism programs existed in the individual budgets of 45 departments and agencies of the federal government.

The Gilmore Commission recommended that the National Office for Combating Terrorism should have a broad and comprehensive scope, with responsibility for the full range of deterring, preventing, preparing for, and responding to international as well as domestic terrorism. The director of the office should be the principal spokesman of the Executive Branch on all matters related to federal programs for combating terrorism and should be appointed by the President and confirmed by the Senate. The office should have a substantial and professional staff, drawn from existing National Security Council offices and other relevant agencies. The Gilmore Commission argued that the office should have at least five major sections, each headed by an Assistant Director:

1. Domestic Preparedness Programs
2. Intelligence
3. Health and Medical Programs
4. Research, Development, Test, and Evaluation (RDT&E), and National Standards
5. Management and Budget[7]

The Hart-Rudman Commission decried the fact that responsibility for homeland security resided at all levels of the U.S. government—local, state, and federal. That within the federal government, almost every agency and department was involved in some aspect of homeland security, but none was organized to focus on the scale of the contemporary threat to the homeland. The Hart-Rudman Commission recommended an organizational realignment that:

- Designated a single person, accountable to the President, to be responsible for coordinating and overseeing various U.S. government activities related to homeland security;
- Consolidated certain homeland security activities to improve their effectiveness and coherence;
- Established planning mechanisms to define clearly specific responses to specific types of threats; and
- Ensured that the appropriate resources and capabilities were available.

In February 2001, the Hart-Rudman Commission recommended the creation of a National Homeland Security Agency (NHSA) with responsibility for planning, coordinating, and integrating various U.S. government activities involved in homeland security.[8]

On October 8th, 2001, President George W. Bush issued Executive Order 13228, establishing the Office of Homeland Security within the Executive Office of the President to coordinate a comprehensive national strategy to secure the United States from terrorist threats and attacks.

Impetus for Change

On September 20th, 2001, the General Accounting Office completed an independent analysis of the national framework for combating terrorism and issued the following recommendations:

> *"Based upon numerous evaluations, the identification of recurring problems in the overall leadership and coordination programs, and an analysis of various proposals, GAO believes a single focal point, with all critical functions and responsibilities, should be assigned to lead and coordinate these programs. This focal point, for example, could be an individual, an executive office, or a council. Furthermore, this focal point should be in the Executive Office of the President and be independent of any existing federal agency. A focal point within the Executive Office of the President would be independent above the interests of any of several individual agencies involved. The focal point needs to have the time, responsibility, authority, and resources for coordinating both crisis management and consequence management activities. Current proposals to create a new agency to combine functions currently in several agencies still would not contain all the government agencies and functions needed to combat terrorism. While not endorsing any specific organizational structure for the single focal point, GAO has identified basic functions that any focal point should perform."*[9]

On October 8th, 2001, President George W. Bush issued Executive Order 13228, establishing the Office of Homeland Security within the Executive Office of the President to coordinate a comprehensive national strategy to secure the United States from terrorist threats and attacks. Thomas Ridge, former Governor of Pennsylvania, was appointed Assistant to the President.

Immediately following the 9-11 the attacks, many Members of Congress sought to address the government's organizational problems by introducing legislation to rearrange the federal government. However, the President preferred instead to focus on faster ways to improve coordination. He established the Office of Homeland Security and initiated a strategic assessment of U.S. capabilities for security of the homeland.

Congress's deliberations on reorganizing the government's homeland security functions were largely built on the recommendations of the U.S. Commission on National Security for the 21st Century (Hart-Rudman Commission) which proposed creating a new federal agency by consolidating the Coast Guard, the Customs Service, the Immigration and Naturalization Service (INS) and FEMA into a new National Homeland Security Agency.

In April 2001, Representative William (Mac) Thornberry (R-TX) introduced HR 1158 to create that agency. Shortly after September 11, Senator Joseph Lieberman (D-CT) proposed similar legislation (S. 1534) to create a National Homeland Security Department (NHSD). Other Members, such as Representative Alcee Hastings (D-FL) and Senator Bob Graham (D-FL) promoted the findings of the Advisory Panel to Assess Domestic Response Capabilities for Terrorism Involving Weapons of Mass Destruction (Gilmore Commission) in HR 3078. The Gilmore Commission had concluded that a White House office with detailed statutory authority, modeled after the Office of National Drug Control Policy (ONDCP), would be best situated to solve the federal government's coordination problems.

On June 6, 2002, President Bush proposed establishment of a Cabinet-level Department of Homeland Security (DHS).

After introducing HR 1158 and S. 1534, Representative Thornberry and Senator Lieberman refined their proposals to gain the support of more Members of Congress, and in May 2002 introduced the National Homeland Security and Combating Terrorism Act of 2002 (HR 4660).[10] The new bill chose to exclude the Transportation Security Administration (TSA) in the reorganization, and focused more narrowly on border security and emergency preparedness and response. [11]

On June 6, 2002, President Bush proposed establishment of a Cabinet-level Department of Homeland Security (DHS). His initiative called for consolidating most federal agencies with homeland security missions in one department to focus the government's resources more efficiently and effectively on domestic security. The President's plan built on the recommendations of the various national commissions and legislative proposals already submitted before Congress.

Following President Bush's call to Congress, Representative Richard Armey (R-TX) submitted House Resolution 5005 (HR 5005) calling for the establishment of a Department of Homeland Security, June 24th, 2002. HR 5005 incorporated most provisions set forth in HR 4660, plus the President's request to transfer TSA from the Department of Transportation (DOT) to DHS. HR 5005 passed the House July 26th, and was handed over to the Senate on July 30th. HR 5005 wasn't without its detractors, and stalled in the Senate.[12]

Controversy centered on whether the FBI and the CIA should be incorporated in part or in whole (both were not). The bill itself was also controversial for the presence of unrelated riders, as well as eliminating some standard civil service and labor protections from employees of the department. President Bush wanted the right to fire an employee within Homeland Security immediately for security reasons, for incompetence, or insubordination. Senate Minority Leader Tom Daschle wanted an appeals process that could take up to 18 months or as little as one month.[13]

The impasse was broken when both the House and Senate agreed to a compromise resolution, HR 5710 incorporating provisions by Senator Joseph Lieberman authorizing the President to bypass traditional civil service procedures provided he first consult with Congress and mediate with the federal employees union.[14]

Conclusion

President Bush signed [the Homeland Security Act establishing the Department of Homeland Security], Public Law 107-296, November 25th, 2002.

On November 20th 2002, the Senate passed HR 5005 by a vote of 90-9 authorizing the creation of a Department of Homeland Security consolidating 22 federal agencies under a single executive department with an initial budget appropriation of $34 billion.

President Bush signed the bill into law, Public Law 107-296, November 25th, 2002. Tom Ridge was made secretary of the new department. President Bush signed Executive Order 13284 activating the Department of Homeland Security effective January 23rd, 2003.

Questions

1. What is the difference between crisis management and consequence management?
2. What was perceived as the biggest impediment to anti-terrorist activity prior to 9-11?
3. What was the purpose for establishing the Department of Homeland Security?

Chapter 11

Homeland Security Strategy

Objectives

- Comprehend the relationship between homeland security and national security.
- Understand the purpose of homeland security.
- Know the critical mission areas identified in the 2002 National Strategy for Homeland Security.
- Describe how and why homeland security strategy was revised in 2007.

Introduction

In the wake of the attacks of September 11th, President George W. Bush issued Executive Order 13228 October 8th 2001 establishing the Office of Homeland Security within the Executive Office of the President to coordinate the implementation of a comprehensive national strategy to secure the United States from terrorist threats or attacks. As HR 5005 went before Congress seeking to establish the Department of Homeland Security, the Office of Homeland Security under the direction of Tom Ridge issued the nation's first National Strategy for Homeland Security July 16th, 2002.

Homeland Security and National Security

The Preamble to the Constitution defines our federal government's basic purposes as "*... to form a more perfect Union, establish justice, insure domestic Tranquility, provide for the common defense, promote the general Welfare, and secure the Blessings of Liberty to ourselves and our Posterity.*" The requirement to provide for the common defense remains as fundamental today as it was when these words were written, more than two hundred years ago.

For six decades, National Security Strategy has sought to protect America's sovereignty and independence through global presence and engagement. Unable to match our great power, our enemies have sought to take advantage of America's freedom and openness to attack her from within. Homeland Security Strategy seeks to deny this avenue of attack to our enemies, and thus to provide a secure foundation for America's ongoing global engagement.

Since 1986 Congress has required the President to enunciate the National Security Strategy of the United States detailing how he aims to guarantee the sovereignty and independence of the United States. The National Security Strategy provides a framework for creating and seizing opportunities that strengthen our security and prosperity. The National Strategy for Homeland Security complements the National Security Strategy of the United States by addressing a very specific and uniquely challenging threat – terrorism in the United States – and by providing a comprehensive framework for organizing the efforts of federal, state, local and private organizations whose primary functions are often unrelated to national security.

The link between national security and homeland security is a subtle but important one. For more than six decades, America has sought to protect its own sovereignty and independence through a strategy of global presence and engagement. In so doing, America has helped many other countries and peoples advance along the path of democracy, open markets, individual liberty, and peace with their neighbors. Yet there are those who oppose America's role in the world, and who are willing to use violence against us and our friends. Our great power leaves these enemies with few conventional options for doing us harm. One such option is to take advantage of our freedom and openness by secretly inserting terrorists into our country to attack our homeland. Homeland security seeks to deny this avenue of attack to our enemies and thus to provide a secure foundation for America's ongoing global engagement. Thus the National Security Strategy of the United States and National Strategy for Homeland Security work as mutually supporting documents, providing guidance to the executive branch departments and agencies.

There are also a number of other, more specific strategies maintained by the United States that are subsumed within the twin concepts of national security and homeland security. The National Strategy for Combating Terrorism defines the U.S. war plan against international terrorism. The National Strategy to Combat Weapons of Mass Destruction coordinates America's many efforts to deny terrorists and states the materials, technology, and expertise to make and deliver weapons of mass destruction. The National Strategy to Secure Cyberspace describes our initiatives to secure our information systems against deliberate, malicious disruption. The National Money Laundering Strategy aims to undercut the illegal flow of money that supports terrorism and international criminal activity. The National Defense Strategy sets priorities for our most powerful national security instrument. The National Drug Control Strategy lays out a comprehensive U.S. effort to combat drug smuggling and consumption. All of these documents fit into the framework established by the National Security Strategy of the United States and National Strategy for Homeland Security, which together take precedence over all other national strategies, programs, and plans.

Securing the Homeland

Homeland security is a concerted national effort to prevent terrorist attacks within the United States, reduce America's vulnerability to terrorism, and minimize the damage and recover from attacks that do occur.

Homeland security is a concerted national effort to prevent terrorist attacks within the United States, reduce America's vulnerability to terrorism, and minimize the damage and recover from attacks that do occur.

The National Strategy for Homeland Security establishes the foundation for organizing efforts and prioritizing work to:

1. Prevent terrorist attacks within the United States.
2. Reduce America's vulnerability to terrorism.
3. Minimize the damage and recover from attacks that do occur.

The National Strategy for Homeland Security aligns and focuses homeland security functions into six critical mission areas:

1. Intelligence and Warning.
2. Border and Transportation Security.
3. Domestic Counterterrorism.
4. Protecting Critical Infrastructure.
5. Defending Against Catastrophic Terrorism.
6. Emergency Preparedness and Response.

The first three mission areas focus primarily on preventing terrorist attacks; the next two on reducing the nation's vulnerabilities, and the final one on minimizing the damage and recovering from attacks that do occur. The Strategy provides a framework to align the resources of the federal budget directly to the task of securing the homeland.

Intelligence and Warning

Terrorism depends on surprise. With it, a terrorist attack has the potential to do massive damage to an unwitting and unprepared target. Without it, the terrorists stand a good chance of being preempted by authorities, and even if they are not, the damage that results from their attacks is likely to be less severe. The United States needs an intelligence and warning system that can detect terrorist activity before it manifests itself in an attack so that proper preemptive, preventative, and protective action can be taken. The National Strategy for Homeland Security identifies five major initiatives in this area:

1. Enhance the analytic capabilities of the FBI.
2. Build new capabilities through the Information Analysis and Infrastructure Protection Division of the Department of Homeland Security.
3. Implement the Homeland Security Advisory System.
4. Utilize dual-use analysis to prevent attacks.
5. Employ "red team" techniques.

The National Strategy for Homeland Security aligns and focuses homeland security functions into six critical mission areas:

1. Intelligence and Warning
2. Border and Transportation Security
3. Domestic Counterterrorism
4. Protecting Critical Infrastructure
5. Defending Against Catastrophic Terrorism
6. Emergency Preparedness and Response

Border and Transportation Security

America historically has relied heavily on two vast oceans and two friendly neighbors for border security, and on the private sector for most forms of domestic transportation security. The increasing mobility and destructive potential of modern terrorism has required the United States to conceive of border security and transportation security as fully integrated requirements because our domestic transportation systems are inextricably intertwined with the global transport infrastructure. Virtually every community in America is connected to the global transportation network by the seaports, airports, highways, pipelines, railroads, and waterways that move people and goods into, within, and out of the nation. It is necessary therefore to promote the efficient and reliable flow of people, goods, and services across borders, while preventing terrorists from using transportation conveyances or systems to deliver implements of destruction. The National Strategy for Homeland Security identifies six major initiatives in this area:

1. Ensure accountability in border and transportation security.
2. Create "smart borders".
3. Increase the security of international shipping containers.
4. Implement the Aviation and Transportation Security Act of 2001.
5. Recapitalize the U.S. Coast Guard.
6. Reform immigration services.

Domestic Counterterrorism

The attacks of September 11 and the catastrophic loss of life and property that resulted have redefined the mission of federal, state, and local law enforcement authorities. While law enforcement agencies will continue to investigate and prosecute criminal activity, they should now assign priority to preventing and interdicting terrorist activity within the United States. The nation's state and local law enforcement officers will be critical to this effort. Our nation will use all legal means—both traditional and nontraditional—to identify, halt, and where appropriate, prosecute terrorists in the United States. We will pursue not only the individuals directly involved in terrorist activity but also their sources of support: the people and organizations that knowingly fund the terrorists and those that provide them with logistical assistance.

Effectively reorienting law enforcement organizations to focus on counterterrorism objectives requires decisive action in a number of areas. The National Strategy for Homeland Security identifies six major initiatives in this area:

1. Improve intergovernmental law enforcement coordination.
2. Facilitate apprehension of potential terrorists.
3. Continue ongoing investigations and prosecutions.
4. Complete FBI restructuring to emphasize prevention of terrorist attacks.
5. Target and attack terrorist financing.
6. Track foreign terrorists and bring them to justice.

Protecting Critical Infrastructure and Key Assets

American society and modern way of life are dependent on networks of infrastructure—both physical networks such as energy and transportation systems, and virtual networks such as the Internet. If terrorists attack one or more pieces of critical infrastructure, they may disrupt entire systems and cause significant damage to the nation. It is important therefore to improve protection of the individual pieces and interconnecting systems that make up the critical infrastructure. Protecting America's critical infrastructure and key assets will not only make us more secure from terrorist attacks, but will also reduce our vulnerability to natural disasters, organized crime, and computer hackers.

America's critical infrastructure encompasses a large number of sectors. The U.S. government will seek to deny terrorists the opportunity to inflict lasting harm to our nation by protecting the assets, systems, and functions vital to our national security, governance, public health and safety, economy, and national morale.

The National Strategy for Homeland Security identifies eight major initiatives in this area:

1. Unify America's infrastructure protection effort in the Department of Homeland Security.

2. Build and maintain a complete and accurate assessment of America's critical infrastructure and key assets.
3. Enable effective partnership with state and local governments and the private sector.
4. Develop a national infrastructure protection plan.
5. Secure cyberspace.
6. Harness the best analytic and modeling tools to develop effective protective solutions.
7. Guard America's critical infrastructure and key assets against "inside" threats.
8. Partner with the international community to protect our transnational infrastructure.

Defending Against Catastrophic Threats

The expertise, technology, and material needed to build the most deadly weapons known to mankind—including chemical, biological, radiological, and nuclear weapons—are spreading inexorably. If our enemies acquire these weapons, they are likely to try to use them. The consequences of such an attack could be far more devastating than those we suffered on September 11—a chemical, biological, radiological, or nuclear terrorist attack in the United States could cause large numbers of casualties, mass psychological disruption, contamination, and significant economic damage, and could overwhelm local medical capabilities.

Currently, chemical, biological, radiological, and nuclear detection capabilities are modest and response capabilities are dispersed throughout the country at every level of government. While current arrangements have proven adequate for a variety of natural disasters and even the September 11 attacks, the threat of terrorist attack using chemical, biological, radiological, and nuclear weapons requires new approaches, a focused strategy, and a new organization.

The National Strategy for Homeland Security identifies six major initiatives in this area:

1. Prevent terrorist use of nuclear weapons thorough better sensors and procedures.
2. Detect chemical and biological materials and attacks.
3. Improve chemical sensors and decontamination.
4. Develop broad spectrum vaccines, antimicrobials, and antidotes.
5. Harness the scientific knowledge and tools to counter terrorism.
6. Implement the Select Agent Program.

Emergency Preparedness and Response

The United States must prepare to minimize the damage and recover from any future terrorist attacks that may occur despite our best efforts at prevention. An effective response to a major terrorist incident—as well as a natural disaster—depends on being prepared. Therefore, we need a comprehensive national system to bring together and coordinate all necessary response assets quickly and effectively. We must plan, equip, train, and exercise many different response units to mobilize without warning for any emergency.

Many pieces of this national emergency response system are already in place. America's first line of defense in the aftermath of any terrorist attack is its first responder community—police officers, firefighters, emergency medical providers, public works personnel, and emergency management officials. Nearly three million state and local first responders regularly put their lives on the line to save the lives of others and make our country safer.

Yet multiple plans currently govern the federal government's support of first responders during an incident of national significance. These plans which form the government's overarching policy for counterterrorism are based on an artificial and unnecessary distinction between "crisis management" and "consequence management." Under the President's proposal, the Department of Homeland Security will consolidate federal response plans and build a national system for incident management in cooperation with state and local government. Our federal, state, and local governments would ensure that all response personnel and organizations are properly equipped, trained, and exercised to respond to all terrorist threats and attacks in the United States. Our emergency preparedness and response efforts would also engage the private sector and the American people.

The National Strategy for Homeland Security identifies twelve major initiatives in this area:

1. Integrate separate federal response plans into a single all-discipline incident management plan.
2. Create a national incident management system.
3. Improve tactical counterterrorist capabilities.
4. Enable seamless communication among all responders.
5. Prepare health care providers for catastrophic terrorism.
6. Augment America's pharmaceutical and vaccine stockpiles.
7. Prepare for chemical, biological, radiological, and nuclear decontamination.
8. Plan for military support to civil authorities.
9. Build the Citizen Corps.
10. Implement the First Responder Initiative of Fiscal Year 2003 Budget.
11. Build a national training and evaluation system.
12. Enhance the victim support system.

Foundations for Homeland Security

The National Strategy for Homeland Security describes four foundations—unique American strengths that cut across all of the mission areas, across all levels of government, and across all sectors of our society:

1. Law
2. Science and Technology
3. Information Sharing and Systems
4. International Cooperation

These foundations provide a useful framework for evaluating homeland security investments across the federal government.

Law

Throughout our nation's history, we have used laws to promote and safeguard our security and our liberty. The law will both provide mechanisms for the government to act and will define the appropriate limits of action.

The National Strategy for Homeland Security outlines legislative actions that would help enable our country to fight the war on terrorism more effectively. New federal laws should not preempt state law unnecessarily or overly federalize the war on terrorism. We should guard scrupulously against incursions on our freedoms.

The Strategy identifies twelve major initiatives in this area:

Federal Level

1. Enable critical infrastructure information sharing.
2. Streamline information sharing among intelligence and law enforcement agencies.
3. Expand existing extradition authorities.
4. Review authority for military assistance in domestic security.
5. Revive the President's reorganization authority.
6. Provide substantial management flexibility for the Department of Homeland Security.

State Level

7. Coordinate suggested minimum standards for state driver's licenses.
8. Enhance market capacity for terrorism insurance.
9. Train for prevention of cyber attacks.
10. Suppress money laundering.

11. Ensure continuity of the judiciary.
12. Review quarantine authorities.

Science and Technology

The nation's advantage in science and technology is a key to ensuring the safety of the homeland. New technologies for analysis, information sharing, detection of attacks, and countering chemical, biological, radiological, and nuclear weapons will help prevent and minimize the damage from future terrorist attacks. Just as science has helped us defeat past enemies overseas, so too will it help us defeat the efforts of terrorists to attack our homeland and disrupt our way of life.

The federal government is launching a systematic national effort to harness science and technology in support of homeland security. We will build a national research and development enterprise for homeland security sufficient to mitigate the risk posed by modern terrorism. The federal government will consolidate most federally funded homeland security research and development under the Department of Homeland Security to ensure strategic direction and avoid duplicative efforts. We will create and implement a long-term research and development plan that includes investment in revolutionary capabilities with high payoff potential. The federal government will also seek to harness the energy and ingenuity of the private sector to develop and produce the devices and systems needed for homeland security.

The National Strategy for Homeland Security identifies eleven major initiatives in this area:

1. Develop chemical, biological, radiological, and nuclear countermeasures.
2. Develop systems for detecting hostile intent.
3. Apply biometric technology to identification devices.
4. Improve the technical capabilities of first responders.
5. Coordinate research and development of the homeland security apparatus.
6. Establish a national laboratory for homeland security.
7. Solicit independent and private analysis for science and technology research.
8. Establish a mechanism for rapidly producing prototypes.
9. Conduct demonstrations and pilot deployments.
10. Set standards for homeland security technology.
11. Establish a system for high-risk, high-payoff homeland security research.

Information Sharing and Systems

Information systems contribute to every aspect of homeland security. Although American information technology is the most advanced in the world, our country's information systems have not adequately supported the homeland security mission. Databases used for federal law enforcement, immigration, intelligence, public health surveillance, and emergency management have not been connected in ways that allow us to comprehend where information gaps or redundancies exist. In addition, there are deficiencies in the communications systems used by states and municipalities throughout the country; most state and local first responders do not use compatible communications equipment. To secure the homeland better, we must link the vast amounts of knowledge residing within each government agency while ensuring adequate privacy.

The National Strategy for Homeland Security identifies five major initiatives in this area:

1. Integrate information sharing across the federal government
2. Integrate information sharing across state and local governments, private industry, and citizens
3. Adopt common "meta-data" standards for electronic information relevant to homeland security
4. Improve public safety emergency communications
5. Ensure reliable public health information

International Cooperation

In a world where the terrorist threat pays no respect to traditional boundaries, the strategy for homeland security cannot stop at the borders. America must pursue a sustained, steadfast, and systematic international agenda to counter the global terrorist threat and improve our homeland security. Our international anti-terrorism campaign has made significant progress since September 11.

The National Strategy for Homeland Security identifies nine major initiatives in this area:

1. Create "smart borders".
2. Combat fraudulent travel documents.
3. Increase the security of international shipping containers.
4. Intensify international law enforcement cooperation.
5. Help foreign nations fight terrorism.
6. Expand protection of transnational critical infrastructure.
7. Amplify international cooperation on homeland security science and technology.

8. Improve cooperation in response to attacks.
9. Review obligations to international treaties and law.[1]

Revising Homeland Security Strategy

In the years following 9/11, the nation made extraordinary progress in the full range of homeland security activities through effective national and international partnerships:

- Constrained the ability of al Qaeda to attack the Homeland and disrupted multiple potentially deadly plots against the United States.
- Instituted an active, multi-layered approach to securing the Homeland integrating the capabilities of local, Tribal, State, and Federal governments, as well as those of the private and non-profit sectors, in order to secure the land, maritime, air, space, and cyber domains.
- Made borders more secure and developed an effective system of layered defense by strengthening the screening of people and goods overseas and by tracking and disrupting the international travel of terrorists.
- Enhanced homeland security and counterterrorism through the creation of the Department of Homeland Security, the Office of the Director of National Intelligence, the Homeland Security Council, the National Counterterrorism Center, and U.S. Northern Command.
- Made the prevention of terrorist attacks the highest priority at the Federal Bureau of Investigation (FBI) and the Department of Justice (DOJ) , as evidenced by the creation of the FBI's new National Security Branch and DOJ's new National Security Division. We also more effectively leveraged State, local, and Tribal law enforcement efforts as part of our national homeland security enterprise.
- Enhanced State, local, and tribal homeland security training and equipment, emergency management capabilities, and communications interoperability through targeted, risk-based delivery of Federal grant funding and technical assistance.
- Developed and procured medical countermeasures against bioterrorism and pandemic threats; improved capabilities for the detection of and response to biological attacks; and supported State, local, and Tribal preparedness efforts through funding and guidance.
- Implemented and renewed key legal reforms – such as the USA PATRIOT Act, the Intelligence Reform and Terrorism Prevention Act of 2004, and the Protect America Act of 2007 – which promote security and help to implement both the 9/11 Commission and the WMD Commission recommendations while protecting our fundamental liberties. Furthermore, with the Military Commissions Act of 2006, the United States can prosecute captured terrorists for war crimes through full and fair trials.

- Established the Privacy and Civil Liberties Oversight Board as an integral part of the Executive Branch, and further established privacy officers in departments and agencies across the Federal Government – all to ensure that the rights of American citizens are considered and respected in our counterterrorism efforts.
- Created a full-scale, comprehensive National Exercise Program to increase our preparedness to respond to the consequences of terrorist attacks and natural disasters.

While America is safer, we are not yet safe. Because of determined terrorist enemies and nature's unyielding power, significant challenges remain, including:

- The War on Terror remains a generational struggle, and our entire Nation must be engaged and prepared to participate in this effort.
- Terrorists have declared their intention to acquire and use weapons of mass destruction to inflict catastrophic attacks against the United States and our allies, partners, and other interests.
- Our vast land and maritime borders make it difficult to completely deny terrorists and their weapons access to the Homeland.
- The United States is not immune to the emergence of homegrown radicalization and violent Islamic extremism.
- We must counter potential waning in the sense of urgency and levels of international cooperation as September 11 becomes a more distant memory and perceptions of the terrorist threat diverge.
- We must guard against complacency and balance the sense of optimism that is fundamental to the American character with the sober recognition that despite our best efforts, future catastrophes – natural and man-made – will occur, and thus we must always remain a prepared Nation.
- Although we have substantially improved our cooperation and partnership among all levels of government, private and non-profit sectors, communities, and individual citizens we must continue to strengthen efforts to achieve full unity of effort through a stronger and further integrated national approach to homeland security.
- Although we have improved our ability to manage the risks that we face in the 21st century global security environment, we must enhance our ability to measure risk in a consistent and commonly accepted fashion and allocate finite resources accordingly.
- We must make additional reforms to the Foreign Intelligence Surveillance Act (FISA) and ensure that the statute is permanently amended so that intelligence professionals continue to have the legal tools they need to gather information about the intentions of our enemies while protecting the civil liberties of Americans.
- While our information sharing capabilities have improved significantly, substantial obstacles remain. We must continue to break down informa-

tion barriers among Federal, State, local, and Tribal partners and the private sector.

- Congress must better align its oversight and committee structure in order to reflect the need for streamlined and effective legislative action that supports a unified approach to securing the Nation.

In recognition of these challenges, in 2007, the Bush administration updated homeland security strategy to reflect increased understanding of the terrorist threats confronting the United States, incorporate lessons learned from exercises and real-world catastrophes – including Hurricane Katrina – and propose new initiatives and approaches to enable the nation to achieve its homeland security objectives.

The **2007 National Strategy for Homeland Security** provides a common framework focusing the nation's efforts on the following four goals:

- **Prevent** and disrupt terrorist attacks;
- **Protect** the American people, critical infrastructure, and key resources;
- **Respond** to and recover from incidents that do occur; and
- **Continue** to strengthen the foundation to ensure long-term success.

While the first three goals help to organize national efforts, the last goal entails creating and transforming homeland security principles, systems, structures, and institutions. This includes applying a comprehensive approach to risk management, building a culture of preparedness, developing a comprehensive Homeland Security Management System, improving incident management, better utilizing science and technology, and leveraging all instruments of national power and influence.[2]

Conclusion

Homeland security requires a truly national effort, with shared goals and responsibilities for protecting and defending the Homeland. Homeland security strategy leverages the unique strengths and capabilities of all levels of government, the private and non-profit sectors, communities, and individual citizens. Mindful that many threats do not recognize geographic boundaries, we must continue to work closely with our international partners throughout the world.[3]

Questions

1. What is the relationship between homeland security and national security?
2. What is the purpose of homeland security?
3. List the six critical mission areas identified in the National Strategy for Homeland Security.
4. Identify at least one significant change since 9/11 prompting a revision of homeland security strategy.

Chapter 12

DHS Organization

Objectives

- Know the mission of DHS.
- Describe the relationship between HSC and DHS.
- Understand the basic structure of DHS.
- Compare the initial DHS structure with 2002 National Strategy for Homeland Security.
- Explain what forces have influenced changes to DHS since it's inception.
- Describe FEMA's evolving authority within DHS.

Introduction

The U.S. Department of Homeland Security (DHS or Department) was established by the Homeland Security Act of 2002 (the Act), Public Law 107-296 (the Law), dated November 25, 2002, as an executive department of the United States government with the following mission:

- Prevent terrorist attacks within the United States;
- Reduce the vulnerability of the United States to terrorism;
- Minimize the damage, and assist in the recovery, from terrorist attacks and natural disasters that occur within the United States;
- Carry out all functions of entities transferred to the Department, including acting as a focal point regarding natural and manmade crises and emergency planning;
- Ensure that the functions of the agencies and subdivisions within the Department that are not related directly to securing the homeland are not diminished or neglected except by a specific, explicit Act of Congress;
- Ensure that the overall economic security of the United States is not diminished by efforts, activities, and programs aimed at securing the homeland; and
- Monitor connections between illegal drug trafficking and terrorism, coordinate efforts to sever such connections, and otherwise contribute to efforts to interdict illegal drug trafficking.[1]

DHS Mission:

1. *Prevent terrorist attacks within the United States;*
2. *Reduce the vulnerability of the United States to terrorism;*
3. *Minimize the damage, and assist in the recovery, from terrorist attacks and natural disasters that occur within the United States;*

To perform its mission, the Department of Homeland Security is staffed with 230,000 employees in jobs ranging from aviation and border security to emergency response, from cybersecurity analyst to chemical facility inspector. DHS' duties are wide-ranging, but the goal is clear - keeping America safe. Within its current mission set, DHS has five main areas of responsibility:

1. Guarding against Terrorism
2. Securing Borders
3. Enforcing Immigration Laws
4. Improving Readiness for, Response to and Recovery from Disasters
5. Maturing and Unifying the Department

To achieve its goals, DHS must continually strive to strengthen partnerships with communities, first responders, law enforcement, and government agencies at the state, local, tribal, federal and international levels. Employing science, technology, and innovation, the Department seeks to secure the nation by becoming leaner, smarter, and more efficient, ensuring that every security resource is used as effectively as possible.[2]

Homeland Security Policy Guidance

Even after creation of the new Department, homeland security would still involve the efforts of other Cabinet departments. The Department of Justice (DoJ) and the FBI would remain the lead law enforcement agencies for preventing terrorist attacks. The Department of Defense (DoD) would continue to play a crucial support role in the case of a catastrophic incident. The Department of Transportation (DoT) would continue to be responsible for highway and rail safety, and air traffic control. The Central Intelligence Agency (CIA) would continue to gather and analyze overseas intelligence. Homeland security would continue to require interagency coordination, and the President would need a close advisor on homeland security related issues.

Executive Order 13228, issued on October 8, 2001, established two entities within the White House to guide homeland security policy:

1. The Office of Homeland Security (OHS) within the Executive Office of the President is tasked to develop and implement a national strategy to coordinate federal, state, and local counterterrorism efforts to secure the country from, and respond to terrorist threats or attacks.
2. The Homeland Security Council (HSC) is responsible for monitoring homeland security-related activities and advising the President on homeland security matters, mirroring the role the National Security Council (NSC).

The Homeland Security Council (HSC) is responsible for monitoring homeland security-related activities and advising the President on homeland security matters.

Later, President Bush issued Executive Order 13260 establishing the President's Homeland Security Advisory Council (PHSAC). Members of the PHSAC advise the President on homeland security matters and represent the private sector, academia, professional service associations, federally funded research and development centers, nongovernmental organizations, state and local governments, and other related professions and communities. EO 13260 requires the PHSAC to renew its charter every two years. After the creation of DHS in 2003, the Council rechartered itself as the Homeland Security Advisory Council (HSAC) and became an advisory committee to the Secretary of Homeland Security.[3]

In May 2009 the Obama Administration announced its intention to integrate the staffs of the National Security Council with the Homeland Security Council into a single National Security Staff, with the goal of ending "the artificial divide between White House staff who have been dealing with national security and homeland security issues.". The position of Assistant to the President for Homeland Security will be retained "with direct and immediate access" to the President, but the incumbent would organizationally report to the National Security Advisor.[4]

Homeland Security Implementation

The Department of Homeland Security stood up March 1, 2003, to coordinate the efforts of the federal, state, and local government, the private sector, and the American people to protect the nation against terrorism.[5] The Naval Security Station, known as the Nebraska Avenue complex, located at Nebraska and

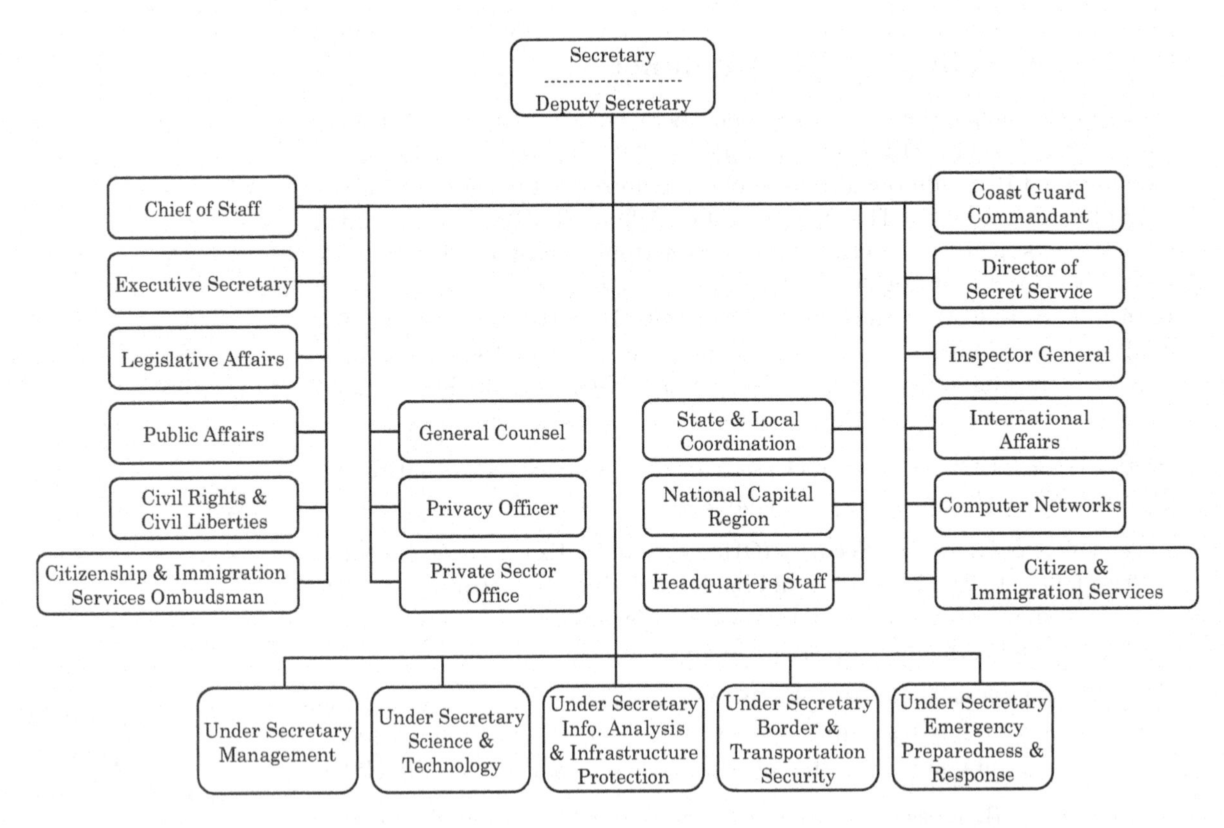

Figure 12.1: Organization of the Department of Homeland Security, March 2003.

The initial organization structure was meant to mirror the critical mission areas established in the 2002 National Strategy for Homeland Security.

Massachusetts Avenues in Washington DC, was chosen as the new home for the newest executive agency.[6] While the new headquarters underwent extensive renovation and construction, the Department lost no time consolidating its new organization. With the exception of the new headquarters management staff, most DHS elements remained in place; there wasn't a massive shift of personnel or resources to Washington DC. The transition, for the most part, involved transferring lines of authority to the new Secretary of Homeland Security.

An orderly transition was facilitated by the November 25, 2002 Reorganization Plan. The plan directed the transfer of personnel, facilities, records, assets (including technology systems), obligations, and functions (e.g., authorities, powers, rights, privileges, immunities, programs, projects, activities, duties and responsibilities) from 22 existing Federal agencies and programs to the Secretary of Homeland Security. Within nine months, the fledgling Department overcame unprecedented challenges to consolidate 180,000 employees, numerous financial management systems, compensation structures, and information systems into a single agency.[7] The incoming components were parceled among four major directorates:

1. Border & Transportation Security
2. Emergency Preparedness & Response
3. Science and Technology

4. Information Analysis and Infrastructure Protection

The initial organization structure was meant to mirror the critical mission areas established in the 2002 National Strategy for Homeland Security. This was accomplished not without some controversy, as the Federal Emergency Management Agency was subordinated under the Preparedness Directorate, losing its direct line to the President. While the new Department succeeded in implementing many homeland security policy objectives, including consolidation of all federal response plans into a single National Response Plan, and adoption of the Incident Command System and National Incident Management System across the nation, DHS was caught short by Hurricane Katrina in 2005.

Hurricane Katrina

Hurricane Katrina struck the Gulf Coast states of Louisiana, Alabama, and Mississippi on August 29, 2005, resulting in severe and widespread damage to the region. The response of the federal government, especially the Federal Emergency Management Agency (FEMA), in the aftermath of the storm has been a matter of considerable controversy among elected officials and in the media. Some of the criticism has focused on FEMA's organizational arrangements at the time of the disaster. Prior to these events, in July 2005, Secretary Michael Chertoff had announced a reorganization of the Department of Homeland Security (DHS), including FEMA. In the aftermath of Hurricane Katrina, the Bush Administration proceeded with the reorganization initiative after Congress signaled its approval.[8]

Hurricane Katrina struck the Gulf Coast states of Louisiana, Alabama, and Mississippi on August 29, 2005, resulting in severe and widespread damage to the region.

DHS & FEMA

The Homeland Security Act of 2002 establishing the Department of Homeland Security included the Emergency Preparedness and Response (EPR) Directorate. Title V of the act transferred the functions, personnel, resources, and authorities of six existing entities, the largest of which was FEMA, into EPR. Section 507 of the act specifically charged FEMA with "carrying out its mission to reduce the loss of life and property and protect the Nation from all hazards by leading and supporting the Nation in a comprehensive, risk-based emergency management program." Although all of FEMA was transferred into the new department, it was not defined as an autonomous or distinct entity within its parent organization. The act explicitly gave the President and Secretary significant discretion in reorganizing the department, including FEMA.

FEMA functions were transferred to DHS on March 1, 2003.76 The following January, Secretary Tom Ridge used his reorganization authority to consolidate organizational units and reallocate functions within DHS. Among other changes, "select grant award functions [then] exercised by the Under Secretary for Emergency Preparedness and Response," under Sections 502 and 503 of the Homeland Security Act, were consolidated within the Office of State and Local Government Coordination and Preparedness, an office that would report directly to the Secretary.

The organizational components changed again in 2005. Upon his appointment as Secretary of Homeland Security, Michael Chertoff launched a "systematic evaluation of the Department's operations, policies and structures." This initiative, which came to be known as the Second Stage Review (2SR), led to a department wide reorganization, which Chertoff announced on July 13, 2005. As part of this reorganization, most preparedness functions housed in the EPR Directorate were to be transferred to a newly created Preparedness Directorate. The remaining components of EPR and FEMA (the names were used interchangeably) were to focus on response and recovery, not on preparation.

Chertoff implemented the reorganization proposal, but it was not universally accepted. For example, the National Emergency Management Association (NEMA), composed of state emergency directors, criticized the proposed reorganization of DHS in a July 27, 2005, letter to House and Senate committees. The association said it would be a mistake to separate disaster planning from response, and that it would "result in a disjointed response and adversely impact the effectiveness of departmental operations." The director of Florida's Division of Emergency Management said the plan would recreate the fragmentation that occurred prior to 1979 when FEMA was formed. Concerned about the increased separation between the preparedness, response, and recovery functions, on August 22 and 23, 2005, state emergency management directors from across the country met with Chertoff and his senior staff in Washington to discuss the proposed DHS reorganization.[9]

In the aftermath of Hurricane Katrina, committees in both chambers of Congress and the Bush Administration conducted investigations into governmental failures during the preparation for and response to the disaster.

Hurricane Katrina Implications

In the aftermath of Hurricane Katrina, committees in both chambers of Congress and the Bush Administration conducted investigations into governmental failures during the preparation for and response to the disaster. The House Select Bipartisan Committee to Investigate the Preparation for and Response to Hurricane Katrina held nine hearings and, on February 15, 2006, issued a report of its findings. Among other findings, the report noted the role of organizational problems at FEMA and DHS in Katrina failures:

> "For years emergency management professionals have been warning that FEMA's preparedness has eroded. Many believe this erosion is a result of the separation of the preparedness function from FEMA, the drain of long-term professional staff along with their institutional knowledge and expertise, and the inadequate readiness of FEMA's national emergency response teams. The combination of these staffing, training, and organizational structures made FEMA's inadequate performance in the face of a disaster the size of Katrina all but inevitable."

The House Select Committee report did not, however, make any recommendations.

The White House's Katrina assessment, which focused solely on the federal level of government, also led to the production of a final report, on February 23, 2006. Although the report provided some assessment of failures of the governmental response to Katrina, it focused primarily on developing recommended changes based on the "lessons learned" from this event. The report appeared to assume a continuation of the basic emergency management organizational arrangements growing out of Secretary Chertoff's 2SR initiative. Several of the report's 125 recommendations, however, would make further adjustments to that organizational structure and distribution of functions. For example, the White House report recommended that

- in order to "[i]ntegrate and synchronize the preparedness functions," DHS "should consider adding an Assistant Secretary for Preparedness Programs and an Assistant Secretary for Operational Plans, Training and Exercises, and an Executive Director for Public and Citizen Preparedness to the Undersecretary of Preparedness' senior staff";
- DHS should also have a "unified departmental external affairs office ... that combines legislative affairs, intergovernmental affairs, and public affairs as a critical component of the preparedness and response cycle";
- a National Operations Center should be established, and it should "combine, co-locate, and replace the situational awareness mission of the Homeland Security Operations Center ..., the operational mission of the National Response Coordination Center ... and the role of the [Interagency Incident Management Group], and be staffed with full time detailed employees assigned to a planning cell from relevant departments and agencies";
- legislation be proposed that would transfer the National Disaster Medical System from FEMA to the Department of Health and Human Services;
- the Department of Housing and Urban Development be designated "as the lead Federal agency for the provision of temporary housing";
- DHS "should establish an office with responsibility for integrating nongovernmental and other volunteer resources into Federal, State, and local emergency response plans and mutual aid agreements [and] a distinct organizational element to assist faith-based organizations"; and
- DHS "should consolidate homeland security related training and exercise assets in a new Office of Training, Exercises and Lessons Learned (TELL)," within the Preparedness Directorate, during FY2006.

Secretary Chertoff also conducted an internal review and, in a speech to the National Emergency Management Association (NEMA), described changes to be implemented at DHS in response to the Katrina failures.

Secretary Chertoff also conducted an internal review and, in a speech to the National Emergency Management Association (NEMA), described changes to be implemented at DHS in response to the Katrina failures. He did not call for any basic organizational structure changes in his speech, but discussed adjustments to the existing arrangements. He called for the "integration of a unified incident command," updating of the department's operational capabilities, and improved human resources development.

The Senate Committee on Homeland Security and Governmental Affairs conducted 22 public hearings and, in May 2006, released a report of their findings and recommendations. The committee investigation "explored several reasons for FEMA's lack of preparedness, including unqualified political leadership, budget shortages, inadequate workforce, FEMA's inclusion within DHS, and underdeveloped and inadequate response capabilities." As a result of this investigation, the report included the following recommendations (part of the report's "foundational" recommendations) regarding FEMA's organization:

- FEMA should be abolished and replaced with a "stronger, more capable structure," which would be known as the National Preparedness and Response Authority (NPRA). NPRA should be a "distinct entity" within DHS.
- The NPRA leader should be at the deputy secretary level, serve as an advisor to the President on national emergency management issues, and should have direct communication with the President during catastrophes.
- Senior NPRA leaders should be drawn from a pool of individuals with crisis management, substantial management, and leadership experience.
- The new organization should be vested with the "four central functions of comprehensive emergency management — mitigation, preparedness, response and recovery."
- The new organization should also be responsible for "overseeing protection of critical infrastructure."
- NPRA should have ten regional offices based on FEMA's regional offices and better coordination across agencies and levels of government. Regional offices should form interdisciplinary, interagency "Strike Teams" that could "be the federal government's first line of response to a disaster."
- One federal coordinating structure — the National Operations Center — should replace the three existing entities.[10]

2005 Second Stage Review

The Second Stage Review began in October 2005 when more than 250 Department members formed into 18 action teams to develop a new organizational plan in consultation with public and private partners at the federal, state, local, tribal, and international levels. The resulting plan, called the Six Point Agenda, abolished the Directorates for Border and Transportation Security, Information Analysis and Infrastructure Protection, and Emergency Preparedness and Response. Formerly subordinate agencies, including FEMA, Customs and Border Protection (CBP), Transportation Security Administration (TSA), Immigration and Customs Enforcement (ICE), and others were elevated to now report directly to the Secretary. The 24-hour Homeland Security Operations Center (HSOC) was renamed the National Operations Center (NOC), and the Interagency Incident Management Group (IIMG) advising the President was renamed the Domestic Readiness Group (DRG).

While the 2SR dismantled three directorates, it also created two new directorates. The Policy Directorate took on most of the policy responsibilities from the former Assistant Secretary for Policy and Planning in the Border and Transportation Security Directorate, and created new branches for the Assistant Secretaries for Legislative and Intergovernmental Affairs, Strategic Plans,

Private Sector, and International Affairs. The new Preparedness Directorate assumed some functions transferred from FEMA, but also accommodated the U.S. Fire Administration, the Office of National Capitol Region, the Office of Infrastructure Preparedness, functions from the Office of State and Local Government Coordination, the new offices of the Assistant Secretary for Grants and Training, and the Chief Medical Officer.

The Second Stage Review also incorporated changes from previous mandates. The position of the Director of the Office of Counternarcotics Enforcement was created on December 17, 2004, by the Intelligence Reform and Terrorism Prevention Act of 2004 (Public Law 108-458) and the Domestic Nuclear Detection Office was established on April 15, 2005.

The Federal Coordinator for Gulf Coast Rebuilding was created by Executive Order 13390, November 1, 2005. Its mission is to manage the long-term post-Katrina Federal rebuilding efforts by working with state and local officials to reach consensus on their vision for the region.

2006 Post-Katrina Emergency Reform Act

While the self-initiated Second Stage Review addressed many of the criticisms stemming from Hurricane Katrina, Congress forced additional changes in the FY2007 Appropriations Bill (Public Law 109-295), signed into law as the Post-Katrina Emergency Reform Act. The Act established new leadership positions within the Department, brought additional functions into the Federal Emergency Management Agency (FEMA), and created and reallocated functions within the Department.

While the self-initiated Second Stage Review addressed many of the criticisms stemming from Hurricane Katrina, Congress forced additional changes in the FY2007 Appropriations Bill (Public Law 109-295), signed into law as the Post-Katrina Emergency Reform Act.

Specifically, the Act renamed the Under Secretary for Federal Emergency Management the FEMA Administrator, and designated them the principal advisor to the President for all matters relating to emergency management. Furthermore, FEMA was legislatively protected as a distinct entity within the Department, and exempt from reorganization except by statute. FEMA's direct line to the President was restored.

The Post-Katrina Emergency Management Reform Act also restored many functions of the Preparedness Directorate to FEMA, including the Office of Grants and Training, the US Fire Administration, and the Office of National Capital Region Coordination. After these changes, the Preparedness Directorate retained the Office of Infrastructure Protection, the National Communications System, the National Cybersecurity Division, and the Office of the Chief Medical Officer.

FEMA was further augmented by the SAFE Port Act of 2006 (Public Law 109-347). The act transferred the Radiological Preparedness Program and the Chemical Stockpile Emergency Preparedness Program to FEMA. The SAFE Port Act also authorized creation of the Domestic Nuclear Detection Office (DNDO) within the Department of Homeland Security.

In the aftermath of the Post-Katrina Management Reform Act and the SAFE Port Act reformations, DHS created a new National Preparedness Division within FEMA. The National Preparedness Division assumed responsibility for policy, contingency planning, exercise coordination and evaluation, emergency management training, and hazard mitigation. Both disaster and non-disaster grant programs within FEMA were co-located within a Grant Program Directorate.

What remained of the Preparedness Directorate was renamed the National Protection and Programs Directorate (NPPD). It retained some preparedness elements not transferred to FEMA, including the Office of Infrastructure Protection, the newly consolidated Office of Cyber Security and Communications, and the Office for State and Local Government Coordination now named the Office of Intergovernmental Programs. Additionally the new Directorate contains US-VISIT and the Office of Risk Management and Analysis, formerly a part of the Office of Infrastructure Protection.

The Chief Medical Officer did not transfer to the National Protection and Programs Division; instead, the reorganization created a new Office of Health Affairs led by an Assistant Secretary/Chief Medical Officer. The changes to the Department became effective on March 31, 2007.

Implementing Recommendations of the 9/11 Commission Act of 2007

The Implementing Recommendations of the 9/11 Commission Act of 2007 (Public Law 110-53), enacted August 7, 2007, built on the Post-Katrina Emergency Management Reform Act of 2006, focusing on the reorganization of the grant processes administered by FEMA. The Act also reorganized intelligence operations at the Department, elevating the Assistant Secretary for Intelligence and Analysis to the Under Secretary level, requiring Senate confirmation.

HSPD-23

On January 8, 2008, President Bush issued Homeland Security Presidential Directive 23 (HSPD-23), creating a National Cyber Security Center (NCSC) within the Department. The NCSC is responsible for coordinating cybersecurity efforts and improving situational awareness and information sharing across the federal government.[11]

The Department of Homeland Security

The Department of Homeland Security leverages resources within federal, state, and local governments, coordinating the transition of multiple agencies and programs into a single, integrated agency focused on protecting the American people and their homeland. More than 87,000 different governmental jurisdictions at the federal, state, and local level have homeland security responsibilities. The comprehensive national strategy seeks to develop a complementary system connecting all levels of government without duplicating effort.[12]

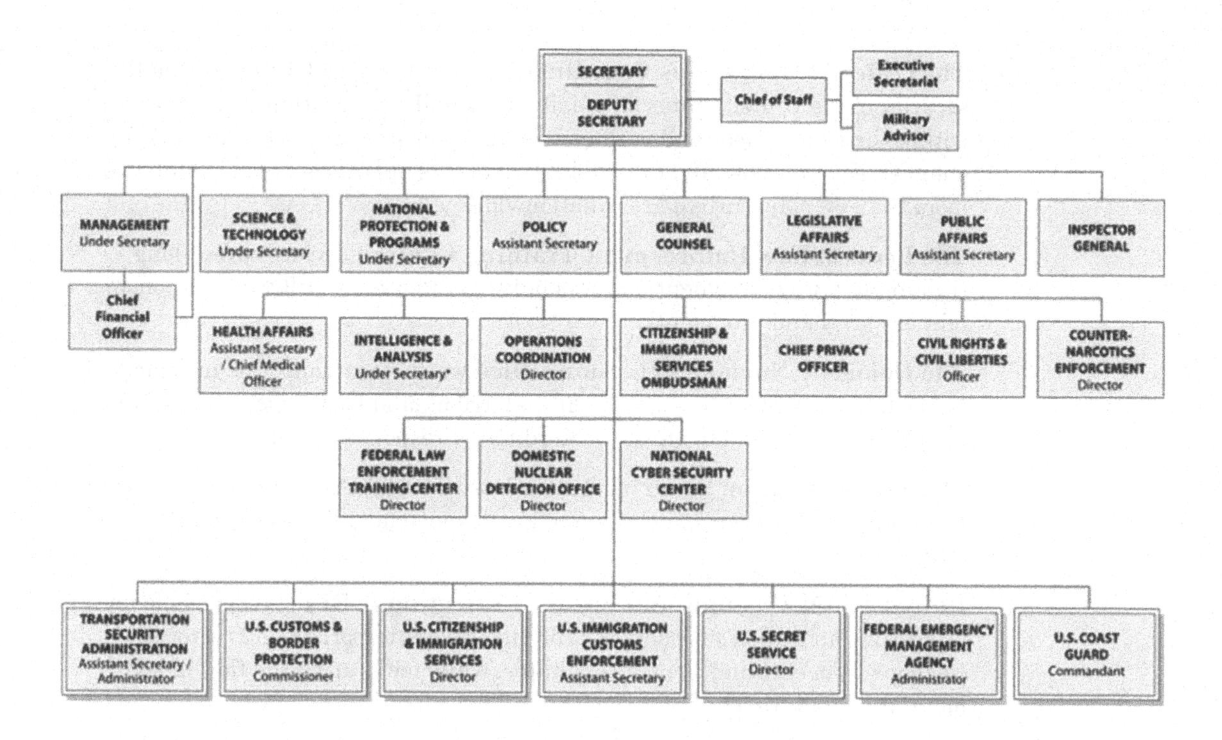

Figure 12.2: Organization of the Department of Homeland Security, March 2007.

Department Components

The Directorate for National Protection and Programs works to advance the Department's risk-reduction mission. Reducing risk requires an integrated approach that encompasses both physical and virtual threats and their associated human elements.

The Directorate for Science and Technology is the primary research and development arm of the Department. It provides federal, state and local officials with the technology and capabilities to protect the homeland.

The Directorate for Management is responsible for Department budgets and appropriations, expenditure of funds, accounting and finance, procurement; human resources, information technology systems, facilities and equipment, and the identification and tracking of performance measurements.

The Office of Policy is the primary policy formulation and coordination component for the Department of Homeland Security. It provides a centralized, coordinated focus to the development of Department-wide, long-range planning to protect the United States.

The Office of Health Affairs coordinates all medical activities of the Department of Homeland Security to ensure appropriate preparation for and response to incidents having medical significance.

The Office of Intelligence and Analysis is responsible for using information and intelligence from multiple sources to identify and assess current and future threats to the United States.

The Office of Operations Coordination is responsible for monitoring the security of the United States on a daily basis and coordinating activities within the Department and with governors, Homeland Security Advisors, law enforcement partners, and critical infrastructure operators in all 50 states and more than 50 major urban areas nationwide.

The Federal Law Enforcement Training Center provides career-long training to law enforcement professionals to help them fulfill their responsibilities safely and proficiently.

The Domestic Nuclear Detection Office works to enhance the nuclear detection efforts of federal, state, territorial, tribal, and local governments, and the private sector and to ensure a coordinated response to such threats.

The Transportation Security Administration (TSA) protects the nation's transportation systems to ensure freedom of movement for people and commerce.

United States Customs and Border Protection (CBP) is responsible for protecting our nation's borders in order to prevent terrorists and terrorist weapons from entering the United States, while facilitating the flow of legitimate trade and travel.

United States Citizenship and Immigration Services is responsible for the administration of immigration and naturalization adjudication functions and establishing immigration services policies and priorities.

United States Immigration and Customs Enforcement (ICE), the largest investigative arm of the Department of Homeland Security, is responsible for identifying and shutting down vulnerabilities in the nation's border, economic, transportation and infrastructure security.

The United States Coast Guard protects the public, the environment, and U.S. economic interests—in the nation's ports and waterways, along the coast, on international waters, or in any maritime region as required to support national security.

The Federal Emergency Management Agency (FEMA) prepares the nation for hazards, manages Federal response and recovery efforts following any national incident, and administers the National Flood Insurance Program.

The United States Secret Service protects the President and other high-level officials and investigates counterfeiting and other financial crimes, including financial institution fraud, identity theft, computer fraud; and computer-based attacks on our nation's financial, banking, and telecommunications infrastructure.

Office of the Secretary

The Office of the Secretary oversees activities with other federal, state, local, and private entities as part of a collaborative effort to strengthen our borders, provide for intelligence analysis and infrastructure protection, improve the use of science and technology to counter weapons of mass destruction, and to create a comprehensive response and recovery system. The Office of the Secretary includes multiple offices that contribute to the overall Homeland Security mission.

The Privacy Office works to preserve and enhance privacy protections for all individuals, to promote transparency of Department of Homeland Security operations, and to serve as a leader in the privacy community.

The office for Civil Rights and Civil Liberties provides legal and policy advice to Department leadership on civil rights and civil liberties issues, investigates and resolves complaints, and provides leadership to Equal Employment Opportunity Programs.

The Office of Inspector General is responsible for conducting and supervising audits, investigations, and inspections relating to the programs and operations of the Department, recommending ways for the Department to carry out its responsibilities in the most effective, efficient, and economical manner possible.

The Citizenship and Immigration Services Ombudsman provides recommendations for resolving individual and employer problems with the United States Citizenship and Immigration Services in order to ensure national security and the integrity of the legal immigration system, increase efficiencies in administering citizenship and immigration services, and improve customer service.

The Office of Legislative Affairs serves as primary liaison to members of Congress and their staffs, the White House and Executive Branch, and to other federal agencies and governmental entities that have roles in assuring national security.

The Office of the General Counsel integrates approximately 1700 lawyers from throughout the Department into an effective, client-oriented, full-service legal team and comprises a headquarters office with subsidiary divisions and the legal programs for eight Department components. The Office of the General Counsel includes the ethics division for the Department.

The Office of Public Affairs coordinates the public affairs activities of all of the Department's components and offices, and serves as the federal government's lead public information office during a national emergency or disaster. Led by the Assistant Secretary for Public Affairs, it comprises the press office, incident and strategic communications, speechwriting, Web content management, and employee communications.

The Office of Counternarcotics Enforcement (CNE) coordinates policy and operations to stop the entry of illegal drugs into the United States, and to track and sever the connections between illegal drug trafficking and terrorism.

The Office of the Executive Secretariat (ESEC) provides all manner of direct support to the Secretary and Deputy Secretary, as well as related support to leadership and management across the Department. This support takes many forms, the most well known being accurate and timely dissemination of information and written communications from throughout the Department and our homeland security partners to the Secretary and Deputy Secretary.

The Military Advisor's Office advises on facilitating, coordinating and executing policy, procedures, preparedness activities and operations between the Department and the Department of Defense.

Office of Intergovernmental Affairs (IGA) has the mission of promoting an integrated national approach to homeland security by ensuring, coordinating, and advancing federal interaction with state, local, tribal, and territorial governments.

Advisory Panels and Committees

The Homeland Security Advisory Council provides advice and recommendations to the Secretary on matters related to homeland security. The Council is comprised of leaders from state and local government, first responder communities, the private sector, and academia.

The National Infrastructure Advisory Council provides advice to the Secretary of Homeland Security and the President on the security of information systems for the public and private institutions that constitute the critical infrastructure of our nation's economy.

The Homeland Security Science and Technology Advisory Committee serves as a source of independent, scientific and technical planning advice for the Under Secretary for Science and Technology.

The Critical Infrastructure Partnership Advisory Council was established to facilitate effective coordination between Federal infrastructure protection programs with the infrastructure protection activities of the private sector and of state, local, territorial and tribal governments.

The Interagency Coordinating Council on Emergency Preparedness and Individuals with Disabilities was established to ensure that the federal government appropriately supports safety and security for individuals with disabilities in disaster situations.

The Task Force on New Americans is an inter-agency effort to help immigrants learn English, embrace the common core of American civic culture, and become fully American.[13]

Conclusion

The Department of Homeland Security was designed to make Americans safer by providing the Nation with:

- One department whose primary mission is to protect the American homeland;
- One department to secure our borders, transportation sector, ports, and critical infrastructure;
- One department to synthesize and analyze homeland security intelligence from multiple sources;
- One department to coordinate communications with state and local governments, private industry, and the American people about threats and preparedness;
- One department to coordinate our efforts to protect the American people against bioterrorism and other weapons of mass destruction;
- One department to help train and equip for first responders;
- One department to manage federal emergency response activities; and
- More security officers in the field working to stop terrorists and fewer resources in Washington managing duplicative and redundant activities that drain critical homeland security resources.[14]

Questions

1. What is the purpose and mission of DHS?
2. Why do we still need an HSC?
3. How did the initial DHS organization mirror the 2002 National Strategy for Homeland Security?
4. Why did Hurricane Katrina prompt major changes to DHS?
5. How did FEMA's authority evolve within DHS?

Part III: Critical Mission Areas

Chapter 11

Intelligence & Warning

Objectives

- Explain the rationale for creating a DHS intelligence and warning capability.
- Describe the Homeland Security Advisory System and some of the issues related to it.
- Understand the relationship between DHS and the National Counterterrorism Center.
- Explain the risk to civil liberties posed by increased intelligence activities.

Intelligence and Warning. Terrorism depends on surprise. With it, a terrorist attack has the potential to do massive damage to an unwitting and unprepared target. Without it, the terrorists stand a good chance of being preempted by authorities, and even if they are not, the damage that results from their attacks is likely to be less severe. The United States will take every necessary action to avoid being surprised by another terrorist attack. We must have an intelligence and warning system that can detect terrorist activity before it manifests itself in an attack so that proper preemptive, preventive, and protective action can be taken.

— *Critical Mission Area #1, National Strategy for Homeland Security, July 2002*

Introduction

Better intelligence is held by many observers to be a crucial factor in preventing terrorist attacks.

Better intelligence is held by many observers to be a crucial factor in preventing terrorist attacks. Concerns have been expressed that no single agency or office in the federal government prior to September 11, 2001 was in a position to "connect the dots" between diffuse bits of information that might have provided clues to the planned attacks. Testimony before the two intelligence committees' Joint Inquiry on the September 11 attacks indicated that significant information in the possession of intelligence and law enforcement agencies was not fully shared with other agencies and that intelligence on potential terrorist threats against the United States was not fully exploited.

For many years, the sharing of intelligence and law enforcement information was circumscribed by administrative policies and statutory prohibitions. Beginning in the early 1990s, however, much effort has gone into improving interagency coordination.

After the September 11 attacks, a number of statutory obstacles were addressed by the USA-Patriot Act of 2001 and other legislation. Nevertheless, there has been no one place where the analytical effort is centered; the Department of Homeland Security (DHS) was designed to remedy that perceived deficiency as is the new National Counterterrorism Center (NCTC).[1]

DHS Intelligence Enterprise

DHS has had an intelligence component since its inception in 2003. The Homeland Security Act of 2002 assigned the original DHS intelligence component—the Directorate of Information Analysis and Infrastructure Protection—with responsibility to receive, analyze, and integrate law enforcement and intelligence information in order to "(A) identify and assess the nature and scope of terrorist threats to the homeland; (B) detect and identify threats of terrorism against the United States; and (C) understand such threats in light of actual and potential vulnerabilities of the homeland."

Congress also made information sharing a top priority of the new DHS intelligence organization, requiring it "to disseminate, as appropriate, information analyzed by the Department within the Department, to other agencies of the Federal government with responsibilities related to homeland security, and to agencies of State and local government and private sector entities, with such responsibilities in order to assist in the deterrence, prevention, preemption of, or response to, terrorist attacks against the United States."

Following the release of the 9/11 Commission Report in 2004, which identified a breakdown in information sharing as a key factor contributing to the failure to prevent the September 11, 2001 attacks, Congress underscored the importance it attached to information sharing at all levels of government. The Intelligence Reform and Terrorism Prevention Act of 2004 required the President to "create an information sharing environment for the sharing of terrorism information in a manner consistent with national security and with applicable legal standards relating to privacy and civil liberties," and "to designate an individual as the program manager responsible for information sharing across the Federal Government."

In July 2005, following "a systematic evaluation of the Department's operations, policies and structures" (commonly called the Second Stage Review or "2SR"), former Secretary of Homeland Security, Michael Chertoff, initiated a major reorganization of DHS. In his remarks describing the reorganization, he noted that "...intelligence lies at the heart of everything that we do." In an effort to improve how DHS manages its intelligence and information sharing responsibilities, he established a strengthened Office of Intelligence and Analysis (I&A) and made the Assistant Secretary for Information Analysis (now Under Secretary for Intelligence and Analysis) the Chief Intelligence Officer (CINT) for the Department. He also tasked I&A with ensuring that intelligence is coordinated, fused, and analyzed within the Department to provide a common operational picture; provide a primary connection between DHS and the Intelligence Community (IC) as a whole; and to act as a primary source of information for state, local and private sector partners.

"...intelligence lies at the heart of everything that we do."

- Secretary Chertoff

Since the 2SR reorganization, Congress imposed additional requirements on DHS through the Implementing Recommendations of the 9/11 Commission Act of 2007:

- Integrate information and standardize the format of intelligence products produced within DHS and its components.
- Establish department-wide procedures for review and analysis of information provided by state, local, tribal, and private sector elements; integrate that information into DHS intelligence products, and disseminate to Federal partners within the Intelligence Community.
- Evaluate how DHS components are utilizing homeland security information and participating in the Information Sharing Environment.
- Establish a comprehensive information technology network architecture to connect various DHS elements and promote information sharing.
- Establish a DHS State, Local, and Regional Fusion Center Initiative to establish partnerships with state, local, and regional fusion centers.
- Coordinate and oversee the creation of an Interagency Threat Assessment and Coordination Group that will bring state, local, and tribal law enforcement and intelligence analysts "to work in the National Counterterrorism

> Center (NCTC)19 with Federal intelligence analysts for the purpose of integrating, analyzing and assisting in the dissemination of federally-coordinated information...."

The Department of Homeland Security Intelligence Enterprise consists of those elements within DHS that have an intelligence mission. At the outset of the new Administration, it consists of I&A, the Homeland Infrastructure Threat and Risk Analysis Center, and the Intelligence Division of the Office of Operations Coordination and Planning (all located at the DHS headquarters), and the intelligence elements of six operational components: U.S. Customs and Border Protection (CBP), U.S. Immigration and Customs Enforcement (ICE), U.S. Citizenship and Immigration Services (USCIS), Transportation Security Administration (TSA), U.S. Coast Guard (USCG), and U.S. Secret Service (USSS). The Department and USCG are statutory members of the IC.[2]

I&A Organization

I&A is led by an Under Secretary, a position subject to Senate confirmation. The Under Secretary also serves as the department's Chief Intelligence Officer and is supported by a Principal Deputy Under Secretary.

The Department of Homeland Security Intelligence Enterprise consists of those elements within DHS that have an intelligence mission.

The Deputy Under Secretary for Intelligence (DU/S-I) is responsible for the analytic mission of I&A. The office has been focused on five "analytic thrusts" aligned with the principal threats to the Homeland: 1) border security, including narcotics trafficking, alien and human smuggling, and money laundering; 2) radicalization and extremism; 3) particular groups entering the United States that could be exploited by terrorists or criminals; 4) critical infrastructure and key resources; and 5) weapons of mass destruction (WMD) and health threats.

There are five divisions within the DU/S-I organization that are engaged in the analytic effort.

1. The Homeland Environment Threat Analysis Division identifies and assesses major threats originating from demographic instabilities, domestic and international radicalization, and future strategic future threats for which DHS must prepare and respond.
2. The Critical Infrastructure Threat Analysis Division integrates all source intelligence from the Intelligence Community with information from critical infrastructure owners and operators, and, collaboratively with state and local intelligence fusion centers to provide a comprehensive tactical and strategic understanding of physical and cyber threats to the critical infrastructure, including threats from nation-states, international and domestic terrorism, and criminal enterprises.
3. The Borders, WMD, and Health Threat Analysis Division monitors, assesses, and reports the threats posed to U.S. borders and to the U.S. population by dangerous people and dangerous things. The Borders branch of this division not only tracks terrorists, but also special interest aliens, transnational gangs such as alien smugglers and narcotics traffickers and how they move their money.

4. The Collection Requirements Division is the focal point for all collection requirements in an effort to ensure that the intelligence needs of DHS components and customers are articulated, clarified, assigned, and fulfilled. This division represents DHS at IC collection requirement committees. It also manages the DHS Open Source Program which produces domestic open source intelligence (OSINT).

5. The Reporting and Production Division integrates DHS and state and local law enforcement information into the IC through Homeland Intelligence Reports. It is also the single point of service across DHSI for state, local, and tribal support requests as well as the central point for dissemination of I&A's finished products.[3]

Homeland Security Intelligence Mission

The mission of the Office of Intelligence and Analysis (I&A) is to "ensure that information related to homeland security threats is collected, analyzed, and disseminated to the full spectrum of homeland security customers in the Department, at state, local, and tribal levels, in the private sector, and in the IC." The Under Secretary for I&A is the Chief Intelligence Officer for the Department and is responsible to lead I&A and the entire DHSI enterprise. The Under Secretary is also the Department's chief information sharing officer and is responsible for implementing the objectives of the PM-ISE within DHS.

The mission of the Office of Intelligence and Analysis (I&A) is to ensure that information related to homeland security threats is collected, analyzed, and disseminated to the full spectrum of homeland security customers in the Department, at state, local, and tribal levels, in the private sector, and in the Intelligence Community.

To accomplish its mission, I&A participates in all aspects of the intelligence cycle—"the process by which information is acquired, converted into finished intelligence, and made available to policymakers. Generally the cycle comprises five steps: planning and direction, collection, processing, analysis, and production and dissemination." It is an iterative process in which collection requirements based on national security threats are developed, and intelligence is collected, analyzed, and disseminated to a broad range of consumers.

DHS does not generally engage in traditional foreign intelligence collection activities such as imagery intelligence, signals intelligence, human intelligence, measurement and signatures intelligence, and foreign open source intelligence. But, as former Secretary Chertoff has noted:

> *"Intelligence, as you know, is not only about spies and satellites. Intelligence is about the thousands and thousands of routine, everyday observations and activities. Surveillance, interactions—each of which may be taken in isolation as not a particularly meaningful piece of information, but when fused together, gives us a sense of the patterns and the flow that really is at the core of what intelligence analysis is all about.... "*

I&A combines the unique information collected by DHS components as part of their operational activities (e.g., at airports, seaports, and the border) with foreign intelligence from the IC; law enforcement information from Federal, state, local, and tribal sources; private sector data about critical infrastructure and key resources; and information from domestic open sources to develop homeland security intelligence. This encompasses a broad range of homeland security threats. It includes border security information to counter human smuggling and trafficking, cargo data to prevent the introduction of dangerous items, information to protect critical infrastructure against all hazards, information about infectious diseases, and demographic data and other research about 'violent radicalization.[4]

I&A Customers

I&A's "customer set" is broad. Former Under Secretary Charles Allen saw the Department—both headquarters and the operational components—as I&A's primary customer. "Virtually any terrorist attack on the homeland that one can imagine must exploit a border crossing, a port of entry, a critical infrastructure, or one of the other domains that the department has an obligation to secure. DHS Intelligence must learn and adapt faster than the enemy, so that our department with all its partners in the federal, state, and local levels of government and the private sector have the information edge they need to secure our nation." Accordingly, I&A's DHS customers range from the Secretary of Homeland Security all the way to individual border patrol agents, Coast Guard seamen, and airport screeners.

I&A's DHS customers range from the Secretary of Homeland Security all the way to individual border patrol agents, Coast Guard seamen, and airport screeners.

I&A is also a full partner within the IC and represents DHS on several IC committees. The Under Secretary, for example, is a member of the Director of National Intelligence (DNI) Executive Committee. I&A contributes analytic staff to the National Counterterrorism Center (NCTC).

The office also contributes items to the President's Daily Brief providing a homeland security perspective on terrorism and other threats to the United States to the nation's leaders.

State, local, and tribal law enforcement—often described as the "first preventers" of terrorism— are another important set of customers. They require timely and actionable intelligence to respond to threats. They also need intelligence about the latest terrorist tactics and techniques so that they know what to look for and what to do when they encounter suspicious behavior or dangerous items. Finally, I&A is charged with supporting the operators of the nation's publicly and privately-owned critical infrastructure with threat information and other intelligence that supports their risk management decision making.[5]

I&A Intelligence Products

I&A produces numerous products for its customers. In 2008, there was a realignment and standardization of the I&A finished intelligence product line which now include:

- **Homeland Security Threat Assessment (HSTA).** This is an annual threat assessment that represents the analytical judgments of DHS and assesses the major threats to the homeland for which the nation must prepare and respond. This includes the actions, capabilities, and intentions of domestic and foreign terrorists and extremists and the possible occurrence of systemic threats. It focuses on domestic extremists, international terrorists operating in the homeland or directing attacks against it, and systemic threats such as pandemics and transnational criminal organizations.44 The HSTA is produced in classified and "Unclassified/For Official Use Only" versions.

- **Intelligence Warning**. Contains urgent intelligence.
- **Intelligence Note**. Contains timely information or analysis on a current topic.
- **Homeland Security Assessment**. Consists of in-depth analysis on a topic.
- **Homeland Security Monitors**. These are produced monthly in collaboration with the components and may be classified or unclassified. Examples include:
- **Border Security Monitor**
- **Cyber Security Monitor**
- **Cuba-Gram**
- **Reference Aids**. These are less analytical and more descriptive. For example, they might describe what an anthrax lab looks like or the latest on improvised explosive devices (IED) and fuses. They contain photos and diagrams and inform law enforcement and first responders what to look for and what actions to take if they are encountered.
- **Perspective**. These are longer term analytic pieces.
- **Joint Homeland Security Assessment/FBI Intelligence Bulletin**. These are joint reports done in conjunction with the FBI.

I&A makes the products of its analysis available to state and local officials through classified and unclassified intelligence networks:
- *HSIN*
- *HSDN*

I&A also produces Homeland Intelligence Reports (HIR) which contain information that has yet to be fully evaluated. These are similar to the Intelligence Information Report (IIR) produced by other IC agencies. An HIR could contain information related to border encounters, information shared by a state or local fusion center, or other information of homeland security interest. There are also Homeland Security Intelligence Reports (HSIR) that are produced by the DHS component agencies. HSIR's, however, do contain some analysis.

I&A makes the products of its analysis available to state and local officials through classified and unclassified intelligence networks: The Homeland Security Information Network (HSIN) is a secured, web-based platform that facilitates Sensitive But Unclassified information sharing and collaboration between federal, state, local, tribal, private sector, and international partners. It is managed by the DHS Directorate of Operations Coordination and Planning. The HSIN platform was created to interface with existing information sharing networks to support the diverse communities of interest engaged in preventing, protecting from, responding to, and recovering from all threats, hazards and incidents under the jurisdiction of DHS. It provides real-time, interactive connectivity between states and major urban areas and the National Operations Center (NOC).

The Homeland Secure Data Network (HSDN) provides access to collateral Secret-level terrorism related information. This includes NCTC Online, a classified repository that serves as the counterterrorism community's library of terrorism information.49 I&A has deployed HSDN terminals to more than 30 state and local fusion centers and intends to install terminals in all of the fusion centers as soon as security requirements are met.[6]

Intelligence Support To State, Local, Tribal Officials, and the Private Sector

There has been some criticism about the focus of I&A analysis and the relevance of its products to state, local, tribal, and private sector customers. For example, at a homeland security forum in early 2008, some state and local participants expressed unhappiness with the flow of intelligence from DHS. According to the forum's findings, published in the journal Homeland Security Affairs, "[t]he Department had become 'irrelevant' to states and localities as a source of intelligence, because that intelligence lacks timeliness and adds so little value to local terrorism efforts. Another participant noted that 'the stream of intelligence from DHS is useless ... '" However, later in 2008, state and local officials interviewed by CRS for this report expressed the general view that although this critique may have been true a couple of years ago, it was not true now.

In 2006, former Under Secretary Allen established a State and Local Fusion Center (SLFC) Pilot Project Team to work with six fusion centers in five states to enhance DHS support. At the outset, the team "found a substantial gap still exists between the kind of support the pilot sites said they need and the kind of support they have been receiving from DHS across a range of issues, including the three focus areas of the project." Moreover, they found in their "discussions at the pilot sites, that the quality of intelligence support in the wake of critical domestic and international homeland security-related incidents is a top priority for state and local fusion center leaders and a key determinant of how they evaluate DHS analytic support."

The pilot project team focused on improving DHS response to SLFC requests for information (RFI), improving reporting and analysis that responds to SLFC mission-critical needs, and assisting the centers with their open source exploitation capabilities. Upon completion of the pilot project in late 2007, the team reported enhancements that 'markedly improved DHS SLFC support efforts' at the pilot sites. They also reported that they had worked with I&A officers to develop a proposed action plan involving six core initiatives to implement these enhancements on a nationwide basis.

One of pilot team's recommendations was to establish a staff element that will serve as focal point for all SLFC RFI's. The Director of the State and Local Program Office (SLPO) reported that in January 2008, I&A established a "Single Point of Service" program to give state and local customers "a 24-hour, one stop shopping resource to request support, communicate product requirements, and share critical information with DHS and its components." In the last quarter of 2008, that team serviced 659 support requests from 36 states.[7]

Homeland Security Advisory System

The Homeland Security Advisory System (HSAS), established on March 12, 2002, is a color-coded terrorist threat warning system administered by the Department of Homeland Security (DHS). The system, which federal departments and agencies are required to implement and use, provides recommended protective measures for federal departments and agencies to prevent, prepare for, mitigate against, and respond to terrorist attacks.[8]

President Bush signed Homeland Security Presidential Directive 3 (HSPD-3), creating the Homeland Security Advisory System (HSAS). Initially, the Attorney General was responsible for developing, implementing and managing the system.[9]

Within DHS, the Undersecretary for Information Assurance and Infrastructure Protection — as head of the Information Assurance and Infrastructure Protection directorate (IAIP) — is responsible for administering the HSAS. Specifically, IAIP is responsible for providing, in coordination with other agencies of the federal government, specific warning information and advice about appropriate protective measures and countermeasures to state and local government agencies and authorities, the private sector, other entities, and the public.[10]

DHS disseminates HSAS terrorist threat warnings to federal departments, state and local agencies, the public, and private-sector entities. DHS, however, only provides protective measures for federal departments. This dissemination of warnings is conducted through multiple communication systems and public announcements.

HSAS has five threat levels: low, guarded, elevated, high, and severe. From March 2002 to the present, the HSAS threat level has been no lower than elevated, raised to high seven times, and raised to severe once. The first time it was raised to high was on September 10, 2002, due to the fear of terrorist attacks on the anniversary of the terrorist attacks of September 11, 2001. The most recent time it was raised to high was on July 7, 2005, due to terrorist bombings of the London mass transit systems. DHS raised the threat level for mass transit systems only. The only time HSAS has been raised to severe (red) was on August 10, 2006, due to a terrorist plan to bomb flights originating in the United Kingdom. DHS raised the threat level for the aviation sector only.[11]

HSAS Issues

Since the creation of the HSAS, a number of issues have arisen, among which are: the vagueness of warnings disseminated by the system; the system's lack of protective measures recommended for state and local governments, and the public; the perceived inadequacy of disseminating threats to state and local governments, the public, and the private sector; and how best to coordinate HSAS with other existing warning systems.

Vagueness of Warnings. The HSAS threat level has been raised seven times from "yellow" to "orange" since its activation on March 12, 2002, and once to "red" on August 10, 2006. With each change, the Attorney General or DHS Secretary cited intelligence information but offered little specificity, except on August 1, 2004, when former DHS Secretary Ridge identified financial institutions in New York, Washington, DC, and New Jersey as being targeted by Al Qaeda. The only other time any specifics were given on possible terrorist attack targets was on February 7, 2003, when former DHS Secretary Ridge cited intelligence reports suggesting Al Qaeda attacks on apartment buildings, hotels, and other soft skin targets.19 But in this case, no region, state, or city was identified as possible locations of attacks. Moreover, DHS has never explained the sources and quality of intelligence upon which the threat levels were based.[12]

The HSOC is in constant communication with the White House, acting as the situational awareness conduit for the White House Situation Room by providing information needed to make decisions and define courses of action.

Lack of Specific Protective Measures for State and Local Governments, the Public, and the Private Sector. The HSAS provides a set of protective measures for each threat condition, but these protective measures are identified only for federal agencies. DHS only recommends protective measures for states, localities, the public, or the private sector, however, the recommended protective measures are the same ones issued to federal agencies. These recommended protective measures provide no specificity for states, localities, the public, or the private sector.[13]

Communication of Terrorist Threats to State and Local Governments, the Public, and the Private Sector. DHS uses a variety of communications systems to provide terrorist threat warnings to states, localities, the public, and the private sector. These systems include, for an example, conference calls, public announcements, CEO COM LINK (a secure telecommunications bridge that enables senior federal officials and CEOs to exchange timely information in the event of a threat or a crisis), and National Law Enforcement Telecommunications System (NLETS), but DHS has no single communication system it uses to issue HSAS terrorist warnings.[14]

Coordination of HSAS with Other Warning Systems HSAS is not the only federal warning system; eight separate systems exist to provide timely notification about imminent and potentially catastrophic threats to health and safety. The types of hazards covered by these systems include severe weather, contamination from chemical and biological weapon stockpiles scheduled for destruction, terrorist attacks, and any other emergency or hazard the President decides is significant enough to warrant public notification.[15]

Cost of Threat Level Changes An increase in the HSAS threat level imposes both direct and indirect costs on federal, state, and local governments, the private sector, and the public. These costs include the increased security measures undertaken by states and localities, loss to tourism, and the indirect cost on the economy during a period of heightened threat level. In FY2003, the Office for Domestic Preparedness (renamed the Office of Grant Programs in FY2007) Critical Infrastructure Protection grant program authorized state and local governments to use allocated grants to fund overtime costs associated with heightened threat levels. According to the Office of Grant Program's State Homeland Security Grant and Urban Area Security Initiative grant programs guidance, overtime is an authorized expenditure only associated with training or exercises. Office of Grant Program's Law Enforcement Terrorism Prevention Program, however, does allow overtime costs specifically related to homeland security efforts.[16]

On July 14, 2009, DHS Secretary Napolitano established a task force to conduct a review of the effectiveness of the Homeland Security Advisory System. While the subsequent report offered suggestions to improve the system, but councilmember's unanimously concluded that the advisory system in its current form is integral to counterterrorism efforts in the United States.

The Task Force members agreed that there are two primary audiences for the Homeland Security Advisory System. Institutions including the federal government, state and local governments, and the private sector have used the Advisory System for planning and for calibrating responses. They determined that the current system has functioned reasonably well for this audience, especially as alerts have become more targeted geographically and to specific sectors; however, improvements are needed. The system's ability to communicate useful information in a credible manner to the public is poor. Significant rethinking of how to communicate to this audience is warranted.

Raising the threat condition has economic, physical, and psychological effects on the nation.

The Task Force members also agreed that, at its best, there is currently indifference to the Homeland Security Advisory System and, at worst, there is a disturbing lack of public confidence in the system that must be remedied.[17] The Task Force recommends that the Secretary consider the measures below to restore confidence in the Advisory System. These include:

- A discipline of more narrowly targeting the specific region and sector under threat, avoiding elevating the alert status of the nation as a whole.
- A practice of providing more specific information on new threats: including information on the type of threat, the credibility of the source of the information, and the steps the government is taking to mitigate the vulnerability.
- A practice of accompanying new alerts with actionable steps the public can take.
- An acknowledgment that the new baseline for the United States is guarded. We remain a nation confronting the threat of terrorist attack, but given that we remain ever on guard, the number of levels can be reduced from five to three.
- As disciplined a focus on lowering the alert status as now goes into raising it.

- A practice of debriefing the nation after alerts have been issued -what happened to the threat, can we now return to (what we recommend to be termed) "guarded" status?[18]

National Counterterrorism Center

Even though the Homeland Security Act (P.L. 107-296), enacted on November 25, 2002, provided the new Department of Homeland Security with a specific mandate for an Under Secretary for Information Analysis and Infrastructure Protection, concern that DHS, as a new agency and not a longtime member of the Intelligence Community, would not be the best place for the integration of highly sensitive information from multiple government agencies. In the 2003 State of the Union address, President Bush revealed his instructions to "the leaders of the FBI, the CIA, the Homeland Security and the Department of Defense to develop a Terrorist Threat Integration Center, to merge and analyze all threat information in a single location." Despite the statutory responsibilities of DHS for threat integration, in May 2003 the Terrorist Threat Integration Center (TTIC) was established (without a statutory mandate) to merge all threat information in a single location. Some Members of Congress expressed concerns about the possibility that the roles of the DHS intelligence analysis office and TTIC might be confused, but DHS was a partner in TTIC and gradually came to concentrate on serving as a bridge between the national intelligence community and state, local, and tribal law enforcement agencies that had never been components of the national Intelligence Community.

In August 2004, President Bush issued Executive Order 13354, establishing the National Counterterrorism Center (NCTC) to serve as the primary organization of the Federal Government for analyzing and integrating all intelligence pertaining to terrorism or counterterrorism and serve as the central and shared knowledge bank on known and suspected terrorists.

A year later, in July 2004, the 9/11 Commission (the National Commission on Terrorist Attacks Upon the United States), noting the existence of a number of various centers in different parts of the government assigned to combine disparate pieces of intelligence, called for the establishment of a National Counterterrorism Center built on the foundation of TTIC but having a responsibility for joint planning for responding to terrorist plots in addition to assessing intelligence from all sources. The NCTC would, according to the 9/11 Commission, compile all-source information on terrorism but also undertake planning of counterterrorism activities, assigning operational responsibilities to lead agencies throughout the Government.

In August 2004 shortly after publication of the 9/11 Commission Report, President Bush issued Executive Order 13354, based on constitutional and statutory authorities, that established the National Counterterrorism Center as a follow-on to TTIC. The NCTC was to serve as the primary organization of the Federal Government for analyzing and integrating all intelligence possessed or acquired pertaining to terrorism or counterterrorism (except purely domestic terrorism) and serve as the central and shared knowledge bank on known and suspected terrorists. The NCTC would not just have the analytical responsibilities TTIC had possessed; it would also assign operational responsibilities to lead agencies for counterterrorism activities, but NCTC would not direct the execution of operations. The Director of the NCTC would be appointed by the Director of Central Intelligence (DCI) with the approval of the President.

Some Members of Congress, however, remained concerned about the status of NCTC, the likelihood that Congress would have no role in the appointment of its leadership, and the possibility that an interagency entity might not be responsive to congressional oversight committees. In December 2004 the Intelligence Reform and Terrorism Prevention Act (P.L. 108- 458), implemented many of the 9/11 Commission's recommendations. The Act established the position of Director of National Intelligence (DNI) along with the Office of the DNI (ODNI) and it created an NCTC with a statutory charter and placed it within the ODNI.

In accordance with the 2004 Intelligence Reform Act and Terrorism Prevention Act, the Director of the NCTC was henceforth to be appointed by the President with the advice and consent of the Senate. The position of the NCTC Director is unusual, if not unique, in government; he reports to the DNI for analyzing and integrating information pertaining to terrorism (except domestic terrorism), for NCTC budget and programs; for planning and progress of joint counterterrorism operations (other than intelligence operations) he reports directly to the President. In practice, the NCTC Director works through the National Security Council and its staff in the White House.[19]

NCTC Activities

According to publicly available information, NCTC provides intelligence in a number of ways— items for the President's Daily Brief and the National Terrorism Bulletin both of which are classified. NCTC claims to provide the Intelligence Community with 24/7 situational awareness, terrorism threat reporting and tracking. According to one media report, "agency-integrated teams [are] assigned by subject matter and geography [to] turn out reports disseminated to thousands of policy and intelligence officials across the government. Agency representatives sit around a table three times daily—at 8 a.m., 3 p.m. and 1 a.m.—to update the nation's threat matrix."

NCTC maintains databases of information on international terrorist identities (in a system known as the Terrorist Identities Datamart Environment (TIDE)) to support the Government's watchlisting system designed to identify potential terrorists. NCTC products are available to some 75 government agencies and other working groups and facilitates information sharing with state, local, tribal, and private partners.

NCTC has also established Intelligence Community-wide working groups—a Radicalization and Extremist Messaging Group and a Chemical, Biological, Radiological, Nuclear Counterterrorism Group and a working group for alternative analysis as part of an effort to improve the rigor and quality of terrorism analysis. NCTC also coordinates the DNI Homeland Threat Task Force that examines threats to the US from al Qaeda, other groups and homegrown violent extremists.

Public information on NCTC's planning responsibilities is limited. One press account describes a National Implementation Plan for the National Strategy for Combating Terrorism prepared in June 2006. The Plan identified major objectives with more than 500 discrete counterterrorism tasks to be carried out by designated agencies. The objectives included disrupting terrorist groups, protecting and defending the homeland, and containing violent extremism. Observers suggest that the primary benefit of such generalized planning is requiring agencies to coordinate their initiatives and providing an opportunity to reduce duplication of effort and ensure that specific tasks are not neglected. The 2006 implementation plan has reportedly been updated but no details have been made public.[20]

Assessments of NCTC

From information available on the public record, NCTC appears to be structured to fulfill the mission it was assigned by the Intelligence Reform and Terrorism Prevention Act and other legislation. Most, if not all, congressional observers apparently believe, that NCTC's authorities are both appropriate and adequate. NCTC's organization reflects the determination to create, within the Intelligence Community, an office that could gather information from all government agencies and from open sources, analyze the data, and provide policymakers with greater situational awareness and warning of planned attacks. According to all available reports, NCTC has access to the databases of all intelligence agencies and it can draw upon analytical resources throughout the government to supplement its own files, but it is unclear to what extent the disparate databases are technically compatible or whether they are, or can be, linked in ways that permit simultaneous searching.

One assessment of the NCTC undertaken by a student at the Army War college in 2007 concluded that "More than two years since its inception, however, the NCTC has arguably achieved neither an acceptable level of effectiveness nor efficiency in performing its intended role." The author, Army Col. Brian R. Reinwald, argued that in focusing on consolidating information from other agencies, the NCTC demonstrated "a seeming unwillingness to take a bold implementation approach and a preference to avoid bureaucratic conflict." Its "vision statement inauspiciously paints a picture of a non-confrontational think tank that identified issues, and attempts to merely influence the greater governmental efforts against counterterrorism." In sum, Reinwald argued that NCTC's approach "does not capture the literal roles and mission assigned by Congress, to plan, to integrate, delineate responsibility, and monitor." Moreover, the large percentage of detailees from other agencies in NCTC "sustains an environment that fosters continued loyalty of NCTC employees to their parent agencies rather than the NCTC itself." The author, taking an expansive view of the NCTC's role argues that "The U.S. requires a single federal entity focused on GWOT [Global War on Terror] counterterrorism strategy with the necessary authorities to integrate intelligence, conduct comprehensive interagency planning, compel specific action when required, and coordinate and synchronize the elements of national power for successful operations."

Members of Congress have taken note of NCTC's ability to gather information from a variety of agencies and its contributions to preventing specific terrorist attacks. There remain concerns that the threat from Al Qaeda and other groups has not diminished. In a visit to NCTC in October 2009, President Obama addressed the representatives, "it's clear for all to see—that you are one team—that you are more integrated and more collaborative and more effective than ever before."

For NCTC as for the Intelligence Community as a whole, in many cases the successes go unreported while the failures are trumpeted. However, two incidents in late 2009 led to widespread publicity about information sharing and counterterrorism analysis that led to significant congressional interest. Reports of the multiple assassinations that occurred in Fort Hood Army Base in Texas on November 5, 2009 led to expressions of concern about the Government's counterterrorism capabilities. The extent of NCTC's role, if any, in gathering information about Major Nidal M. Hasan prior to the incident has not been made available publicly. As Major Hasan was both a U.S. citizen and a commissioned officer much relevant information would have come from internal DOD information that would not necessarily be shared with NCTC. Press reports indicate, however, that he had been in contact with a known terrorist living in Yemen. This type of information might have come to the attention of law enforcement and intelligence agencies and could have been available to NCTC. Whether NCTC did access such information and whether it notified the Army or other DOD elements is unknown. Ongoing investigations will probably provide more background on NCTC's role, but Congress may move to undertake its own assessment.

The December 25, 2009 incident in which a Nigerian traveler, Umar Farouk Abdulmutallab, attempted to set off an incendiary device onboard an aircraft approaching Detroit was a more straightforward foreign intelligence problem. It did not involve a U.S. citizen nor was he an employee of the US Government. In this case, according to the Obama Administration, it was not the availability or the interagency sharing of data that was the problem; there were no major difficulties in collecting or sharing information (as had been the case prior to 9/11). The problem in December 2009 was inadequate analysis. Despite the information "available to all-source analysts at the CIA and the NCTC prior to the attempted attack, the dots were never connected and, as a result, the problem appears to be more about a component failure to 'connect the dots,' rather than a lack of information sharing." The Obama Administration has pointed to several specific failures by the counterterrorism community generally and NCTC in particular:

> *"NCTC and CIA personnel who are responsible for watchlisting did not search all available databases to uncover additional derogatory information that could have been correlated with Mr. Abdulmutallab."*

Further, "A series of human errors occurred—delayed dissemination of a finished intelligence report and what appears to be incomplete/faulty database searches on Mr. Abdulmutallab's name and identifying information." There was not a process for tracking reports and actions taken in response and there appears to have been a greater concern with the threat posed to American interests in Yemen than to the possibility of an attack by Al Qaeda in the Arabian Peninsula (AQAP) on the US Homeland. The extent to which such failings belong solely or even significantly to NCTC as opposed to other agencies is as yet undetermined.[21]

Freedom Versus Security

Homeland security measures often involve striking a balance between greater safety and infringements on civil liberties, such as invasions of privacy, discrimination, and other curtailments of individual freedom. As USA Today's Gene Stephens explains, "*We cannot truly be free unless we have a reasonable degree of safety, but we cannot truly feel safe unless we are also secure from undue prying into our personal lives.*" Baggage searches at airports, for example, may deter potential hijackers, but they also invade the privacy of countless non-terrorists. Similarly, granting broader investigative powers to the FBI could help thwart future attacks but may also result in unwarranted government surveillance or harassment of many innocent people. Evaluating homeland security efforts thus becomes a question of trade-offs; security experts must decide to what degree civil liberties should be curtailed in order to strengthen homeland security.

While homeland security encompasses a vast array of efforts at the local, state, and national levels, three centerpieces of the federal government's homeland security strategy have been intelligence gathering, intelligence sharing, and immigration control. The Bush administration's efforts to improve the government's capabilities in each of these three areas have been among the most controversial issues surrounding homeland security.

"We cannot truly be free unless we have a reasonable degree of safety, but we cannot truly feel safe unless we are also secure from undue prying into our personal lives."

- Gene Stephens
USA Today

Intelligence Gathering

In the aftermath of September 11, a consensus quickly emerged that the tragedies were due in part to a breakdown in intelligence. Leaders from across the political spectrum questioned how al Qaeda—a known terrorist network—had been able to plan and execute the September 11 attacks without attracting the attention of the CIA, the FBI, the National Security Agency, the Department of Defense, and other agencies charged with tracking terrorist threats. A key to preventing future attacks, it seemed, was to revitalize U.S. intelligence efforts.

To this end Congress passed, and President George W. Bush signed, the USA Patriot Act on October 26, 2001. The act gave new investigative powers to domestic law enforcement and international intelligence agencies. For example, it expanded federal agents' power to conduct telephone and e-mail surveillance of suspected terrorists—measures that have alarmed some civil libertarians and privacy advocates.

Controversy over the Patriot Act highlights a fundamental theme in homeland security debates: In general Americans want the government to use its power to investigate and avert terrorist threats, but at the same time they oppose the idea of a "police state" in which the government continuously monitors average people. The challenge facing the government, according to William Webster, former FBI director and CIA chief, is *"getting as much information as possible without impairing the rights of privacy that Americans have always considered dear. Everyone has a right to question, 'Why are they doing these things?'"*

Intelligence Sharing

Related to, but distinct from, the challenge of intelligence gathering is the issue of intelligence sharing. Critics of the government's counterterrorism measures have laid part of the blame for September 11 on a lack of communication between the FBI, CIA, and other federal agencies. According to this view, there were significant warning signs that, had they been heeded, could have averted the September 11 attacks. However, because of the compartmentalized nature of the U.S. intelligence apparatus, the various agencies charged with tracking terrorist threats were unable to recognize the warning signs because they were not communicating with one another. As former FBI agent David Major put it, "*If you don't share intelligence, you don't connect the dots.*"

To better "connect the dots"—the countless bits of information gathered through separate intelligence operations—Congress passed the Homeland Security Act, which became law on November 25, 2002. The act created a new cabinet-level agency, the Department of Homeland Security (DHS), to coordinate homeland security efforts. The DHS incorporated twenty-two federal agencies, including the Immigration and Naturalization Service, Coast Guard, and the Border Patrol—but not the FBI or CIA—and constitutes the biggest reorganization in the federal government since the Department of Defense was created in 1947. One of the primary roles of the DHS is to collect and coordinate intelligence from the FBI, CIA, NSA, and other agencies so that they can more easily recognize patterns and threats.

From a civil libertarian point of view, the problem with intelligence sharing—as with intelligence gathering—is its potential for abuse.

From a civil libertarian point of view, the problem with intelligence sharing—as with intelligence gathering—is its potential for abuse. By its very nature intelligence gathering—or more colloquially, spying—involves invasions of privacy that run counter to the Fourth Amendment's protection against unwarranted government searches. For this reason, spying has historically been justified as a tool of national security rather than law enforcement, to be used against foreign governments rather than U.S. citizens. Domestic law enforcement agencies, such as the FBI, who wish to conduct wiretaps or property searches in criminal investigations must obtain warrants and observe other rules of procedure that foreign intelligence agencies such as the CIA do not. The CIA, in turn, is prohibited from engaging in law enforcement or internal security functions. Many analysts worry that the DHS's emphasis on intelligence sharing may serve to remove the prohibitions on domestic spying and erode the regulatory framework that governs the use of sensitive information gained through intelligence operations.[22]

Conclusion

Legislation creating a homeland security department recognized the crucial importance of intelligence to the counterterrorist effort. It proposed an analytical office within DHS that would be able to draw upon the information gathering resources of other government agencies and of the private sector. It envisioned the DHS information analysis entity working closely with other DHS offices, other federal agencies, state and local officials, and the private sector to devise strategies and programs to protect U.S. vulnerabilities and to provide warning of specific attacks.[23]

Concerned that DHS would not be the best place for the integration of highly sensitive information from multiple government agencies, the National Counterterrorism Center was eventually established by the 2004 Intelligence Reform and Terrorism Prevention Act to compile all-source information on terrorism and plan counterterrorism activities. The NCTC Director is appointed by the President with the advice and consent of the Senate, and works through the National Security Council and its staff in the White House. DHS remains a partner in in the NCTC and serves as a bridge between the national intelligence community and state, local, and tribal law enforcement agencies that had never previously been components of the national Intelligence Community.

Questions

1. Why did DHS incorporate an information analysis and warning capability?
2. How does the Homeland Security Advisory System work?
3. What is the relationship between DHS and NCTC?
4. What are the advantages and disadvantages of increased intelligence activities?

Chapter 14

Border & Transportation Security

Objectives

- Know the three subcomponents of Border and Transportation Security.
- Know the purpose of the CBP, TSA, and ICE.
- Explain the U.S. Coast Guard's role in border security.
- Understand the importance of security and trade issues in BTS.

America historically has relied heavily on two vast oceans and two friendly neighbors for border security, and on the private sector for most forms of domestic transportation security. The increasing mobility and destructive potential of modern terrorism has required the United States to rethink and renovate fundamentally its systems for border and transportation security... We must therefore promote the efficient and reliable flow of people, goods, and services across borders, while preventing terrorists from using transportation conveyances or systems to deliver implements of destruction.

— Critical Mission Area #2, National Strategy for Homeland Security, July 2002

Introduction

Securing the borders of the United States has long been a contentious political issue. Although the United States is often described as "a country of immigrants" and a "melting pot," highlighting the relative openness of its borders, the borders have also served as a line of protection against external security threats. Such threats can take many shapes, but in recent years they have mainly included illegal immigration, smuggling and trafficking, and terrorism.

Secure, well-managed borders must not only protect the United States against threats from abroad; they must also expedite the safe flow of lawful travel and commerce.

To that end, globalization has produced increasing transnational threats to the United States and the pressure to use the border as a protection mechanism has grown. Since at least the 1980s, the border has played a central role in the debate over how to provide domestic security in the United States. The terrorist attacks of September 11, 2001 (and subsequent attempts on U.S. soil), the significant domestic population of unauthorized aliens, and recent concerns over drug-trafficking-related violence in Mexico and the potential for spillover into the United States have all continued to fuel this debate.[1]

A safe and secure homeland requires that we maintain effective control of our air, land, and sea borders. Secure, well-managed borders must not only protect the United States against threats from abroad; they must also expedite the safe flow of lawful travel and commerce.[2] There is consensus that Border and Transportation Security (BTS) is a pivotal function in protecting the American people from terrorists and their instruments of destruction. The adequate provision of BTS is an extremely complex endeavor given the scope of U.S. borders, and the volume of traffic flowing across them. As described by Admiral James Loy, former Deputy Secretary of the Department of Homeland Security (DHS):

> We must secure nearly 7,500 miles of land border with Canada and Mexico, across which more than 500 million people, 130 million motor vehicles, and 2.5 million rail cars pass every year. We also patrol almost 95,000 miles of shoreline and navigable waters, and 361 ports that see 8,000 foreign flag vessels, 9 million containers of cargo, and nearly 200 million cruise and ferry passengers every year. We have some 422 primary airports and another 124 commercial service airports that see 30,000 flights and 1.8 million passengers every day. There are approximately 110,000 miles of highway and 220,000 miles of rail track that cut across our nation, and 590,000 bridges dotting America's biggest cities and smallest towns. That is just a thumbnail

> of the vast infrastructure that supports the largest and most efficient economy in the world — with more than $11 trillion in Gross Domestic *Product.*[3]

The Department's first priority then is to prevent the entry of terrorists and the instruments of terrorism while simultaneously ensuring the efficient flow of lawful traffic and commerce. BTS manages and coordinates port of entry activities and leads efforts to create a border of the future that provides greater security through better intelligence, coordinated national efforts, and international cooperation against terrorists, the instruments of terrorism, and other international threats.[4]

To carry out its mission, the BTS organizes these capabilities under three major subcomponents:

1. Customs and Border Protection (CBP)
2. Transportation Security Administration (TSA)
3. Immigration and Customs Enforcement (ICE)

Conceptually speaking, CBP is responsible for protecting our nation's borders while facilitating the flow of legitimate trade and travel. TSA is charged with protecting the nation's transportation systems to ensure freedom of movement for people and commerce, and ICE serves an important border security function by identifying and shutting down vulnerabilities in the nation's border, economic, transportation, and infrastructure security.[5] In addition, the U.S. Coast Guard plays a key role in protecting the nation's borders.

At official ports of entry, CBP officers are responsible for conducting immigrations, customs, and agricultural inspections on entering aliens.

Customs and Border Protection

The U.S. Customs and Border Protection (CBP) is the unified border agency within the Department of Homeland Security. CBP combined portions of the previous border law enforcement agencies under one administrative umbrella. This involved absorbing employees from the Immigration and Naturalization Service (INS), the Border Patrol, the Customs Service, and the Department of Agriculture. CBP's mission is to prevent terrorists and terrorist weapons from entering the country, provide security at U.S. borders and ports of entry, apprehend illegal immigrants, stem the flow of illegal drugs, and protect American agricultural and economic interests from harmful pests and diseases. As it performs its official missions, CBP maintains two overarching and sometimes conflicting goals: increasing security while facilitating legitimate trade and travel. CBP includes more than 58,000 employees to manage, control, and protect the Nation's borders, at and between official points of entry.

At official ports of entry, CBP officers are responsible for conducting immigrations, customs, and agricultural inspections on entering aliens. As a result of the "one face at the border" initiative, CBP inspectors are being cross-trained to perform all three types of inspections in order to streamline the border crossing process. This initiative unifies the prior inspections processes, providing entering aliens with one primary inspector who is trained to determine whether a more detailed secondary inspection is required.

Between official ports of entry, the U.S. Border Patrol (USBP)—a component of CBP—enforces U.S. immigration law and other federal laws along the border. As currently comprised, the USBP is a uniformed law enforcement arm of the Department of Homeland Security. Its primary mission is to detect and prevent the entry of terrorists, weapons of mass destruction, and unauthorized aliens into the country, and to interdict drug smugglers and other criminals. In the course of discharging its duties the USBP patrols over 8,000 miles of our international borders with Mexico and Canada and the coastal waters around Florida and Puerto Rico.

CBP inspectors enforce immigration law by examining and verifying the travel documents of incoming international travelers to ensure they have a legal right to enter the country. On the customs side, CBP inspectors ensure that all imports and exports comply with U.S. laws and regulations, collect and protect U.S. revenues, and guard against the smuggling of contraband. Additionally, CBP is responsible for conducting agricultural inspections at ports of entry in order to enforce a wide array of animal and plant protection laws. In order to carry out these varied functions, CBP inspectors have a broad range of powers to inspect all persons, vehicles, conveyances, merchandise, and baggage entering the United States from a foreign country.[6]

Between official ports of entry, the U.S. Border Patrol—a component of CBP—enforces U.S. immigration law and other federal laws along the border.

Transportation Security Administration

The Transportation Security Administration (TSA) was created as a direct result of the events of September 11 and is charged with protecting the United States' air, land, and rail transportation systems to ensure freedom of movement for people and commerce. The Aviation and Transportation Security Act (ATSA, P.L. 107-71, November 19, 2001) created the TSA and included provisions that established a federal baggage screener workforce, required checked baggage to be screened by explosive detection systems, and significantly expanded the Federal Air Marshal Service (FAMS). In 2002, TSA was transferred to the newly formed DHS from the Department of Transportation. Then, in 2003, the Federal Air Marshal program was taken out of TSA and transferred to ICE. As a result of the Second Stage Review (2SR) initiative, the Federal Air Marshalls (FAMS) program was transferred back to TSA in 2006 where it currently resides.[7]

TSA is most commonly known for its aviation security role, particularly the security screening of airline passengers and their baggage. However, the Aviation Transportation Security Act assigned the Assistant Secretary for TSA responsibility for security in all modes of transportation – aviation, maritime, mass transit, highway and motor carrier, freight rail, and pipeline. These modes form a transportation network that is central to the American economy. That network connects cities, towns, and farms, and moves millions of people and millions of tons of goods. The majority of transportation infrastructure in the United States is privately-owned. The remainder is owned and operated by state, local, or regional entities.

The size of the transportation sector in the United States makes it impossible for the Federal government to provide security for all modes. The exception is the commercial aviation sector. But, TSA does provide threat and other intelligence information to support security programs for each sector. In addition, TSA collaborates with industry and government operators and other stakeholders to develop strategies, policies, and programs to reduce security risks and vulnerabilities within each mode. Finally, it seeks to enhance capabilities to detect, deter, and prevent terrorist attacks and respond to and recover from attacks and security incidents, should they occur.

TSA recognizes the unique attributes of each transportation mode and is committed to ensuring passenger and cargo security and preserving public confidence in the security of the U.S. transportation system. TSA's specific responsibilities include:

- Ensuring a thorough and efficient screening of all aviation passengers and baggage;
- Promoting confidence by deploying Federal Air Marshals to detect, deter, and defeat hostile acts targeting air carriers;
- Managing security risks of the surface transportation systems by establishing clear lines of communication and collaborative working relationships with federal, local and private stakeholders, providing support and programmatic direction, conducting on-site inspections, and developing security programs; and
- Developing and implementing more efficient, reliable, integrated, and cost effective terrorist-related screening programs.[9]

The size of the transportation sector in the United States makes it impossible for the Federal government to provide security for all modes... But, TSA does provide threat and other intelligence information to support security programs for each sector.

Immigration and Customs Enforcement

The U.S. Immigration and Customs Enforcement (ICE) is the largest investigative agency in the Department of Homeland Security (DHS). With more than 20,000 employees in over 400 offices nationwide and around the world, ICE is a key component of the DHS layered defense approach to protecting the United States.[10] ICE merged the investigative functions of the former Immigration and Naturalization Service (INS) and the Customs Service, the INS detention and removal functions, most INS intelligence operations, and the Federal Protective Service (FPS). This makes ICE the principal investigative arm for DHS. ICE's mission is to detect and prevent terrorist and criminal acts by targeting the people, money, and materials that support terrorist and criminal networks.[11] As such they are an important component of our nation's border security network even though their main focus is on interior enforcement.

Unlike CBP, whose jurisdiction is confined to law enforcement activities along the border, ICE special agents investigate immigrations and customs violations in the interior of the United States. ICE's mandate includes uncovering national security threats such as weapons of mass destruction or potential terrorists, identifying criminal aliens for removal, probing immigration-related document and benefit fraud, investigating work-site immigration violations, exposing alien and contraband smuggling operations, interdicting narcotics shipments[12] and detaining illegal immigrants and ensuring their departure (or removal) from the United States.[13] ICE is also responsible for the collection, analysis and dissemination of strategic and tactical intelligence data pertaining to homeland security, infrastructure protection, and the illegal movement of people, money, and cargo within the United States.[14]

Formed in 2003 as part of the federal government's response to the 9/11 attacks, ICE's mission is to protect the security of the American people and homeland by vigilantly enforcing the nation's immigration and customs laws.

ICE combines innovative investigative techniques, new technological resources and a high level of professionalism to provide a wide range of resources to the public and to our federal, state and local law enforcement partners.[15]

U.S. Coast Guard

The U.S. Coast Guard (USCG) plays a pivotal role in securing the nation's borders and maritime transportation. The USCG was incorporated into DHS as a standalone agency by P.L. 107-296. The Coast Guard's overall mission is to protect the public, the environment, and U.S. economic interests in maritime regions—at the nation's ports and waterways, along the coast, and in international waters. The Coast Guard is thus the nation's principal maritime law enforcement authority and the lead federal agency for the maritime component of homeland security, including port security.

Unlike CBP, whose jurisdiction is confined to law enforcement activities along the border, ICE special agents investigate immigrations and customs violations in the interior of the United States.

Among other things, the Coast Guard is responsible for evaluating, boarding, and inspecting commercial ships as they approach U.S. waters; countering terrorist threats in U.S. ports; and for helping to protect U.S. Navy ships in U.S. ports. A high-ranking Coast Guard officer in each port area serves as the Captain of the Port and is the lead federal official responsible for the security and safety of the vessels and waterways in their geographic zone.

The Coast Guard is at a heightened state of alert protecting more than 361 ports and 95,000 miles of coastline. The Coast Guard's homeland security role includes protecting ports, the flow of commerce, and the marine transportation system from terrorism; maintaining maritime border security against illegal drugs, illegal aliens, firearms, and weapons of mass destruction; ensuring that the U.S. can rapidly deploy and resupply military assets by maintaining the Coast Guard at a high state of readiness as well as by keeping marine transportation open for the other military services; protecting against illegal fishing and indiscriminate destruction of living marine resources; preventing and responding to oil and hazardous material spills; and coordinating efforts and intelligence with federal, state, and local agencies.[16]

Security vs Trade

The overarching border security issue is how to balance two competing public policy goals: (1) the need to enhance border security with (2) an equally compelling requirement to facilitate legitimate trade and travel. This requires a sophisticated border management system that identifies and intercepts dangerous or unwanted (high-risk) people or goods, while facilitating access for legitimate (low-risk) travelers and commerce without excessive infringement on privacy or civil liberties. Another policy challenge is how to balance competing demands for resources, concentrating them on higher-risk areas while also providing security to lower-risk areas. A variety of legislative and oversight issues flow from this framework to address:

- Passenger Screening, Immigration Enforcement, and Improving Infrastructure at Ports of Entry. A number of issues have been widely debated in the years since the 9/11 attacks. One such issue is the most effective way to identify and intercept high-risk individuals. To accomplish this, Customs and Border Protection deploys resources to the ports of entry, including its officers, the US-VISIT entry-exit control system, and detection systems. While the US-VISIT system was identified as "an essential investment in our national security" by the 9/11 Commission report, the exit component has yet to be implemented and its entry functions have yet to be deployed during primary inspection at land POE. This means that DHS has no easy way to identify those individuals who have overstayed their visas and remain in the United States illegally. Other passenger screening issues include enforcement of Visa Waiver program requirements, the implementation of the Western Hemisphere Travel Initiative, and the continuing efforts to implement the integrated terrorist watch-list. Projected increases in the volume of people and goods flowing through the nation's ports of entry present added challenges to policy makers. Personnel, port design, and new technologies designed to inspect people and goods are particularly important issues due to the infrastructure and resource stresses that have arisen at POE.
- Securing the Physical Border and Improving Infrastructure Between Ports of Entry. Effective border security entails promoting policies that can effectively manage the flow of people and goods crossing the border not only at POE, but also between POE. The main oversight issue will continue to be what the appropriate mix of technology, infrastructure, and personnel should be to detect and interdict illegal entries along the international land border. The operation of the Secure Border Initiative (SBI), the latest DHS effort to gain operational control of the land borders, will continue to be of interest to Congress. Other issues concern the expansion of authorized and partly funded border fencing, including the acquisition of land for the fence; identification of where fencing should be constructed; and how best to balance environmental concerns with the prerogative to secure the border.
- Drug-Related Violence along the Southwest Border. There has been a recent increase in the level of drug-related violence within and between the drug trafficking organizations in Mexico—a country with which the United States shares a nearly 2,000-mile border. Some estimates have placed the number of drug trafficking-related deaths in Mexico since January 2007 at nearly 10,000. In 2008, over 60% of these murders took place in three Mexican states bordering the United States: Baja California, Sinaloa, and Chihuahua. This violence has generated concern among U.S. policy makers that the violence in Mexico might spill over into the United States. Currently, U.S. federal officials deny that the recent increase in drug trafficking-related violence in Mexico has resulted in a spillover into the

United States, but they acknowledge that the prospect is a serious concern. In response to the possibility of violence spillover, the U.S. government is supporting Mexico's crackdown campaign against drug cartels in Mexico through the Mérida Initiative. It is also enhancing border security programs and reducing the movement of contraband (drugs, money, and weapons) in both directions across the Southwest border. Congress held a number of hearings on this issue in the first session of the 111th Congress, and the issue will continue to generate legislative activity throughout the course of the second session as Congress grapples with various policy responses to this issue.

- Cargo and Container Security. The key question in the debate over cargo security is how an inspector can know what is inside a container. This involves: (1) breadth (what and how much should be inspected); (2) depth (intensity of the inspection); (3) jurisdiction (what entity is responsible for conducting the inspection); and (4) technology, such as cargo inspection technology, smart containers, biometric identification for transportation workers, and hazardous materials detection equipment. Debate has thus far focused primarily on containerized cargo, although the security of other forms of imported cargo has also been an issue. Other policy questions include whether or not each cargo container needs to be physically inspected, how to secure the areas through which the container passes, and how to secure the people who come in contact with containers.

- Managing International and Private Sector Partnerships. Since 9/11, the United States has developed several initiatives that require the assistance of other governments or the private sector. These programs seek to "push back the border" to give U.S. agencies multiple opportunities to identify and intercept high-risk cargo and people, and to engage other countries and entities in security efforts that extend beyond the jurisdiction of the U.S. government. U.S. efforts include the Container Security Initiative (CSI), which provides the opportunity to inspect U.S.-bound containers in overseas ports, and the Customs-Trade Partnership Against Terrorism (C-TPAT), which encourages private entities to secure their supply chains from origin to destination, and advance manifest and entry data rules that mandate the submission of cargo information in advance of lading for security screening. As other countries and non-governmental organizations develop cargo and supply chain security initiatives, issues will arise relating to the management of these new initiatives, such as reciprocity, standards, validations (conducted either by private third parties or other governments), funding assistance, and jurisdictional issues relating to inspections.[17]

Conclusion

The four main agencies within the DHS charged with securing our nation's borders are the CBP, TSA, ICE, and the U.S. Coast Guard. It should be noted, however, that although the Homeland Security Act of 2002 consolidated all the agencies with primary border security roles in DHS, many other federal agencies are involved in the difficult task of securing our nation's borders.

The current border protection framework can be understood as consisting of a mission, three goals, and five strategic elements. The mission is securing and managing the U.S. border. The current border protection framework can be summarized as obtaining effective control of the borders, safeguarding lawful trade and travel, and identifying and disrupting transnational criminal organizations. Finally, the five strategic elements to achieve these goals consist of Department of Homeland Security leadership, deployment of layered security, maximizing domain awareness, promotion of a shared agency culture, and expansion of the border through international and domestic partnerships.[18]

To achieve effective control of the physical borders and approaches to the United States, it is imperative that efforts address prevention of illegal entry of inadmissible persons and contraband and the illegal exit of dangerous goods, proceeds of crime, and malicious actors, but also a securely expedited cross-border flow of lawful immigration, travel, and commerce at our nation's borders. Indeed, these "twin goals" mutually reinforce each other. Increased use of technology, information, and training to support operations that identify and expedite lawful travel and commerce across our borders, allows officials at the border to better focus on the known threats that require more scrutiny. We must and can achieve both greater security and greater interchange with the world.[19]

The current border protection framework can be summarized as obtaining effective control of the borders, safeguarding lawful trade and travel, and identifying and disrupting transnational criminal organizations.

Questions

1. How do the three subcomponents of Border and Transportation Security work together to increase homeland security and effective commerce?
2. How does the U.S. Coast Guard address border security issues?
3. How do efforts at and between ports of entry contribute to the overall effectiveness of the CBP?
4. What are the major goals of the TSA?
5. How does ICE's mandate relate to law enforcement and intelligence functions?
6. What are the goals that address border security and the facilitation of legitimate trade?

Chapter 15

Domestic Counterterrorism

Objectives

- Describe how the CIA and FBI missed capturing two of the 9/11 hijackers.
- Explain how the USA PATRIOT Act might have helped the FBI stop 9/11.
- Assess DHS' role in domestic counterterrorism.

The attacks of September 11 and the catastrophic loss of life and property that resulted have redefined the mission of federal, state, and local law enforcement authorities. While law enforcement agencies will continue to investigate and prosecute criminal activity, they should now assign priority to preventing and interdicting terrorist activity within the United States. The Nation's state and local law enforcement officers will be critical in this effort. Our Nation will use all legal means—both traditional and nontraditional—to identify, halt, and, where appropriate, prosecute terrorists in the United States.

— Critical Mission Area #3, National Strategy for Homeland Security, July 2002

Blinking Red

Khalid Sheikh Mohammed (KSM) started to think about attacking the United States shortly after the 1993 World Trade Center bombing. KSM claims that the earlier bombing of the World Trade Center taught him that bombs and explosives could be problematic, and that he needed to graduate to a more novel form of attack. He maintains that he began thinking about using aircraft as weapons and speculated about striking the World Trade Center and CIA headquarters as early as 1995. Indeed, KSM describes a grandiose original plan: a total of ten aircraft to be hijacked, nine of which would crash into targets on both coasts—they included those eventually hit on September 11 plus CIA and FBI headquarters, nuclear power plants, and the tallest buildings in California and the state of Washington. KSM himself was to land the tenth plane at a U.S. airport and, after killing all adult male passengers on board and alerting the media, deliver a speech excoriating U.S. support for Israel, the Philippines, and repressive governments in the Arab world.

KSM concedes that this proposal received a lukewarm response from al Qaeda leaders skeptical of its scale and complexity. Bin Ladin summoned KSM to Kandahar in March or April 1999 to tell him that al Qaeda would support his proposal. The plot was now referred to within al Qaeda as the "planes operation."

Bin Ladin reportedly discussed the planes operation with KSM in a series of meetings in the spring of 1999 at the al Matar complex near Kandahar. KSM's original concept of using one of the hijacked planes to make a media statement was scrapped, but Bin Ladin considered the basic idea feasible. Bin Ladin and KSM developed an initial list of targets. These included the White House, the U.S. Capitol, the Pentagon, and the World Trade Center. According to KSM, Bin Ladin wanted to destroy the White House and the Pentagon, KSM wanted to strike the World Trade Center, and all of them wanted to hit the Capitol. Bin Ladin also soon selected four individuals to serve as suicide operatives: Khalid al Mihdhar, Nawaf al Hazmi, Khallad, and Abu Bara al Yemeni.

Hazmi and Mihdhar were Saudi nationals, born in Mecca. Like the others in this initial group of selectees, they were already experienced mujahideen. They had traveled together to fight in Bosnia in a group that journeyed to the Balkans in 1995. By the time Hazmi and Mihdhar were assigned to the planes operation in early 1999, they had visited Afghanistan on several occasions.

Bin Laden boasted that Mihdhar and Hazmi were so eager to participate in an operation against the United States that they had already obtained U.S. visas

Hazmi and Mihdhar came to the United States to learn English, take flying lessons, and become pilots as quickly as possible. After arriving in California, Hazmi and Mihdhar sought out and found a group of young and ideologically like-minded Muslims with roots in Yemen and Saudi Arabia. The al Qaeda operatives lived openly in San Diego under their true names, listing Hazmi in the telephone directory. They managed to avoid attracting much attention. They turned out, however, to have no aptitude for English. Even with help and tutoring from friends, Hazmi and Mihdhar's efforts to learn proved futile. This lack of language skills in turn became an insurmountable barrier to learning how to fly. Instructors who worked with Hazmi and Mihdhar remember them as poor students who focused on learning to control the aircraft in flight but took no interest in takeoffs or landings. By the end of May 2000, Hazmi and Mihdhar had given up on learning how to fly.

Mihdhar abandoned Hazmi in San Diego in June 2000 and returned to his family in Yemen. Mihdhar reportedly stayed in Yemen for about a month before being persuaded to return to Afghanistan. In February 2001, Khalid al Mihdhar may have taken a flight from Syria to Iran, and then traveled further within Iran to a point near the Afghan border . Mihdhar met with KSM,who was annoyed at his decision to go absent. But Kim's desire to drop him from the operation yielded to Bin Ladin's insistence to keep him. On July 4, 2001, Mihdhar left Saudi Arabia to return to the United States, arriving at John F. Kennedy International Airport in New York. He then rejoined Nawaf al Hazmi and four other hijackers in a rented one-room apartment in Paterson New Jersey. With two months remaining, all 19 hijackers were in the United States and ready to take the final steps toward carrying out the attacks.

Mihdhar had been a weak link in al Qaeda's operational planning.

Mihdhar had been a weak link in al Qaeda's operational planning. He had left the United States in June 2000, a mistake KSM realized could endanger the entire plan—for to continue with the operation, Mihdhar would have to travel to the United States again. And unlike other operatives, Mihdhar was not "clean": he had jihadist connections. It was just such connections that had brought him to the attention of U.S. officials.

In late 1999, the National Security Agency (NSA) analyzed communications associated with a suspected terrorist facility in the Middle East, indicating that several members of "an operational cadre" were planning to travel to Kuala Lumpur in early January 2000. Initially, only the first names of three were known—"Nawaf," "Salem," and "Khalid." The CIA soon identified " Khalid" as Khalid al Mihdhar. He was located leaving Yemen and tracked until he arrived in Kuala Lumpur on January 5, 2000. Other Arabs, unidentified at the time, were watched as they gathered with him in the Malaysian capital. On January 8, the surveillance teams reported that three of the Arabs had suddenly left Kuala Lumpur on a short flight to Bangkok. In Bangkok, CIA officers received the information too late to track the three men as they came in, and the travelers disappeared into the streets.

In early March 2000, Bangkok reported that Nawaf al Hazmi, now identified for the first time with his full name, had departed on January 15 on a United Airlines flight to Los Angeles. As for Khalid al Mihdhar, there was no report of his departure even though he had accompanied Hazmi on the United flight to Los Angeles. No one outside of the CIA Counterterrorist Center was told any of this. The CIA did not try to register Mihdhar or Hazmi with the State Department's TIPOFF watchlist—either in January, when word arrived of Mihdhar's visa, or in March, when word came that Hazmi, too, had had a U.S. visa and a ticket to Los Angeles. None of this information—about Mihdhar's U.S. visa or Hazmi's travel to the United States—went to the FBI, and nothing more was done to track any of the three until January 2001, when the investigation of another bombing, that of the USS Cole, reignited interest in Khallad.

By mid-May 2001, as the threat reports were surging, a CIA official detailed to the International Terrorism Operations Section at the FBI wondered where the attacks might occur. Following good instinct, but not as part of any formal assignment, he asked an FBI analyst detailed to the CIA's Bin Ladin unit, to review all the Kuala Lumpur materials one more time. On July 24, she found the cable reporting that Mihdhar had a visa to the United States. A week later, she found the cable reporting that Mihdhar's visa application—what was later discovered to be his first application—listed New York as his destination. On August 21, she located the March 2000 cable that "noted with interest" that Hazmi had flown to Los Angeles in January 2000. She immediately grasped the significance of this information. On August 22, the Immigration and Naturalization Service (INS) confirmed that Mihdhar had entered the United States on January 15, 2000, and again on July 4, 2001. The FBI agent asked the CIA Bin Ladin unit to draft a cable requesting that Mihdhar and Hazmi be put on the TIPOFF watchlist. Both Hazmi and Mihdhar were added to this watchlist on August 24.

It was decided that if Mihdhar was in the United States, he should be found.

It was decided that if Mihdhar was in the United States, he should be found. Another FBI agent, one assigned to the Cole investigation, took responsibility for the search effort inside the United States. As the information indicated that Mihdhar had last arrived in New York, she began drafting what is known as a lead for the FBI's New York Field Office. A lead relays information from one part of the FBI to another and requests that a particular action be taken. She called an agent in New York to give him a "headsup" on the matter, but her draft lead was not sent until August 28. Her email told the New York agent that she wanted him to get started as soon as possible, but labeled the lead as "Routine"—a designation that informs the receiving office that it has 30 days to respond.

The agent who received the lead forwarded it to his squad supervisor. That same day, the supervisor forwarded the lead to an intelligence agent to open an intelligence case—an agent who thus was behind "the wall" keeping FBI intelligence information from being shared with criminal prosecutors. He also sent it to the Cole case agents and an agent who had spent significant time in Malaysia searching for another Khalid: Khalid Sheikh Mohammad. Sheikh Mohammad.

One of the Cole case agents read the lead with interest, and asked for more information. He was told that because he was a "criminal" FBI agent, not an "intelligence" FBI agent, the wall kept him from participating in any search for Mihdhar. He later received an email explaining that according to the FBI National Security Law Unit (NSLU), the case could be opened only as an intelligence matter, and that if Mihdhar was found, only designated intelligence agents could conduct or even be present at any interview.

As a result, the search was assigned to another FBI agent in New York; it was his very first counterterrorism lead. Because the lead was "routine," he was given 30 days to open an intelligence case and make some unspecified efforts to locate Mihdhar. He started the process a few days later. He checked local New York databases for Mihdhar's U.S. entry form. Finally, because Mihdhar had initially arrived in Los Angeles, on September 11 the agent sent a lead to Los Angeles.

According to the 9/11 Commission Report, everyone involved was confused about the rules governing the sharing and use of information gathered in intelligence channels. Because Mihdhar was being sought for his possible connection to or knowledge of the Cole bombing, he could be investigated or tracked under the existing Cole criminal case. No new criminal case was needed for the criminal agent to begin searching for Mihdhar. And as NSA had approved the passage of its information to the criminal agent, he could have conducted a search using all available information. As a result of this confusion, the criminal agents who were knowledgeable about al Qaeda and experienced with criminal investigative techniques, including finding suspects and possible criminal charges, were thus excluded from the search.

The 9/11 Commission further contends that if, in January 2001, the CIA had resumed its search for Mihdhar, placed him on the State Department's TIPOFF watchlist, or provided the FBI with the information, he might have been found—either before or at the time he applied for a new visa in June 2001, or when he returned to the United States on July 4.

The 9/11 Commission believes that if more resources had been applied and a significantly different approach taken, Mihdhar and Hazmi might have been found. They had used their true names in the United States. Still, the investigators would have needed luck as well as skill to find them prior to September 11 even if such searches had begun as early as August 23, when the lead was first drafted.

Many FBI witnesses have suggested that even if Mihdhar had been found, there was nothing the agents could have done except follow him onto the planes. The 9/11 Commission believes this is incorrect. Both Hazmi and Mihdhar could have been held for immigration violations or as material witnesses in the Cole bombing case. Investigation or interrogation of them, and investigation of their travel and financial activities, could have yielded evidence of connections to other participants in the 9/11 plot. The simple fact of their detention could have derailed the plan.[1]

The 9/11 Commission believes both Hazmi and Mihdhar could have been held for immigration violations or as material witnesses in the Cole bombing case. Investigation or interrogation of them, and investigation of their travel and financial activities, could have yielded evidence of connections to other participants in the 9/11 plot. The simple fact of their detention could have derailed the plan.

2002 Homeland Security Objectives

We will redefine our law enforcement mission to focus on the prevention of all terrorist acts within the United States, whether international or domestic in origin. We will use all legal means— both traditional and non-traditional—to identify, halt, and, where appropriate, prosecute terrorists in the United States. We will prosecute or bring immigration or other civil charges against such individuals where appropriate and will utilize the full range of our legal authorities. We will pursue not only the individuals directly engaged in terrorist activity, but also their sources of support: the people and organizations that knowingly fund the terrorists and those that provide them with logistical assistance.

To achieve these aims, we will strengthen our federal law enforcement community. In addition, we will augment the scope and quality of information available to all law enforcement. In that regard, we will build and continually update a fully integrated, fully accessible terrorist watch list. When we have identified any suspected terrorist activities, we will then use all the tools in our Nation's legal arsenal, including investigative, criminal, civil, immigration, and regulatory powers to stop those who wish to do us harm.

The Intelligence Community, including the FBI was criticized for failing to warn of the attacks of September 11, 2001.

Our Nation's highest law enforcement objective must be the prevention of terrorist acts—a significant shift from pre-September 11 objectives. In order to focus the mission of the federal law enforcement community on prevention, the federal government, working with Congress, needs to restructure the FBI and other federal law enforcement agencies, reallocating certain resources and energies to the new prevention efforts.[2]

FBI Reform

The Intelligence Community, including the FBI was criticized for failing to warn of the attacks of September 11, 2001. In a sweeping indictment of the FBI's intelligence activities relating to counterterrorism and September 11, the 9/11 Commission, singled out the FBI in a significant manner for failing to focus on the domestic terrorist threat; collect useful intelligence; analyze strategic intelligence; and to share intelligence internally and with other members of the Intelligence Community. The Joint Inquiry concluded that the FBI was seriously deficient in identifying, reporting on, and defending against the foreign terrorist threat to the United States.

The FBI responded by attempting to transform itself into an agency that can prevent terrorist acts, rather than react to them as crimes. The major component of this effort is restructuring and upgrading of its various intelligence support units into a formal and integrated intelligence program, which includes the adoption of new operational practices, and the improvement of its information technology. FBI Director Robert S. Mueller, III, introduced reforms to curb the autonomy of the organization's 56 field offices by consolidating and centralizing FBI Headquarters control over all counterterrorism and counterintelligence cases. He also established (1) an Executive Assistant Director for Intelligence (EAD-I); (2) an Office of Intelligence to exercise control over the FBI's historically fragmented intelligence elements; and (3) field intelligence groups to collect, analyze, and disseminate intelligence.

Reactions to these FBI reforms are mixed. Critics contend the reforms are too limited and have implementation problems. More fundamentally, they argue that the gulf between law enforcement and intelligence cultures is so wide, that the FBI's reforms, as proposed, are unlikely to succeed. They believe the FBI will remain essentially a reactive law enforcement agency, significantly constrained in its ability to collect and exploit effectively intelligence in preventing terrorist acts.

Supporters counter that the FBI can successfully address its deficiencies, particularly its intelligence shortcomings, and that the Director's intelligence reforms are appropriate for what needs to be done. The 9/11 Commission concluded that the FBI has made significant progress in improving its intelligence capabilities, and generally endorsed Director Mueller's reforms, rejecting the creation of a new domestic intelligence agency.[3]

USA PATRIOT Act

The USA PATRIOT Act, signed into law October 26, 2001, and reauthorized March 9, 2006. The Act gives federal officials greater authority to track and intercept communications, both for law enforcement and foreign intelligence gathering purposes. It vests the Secretary of the Treasury with regulatory powers to combat corruption of U.S. financial institutions for foreign money laundering purposes. It seeks to further close our borders to foreign terrorists and to detain and remove those within our borders. It creates new crimes, new penalties, and new procedural efficiencies for use against domestic and international terrorists. Although it is not without safeguards, critics contend some of its provisions go too far. Although it grants many of the enhancements sought by the Department of Justice, others are concerned that it does not go far enough.

The USA PATRIOT Act gives federal officials greater authority to track and intercept communications, both for law enforcement and foreign intelligence gathering purposes. It vests the Secretary of the Treasury with regulatory powers to combat corruption of U.S. financial institutions for foreign money laundering purposes. It seeks to further close our borders to foreign terrorists and to detain and remove those within our borders.

Criminal Investigations: Tracking and Gathering Communications

Federal communications privacy law features a three tiered system, erected for the dual purpose of protecting the confidentiality of private telephone, face-to-face, and computer communications while enabling authorities to identify and intercept criminal communications. Title III of the Omnibus Crime Control and Safe Streets Act of 1968 supplies the first level. It prohibits electronic eavesdropping on telephone conversations, face-to-face conversations, or computer and other forms of electronic communications in most instances. It does, however, give authorities a narrowly defined process for electronic surveillance to be used as a last resort in serious criminal cases. When approved by senior Justice Department officials, law enforcement officers may seek a court order authorizing them to secretly capture conversations concerning any of a statutory list of offenses (predicate offenses). Title III court orders come replete with instructions describing the permissible duration and scope of the surveillance as well as the conversations which may be seized and the efforts to be taken to minimize the seizure of innocent conversations. The court notifies the parties to any conversations seized under the order after the order expires.

Below Title III, the next tier of privacy protection covers telephone records, e-mail held in third party storage, and the like, 18 U.S.C. 2701-2709 (Chapter 121). Here, the law permits law enforcement access, ordinarily pursuant to a warrant or court order or under a subpoena in some cases, but in connection with any criminal investigation and without the extraordinary levels of approval or constraint that mark a Title III interception.

Least demanding and perhaps least intrusive of all is the procedure that governs court orders approving the government's use of trap and trace devices and pen registers, a kind of secret "caller id.", which identify the source and destination of calls made to and from a particular telephone, 18 U.S.C. 3121-3127 (Chapter 206). The orders are available based on the government's certification, rather than a finding of a court, that use of the device is likely to produce information relevant to the investigation of a crime, any crime. The devices record no more than identity of the participants in a telephone conversation, but neither the orders nor the results they produce need ever be revealed to the participants.

The PATRIOT Act modifies the procedures at each of the three levels. It:

- permits pen register and trap and trace orders for electronic communications (e.g., e-mail);
- authorizes nationwide execution of court orders for pen registers, trap and trace devices, and access to stored e-mail or communication records;
- treats stored voice mail like stored e-mail (rather than like telephone conversations);
- permits authorities to intercept communications to and from a trespasser within a computer system (with the permission of the system's owner);
- adds terrorist and computer crimes to Title III's predicate offense list;
- reinforces protection for those who help execute Title III, ch. 121, and ch. 206 orders;
- encourages cooperation between law enforcement and foreign intelligence investigators;
- establishes a claim against the U.S. for certain communications privacy violations by government personnel; and
- terminates the authority found in many of these provisions and several of the foreign intelligence amendments with a sunset provision (Dec. 31, 2005).

Foreign Intelligence Investigations

The PATRIOT Act eases some of the restrictions on foreign intelligence gathering within the United States, and affords the U.S. intelligence community greater access to information unearthed during a criminal investigation, but it also establishes and expands safeguards against official abuse. More specifically, it:

- permits "roving" surveillance (court orders omitting the identification of the particular instrument, facilities, or place where the surveillance is to occur when the court finds the target is likely to thwart identification with particularity);
- increases the number of judges on the Foreign Intelligence Surveillance Act (FISA) court from 7 to 11;
- allows application for a FISA surveillance or search order when gathering foreign intelligence is a significant reason for the application rather than the reason;
- authorizes pen register and trap & trace device orders for e-mail as well as telephone conversations;
- sanctions court ordered access to any tangible item rather than only business records held by lodging, car rental, and locker rental businesses;
- carries a sunset provision;
- establishes a claim against the U.S. for certain communications privacy violations by government personnel; and
- expands the prohibition against FISA orders based solely on an American's exercise of his or her First Amendment rights.

In federal law, money laundering is the flow of cash or other valuables derived from, or intended to facilitate, the commission of a criminal offense.

Money Laundering

In federal law, money laundering is the flow of cash or other valuables derived from, or intended to facilitate, the commission of a criminal offense. It is the movement of the fruits and instruments of crime. Federal authorities attack money laundering through regulations, criminal sanctions, and forfeiture. The Act bolsters federal efforts in each area.

Regulation: The PATRIOT Act expands the authority of the Secretary of the Treasury to regulate the activities of U.S. financial institutions, particularly their relations with foreign individuals and entities. He is to promulgate regulations:

- under which securities brokers and dealers as well as commodity merchants, advisors and pool operators must file suspicious activity reports (SARs);
- requiring businesses, which were only to report cash transactions involving more than $10,000 to the IRS, to file SARs as well;
- imposing additional "special measures" and "due diligence" requirements to combat foreign money laundering;

- prohibiting U.S. financial institutions from maintaining correspondent accounts for foreign shell banks;
- preventing financial institutions from allowing their customers to conceal their financial activities by taking advantage of the institutions' concentration account practices;
- establishing minimum new customer identification standards and recordkeeping and recommending an effective means to verify the identity of foreign customers;
- encouraging financial institutions and law enforcement agencies to share information concerning suspected money laundering and terrorist activities; and
- requiring financial institutions to maintain anti-money laundering programs which must include at least a compliance officer; an employee training program; the development of internal policies, procedures and controls; and an independent audit feature.

Crimes

The PATRIOT Act contains a number of new money laundering crimes, as well as amendments and increased penalties for earlier crimes. It:

- outlaws laundering (in the U.S.) any of the proceeds from foreign crimes of violence or political corruption;
- prohibits laundering the proceeds from cybercrime or supporting a terrorist organization;
- increases the penalties for counterfeiting;
- seeks to overcome a Supreme Court decision finding that the confiscation of over $300,000 (for attempt to leave the country without reporting it to customs) constituted an unconstitutionally excessive fine;
- provides explicit authority to prosecute overseas fraud involving American credit cards; and
- endeavors to permit prosecution of money laundering in the place where the predicate offense occurs.

Forfeiture

The Act creates two types of forfeitures and modifies several confiscation related procedures. It allows confiscation of all of the property of any individual or entity that participates in or plans an act of domestic or international terrorism; it also permits confiscation of any property derived from or used to facilitate domestic or international terrorism. The Constitution's due process, double jeopardy, and ex post facto clauses may limit the anticipated breadth of these provisions. Procedurally, the Act:

- establishes a mechanism to acquire long arm jurisdiction, for purposes of forfeiture proceedings, over individuals and entities;
- allows confiscation of property located in this country for a wider range of crimes committed in violation of foreign law;
- permits U.S. enforcement of foreign forfeiture orders;
- calls for the seizure of correspondent accounts held in U.S. financial institutions for foreign banks who are in turn holding forfeitable assets overseas; and
- denies corporate entities the right to contest a confiscation if their principal shareholder is a fugitive.

Alien Terrorists and Victims

The Act contains a number of provisions designed to prevent alien terrorists from entering the United States, particularly from Canada; to enable authorities to detain and deport alien terrorists and those who support them; and to provide humanitarian immigration relief for foreign victims of the attacks on September 11.

Other Crimes, Penalties, & Procedures

The Act creates new federal crimes for terrorist attacks on mass transportation facilities, for biological weapons offenses, for harboring terrorists, for affording terrorists material support, for misconduct associated with money laundering already mentioned, for conducting the affairs of an enterprise which affects interstate or foreign commerce through the patterned commission of terrorist offenses, and for fraudulent charitable solicitation. Although strictly speaking these are new federal crimes, they generally supplement existing law by filling gaps and increasing penalties.

The Act increases the penalties for acts of terrorism and for crimes which terrorists might commit. More specifically it establishes an alternative maximum penalty for acts of terrorism, raises the penalties for conspiracy to commit certain terrorist offenses, envisions sentencing some terrorists to life-long parole, and increases the penalties for counterfeiting, cybercrime, and charity fraud.

Other Procedural Adjustments: In other procedural adjustments designed to facilitate criminal investigations, the Act:

- increases the rewards for information in terrorism cases;
- expands the Posse Comitatus Act exceptions;
- authorizes "sneak and peek" search warrants;
- permits nationwide and perhaps worldwide execution of warrants in terrorism cases;
- eases government access to confidential information;
- allows the Attorney General to collect DNA samples from prisoners convicted of any federal crime of violence or terrorism;
- lengthens the statute of limitations applicable to crimes of terrorism;
- clarifies the application of federal criminal law on American installations and in residences of U.S. government personnel overseas; and
- adjusts federal victims' compensation and assistance programs.[4]

Conclusion

The FBI has made or is in the process of making substantial organizational, business process, and resource allocation changes to enhance its ability to deter, detect, neutralize and prevent acts of terrorism or espionage directed against the United States. Some experts believe that the remedial measures currently being taken by the FBI, to include a centralization of national security-related cases, enhanced intelligence training for agents and analysts, increased recruitment of intelligence analysts, and the development of a formal and integrated intelligence cycle are all appropriate and achievable. Other experts are more critical of the current intelligence reforms believing that the culture of the FBI, including its law enforcement-oriented approach to intelligence, may prove to be an insurmountable obstacle to necessary intelligence reforms. Some argue that the pace and scope of reform may be too slow and not radical enough. One of the central points of distinction between supporters and critics of the current FBI intelligence reforms is the extent to which they believe that the two disciplines of law enforcement and intelligence are synergistic, that is that the commonalities among them would benefit from continued integration. In general, those believing that law enforcement and intelligence should be integrated argue for the status quo. However, other experts believe that given the conceptual and operational differences between law enforcement and intelligence, the national interest would be best served by having them located in separate organizations with systematic and formal mechanisms in place to share information and protect civil liberties.[5]

Questions

1. How could the CIA and FBI have better collaborated to possibly prevent 9/11?
2. How does the USA PATRIOT Act attempt to fix the FBI's mistakes from 9/11?
3. What is DHS' role in domestic counterterrorism?

Chapter 16

Critical Infrastructure Protection

Objectives

- Describe what is meant by "critical infrastructure".
- Know the national strategy for protecting critical infrastructure.
- Understand the role of DHS in protecting critical infrastructure.
- Describe the mission of the National Cyber Security Division.

Protecting Critical Infrastructure and Key Assets. Our society and modern way of life are dependent on networks of infrastructure—both physical networks such as our energy and transportation systems and virtual networks such as the Internet. If terrorists attack one or more pieces of our critical infrastructure, they may disrupt entire systems and cause significant damage to the Nation. We must therefore improve protection of the individual pieces and interconnecting systems that make up our critical infrastructure. Protecting America's critical infrastructure and key assets will not only make us more secure from terrorist attack, but will also reduce our vulnerability to natural disasters, organized crime, and computer hackers.

— Critical Mission Area #4, National Strategy for Homeland Security, July 2002

Introduction

The Homeland Security Act of 2002 created DHS and gave the department wide-ranging responsibilities for, among other things, leading and coordinating the overall national critical infrastructure protection effort. The act required DHS to (1) develop a comprehensive national plan for securing the nation's critical infrastructures and key resources (CIKR) and (2) recommend measures to protect CIKR in coordination with other agencies of the federal government and in cooperation with state and local government agencies and authorities, the private sector, and other entities. Homeland Security Presidential Directive 7 (HSPD-7) further defined critical infrastructure protection responsibilities for DHS and those federal agencies—known as sector-specific agencies (SSA)—responsible for particular industry sectors, such as transportation, energy, and communications.[1]

Definitions

The USA PATRIOT Act defines **critical infrastructure** as those "systems and assets, whether physical or virtual, so vital to the United States that the incapacity or destruction of such systems and assets would have a debilitating impact on security, national economic security, national public health or safety, or any combination of those matters."[2]

As defined in the Homeland Security Act, **key resources** are publicly or privately controlled resources essential to the minimal operations of the economy and government.[3]

Background

HSPD-7 directed DHS to establish uniform policies, approaches, guidelines, and methodologies for integrating federal infrastructure protection and risk management activities within and across 17 sectors. The directive also gave DHS the authority to establish additional sectors and in 2008, DHS created an 18th sector for critical manufacturing.

In accordance with the Homeland Security Act and in response to HSPD-7, DHS issued, in June 2006, the first National Infrastructure Protection Plan (NIPP), which provides the overarching approach for integrating the nation's CIKR protection initiatives in a single effort. DHS issued a revised NIPP in January 2009.

The NIPP provides the framework for developing, implementing, and maintaining a coordinated national effort to protect CIKR in the 18 sectors. Each of the CIKR sectors is represented in the federal planning process by a Sector-Specific Agency; a Government Coordinating Council to represent each sector's interests among government agencies; and a Sector Coordinating Council that includes private sector representatives of the sector.

Each sector is responsible for developing Sector-Specific Plans (SSPs) and Sector Annual Reports (SARs). In 2007, each SSA then operating published an SSP that mirrored and applied the NIPP framework. SSPs are to be updated, like the NIPP, every 3 years. In addition, beginning in 2006 each sector then operating was to produce a SAR that is expected to focus on sector goals, priorities, and SSP implementation.[4]

National Infrastructure Protection Plan

The NIPP outlines the roles and responsibilities of DHS and other security partners—including other federal agencies, state, territorial, local, and tribal governments, and private companies. Within the NIPP framework, DHS is responsible for leading and coordinating the overall national effort to enhance protection via 18 CIKR sectors. The NIPP is prepared by the NIPP Program Management Office (PMO) within the Infrastructure Protection office of the National Preparedness and Protection Directorate of DHS. The NIPP PMO has the responsibility for coordinating and ensuring development, implementation, and maintenance of the NIPP and the associated sector-specific plans.[5]

Roles & Responsibilities

Department of Homeland Security: Coordinates the Nation's overall CIKR protection efforts and oversees NIPP development, implementation, and integration with national preparedness initiatives.

Sector-Specific Agencies: Implement the NIPP framework and guidance as tailored to the specific characteristics and risk landscapes of each of the CIKR sectors.

Other Federal Departments, Agencies, and Offices: Implement specific CIKR protection roles designated in HSPD-7 or other relevant statutes, executive orders, and policy directives.

State, Local, Tribal, and Territorial Governments: Develop and implement a CIKR protection program, in accordance with the NIPP risk management framework, as a component of their overarching homeland security programs.

Regional Partners: Use partnerships that cross jurisdiction-al and sector boundaries to address CIKR protection within a defined geographical area.

Boards, Commissions, Authorities, Councils, and Other Entities: Perform regulatory, advisory, policy, or business oversight functions related to various aspects of CIKR operations and protection within and across sectors and jurisdictions.

Private Sector Owners and Operators: Undertake CIKR protection, restoration, coordination, and cooperation ac-tivities, and provide advice, recommendations, and subject matter expertise to all levels of government.

Homeland Security Advisory Councils: Provide advice, recommendations, and expertise to the government re-garding protection policy and activities.

Academia and Research Centers: Provide CIKR protection subject matter expertise, independent analysis, research and development (R&D), and educational programs.[6]

Sector-Specific Agencies

HSPD-7 and the NIPP assign responsibility for CIKR sectors to Sector-Specific Agencies. As an SSA, DHS has direct responsibility for leading, integrating, and coordinating efforts of sector partners to protect 11 CIKR sectors. The remaining sectors are coordinated by eight other federal agencies.[7]

Sector-Specific Agency	Responsible CIKR Sector
Department of Agriculture & Dept. of Health & Human Services	1. Agriculture & Food
Department of Defense	2. Defense Industrial Base
Department of Energy	3. Energy
Department of Health & Human Services	4. Healthcare & Public Health
Department of the Interior	5. National Monuments & Icons
Department of the Treasury	6. Banking & Finance
Environmental Protection Agency	7. Water
Department of Homeland Security	
Office of Infrastructure Protection	8. Commercial Facilities
	9. Critical Manufacturing
	10. Emergency Services
	11. Nuclear Reactors, Materials, & Waste
	12. Dams
	13. Chemical Sector
Office of Cybersecurity & Comm.	14. Information Technology
	15. Communications
Transportation Security Administration	16. Postal & Shipping
Transportation Security Administration & United States Coast Guard	17. Transportation Systems
Federal Protective Service	18. Government Facilities

Table 16.1: Sector-Specific Agencies & CIKR Sectors.

Sector-Specific Plans

The NIPP depends on supporting Sector Specific Plans (SSPs) for full implementation of this framework within and across CIKR sectors. Sector-Specific Plans are developed by the Sector-Specific Agencies designated in HSPD-7 in close collaboration with sector partners, including sector and government coordinating councils.

These SSPs contain the plan to identify and address the risks to CIKR specific to each sector and are reviewed by DHS for adherence to DHS guidance which follows the format of the NIPP.[8]

CIKR Protection Strategy

The cornerstone of the NIPP is its risk analysis and management framework that establishes the processes for combining consequence, vulnerability, and threat information to produce assessments of national or sector risk. The risk management framework is structured to promote continuous improvement to enhance CIKR protection by focusing activities on efforts to:

The risk management framework is structured to promote continuous improvement to enhance CIKR protection.

- set goals and objectives;
- identify assets, systems, and networks;
- assess risk based on consequences, vulnerabilities, and threats;
- establish priorities based on risk assessments and, increasingly, on return-on-investment for mitigating risk;
- implement protective programs and resiliency strategies; and measure effectiveness.

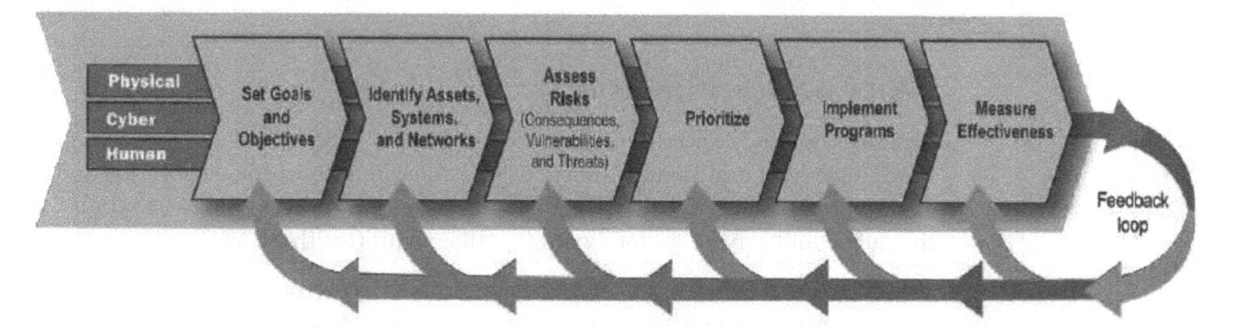

Figure 16.1: National Infrastructure Protection Plan Risk Management Framework.

The results of these processes drive CIKR risk-reduction and management activities. The NIPP risk management framework is tailored to and applied on an asset, system, network, or mission essential function basis, depending on the fundamental characteristics of the individual CIKR sectors. DHS, the Sector-Specific Agencies, and other CIKR partners share responsibilities for implementing the risk management framework.[9]

Assessing Risk

The NIPP framework calls for CIKR partners to assess risk from any scenario as a function of consequence, vulnerability, and threat. It is important to think of risk as influenced by the nature and magnitude of a threat, the vulnerabilities to that threat, and the consequences that could result:

$$R = f(C, V, T)$$

Consequence: The effect of an event, incident, or occurrence; reflects the level, duration, and nature of the loss resulting from the incident. For the purposes of the NIPP, consequences are divided into four main categories: public health and safety (i.e., loss of life and illness); economic (direct and indirect); psychological; and governance/mission impacts.

Vulnerability: Physical feature or operational attribute that renders an entity open to exploitation or susceptible to a given hazard. In calculating the risk of an intentional haz-ard, a common measure of vulnerability is the likelihood that an attack is successful, given that it is attempted.

The NIPP framework calls for CIKR partners to assess risk from any scenario as a function of consequence, vulnerability, and threat.

Threat: Natural or manmade occurrence, individual, entity, or action that has or indicates the potential to harm life, information, operations, the environment, and/or prop-erty. For the purpose of calculating risk, the threat of an intentional hazard is generally estimated as the likelihood of an attack being attempted by an adversary; for other hazards, threat is generally estimated as the likelihood that a hazard will manifest itself. In the case of terrorist attacks, the threat likelihood is estimated based on the intent and capability of the adversary.[10]

CIKR Protection Partnership

Because the private sector owns approximately 85 percent of the nation's CIKR—banking and financial institutions, telecommunications networks, and energy production and transmission facilities, among others—it is vital that the public and private sectors work together to protect these assets.[11]

The distributed character of our national protective architecture, and the uncertain nature of the terrorist threat and other manmade or natural disasters make the effective implementation of protection and resiliency efforts a great challenge. To be effective, the National Infrastructure Protection Plan must be implemented using organizational structures and partnerships committed to sharing and protecting the information needed to achieve the NIPP goal and supporting objectives.[12]

The NIPP goal is to build a safer, more secure, and more resilient America by preventing, deterring, neutralizing, or mitigating the effects of deliberate efforts by terrorists to destroy, incapacitate, or exploit elements of our Nation's CIKR and to strengthen national preparedness, timely response, and rapid recovery of CIKR in the event of an attack, natural disaster, or other emergency.[13]

Sector-specific planning and coordination are addressed through coordinating councils that are established for each sector.

- Sector Coordinating Councils (SCCs) are comprised of representative owners and operators, generally from the private sector.
- Government Coordinating Councils (GCCs) are comprised of Sector-Specific Agency representatives from Federal, State, local, tribal, and territorial governments.

These councils create a structure through which representative groups from all levels of government and the private sector can collaborate or share existing approaches to CIKR protection and work together to advance capabilities. Engaging and coordinating with foreign governments and international organizations are also essential to ensuring the protection and resiliency of U.S. CIKR, both at home and abroad.

The NIPP goal is to build a safer, more secure, and more resilient America by preventing, deterring, neutralizing, or mitigating the effects of deliberate efforts by terrorists to destroy, incapacitate, or exploit elements of our Nation's CIKR and to strengthen national preparedness, timely response, and rapid recovery of CIKR in the event of an attack, natural disaster, or other emergency.

Cross-sector issues and interdependencies are addressed among the Sector Coordinating Counciles through the CIKR Cross-Sector Council. Cross-sector issues are challenging to identify and assess comparatively. Interdependency analysis is often so complex that modeling and simulation capabilities must be brought to bear. [14]

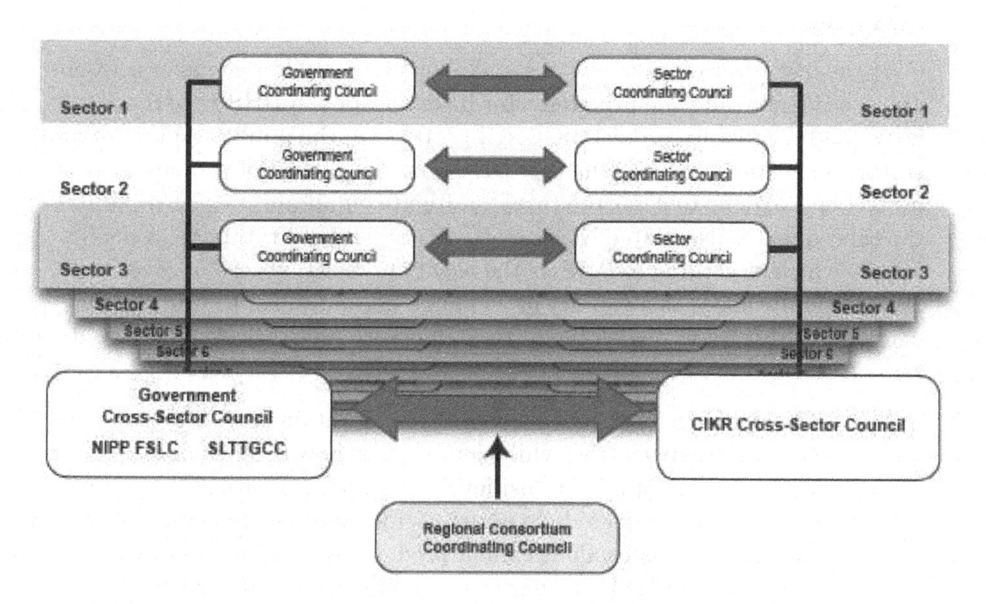

Figure 16.2: CIKR Protection Partnership.

Family of Plans

To be effective, the National Infrastructure Protection Plan must complement other plans designed to help prevent, prepare for, protect against, respond to, and recover from terrorist attacks, natural disasters, and other emergencies. Homeland security plans and strategies at the Federal, State, local, tribal, and territorial levels of government address CIKR protection within their respective jurisdictions. Similarly, CIKR owners and operators have responded to the increased threat environment by instituting a range of CIKR protection-related plans and programs, including business continuity and resilience and response measures. Implementation of the NIPP is coordinated among CIKR partners to ensure that it does not result in the creation of duplicative or costly risk management requirements that offer little enhancement of CIKR protection.

The NIPP, the National Preparedness Guidelines (NPG), and the National Response Framework (NRF) together provide a comprehensive, integrated approach to the homeland security mission. The NIPP establishes the overall risk-informed approach that defines the Nation's CIKR protection posture, while the NRF provides the approach for domestic incident management. The NPG sets forth national priorities, doctrine, and roles and responsibilities for building capabilities across the prevention, protection, response, and recovery mission areas. Increases in CIKR protective measures in the context of specific threats or that correspond to the threat conditions established in the Homeland Security Advisory System (HSAS) provide an important bridge between NIPP steady-state protection and the incident management activities under the NRF.[15]

The NIPP, the National Preparedness Guidelines (NPG), and the National Response Framework (NRF) together provide a comprehensive, integrated approach to the homeland security mission.

Assessment

Over the last several years, various stakeholders, including members of Congress, academia, and the private sector have questioned DHS's approach to critical infrastructure protection. CIKR partners in the public and the private sector have expressed concerns that DHS has placed most of its emphasis on protection—actions to deter the threat, mitigate vulnerabilities, or minimize the consequences associated with an attack or disaster—rather than resiliency—which, according to DHS, is the ability to resist, absorb, recover from, or successfully adapt to adversity or a change in conditions. In framing the debate over this issue, the National Infrastructure Advisory Council stated that:

> "The challenge facing government is to maintain its role in protecting critical infrastructures, while determining how best to encourage market forces to improve the resilience of companies, provide appropriate incentives and tools to help entire sectors become resilient, and step in when market forces alone cannot produce the level of infrastructure security needed to protect citizens, communities, and essential economic systems."[16]

DHS increased its emphasis on resiliency in the 2009 NIPP by discussing it with the same level of importance as protection. While the 2009 NIPP uses much of the same language as the 2006 NIPP to describe resiliency, the 2006 NIPP primarily treated resiliency as a subset of protection while the 2009 NIPP generally referred to resiliency alongside protection. DHS officials stated that these changes are not a major shift in policy; rather they are intended to raise awareness about resiliency as it applies within individual sectors. Furthermore, they stated that there is a greater emphasis on resilience in the 2009 NIPP to encourage more sector and cross-sector activities to address a broader spectrum of risks, such as cyber security. DHS officials also used guidance to encourage SSAs to devote more attention to resiliency. For example, in the 2009 guidance, SSAs are advised that in sectors where infrastructure resiliency is as or more important than physical security, they should focus on describing the resiliency measures and strategies being used by the sector.

Compared to the 2006 NIPP, DHS's 2009 update also placed greater emphasis on regional CIKR protection planning and updates to DHS's overall risk management framework, such as instructions for sectors to develop metrics to gauge how well programs reduced the risk to their sector. DHS officials said that the changes highlighted in the 2009 NIPP were the result of knowledge gained and issues raised during discussions with partners and outside organizations.[17]

Securing Cyberspace

Cyberspace is the nervous system—the control system of our country... Thus, the healthy functioning of cyberspace is essential to our economy and our national security.

The Nation's critical infrastructures are composed of public and private institutions in the sectors of agriculture, food, water, public health, emergency services, government, defense industrial base, information and telecommunications, energy, transportation, banking and finance, chemicals and hazardous materials, and postal and shipping. Cyberspace is their nervous system—the control system of our country. Cyberspace is composed of hundreds of thousands of interconnected computers, servers, routers, switches, and fiber optic cables that allow our critical infrastructures to work. Thus, the healthy functioning of cyberspace is essential to our economy and our national security.

National Strategy to Secure Cyberspace

The National Strategy to Secure Cyberspace is part an implementing component of the National Strategy for Homeland Security complemented by the National Strategy for the Physical Protection of Critical Infrastructures and Key Assets. The purpose of the Strategy is to engage and empower Americans to secure the portions of cyberspace that they own, operate, control, or with which they interact. Securing cyberspace is a difficult strategic challenge that requires coordinated and focused effort from our entire society—the federal government, state and local governments, the private sector, and the American people.

The National Strategy to Secure Cyberspace outlines an initial framework for both organizing and prioritizing efforts. It provides direction to the federal government departments and agencies that have roles in cyberspace security. It also identifies steps that state and local governments, private companies and organizations, and individual Americans can take to improve our collective cybersecurity. The Strategy highlights the role of public-private engagement. The document provides a framework for the contributions that we all can make to secure our parts of cyberspace. The dynamics of cyberspace will require adjustments and amendments to the Strategy over time.

Cyber Threat

The speed and anonymity of cyber attacks makes distinguishing among the actions of terrorists, criminals, and nation states difficult, a task which often occurs only after the fact, if at all. Therefore, the National Strategy to Secure Cyberspace helps reduce our Nation's vulnerability to debilitating attacks against our critical information infrastructures or the physical assets that support them.

Consistent with the National Strategy for Homeland Security, the strategic objectives of this National Strategy to Secure Cyberspace are to:

- Prevent cyber attacks against America's critical infrastructures;
- Reduce national vulnerability to cyber attacks; and
- Minimize damage and recovery time from cyber attacks that do occur.

The strategic objectives of this National Strategy to Secure Cyberspace are to:

1. *Prevent cyber attacks against America's critical infrastructures;*
2. *Reduce national vulnerability to cyber attacks; and*
3. *Minimize damage and recovery time from cyber attacks that do occur.*

Our economy and national security are fully dependent upon information technology and the information infrastructure. At the core of the information infrastructure upon which we depend is the Internet, a system originally designed to share unclassified research among scientists who were assumed to be uninterested in abusing the network. It is that same Internet that today connects millions of other computer networks making most of the nation's essential services and infrastructures work. These computer networks also control physical objects such as electrical transformers, trains, pipeline pumps, chemical vats, radars, and stock markets, all of which exist beyond cyberspace.

A spectrum of malicious actors can and do conduct attacks against our critical information infrastructures. Of primary concern is the threat of organized cyber attacks capable of causing debilitating disruption to our Nation's critical infrastructures, economy, or national security. The required technical sophistication to carry out such an attack is high—and partially explains the lack of a debilitating attack to date.

We should not, however, be too sanguine. There have been instances where organized attackers have exploited vulnerabilities that may be indicative of more destructive capabilities.

Uncertainties exist as to the intent and full technical capabilities of several observed attacks. Enhanced cyber threat analysis is needed to address long-term trends related to threats and vulnerabilities. What is known is that the attack tools and methodologies are becoming widely available, and the technical capability and sophistication of users bent on causing havoc or disruption is improving.

In peacetime America's enemies may conduct espionage on our Government, university research centers, and private companies. They may also seek to prepare for cyber strikes during a confrontation by mapping U.S. information systems, identifying key targets, and lacing our infrastructure with back doors and other means of access. In wartime or crisis, adversaries may seek to intimidate the Nation's political leaders by attacking critical infrastructures and key economic functions or eroding public confidence in information systems.

Cyber Security

Cyber attacks on United States information networks can have serious consequences such as disrupting critical operations, causing loss of revenue and intellectual property, or loss of life. Countering such attacks requires the development of robust capabilities where they do not exist today if we are to reduce vulnerabilities and deter those with the capabilities and intent to harm our critical infrastructures.

In general, the private sector is best equipped and structured to respond to an evolving cyber threat. There are specific instances, however, where federal government response is most appropriate and justified. Looking inward, providing continuity of government requires ensuring the safety of its own cyber infrastructure and those assets required for supporting its essential missions and services. Externally, a government role in cybersecurity is warranted in cases where high transaction costs or legal barriers lead to significant coordination problems; cases in which governments operate in the absence of private sector forces; resolution of incentive problems that lead to under provisioning of critical shared resources; and raising awareness.

In general, the private sector is best equipped and structured to respond to an evolving cyber threat... A federal role in these and other cases is only justified when the benefits of intervention outweigh the associated costs.

Public-private engagement is a key component of our Strategy to secure cyberspace. This is true for several reasons. Public-private partnerships can usefully confront coordination problems. They can significantly enhance information exchange and cooperation. Public-private engagement takes a variety of forms and addresses awareness, training, technological improvements, vulnerability remediation, and recovery operations.

A federal role in these and other cases is only justified when the benefits of intervention outweigh the associated costs. This standard is especially important in cases where there are viable private sector solutions for addressing any potential threat or vulnerability. For each case, consideration should be given to the broad based costs and impacts of a given government action, versus other alternative actions, versus non-action, taking into account any existing or future private solutions.

Federal actions to secure cyberspace are warranted for purposes including: forensics and attack attribution, protection of networks and systems critical to national security, indications and warnings, and protection against organized attacks capable of inflicting debilitating damage to the economy. Federal activities should also support research and technology development that will enable the private sector to better secure privately-owned portions of the Nation's critical infrastructure.[18]

National Cyber Security Division

The Department of Homeland Security (DHS) in implementing the President's National Strategy to Secure Cyberspace and the Homeland Security Act of 2002, created the National Cyber Security Division (NCSD) under the Department's Information Analysis and Infrastructure Protection Directorate, June 6, 2003. The NCSD provides for 24 x7 functions, including conducting cyberspace analysis, issuing alerts and warning, improving information sharing, responding to major incidents, and aiding in national-level recovery efforts. This Division represents a significant step toward advancing the Federal government's interaction and partnership with industry and other organizations in this critical area.

The NCSD identifies, analyzes and reduces cyber threats and vulnerabilities; disseminate threat warning information; coordinates incident response; and provides technical assistance in continuity of operations and recovery planning.

The NCSD builds upon the existing capabilities transferred to DHS from the former Critical Infrastructure Assurance Office, the National Infrastructure Protection Center, the Federal Computer Incident Response Center, and the National Communications System. The creation of the NCSD both strengthens government-wide processes for response and improves protection of critical cyber assets through maximizing and leveraging the resources of these previously separate offices.

With 60 employees, the Division is organized around three units designed to:

- Identify risks and help reduce the vulnerabilities to government's cyber assets and coordinate with the private sector to identify and help protect America's critical cyber assets;
- Oversee a consolidated Cyber Security Tracking, Analysis, & Response Center (CSTARC), which will detect and respond to Internet events; track potential threats and vulnerabilities to cyberspace; and coordinate cyber security and incident response with federal, state, local, private sector and international partners; and
- Create, in coordination with other appropriate agencies, cyber security awareness and education programs and partnerships with consumers, businesses, governments, academia, and international communities.

Consistent with law and policy, DHS's NCSD coordinates closely with the Office of Management and Budget and National Institute of Standards and Technology regarding the security of Federal systems, and coordinates with Federal law enforcement authorities, as appropriate. NCSD leverages other DHS components including the Science and Technology Directorate, the U.S. Secret Service and the Department's Privacy Officer.

The NCSD works closely with the DHS Science & Technology (S&T) Directorate to implement all required programs for research and development in cyber security. While S&T provides the actual research and development functions and execution, the NCSD provides detailed requirements into the direction of this R&D in response to needs of our public and private sectors partners.[19]

Conclusion

Terrorists are opportunistic. They exploit vulnerabilities we leave exposed, choosing the time, place, and method of attack according to the weaknesses they observe or perceive. Protecting America's critical infrastructure and key assets is thus a formidable challenge. Our open and technologically complex society presents an almost infinite array of potential targets, and our critical infrastructure changes as rapidly as the marketplace. It is impossible to protect completely all targets, all the time. On the other hand, we can help deter or deflect attacks, or mitigate their effects, by making strategic improvements in protection and security. Thus, while we cannot assume we will prevent all terrorist attacks, we can substantially reduce America's vulnerability, particularly to the most damaging attacks.

All elements of our society have a crucial stake in reducing our vulnerability to terrorism; and all have highly valuable roles to play. Protecting America's critical infrastructure and key assets requires an unprecedented level of cooperation throughout all levels of government-with private industry and institutions, and with the American people. The federal government has the crucial task of fostering a collaborative environment, and enabling all of these entities to work together to provide America the security it requires.[20]

Questions

1. What is “critical infrastructure”?
2. Why must we protect it?
3. What is the role of DHS in protecting our nation’s critical infrastructure?
4. What is the mission of the National Cyber Security Division?

Chapter 17

Defending Against Catastrophic Terrorism

Objectives

- Describe the different effects of biological, chemical, and nuclear attacks.
- Explain the consequences of attacking U.S. agriculture.
- Identify significant efforts since 9/11 to mitigate WMD threats.
- Know the role of state and local government in responding to WMD threats.
- Understand how DHS helps state and local governments prepare for WMD incidents.
- Describe the nation's current state of readiness with respect to WMD threats.

"America will have a coordinated national effort to prepare for, prevent, and respond to chemical, biological, radiological, and nuclear terrorist threats to the homeland. We will seek to detect chemical, biological, radiological, or nuclear weapons and prevent their entry into the United States. If terrorists use chemical, biological, radiological, or nuclear weapons, our communities and emergency personnel will be organized, trained, and equipped to detect and identify dangerous agents, respond rapidly, treat those who are harmed, contain the damage, and decontaminate the area."

— Critical Mission Area #5, National Strategy for Homeland Security, July 2002

Introduction

In 2001, chemical, biological, radiological, and nuclear detection capabilities were modest and response capabilities dispersed throughout the country at every level of government. Responsibility for chemical, biological, radiological, and nuclear surveillance as well as for initial response efforts often rested with state and local hospitals and public health agencies.[1] The widespread public unease following the anthrax mailings and the continued concern regarding possible terrorist use of weapons of mass destruction – nuclear, chemical, biological, or radiological – have highlighted the potential these weapons may have to a terrorist group.[2]

On November 25, 2002, President Bush signed into law the Homeland Security Act of 2002 (P.L. 107-296). This act created the Department of Homeland Security (DHS), which has the primary mission of preventing terrorist attacks in the United States, reducing national terrorism vulnerability, and minimizing damage and aiding in recovery from attacks. DHS coordinates federal preparedness and response to chemical and biological terrorism, the latter in conjunction with the Department of Health and Human Services. DHS has extended grants to local first responders to increase local preparedness against chemical or biological weapons use, and also has established, through the Science and Technology directorate, its own programs for funding research into chemical and biological defense. The DHS has also developed and deployed the BioWatch program, which aims to detect releases of biological weapons in urban areas.[3]

Bioterrorism

Unlike most other terrorist attacks, a bioterrorism attack may not be immediately apparent. Victims may not develop symptoms for days or weeks following exposure. The first indication of a successful bioterrorism attack might be the discovery of infected individuals by health practitioners. The Bush Administration prioritized the development and deployment of biosurveillance technologies in an attempt to identify a bioterrorism attack as soon after an attack as possible. The earlier an attack could be identified, the earlier treatment of the exposed individuals could begin. Earlier treatment generally increases the likelihood of individual recovery and survival.[4]

Federal efforts to combat the threat of bioterrorism predate the anthrax attacks of 2001, but have significantly increased since then. These efforts have been developed as part of and in parallel with other defenses against conventional terrorism.[5]

Congress and the Bush Administration established DHS as a focal point in the federal preparedness, response, and recovery to terrorism and imbued it with a variety of new authorities. In addition, the Bush Administration developed a series of national strategies and other guidance documents for homeland security generally and biodefense in specific. Beyond these cross-governmental strategy documents, many agencies developed more focused strategic plans for their individual operations against bioterrorism. The Obama Administration has continued this focus on bioterrorism by issuing additional guidance and directives. Congress has acted to require federal strategic planning activities through provisions of the Homeland Security Act of 2002 and other legislation. As well as establishing DHS, Congress has created offices and agencies within other Cabinet departments and assigned them specific planning activities. Finally, Congress established an office within the Executive Office of the President charged with preventing WMD proliferation and terrorism.[6]

The federal government's biodefense efforts span many different agencies and vary widely in their resources, scope, and approach. For example, the Departments of State and Defense have engaged in nonproliferation and counterproliferation efforts. The Departments of State and Commerce have strengthened export controls of materials that could be used for bioterrorism. The Department of Health and Human Services (HHS) has made investments in public health preparedness; response planning; and research, development, and procurement of medical countermeasures against biological terrorism agents. The intelligence community has engaged in intelligence gathering and sharing regarding bioterrorism. The Department of Justice performs background checks on people who want to possess certain dangerous pathogens. The Department of Homeland Security has engaged in preparedness, response, and recovery related activities, developed increased capabilities in environmental biosurveillance, and invested in expanding domestic bioforensics capabilities. The Environmental Protection Agency (EPA) has explored post-event infrastructure decontamination. Many agencies, jointly or separately, have invested in expanded biodefense infrastructure, including public and private high containment laboratories for research, diagnostic, and forensics purposes. Lastly, White House-led efforts and other coordinating groups have engaged in risk assessment and strategic planning exercises to coordinate and optimize federal investment against bioterrorism and response capabilities.[7]

The federal government's biodefense efforts span many different agencies and vary widely in their resources, scope, and approach.

Biosurveillance

Biosurveillance is the process of gathering, analyzing, and interpreting data in order to achieve early detection and warning and overall situational awareness of biological events with the potential to have catastrophic human and economic consequences.[8]

The Bush Administration implemented a number of different detection approaches, including environmental detection, syndromic surveillance, and information sharing. Through these efforts, the federal government aims to identify bioterrorism events at various scales, ranging from large, aerially disseminated releases to smaller releases infecting only a few individuals. The federal government, in collaboration with state and local jurisdictions, enhanced the existing network of public health laboratories to ensure that diagnostic laboratories could correctly handle and analyze clinical samples related to potential bioterrorism events. Similarly, the federal government has continued to invest in some global health activities partly in order to help identify when an emerging disease might pose a threat to the United States.[9]

Widespread deployment of environmental biosurveillance technologies began after the2001 anthrax mailings, and federal efforts to further develop these technologies have also increased. Questions remain regarding the effectiveness of their detection ability, especially in comparison to the innate detection ability of the medical system through astute physicians. A repeated criticism of biosurveillance activities is that the detection system may not be sufficiently sensitive and dependable to allow for a federal response following detection of a bioterrorism event. Technical difficulties persist in making a detection system sufficiently sensitive to detect very low levels of pathogens while maintaining a very low number of false alarms. Frequent false alarms pose a high cost in terms of resource consumption and responder opportunity costs. Additionally, frequent false alarms may lead responders and the public to assume that all alarms are likely to be false and thus they may not take alarms seriously. Other widely discussed issues include the extent to which the federal government should protect the population of the United States with such systems, through environmental sensing or other methods, and how the federal government should deploy systems that are only available in limited numbers.[10]

Frequent false alarms pose a high cost in terms of resource consumption and responder opportunity costs. Additionally, frequent false alarms may lead responders and the public to assume that all alarms are likely to be false and thus they may not take alarms seriously.

BioWatch

DHS, through the Science & Technology Directorate, provides management oversight to BioWatch, an early warning system designed to detect the release of biological agents in the air through a comprehensive protocol of monitoring and laboratory analysis. The goals of BioWatch are to:

- Provide early warning of a biological attack by expeditiously identifying the bio-agent, therby minimizing casualties in an affected area;
- Assist in establishing forensic evidence on the source, nature, and extent of biological attack to aid law enforcement agents in identifying the perpetrators; and
- Determine a preliminary spatial distribution of biological contamination, including what populations may have been expose.

DHS manages the program in cooperation with its federal partners, the Environmental Protection Agency and the Centers for Disease Control and Prevention (CDC), a Department of Health and Human Services agency.[11]

BioWatch was rolled out in just under 80 days from late January 2003 to mid-April 2003.[12] BioWatch is comprised of three main components: environmental aerosol sampling using stationary monitors, sample analysis, and response to a positive result. EPA is principally responsible for the aerosol sampling component of BioWatch. Current environmental aerosol sampling equipment is reportedly based on the Biological Aerosol Sentry and Information System (BASIS) developed by Lawrence Livermore National Laboratory and the Los Alamos National Laboratory. These aerosol samplers now are deployed in and around at least 30 major cities, and share site locations with EPA air quality monitors. The samplers collect airborne particles, including bacteria and viral particles, onto solid filters using a vacuum system. The sampler filters are manually collected at 24-hour intervals and transported to a nearby laboratory member of the Laboratory Response Network (LRN) for analysis. Established in 1999 by the CDC, the LRN is a national network of approximately 150 federal, state, and local laboratories equipped to promptly identify biological agents. BioWatch is configured to identify highly pathogenic species selected from the CDC's Category A and Category B lists of select agents.

A number of factors inhibit the effectiveness of the BioWatch program in its current form. Because filter retrieval, transport, and analysis are all performed manually, pathogen identification requires up to 36 hours from the time of particle capture, assuming a 24-hour filter collection interval. Perhaps most importantly, the entire collection/analysis process is labor intensive and requires substantial human resources. According to DHS, labor costs dominate the operational budget of BioWatch, and impose practical and financial limits on the number of aerosol samplers that the program is able to deploy. Ultimately, BioWatch will form one component of a more comprehensive interagency surveillance system designed to identify and respond to pathogen outbreaks. This system, known as the National Bio-Surveillance Integration System (NBIS) is in its infancy and remains under development.[13]

National Bio-Surveillance Integration System

In 2004, President Bush issued two directives aimed at improving coordination across all federal agency bio-awareness programs. Specifically, Homeland Security Presidential Directive (HSPD) 9, Defense of United States Agriculture and Food, dated January 30, 2004, charges federal agencies to create a new biological threat awareness capacity. HSPD-9 directs the Secretary of Homeland Security to coordinate with cross-federal efforts to build an updated and improved surveillance system and create a new biological threat awareness capacity that will enhance detection and characterization of an attack. Further, HSPD-10, Biodefense for the 21st Century, dated April 28, 2004, calls for an integrated and comprehensive attack warning system that will assist in recognizing and responding to biological attacks on humans, animals, food, water, agriculture, and environmental resources. HSPD-10 directs the Secretary of Homeland Security to integrate all federal agency efforts to create a national bioawareness system that will detect a biological attack at the earliest possible moment and permit initiation of a robust response to prevent unnecessary loss of life, economic impact, and social disruption. In addition, in November 2005, President Bush issued the National Strategy for Pandemic Influenza, which outlines the need for an early warning system to identify possible pandemic outbreaks.

DHS' Science and Technology Directorate began the NBIS program in 2004 as a means of integrating bio-surveillance information across government. The program essentially is composed of three parts:

- A robust information management system capable of handling large quantities of structured and unstructured data;
- A corps of specially skilled subject matter experts responsible for analyzing the data and providing situational awareness; and
- A culture of cooperation among interagency partners.

In addition to integrating disparate agency systems, NBIS was designed to bring together bio-surveillance data from the various sector-specific systems used for human, animal, and plant health surveillance; environmental monitoring of air, agriculture, water, and food; and intelligence and threat analysis. Such data will be digitally fed into the system, integrated and illustrated based on defined ontologies, analyzed using specific analytical tools, and then disseminated via a web portal. The data flow will be bidirectional, taking the sector-specific information from the relevant agencies and fusing it to provide comprehensive situational awareness back to the agencies. By correlating "subthreshold" data across the various sectors, NBIS can help ensure earlier recognition of biologically significant information and events that otherwise might not be reported beyond the originating agency.[14]

Beginning in 2004, DHS managed the NBIS and developed an information technology system to manage other agencies' biosurveillance information. In 2007, DHS created the Office of Health Affairs, headed by the DHS Chief Medical Officer, to lead DHS's biodefense activities and provide timely incident-specific management guidance for the medical consequences of disasters. At that time, DHS placed NBIS in the Office of Health Affairs.[15]

DHS BioDefense

The Office of Health Affairs' (OHA) WMD and Biodefense Office leads the Department's biological and chemical defense activities in coordination with other Departments and agencies across the federal government. WMD and Biodefense integrates the bio-monitoring activities of executive branch departments that include biosurveillance, aerosol detection, environmental animal surveillance, clinical syndrome detection, mail room observation, and suspicious substance management. With the Directorate of Science and Technology, WMD and Biodefense leads the Department's efforts for veterinary and agrodefense activities, covering animal and zoonotic diseases and agricultural security issues related to livestock, food, and water. The WMD and Biodefense Office comprises five parts:

1. National Biosurveillance Integration Center (NBIC)
2. Food, Agriculture, and Veterinary (FAV) defense
3. Threats and countermeasures
4. Early detection
5. Chemical defenses

In August 2007, the 9/11 Commission Act established **National Biosurveillance Integration Center (NBIC)** within DHS to contribute to the nation's biosurveillance capability by enhancing the ability of the federal government to rapidly identify, characterize, localize, and track biological events of national concern through integration and analysis of data relating to human health, animal, plant, food, and environmental monitoring systems (both national and international).[16] The NBIC integrates bio-monitoring activities of executive branch departments to provide a biological common operating picture and facilitate earlier detection of adverse events and trends. This Center fuses information from more than 12 federal agencies and state, local, private sector, and international sources of biosurveillance data on human, animal, plant, and environmental health to provide early warnings of a possible biological attack or a pandemic.[17] Once a potential event is detected, NBIC disseminates alerts to enable response to a biological event of national concern. To achieve these objectives, NBIC is to coordinate with federal and other stakeholders that have information that can be used to enhance the safety and security of the United States against potential biological events of national significance. This community of federal stakeholders is known as the NBIS.[18]

Food, Agriculture, and Veterinary (FAV) Defense coordinates with federal partners and other public and private entities to ensure awareness, readiness, and response to all disasters related to food, animals, agriculture, and their impact on public health. FAV provides advice to Department leadership on all security issues regarding food, water, agro-defense, veterinary and zoonotic diseases (public health). For example, FAV—in conjunction with other OHA and Department components, as well as various federal agencies—seeks to identify the course of events and determine the effects on the nation in regards to animal diseases such as Foot and Mouth Disease, Avian Influenza, Rift Valley Fever, and Wheat Rust, as well as nationwide food contamination events.

The NBIC integrates bio-monitoring activities of executive branch departments to provide a biological common operating picture and facilitate earlier detection of adverse events and trends. This Center fuses information from more than 12 federal agencies and state, local, private sector, and international sources of biosurveillance data on human, animal, plant, and environmental health to provide early warnings of a possible biological attack or a pandemic.

Threats and Countermeasures helps to advance the effectiveness of Project BioShield, in conjunction with the Department of Health and Human Services, through utilization of information derived from the Material Threat Determinations and Population Threat Assessments to identify medical countermeasures. This division also seeks to better understand the risk of current and emerging biological and chemical threats.

Early Detection provides a bio-aerosol environmental monitoring system to our nation's largest population centers for early detection of biological agents. Currently operational in over 30 urban metropolitan areas, BioWatch is a collaborative effort of health personnel at all levels of government. As S&T's research and development personnel continue to improve current technologies, OHA will incorporate these enhancements for greater detection and cost efficiencies. BioWatch also works closely with its federal, state and local partners, providing the infrastructure needed to further the Department's biodefense mission.

Chemical Defense seeks to save lives and expedite support to limit suffering and illness in the event of a catastrophic chemical attack. This division provides leadership and direction to assist in the nation's preparedness against a chemical attack and ensure the execution of an effective response. As part of the mission, the division deploys the Rapidly Deployable Chemical Detection System at various public events.[19]

National Biodefense Analysis and Countermeasures Center

The National Biodefense Analysis and Countermeasures Center (NBACC) applies science to challenges critical to defending the nation against bioterrorism. The Department of Homeland Security's Directorate for Science and Technology established the NBACC to be a national resource to understand the scientific basis of the risks posed by biological threats and to attribute their use in bioterrorism or biocrime events.

NBACC's National Bioforensic Analysis Center (NBFAC) conducts bioforensic analysis of evidence from a biocrime or terrorist attack to attain a "biological fingerprint" to help investigators identify perpetrators and determine the origin and method of attack. NBFAC is designated by Presidential Directive to be the lead federal facility to conduct and facilitate the technical forensic analysis and interpretation of materials recovered following a biological attack in support of the appropriate lead federal agency.

NBFAC maintains accreditation to a rigorous international standard of testing and calibration, and has established itself as a model for bioforensic laboratory practices.

The goal of agroterrorism is not to kill cows or plants. These are the means to the end of causing economic damage, social unrest, and loss of confidence in government.

NBACC's National Biological Threat Characterization Center (NBTCC) conducts studies and laboratory experiments to fill in information gaps to better understand current and future biological threats; to assess vulnerabilities and conduct risk assessments; and to determine potential impacts to guide the development of countermeasures such as detectors, drugs, vaccines, and decontamination technologies.

In 2008, NBTCC supported the Department's delivery to the President of the second Bioterrorism Risk Assessment - a comprehensive evaluation of the risks posed from biological threat agents in the hands of a terrorist.

NBACC is operated as a Federally Funded Research and Development Center for the Department by the Battelle National Biodefense Institute, LLC.[20]

Agro-Terrorism

The potential for terrorist attacks against agricultural targets (agroterrorism) is increasingly recognized as a national security threat, especially after the events of September 11, 2001. Agroterrorism is a subset of bioterrorism, and is defined as the deliberate introduction of an animal or plant disease with the goal of generating fear, causing economic losses, and/or undermining social stability.

The goal of agroterrorism is not to kill cows or plants. These are the means to the end of causing economic damage, social unrest, and loss of confidence in government. Human health could be at risk if contaminated food reaches the table or if an animal pathogen is transmissible to humans (zoonotic). While agriculture may not be a terrorist's first choice because it lacks the "shock factor" of more traditional terrorist targets, many analysts consider it a viable secondary target.

Agriculture has several characteristics that pose unique vulnerabilities. Farms are geographically disbursed in unsecured environments. Livestock are frequently concentrated in confined locations, and transported or commingled with other herds. Many agricultural diseases can be obtained, handled, and distributed easily. International trade in food products often is tied to disease-free status, which could be jeopardized by an attack. Many veterinarians lack experience with foreign animal diseases that are eradicated domestically but remain endemic in foreign countries.

In the past five years, "food defense" has received increasing attention in the counterterrorism and bioterrorism communities. Laboratory and response capacity are being upgraded to address the reality of agroterrorism, and national response plans now incorporate agroterrorism.[21]

Agriculture and the food industry are very important to the social, economic, and arguably, the political stability of the United States. Although farming employs less than 2% of the of the country's workforce, 16% of the workforce is involved in the food and fiber sector, ranging from farmers and input suppliers, to processors, shippers, grocers, and restauranteurs. In 2002, the food and fiber sector contributed $1.2 trillion, or 11% to the gross domestic product (GDP), even though the farm sector itself contributed less than 1%.

Agriculture in the U.S. is technologically advanced and efficient. This productivity allows Americans to spend only about 10% of their disposable income on food (both at home and away from home). Productivity increases over time have allowed the share of disposable income spent on food in the U.S. to fall from 23% in 1929 to 10% in 2003. The United States has the lowest spending on food prepared at home (6.5%) compared to the rest of the world, which ranges from 10%-15% for most developed countries and 30% or higher for some developing countries.[22]

The United States has the lowest spending on food prepared at home (6.5%) compared to the rest of the world, which ranges from 10%-15% for most developed countries and 30% or higher for some developing countries.

The U.S. produces and exports a large share the world's grain. In 2003, the U.S. share of world production was 42% for corn, 35% for soybeans, and 12% for wheat. Of global exports, the U.S. accounted for 65% for corn, 40% for soybeans, and 32% for wheat. If export markets were to decline following an agroterrorism event, U.S. markets could be severely disrupted since 21% of U.S. agricultural production is exported (10.5% of livestock, and 22% of crops). The U.S. exported nearly $60 billion of agricultural products (8% of all U.S. exports), and imported $47 billion of agricultural products (4% of all U.S. imports), making agriculture a positive contributor to the country's balance of trade.[23]

Economic losses from an agroterrorist incident could be large and widespread.

- First, losses would include the value of lost production, the cost of destroying diseased or potentially diseased products, and the cost of containment (drugs, diagnostics, pesticides, and veterinary services).
- Second, export markets could be lost if importing countries place restrictions on U.S. products to prevent possibilities of the disease spreading. Sanitary and phytosanitary rules in international trade agreements would be important for maintaining export markets.

- Third, multiplier effects could ripple through the economy due to decreased sales by agriculturally dependent businesses (farm input suppliers, food manufacturing, transportation, retail grocery, and food service). Tourism can be affected of access to certain destinations within the country is limited or perceptions of food or personal safety falter.
- Fourth, federal and state governments could bear significant costs, including eradication and containment costs, and compensation to producers for destroyed animals.

Depending on the erosion of consumer confidence and export sales, market prices of the affected commodities may drop. This would affect producers whose herds or crops were not directly infected, making the event national in scale even if the disease itself were contained to a small region.[24]

Consumer confidence in government may also be tested depending on the scale of the eradication effort and means of destroying animals or crops. The need to slaughter perhaps hundreds of thousands of cattle (or tens of millions of poultry) could generate public criticism if depopulation methods are considered inhumane or the destruction of carcases is questioned environmentally. For example, during the United Kingdom's foot-and-mouth (FMD) outbreak in 2001, euthanizing thousands of cattle and incinerating the carcasses in huge open air pyres provided poignant television images and difficult public relations situations for the agriculture ministry. Dealing with these concerns can add to the cost for both government and industry.[25]

The Public Health Security and Bioterrorism Preparedness and Response Act (P.L. 107-188, June 12, 2002) was enacted in response to vulnerabilities identified following September 11, 2001. Among many provisions affecting public health and general preparedness, the act contained several provisions important to agriculture. These provisions accomplish the following:

- Expand Food and Drug Administration (FDA) authority over food manufacturing and imports (particularly in sections 303-307). Tighten control of biological agents and toxins ("select agents" in sections 211-213, the "Agricultural Bioterrorism Protection Act of 2002") under rules by the Animal and Plant Health Inspection Service (APHIS) and Centers for Disease Control and Prevention.
- Authorize expanded agricultural security activities and security upgrades at USDA facilities (sections 331-335).
- Address criminal penalties for terrorism against animal enterprises (section 336) and violation of the select agent rules (section 231).[26]

The Animal Enterprise Terrorism Act (P.L. 109-374, Nov. 27, 2006) was enacted to expand criminal consequences for damaging or interfering with the operations of an animal enterprise. The Bioterrorism Preparedness Act (P.L. 107- 188, Sec. 336) contained less extensive penalties for animal enterprise terrorism.

P.L. 109-374 prescribes penalties and restitution in Title 18 of the U.S. Code for varying levels of economic damage and personal injury involving threats, acts of vandalism, property damage, criminal trespass, harassment, or intimidation. The act covers enterprises that use, sell, or raise animals (or animal products) for profit or educational purposes. With this broad definition, the law applies to both bioterrorism (from foreign sources) and eco-terrorism (from domestic animal rights activist groups).[27]

In December 2002, the USDA Animal and Plant Health Inspection Service (APHIS) issued regulations to reduce the threat that certain biological agents and toxins could be used in domestic or international terrorism. APHIS determined that the "select agents" on the list have the potential to pose a severe threat to agricultural production or food products.

The select agent regulations (9 CFR 121 for animals, 7 CFR 331 for plants) establish the requirements for possession, use, and transfer of the listed pathogens. The rules affect many research institutions including federal, state, university, and private laboratories, as well as firms that transport such materials. The laboratories have had to assess security vulnerabilities and upgrade physical security, often without additional financial resources. Some have been concerned that certain research programs may be discontinued or avoided because of regulatory difficulties in handling the select agents.[28]

DHS Agro Responsibilities

Plum Island Animal Disease Center (PIADC), located on an island off the northeastern tip of Long Island, NY is currently the premier U.S. facility for research on foreign animal diseases. ht Sidebar

With passage of the Homeland Security Act of 2002 (P.L. 107-296, November 25, 2002), the law made two major changes to the facilities and functions of the U.S. Department of Agriculture. The Homeland Security Act transferred:

- personnel and responsibility for agricultural border inspections from USDA to DHS (specifically, from the USDA Animal and Plant Health Inspection Service (APHIS) to DHS Customs and Border Protection (CBP)), and
- possession of the Plum Island Animal Disease Center in New York from USDA to DHS.[29]

Plum Island Animal Disease Center (PIADC), located on an island off the northeastern tip of Long Island, NY is currently the premier U.S. facility for research on foreign animal diseases. The property of Plum Island was transferred from USDA to DHS in the Homeland Security Act (P.L. 107-296), although personnel from both USDA and DHS still conduct research there. Built in the 1950s, many experts agree that the 50-year old Plum Island facility is nearing the end of its useful life and unable to provide the necessary capacity for current biosecurity research. Plum Island is the only facility in the United States that is currently approved to study high-consequence foreign livestock diseases, such as foot-and-mouth disease (FMD), because its laboratory has been equipped with a specially designed bio-safety level 3 (BSL-3) biocontainment area for large animals that meets specific safety measures. Live FMD virus may be used only at coastal islands such as Plum Island, unless the Secretary of Agriculture specifically authorizes the use of the virus on the U.S. mainland (21U.S.C. 113a).[30]

The Department of Homeland Security is proceeding with plans to replace the aging Plum Island Animal Disease Center with a new National Bio and Agro-Defense Facility (NBAF).[31] This facility will house high biocontainment laboratories able to hold the pathogens currently under investigation at PIADC, as well as other pathogens of interest. The DHS has selected Manhattan, Kansas, as the NBAF site and plans to open the facility in 2015. The DHS estimates the final, total facility construction cost as $725 million, significantly exceeding earlier projections. Additional expenses, such as equipping the new facility, relocating existing personnel and programs, and preparing the Plum Islan Animal Disease Center facility for disposition, are expected to add $190 million.[32]

In terms of protecting critical infrastructure, agriculture was added to the list in December 2003 by Homeland Security Presidential Directive 7 (HSPD-7), "Critical Infrastructure Identification, Prioritization, and Protection." This directive replaces the 1998 Presidential Decision Directive 63 (PDD-63) that omitted agriculture and food. Both of these critical infrastructure directives designate the physical systems that are vulnerable to terrorist attack and are essential for the minimal operation of the economy and the government.

These directives instruct agencies to develop plans to prepare for and counter the terrorist threat. HSPD-7 mentions the following industries: agriculture and food; banking and finance; transportation (air, sea, and land, including mass transit, rail, and pipelines); energy (electricity, oil, and gas); telecommunications; public health; emergency services; drinking water; and water treatment.

More significant recognition came on January 30, 2004, when the White House released Homeland Security Presidential Directive 9 (HSPD-9), "Defense of United States Agriculture and Food." This directive establishes a national policy to protect against terrorist attacks on agriculture and food systems. HSPD-9 generally instructs the Secretaries of Homeland Security (DHS), Agriculture (USDA), and Health and Human Services (HHS), the Administrator of the Environmental Protection Agency (EPA), the Attorney General, and the Director of Central Intelligence to coordinate their efforts to prepare for, protect against, respond to, and recover from an agroterrorist attack. In some cases, one department is assigned primary responsibility, particularly when the intelligence community is involved. In other cases, only USDA, HHS, and/or EPA are involved regarding industry or scientific expertise.[33]

Finally, Homeland Security Presidential Directive 5 (HSPD-5) called for a National Response Plan (NRP) to coordinate federal bureaucracies, capabilities, and resources into a unified, all-discipline, and all-hazards approach to manage domestic incidents, both for terrorism and natural disasters. The National Response Plan, developed by DHS, was unveiled in December 2004.

The NRP addresses agriculture and food in two annexes at the end of the plan. The first is in terms of emergency support. The Emergency Support Function (ESF) annexes to the NRP seek to coordinate federal interagency support by describing the roles and responsibilities of departments and agencies. USDA is the coordinator and primary responding agency for ESF #11, the "Agriculture and Natural Resources Annex," which addresses:

- Provision of nutrition assistance by determining nutrition assistance needs in disaster areas, obtaining appropriate food supplies, arranging for delivery of the supplies, and authorizing disaster food stamps,
- Control and eradication of animal and plant pests and diseases,
- Assurance of food safety and food security, including food safety inspection at processing plants, distribution, retail sites, and ports of entry; laboratory analysis of food samples; food borne disease surveillance; and field investigations, and
- Protection of natural and cultural resources and historic properties.

HHS is the coordinating agency for food inspected by the FDA beyond the farm gate (all domestic and imported food except meat, poultry and egg products), animal feed, and animal drugs. USDA is the coordinating agency for food inspected by the Food Safety Inspection Service (FSIS) such as processed meat, poultry and egg products, and for coordinating the response to animal and plant diseases and pests. EPA is identified in the annex to provide expedited assistance for approving particular types of pesticide applications, and to provide technical assistance for decontamination and disposal efforts. DHS appears to be involved to the extent that other parts of the NRP are activated by the agriculture and food incident, especially when law enforcement, investigative, or border inspection activities are involved.[34]

Federal response roles and responsibilities remained essentially the same when the NRP was replaced in 2008 by the National Response Framework (NRF).

Chemical weapons, with their quick acting effects, must be treated as promptly as possible.

Chemical & Toxin Weapons

Chemical weapons are chemical compounds that have a strong, deleterious effect on the human body, even when encountered in small doses. The different types of chemical weapons include vesicants, which blister and burn on contact; choking agents, which cause lung damage; and nerve agents, which interfere with the nervous system and may lead to death. The effects from chemical weapons may occur very quickly after exposure, on the order of minutes to hours.

Toxin weapons are primarily illness-inducing chemicals formed from living creatures, such as bacteria, fungi, plants, and animals. Toxins range in effect from disabling to acutely toxic. The most deadly compound currently known, botulinum toxin, is a bacterial toxin. Toxins are more potent than chemical weapons, requiring less material to produce equivalent casualties, but they are not self-reproducing, so more material is required than for a biological weapon. Symptoms from toxin exposure typically occur on a timescale intermediate between chemical and biological weapons, generally appearing over the course of several hours.[35]

Chemical weapons, with their quick acting effects, must be treated as promptly as possible. Because of the large range of potential effects caused by chemical weapons, there is no universal treatment for chemical weapon exposure. Exposure to nerve agents can be directly treated with medication to prevent or reduce symptoms. Exposure to vesicants, such as mustard gas, is generally untreatable; most people exposed will exhibit the agent's effects. The effects from vesicant exposure, primarily blisters and lesions, can be treated. In addition, injury from exposure to choking agents, such as chlorine, can be ameliorated by prompt medical treatment to limit permanent lung damage.[36]

Treatment of injuries sustained from toxin weapons may be more complicated. Anti-toxins and toxoid vaccines can be developed against toxin weapons, but the process for doing so is involved and time-consuming. Consequently, stores of these medicines are limited in scope, and a large number of toxin weapon casualties could exhaust local supplies. Some toxins, such as botulinum toxin, cause death by paralyzing the muscles used for breathing. These toxins can be treated with supportive care, through artificial ventilation and other means, until the patients recover.[37]

The use of chemical, biological, or toxin weapons in terror attacks could complicate emergency response due to the need to establish special care facilities for the victims, such as decontamination areas, and the need to protect first responders from the weapon's effects. If first responders became victims through inadequate personal protective equipment or contamination of emergency vehicles, increased casualties and greater social disruption could result.

Anti-toxins and toxoid vaccines can be developed against toxin weapons, but the process for doing so is involved and time-consuming.

The use of chemical or toxin weapons could generate a disproportionate public response because of a broad public perception that their use is akin to poisoning. According to experts, there has long been fear of and antipathy towards the use of poison. It is especially frightening to the victim, as the symptoms may seem to appear from nowhere. Poisons lacking an antidote may raise concerns further, as the victim perceives that there is no recourse or cure available. The dread generated from the inability to control the situation, and often times one's own bodily safety, is common to victims of chemical weapons, and multiplies anxieties related to these weapons' use.[38]

Public panic might have weighty ramifications. If a chemical or biological weapon was disseminated widely, especially in the case of a contagious pathogen, there might be government intervention to quarantine individuals or groups of individuals. Panicked flight from areas of perceived danger could complicate response efforts. Additionally, due to the newsworthy aspects of a chemical, biological, and toxin weapon attack, public panic could propagate through media reports to locations not affected by the attack.

While hysterical, widespread panic is cited as a potential public response to mass dissemination of a chemical, biological, or toxin weapon, it is not clear if this is a likely outcome. The loss of public confidence and angry, perhaps violent, competition for medical treatment have been suggested as possible results from a chemical or biological weapon attack. On the other hand, public response after natural disasters has not generally led to public hysteria or unreasoned aggression, even when there has been significant anger directed towards government officials. In previous crises, public anxiety has been successfully reduced by government response.[39]

Federal policymakers have addressed reducing terrorist use of chemical, biological, and toxin weapons through programs ameliorating these weapons' destructive aspects and through increased vigilance in detecting and preventing terror attacks in general. Local response to terrorist attack has been further developed through federal programs providing state health departments grant-based funding in order to address vulnerable aspects of their response system. These improvements include further development of hospital and laboratory capacity; development of response networks for timely communication during a bioterror event; development of protocols for communicating between local, state, and federal responders; and improved education of physicians and health care providers. A concerted federal effort is underway to develop emergency reserves of medicines to combat chemical, biological, and toxin casualties. Additionally, research proposals have been funded in the areas of detection systems and enhanced epidemiological surveillance, to detect chemical, biological, or toxin use as early as possible.

Federal law enforcement agencies now have greater power to gather intelligence on terror groups and their members. Increased information about terrorist groups, combined with apprehension of any who have chemical, biological, or toxin weapons, may provide further barriers to terrorist acquisition and use of these weapons. A registration system for researchers and facilities possessing select agents has been developed by the Department of Health and Human Services, and additional restrictions regarding access to these agents have been made law.[40]

State & Local Preparedness

Initial response to a public health emergency of any type, including a bioterrorist attack, is generally a local responsibility that could involve multiple jurisdictions in a region, with states providing additional support when needed.

Initial response to a public health emergency of any type, including a bioterrorist attack, is generally a local responsibility that could involve multiple jurisdictions in a region, with states providing additional support when needed. The federal government could also become involved in investigating or responding to an incident. In addition, the federal government provides funding and resources to state and local entities to support preparedness and response efforts. Having the necessary resources immediately available at the local level to respond to an emergency can minimize the magnitude of the event and the cost of remediation.[41]

While the federal government has resources at hand for responding to terrorist attacks, the proximity of state and local responders ensures they will almost always be the first to arrive at the site of an attack. For this reason, the preparedness of state and local governments has become a salient national issue.

Preparedness is one of four phases of comprehensive emergency management (CEM). The other three phases are response, recovery, and mitigation. CEM offers emergency managers a framework for classifying and planning not only preparedness activities, but all emergency management activities. Preparedness involves a wide range of activities such as developing flexible response plans, training and equipping responders, and assessing a community's vulnerabilities.

Congress has addressed the preparedness phase of emergency management by authorizing several training and grant programs designed to help states and localities enhance their response capabilities, particularly for terrorist attacks involving weapons of mass destruction (WMD). Federal programs cover a range of activities, including emergency management and planning; training and equipment; preparation forWMD attacks; law enforcement; and public health.[42]

Since the September attacks, however, emergency managers and analysts have asked Congress to address several issues in federal policy on state and local preparedness. Some frequently mentioned policy issues are:

- Amount and Uses of Federal Assistance—Observers have urged Congress to increase levels of financial and technical assistance available to states and localities. Some observers have also asked for more flexibility with federal funds.
- Coordination of Federal Assistance—Preparedness programs administered by various federal agencies often are not well coordinated, causing frustration among state and local officials seeking assistance. Some call for one federal office to coordinate the content and availability of preparedness programs.

The Homeland Security Grant Program is a primary funding mechanism for building and sustaining national preparedness capabilities.

- Preparedness Standards—Nongovernmental organizations working with FEMA have developed voluntary standards for emergency preparedness. Some observers have urged Congress to support the use of standards by instructing FEMA to undertake more research on preparedness standards and provide more assistance to governments attempting to meet standards.
- Preparedness of the Medical Community—Observers have emphasized the need to give public health agencies and hospitals a greater role in emergency planning and increase their capability to respond to weapons of mass destruction.
- Mutual Aid Compacts—Compacts are not uncommon, but some observers believe states and localities need to formalize and update their compacts.
- Joint Training Exercises—Observers argue that more joint training exercises are needed to adequately prepare local, state, and federal responders for terrorist attacks.
- Communications Infrastructure and Other Equipment—First responders may need specialized equipment to respond to a terrorist attack, including an interoperable communications system.[43]

Homeland Security Grant Program

The HSGP is a primary funding mechanism for building and sustaining national preparedness capabilities and is comprised of five interconnected grant programs: the State Homeland Security Program (SHSP), the Urban Areas Security Initiative (UASI), Operation Stonegarden (OPSG), the Metropolitan Medical Response System (MMRS) and the Citizen Corps Program (CCP). Together, these grant programs fund a range of preparedness activities, including planning, organization, equipment purchase, training, exercises and management and administration.[44]

State Homeland Security Program. This core assistance program provides funds to build capabilities at the state and local levels and to implement the goals and objectives included in state homeland security strategies and initiatives in their State Preparedness Report. Consistent with the Implementing Recommendations of the 9/11 Act of 2007 (Public Law 110-53) (9/11 Act), states are required to ensure that at least 25 percent of SHSP appropriated funds are dedicated towards law enforcement terrorism prevention-oriented planning, organization, training, exercise, and equipment activities, including those activities which support the development and operation of fusion centers.

Urban Areas Security Initiative. The UASI program focuses on enhancing regional preparedness in major metropolitan areas. The UASI program directly supports the National Priority on expanding regional collaboration in the National Preparedness Guidelines and is intended to assist participating jurisdictions in developing integrated regional systems for prevention, protection, response, and recovery. Consistent with the 9/11 Act, states are required to ensure that at least 25 percent of UASI appropriated funds are dedicated towards law enforcement terrorism prevention-oriented planning, organization, training, exercise, and equipment activities, including those activities which support the development and operation of fusion centers.

Operation Stonegarden. The intent of OPSG is to enhance cooperation and coordination among local, state and federal law enforcement agencies in a joint mission to secure the United States borders along routes of ingress from international borders to include travel corridors in states bordering Mexico and Canada, as well as states and territories with international water borders.

Metropolitan Medical Response System. The MMRS program supports the integration of emergency management, health, and medical systems into a coordinated response to mass casualty incidents caused by any hazard. Successful MMRS grantees reduce the consequences of a mass casualty incident during the initial period of a response by having augmented existing local operational response systems before the incident occurs.

Citizen Corps Program. The Citizen Corps mission is to bring community and government leaders together to coordinate community involvement in emergency preparedness, planning, mitigation, response and recovery.[45]

Rabiological & Nuclear Threats

The federal government has implemented a series of programs focused on detecting the illicit shipment of nuclear and radiological materials and protecting and securing nuclear weapons and material. Following the events of September 11, 2001, these programs were augmented by new programs focusing on preventing radiological and nuclear terrorism within the United States. Some of these new and existing efforts had overlapping goals, but they generally used different approaches to improve the detection and security of nuclear materials. These programs largely reside within the Departments of Defense, Energy, and State; agencies that became part of the Department of Homeland Security (DHS) upon its creation in 2002; and the Nuclear Regulatory Commission. Many of these agencies have both national and international roles in nuclear defense, protecting domestic nuclear assets while aiding in securing or detecting the transport of foreign nuclear material.

Programs established by the Departments of Defense and Energy and the Nuclear Regulatory Commission have focused on the security of nuclear and radiological materials. For example, the Department of Energy (DOE) International Nuclear Materials Protection and Cooperation program aids in securing foreign special nuclear material. The Department of Defense (DOD), through the Defense Threat Reduction Agency (DTRA), has enhanced the security and safety of fissile material storage and transportation in the former Soviet Union while dismantling and destroying associated infrastructure.[46]

Other programs have focused on detection of nuclear and radiological materials in transit, in order to detect attempts to illicitly transport a nuclear weapon or special nuclear material across borders. The DOE Second Line of Defense (SLD) program aids in establishing capabilities to detect nuclear and radiological materials in foreign countries at ports of entry, border crossings, and other designated locations. The Department of State Export Control and Related Border Security Assistance Program undertakes similar efforts to provide radiation detection capabilities at border crossings. Other programs are designed to detect nuclear and radiological materials in transit towards the United States, through screening either at foreign ports or at the U.S. border. For example, U.S. Customs and Border Protection uses both handheld and portal-based radiation monitoring to detect nuclear and radiological materials entering the United States.

Once created, DHS expanded the deployment of radiation detectors, both portal monitors through the Radiation Portal Monitor (RPM) program and handheld and portable detectors through the U.S. Coast Guard and Customs and Border Protection. The DHS Science and Technology (S&T) Directorate began research and development activities to develop an improved radiation detection portal and an integrated plan and structure for the use of federal radiation detection equipment. Additionally, DHS developed several overarching initiatives, such as the Container Security Initiative and the Secure Freight Initiative, to increase the likelihood that nuclear and radiological material or a nuclear weapon would be detected, identified, and interdicted during shipping. These initiatives built on other federal efforts, such as the DOE Megaports Initiative, which deploys radiation detection equipment and aims to increase detection of nuclear materials at ports of departure rather than at ports of entry.

The early post-September 11, 2001, efforts of the federal government, taking place in several agencies and departments, were criticized by experts who perceived these activities as uncoordinated and insufficient to protect the United States from nuclear terrorism. The Defense Science Board, among others, recommended that the federal government make a greater, more organized effort to protect the United States against the nuclear terrorism threat.[47]

Domestic Nuclear Detection Office

In April 15, 2005, the Domestic Nuclear Detection Office (DNDO) was established within the Department of Homeland Security to centralize coordination of the federal response to an unconventional nuclear threat. The office was codified in 2006 through the passage of the SAFE Port Act (P.L. 109-347) and given specific statutory responsibilities to protect the United States against radiological and nuclear attack:[48]

- Develop the global nuclear detection and reporting architecture
- Develop, acquire, and support the domestic nuclear detection and reporting system
- Fully characterize detector system performance before deployment
- Establish situational awareness through information sharing and analysis
- Establish operation protocols to ensure detection leads to effective response
- Conduct a transformational research and development program
- Establish the National Technical Nuclear Forensics Center to provide planning, integration, and improvements to USG nuclear forensics capabilities[49]

The Domestic Nuclear Detection Office was established within the Department of Homeland Security to centralize coordination of the federal response to an unconventional nuclear threat.

Initially placed under the S&T Directorate, DNDO was subsequently established as an independent office whose Director reports directly to the Secretary. The SAFE Port Act (P.L. 109- 347) gave the office statutory authority and specific responsibilities to protect the United States against radiological and nuclear attack. Among these responsibilities is to:

> develop, with the approval of the Secretary and in coordination with the Attorney General, the Secretary of State, the Secretary of Defense, and the Secretary of Energy, an enhanced global nuclear detection architecture with implementation under which (A) the Office will be responsible for the implementation of the domestic portion of the global architecture; (B) the Secretary of Defense will retain responsibility for implementation of Department of Defense requirements within and outside the United States; and (C) the Secretary of State, the Secretary of Defense, and the Secretary of Energy will maintain their respective responsibilities for policy guidance and implementation of the portion of the global architecture outside the United States, which will be implemented consistent with applicable law and relevant international arrangements.

The development and implementation of a global nuclear detection architecture is a challenging endeavor. Because federal efforts to protect against nuclear attack are spread among multiple agencies, determining the full range of existing efforts, coordinating the outcomes of these efforts, identifying any overlaps and gaps between them, and developing an architecture integrating current and future efforts are likely to be evolving, ongoing tasks.[50]

Global Nuclear Detection Architecture

The SAFE Port Act requires that DNDO establish an "enhanced global nuclear detection architecture," but it does not define this term. The DNDO describes the global nuclear detection architecture as comprising several key elements: "a multi-layered structure of radiological/nuclear (rad/nuc) detection systems, deployed both domestically and overseas; a well-defined and carefully coordinated network of interrelationships among them; and a set of systems engineering-based principles and guidelines governing the architecture's design and evolution over time." In implementing this definition, DNDO solicited information about existing programs from agencies involved in nuclear detection. The DNDO then performed a "net assessment" of federal nuclear detection capabilities. This assessment determined that 72 programs contributed in whole or in part to the existing global nuclear detection architecture, with total funding of more than $2.2 billion in FY2006. This existing global nuclear detection architecture includes programs at DHS, the Department of Defense (DOD), the Department of Energy (DOE), the Department of State (DOS), and other agencies. According to DHS, before the formation of DNDO these programs were "a disparate patchwork of systems, distributed and implemented in recent years across multiple departments, jurisdictions and locations without any degree of coordination." The DNDO has organized these programs into a global nuclear detection architecture framework, a combined system of systems, which relies heavily on its technological component. The deployment of radiation detectors at points of entry, commercial ports, and other border crossings is key to its effectiveness.

Although much focus has been given to technologies to detect nuclear or radiological material that have been developed or procured by DNDO, the global nuclear detection architecture encompasses more than just these sensors. Other elements include site security of known nuclear or radiological material, use of sensor data to inform decision makers, effective reaction to a detection event, and interdiction following detection. According to the Government Accountability Office, "combating nuclear smuggling requires an integrated approach that includes equipment, proper training of border security personnel in the use of radiation detection equipment, and intelligence gathering on potential nuclear smuggling operations." Other experts have concluded that the deployment of radiation detectors needs to be highly integrated with other federal efforts, prioritized on identified threats, configured for flexibility and efficiency, and organized as a global approach including international institutions.

The DNDO has attempted to align existing federal programs so that their capabilities can be compared and integrated into an organizing framework that can help identify gaps and duplication.[51]

Layered Defense

A layered, defense-in-depth approach to a global nuclear detection architecture was recommended by the Defense Science Board when considering how to protect DoD assets against unconventional nuclear threats. Successful application of a layered defense provides multiple opportunities to detect and interdict threats. According to DNDO, "It is recognized that no single layer of protection can ever be one hundred percent successful," and a layered defense strategy acknowledges this difficulty. If one sublayer fails to detect a threat, the next may succeed.

This increase in the likelihood of detection occurs in two different ways. In one case, a threat may avoid the detector in an outer layer, but then encounter a detector in an inner layer. In this case, having more detection opportunities makes it more likely that a detector is encountered. An example of this approach could be the use of detection technology at U.S. borders coupled with random truck screening at weigh stations on interstate highways. The DNDO has explicitly attempted to incorporate such redundancy into its global nuclear detection architecture, identifying numerous areas where detection capabilities might be integrated into existing operations:

Examples include, but are not limited to, fixed and mobile detection systems integrated into commercial vehicle inspection activities, detection enabled law enforcement, and screening conducted for special events. Capabilities that may require additional operational costs include mobile teams sweeping of areas of concern, chokepoint screening at bridges and tunnels, roadway monitoring concepts, and options for reducing the risk posed by the small maritime craft pathway.

A layered, defense-in-depth approach to a global nuclear detection architecture was recommended by the Defense Science Board when considering how to protect DoD assets against unconventional nuclear threats. Successful application of a layered defense provides multiple opportunities to detect and interdict threats.

Alternatively, a threat may encounter a detector in an outer layer that fails to detect it, but then may encounter a different type of detector in an inner layer that is more successful. In this case, it is the use of different detection technologies or procedures that provides the increased likelihood of success. Examples might include the screening of manifest information for shipments entering the United States, followed by the use of radiation detection equipment; the use of both radiation detectors and non-intrusive imaging technologies; or the physical search of a vehicle triggered by suspicious behavior even though a radiation detector did not detect any emitted radioactivity. Prior experience has shown that nuclear smuggling detection occurs not only through the raising of alarms by radiation detection equipment at borders, but also by intelligence information and through police investigations.

An additional advantage to a layered system is that its multiple detection and interdiction opportunities may increase the number of steps that a terrorist group must take to evade detection. Because of these additional steps, the group may be more likely to be detected by other means unrelated to the global nuclear detection architecture. For example, if it is necessary to disassemble a nuclear device to avoid detection, the reassembly of the device within the United States might be prevented by unrelated law enforcement activities. Even better, the increased complexity of evading detection might deter an attacker from even attempting a particular type of attack.

The ability to correlate information from different layers may also enhance the detection capability of the global nuclear detection architecture. Fusion of data from the different layers may reveal patterns or information not apparent in any single layer. It is the intent of the global nuclear detection architecture to integrate detection and notification systems at the federal, state, and local level, but accomplishing that goal may take significant time and effort, as procedures, technology, and data formats may need to be harmonized to allow easy information exchange.[52]

Report Card

In December 2008 in accordance with the Implementing Recommendations of the 9/11 Commission Act of 2007 (P.L. 110-53), the Commission on the Prevention of Weapons of Mass Destruction Proliferation and Terrorism submitted its report, World at Risk. That report assessed the nation's activities, initiatives, and programs to prevent weapons of mass destruction proliferation and terrorism and provided concrete recommendations to address these threats. The Commission found several areas where the risks to the United States are increasing: the crossroads of terrorism and proliferation in the poorly governed regions of Pakistan, the proliferation of biological and nuclear materials, and technology, and the potential erosion of international nuclear security, treaties, and norms as we enter a nuclear energy renaissance.

Unless the world community acts decisively and with great urgency, it is more likely than not that a weapon of mass destruction (WMD) will be used in a terrorist attack somewhere in the world by the end of 2013. That weapon is more likely to be biological than nuclear.

In 2009, the Commission was authorized for an additional year of work, to assist Congress and the Obama Administration to improve understanding of its findings and turn its concrete recommendations into actions. In accordance with that authorization, the Chair and Vice Chair of the Commission, based upon close consultation with Commissioners, submitted a report card assessing the U.S. Government's progress in protecting the United States from weapons of mass destruction proliferation and terrorism.[53]

In December 2008, the Commission released a unanimous threat assessment: Unless the world community acts decisively and with great urgency, it is more likely than not that a weapon of mass destruction (WMD) will be used in a terrorist attack somewhere in the world by the end of 2013. That weapon is more likely to be biological than nuclear.

Less than a month after this assessment, then Director of National Intelligence Mike McConnell publicly endorsed it.

The assessment was based on four factors.

1. First, there is direct evidence that terrorists are trying to acquire weapons of mass destruction.
2. Second, acquiring WMD fits the tactical profile of terrorists. They understand the unique vulnerability of first-world countries to asymmetric weapons—weapons that have a far greater destructive impact than the power it takes to acquire and deploy them. The airplanes that al Qaeda flew into the World Trade Center were asymmetric weapons.

3. Third, terrorists have demonstrated global reach and the organizational sophistication to obtain and use WMD. As recent actions by al Qaeda in the Arabian Peninsula demonstrate, the al Qaeda network is expanding through international partnerships. In particular, it is well within their present capabilities to develop and use bioweapons. As the Commission's report, World at Risk, found, if al Qaeda recruits skilled bioscientists, it will acquire the capability to develop and use biological weapons.
4. Fourth, the opportunity to acquire and use such weapons is growing exponentially because of the global proliferation of nuclear material and biological technologies.

Since this report was released, the risk has continued to grow.

This is not meant to question the good faith or deny the dedication of anyone in the government. The fact is that first-world democracies are particulary vulnerable to asymmetric attack, especially from organizations that have no national base and therefore, are undeterred by the threat of retaliation. So although everyone wants to prevent such attacks, and the government made progress toward that end in certain areas, the forces and factors that imperil the country have been outracing defensive efforts and overwhelming good intentions.

While the government has made progress on preventing such attacks, it is simply not paying consistent and urgent attention to the means of responding quickly and effectively so that they no longer constitute a threat of mass destruction.

It is possible that fortuitous circumstances may reduce the anticipated risk. Outside forces may change and render more benign the groups that are working against us, or as in the case of the Detroit-bound flight on Christmas Day, an attack may occur but fail in execution to the point that the destructive impact is minimal.

But the United States cannot count on such good fortune. Plans must be based on the assumption that what is likely to occur, given the current trajectory of risk, WILL occur, unless the trajectory is reversed. And on the current course, what is likely to occur within a very few years is an attack using weapons of mass destruction—probably a bioweapon—that will fundamentally change the character of life for the world's democracies.

In reaction to the Christmas Day attack, President Barack Obama stated that he would do everything in his power to support the men and women in intelligence, law enforcement and homeland security to ensure they have the tools and resources to keep America safe. He promised to "leave no stone unturned in seeking better ways to protect the American people." It is in this spirit of protecting America that the Commission made its recommendations, and it is in this spirit that the report card was developed.

The assessment is not a good one, particularly in the area of biological threats. While the government has made progress on preventing such attacks, it is simply not paying consistent and urgent attention to the means of responding quickly and effectively so that they no longer constitute a threat of mass destruction. The failures did not begin with the current group of leaders. Each of the last three Administrations has been slow to recognize and respond to the biothreat. The difference is that the danger has grown to the point that we no longer have the luxury of a slow learning curve. The clock is ticking, and time is running out.

Failure to Understand Nature of Biothreat

The evolution of the nature of the threat is nowhere more pronounced than in the area of biological weapons. A revolution in biotechnology continues, expanding potentially dangerous dual-use capabilities across the globe. As the delayed response to H1N1 has demonstrated, the United States is woefully behind in its capability to rapidly produce vaccines and therapeutics, essential steps for adequately responding to a biological threat, whether natural or man-made.

H1N1 came with months of warning. But even with time to prepare, the epidemic peaked before most Americans had access to vaccine. A bioattack will come with no such warning. Response is a complex series of links in a chain of resilience necessary to protect the United States from biological attacks. Rapid detection and diagnosis capabilities are the first links, followed by providing actionable information to federal, state, and local leaders and the general public; having adequate supplies of appropriate medical countermeasures; quickly distributing those countermeasures; treating and isolating the sick in medical facilities; protecting the well through vaccines and prophylactic medications; and in certain cases, such as anthrax, environmental cleanup. We conclude that virtually all links are weak, and require the highest priority of attention from the Administration and Congress.

H1N1 came with months of warning. But even with time to prepare, the epidemic peaked before most Americans had access to vaccine. A bioattack will come with no such warning.

The Chair and Vice Chair believe that this lack of preparedness and a consistent lack of action, even on fundamental issues like provision of adequate high-level expertise and investment in medical countermeasures, is a symptom of a failure of the U.S. government to grasp the threat of biological weapons.

Whereas the Obama Administration has demonstrated a keen understanding of the nuclear threat and has set in motion a series of policies that all hope will bear fruit, there has been no equal sense of urgency displayed towards the threat of a large-scale biological weapons attack.

Positive Strides to Address Nuclear Threat

President Obama has undertaken substantial effort to bolster the nonproliferation regime. From his April 2009 speech in Prague to his chairmanship of a United Nations Security Council meeting on the subject and plans for a Global Summit on Nuclear Security, he is attempting to bend current trend lines.

We have some concerns in the nuclear arena, particularly regarding the Administration's failure to prevent the lapse of verification mechanisms established under the START treaty. Ensuring their continuation was very important and insufficient attention was paid to it.

The U.S. government has placed priority on Iran and North Korea, and much attention and resources have been spent on Pakistan, but progress has been slow. The Chair and Vice Chair are gravely concerned about these regions. Recognizing the limited leverage the United States has in addressing them and the time-consuming nature of diplomacy, as the Administration works to deepen global resolve to act, we underscore the unacceptable consequences of failure.

The U.S. government must strengthen the nonproliferation regime, develop more effective policies to eliminate terrorist havens in Pakistan, and galvanize allies to stop the Iranian and North Korean nuclear weapons programs.

Failure on Government Reform and Building a National Security Workforce

As former members of the U.S. Senate, the Chair and Vice Chair are enormously frustrated at the inability of Congress to reform its own oversight of the nation's homeland security agency.

The Chair and Vice Chair recognize the immense domestic challenges faced by Congress and the new Administration over the past year, including the financial crisis and health care reform, but believes that there should have been room for the structural procedures necessary to face the critical national security issue of protecting Americans from WMD threats.

As an independent branch of the U.S. government, Congress has an essential role to play in ensuring our national security—through authorization, appropriation, and oversight. It is essential to the safety of the American citizen that these functions are carried out competently.

For instance, the authorization, appropriation, and oversight for the U.S. Department of Homeland Security (DHS) are spread across more than 80 committees and subcommittees. This ensures that Congress will continue to lack a deep understanding of the important and interrelated security and intelligence policy issues that face the nation. This fragmentation guarantees that much of what Congress does will be duplicative and disjointed.

The authorization, appropriation, and oversight for DHS are spread across more than 80 committees and subcommittees. This ensures that Congress will continue to lack a deep understanding of the important and interrelated security and intelligence policy issues that face the nation.

Oversight of DHS should be removed from legacy committees and focused within the House and Senate Homeland Security Committees.

The refusal of Congress, as the nation's elected representatives, to pull congressional authority together into one coherent oversight body is both self-serving and conspicuous, suggesting that individual concerns for "turf" supersede the legislature's willingness to assume responsibility to ensure national security.

Although the executive branch has made improvements in integrating the efforts of various departments and agencies, much work remains, as demonstrated by the Detroit-bound flight on Christmas Day. That thwarted attack exposed not only the inability of various intelligence agencies to provide protection, but also the inability of Congress to provide oversight.

In addition, both the Administration and Congress are well aware of the need to substantially improve how our federal departments, agencies, and the national laboratories hire and retain highly skilled personnel. The aging of our national security workforce has been a growing problem for over a decade, and yet little has been done by either branch of government.

If these long-standing deficiencies in executive agency operations and congressional oversight of homeland security, intelligence, and other crosscutting 21st century issues are not corrected, the United States will remain woefully underprepared to respond to the growing WMD threat.

The Commission emphasized in World at Risk that there is a vital connection between the process of making decisions and decisions made, or not made. In other words, if the process is balkanized; if there are no "integrators" to make sure agencies or committees work together; if experienced, senior officials are not put into the crucial positions, then the people can expect that little or nothing will be done—despite the good will of top authorities.

Progress on Citizen and Community Preparedness

A well-informed, organized, and engaged citizenry remains the country's greatest resource. The federal government has made some progress in supporting the development of preparedness and resilience of state and local governments, business and non-profit communities, and individual citizens. Efforts, such as development of a checklist that citizens can use to ensure the readiness of their local governments, need to be expanded to ensure that all communities and citizens are prepared in the event of a WMD attack.[54]

Conclusion

The expertise, technology, and material needed to build the most deadly weapons known to mankind—including chemical, biological, radiological, and nuclear weapons —are spreading inexorably. If our enemies acquire these weapons, they are likely to try to use them. The consequences of such an attack could be far more devastating than those we suffered on September 11— a chemical, biological, radiological, or nuclear terrorist attack in the United States could cause large numbers of casualties, mass psychological disruption, contamination and significant economic damage, and could overwhelm local medical capabilities.[55]

Questions

1. How are the effects of a biological attack significantly different than a chemical or nuclear attack?
2. How could a catastrophic attack on U.S. agriculture potentially cripple the nation?
3. How has Bio-Watch proven ineffective?
4. How does DHS help state and local governments prepare for potential WMD attack?
5. Assess post-9/11 efforts to protect the U.S. from WMD threats.

Chapter 18

Emergency Preparedness & Response

Objectives

- Understand the purpose and evolution of the National Response Framework (NRF).
- Understand the purpose and function of Emergency Support Functions (ESFs).
- Understand the purpose and function of the National Incident Management System (NIMS).
- Understand the purpose and function of the National Exercise Program (NEP).
- Explain the relation between NRF, NIMS, and NEP.

"We must prepare to minimize the damage and recover from any future terrorist attacks that may occur despite our best efforts at prevention. Past experience has shown that preparedness efforts are key to providing an effective response to major terrorist incidents and natural disasters. Therefore, we need a comprehensive national system to bring together and command all necessary response assets quickly and effectively. We must equip, train, and exercise many different response units to mobilize for any emergency without warning. Under the President's proposal, the Department of Homeland Security, building on the strong foundation already laid by the Federal Emergency Management Agency (FEMA), will lead our national efforts to create and employ a system that will improve our response to all disasters, both manmade and natural."

— *Critical Mission Area #5, National Strategy for Homeland Security, July 2002*

Introduction

In a serious emergency, the federal government augments state and local response efforts. FEMA, a key component of the Department of Homeland Security, provides funding and command and control support. A number of important specialized federal emergency response assets that are housed in various departments also fall under the Secretary of Homeland Security's authority for responding to a major terrorist attack. Because response efforts to all major incidents entail the same basic elements, it is essential that federal response capabilities for both terrorist attacks and natural disasters remain in the same organization. This ensures the most efficient provision of federal support to local responders by preventing the proliferation of duplicative "boutique" response entities.[1]

The 2002 National Strategy for Homeland Security set a goal to enhance capabilities for responding to a terrorist attack all across the country. Initially, many geographic areas had little or no capability to respond to a terrorist attack using weapons of mass destruction. Even the best prepared states and localities did not possess adequate resources to respond to the full range of terrorist threats we face. Many did not have in place mutual aid agreements to facilitate cooperation with their neighbors in time of emergency. Until recently, federal support for domestic preparedness efforts had been relatively small and disorganized, with eight different departments and agencies providing money in a tangled web of grant programs.

From the outset, one of the major objectives for the Department of Homeland Security was to create a fully integrated national emergency response system that is adaptable enough to deal with any terrorist attack, no matter how unlikely or catastrophic, as well as all manner of natural disasters. Among the first tasks of DHS was to consolidate federal response plans and build a national system for incident management. The Department would aim to ensure that leaders at all levels of government have complete incident awareness and can communicate with and command all appropriate response personnel. Federal, state, and local governments ensure that all response personnel and organizations—including law enforcement, military, emergency response, health care, public works, and environmental communities—are properly equipped, trained, and exercised to respond to all terrorist threats and attacks in the United States.[2]

National Response Framework

The Robert T. Stafford Disaster Relief and Emergency Assistance Act (Stafford Act) establishes the programs and processes by which the federal government provides emergency and major disaster assistance to states and localities, individuals, and qualified private nonprofit organizations. Section 611 of the Stafford Act authorizes the Director of FEMA to prepare federal response plans and programs and to coordinate these plans with state efforts. Consistent with this authorization, FEMA released the Federal Response Plan in April 1992. The primary purpose of the Federal Response Plan was to maximize the availability of federal resources to support response and recovery efforts taken by state and local emergency officials.

After the terrorist attacks of September 11, Congress passed the Homeland Security Act of 2002 (P.L. 107-296). Subsection 502(6) required the consolidation of "existing federal government emergency response plans into a single, coordinated national response plan." The Homeland Security Act also created DHS, consolidating over 20 agencies, including FEMA, into a single department. Under DHS, FEMA retained both its authority to administer the provisions of the Stafford Act and its designation as the lead agency for the nation's response plan.

The Robert T. Stafford Disaster Relief and Emergency Assistance Act establishes the programs and processes by which the federal government provides emergency and major disaster assistance to states and localities.

On February 28, 2003, President Bush issued HSPD-5. Section 16 of HSPD-5 directed the Secretary to develop and submit for review to the Homeland Security Council a national response plan. Section 16 also mandated that the plan use an "all discipline" and "all-hazards" approach in preparing for, responding to, and recovering from domestic incidents. In December 2004, through the primary guidance and authorization of the Stafford Act, the Homeland Security Act, and HSPD-5, DHS issued a successor to the Federal Response Plan, which was entitled the National Response Plan (NRP).[3]

The NRP was in place and implemented for the Hurricane Katrina response in August 2005. The problems that arose from Hurricane Katrina prompted numerous studies. Some of these studies attributed the poor response, in part, to the implementation of the NRP. Concerned by perceived deficiencies in the NRP, Congress sought a remedy through legislation in the Post- Katrina Act. The Post-Katrina Act provides the most comprehensive legislation concerning the NRP (or any subsequent plans) by mandating numerous adjustments to the NRP as well as mechanisms for oversight. Section 642 amended the Stafford Act and the Homeland Security Act to mandate that the President develop a national preparedness system. Section 643 further establishes that the President shall, through the Administrator of FEMA "complete, revise, and update, as necessary, a national preparedness goal... to ensure the Nation's ability to prevent, respond to, recover from, and mitigate against natural disasters, acts of terrorism, and other manmade disasters." It further states that the national preparedness goal, to the extent possible, should be consistent with NIMS and the NRP.

Section 649(b) of the Post-Katrina Act requires that the national preparedness goal, NIMS, and the NRP be subjected to clear and quantifiable performance measures to ensure they are continuously revised and updated. Section 652 of the act establishes annual reporting requirements concerning preparedness capabilities. Section 652(c) requires the reporting of state compliance with the NRP. Finally, Section 653 requires the president to ensure that federal agencies assigned with responsibilities in the NRP have the capability to meet the national preparedness goal, and develop plans to "respond effectively to natural disasters, acts of terrorism, and other man-made disasters in support of the National Response Plan to ensure a coordinated federal response."

In response to the Post-Katrina legislation and perceived problems with the implementation of the NRP, DHS revised the plan and issued the NRF. In January 2008, DHS issued the NRF,[4] which took effect in March 2008. Since that time, the NRF has been the nation's core response document, providing a structure for the response to such disasters as the 2008 Midwest floods and California wildfires, as well as Hurricanes Gustav and Ike.[5]

NRF Overview

The National Response Framework provides the doctrine and guiding principles for a unified response from all levels of government, and all sectors of communities, to all types of hazards regardless of their origin.

The NRF is part of a national strategy for homeland security. It provides the doctrine and guiding principles for a unified response from all levels of government, and all sectors of communities, to all types of hazards regardless of their origin. Although the primary focus of the NRF is on response and short-term recovery, the document also defines the roles and responsibilities of the various actors involved in all phases of emergency management. The NRF is not an operational plan that dictates a step-by-step process for responding to hazards. Rather, the NRF appears to be an attempt to build flexibility into response efforts by setting up a framework that DHS believes is necessary for responding to hazards. Within this framework, the NRF gives users a degree of discretion as to how they choose to respond to the incident.[6]

The National Response Framework is a guide to how the Nation conducts all-hazards response. It is built upon scalable, flexible, and adaptable coordinating structures to align key roles and responsibilities across the Nation. It describes specific authorities and best practices for managing incidents that range from the serious but purely local, to large-scale terrorist attacks or catastrophic natural disasters.

The term "response" includes immediate actions to save lives, protect property and the environment, and meet basic human needs. Response also includes the execution of emergency plans and actions to support short-term recovery. The Framework is always in effect, and elements can be implemented as needed on a flexible, scalable basis to improve response.[7]

The responsibility for responding to incidents, both natural and manmade, begins at the local level – with individuals and public officials in the county, city, or town affected by the incident. Local leaders and emergency managers prepare their communities to manage incidents locally. The Framework's response doctrine plays a key role in helping community leaders to coordinate resources within jurisdictions, among adjacent jurisdictions, and with the private sector and non-government organizations (NGOs) such as the American Red Cross.[8]

A primary role of State government is to supplement and facilitate local efforts before, during, and after incidents. The State provides direct and routine assistance to its local jurisdictions through emergency management program development and by routinely coordinating these efforts with Federal officials. States must be prepared to maintain or accelerate the provision of commodities and services to local governments when local capabilities fall short of demands.

Under the Framework, the term "State" and discussion of the roles and responsibilities of States typically also include similar responsibilities that apply to U.S. territories and possessions and tribal governments. Under the Stafford Act, States are also responsible for requesting Federal emergency assistance for communities and tribal governments within their jurisdiction. In response to an incident, the State helps coordinate and integrate resources and applies them to local needs.[9]

When an incident occurs that exceeds or is anticipated to exceed local or State resources – or when an incident is managed by Federal departments or agencies acting under their own authorities – the Federal Government uses the Framework to involve all necessary department and agency capabilities, organize the Federal response, and ensure coordination with response partners.

Overall coordination of Federal response activities is implemented through the Secretary of Homeland Security consistent with HSPD-5.

The President leads the Federal Government response effort to ensure that the necessary coordinating structures, leadership, and resources are applied quickly and efficiently to large-scale and catastrophic incidents. The President's Homeland Security Council and National Security Council, which bring together Cabinet officers and other department or agency heads as necessary, provide national strategic and policy advice to the President during large-scale incidents that affect the Nation.

Federal disaster assistance is often thought of as synonymous with Presidential declarations and the Stafford Act. The fact is that Federal assistance can be provided to State, tribal, and local jurisdictions, and to other Federal departments and agencies, in a number of different ways through various mechanisms and authorities. Often, Federal assistance does not require coordination by DHS and can be provided without a Presidential major disaster or emergency declaration. Examples of these types of Federal assistance include that described in the National Oil and Hazardous Substances Pollution Contingency Plan, the Mass Migration Emergency Plan, the National Search and Rescue Plan, and the National Maritime Security Plan. These and other supplemental agency or interagency plans, compacts, and agreements may be implemented concurrently with the Framework, but are subordinated to its overarching coordinating structures, processes, and protocols.

When the overall coordination of Federal response activities is required, it is implemented through the Secretary of Homeland Security consistent with HSPD-5. Other Federal departments and agencies carry out their response authorities and responsibilities within this overarching construct.[10]

Requesting Federal Assistance

When it is clear that State capabilities will be exceeded, the Governor can request Federal assistance, including assistance under the Stafford Act. The Stafford Act authorizes the President to provide financial and other assistance to State and local governments, certain private nonprofit organizations, and individuals to support response, recovery, and mitigation efforts following Presidential emergency or major disaster declarations.

Ordinarily, only a Governor can initiate a request for a Presidential emergency or major disaster declaration. In extraordinary circumstances, the President may unilaterally declare a major disaster or emergency. This request is made through the FEMA Regional Administrator and based on a finding that the disaster is of such severity and magnitude that effective response is beyond the capabilities of the State and affected local governments, and that Federal assistance is necessary.

The completed request, addressed to the President, is submitted through the FEMA Regional Administrator, who evaluates the damage and requirements for Federal assistance and makes a recommendation to the FEMA Administrator. The FEMA Administrator, acting through the Secretary of Homeland Security, may then recommend a course of action to the President. The Governor, appropriate Members of Congress, and Federal departments and agencies are immediately notified of a Presidential declaration.[11]

When it is clear that State capabilities will be exceeded, the Governor can request Federal assistance, including assistance under the Stafford Act.

The Stafford Act is triggered by a Presidential declaration of a major disaster or emergency.[12] If declared, funding comes from the President's Disaster Relief Fund, which is managed by FEMA, and the disaster aid programs of other participating Federal departments and agencies. A Presidential major disaster declaration triggers long-term Federal recovery programs, some of which are matched by State programs, and designed to help disaster victims, businesses, and public entities. An emergency declaration is more limited in scope and without the long-term Federal recovery programs of a major disaster declaration. Generally, Federal assistance and funding are provided to meet a specific emergency need or to help prevent a major disaster from occurring.[13]

In many cases, assistance may be obtained from the Federal Government without a Presidential declaration. For example, FEMA places liaisons in State EOCs and moves commodities near incident sites that may require Federal assistance prior to a Presidential declaration. Additionally, some types of assistance, such as Fire Management Assistance Grants – which provide support to States experiencing severe wildfires – are performed by Federal departments or agencies under their own authorities and do not require Presidential approval. Finally, Federal departments and agencies may provide immediate lifesaving assistance to States under their own statutory authorities without a formal Presidential declaration.[14]

Responding Federal departments and agencies respect the sovereignty and responsibilities of local, tribal, and State governments while rendering assistance. The intention of the Federal Government in these situations is not to command the response, but rather to support the affected local, tribal, and/or State governments.[15]

NRF Response

The DHS National Operations Center (NOC) serves as the national fusion center, collecting and synthesizing all-source information, including information from State fusion centers, across all-threats and all-hazards information covering the spectrum of homeland security partners. Federal departments and agencies report information regarding actual or potential incidents requiring a coordinated Federal response to the NOC.[16]

The primary reporting method for information flow is the Homeland Security Information Network (HSIN). Additionally, there are threat reporting mechanisms in place through the FBI where information is assessed for credibility and possible criminal investigation.[17]

When notified of a threat or an incident that potentially requires a coordinated Federal response, the NOC evaluates the information and notifies appropriate senior Federal officials and Federal operations centers: the FEMA National Response Coordination Center (NRCC), the FBI Strategic Information Operations Center (SIOC), the National Counterterrorism Center (NCTC), and the National Military Command Center (NMCC). The NOC serves as the primary coordinating center for these and other operations centers.[18]

The Stafford Act is triggered by a Presidential declaration of a major disaster or emergency.

After being notified, departments and agencies should:

- Identify and mobilize staff to fulfill their department's or agency's responsibilities, including identifying appropriate subject-matter experts and other staff to support department operations centers.
- Identify staff for deployment to the NOC, the NRCC, FEMA Regional Response Coordination Centers (RRCCs), or other operations centers as needed, such as the FBI's Joint Operations Center. These organizations have standard procedures and call-down lists, and will notify department or agency points of contact if deployment is necessary.
- Identify staff that can be dispatched to the Joint Field Office (JFO), including Federal officials representing those departments and agencies with specific authorities, lead personnel for the JFO Sections (Operations, Planning, Logistics, and Administration and Finance) and the ESFs.
- Begin activating and staging Federal teams and other resources in support of the Federal response as requested by DHS or in accordance with department or agency authorities.
- Execute pre-scripted mission assignments and readiness contracts, as directed by DHS.[19]

The FEMA Regional Administrator deploys a liaison to the State Emergency Operations Center (SEOC) to provide technical assistance and also activates the Regional Response Coordination Center. Federal department and agency personnel, including Emergency Support function (ESF) primary and support agency personnel, staff the RRCC as required. The RRCCs:

- Coordinate initial regional and field activities.

- In coordination with State, tribal, and local officials, deploy regional teams to assess the impact of the event, gauge immediate State needs, and make preliminary arrangements to set up operational field facilities.
- Coordinate Federal support until a Joint Field Office (JFO) is established.
- Establish a Joint Information Center (JIC) to provide a central point for coordinating emergency public information activities.

In coordination with the RRCC and the State, FEMA may deploy an Incident Management Assistance Team (IMAT). IMATs are interagency teams composed of subject-matter experts and incident management professionals. IMAT personnel may be drawn from national or regional Federal department and agency staff according to established protocols. IMAT teams make preliminary arrangements to set up Federal field facilities and initiate establishment of the Joint Field Office.[20]

Emergency Support Functions

FEMA coordinates response support from across the Federal Government and certain NGOs by calling up, as needed, one or more of 15 Emergency Support Functions.

FEMA coordinates response support from across the Federal Government and certain NGOs by calling up, as needed, one or more of 15 Emergency Support Functions. The ESFs are coordinated by FEMA through its NRCC. During a response, ESFs are a critical mechanism to coordinate functional capabilities and resources provided by Federal departments and agencies, along with certain private-sector and nongovernmental organizations. They represent an effective way to bundle and funnel resources and capabilities to local, tribal, State, and other responders. These functions are coordinated by a single agency but may rely on several agencies that provide resources for each functional area. The mission of the ESFs is to provide the greatest possible access to capabilities of the Federal Government regardless of which agency has those capabilities.

The ESFs serve as the primary operational-level mechanism to provide assistance in functional areas such as transportation, communications, public works and engineering, firefighting, mass care, housing, human services, public health and medical services, search and rescue, agriculture and natural resources, and energy.[21]

Each ESF is comprised of a coordinator and primary and support agencies. The Framework identifies primary agencies on the basis of authorities, resources, and capabilities. Support agencies are assigned based on resources and capabilities in a given functional area. The resources provided by the ESFs are consistent with resource-typing categories identified in the NIMS.

ESFs may be selectively activated for both Stafford Act and non-Stafford Act incidents under circumstances as defined in HSPD-5. Not all incidents requiring Federal support result in the activation of ESFs. FEMA can deploy assets and capabilities through ESFs into an area in anticipation of an approaching storm or event that is expected to cause a significant impact and result. This coordination through ESFs allows FEMA to position Federal support for a quick response, though actual assistance cannot normally be provided until

#	ESF	Coordinator
1	Transportation	Dept. Transportation
2	Communications	DHS
3	Public Works & Engineering	Army Corps of Engineers
4	Firefighting	US Forest Service
5	Emergency Management	FEMA
6	Mass Care, Emergency Assistance, Housing, & Human Services	FEMA
7	Logistics Management & Resource Support	General Services Administration & DHS
8	Public Health & Medical Services	Dept. Health & Human Services
9	Search & Rescue	FEMA
10	Oil & Hazardous Materials Response	Environmental Protection Agency
11	Agriculture & Natural Resources	Dept. Agriculture
12	Energy	Dept. Energy
13	Public Safety & Security	Dept. Justice
14	Long-Term Community Recovery	FEMA
15	External Affairs	DHS

Table 18.1: NRF Emergency Support Functions

the Governor requests and receives a Presidential major disaster or emergency declaration. Many States have also organized an ESF structure along this approach.

When ESFs are activated, they may have a headquarters, regional, and field presence. At FEMA headquarters, the ESFs support decisionmaking and coordination of field operations within the NRCC. The ESFs deliver a broad range of technical support and other services at the regional level in the Regional Response Coordination Centers, and in the Joint Field Office and Incident Command Posts, as required by the incident. At all levels, FEMA issues mission assignments to obtain resources and capabilities from across the ESFs in support of the State.

The ESFs plan and support response activities. At the headquarters, regional, and field levels, ESFs provide staff to support the incident command sections for operations, planning, logistics, and finance/administration, as requested. The incident command structure enables the ESFs to work collaboratively. For example, if a State requests assistance with a mass evacuation, the Joint Field Office would request personnel from ESF #1 (Transportation), ESF #6 (Mass Care, Emergency Assistance, Housing, and Human Services), and ESF #8 (Public Health and Medical Services). These would then be integrated into a single branch or group within the Operations Section to ensure effective coordination of evacuation services. The same structures are used to organize ESF response at the field, regional, and headquarters levels.

To support an effective response, all ESFs are required to have both strategic and more-detailed operational plans that include all participating organizations and engage the private sector and NGOs as appropriate. The ongoing support, coordination, and integration of ESFs and their work are core responsibilities of FEMA in its response leadership role for DHS.[22]

NRF Review

Several emergencies and disasters have taken place since implementation of the NRF. In general, responses to the NRF have been mixed. Some have indicated that its implementation has been successful. One observer stated that coordination among federal, state, and local governments has improved. In the case of Hurricanes Gustav and Ike, officials in Texas related that the federal response to the hurricanes was good. Other officials have been ambivalent regarding the NRF's implementation, noting that the scale of recent disasters has not warranted enough federal involvement to understand how well the NRF works.

A review of various reports may hint at some problems, however. For instance, during Hurricanes Gustav and Ike, state officials in Texas said it was the local government's responsibility to set up distribution points for supplies. However, the local government claimed it was unaware of this responsibility. Such confusion may indicate that the NRF still does not clearly articulate the roles and responsibilities of state and local governments during emergencies and disasters.[23]

The National Incident Management System provides standard command and management structures that apply to response activities.

National Incident Management System

The National Incident Management System (NIMS) is a companion to the National Response Framework that provides standard command and management structures that apply to response activities. This system provides a consistent, nationwide template to enable Federal, State, tribal, and local governments, the private sector, and NGOs to work together to prepare for, prevent, respond to, recover from, and mitigate the effects of incidents regardless of cause, size, location, or complexity. This consistency provides the foundation for utilization of the NIMS for all incidents, ranging from daily occurrences to incidents requiring a coordinated Federal response.[24]

Much of NIMS is built upon Incident Command System (ICS), which was developed by the Federal, State, and local wildland fire agencies during the 1970s. ICS is normally structured to facilitate activities in five major functional areas: command, operations, planning, logistics, and finance/administration. In some circumstances, intelligence and investigations may be added as a sixth functional area.[25]

ICS is a management system designed to enable effective incident management by integrating a combination of facilities, equipment, personnel, procedures and communications operating within a common organizational structure. A basic strength of ICS is that it is already widely adopted. It is used to organize both near-term and long-term field-level operations for a broad spectrum of incidents.[26]

The Incident Commander is the individual responsible for all response activities, including the development of strategies and tactics and the ordering and release of resources. The Incident Commander has overall authority and responsibility for conducting incident operations and is responsible for the management of all incident operations at the incident site. When multiple command authorities are involved, the incident may be led by a unified command comprised of officials who have jurisdictional authority or functional responsibility for the incident under an appropriate law, ordinance, or agreement. The unified command provides direct, on-scene control of tactical operations.

At the tactical level, on-scene incident command and management organization are located at an Incident Command Post, which is typically comprised of local and mutual aid responders.

If the Incident Commander determines that additional resources or capabilities are needed, he or she will contact the local Emergency Operations Center (EOC) and relay requirements to the local emergency manager. Local EOCs are the physical locations where multiagency coordination occurs. EOCs help form a common operating picture of the incident, relieve on-scene command of the burden of external coordination, and secure additional resources. The core functions of an EOC include coordination, communications, resource allocation and tracking, and information collection, analysis, and dissemination.[27]

EOCs may be permanent organizations and facilities that are staffed 24 hours a day, 7 days a week, or they may be established to meet short-term needs. Standing EOCs (or those activated to support larger, more complex incidents) are typically established in a central or permanently established facility. Such permanent facilities in larger communities are typically directed by a full-time emergency manager. EOCs may be organized by major discipline (fire, law enforcement, medical services, etc.), by jurisdiction (city, county, region, etc.), by Emergency Support Function (communications, public works, engineering, transportation, resource support, etc.) or, more likely, by some combination thereof.

The Incident Commander has overall authority and responsibility for conducting incident operations and is responsible for the management of all incident operations at the incident site.

During an incident, the local emergency manager ensures the EOC is staffed to support the incident command and arranges needed resources. The chief elected or appointed official provides policy direction and supports the Incident Commander and emergency manager, as needed.

State EOCs are the physical location where multiagency coordination occurs. Every State maintains an EOC configured to expand as necessary to manage events requiring State-level assistance.

The local incident command structure directs on-scene emergency management activities and maintains command and control of on-scene incident operations. State EOCs are activated as necessary to support local EOCs. Therefore, the State EOC is the central location from which off-scene activities supported by the State are coordinated. Chief elected and appointed officials are located at the State EOC, as well as personnel supporting core functions. The key function of State EOC personnel is to ensure that those who are located at the scene have the resources (e.g., personnel, tools, and equipment) they need for the response.[28]

The Governor is responsible for requesting Federal assistance for incidents within his or her State. The Governor of the affected State appoints a State

Coordinating Officer (SCO), and lines of authority flow from the Governor to the SCO, following the State's policies and laws. The SCO plays a critical role in managing the State response and recovery operations following Stafford Act declarations. For certain anticipated events in which a Stafford Act declaration is expected, such as an approaching hurricane, the Secretary of Homeland Security or the FEMA Administrator may pre-designate one or more Federal officials to coordinate with the SCO to determine resources and actions that will likely be required, and begin deployment of assets.

Overall, Federal incident support to the State is generally coordinated through a Joint Field Office (JFO). The JFO provides the means to integrate diverse Federal resources and engage directly with the State. Using unified command principles, a Unified Coordination Group comprised of senior officials from the State and key Federal departments and agencies is established at the JFO. This group of senior officials provides the breadth of national support to achieve shared objectives.[29]

Overall, Federal incident support to the State is generally coordinated through a Joint Field Office.

The Joint Field Office is the primary Federal incident management field structure. The JFO is a temporary Federal facility that provides a central location for the coordination of Federal, State, tribal, and local governments and private-sector and nongovernmental organizations with primary responsibility for response and recovery. Although the JFO uses an ICS structure, the JFO does not manage on-scene operations. Instead, the JFO focuses on providing support to on-scene efforts and conducting broader support operations that may extend beyond the incident site.

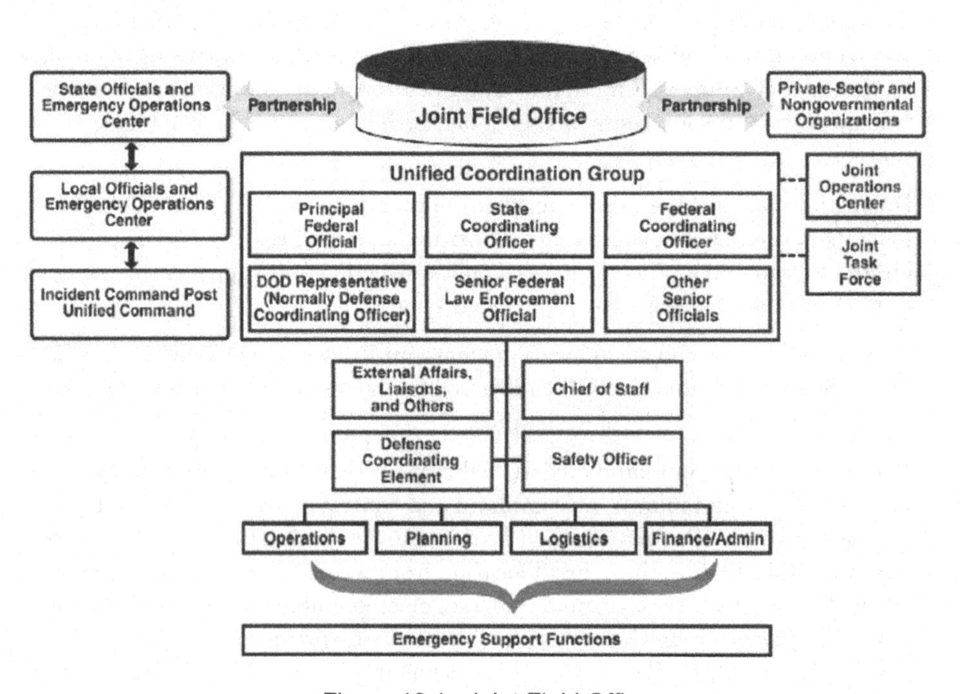

Figure 18.1: Joint Field Office

Personnel from Federal and State departments and agencies, other jurisdictional entities, the private sector, and NGOs may be requested to staff various levels of the JFO, depending on the requirements of the incident. When incidents impact the entire Nation or multiple States or localities, multiple JFOs may be established. As the primary field structure, the JFO provides the organizing structure to integrate diverse Federal authorities and capabilities and coordinate Federal response and recovery operations.[30]

The JFO is led by the Unified Coordination Group, which is comprised of specified senior leaders representing State and Federal interests, and in certain circumstances tribal governments, local jurisdictions, the private sector, or nongovernmental organizations. The Unified Coordination Group typically consists of the FEMA Federal Coordinating Officer (FCO), State Coordinating Officer, and senior officials from other entities with primary statutory or jurisdictional responsibility and significant operational responsibility for an aspect of an incident (e.g., the Senior Health Official, Department of Defense representative, or Senior Federal Law Enforcement Official if assigned). Within the Unified Coordination Group, the FCO is the primary Federal official responsible for coordinating, integrating, and synchronizing Federal response activities.[31]

The Federal Coordinating Officer executes Stafford Act authorities, including commitment of FEMA resources and the mission assignment of other Federal departments or agencies via ESFs.

For Stafford Act incidents (i.e., emergencies or major disasters), upon the recommendation of the FEMA Administrator and the Secretary of Homeland Security, the President appoints an FCO. The FCO is a senior FEMA official trained, certified, and well experienced in emergency management, and specifically appointed to coordinate Federal support in the response to and recovery from emergencies and major disasters. The FCO executes Stafford Act authorities, including commitment of FEMA resources and the mission assignment of other Federal departments or agencies via ESFs. If a major disaster or emergency declaration covers a geographic area that spans all or parts of more than one State, the President may decide to appoint a single FCO for the entire incident, with other individuals as needed serving as Deputy FCOs.

In all cases, the FCO represents the FEMA Administrator in the field to discharge all FEMA responsibilities for the response and recovery efforts underway. For Stafford Act events, the FCO is the primary Federal representative with whom the SCO and other State, tribal, and local response officials interface to determine the most urgent needs and set objectives for an effective response in collaboration with the Unified Coordination Group.

In Stafford Act incidents, the FCO is the focal point of coordination within the Unified Coordination Group, ensuring overall integration of Federal emergency management, resource allocation, and seamless integration of Federal activities in support of, and in coordination with, State, tribal, and local requirements.[32]

In non-Stafford Act situations, when a Federal department or agency acting under its own authority has requested the assistance of the Secretary of Homeland Security to obtain support from other Federal departments and agencies, DHS may designate a Federal Resource Coordinator (FRC). In these situations, the FRC coordinates support through interagency agreements and memorandums of understanding. Relying on the same skill set, DHS may select the FRC from the FCO cadre or other personnel with equivalent knowledge, skills, and abilities. The FRC is responsible for coordinating timely delivery of resources to the requesting agency.

Meanwhile, DoD has appointed 10 Defense Coordinating Officers (DCOs) and assigned one to each FEMA region. If requested and approved, the DCO serves as DoD's single point of contact at the Joint Field Office for requesting assistance from DoD. With few exceptions, requests for Defense Support of Civil Authorities (DSCA) originating at the JFO are coordinated with and processed through the DCO. The DCO may have a Defense Coordinating Element consisting of a staff and military liaison officers to facilitate coordination and support to activated Emergency Support Functions.

Specific responsibilities of the DCO (subject to modification based on the situation) include processing requirements for military support, forwarding mission assignments to the appropriate military organizations through DoD-designated channels, and assigning military liaisons, as appropriate, to activated ESFs.

With few exceptions, requests for Defense Support of Civil Authorities (DSCA) originating at the JFO are coordinated with and processed through the Defense Coordinating Officer.

The Senior Federal Law Enforcement Officer (SFLEO) is an official appointed by the Attorney General during an incident requiring a coordinated Federal response to coordinate all law enforcement, public safety, and security operations with intelligence or investigative law enforcement operations directly related to the incident. The SFLEO is a member of the Unified Coordination Group and, as such, is responsible to ensure that allocation of law enforcement requirements and resource allocations are coordinated as appropriate with all other members of the Group. In the event of a terrorist incident, the SFLEO will normally be a senior FBI official who has coordinating authority over all law enforcement activities related to the incident, both those falling within the Attorney General's explicit authority as recognized in HSPD-5 and those otherwise directly related to the incident itself.

Based on the complexity and type of incident, and the anticipated level of Department of Defense resource involvement, DoD may elect to designate a Joint Task Force to command Federal (Title 10) military activities in support of the incident objectives. If a JTF is established, consistent with operational requirements, its command and control element will be co-located with the senior on-scene leadership at the Joint Field Office to ensure coordination and unity of effort. The co-location of the JTF command and control element does not replace the requirement for a DCO/Defense Coordinating Element as part of the JFO Unified Coordination Staff. The DCO remains the DOD single point of contact in the JFO for requesting assistance from DoD.[33]

The JTF Commander exercises operational control of Federal military personnel and most defense resources in a Federal response. Some DoD entities, such as the U.S. Army Corps of Engineers, may respond under separate established authorities and do not provide support under the operational control of a JTF Commander. Unless federalized, National Guard forces remain under the control of a State Governor. Close coordination between Federal military, other DoD entities, and National Guard forces in a response is critical.

Based on the scope and nature of an incident, senior officials from other Federal departments and agencies, State, tribal, or local governments, and the private sector or NGOs may participate in a Unified Coordination Group. Usually, the larger and more complex the incident, the greater the number of entities represented.[34]

National Exercise Program

While training and exercises are longstanding components of government preparedness efforts, a program of national exercises that attempts to coordinate and synchronize federal exercise activities, and incorporate state, territorial, local, and tribal governments and the private sector, arguably has emerged only in the past decade. A product of congressional and executive branch mandates, the program appears to have been motivated in part by perceived shortcomings in previous exercise efforts as well as deficiencies perceived in response to actual incidents.[35]

Impetus for an exercise of national scope came in 1998. The Senate Committee on Appropriations, noting that "few of the top officials of agencies have ever fully participated" in ongoing preparedness exercises, directed in report language "that an exercise be conducted in fiscal year 1999 with the participation of all key personnel who would participate in the consequence management of ... an actual terrorist event." The result was the Top Officials (TOPOFF) exercise, the first of what was to be a series of four full-scale simulation exercises. The series appears to have been a de facto national program of exercises held biennially to "assess the nation's crisis and consequence management capacity under extraordinary conditions." TOPOFF exercises enabled high level federal officials and relevant participants to "practice different courses of action, gain and maintain situational awareness, and assemble appropriate resources."

The National Exercise Program attempts to coordinate and synchronize federal exercise activities, and incorporate state, territorial, local, and tribal governments and the private sector.

TOPOFF exercise scenarios attempted to address several objectives, and typically included several incidents occurring at multiple geographic locations. First, they were designed to reveal potential emergency response vulnerabilities so that any identified deficiencies could be addressed before an actual incident occurred. Second, TOPOFFs were used to observe how national, state, and local levels of government, as well as public and private organizations, might interact and coordinate their emergency responses. Finally, it has been pointed out that TOPOFFs might also have served other, more subtle objectives, including assuring the public of the ability of the government to respond to the results of attacks, and to communicate a message of deterrence to potential enemies.[36]

Citing paragraph 18 of HSPD-8 and section 648 of the Post-Katrina Emergency Management Reform Act, the National Exercise Program (NEP) Implementation Plan, issued in June 2008, formally establishes the NEP "under the leadership of the Secretary of Homeland Security." According to the plan, the "principal focus of the NEP is to coordinate, design and conduct a program of exercises designed for the participation of Federal department and agency principals and other key officials...." The NEP implementation plan states that the "DHS-led program required pursuant to" the Post-Katrina Emergency Management Reform Act and HSPD-8 "has been renamed the Homeland Security Exercise and Evaluation Program (HSEEP)," with the NEP serving as "the overarching exercise program directed at principals" of federal agencies and other officials "...to ensure the United States Government (USG) has a single, comprehensive exercise program." The NEP is used to examine and evaluate national policy issues and guidance, including the National Preparedness Guidelines, National Incident Management System, National Response Framework, and other related plans and strategies to provide domestic incident management, "either for terrorism or non-terrorist catastrophic events."[37]

Within the White House, the NEP is managed through an interagency process overseen by the Homeland Security Council and the National Security Council. Day-to-day coordination of the program is carried out by the White House Domestic Readiness Group exercise and evaluation policy coordinating subcommittee (DRG E&E Sub-PCC). A steering committee is responsible for staff-level coordination of the NEP. The steering committee also frames issues and recommendations for the DRG E&E Sub-PCC on exercise themes, goals, objectives, scheduling and corrective actions. The steering committee is chaired and facilitated by FEMA's National Exercise Division, with staff support provided by agencies that sit on the steering committee. HSC, NSC, and the Office of Management and Budget (OMB) participate in the steering committee in a non-voting, oversight capacity.[38]

The strategic objectives of the NEP charter are to:

- Exercise senior USG officials;
- Examine and evaluate emerging national level policy issues;
- Practice efforts to prevent, prepare for, respond to and recover from terrorist attacks, major disasters, and other emergencies in an integrated fashion from the federal level down to state, local, and private sector level; and
- Identify and correct national-level issues, while avoiding repetition of mistakes.[39]

Generally, the NEP implementation plan requires all federal executive agencies to:

- provide resource and budget support for the planning and conduct of certain NEP exercises unless specifically relieved of this requirement by both the Assistant to the President for National Security Affairs (APNSA) and the Assistant to the President for Homeland Security and Counterterrorism (APHS/CT);
- provide principal- or deputy-level support to national and principal level exercises;
- participate in the planning and conduct of certain DHS- led NEP national and regional simulation requirements;
- designate an exercise and evaluation point of contact (POC) for coordination with the NEP ESC;

- submit annually to the NEP ESC a prioritized list of exercise objectives and capabilities they wish to exercise and evaluate;
- maintain a corrective action program (CAP) that can generate input for, and track assignments from, an interagency NEP corrective action program, described below;
- report their sponsored exercise activities to a national exercise schedule;
- have an exercise participation decision process that accords priority to certain NEP events;
- and develop and report on output, outcome and efficiency measures to guide evaluation of exercise and related training programs as they relate to the NEP. The results of the report shall be submitted to OMB concurrently with the agencies' annual budget submissions.[40]

The NEP implementation plan requires the establishment of a corrective action program (NEP CAP), administered by DHS in support of HSC and NSC, to provide a government-wide process for identifying, assigning, and tracking remediation of interagency issues identified through exercises.[41]

A National Level Exercise (NLE) is an annual operations-based exercise focused on White House directed, government-wide strategy and policy-related issues.

NEP Exercises

The National Exercise Program implementation plan describes three broad categories of exercises — national level exercise (NLE), principal level exercises (PLE), and NEP classified exercises.[42]

National Level Exercise. The NEP implementation plan describes an NLE as the single, annual operations-based exercise focused on White House directed, government-wide strategy and policy-related issues. An NLE requires the participation of all appropriate department and agency principals or their deputies, other key officials, and all related staff, operations and facilities at national, regional and local levels. NLEs examine the preparation of the government and its officers and other officials to prevent, respond to, or recover from threatened or actual terrorist attacks, particularly those involving weapons of mass destruction (WMD), major disasters, and other emergencies. NLEs address strategic- and policy- level objectives intended to challenge the national preparedness of the United States. Federal executive agency exercise planning activities that support national priorities and objectives, specified in various Presidential directives, may be incorporated into NLEs. An NLE may involve all levels of federal, state, and local authorities and may involve critical private-sector entities, or international partners, as appropriate.

NLE scenarios are based on the response requirements of one of 15 National Planning Scenarios (NPS), and one of the components of the NPG. The NPS are high-consequence threat scenarios of both potential terrorist attacks and natural disasters that could necessitate emergency response. DHS argues that they are designed to focus contingency planning for homeland security preparedness work at all levels of government and the private sector.[43]

Principal Level Exercise. PLEs address emerging threats and issues requiring senior-level attention, and establish and clarify roles and responsibilities, as well as strategy and policy, for government-wide activities. The NEP includes four discussion-based PLEs per year, and requires the participation of all appropriate department and agency principals or their deputies. One PLE serves as a preparatory event for the annual NLE. The topic for one of the PLEs is not decided until the year it is conducted. DHS conducts PLEs in consultation with HSC and NSC staffs. DoD provides technical assistance, while "all other departments and agencies" provide "appropriate assistance."

NEP Classified Exercises. Some aspects of federal executive branch efforts to prevent and respond to threatened or actual terrorist attacks, major disasters, and other emergencies are national security classified, restricted to select executive agencies, and must be exercised and evaluated within the context of ongoing exercise prevention or response operations. Classified exercise activities are incorporated into some NEP exercises. The NEP implementation plan notes that classified exercises "should be a logical component of the exercise scenario and aligned with exercise objectives."[44]

Exercise Levels

The NEP categorizes exercise activities into four tiers reflecting the priority for national and regional federal interagency participation. Exercises are assigned to tiers according to a consensus interagency judgment expressed in the DRG E&E Sub-PCC of how closely they align to government-wide strategic and policy priorities. The four tiers, numbered I through IV, are as follows:

Tier I. Tier I exercises include an annual National Level Exercise and four quarterly Principal Level Exercises. The exercises are centered on White House directed, government-wide strategy and policy-related issues; federal executive agency participation is required. FEMA's National Exercise Division is the lead planning agent for the NEP Tier I exercises, unless otherwise stipulated by the Domestic Readiness Group.

Tier II. Tier II exercises include federal executive agency exercises that focus on government strategy, policy and procedural issues meriting priority for national and regional federal interagency participation. Tier II exercises may be carried out through the National Simulation Center, or as determined by a sponsoring agency's leadership. A federal executive agency that sponsors a Tier II exercise is responsible for leading the coordination, planning, conduct, and evaluation of the exercise. FEMA's National Exercise Division is responsible for coordinating federal, national interagency simulation of exercises. This may be accomplished through the National Simulation Center, or by coordinating federal regional simulation as required to support an exercise. The DRG E&E Sub-PCC shall recommend no more than three Tier II exercises each year for federal, national, and regional interagency participation.

Tier III. Tier III exercises include other federal exercises focused on regional plans, policies and procedures. The exercises may focus on operational, tactical, or organization-specific objectives that do not require broad interagency headquarters-level involvement to achieve their stated exercise or training objectives. Participation in Tier III exercises by national level assets is at the discretion of each federal executive agency. Tier II exercises take precedence over Tier III exercises in the event of resource conflicts.

Tier IV. Tier IV exercises are exercises in which state, territorial, local, or tribal governments and private sector entities are the primary audience or subject of evaluation.[45]

Exercise Scheduling

The NEP implementation plan requires the development and annual revision of a five-year schedule of exercises by the Secretary of Homeland Security, in coordination with the principals of other relevant departments and agencies. As part of an annual scheduling process, federal executive agencies may nominate an exercise for consideration as a Tier II exercise.

The NEP implementation plan appears to be unclear whether participating agencies are required to fit their entire exercise programs into the NEP framework. When they participate in NLEs, however, agencies are expected to shape their participation to fit the themes and schedules of NLE scenarios. In a preliminary example of this approach, during NLE 1-08, a Tier I exercise, TOPOFF 4 ran simultaneously with DOD- and Department of Health and Human Services (HHS)- based exercises. In NLE 2-08, a tier II exercise, two FEMA exercises, Eagle Horizon 08, designed to exercise the continuity of operations (COOP) capabilities of federal agencies in the National Capital Region (NCR), and Hurricane Prep 08, designed to test FEMA response to a hurricane, exercised under the same scenario. Both exercises incorporated some of the simulated intelligence materials established for three DOD conducted exercises held during NLE 2-08: Positive Response 08-2; Ardent Sentry 08; and Ultimate Caduceus 08.

Tier IV exercises are exercises in which state, territorial, local, or tribal governments and private sector entities are the primary audience or subject of evaluation.

Emergency management staff in DHS and DoD indicate that exercise activities carried out during FY2007 and FY2008 reflected a period of transition to the NEP. Scheduled and planned prior to the implementation of the National Exercise Schedule (NEXS) and NLE processes, the exercises were somewhat less unified in terms of exercise scenarios and objectives than those anticipated by the NEP. The individual exercise components of NLE 2-08 appear to have been carried out essentially independently by DHS and DOD components, and the extent of interactions of players from different agencies is unclear. On the other hand, some interagency coordination occurred at higher, more strategic levels. During the NLE 2-08 planning process, DOD and DHS held joint planning conferences. Further, DOD provided some logistical support to the DHS Eagle Horizon continuity exercise, which based its exercise control cell and some evaluation components at DOD's Joint Warfighting Center (JWFC). Both agencies anticipate future NLEs will be carried out according to timing specified in the NEP implementation plan, based on common exercise scenarios and coordinated response activities.[46]

Exercise Findings

Many hospitals, police and fire departments cannot meet the level of demand a disaster or large-scale emergency places on them. Maintaining facilities and staffing at a disaster level for long periods of time is unlikely since it would be cost prohibitive for most organizations. At the same time, a scalable response process capable of evolving with a disaster has not been identified by public health practitioners. Overcoming surge capacities and related workforce shortages may require additional funding or more creative resource allocation practices to develop adequate capacity.

During incident response, it is often necessary to deliver response resources across state lines. One concern identified by private sector players in the Oregon venue of TOPOFF 4 was the ability of commercial vehicles involved in emergency response to travel into states in which they are not registered. Currently, the Federal Motor Carrier Safety Administration (FMCSA) may waive certain federal regulations (e.g., limiting hours of service) governing commercial vehicles during emergencies. State governors may waive certain state regulations governing vehicles traveling in their jurisdictions (e.g., limitations on vehicle length and weight) pursuant to their authorities. Federal and state waivers are typically issued for limited periods of time, and apply only to vehicles involved in responding to a state or federally declared emergency. Observers argue that the lack of common vehicle standards from state to state, and the potential need to obtain waivers and proper credentials for vehicles traveling through two or more states en route to an incident, could impair the speed of emergency response. Congress might consider oversight approaches that could define and address the extent of this potential challenge, or legislative options that could address concerns that are identified.[47]

National Preparedness Goal

Homeland Security Presidential Directive-8 (HSPD-8) of December 17, 2003 ("National Preparedness") directed the Secretary of Homeland Security to develop a national domestic all-hazards preparedness goal. As part of that effort, in March 2005 the Department of Homeland Security (DHS) released the Interim National Preparedness Goal. The National Preparedness Guidelines, published in September 2007, supersede the Interim National Preparedness Goal and defines what it means for the Nation to be prepared for all hazards. There are four critical elements of the Guidelines:

1. The National Preparedness Vision, which provides a concise statement of the core preparedness goal for the Nation: "A Nation prepared with coordinated capabilities to prevent, protect against, respond to, and recover from all hazards in a way that balances risk with resources and need."
2. The National Planning Scenarios, which depict a diverse set of high-consequence threat scenarios of both potential terrorist attacks and natural disasters. Collectively, the 15 scenarios are designed to focus contingency planning for homeland security preparedness work at all levels of government and with the private sector. The scenarios form the basis for coordinated Federal planning, training, exercises, and grant investments needed to prepare for emergencies of all types.
3. The Universal Task List (UTL), which is a menu of some 1,600 unique tasks that can facilitate efforts to prevent, protect against, respond to, and recover from the major events that are represented by the National Planning Scenarios. It presents a common vocabulary and identifies key tasks that support development of essential capabilities among organizations at all levels. Of course, no entity will perform every task.
4. The Target Capabilities List (TCL), which defines 37 specific capabilities that communities, the private sector, and all levels of government should collectively possess in order to respond effectively to disasters.

The National Preparedness Goal defines what it means for the Nation to be prepared for all hazards.

The Guidelines reinforce the fact that preparedness is a shared responsibility. They were developed through an extensive process that involved more than 1,500 Federal, State, and local officials and more than 120 national associations. They also integrate lessons learned following Hurricane Katrina and a 2006 review of States' and major cities' emergency operations and evacuation plans.[48]

Conclusion

Effective response begins with a host of preparedness activities conducted well in advance of an incident. Preparedness involves a combination of planning, resources, training, exercising, and organizing to build, sustain, and improve operational capabilities. Preparedness is the process of identifying the personnel, training, and equipment needed for a wide range of potential incidents, and developing jurisdiction-specific plans for delivering capabilities when needed for an incident. Preparedness activities should be coordinated among all involved agencies within the jurisdiction, as well as across jurisdictions.[49] Effective response to an incident is a shared responsibility of governments at all levels, the private sector and NGOs, and individual citizens. The National Response Framework commits the Federal Government, in partnership with local, tribal, and State governments and the private sector, to complete both strategic and operational plans.[50] The National Incident Management System provides standard command and management structures that apply to response.[51] Finally, all stakeholders should regularly exercise their incident management and response capabilities and procedures to ensure that they are fully capable of executing their response responsibilities.[52]

Questions

1. What is the purpose of the National Response Framework?
2. How are federal resources organized and delivered?
3. What is the purpose of the National Incident Management System?
4. How is federal support requested under NRF/NIMS?
5. Why do we need a National Exercise Program?

Part IV: Critical Mission Components

Chapter 19

U.S. Secret Service

Objectives

- Know the two primary missions of the Secret Service.
- Describe the investigative missions of the Secret Service.
- Understand the Secret Service's role in the National Threat Assessment Center.

Introduction

The United States Secret Service is mandated by statute and executive order to carry out two significant missions: protection and criminal investigations. The Secret Service protects the President and Vice President, their families, heads of state, and other designated individuals; investigates threats against these protectees; protects the White House, Vice President's Residence, Foreign Missions, and other buildings within Washington, D.C.; and plans and implements security designs for designated National Special Security Events (NSSEs). The Secret Service also investigates violations of laws relating to counterfeiting of obligations and securities of the United States; financial crimes that include, but are not limited to, access device fraud, financial institution fraud, identity theft, computer fraud; and computer-based attacks on our nation's financial, banking, and telecommunications infrastructure.

Protective Mission

After the assassination of President William McKinley in 1901, Congress directed the Secret Service to protect the President of the United States. Protection remains the primary mission of the United States Secret Service.

The United States Secret Service is mandated by statute and executive order to carry out two significant missions: protection and criminal investigations.

Today, the Secret Service is authorized by law to protect:

- The President, the Vice President, (or other individuals next in order of succession to the Office of the President), the President-elect and Vice President-elect;
- The immediate families of the above individuals;
- Former Presidents, their spouses for their lifetimes, except when the spouse re-marries. In 1997, Congressional legislation became effective limiting Secret Service protection to former Presidents for a period of not more than 10 years from the date the former President leaves office.
- Children of former presidents until age 16;
- Visiting heads of foreign states or governments and their spouses traveling with them, other distinguished foreign visitors to the United States, and official representatives of the United States performing special missions abroad;
- Major Presidential and Vice Presidential candidates, and their spouses within 120 days of a general Presidential election.[1]

Investigative Mission

The Secret Service was established as a law enforcement agency in 1865. While most people associate the Secret Service with Presidential protection, the original mandate was to investigate the counterfeiting of U.S. currency—which they still do. Today the primary investigative mission is to safeguard the payment and financial systems of the United States. This has been historically accomplished through the enforcement of the counterfeiting statutes to preserve the integrity of United States currency, coin and financial obligations. Since 1984, investigative responsibilities have expanded to include crimes that involve financial institution fraud, computer and telecommunications fraud, false identification documents, access device fraud, advance fee fraud, electronic funds transfers, and money laundering as it relates to core violations.

The Secret Service believes that its primary enforcement jurisdictions will only increase in significance in the 21st Century. For this reason, the Secret Service has adopted a proactive approach to monitor the development of technology and continue to use it in the interest of federal, state, and local law enforcement. There are three Investigative Missions: Counterfeit, Financial Crimes, and Forensic Services.[2]

Counterfeit Division

The Secret Service has exclusive jurisdiction for investigations involving the counterfeiting of United States obligations and securities. This authority to investigate counterfeiting is derived from Title 18 of the United States Code, Section 3056. Some of the counterfeited United States obligations and securities commonly dealt with by the Secret Service include U.S. currency and coins; U.S. Treasury checks; Department of Agriculture food coupons and U.S. postage stamps. The Secret Service remains committed to the mission of combating counterfeiting by working closely with state and local law enforcement agencies, as well as foreign law enforcement agencies, to aggressively pursue counterfeiters. To perform at the highest level, the Secret Service constantly reviews the latest reprographic/lithographic technologies to keep a step ahead of the counterfeiters. The Secret Service maintains a working relationship with the Bureau of Engraving and Printing and the Federal Reserve System to ensure the integrity of our currency.

The counterfeiting of money is one of the oldest crimes in history. At some periods in early history, it was considered treasonous and was punishable by death.

History of Counterfeiting

The counterfeiting of money is one of the oldest crimes in history. At some periods in early history, it was considered treasonous and was punishable by death.

During the American Revolution, the British counterfeited U.S. currency in such large amounts that the Continental currency soon became worthless. "Not worth a Continental" became a popular expression that is still heard today.

During the Civil War, one-third to one-half of the currency in circulation was counterfeit. At that time, approximately 1,600 state banks designed and printed their own bills. Each bill carried a different design, making it difficult to detect counterfeit bills from the 7,000 varieties of real bills.

A national currency was adopted in 1862 to resolve the counterfeiting problem. However, the national currency was soon counterfeited and circulated so extensively that it became necessary to take enforcement measures. Therefore, on July 5, 1865, the United States Secret Service was established to suppress preserve the integrity of United States currency, coin and financial obligations. Since 1984, investigative responsibilities have expanded to include crimes that involve financial institution fraud, computer and telecommunications fraud, false identification documents, access device fraud, advance fee fraud, electronic funds transfers, and money laundering as it relates to core violations.

The Secret Service believes that its primary enforcement jurisdictions will only increase in significance in the 21st Century. For this reason, the Secret Service has adopted a proactive approach to monitor the development of technology and continue to use it in the interest of federal, state, and local law enforcement. There are three Investigative Missions: Counterfeit, Financial Crimes, and Forensic Services.[3]

Financial Crimes Division

The Secret Service investigates crimes associated with financial institutions. Today, this jurisdiction includes bank fraud, access device fraud involving credit and debit cards, telecommunications and computer crimes, fraudulent identification, fraudulent government and commercial securities, and electronic funds transfer fraud.

The Secret Service has concurrent jurisdiction with the Department of Justice to investigate fraud, both civil and criminal, against federally insured financial (FIF) institutions.

Financial Institution Fraud (FIF)

On November 5, 1990, Congress enacted legislation that gave the Secret Service concurrent jurisdiction with the Department of Justice to investigate fraud, both civil and criminally against any federally insured financial institution or the Resolution Trust Corporation. Annually, agents of the Secret Service review thousands of criminal referrals submitted by Treasury Department regulators. The Secret Service promotes an aggressive policy toward conducting these investigations in an effort to safeguard the soundness of our financial institutions.

The Secret Service has concurrent jurisdiction with the Department of Justice to investigate fraud, both civil and criminal, against federally insured financial (FIF) institutions. The Crime Bill of 1994 extended FIF investigative authority to the year 2004.

The FIF program distinguishes itself from other such programs by recognizing the need to balance traditional law enforcement operations with a program management approach designed to prevent recurring criminal activity.

A recent American Banking Association (ABA) survey concluded that the two major problems in the area of bank fraud today are: (1) the fraudulent production of negotiable instruments through the use of what has become known as "desktop publishing," and (2) access device fraud.

Recent Secret Service investigations indicate that there has been an increase in credit card fraud, fictitious document fraud, and fraud involving the counterfeiting of corporate checks and other negotiable instruments, as well as false identification documents created with the use of computer technology.

Title 18 United States Code, Section 514 was enacted into law in 1996 to prevent the increasing amount of fraud through the use of fictitious instruments. Congress passed this law through the joint efforts of the Department of Justice and the Department of Treasury. The Financial Crimes Division (FCD) is responsible for the investigations of Title 18, United States Code Section 514 (Fictitious Instruments).

Access Device Fraud

Financial industry sources estimate that losses associated with credit card fraud are in the billions of dollars annually. The Secret Service is the primary federal agency tasked with investigating access device fraud and its related activities under Title 18, United States Code, Section 1029. Although it is commonly called the credit card statute, this law also applies to other crimes involving access device numbers including debit cards, automated teller machine (ATM) cards, computer passwords, personal identification numbers (PINs) used to activate ATMs, credit card or debit card account numbers, long-distance access codes, and the computer chips in cellular phones that assign billing. During fiscal year 1996, the Secret Service opened 2,467 cases, closed 2,963 cases, and arrested 2,429 individuals for access device fraud. Industry sources estimate that losses associated with credit card fraud are in the billions of dollars annually.

The Secret Service is the primary federal agency tasked with investigating access device fraud involving debit cards, automated teller machine (ATM) cards, computer passwords, personal identification numbers (PINs) used to activate ATMs, credit card or debit card account numbers, long-distance access codes, and the computer chips in cellular phones that assign billing.

Counterfeit and Fraudulent Identification

Since 1982, the Secret Service has enforced laws involving counterfeit and fraudulent identification. Title 18, United States Code, Section 1028, defines this criminal act as someone who knowingly and without lawful authority produces, transfers, or possesses a false identification document to defraud the U.S. Government. The use of desktop publishing software/hardware to counterfeit and produce different forms of identification used to obtain funds illegally remains one of the Secret Service's strongest core violations.

Money Laundering

The Money Laundering Control Act makes it a crime to launder proceeds of certain criminal offenses called "specified unlawful activities" (SUA), which are defined in Title 18, United States Code,1956, 1957 and Title 18,United States Code, 1961, the Racketeer Influenced and Corrupt Organizations Act (RICO).

The Secret Service has observed an increase in money laundering activities as they relate to these specified unlawful activities. This is especially true in the area of financial institution fraud, access device fraud (credit card, telecommunications and computer investigations), food stamp fraud, and counterfeiting of U.S. currency.

Computer Fraud

In 1986, Congress revised Title 18 of the United States Code to include the investigation of fraud and related activities concerning computers that were described as "federal interest computers," as defined in Title 18, United States Code, Section 1030. The Secret Service has also investigated cases where computer technology has been used in traditional Secret Service violations, such as counterfeiting and the creation of false identification documents.

Computers are being used extensively in financial crimes, not only as an instrument of the crime, but to "hack" into databases to retrieve account information; store account information; clone microchips for cellular telephones; and scan corporate checks, bonds and negotiable instruments, that are later counterfeited using desktop publishing methods.

Because computers are a tremendous source of both investigative leads and evidentiary material, the Secret Service has established the Electronic Crimes Special Agent Program (ECSAP), that trains agents to conduct forensic examinations of computers that were used in criminal endeavors. So trained, these agents can preserve any investigative leads within the computer, as well as any evidence needed for subsequent prosecutions.

The Secret Service has become the recognized law enforcement expert in the field of telecommunications fraud.

Telecommunications Fraud

Telecommunication fraud losses are estimated at more than a billion dollars yearly. One of the largest "markets" for this type of fraud is the cloning of cellular telephones, a relatively simple procedure that can be done with the purchase of over-the-counter electronic equipment. When an individual transmits with a cellular telephone, the telephone emits a burst of electronic information. Within this burst of information is the electronic serial number (ESN), the mobile identification number (MIN) and other electronic identification signals, all of which can be illegally captured through the use of an ESN reader. Once captured, this information is transported through a computer onto microchips in the cellular telephones. These new telephones can be used for up to 30 days before the fraudulent charges are discovered. Cell telephones are being used extensively by organized criminal groups and drug cartels, as well as several Middle Eastern groups. Using acquired investigative expertise and state-of-the-art electronic equipment, the Secret Service now has the ability to effectively investigate the use of such telephones. This is another example of law enforcement using technology to target criminal enterprise.

The Secret Service has become the recognized law enforcement expert in the field of telecommunications fraud. It works closely with other law enforcement agencies, as well as representatives of the telecommunications industry in conducting telecommunications fraud investigations. These types of investigations, in many instances, act as a nexus to other criminal enterprises, such as access device fraud, counterfeiting, money laundering, and the trafficking of narcotics. During fiscal year 1996, the Secret Service opened 555 cases and arrested 556 individuals for telecommunications fraud.

Electronic Benefits Transfer (EBT) Card

The Vice President's National Performance Review designated the Electronic Benefits Transfer (EBT) card as the method of payment for the delivery of recurring government cash benefit payments to individuals without a bank account and for the delivery of non-cash benefits such as Food Stamps. For individuals with bank accounts, Electronic Funds Transfer will continue as the preferred method of making federal benefit payments. As with any recurring payment system, EBT is open to a wide variety of fraud, including multiple false applications for benefits, counterfeiting of the EBT card and trafficking of non-cash benefits for cash or contraband. The Financial Crimes Division is taking a proactive approach by recommending fraud deterrent features to this new system as it is designed.

In an attempt to combat potential attacks, Financial Crimes Division has suggested the use of: biometric identifiers to verify applicants' identities and prevent application fraud; counterfeit deterrents such as four-color graphics and fine-line printing, and the use of holograms and embossing in the design of the card; and features that allow investigators to monitor transactions and use the audit trail to identify criminals who illegally traffic food benefit payments.[4]

Forensic Services Division

Forensic examiners in the Secret Service Forensic Services Division (FSD) provide analysis for questioned documents, fingerprints, false identification, credit cards, and other related forensic science areas.

Forensic examiners in the Secret Service Forensic Services Division (FSD) provide analysis for questioned documents, fingerprints, false identification, credit cards, and other related forensic science areas. Examiners use both instrumental and chemical analysis when reviewing evidence. FSD also manages the Secret Service's polygraph program nationwide. The division coordinates photographic, graphic, video, and audio and image enhancement service, as well as the Voice Identification Program. In addition, FSD is responsible for handling the Forensic Hypnosis Program. Much of the forensic assistance the Secret Service offers is unique technology operated in this country only by FSD.

Instrument Analysis Services Section

The Instrument Analysis Services Section houses the International Ink Library - the most complete forensic collection of writing inks world-wide that contains over 7,000 samples. This collection is used to identify the source of suspect writing by not only providing the type and brand of writing instrument, but the earliest possible date that a document could have been produced. This Section also maintains a watermark collection of over 22,000 images as well as collections of plastics, toners and computer printer inks.

Fingerprint Identification Services Section

FSD also operates a hybrid Automated Fingerprint Identification System (AFIS). As of 1999, this network is the largest of its kind and is composed of remote latent fingerprint terminals providing a connection to fingerprint databases with access to more than 30 million fingerprints. This enables the fingerprint specialist to digitize a single latent fingerprint from an item of evidence and to search for its likeness from fingerprint databases throughout the country. These findings often provide the investigator with a suspect's name.

Polygraph Examination Program

The Polygraph Examination Program is known as a forerunner in the law enforcement community for advancing the fine art of physiologically detecting deception. Polygraph examinations are a major investigative tool for all cases under the Secret Service jurisdiction. Through proper use of the polygraph, the agency maintains a high resolution of its investigations, resulting in a significant savings in the expenditure of man-hours, equipment, and money. The Polygraph Program has a host of examiners who are highly trained in interview and interrogation techniques. Each examiner is capable of conducting a reliable polygraph examination on issues involving criminal, national security, and employee-screening matters.[5]

Origin of the U.S. Secret Service

The U.S. Secret Service, one of the nation's oldest federal investigative law enforcement agencies, was founded in 1865 as a branch of the U.S. Treasury Department.

The U.S. Secret Service, one of the nation's oldest federal investigative law enforcement agencies, was founded in 1865 as a branch of the U.S. Treasury Department. The original mission was to investigate counterfeiting of U.S. currency. It was estimated that one-third to one-half of the currency in circulation at that time was counterfeit. In 1901, following the assassination of President William McKinley in Buffalo, New York, the Secret Service was assigned the responsibility of protecting the President. Today, the Secret Service's mission is two fold: protection of the President, Vice President and others; and protection of our nation's financial system.

Legal Authority

Under Title 18, Section 3056, United States Code, agents and officers of the Secret Service can carry firearms; execute warrants issued under the laws of the United States; make arrests without warrants for any offense against the United States committed in their presence, or for any felony recognizable under the laws of the United States if they have reasonable grounds to believe that the person to be arrested has committed such felony; offer and pay rewards for services and information leading to the apprehension of persons involved in the violation of the law that the Secret Service is authorized to enforce; investigate fraud in connection with identification documents, fraudulent commerce, fictitious instruments and foreign securities; perform other functions and duties authorized by law. The Secret Service works closely with the United States Attorney's Office in both protective and investigative matters.

Title 18, United States Code, Section 504 permits black and white reproductions of currency and other obligations, provided such reproductions meet the size requirement.[6]

The Patriot Act (Public Law 107-56, October 26, 2001) increased the Secret Service's role in investigating fraud and related activity in connections with computers. In addition it authorized the Director of the Secret Service to establish nationwide electronic crimes taskforces to assist the law enforcement, private sector and academia in detecting and suppressing computer-based crime; increased the statutory penalties for the manufacturing, possession, dealing and passing of counterfeit U.S. or foreign obligations; and allowed enforcement action to be taken to protect our financial payment systems while combating transnational financial crimes directed by terrorists or other criminals.[7]

Protection of Former Presidents

In 1965, Congress authorized the Secret Service (Public Law 89-186) to protect a former president and his/her spouse during their lifetime, unless they decline protection. Congress recently enacted legislation that limits Secret Service protection for former presidents to ten years after leaving office. Under this new law, individuals who are in office before January 1, 1997, will continue to receive Secret Service protection for their lifetime. Individuals elected to office after that time will receive protection for ten years after leaving office. Therefore, former president Clinton will be the last President to receive lifetime protection.

The goal of the Secret Service's threat assessment efforts is to identify, assess, and manage persons who have the interest and ability to mount attacks against Secret Service protectees.

Title 18, Section 3056 of the U.S. Code states, "The United States Secret Service is authorized to protect former presidents and their spouses for their lifetimes, except that protection of a spouse shall terminate in the event of remarriage unless the former president did not serve as president prior to January 1, 1997, in which case, former president and their spouses for a period of not more than ten years from the date a former president leaves office, except that—

Protection of a spouse shall terminate in the event of remarriage or the divorce from, or death of a former president; and

Should the death of a president occur while in office or within one year after leaving office, the spouse shall receive protection for one year from the time of such death.

Children of a former president who are under 16 years of age for a period not to exceed ten years or upon the child becoming 16 years of age, whichever comes first."

National Threat Assessment Center

As part of its protective responsibilities, the United States Secret Service has long held the view that the best protective strategy is prevention. The goal of the Secret Service's threat assessment efforts is to identify, assess, and manage persons who have the interest and ability to mount attacks against Secret Service protectees.

After the completion of the Secret Service's first operationally-relevant study on assassins and near-assassins (i.e., the Exceptional Case Study Project) in 1998, the agency created the National Threat Assessment Center (NTAC). The mission of NTAC is to provide guidance on threat assessment, both within the Secret Service and to its law enforcement and public safety partners. Through the Presidential Threat Protection Act of 2000, Congress formally authorized NTAC to provide assistance in the following functional areas:

- Research on threat assessment and various types of targeted violence.
- Training on threat assessment and targeted violence to law enforcement officials and others with protective and public safety responsibilities.
- Information-sharing among agencies with protective and/or public safety responsibilities.
- Programs to promote the standardization of federal, state, and local threat assessment and investigations involving threats.

In addition to internal research conducted to support the protective mission of the Secret Service, NTAC publishes research to advance the field of threat assessment more generally. These projects are described below.

Exceptional Case Study Project

The Exceptional Case Study Project (ECSP) led to the creation of NTAC. The ECSP was a five-year operational analysis of the thinking and behavior of individuals who assassinated, attacked or approached to attack a prominent person of public status in the United States. It employed an incident-focused, behaviorally-based approach consisting of a systematic analysis of investigative reports, criminal justice records, medical records, and other source documents, as well as in-depth interviews with subjects.

Completed in 1998, the ECSP identified and analyzed 83 persons known to have engaged in 73 incidents of assassination, attack, and near-attack behaviors from 1949 to 1995. The findings indicated that there is no "profile" of an assassin; however, subjects exhibited a common set of "attack-related behaviors." They further revealed that assassination is an often discernable process of thinking and behavior. Assassins and attackers plan their attacks and are motivated by a wide range of issues. They consider several targets before acting but rarely direct threats either to the target or to law enforcement.

Based on these findings, the Secret Service implemented significant policy changes in protective intelligence investigations. The agency also developed key investigative questions and training materials which provide a framework for law enforcement to utilize in conducting threat assessment investigations at the federal, state, and local levels.

Targeted School Violence

In response to the Virginia Tech shooting on April 16, 2007, former Cabinet Secretaries Michael Leavitt and Margaret Spellings, and former Attorney General Alberto Gonzales submitted a Report to the President on Issues Raised by the Virginia Tech Tragedy dated June 13, 2007. The report included a recommendation that the U.S. Secret Service, U.S. Department of Education, and the Federal Bureau of Investigation explore the issue of violence at institutions of higher education. Accordingly, the three agencies initiated a collaborative effort, the goal of which was to understand the scope of the problem of targeted violence at these institutions in the United States.

In total, 272 incidents were identified through a comprehensive search of open-source reporting from 1900 to 2008. The incidents studied include various forms of targeted violence, ranging from domestic violence to mass murder. The findings should be useful for campus safety professionals charged with identifying, assessing, and managing violence risk at institutions of higher education.

The Safe School Initiative

The Safe School Initiative study found that school-based attacks are rarely impulsive acts. Rather, they are typically thought out and planned in advance.

In 2002, NTAC completed the Safe School Initiative (SSI), a study of attacks at K-12 schools. Conducted in collaboration with the U.S. Department of Education, the study examined incidents in the United States from 1974 through May 2000, analyzing a total of 37 incidents involving 41 student attackers. The study involved extensive review of police records, school records, court documents, and other source materials, and included interviews with 10 school shooters. The focus of the study was on developing information about pre-attack behaviors and communications to identify information that may be identifiable or noticeable before such incidents occur.

The SSI found that school-based attacks are rarely impulsive acts. Rather, they are typically thought out and planned in advance. Almost every attacker had engaged in behavior before the shooting that seriously concerned at least one adult - and for many had concerned three or more adults. In addition, prior to most of the incidents, other students knew the attack was to occur but did not alert an adult. Rarely did the attackers direct threats to their targets before the attack. The study's findings also revealed that there is no "profile" of a school-based attacker; instead, the students who carried out the attacks differed from one another in numerous ways.

The findings from the study suggest that some school-based attacks may be preventable, and that students can play an important role in prevention efforts. Using the study's findings, the Secret Service and U.S. Department of Education modified the Secret Service's threat assessment approach for use in schools in order to give school and law enforcement professionals tools for investigating threats in schools, managing situations of concern, and creating safe school climates.

Bystander Study

This study served as a follow-up to the Safe School Initiative (SSI). One of the most significant findings from the SSI is that prior to most school-based attacks, other children knew what was going to happen. In collaboration with the U.S. Department of Education and McLean Hospital (a Harvard Medical School affiliate), NTAC interviewed friends, classmates, siblings, and others in whom school attackers confided their ideas and plans prior to their incidents. Other interviews included students who came forward with information regarding a planned school-based attack, and are believed to have prevented an attack from happening. The goal of the study was to provide information to school administrators and educators regarding possible barriers that may prevent children who have information about a potential incident from reporting that information to a responsible adult.

The Insider Threat Study

In 2002, NTAC partnered with Carnegie Mellon University's Computer Emergency Response Team (CERT) Program to conduct the Insider Threat Study (ITS), which also received financial support from the Department of Homeland Security's Science and Technology Directorate.

The Secret Service and CERT have a longstanding relationship dedicated to addressing cyber security issues that have implications for the nation's critical infrastructure sectors or national security. Incidents of illicit insider cyber activity are of concern to the Secret Service as they often involve criminal activity the agency investigates including financial fraud, computer fraud, electronic crimes, identity theft, and computer-based attacks on the nation's financial, banking and telecommunications infrastructures. Insider incidents may impact not only the targeted organization but also industries, critical infrastructure sectors, and national security.

The ITS examined organizational insiders - current, former or contract employees - who perpetrated harm to their organizations via a computer or system/network for purposes of intellectual property theft, fraud, and acts of sabotage. The study identified and analyzed insiders' behaviors (physical, social, and online) that may be detectable prior to an incident. The goal was to develop information to help private industry, government, and law enforcement better understand, detect, and ultimately prevent harmful insider activity by enhancing their threat assessment processes.

Analyzed from both behavioral and technical perspectives, the incidents included in the study involved companies/organizations, within various critical infrastructure sectors, that took place between 1996 and 2002. Findings from the ITS underscore the importance of organizations' technology, policies, and procedures in securing their networks against insider threats.[8]

Conclusion

The primary mission of the United States Secret Service is to protect the President, Vice President, and other national leaders. The Service also contributes its specialized protective expertise to planning for events of national significance (National Special Security Events). In addition, the Service combats counterfeiting, cyber-crime, identity fraud, and access device fraud, all closely tied to the terrorist threat. The Homeland Security Act of 2002 transferred the Secret Service from the Treasury Department to the Department of Homeland Security. The Service remained intact and was not merged with any other Department function to take advantage of the Service's unique and highly specialized expertise to complement the core mission of the new Department.

Protecting the nation's financial infrastructure is increasingly complicated as counterfeit currency, financial crimes and electronic crimes have become more complex and transnational. To effectively detect, investigate and prevent these crimes, the Secret Service will continue developing, acquiring and deploying cutting-edge scientific tools and technology. The Secret Service workforce is essential to the investigative mission; therefore, the Secret Service will continue to train and develop personnel in investigative techniques and continue to partner with federal, state, local and international law enforcement, private industry and academia.

Protecting national leaders, visiting heads of state and government, designated sites and National Special Security Events has become more complex with the evolution of conventional and non-conventional weapons and technology. In meeting new challenges, the Secret Service will continue to provide progressive training, devise and implement sound security plans, measures, equipment and systems to ensure the safety of individuals, sites and events under Secret Service protection. The Secret Service's unique investigative and protective mission is sustained by a strong, multi-tiered infrastructure of science, technology and information systems; administrative, professional and technical expertise; and management systems and processes. The Secret Service's diverse and talented workforce develops and employs sophisticated science and technology, workforce planning strategies, and business and management practices to propel operational programs. To promote innovation, diversity, mutual respect and teamwork, the Secret Service will continue to foster open communication both internally and with partners at the departmental, federal, state, local and international levels. To demonstrate a steadfast commitment to excellence, the Secret Service will continue to infuse a high level of accountability throughout its business practices, as well as investigative and protective operations.[9]

Questions

1. What are the two primary missions of the Secret Service?
2. What are the three investigative missions of the Secret Service?
3. How have the studies conducted by the NTAC contributed to the overall mission of the Secret Service?

Chapter 20

U.S. Coast Guard

Objectives

- Describe the organization of the United States Coast Guard.
- Explain the three major roles of the United States Coast Guard.
- Explain how the Coast Guard is unique among the uniform services.

Introduction

The Coast Guard is the lead federal agency for maritime homeland security. Section 888(a)(2) of The Homeland Security Act of 2002 (P.L. 107-296 of November 25, 2002) specifies five homeland security missions for the Coast Guard: (1) ports, waterways, and coastal security, (2) drug interdiction, (3) migrant interdiction, (4) defense readiness, and (5) other law enforcement. Under the Ports and Waterways Safety Act of 1972 (P.L. 92-340) and the Maritime Transportation Security Act (MTSA) of 2002 (P.L. 107-295 of November 25, 2002), the Coast Guard has responsibility to protect vessels and harbors from subversive acts. With regard to port security, the Coast Guard is responsible for evaluating, boarding, and inspecting commercial ships approaching U.S. waters, countering terrorist threats in U.S. ports, and helping protect U.S. Navy ships in U.S. ports. A Coast Guard officer in each port area is the Captain of the Port (COTP), who is the lead federal official for security and safety of vessels and waterways in that area.[1]

Maritime Guardian

Since 1915, when the Coast Guard was established by law as an armed force, USCG has been a military, multi-mission, maritime force offering a unique blend of military, law enforcement, humanitarian, regulatory, and diplomatic capabilities.

America's enduring maritime interests—its reliance on the seas for commerce, sustenance, and defense—have changed little since colonial days. The U.S. Coast Guard exists to address these interests. The United States is a maritime country, with extensive interests in the seas around us and far beyond. Having 95,000 miles of shoreline and nearly 3.4 million square miles of Exclusive Economic Zones (EEZ), the United States will always remain tied to the sea. The seas link the Nation with world trade and commerce. They allow us to project military power beyond our shores to protect important U.S. interests, and to assist allies or friends. Regrettably, however, the seas also serve as highways for criminal and terrorist threats that honor no national borders.

The Coast Guard is one of the five military services which make up the Armed Forces of the United States of America. As such, the Coast Guard exists to defend and preserve the United States as a free nation. USCG also protects important interests of the United States— the personal safety and security of our population; the marine transportation system and critical infrastructure; our natural and economic resources; and the territorial integrity of our nation—from both internal and external threats, natural and man-made. The Coast Guard protects these interests in U.S. ports and inland waterways, along the coasts, on international waters, and in any other maritime region where they may be at risk. Since 1915, when the Coast Guard was established by law as an armed force, USCG has been a military, multi-mission, maritime force offering a unique blend of military, law enforcement, humanitarian, regulatory, and diplomatic capabilities. These capabilities underpin our three broad roles: maritime safety, maritime security, and maritime stewardship.

Each Coast Guard role is composed of 11 missions assigned by the Congress, acting on behalf of the American people. However, most Coast Guard missions support more than one role. For example, the Coast Guard's aids to navigation mission primarily supports maritime stewardship role by preventing pollution from vessel groundings and collisions, while facilitating the movement of people and goods. But this mission also supports maritime safety role by preventing accidents, injuries, and deaths. These interwoven roles and complementary missions call for Coast Guard personnel and resources that are similarly multi-mission capable. This characteristic of USCG people and platforms—their ability to perform multiple missions—brings greater effectiveness, insight, and agility to bear in any situation. It is a fundamental source of the Coast Guard's strength.

Safety	Security
Search & Rescue	Drug Interdiction
Marine Safety	Migrant Interdiction
Stewardship	Defense Readiness
Ice Operations	Ports, Waterways, & Coastal Security
Aids to Navigation	
Marine Environmental Protection	
Living Marine Resources	
Other Law Enforcement	

Table 15.1: Statutory Coast Guard Missions

Following the terrorist attacks of September 11, 2001, Congress passed the Homeland Security and the Maritime Transportation Security Acts of 2002, and transferred the Coast Guard into the Department of Homeland Security. But these actions have not substantially altered the Service's roles and missions. Rather, these developments have brought increased emphasis to the importance of the Coast Guard's multimission work in protecting U.S. maritime borders and enforcing U.S. sovereignty over our coastal waters. As criminals and terrorists try to exploit or blend in with legitimate maritime activity, the Coast Guard's roles of maritime safety, security, and stewardship are increasingly recognized as interrelated and essential to our nation's layered security construct against all threats and all hazards.

Maritime Safety

A fundamental responsibility of the U.S. government is to safeguard the lives and safety of its citizens. In the maritime realm, this duty falls mainly to the Coast Guard. In partnership with other federal agencies, state, local, and tribal governments, marine industries, and individual mariners, the Coast Guard improves safety at sea through complementary programs of mishap prevention, search and rescue, and accident investigation.

Coast Guard prevention activities include the development of standards and regulations, various types of plan review and compliance inspections, and a variety of safety programs designed to protect mariners.

The Coast Guard is America's voice in the International Maritime Organization (IMO), which promulgates measures to improve shipping safety, pollution prevention, mariner training, and certification standards. USCG develops and enforce vessel construction standards as well as domestic shipping and navigation regulations.

To ensure compliance, the Coast Guard reviews and approves plans for ship construction, repair, and alteration. USCG inspects vessels, mobile offshore drilling units, and marine facilities for safety. The Coast Guard's Port State Control program, aimed at eliminating substandard vessels from U.S. ports and waterways, is a key element. This program is critical since the majority of the passenger and cargo ships operating in U.S. waters are foreign flagged.

Nearly all Coast Guard prevention activities are designed to protect mariners. For example, commercial fishing vessel safety programs are designed to safeguard commercial fishermen, many of whom earn their living performing some of the most dangerous work in the world. The Coast Guard operates the International Ice Patrol to protect ships transiting the North Atlantic shipping lanes. We document and admeasure U.S. flag vessels. And, USCG licenses commercial mariners.

The Coast Guard operates the International Ice Patrol to protect ships transiting the North Atlantic shipping lanes.

America has approximately 17 million recreational boats.2 As National Recreational Boating Safety Coordinator, the Coast Guard works to minimize loss of life, personal injury, property damage, and environmental harm associated with this activity. USCG boating safety programs involve public education programs, regulation of boat design and construction, approval of boating safety equipment, and vessel safety checks for compliance with federal and state safety requirements. The all- volunteer Coast Guard Auxiliary plays a central role in this program.

But the maritime domain is large and complex, and the sea is powerful and unforgiving. Despite the best efforts, mariners sometimes find themselves in harm's way. When they do, the Coast Guard has a long heritage and proud tradition of immediate response to save lives and property in peril. As the lead agency for maritime search and rescue (SAR) in U.S. waters, USCG coordinates the SAR efforts of afloat and airborne Coast Guard units with those of other federal, state, and local responders. The Coast Guard also partners with the world's merchant fleet to rescue mariners in distress around the globe through the Automated Mutual- assistance Vessel Rescue (AMVER) system. Using its Captain of the Port (COTP) authorities and responsibilities, the Coast Guard also coordinates response efforts on waterways after an incident or disaster.

In addition to responding to a variety of maritime accidents and emergencies, USCG investigates their causes. The Coast Guard determines whether applicable laws have been violated, or whether changes should be made to improve safety through prevention programs. This work is often done in coordination with the National Transportation Safety Board (NTSB).

Coast Guard activities in support of maritime safety are often inseparable from those performed to protect the marine environment or secure the U.S. Marine Transportation System (MTS). A routine inspection for safety compliance may uncover a serious risk to the environment. Coast Guard vessel traffic services not only reduce the risk of vessel collisions, but also provide maritime domain awareness. This improves security. A buoy tender working an aid to navigation may immediately divert to a search and rescue case. The integration of all Coast Guard missions has saved many thousands of lives, helped secure our citizens, and contributed to our national economic and environmental well-being.

Maritime Security

Maritime law enforcement and border control are the oldest of the Coast Guard's numerous responsibilities. They date back to the Coast Guard's founding as the Revenue Marine in 1790. The First Congress established the Revenue Marine specifically to patrol our coasts and seaports to frustrate smuggling and enforce the customs laws of the fledgling Republic. Over two centuries later, that early challenge has evolved into a global obligation for the maritime security of our nation. USCG's maritime law enforcement and border control duties require the interdiction of ships at sea. This core capability provides the foundation upon which today's broader and more complex maritime security mission set has been built.

As the Nation's primary maritime law enforcement service, the Coast Guard enforces, or assists in enforcing, federal laws and treaties on waters under U.S. jurisdiction, and other international agreements on the high seas. The Coast Guard possesses the civil authority to board any vessel subject to U.S. jurisdiction. Once aboard, USCG can inspect, search, inquire, and arrest. The Coast Guard wields this broad police power with prudence and restraint primarily to suppress violations of U.S. drug, immigration, and fisheries laws, as well as to secure our nation from terrorist threats.

The Coast Guard possesses the civil authority to board any vessel subject to U.S. jurisdiction. Once aboard, USCG can inspect, search, inquire, and arrest.

The Coast Guard is the designated lead agency for maritime drug interdiction under the National Drug Control Strategy and the co-lead agency for air interdiction operations with U.S. Customs and Border Protection. As such, the Coast Guard defends America's seaward frontier against a torrent of illegal drugs. For more than three decades, Coast Guard cutters and aircraft have forward deployed off South America and in the drug transit zone. They have intercepted thousands of tons of cocaine, marijuana, and other illegal drugs that otherwise would have found their way to America's streets.

Coast Guard undocumented migrant interdiction operations are law enforcement missions with an important humanitarian dimension. Migrants often take great risks and endure significant hardships in their attempts to flee their countries and enter the United States. In many cases, migrant vessels interdicted at sea are overloaded and unseaworthy, lack basic safety equipment, and are operated by inexperienced mariners. Many of the undocumented migrant cases USCG handles actually begin as search and rescue incidents. Once again, this illustrates the interweaving of USCG roles and missions. Between 1982 and 2007, the Coast Guard interdicted over 225,000 migrants mostly from Cuba, the Dominican Republic, and Haiti.

Throughout USCG history, the Coast Guard has served with the U.S. Navy to defend our nation. This began with the Quasi- War with France in 1798, and continued through the Civil War, the World Wars, Vietnam, the Persian Gulf War, and Operation Iraqi Freedom.

Today, as a critical component of the U.S. National Fleet, the Coast Guard maintain a high state of readiness to operate as a specialized service alongside the Navy and Marine Corps. The close relationship among the services has evolved over two centuries of cooperation. This enduring relationship is captured in the May 2008 agreement between the Secretaries of Defense and Homeland Security.

The agreement formalizes the use of Coast Guard competencies and resources in support of the National Military Strategy and other national-level defense and security strategies. It lists the following Coast Guard national defense capabilities:

- Maritime interception and interdiction;
- Military environmental response;
- Port operations, security, and defense;
- Theater security cooperation;
- Coastal sea control;
- Rotary wing air intercept;
- Combating terrorism; and
- Maritime Operational Threat Response support

Today, as a critical component of the U.S. National Fleet, USCG maintains a high state of readiness to operate as a specialized service alongside the Navy and Marine Corps.

These support the unified combatant commanders and require the Coast Guard to execute essential military operations in peacetime, crisis, and war.

The Coast Guard's domestic civil law enforcement and port security expertise are uniquely valuable today as combatant commanders work to build foreign nation capacity for security and governance. In recent years, combatant commanders have requested Coast Guard forces to conduct at-sea interception and antipiracy operations, foreign liaison, and other supporting warfare tasks in all key theaters.

The Coast Guard has been responsible for the security of the ports and waterways of the United States during times of war since the enactment of the Espionage Act of 1917. After World War II, the Magnuson Act of 1950 assigned the Coast Guard an ongoing mission to safeguard U.S. ports, harbors, vessels, and waterfront facilities from accidents, sabotage, or other subversive acts.

Following the terrorist attacks of September 11, 2001, these authorities took on grave new importance. This includes denying terrorists the use of the U.S. maritime domain and the U.S. MTS to mount attacks on our territory, population, or critical infrastructure.

Coast Guard authorities were further strengthened with the passage of the Maritime Transportation Security Act of 2002. This designated Coast Guard Captains of the Port as the Federal Maritime Security Coordinators. The Coast Guard thus became the lead agency for coordinating all maritime security planning and operations in our ports and waterways. These activities encompass all efforts to prevent or respond to attacks.

Maritime security is a continuing theme running throughout the Coast Guard's proud history of service to America. It requires a breadth of experience and skills—seamanship, diplomacy, legal expertise, and combat readiness. The Coast Guard has honed these skills for more than two centuries. No other federal agency offers this combination of law enforcement and military capabilities, together with the legal authorities to carry them out.

Maritime Stewardship

Our nation's waters are vital to its well-being and economy. The marine environment of the United States is one of the most valuable natural resources on Earth. It contains one-fifth of the world's fishery resources. It is also a region of extraordinary recreation, energy and mineral resources, and transportation activities. Finally, it is an inseparable part of our national heritage and daily fabric of life in our coastal communities.

The Coast Guard's role in protecting natural resources dates to the 1820s when Congress tasked the Revenue Marine to protect federal stocks of Florida live oak trees. These trees were deemed critical to the security of our young nation because they provided the best wood for shipbuilding.

No other federal agency offers this combination of law enforcement and military capabilities, together with the legal authorities to carry them out.

As the exploitation of the Nation's valuable marine resources— whales, furbearing animals, and fish—increased, USCG was given the duty to protect those resources as well. Today, U.S. waters support commercial and recreational fisheries worth more than $30 billion annually, and serve as the primary agency for at- sea fisheries enforcement. The Coast Guard, in coordination with other federal and state agencies, enforces marine resource management and protection regimes to preserve healthy stocks of fish and other living marine resources.

In 1976, Congress passed what is now known as the Magnuson- Stevens Fishery Conservation and Management Act. By creating an EEZ, this legislation extended our exclusive rights out to 200 nautical miles for fisheries and other natural resources. The Coast Guard patrols these areas to uphold U.S. sovereignty and protect precious resources. Today, international fisheries agreements have extended U.S. jurisdiction to waters beyond the EEZ.

USCG's stewardship role has expanded to include enforcing laws intended to protect the environment for the common good. As a result, the Coast Guard safeguard sensitive marine habitats, mammals, and endangered species. USCG enforces laws protecting our waters from the discharge of oil, hazardous substances, and non-indigenous invasive species.

To do all this, the Coast Guard conducts a wide range of activities. These include education and prevention; law enforcement; emergency response and containment; and disaster recovery. The Coast Guard also provide mission critical command and control support for forces responding to environmental disasters in the maritime domain.

Under the National Contingency Plan, Coast Guard COTPs are the predesignated Federal On-Scene Coordinators (FOSC) for oil and hazardous substance incidents in all coastal and some inland areas. The FOSC is the President's designated on-scene representative and, as such, is responsible for coordinating effective response operations among a diverse group of government and commercial entities in emotion- charged and often dangerous emergency situations.

While the health of our Nation's waters and marine resources is vital to our economy, our waterways are also an economic highway essential to the Nation's access to several billion tons of foreign and domestic freight annually. Waterborne trade generates tens of millions of jobs and contributes hundreds of billions of dollars to the U.S. gross national product each year. The U.S. MTS and its intermodal links support our economic prosperity, military strength, and national security. This complex system includes international and domestic passenger services, commercial and recreational fisheries, and recreational boating.

The Coast Guard carries out numerous port and waterways management tasks. USCG is responsible for providing a safe, efficient, and navigable waterway system to support domestic commerce, international trade, and military sealift requirements for national defense. The Coast Guard provides long and short- range aids to navigation; navigation schemes and standards; support for mapping and charting; tide, current, and pilotage information; vessel traffic services; domestic icebreaking to facilitate commerce; and technical assistance and advice.

The Coast Guard's full-time workforce is made up of approximately 40,000 active duty military personnel and over 7,000 civilian employees.

Finally, the Coast Guard operates the Nation's only Polar icebreakers. This enables USCG to project U.S. presence and protect national interests in the Arctic and Antarctic regions. These Polar vessels are key components in resupplying U.S. Antarctic facilities. They support the research requirements of the National Science Foundation, and protect or advance other U.S. interests in the Polar Regions.[2]

Workforce

Mission success is made possible by the combined activities of Coast Guard operational and support personnel. This teamwork is key to ensuring Coast Guard readiness, agility, and operational excellence. The Coast Guard cannot succeed without the skilled contributions, direct and indirect, of USCG active duty and civilian full-time employees, part-time reservists, and auxiliary volunteers. When appropriate or necessary, the Coast Guard also relies on the help of many federal, state, local, tribal, and private sector partners.

The Coast Guard's full-time workforce is made up of approximately 40,000 active duty military personnel and over 7,000 civilian employees. They are augmented when necessary by small numbers of civilians working under contract. This entire workforce could fit into an average size major league baseball stadium.

The Coast Guard Reserve offers citizens the opportunity to serve in the military part-time while maintaining a separate civilian career. The Reserve provides the Coast Guard highly trained and well qualified personnel for active duty in time of war and national emergency, and for augmentation of Coast

Guard forces during natural or man-made disasters or accidents. The Coast Guard Reserve, numbering over 10,000 members,4 provides the Coast Guard surge capacity and flexibility to respond to all threats and all hazards.

Nearly 30,000 strong, the men and women of the uniformed all-volunteer U.S. Coast Guard Auxiliary spend thousands of hours each year, often on their personal vessels and aircraft, helping to carry out Coast Guard missions. On some waterways, Auxiliarists are the principal Coast Guard personnel serving the public. They are probably best known for their boating safety classes and courtesy vessel safety checks. However, since 1997 they have supported all Coast Guard missions except those involving military operations or law enforcement. The Coast Guard Auxiliary is the only all-volunteer component within the Department of Homeland Security.

All together, this small service with a very big job numbers only about 87,000 personnel. By comparison, the next smallest U.S. armed force is the Marine Corps with over 198,000 active duty members alone.

Operational Force Structure

To understand the Coast Guard's operational structure today, it is helpful to categorize Coast Guard field operational units according to three types of forces.

Multi-Mission Shore-Based Forces

Coast Guard Sector commands focus service delivery on major port regions within the U.S. and its territories. Sector commands are a consolidation of Coast Guard shore-based field operational units. These include boat stations, aids to navigation teams, and prevention and response forces such as vessel inspectors, port operations forces, communications centers, and mission controllers.

Sector Commanders possess specific legal authorities for statutorily defined areas. The most important of these are:

- Captain of the Port (COTP), with authority over maritime commerce;
- Federal Maritime Security Coordinator (FMSC), with authority over maritime security;
- Officer in Charge of Marine Inspection (OCMI), with authority over vessel standards compliance;
- Search and Rescue Mission Coordinator (SMC), with authority over rescue operations; and
- Federal On-Scene Coordinator (FOSC), with authority over oil and hazardous material spill response and preparedness.

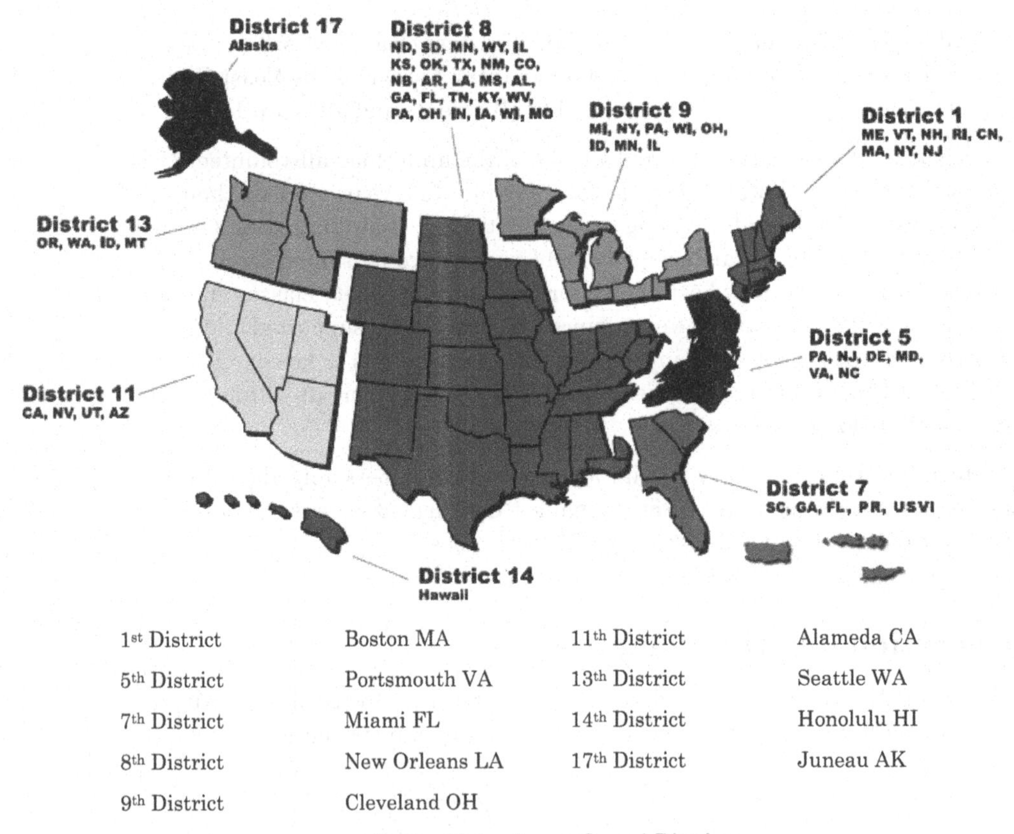

1st District	Boston MA	11th District	Alameda CA
5th District	Portsmouth VA	13th District	Seattle WA
7th District	Miami FL	14th District	Honolulu HI
8th District	New Orleans LA	17th District	Juneau AK
9th District	Cleveland OH		

Table 15.2: Coast Guard Districts.

Coast Guard Sector commands are the principal enforcers of ports, waterways, and coastal laws and regulations. As such, they are the Coast Guard's key operational link to federal, state, local, tribal, and private sector partners.

Maritime Patrol and Interdiction Forces

Coast Guard cutters, aircraft, and their crews make up the second type of forces. These multi-mission platforms are assigned operations domestically or globally, and enable maritime presence, patrol, response, and interdiction throughout the maritime domain. With their military command, control, and communications networks, they allow the Coast Guard to deter criminal activity and respond to threats and natural or man-made emergencies.

The Coast Guard can also provide these uniquely capable forces to the Department of Defense for national security contingencies. USCG's newest cutters and aircraft are highly adaptable and capable of meeting current and future homeland and national security needs around the world. Networked and mobile, USCG cutters and aircraft provide domain awareness and coordinate multi-mission, interagency operations.

Although maritime patrol and interdiction forces work principally in the offshore and international environments, they can also operate near shore or within ports. This is critical following a disaster or major disruption to local command, control, and communications capabilities. As the Nation's only provider of Polar icebreaking capabilities, the Coast Guard enables unique access and capabilities in the Polar Regions.

Deployable Specialized Forces

Deployable Specialized Forces (DSFs) are rapidly transportable elements with specialized skills in law enforcement, military port security, hazardous spill response, and other such missions. These specialized teams provide the Coast Guard with surge capability and flexibility. The Deployable Operations Group (DOG) oversees, coordinates, and integrates Coast Guard DSFs, which include some reserve-based units. The DOG also works with other DHS components and government agencies to develop integrated, multi-agency, force packages to address maritime threats and hazards.

Forces within the DOG include:

- Maritime Safety and Security Teams (MSSTs), which include security and boat forces;
- Maritime Security Response Team (MSRT), which has specialized capabilities for law enforcement;
- Tactical Law Enforcement Teams (TACLETs) and Law Enforcement Detachments (LEDETs), which deploy wherever needed for law enforcement missions;
- Port Security Units (PSUs), which provide expeditionary port security; and
- National Strike Force (NSF), which provides high-end pollution and hazardous material response.[3]

Conclusion

the Coast Guard's ability to fulfill its three broad roles— maritime safety, maritime security, and maritime stewardship— makes us truly a unique instrument of national policy and well-being. More than simply "guarding the coast," the Coast Guard help safeguard the global maritime commons.[4]

Questions

1. What are the three major roles of the United States Coast Guard?
2. What is the Coast Guard's primary role in homeland security?
3. What makes the Coast Guard unique among the uniform services?

Chapter 21

Border Patrol

Objectives

- Be familiar with the history of the Border Patrol.
- Understand the mission and objectives of the Border Patrol.
- Know the functions of the Border Patrol under the Customs and Border Patrol directorate.
- Understand the initiatives of the Border Patrol to facilitate secure travel and trade.

The challenge of our borders is relatively simple on paper. We must allow legal travelers and legal cargo in, and we must keep illegal and potentially dangerous people and cargo out. That simple equation is complicated by the sheer magnitude of the mission.

— Michael Chertoff, Former Secretary, Department of Homeland Security

Introduction

Securing the nation's air, land, and sea borders is a difficult yet critical task. The United States has 5,525 miles of border with Canada and 1,989 miles with Mexico. Our maritime border includes 95,000 miles of shoreline, and a 3.4 million square mile exclusive economic zone. Each year, more than 500 million people cross the borders into the United States, some 330 million of whom are non-citizens.[1]

The United States Border Patrol is the mobile, uniformed law enforcement arm of the U.S. Customs and Border Protection (CBP) within the Department of Homeland Security (DHS). The Border Patrol was officially established on May 28, 1924 by an act of Congress passed in response to increasing illegal immigration. As mandated by this Act, the small border guard in what was then the Bureau of Immigration was reorganized into the Border Patrol. The initial force of 450 officers was given the responsibility of combating illegal entries and the growing business of alien smuggling.

The Border Patrol was officially established on May 28, 1924 by an act of Congress passed in response to increasing illegal immigration.

Since the terrorist attacks of September 11, 2001, the focus of the Border Patrol has evolved to functions of detection, apprehension and/or deterrence of terrorists and terrorist weapons. Although the Border Patrol has changed dramatically since its inception over 80 years ago, its overall mission remains unchanged: to detect and prevent the illegal entry of aliens into the United States. Together with other law enforcement officers, the Border Patrol helps maintain borders that work - facilitating the flow of legal immigration and goods while preventing the illegal trafficking of people and contraband.[2]

History

The United States Border Patrol (USBP) has a long and storied history as our nation's front line in the struggle to secure our borders. Founded in 1924, the U.S. Border Patrol was established in El Paso, Texas, and Detroit, Michigan. The Purpose: To combat the illegal entry of aliens, contraband, and the flow of illicit liquor from Mexico and Canada into the United States. The newly organized El Paso Border Patrol Station was assigned 25 Patrol Inspectors, many of whom were recruited from the ranks of the Texas Rangers. Today, The Border Patrol boasts over 18,000 agents, in 20 sectors, and 164 stations around the nation.

Under the authority of the Immigration Act, approved by Congress on May 28, 1924, the Border Patrol was created as a uniformed law enforcement branch of the Immigration Bureau. This prompted the establishment of the El Paso Border Patrol Sector on July 1, 1924. It was the height of Prohibition in the

United States, and organized crime was a growing concern, as the mafia controlled a majority of the alcohol being smuggled into the United States. As a result, liquor smuggling from Mexico and Canada became a well organized, thriving industry. The opportunity to earn substantial sums of money became a temptation for many illegal aliens that were willing to enter the United States carrying a few crates of contraband.

It wasn't long before gun battles began to erupt between Border Patrolmen, and smugglers attempting to avoid arrest. In February 1927, El Paso Sector experienced one of the bloodiest months for the agency. As old newspapers report, during the entire month, there had not been a 24-hour period of time without a gunfight between smugglers and Patrol Inspectors. These gunfights added to the renown of the Border Patrol, as patrolmen gained a reputation for winning most of these shootouts.

Almost immediately after the establishment of the El Paso Station, a need was seen to have officers at outlying locations. Other stations soon opened within the sector. The Border Patrol began to grow, as the situation along the border was steadily deteriorating.

As the prohibition era reached the peak of its infamy; lawlessness and violence became more common along the water borders of the Detroit Sector. Several Detroit Sector Patrol Inspectors were killed in the line of duty during this period, as smugglers attempting to bring contraband across the border resorted to violence to protect their cargo from the Border Patrol Inspectors.

The USBP was established at the height of the Prohibition Era in 1924.

Eighty-six years later, the Border Patrol has evolved into the finest law enforcement organization in the world. On a daily basis, the Border Patrol is confronted with a large number of threats that would never have been conceived of at the time of the agency's inception. Criminal organizations have evolved as well, adopting a wide variety of weapons and technology to aid them in their efforts to enter the United States while smuggling human cargo and other contraband.

Since 9-11, the agency has had to adapt yet again, to our nation's newest threat; terrorism. The U.S. Border Patrol has proven over its long history that its men and women are up to the task ahead, and stand ready at our nation's borders. [3]

Mission

The USBP's mission has historically been to prevent unauthorized aliens from entering into the country. In the wake of the terrorist attacks of September 11, 2001, the Border Patrol has experienced a tremendous change in its mission. Under the auspices of its new parent agency, U.S. Customs and Border Protection (CBP), the Border Patrol's priority mission is to prevent terrorists and terrorist weapons from entering the United States. The Border Patrol will continue to advance its traditional mission by preventing illegal aliens, smugglers, narcotics, and other contraband from entering the United States as these measures directly impact the safety and security of the United States. To carry out its missions, the Border Patrol has a clear strategic goal: to establish and maintain operational control of the border of the United States.

The Border Patrol's strategy consists of five main objectives :

- Establish substantial probability of apprehending terrorists and their weapons as they attempt to enter illegally between the ports of entry;
- Deter illegal entries through improved enforcement;
- Detect, apprehend, and deter smugglers of humans, drugs, and other contraband;
- Leverage "Smart Border" technology to multiply the deterrent and enforcement effect of the agents; and
- Reduce crime in border communities and consequently improve the quality of life and economic vitality of targeted areas.[4]

These objectives, as part of the National Border Patrol's Strategy, specifically address three of CBP's overarching goals:

- Preventing Terrorism: Detect and prevent terrorists and terrorist weapons, including weapons of mass effect, from entering the United States.
- Strengthening Control of the United States Borders: Strengthen national security between the ports of entry to prevent the illegal entry of terrorists, terrorist weapons, contraband, and illegal aliens into the United States.
- Protecting America and its Citizens: Contribute to a safer America by prohibiting the introduction of illicit contraband, including illegal drugs, and other harmful materials and organisms, into the United States.[5]

Line Watch

In order to apply the Border Patrol's objectives, one of the most important activities of a Border Patrol Agent is the "line watch." This involves the detection, prevention and apprehension of terrorists, undocumented aliens and smugglers of aliens at or near the land border by maintaining surveillance from a covert position, following up leads, responding to electronic sensor television systems, aircraft sightings, and interpreting and following tracks, marks and other physical evidence. Some of the major activities are traffic check, traffic observation, city patrol, transportation check, administrative, intelligence, and anti-smuggling activities.[6]

Organization

The USBP's statutory authority for border enforcement powers derives from section 287 of the Immigration and Nationality Act (INA). The INA gives immigration officers (as designated by federal regulations) the statutory authority to search, interrogate, and arrest unauthorized aliens and all others who are violating immigration laws. The INA also bequeaths immigration officers a broader statutory authority to make arrests for any felony cognizable under the laws of the United States. Federal regulations then designate USBP agents as immigration officers capable of wielding the above mentioned powers. This means that the USBP is not a statutorily defined agency, instead its role is delineated through federal regulations.[7]

In the course of discharging its duties, the USBP patrols over 8,000 miles of American international borders with Mexico and Canada and the coastal waters around Florida and Puerto Rico. However, there are significant geographic, political, and immigration-related differences between the northern border with Canada and the southwest border with Mexico. Accordingly, the USBP deploys a different mix of personnel and resources along the two borders. With over 97% of unauthorized migrant apprehensions occurring along the southwest border, the USBP deploys over 90% of its agents there to deter illegal immigration. The northern border is more than two times longer than the southwest border, features far lower numbers of aliens attempting to enter illegally, but may be more vulnerable to terrorist infiltration. As a consequence of this, the USBP has focused its northern border efforts on deploying technology and cooperating closely with Canadian authorities through the creation of International Border Enforcement Teams.

The Border Patrol's National Strategy (BPNS) is an attempt to lay the foundation for achieving operational control over the border. The strategy thus places greater emphasis on a hierarchical and vertical command structure, featuring a direct chain of command from HQ to the field. The BPNS builds on the "Prevention Through Deterrence" strategy, but places added emphasis on enhancing the Border Patrol's ability to rapidly deploy its agents to respond to emerging threats.

In order to effectively apply its mission across the border coverage area, the USBP is broken down into 20 separate sectors and their respective duty stations that span across the Canadian and Mexican borders as well as protecting the shorelines of Florida and Puerto Rico, each headed up by a sector chief patrol agent.[8]

The Border Patrol also recognizes the need for specialized teams capable of handling uncommon and dangerous situations. The Special Operations Group (SOG) provides the Department of Homeland Security, CBP and the Border Patrol with specially-trained and equipped teams capable of rapid response to emergent and uncommon law enforcement situations requiring special tactics and techniques, search and rescue, and medical response capabilities. As a highly mobile, rapid response tool, SOG significantly increases the ability of DHS to respond operationally to specific terrorist threats and incidents, as well as supporting traditional Border Patrol operations. SOG is comprised of three unique, specially-trained units: The Border Patrol Tactical Unit; Border Patrol Search, Trauma, and Rescue Unit; and the Border Patrol Special Response Team. Each component possesses its own history and specialized field of expertise.[9]

Operational Objectives

Tactical, operational, and strategic intelligence is critical to this new emphasis on rapid deployment, as it will allow the Border Patrol to assess risk and target its enforcement efforts. The Border Patrol believes that much of this intelligence will be generated through the use of next generation surveillance systems, including cameras, sensors, and other technologies. However, recent pilot programs of these next-generation technologies have yielded mixed results. Additionally, the Border Patrol will coordinate closely with CBP's Office of Intelligence and other DHS and Federal agencies' intelligence apparatuses.[10]

Therefore, the Border Patrol has primary responsibility for monitoring and responding to illicit border intrusions across thousands of miles of border between U.S. ports of entry. Prior to the terrorist attacks of 9/11, the primary focus of the Border Patrol was on illegal aliens, alien smuggling, and narcotics interdiction. The Border Patrol arrests over one million illegal aliens annually, and routinely seizes over 1 million pounds of marijuana and 15 - 20 tons of cocaine every year. After 9/11, it was apparent that smugglers' methods, routes, and modes of transportation are potential vulnerabilities that can be exploited by terrorists and result in terrorist weapons illegally entering the United States.

The Border Patrol's expertise in countering this threat is critical to ensuring the security of the United States. Although the threat and strategic response vary across the Northern, Southern and Coastal Borders, the potential exists for a single individual or small group to cross the border undetected with biological or chemical weapons, weapons of mass effect, or other implements of terrorism. The CBP's National Border Patrol Strategy has been developed with measures and initiatives designed to eliminate or mitigate this threat.

The Border Patrol will address a wide variety of threats and vulnerabilities by deploying an appropriate mix of personnel, equipment, technology, and border infrastructure. The differing threat locations outlined below result from the geographical diversity of the border and from other related factors, such as differences in population centers, routes of ingress and egress from the border, economic stability of neighboring countries, and immigration patterns. These differences are wide-ranging and require the Border Patrol to maintain a high degree of flexibility in its approach to the border security mission.

Southern (U.S.–Mexico) Border

Much of the southern border with Mexico is extremely inhospitable and is surrounded by harsh terrain. Hundreds of aliens die each year as a result of failed smuggling efforts while attempting to cross the southern border. Within a stretch of nearly 2,000 miles of border, there are three primary smuggling corridors: South Texas corridor; West Texas/New Mexico corridor; and California/Arizona corridor. These corridors are largely dictated by transportation routes, geography, and population centers. More than ninety percent of the one million plus annual arrests that the Border Patrol makes occur along the U.S.-Mexico border within these smuggling corridors.

The Border Patrol has experienced success in gaining operational control of the border in some of the highest trafficked areas, such as San Diego, El Paso, and McAllen. However, many other areas along the southwest border are not yet under operational control, and the daily attempts to cross the border by thousands of illegal aliens from countries around the globe continue to present a threat to U.S. national security. Some would classify the majority of these aliens as "economic migrants." However, an ever-present threat exists from the potential for terrorists to employ the same smuggling and transportation networks, infrastructure, drop houses, and other support and then use these masses of illegal aliens as "cover" for a successful cross-border penetration.

The Border Patrol arrests hundreds of aliens each year from "special interest" countries. The State Department has determined that these countries present a potential terrorist threat to U.S. national security. Cross-border illegal penetrations by terrorists and those potentially smuggling terrorist weapons are not mutually exclusive from penetrations by illegal aliens, criminals, and narcotics traffickers.

Past experience has shown that a balanced mix of personnel, technology, and border infrastructure, such as roads, lights, fencing, and facilities, are critical to expanding control over the Southern Border. The Border Patrol builds on the successes won by the deployment of these resources on the Southern Border, and continue to expand state of the art sensoring technologies, intelligence, skills and training, and nationally driven deployment of personnel and material.

Northern (U.S.-Canada) Border:

The U.S.-Canada border consists of many water boundaries and includes the Great Lakes area and surrounding waterways. Some of these waterways freeze during the winter and can easily be crossed on foot or by vehicle or snowmobile. The Border Patrol must also address issues inherent in locations along the Northern Border designated as reservation lands for Native American peoples, that allow more limited access on both the U.S. and Canadian sides of the border.

Further threats result from the fact that over ninety percent of Canada's population lives within one hundred miles of the U.S.-Canada border. Although the U.S. and Canada enjoy an extremely cooperative relationship, intelligence indicates that some individuals and organizations in Canada who reside near the border represent a potential threat to U.S. national security. The northern border also has well-organized smuggling operations, which can potentially support the movement of terrorists and their weapons.

The number of actual illegal border penetrations along the U.S.-Canada border is small in comparison to daily arrests along the U.S.-Mexico border. While resources have been significantly increased since 9/11 from approximately 350 agents to 1,000 agents, the Border Patrol's ability to detect, respond to, and interdict illegal cross-border penetrations along the U.S.-Canada border remains limited. Continued testing, acquisition, and deployment of sensing and monitoring platforms will be key to the Border Patrol's ability to effectively address the Northern Border threat situation.

To identify specific Northern Border threats, the Border Patrol has strengthened its partnerships with Canadian law enforcement and intelligence officials, and with officials from other federal, state, local, and tribal organizations by leveraging information and increasing communication and cooperation. The Integrated Border Enforcement, Maritime, and Intelligence Teams (IBET/IMET/IBIT) are examples of this effort.

Coastal (Caribbean) Borders:

In the U.S. Coastal areas, the Border Patrol works with a variety of law enforcement agencies, such as the U.S. Coast Guard, to address the threat of potential mass migrations, maritime smuggling, and crewman control. While the number of illegal entrants migrating through Coastal areas is currently lower than on the land borders, the threat faced by the Border Patrol is increased by local government corruption and inadequate tracking systems which fail to monitor those who transit those countries.

The proximity of these nations to the United States coastline requires that all CBP components remain vigilant and promote a common operational picture. Therefore, investing in air and maritime assets, continuing partnerships with other DHS components, and leveraging available assets operating in this environment are critical to ensuring that CBP has flexible response capabilities to address the threat in Coastal sectors.[11]

SBI mission is to lead the operational requirements support and documentation as well as the acquisition efforts to develop, deploy, and integrate technology and tactical infrastructure .

Customs and Border Patrol Initiatives

USBP addresses the CBP's National Strategy to prevent terrorism, strengthen control of U.S. borders, and protect America and its citizens by engaging in specific initiatives that include the overarching Secure Border Initiative (SBI) as well as efforts in international cooperation, partnering with the private sector, advanced screening initiatives, and border surveillance systems.

In 2005, the Department of Homeland Security established the Secure Border Initiative (SBI), a comprehensive, multi-year plan to help secure America's borders. The SBI program office within CBP was established to manage the development, deployment, and integration of SBI acquisition programs, and integrate and coordinate border security programs within CBP.

The SBI mission is to lead the operational requirements support and documentation as well as the acquisition efforts to develop, deploy, and integrate technology and tactical infrastructure in support of CBP's efforts to gain and maintain effective control of U.S. land border areas.

Effective control of the border is achieved by knowing what is going on at the border (situational awareness) and having the ability to respond. CBP utilizes a combination of three tools to achieve effective control: personnel, tactical infrastructure, and technology.

SBI supports CBP's front-line agents and officers by deploying an optimal, integrated solution that includes the SBInet, SBI Tactical Infrastructure, and the Northern Border Project.

- SBInet is a major technology effort focused on the areas between the ports-of-entry on the Southwest Border. The goal of the SBInet program is to integrate new and existing border technology into a networked system that will enable CBP personnel to more effectively detect, identify, classify, and respond to incursions at the border.[13]
- SBI Tactical Infrastructure/Border Fence (TIBF), part of the Department's Southwest Border security strategy, originally stood up under the Secure Border Initiative (SBI) in 2007 – developed, installed, operated, and maintained physical components designed to provide persistent impedance of illicit cross-border activity. The success of the TIBF projects directly impacts the Department's goal to achieve effective control of the border. When finished, the TIBF Program will have constructed a total of approximately 670 miles of pedestrian and vehicle fence along the Southwest Border.[14]
- Northern Border Project deploys 16 Remote Video Surveillance Systems (RVSS) in the Buffalo and Detroit Sectors to provide coverage along the Niagara and St. Clair Rivers. CBP chose the Buffalo and Detroit Sectors for this deployment based on the needs of the Border Patrol and the unique operational area which consists of coastal maritime, riverine, urban, and rural environments. The RVSSs provides 17 miles and 35 miles of surveillance coverage along the Niagara and St. Clair Rivers, respectively.[15]

International Cooperation

Smarter borders were created by extending a zone of security beyond our physical borders and creating working groups with foreign counterparts to establish ties, improve security, and facilitate the flow of legitimate travel and trade.

The Container Security Initiative (CSI) pushes the border protection outward by working jointly with host nation counterparts to identify and pre-screen containers that pose a risk at the foreign port of departure before they are loaded on board vessels bound for the U.S. CSI is now implemented in 20 of the largest ports in terms of container shipments to the U.S.

Joint initiatives were also implemented with Canada and Mexico; The Smart Border Declaration and associated 30-Point Action Plan with Canada, and the Smart Border Accord with Mexico work to ensure the secure flow of people and goods across the borders. The Secure Electronic Network for Travelers' Rapid Inspection (SENTRI) allows pre-screened, low-risk travelers from Mexico to be processed in an expeditious manner through dedicated lanes. Similarly, on our northern border with Canada, CBP is engaging in NEXUS to identify and facilitate low-risk travelers. Along both borders, CBP has implemented the Free and Secure Trade (FAST) program. The FAST program utilizes transponder technology and pre-arrival shipment information to process participating trucks as they arrive at the border, expediting trade while better securing our borders.

Other international initiatives to facilitate secure travel and trade include:

- The World Customs Organization harmonizes the advance of electronic cargo information requirements on inbound, outbound and transit shipments; each country that joins the Framework commits to employing a consistent risk management approach to address security threats; at the reasonable request of the receiving nation, based upon a comparable risk targeting methodology, the sending nation's Customs administration will perform an outbound inspection of high-risk containers and cargo, preferably using non-intrusive detection equipment such as large-scale X-ray machines and radiation detectors; and defines benefits that Customs will provide to businesses that meet minimal supply chain security standards and best practices.[16]
- The Customs Mutual Assistance Agreements (CMAA) allow for the exchange of information, intelligence, and documents that will ultimately assist countries in the prevention and investigation of customs offenses. The agreements are particularly helpful for U.S. Attaché offices, as each agreement is tailored to the capacities and national policy of an individual country's customs administration.[17]
- The International Visitors Program (IVP) consists of specially arranged briefings and visits to Customs and Border Protection (CBP) operations in the United States by foreign high-level customs and other law enforcement officials who perform or manage functions similar to those encompassed within CBP's area of responsibility and expertise. The IVP is especially appropriate for government management officials who are new to their positions and are committed to improving the effectiveness and efficiency of their organizations. In addition to affording top managers the opportunity to observe current CBP programs and processes, IVP visits have the objective of encouraging close cooperation in designing and implementing secure government processing systems and processes and encouraging efforts to strengthen supply chain security in the country of the visiting official.[18]

Partnering with Business

Processing the sheer volume of trade entering the U.S. each year requires help from the private sector as well. The Customs-Trade Partnership Against Terrorism (C-TPAT) is a voluntary government-business initiative to build cooperative relationships that strengthen and improve overall international supply chain and U.S. border security. C-TPAT recognizes that U.S. Customs and Border Protection (CBP) can provide the highest level of cargo security only through close cooperation with the ultimate owners of the international supply chain such as importers, carriers, consolidators, licensed customs brokers, and manufacturers. Through this initiative, CBP is asking businesses to ensure the integrity of their security practices and communicate and verify the security guidelines of their business partners within the supply chain.[19]

In addition, the Advanced Trade Data Initiative, known as the 10+2 Initiative effective January 26, 2009, is under way. [20]This program works with the trade community to obtain information on U.S. bound goods at the earliest possible point in the supply chain. Partnering with carriers, importers, shippers and terminal operators, this initiative gathers supply chain data and feeds it into database systems to validate container shipments during the supply process. This information increases CBP's existing ability to zero in on suspect movements and perform any necessary security inspections at the earliest point possible in the supply chain.[21]

Advanced Screening

Given the magnitude of CBP's responsibility, the development and deployment of sophisticated detection technology is essential. Deployment of Non-Intrusive Inspection (NII) technology is increasing and viewed as "force multipliers" that enable CBP officers to screen or examine a larger portion of the stream of commercial traffic. CBP does not rely on any single technology or inspection process. Instead, officers and agents use various technologies in different combinations to substantially increase the likelihood that terrorist weapons including a nuclear or radiological weapon will be detected and interdicted.

Technologies deployed to our nation's land, sea, and airports of entry include large-scale x-ray and gamma-imaging systems. CBP has deployed radiation detection technology including Personal Radiation Detectors (PRDs), radiation isotope identifiers, and radiation portal monitors. CBP uses trained explosive and chemical detector dogs. CBP's Laboratories and Scientific Services Fast Response Team reacts to calls on suspicious containers. The Laboratories and Scientific Services also operates a 24x7x365 hotline at its Chemical, Biological, Radiation, and Nuclear Technical Data Assessment and Teleforensic Center.

U.S. Customs and Border Protection has the authority to search outbound, as well as inbound shipments, and uses targeting to carry out its mission in this area. Targeting of outbound shipments and people is a multi-dimensional effort that is enhanced by inter-agency cooperation. CBP in conjunction with the Department of State and the Bureau of the Census has put in place regulations that require submission of electronic export information on U.S. Munitions List and for technology for the Commerce Control List. This information flows via the Automated Export System (AES). CBP is also working with the Departments of State and Defense to improve procedures on exported shipments of foreign military sales commodities. CBP works with Immigration and Customs Enforcement (ICE) to seize outbound currency, particularly cash and monetary instruments going to the Middle East.

Border Surveillance

U.S. Customs and Border Protection's Border Patrol agents are better securing areas between the ports of entry by implementing a comprehensive border enforcement strategy, expanding, integrating, and coordinating the use of technology and communications through:

- Integrated Surveillance Intelligence System (ISIS) is a system that uses remotely monitored night-day camera and sensing systems to better detect, monitor, and respond to illegal crossings.
- Unmanned Aerial Vehicles (UAVs) are equipped with sophisticated onboard sensors. UAVs provide long-range surveillance and are useful for monitoring remote land border areas where patrols cannot easily travel and infrastructure is difficult or impossible to build.
- Remote Video Surveillance Systems (RVSS) provide coverage 24x7 to detect illegal crossings on both our northern and southern borders.
- Geographic Information System (GIS)—a CBP Border Patrol southwest border initiative to track illegal migration patterns.7
- CBP's Air and Marine Operations Division is responsible for protecting the nation's borders and the American people from the smuggling of people, narcotics, and other contraband and for detecting and deterring terrorist activity with an integrated and coordinated air and marine interdiction force. The Air and Marine Operations Division also supports ICE investigations.[22]

The biometrics technology used by US VISIT includes digital fingerprinting and photographs to identify international travelers.

US-VISIT

US-VISIT supports the Department of Homeland Security's mission to protect our nation by providing biometric identification services to federal, state and local government decision makers to help them accurately identify the people they encounter and determine whether those people pose a risk to the United States.

US-VISIT's most visible service is the collection of biometrics—digital fingerprints and a photograph—from international travelers at U.S. visa-issuing posts and ports of entry. Collecting this information helps immigration officers determine whether a person is eligible to receive a visa or enter the United States. The biometric collection process is simple, convenient and secure.

US-VISIT's innovative use of biometrics prevents identity fraud and deprives criminals and immigration violators of the ability to cross our borders. US-VISIT also supports the Department's ability to identify international travelers who have remained in the United States beyond their period of admission by analyzing biographical information.

By providing decision makers with the information they need where and when they need it, US-VISIT is helping to make U.S. immigration and border management efforts more collaborative, more streamlined and more effective.[23]

Conclusion

The U.S. Border Patrol continues its efforts to control our nation's borders. The 21st century promises to provide enormous leaps in technology that can be applied to border enforcement. The modernization of the Patrol advances at a dizzying rate as new generations of agents develop innovative ways to integrate the contemporary technology into field operations. New and specialized technology is being created within the Border Patrol that holds increasing potential to assist agents in fulfilling the mission of the Patrol. Additionally, cooperation with neighboring countries increases border safety and law enforcement efforts. The future of the U.S. Border Patrol promises to be as exciting and interesting as its past, and will continue to echo the motto that agents have lived by since 1924.[24]

Questions

1. How has the Border Patrol improved border security for the United States?
2. What are the competing factors between securing the Northern Border with Canada and the Southwest Border with Mexico?
3. What role does technology play in securing our Nation's borders?

Chapter 22

Transportation Security Administration

Objectives

- Know the history of the TSA.
- Understand the role and responsibility of the TSA in homeland security efforts.
- Understand the operational objectives of the TSA.
- Know the programs and initiatives under the TSA functions.

Introduction

The Transportation Security Administration (TSA) was created in the wake of 9/11 to strengthen the security of the nation's transportation systems while ensuring the freedom of movement for people and commerce. Within a year, TSA assumed responsibility for security at the nation's airports and deployed a Federal workforce to meet Congressional deadlines for screening all commercial airline passengers and baggage. In March 2003, TSA transferred from the Department of Transportation to the Department of Homeland Security.

TSA employs a risk-based strategy to secure U.S. transportation systems, working closely with stakeholders in aviation, rail, transit, highway, and pipeline sectors, as well as the partners in the law enforcement and intelligence community. The agency continuously sets the standard for excellence in transportation security through its people, processes, technologies and use of intelligence to drive operations.[1]

The TSA employs approximately 51,000 security officers, inspectors, directors, air marshals and managers who protect the nation's transportation systems. They look for bombs at checkpoints in airports, inspect rail cars, patrol subways with our law enforcement partners, and work to make all modes of transportation safe.[2]

History

The Transportation Security Administration (TSA) was created in response to the 9/11 attacks as part of the Aviation and Transportation Security Act (ATSA, Public Law 107-71) passed by the U.S. Congress and signed into law by President George W. Bush on November 19, 2001 which among other things established the new Transportation Security Administration (TSA) within the Department of Transportation.[3] The head of TSA was the Under Secretary of Transportation for Security. Under the Homeland Security Act of 2002, Public Law 107-296, TSA transferred to DHS in March, 2003. The head of TSA is now referred to as the Assistant Secretary of Homeland Security for the Transportation Security Administration.[4] The organization was charged with developing policies to ensure the security of U.S. air traffic and other forms of transportation.

Organization

One of the most significant changes mandated by ATSA was the shift from the use of private-sector screeners to perform airport screening operations to the use of federal screeners (now referred to as TSOs). Prior to ATSA, passenger and checked baggage screening had been performed by private screening companies under contract to airlines. ATSA established TSA and required it to create a federal workforce to assume the job of conducting passenger and checked baggage screening at commercial airports. The federal screener workforce was put into place, as required, by November 2002.[5]

Now, as a federal operation, the TSA is a component of the Department of Homeland Security. With state, local and regional partners, the TSA oversees security for highways, railroads, buses, mass transit systems, pipelines, ports, and 457 U.S. airports. However, the bulk of the TSA's efforts are in aviation security. The TSA employs Transportation Security Officers, colloquially known as screeners as well as Federal Air Marshals, Transportation Security Specialists and Transportation Security Inspectors, and oversees the training and testing of explosives detection canine teams.

- Transportation Security Officer (TSO) also known as a screener who performs security screening of persons and property and controls entry and exit points within an airport. They also practice surveillance of several areas beyond the checkpoint and before it in specialized programs TSA has implemented. Today, approximately 48,000 TSO's serve on TSA's frontline in 457 U.S. airports. They use their training and experience to effectively and efficiently screen approximately 2 million people a day.
- Federal Air Marshal (FAM) federal law enforcement officer who while blending in with passengers, are tasked with detecting, deterring, and defeating terrorist or other criminal hostile acts targeting U.S. air carriers, airports, passengers, crew, and when necessary, other transportation modes within the US's general transportation systems.
- Transportation Security Inspectors (TSIs) conduct comprehensive inspections, assessments and investigations of passenger and cargo transportation systems to determine their security posture. TSA employs roughly 1,000 aviation inspectors,[6] 450 cargo inspectors, and 100 surface inspectors.[7]
- The TSA's National Explosives Detection Canine Team Program prepares dogs and handlers to serve as mobile teams that can quickly locate and identify dangerous materials that may present a threat to transportation systems. As of June 2008, the TSA had trained about 430 canine teams with 370 deployed to airports and 56 deployed to mass transit systems.[8]

Belts, wallets and cell phones are the most common items that alarm on a passenger when passing through the metal detector.

Operations

The focus of TSA is to identify, prioritize, and mitigate risks, ultimately minimizing the impact of potential incidents. Information sharing among agencies and stakeholders – including intelligence information – is a cornerstone of the risk management model.

TSA recognizes the unique attributes of each transportation mode and is committed to ensuring passenger and cargo security and preserving public confidence in the security of the U.S. transportation system. TSA's specific responsibilities include:

- Ensuring a thorough and efficient screening of all aviation passengers and baggage;
- Promoting confidence by deploying Federal Air Marshals to detect, deter, and defeat hostile acts targeting air carriers;

- Managing security risks of the surface transportation systems by establishing clear lines of communication and collaborative working relationships with federal, local and private stakeholders, providing support and programmatic direction, conducting on-site inspections, and developing security programs; and
- Developing and implementing more efficient, reliable, integrated, and cost effective terrorist-related screening programs. [9]

The TSA is responsible for day-to-day Federal security screening operations for passenger air transportation and intrastate air transportation. The TSA develops standards for hiring and retaining security screening personnel; training and testing security screening personnel; and hiring and training personnel to provide security screening at all airports in the United States.

The TSA conducts the following activities to secure the nation's transportation networks:

- Receives, assesses, and distributes intelligence information related to transportation security;
- Assesses threats to transportation;
- Develops policies, strategies, and plans for dealing with threats to transportation security;
- Makes other plans related to transportation security, including coordinating countermeasures with appropriate departments, agencies, and instrumentalities of the United States Government;
- Serves as the primary liaison for transportation security to the intelligence and law enforcement communities;
- Manages and provides operational guidance to the field security resources of the Administration;
- Enforces security-related regulations and requirements;
- Identifies and undertakes research and development activities necessary to enhance transportation security;
- Inspects, maintains, and tests security facilities, equipment, and systems;
- Ensures the adequacy of security measures for the transportation of cargo;
- Oversees the implementation and ensures the adequacy of security measures at airports and other transportation facilities;
- Conducts background checks for airport security screening personnel, individuals with access to secure areas of airports, and other transportation security personnel;
- Works in conjunction with the Federal Aviation Administration with respect to any actions or activities that may affect aviation safety or air carrier operations;
- Works with the International Civil Aviation Organization and appropriate

The average traveler takes up four feet of space at the checkpoint taking roughly 32 seconds to divest their belongings and 42 seconds to compose at the end of the checkpoint. These numbers may seem insignificant for one traveler, but when you consider that about 2 million passengers go through checkpoints everyday it adds up.

aeronautic authorities of foreign governments to address security concerns on passenger flights by foreign air carriers in foreign air transportation;

- Carries out such other duties, and exercise such other powers, relating to transportation security as the TSA considers appropriate.

In times of national emergency, the TSA is granted additional authority to coordinate domestic transportation, including aviation, rail, and other surface transportation, and maritime transportation (including port security), except for that belonging to the Department of Defense and the military departments. TSA also coordinates security alerts and provides threat notices to other departments and agencies of the Federal Government, and appropriate agencies of State and local governments, including departments and agencies for transportation, law enforcement, and border control.[10]

TSA is also tasked with managing the security risk to the US surface transportation system while ensuring freedom of movement of people and commerce. To put the magnitude of the system TSA is protecting into perspective, Americans took 9.8 billion trips using public transportation. Bus travel accounts for 59.7% of the trips and train travel accounts for 28.6% of the trips on public transportation. To support this system, approximately 354,000 workers and 6,429 agencies are responsible for operating the nation's public transportation system.[11]

42% of the checkpoint bottlenecks are caused by delays in composing after screening.

Service to the Public

TSA responsibilities, which span all modes of transportation, ensure the provision of proactive security measures and a quick and efficient response to any threat, including terrorist incidents and natural disasters. TSA is committed to the highest level of transportation security for the United States. Public confidence in the safety and security of the nation's transportation systems ensures the continued success and growth of the transportation industry. The nation's economy depends upon implementation of effective, yet efficient transportation security measures. The U.S. and its citizens remain targets for terrorist and other criminals. Protecting our transportation systems is a national security priority and TSA's goals reflect this responsibility. Federal, state, and local governments and private industry continue to work together to achieve our common goal: safe and secure transportation worldwide. TSA is also engaging the public to enhance security awareness in the transportation system and increase mission performance. The public adds its own significant layer of security by its vigilance in looking for and reporting suspicious behavior. The likelihood that a passenger will take action if an event occurs on an aircraft has increased significantly. [12]

The Transportation Security Administration (TSA) has statutory responsibility for security of all of the nation's airports. Tools it uses include intelligence, regulation, enforcement, inspection, and screening and education of carriers, passengers and shippers. The incorporation of TSA into the Department of Homeland Security allows the Department of Transportation to remain focused on its core mandate of ensuring that the nation has a robust and efficient transportation infrastructure that keeps pace with modern technology and the nation's demographic and economic growth.

Initiatives

The TSA employs several programs and initiatives to achieve its goal of security in all modes of transportation. Using the layered security approach to ensure the security of the traveling public and the Nation's transportation system, the TSA not only uses passenger checkpoints at airports, but includes intelligence gathering and analysis, checking passenger manifests against watch lists, random canine team searches at airports, federal air marshals, federal flight deck officers and more security measures both visible and invisible to the public.[13]

The Secure Flight Program is a behind the scenes program that enhances the security of domestic and international commercial air travel through the use of improved watch list matching. By collecting additional passenger data, it will improve the travel experience for all airline passengers, including those who have been misidentified in the past.

The airline will transmit this information to Secure Flight, who uses it to perform watch list matching. This serves to prevent individuals on the No Fly List from boarding an aircraft and to identify individuals on the Selectee List for enhanced screening. After matching passenger information against government watch lists, Secure Flight transmits the matching results back to airlines.

A new initiative under the Secure Flight Program is the Department of Homeland Security's Travel Redress Inquiry Program (DHS TRIP); a single point of contact for individuals who have inquiries or seek resolution regarding difficulties they experienced during their travel screening at transportation hubs--like airports and train stations--or while crossing U.S. borders. DHS TRIP is part of an effort by the departments of State and Homeland Security to welcome legitimate travelers while still securing our country from those who want to do us harm.[14]

Other TSA initiatives include:

- Airline Security Screening (TSA) provides highly trained Security Officers operating at over 700 security checkpoints and nearly 7,000 baggage screening areas each day. They use the latest technology and equipment combined with continually improving screening techniques.
- Crew Member Self Defense Training Program (TSA) provides basic security training for actively employed flight and cabin crewmembers in order to prepare them for potential threat conditions that may occur onboard an aircraft.
- Federal Air Marshals (TSA) work across several law enforcement organizations, and in the air, they blend in with airline passengers and rely on their extensive training to protect the flying public.
- Federal Flight Deck Officers (TSA) via training by the Federal Air Marshal Service allows eligible airline flight crew members the use of firearms to defend against hijacking attempts and other acts of criminal violence.

- Mass Transit (TSA) seeks to advance mass transit and passenger rail security through a comprehensive strategic approach that enhances capabilities to detect, deter, and prevent terrorist attacks and respond to and recover from attacks and security incidents, should they occur.
- Rail Security (TSA) focuses on greater information sharing, increased training and public awareness, and providing greater assistance and funding for rail transit activities.
- US-VISIT Traveler Information gathers biometric data that is unique and virtually impossible to forge. Collecting biometrics helps the U.S. government prevent people from using fraudulent documents to enter the country illegally. US-VISIT is part of a continuum of security measures that begins overseas and continues through a visitor's arrival in and departure from the United States.
- In 2004, TSA assumed responsibility for the Alien Flight Student Program from the FBI. This program requires FAA-regulated flight schools to notify TSA when a foreign national requests flight training, and requires the candidate to submit to TSA an application that includes identifying information and specific information about their desired training prior to beginning flight training.[15]

Each one of these layers alone is capable of stopping a terrorist attack. In combination their security value is multiplied, creating a much stronger, formidable system. A terrorist who has to overcome multiple security layers in order to carry out an attack is more likely to be pre-empted, deterred, or to fail during the attempt.[16]

Conclusion

The Transportation Security Administration (TSA) was established in 2001 with the mission to protect the transportation network while also ensuring the free movement of people and commerce. Since its inception, TSA has focused much of its efforts on aviation security, and has developed and implemented a variety of programs and procedures to secure commercial aviation.[17] However, the TSA is responsible for oversight of all modes of transportation. The nation's air, land, and marine transportation systems are designed for accessibility and efficiency, two characteristics that make them highly vulnerable to terrorist attack. While hardening the transportation sector from terrorist attack is difficult, reasonable measures can be taken to deter terrorists.[18]

> *TSA has grown from a small cadre of employees to a dedicated workforce of over 50,000 protecting every domestic commercial airport, strengthening our nation's surface transportation modes, and working with our transportation security partners both domestically and around the world. We began with the challenge of hiring, training, and placing the first Federal screeners, known as Transportation Security Officers (TSOs), in airports where they intercepted prohibited items such as guns, knives, and razor blades. Now, TSA employs a highly-trained, professional, multi-skilled TSO workforce that conducts physical and behavioral screening to counter constantly changing threats and operates state-of-the-art screening equipment throughout airports and across multiple modes of transportation.*[19]
>
> — GALE D. ROSSIDES, TSA Acting Administrator

Questions

1. Why was the formulation of the TSA important?
2. 2. What are some inherent public service issues and how might the TSA address them?
3. 3. What is Secure Flight and how does it relate to previous aviation security efforts.
4. 4. How does the TSA manage non-aviation modes of transportation?

Chapter 23

Immigration & Customs

Objectives

- Understand the missions of ICE and USCIS.
- Know the four operational divisions of the Immigration and Customs Enforcement Agency.
- Describe the functions of the USCIS.
- Understand the issues of immigration reform.

"We continue to be a destination that is sought out by immigrants from around the world, who enrich our society."

— National Security Strategy, 2010

Introduction

The United States Government is dedicated to comprehensive reform of America's immigration laws by increasing border security, while maintaining the Nation's tradition of welcoming immigrants who enter the country legally. For immigration reform to succeed, it must be based on five pillars: 1) strengthening security at the borders; 2) substantially increasing enforcement in the interior to remove those who are here illegally, and to prevent employers from deliberately or inadvertently hiring illegal immigrants; 3) implementing a Temporary Worker Program to provide a legal channel for employers to hire foreign workers to do jobs Americans are unwilling to do; 4) addressing the millions of illegal immigrants already in the country; and 5) helping new immigrants assimilate into American society. The plan will deter and apprehend migrants attempting to enter the country illegally and decrease crime rates along the border. The plan also will serve the needs of the economy by allowing employers to hire legal foreign workers on a temporary basis when no American is willing to take the job, bring illegal immigrants out of the shadows without providing amnesty, and restore public confidence in the Federal Government's ability to enforce immigration laws.[1]

The Department of Homeland Security bears responsibility for facilitating legal immigration and welcoming new Americans - as well as providing a range of other immigration services - while cracking down on those who violate our nation's laws.

The Department of Homeland Security (DHS) bears responsibility for facilitating legal immigration and welcoming new Americans - as well as providing a range of other immigration services - while cracking down on those who violate our nation's laws.[2]

U.S. Immigration and Customs Enforcement (ICE), an agency of the Department of Homeland Security (DHS), protects national security and upholds public safety by targeting criminal networks and terrorist organizations that seek to exploit vulnerabilities in our immigration system, in our financial networks, along our border, at federal facilities and elsewhere in order to do harm to the United States. [3]

In addition, DHS, through the U.S. Citizenship and Immigration Services (USCIS), is responsible for providing immigration-related services and benefits such as naturalization and work authorization as well as investigative and enforcement responsibilities for enforcement of federal immigration laws, customs laws and air security laws.[4]

History

Immigration patterns have changed substantially since 1952, when policy makers codifying the

Immigration and Nationality Act (INA) assumed that most aliens becoming legal permanent residents (LPRs) of the United States would be arriving from abroad. In 1975, more than 80% of all LPRs arrived from abroad. By 2005, however, only 34% of all aliens who became LPRs had arrived from abroad; most LPRs adjust status within the United States. That the number of LPRs arriving from abroad has generally remained around 400,000 for the past 30 years while the total number of LPRs now hovers around one million annually highlights the contribution that aliens adjusting to LPR status after being in the United States is making to the growth of permanent legal immigration.

In addition to LPRs, each year millions of foreign nationals come temporarily on nonimmigrant visas (e.g., tourists, foreign students and intra-company business transfers). It is estimated that annually hundreds of thousands of foreign nationals either overstay their nonimmigrant visas or enter the country illegally and thus may become unauthorized aliens. As of March 2008, there were an estimated 11.9 million aliens living here without legal authorization to do so. Almost 40%, an estimated 4.4 million, arrived in the 2000-2005 period.[5]

Immigration & Customs Enforcement

U.S. Immigration and Customs Enforcement (ICE) was formed pursuant to the Homeland Security Act of 2002 following the events of September 11, 2001. With the establishment of the Department of Homeland Security the functions and jurisdictions of several border and revenue enforcement agencies were combined and consolidated into U.S. Immigration and Customs Enforcement. Consequently, ICE is the largest investigative arm of the Department of Homeland Security, and the second largest contributor to the nation's Joint Terrorism Task Force (after the Federal Bureau of Investigation).

It is estimated that annually hundreds of thousands of foreign nationals either overstay their nonimmigrant visas or enter the country illegally and thus may become unauthorized aliens.

The agencies that were either moved entirely or merged in part into ICE included the investigative and intelligence resources of the United States Customs Service, the criminal investigation resources of the Immigration and Naturalization Service, and the United States Federal Protective Service. The Federal Protective Service was transferred from ICE to the National Protection and Programs Directorate effective October 28, 2009. At one point, the Federal Air Marshals Service was moved from the Transportation Security Administration to ICE, but they were eventually moved back to the TSA.[6]

ICE is comprised of four operational divisions:

1. Office of Detention and Removal Operations (DRO)
2. Office of Investigations (OI)
3. Office of Intelligence (Intel)
4. Office of International Affairs (OIA)
5. Office of Detention and Removal Operations

Detention & Removal Operations

The primary responsibility of Detention and Removal Operations (DRO) is to identify, apprehend and remove illegal aliens from the United States. This requires DRO to facilitate the processing of illegal aliens through immigration courts, and to enforce their removal from the United States. Key elements in exercising those responsibilities include: identifying and removing all high-risk illegal alien fugitives and absconders; ensuring that those aliens who have already been identified as criminals are expeditiously removed; and to develop and maintain a robust removals program with the capacity to remove all final order cases - thus precluding growth in the illegal alien absconder population. Simply stated, DRO's ultimate goal is to develop the capacity to identify and remove all removable aliens.

Generally, the Immigration and Nationality Act (INA) grants aliens the right to a removal proceeding before an immigration judge to decide both inadmissibility and deportability. Aliens can be removed for reasons of health, criminal status, economic well-being, national security risks and other reasons of public concern that are specifically defined in the Act. Immigration judges, employed by the Department of Justice, Executive Office for Immigration Review (EOIR) weigh evidence presented by both the alien and ICE, assesses the facts and renders a decision that can be appealed to the Board of Immigration Appeals. If the immigration judge issues a decision ordering the alien removed from the United States, DRO is responsible to enforce the removal order. The process includes coordination and liaison with foreign government officials and embassies to obtain travel documents and country clearances, coordinating complex logistical and transportation issues to repatriate the alien and, if required DRO officers escort the alien to his or her foreign country.

The primary responsibility of Detention and Removal Operations (DRO) is to identify, apprehend and remove illegal aliens from the United States.

The removal of criminal aliens from the United States is a national priority. To address this priority, DRO designed the National Fugitive Operations Program (NFOP). Its mission is to identify, apprehend, and remove from the United States aliens who have failed to surrender for removal or to comply with a removal order. NFOP teams work exclusively on fugitive cases, giving priority to the public safety concerns of criminal aliens cases. The "Absconder Apprehension Initiative" uses the data available from National Crime Information Center databases as a virtual force multiplier. As part of the Alien Absconder Initiative, DRO developed and coordinated the "ICE Most Wanted" program. This program publicizes the names, faces and other identifying features of the 10 most wanted fugitive criminals by ICE.

Intelligence Operations Unit

The Intelligence Operations Unit (IOU) manages the collection and dissemination of law enforcement information and intelligence within the DRO Program. The IOU ensures that all intelligence, developed or received, is evaluated and disseminated to the appropriate ICE operational entity as it pertains to homeland security, criminal activities, infrastructure protection, and the illegal movement of people, money, narcotics, and cargo entering, transiting, or operating within our national borders.

One of the most important ICE mandates is the enhancement of public safety and the security of the American public. The broad authority of ICE allows for the identification and removal of dangerous, often recidivist, criminals engaged in crimes such as murder, predatory sexual offenses, narcotics trafficking, alien smuggling, and a host of other crimes that have a profoundly negative impact on our society. A largely untapped source of information resides in the ICE detainee population. The IOU seeks to dedicate personnel to gather information in detention facilities, organize information, provide information locally, as needed, to avert possible detention riots or other illegal activities within the ICE detainee population and provide the information to the ICE Office of Intelligence for further analysis and assimilation into the "big picture."

The information obtained from aliens can also provide more raw information to:

- provide real time information on particular terrorist threats or organized criminal activities,
- enhance the development of a foreign informant network strategy utilizing alien removals, and
- provide a source of information that can provide the ICE Office of Intelligence with criminal trends and patterns that will allow for the effective use of ICE investigative resources.

In addition to exploiting available intelligence information, the IOU is working in conjunction with other DHS entities to coordinate border security intelligence in achieving the recommendations of the Secure Border Initiative (SBI). The IOU also provides guidance, direction and accountability for DRO intelligence initiatives and exercises oversight over intelligence efforts by all DRO field offices.

The aliens (non-citizens) who are apprehended and not released from custody are placed in detention facilities. Those that cannot be legally released from secure custody constitute DRO's "nondetained" docket. Every case, whether "detained" or "nondetained," remains part of DRO's caseload, actively managed until and unless it is formally closed. DRO processes and monitors detained and nondetained cases as they move through immigration court proceedings to conclusion. At that point, DRO executes the judge's order. Primary healthcare for alien detainees is managed by the Division of Immigration Health Services (DIHS). DRO has defined policy and procedures regarding the proper handling of unaccompanied alien juveniles taken into federal custody as a result of their unlawful immigration status. DHS' juvenile guidelines address the responsibilities related to unaccompanied alien juveniles who enter the United States illegally, violate their legal status or commit a deportable crime. As part of the restructuring of INS, the responsibilities related to the care and custody of unaccompanied alien juveniles has been transferred to HHS, Office of Refugee Resettlement and the Division of Unaccompanied Children Services.

ICE operates eight secure detention facilities called Service Processing Centers (SPCs). They are located in Aguadilla, Puerto Rico; Batavia, New York; El

Centro, California; El Paso, Texas; Florence, Arizona; Miami, Florida; Los Fresnos, Texas; and San Pedro, California. The newest SPC, the Buffalo Federal Detention Facility, is unique because in addition to its 300 beds for detained aliens, it has 150 beds for use by the U.S. Marshals Service. ICE augments its SPCs with seven contract detention facilities. These facilities are located in Aurora, Colorado; Houston, Texas; Laredo, Texas; Seattle, Washington; Elizabeth, New Jersey; Queens, New York; and San Diego, California. ICE also uses state and local jails on a reimbursable detention day basis and has joint federal facilities with the Bureau of Prisons, the Federal Detention Center in Oakdale, Louisiana, and the contractor owned and operated (with the Bureau of Prisons) criminal alien facility in Eloy, Arizona. In addition, major expansion initiatives are underway at several SPCs to enhance DROs detention capabilities.

Office of Investigations

The Office of Investigations (OI) investigates immigration crime, human rights violations, and human smuggling; narcotics, weapons and other types of smuggling; and financial crimes, cybercrime, and export enforcement issues.

The Office of Investigations (OI) is responsible for investigating a range of issues that may threaten national security. OI uses its legal authority to investigate issues such as immigration crime, human rights violations, and human smuggling; narcotics, weapons and other types of smuggling; and financial crimes, cybercrime, and export enforcement issues. ICE special agents also conduct investigations aimed at protecting critical infrastructure industries that are vulnerable to sabotage, attack, or exploitation. OI is a critical asset in this mission, responsible for investigating a wide range of domestic and international activities arising from the illegal movement of people and goods into, within, and out of the United States.

ICE investigations cover a broad range of areas, including national security threats, financial and smuggling violations (including illegal arms exports), financial crimes, commercial fraud, human trafficking, narcotics smuggling, child pornography/exploitation, and immigration fraud. ICE has 26 principal field offices throughout the United States and more than 50 international offices around the world.

Office of Intelligence

The Office of Intelligence (Intel) collects, analyzes and shares strategic and tactical data for use by ICE and DHS management and operational units, as well as to support our federal, state, local and tribal law enforcement partners. ICE's intelligence capabilities play a vital role in supporting investigations related to illegal immigration, financial crime, trade fraud, human smuggling and trafficking, child sex tourism, weapons proliferation, drug smuggling and other criminal activities.

Intel's goal is to provide timely and accurate intelligence in support of law enforcement and homeland security operations. By getting the right information to the right people at the right time, Intel helps to:

- Identify patterns, trends, routes and methods of criminal activity;
- Prioritize current enforcement efforts;

- Predict emerging or future threats;
- Identify potential systemic vulnerabilities;
- Identify methods to mitigate those vulnerabilities; and
- Provide critical information to law enforcement and intelligence community partners.

In order to provide localized support to ICE operations, Intel oversees 26 Field Intelligence Groups (FIGs) co-located in agency field offices alongside other ICE components. These FIGs allow for improved working relationships and information-sharing with each ICE field office and with other government agencies.

Office of International Affairs

The ICE Office of International Affairs (OIA) is a critical asset in this mission, responsible for enhancing national security by conducting and coordinating international investigations involving transnational criminal organizations and serving as ICE's liaison to counterparts in local government and law enforcement.

ICE has 63 offices in 44 countries around the world.

ICE has 63 offices in 44 countries around the world, with more than 300 government and contract personnel and local employees committed to the OIA mission. ICE OIA operations are directed by ICE attachés, whose responsibilities include:

- Coordinating investigations with foreign law enforcement counterparts;
- Acquiring and developing intelligence related to cross-border criminal activities involving people, goods and technology;
- Providing investigative case support to domestic and international ICE offices;
- Referring requests from host country agencies to ICE domestic investigative offices; and
- Assisting in removal operations by coordinating ICE efforts to transport removed aliens to their countries of origin.

United States Citizenship and Immigration Services

The Department of Homeland Security separates immigration services from immigration law enforcement. Immigration and Customs Enforcement (ICE) and Customs and Border Protection (CBP), components within DHS, handle immigration enforcement and border security functions while the U.S. Citizenship and Immigration Services (USCIS) is the government agency that oversees lawful immigration to the United States. On March 1, 2003, USCIS officially assumed responsibility for the immigration service functions of the federal government. The Homeland Security Act of 2002 (Pub. L. No. 107–296, 116 Stat. 2135) dismantled the former Immigration and Naturalization Service (INS) and USCIS was formed to enhance the security and improve the efficiency of national immigration services by exclusively focusing on the administration of benefit applications.

Some of the services provided by the USCIS include:

- Citizenship (Includes the Related Naturalization Process). Individuals who wish to become U.S. citizens through naturalization submit their applications to USCIS who determine eligibility, process the applications and, if approved, schedule the applicant for a ceremony to take the Oath of Allegiance. USCIS also determines eligibility and provides documentation of U.S. citizenship for people who acquired or derived U.S. citizenship through their parents. (See the "Citizenship" link to the right.)
- Immigration of Family Members. USCIS manages the process that allows current permanent residents and U.S. citizens to bring close relatives to live and work in the United States.
- Working in the U.S. USCIS manages the process that allows individuals from other countries to work in the United States. Some of the opportunities are temporary, and some provide a path to a green card (permanent residence).

USCIS manages the system that allows participating employers to electronically verify the employment eligibility of their newly hired employees.

- Verifying an Individual's Legal Right to Work in the United States (E-Verify). USCIS manages the system that allows participating employers to electronically verify the employment eligibility of their newly hired employees.
- Humanitarian Programs. USCIS administers humanitarian programs that provide protection to individuals inside and outside the United States who are displaced by war, famine and civil and political unrest, and those who are forced to flee their countries to escape the risk of death and torture at the hands of persecutors.
- Adoptions . USCIS manages the first step in the process for U.S. citizens to adopt children from other countries. Approximately 20,000 adoptions take place each year.
- Civic Integration. USCIS promotes instruction and training on citizenship rights and responsibilities and provides immigrants with the information and tools necessary to successfully integrate into American civic culture.
- Genealogy. The USCIS Genealogy Program is a fee-for-service program providing family historians and other researchers with timely access to historical immigration and naturalization records.[7]

Immigration Reform

The number of foreign-born people residing in the United States is at the highest level in U.S. history and has reached a proportion of the U.S. population—12.6%—not seen since the early 20th century. Of the 38 million foreign-born residents in the United States, approximately one-third are naturalized citizens, one-third are legal permanent residents, and one-third are estimated to be unauthorized (illegal) residents. Some observers and policy experts maintain that the presence of an estimated 11 million unauthorized residents is evidence of flaws in the legal immigration system as well as failures of immigration control policies and practices.

There is, indeed, a broad-based consensus that the U.S. immigration system is broken. This consensus erodes, however, as soon as the options to reform the U.S. immigration system are debated. Substantial efforts to reform immigration law have failed in the recent past, prompting some to characterize the issue as a "zero-sum game" or a "third rail." The thorniest of these immigration issues centers on policies directed toward unauthorized aliens in the United States.

Although the economy appears to be recovering from the recession and some economic indicators suggest that growth has resumed, unemployment remains high and is projected to remain so for some time. Historically, international migration ebbs during economic crises (e.g., immigration to the United States was at its lowest levels during the Great Depression). While preliminary statistical trends suggest a slowing of migration pressures, it remains unclear how the current economic climate will affect immigration to the United States. Whether the Congress will act to alter immigration policies—either in the form of comprehensive immigration reform or in the form of incremental revisions aimed at strategic changes—is at the crux of the debate. Addressing these contentious policy reforms against the backdrop of economic turbulence sharpens the social and business cleavages and may narrow the range of options.[8]

The number of foreign-born people residing in the United States is at the highest level in U.S. history and has reached a proportion of the U.S. population—12.6%—not seen since the early 20th century.

Conclusion

As the largest investigative arm of the Department of Homeland Security (DHS), U.S. Immigration and Customs Enforcement (ICE) uses its unique immigration and customs authorities to prevent terrorist and criminal activity by targeting the people, money and materials that support terrorist and criminal organizations. ICE protects America and upholds public safety by identifying and dismantling criminal organizations that exploit our nation's borders. ICE makes America safer by identifying, apprehending, and removing criminal and other illegal aliens from the United States.

USCIS ensures that citizenship and immigration information and decisions on immigration benefits are provided to customers in a timely, accurate, consistent, courteous, and professional manner. Over fifty different types of immigration benefits are processed through USCIS. Every case is unique and requires specialized attention from experienced USCIS immigration officers. USCIS is also responsible for strengthening the effectiveness of national security efforts; enhancing the integrity of our country's legal immigration system by deterring, detecting, and pursuing immigration related fraud; and combating unauthorized employment in the workplace. In addition, USCIS provides protection to refugees, both inside and outside of the United States, in accordance with US law and international obligations.[9]

The United States is a nation of immigrants.

The United States is a nation of immigrants. Our ability to innovate, our ties to the world, and our economic prosperity depend on our nation's capacity to welcome and assimilate immigrants, and a visa system which welcomes skilled professionals from around the world. At the same time, effective border security and immigration enforcement must keep the country safe and deter unlawful entry. Indeed, persistent problems in immigration policy consume valuable resources needed to advance other security objectives and make it harder to focus on the most danger-ous threats facing our country. Ultimately, our national security depends on striking a balance between security and openness. To advance this goal, we must pursue comprehensive immigration reform that effectively secures our borders, while repairing a broken system that fails to serve the needs of our nation.[10]

Questions

1. How does each of the operational divisions of ICE address national security and public safety efforts?
2. What is the difference between ICE and USCIS?
3. How does USCIS promote legal immigration efforts?
4. What are the major challenges with immigration reform?

Chapter 24

FEMA

Objectives

- Describe FEMA's mission and organization.
- Understand the disaster declaration process.
- Know the functions of the FEMA directorates and offices.
- Understand the elements of the Preparedness Cycle.

Introduction

The Federal Emergency Management Agency coordinates the federal government's role in preparing for, preventing, mitigating the effects of, responding to, and recovering from all domestic disasters, whether natural or man-made, including acts of terror.[1]

Hurricane Katrina struck the Gulf coasts of Louisiana, Alabama, and Mississippi on August 29, 2005, resulting in severe and widespread damage to the region. The response of the federal government, especially the Federal Emergency Management Agency (FEMA), in the aftermath of the storm has been widely criticized. Some of the criticism has focused on the organizational arrangements involving FEMA and its parent, the Department of Homeland Security (DHS).

One month prior to the hurricane, in July 2005, Secretary of Homeland Security Michael Chertoff announced plans for a reorganization of DHS, including FEMA. Known as the "Second Stage Review," or "2SR," the reorganization transferred emergency preparedness functions from FEMA to a new Preparedness Directorate, among other changes. The Administration began implementation of the reorganization on October 1, 2005. In response to Administration requests, congressional support for the proposal was provided through approval of the FY2006 appropriations legislation.

FEMA coordinates the federal government's role in preparing for, preventing, mitigating the effects of, responding to, and recovering from all domestic disasters, whether natural or man-made.

In the aftermath of the Katrina disaster, administrative structure issues remain a matter of contention. Pending legislation before Congress would make further changes. The release of reports by the House, Senate, and White House on the response to Hurricane Katrina may lead to further examination of the issues.[2]

History

FEMA can trace its beginnings to the Congressional Act of 1803. This act, generally considered the first piece of disaster legislation, provided assistance to a New Hampshire town following an extensive fire. In the century that followed, ad hoc legislation was passed more than 100 times in response to hurricanes, earthquakes, floods and other natural disasters.

By the 1930s, when the federal approach to problems became popular, the Reconstruction Finance Corporation was given authority to make disaster loans for repair and reconstruction of certain public facilities following an earthquake, and later, other types of disasters. In 1934, the Bureau of Public Roads was given authority to provide funding for highways and bridges damaged by natural disasters. The Flood Control Act, which gave the U.S. Army Corps of Engineers greater authority to implement flood control projects, was also passed. This piecemeal approach to disaster assistance was problematic and it prompted legislation that required greater cooperation between federal agencies and authorized the President to coordinate these activities.

The 1960s and early 1970s brought massive disasters requiring major federal response and recovery operations by the Federal Disaster Assistance Administration, established within the Department of Housing and Urban Development (HUD). Hurricane Carla struck in 1962, Hurricane Betsy in 1965, Hurricane Camille in 1969 and Hurricane Agnes in 1972. The Alaskan Earthquake hit in 1964 and the San Fernando Earthquake rocked Southern California in 1971. These events served to focus attention on the issue of natural disasters and brought about increased legislation. In 1968, the National Flood Insurance Act offered new flood protection to homeowners, and in 1974 the Disaster Relief Act firmly established the process of Presidential disaster declarations.

However, emergency and disaster activities were still fragmented. When hazards associated with nuclear power plants and the transportation of hazardous substances were added to natural disasters, more than 100 federal agencies were involved in some aspect of disasters, hazards and emergencies. Many parallel programs and policies existed at the state and local level, compounding the complexity of federal disaster relief efforts. The National Governor's Association sought to decrease the many agencies with which state and local governments were forced to work. They asked President Jimmy Carter to centralize federal emergency functions.

Executive Order 12127

President Carter's 1979 executive order merged many of the separate disaster-related responsibilities into the Federal Emergency Management Agency (FEMA). Among other agencies, FEMA absorbed: the Federal Insurance Administration, the National Fire Prevention and Control Administration, the National Weather Service Community Preparedness Program, the Federal Preparedness Agency of the General Services Administration and the Federal Disaster Assistance Administration activities from HUD. Civil defense responsibilities were also transferred to the new agency from the Defense Department's Defense Civil Preparedness Agency.

John Macy was named as FEMA's first director. Macy emphasized the similarities between natural hazards preparedness and the civil defense activities. FEMA began development of an Integrated Emergency Management System with an all-hazards approach that included "direction, control and warning systems which are common to the full range of emergencies from small isolated events to the ultimate emergency - war."

The new agency was faced with many unusual challenges in its first few years that emphasized how complex emergency management can be. Early disasters and emergencies included the contamination of Love Canal, the Cuban refugee crisis and the accident at the Three Mile Island nuclear power plant. Later, the Loma Prieta Earthquake in 1989 and Hurricane Andrew in 1992 focused major national attention on FEMA. In 1993, President Clinton nominated James L. Witt as the new FEMA director. Witt became the first agency director with experience as a state emergency manager. He initiated sweeping reforms that streamlined disaster relief and recovery operations, insisted on a new emphasis regarding preparedness and mitigation, and focused agency employees on customer service. The end of the Cold War also allowed Witt to redirect more of FEMA's limited resources from civil defense into disaster relief, recovery and mitigation programs.

In 2001, President George W. Bush appointed Joe M. Allbaugh as the director of FEMA. Within months, the terrorist attacks of Sept. 11th focused the agency on issues of national preparedness and homeland security, and tested the agency in unprecedented ways. The agency coordinated its activities with the newly formed Office of Homeland Security, and FEMA's Office of National Preparedness was given responsibility for helping to ensure that the nation's first responders were trained and equipped to deal with weapons of mass destruction.

A New Mission: Homeland Security

Billions of dollars of new funding were directed to FEMA to help communities face the threat of terrorism. Just a few years past its 20th anniversary, FEMA was actively directing its "all-hazards" approach to disasters toward homeland security issues. In March 2003, FEMA joined 22 other federal agencies, programs and offices in becoming the Department of Homeland Security. The new department, headed by Secretary Tom Ridge, brought a coordinated approach to national security from emergencies and disasters - both natural and man-made.

The Robert T. Stafford Disaster Relief and Emergency Assistance Act (referred to as the Stafford Act - 42 U.S.C. 5721 et seq.) authorizes the President to issue "major disaster" or "emergency" declarations before or after catastrophes occur.

On October 4, 2006, President George W. Bush signed into law the Post-Katrina Emergency Reform Act. The act significantly reorganized FEMA, provided it substantial new authority to remedy gaps that became apparent in the response to Hurricane Katrina in August 2005, the most devastating natural disaster in U.S. history, and included a more robust preparedness mission for FEMA.

As it has for almost 30 years, FEMA's mission remains: to lead America to prepare for, prevent, respond to and recover from disasters with a vision of "A Nation Prepared." [3]

Disaster Declaration

The Robert T. Stafford Disaster Relief and Emergency Assistance Act (referred to as the Stafford Act - 42 U.S.C. 5721 et seq.) authorizes the President to issue "major disaster" or "emergency" declarations before or after catastrophes occur. Emergency declarations trigger aid that protects property, public health, and safety and lessens or averts the threat of an incident becoming a catastrophic event. A major disaster declaration, issued after catastrophes occur, constitutes broader authority for federal agencies to provide supplemental assistance to help state and local governments, families and individuals, and certain nonprofit organizations recover from the incident.

The end result of a presidential disaster declaration is well known, if not entirely understood.

Various forms of assistance are provided, including aid to families and individuals for uninsured needs and assistance to state and local governments and certain non-profits in rebuilding or replacing damaged infrastructure. The amount of assistance provided through Presidential disaster declarations has exceeded $100 billion. Often, in recent years, Congress has enacted supplemental appropriations legislation to cover unanticipated costs. While the amounts spent by the federal government on different programs may be reported, and the progress of the recovery can be observed, much less is known about the process that initiates all of this activity. Yet, it is a process that has resulted in an average of more than one disaster declaration a week over the last decade.

The disaster declaration procedure is foremost a process that preserves the discretion of the governor to request assistance and the president to decide to grant, or not to grant, supplemental help. The process employs some measurable criteria in two broad areas: Individual Assistance that aids families and individuals and Public Assistance that is mainly for repairs to infrastructure. The criteria, however, also considers many other factors, in each category of assistance, that help decision makers assess the impact of an event on communities and states. Under current law, the decision to issue a declaration rests solely with the President. Congress has no formal role, but has taken actions to adjust the terms of the process. For example, P.L. 109-295 established an advocate to help small states with the declaration process. More recently, Congress introduced legislation, H.R. 6658, that would direct FEMA to update some of its criteria for considering Individual Assistance declarations.[4]

Organization

For the most part, FEMA is organized functionally on the four phases of emergency management: mitigation, preparedness, response, and recovery.

For the most part, FEMA is organized functionally on the four phases of emergency management: mitigation, preparedness, response, and recovery. The National Advisory Council (NAC) advises the Administrator of the Federal Emergency Management Agency (FEMA) on all aspects of emergency management. The National Advisory Council incorporates State, local and tribal government and private sector input in the development and revision of the national preparedness goal, the national preparedness system, the National Incident Management System, the National Response Framework and other related plans and strategies. FEMA is organized into several directorates, offices, and regions.

Recovery Directorate

The Recovery Directorate ensures that individuals and communities affected by disasters of all sizes are able to return to normal function with minimal suffering and disruption of services. It does this through the following programs: Individual Assistance, which provides or coordinates emergency housing, financial assistance, and unemployment assistance for individuals, families, farmers and businesses; Public Assistance, which helps states, local communities and certain nonprofit groups restore and rebuild public systems and facilities, as well as with debris removal and emergency protective measures; the Federal Coordinating Officer Program; emergency and disaster declaration processing; and National Response Plan Emergency Support Functions # 14 (Long-Term Community Recovery). Victims of disaster may register via InterNet or telephone to access these programs through a network of National Processing Centers managed by the Recovery Directorate.

Disaster Operations Directorate

The Disaster Operations Directorate (DOD) is responsible for coordinating and facilitating the federal disaster response activities needed to save lives, reduce suffering and protect property in communities across the country that have been overwhelmed by a major disaster or emergency. The directorate recently has established a new generation of disaster response teams called Incident Management Assistance Teams (IMATs). IMATs were developed from an expanded concept of the former Emergency Response Teams (ERT) and the Federal Incident Response Support Teams. The new IMATs are full-time, rapid response teams with dedicated staff able to deploy within two hours and arrive at an incident within 12 hours. Their role is to support the local incident commander, coordinate federal response activities and provide information about the situation and current conditions to FEMA leadership. Two national and three regional teams are now operational.

FEMA's DOD has recently enhanced coordination and connectivity with its interagency, military and DHS partners through upgrades to its network of operations centers. Operations centers at the national and regional levels are responsible for coordinating and sustaining response operations; maintaining situational awareness and a common operating picture; facilitating information sharing between FEMA and non-FEMA entities; and providing internal and external stakeholders a consolidated, consistent, and accurate status of on-going incidents, responses or potential events.

Full staffing of the 24/7 National Response Coordination Center (NRCC) Watch Center and the Regional Response Coordination Centers (RRCC), upgrades to information technology and videoteleconferencing capabilities has greatly improved our ability to provide seamless connectivity with all of our partners. It has also increased our effectiveness in coordinating and exchanging information critical to ensuring smooth disaster response operations. DOD's new emphasis on operational planning has been critical to the improvement of the agency's disaster response planning and operations. Operational planners at Headquarters and in the Regions are responsible for horizontal and vertical planning across all levels of government and ensuring continuity between long range planning, current operations planning, and field element incident action planning.

FEMA also has been coordinating closely with its federal partners to expand the number of Mission Assignments that have been prepared in advance to facilitate rapid response to incidents. FEMA now has 236 pre-scripted mission assignments with 33 departments and agencies, up from 44 in 2006.

The Gap Analysis Program (GAP) is another critical operational planning capability designed to identify limitations at the local, state and national levels that could impede response operations.[5]

Grant Programs Directorate

FEMA consolidated multiple legacy grant management organizations to create the new Grant Programs Directorate (GPD) in order to provide a unified, solutions-oriented approach to managing federal financial assistance programs.

GPD is fiscally responsible for approximately 17,000 open grants and is programmatically responsible for more than two-thirds of those grants. GPD subject matter experts provide on-site programmatic monitoring and technical assistance to grantees, while analyzing, evaluating and ensuring accountability and program effectiveness.

GPD awarded and provided oversight over more than $10.6 billion in grants through approximately 50 programs to state, territorial and local communities, and critical infrastructure systems to enhance preparedness, protection, response, recovery and mitigation capabilities throughout the nation.

GPD also instituted a balanced approach to making Homeland Security grant awards to states and high threat urban areas based on risk. While identifying the Nation's highest threat communities, this methodology also recognizes that risks are widespread and all states and many cities have inherent needs for Federal resources.

To achieve its mission, FEMA has forged strong partnerships with many Federal Departments and Agencies to develop and implement the various grant programs. Federal partners include the Department of Commerce, Department of Energy, Department of Health and Human Services, Department of Justice, Department of Transportation, Department of Housing and Urban Development, Department of Agriculture, and the Department of Homeland Security's Office of Infrastructure Protection and Office of Intelligence and Analysis, as well as other components within DHS.

GPD will become the one-stop shop to enhance fiduciary management of FEMA grants through standardization of grants management policies, processes, reporting, and accountability across all FEMA grant programs.

GPD will ensure all preparedness grant programs are aligned to, and are measurable against the National Preparedness Guidelines and the National Priorities as authorized by the 9/11 Recommendations Implementation Act. Another initiative involves the implementation of a program-wide paperless process to increase efficiency and standardize all grant management procedures, from applicant submission to grant closeout.

Logistics Management Directorate

The Logistics Management Directorate (LMD) is a very dynamic Directorate with a business process concept that continues to transform. The LMD mission is to effectively plan, manage and sustain national logistics response and recovery operations, in support of domestic emergencies and special events, acting as the National Logistics Coordinator (NLC) or Single Logistics Integrator for domestic incident support. The NLC establishes national procedures, fostering transparency through collaboration and coordination and, focuses on technology enhancements to expand Region & State level logistics capabilities.

LMD is organized around the following four core competencies:

1. Logistics Operations - Manages and executes the national logistics command and coordination, tracking and reporting for all-hazards operations utilizing the National Logistics Coordinator concept. Operates the Logistics Management Center (LMC) serving as the central reporting element for the National Response Coordination Center on all logistics actions and operational activities. Stores, maintains and deploys Temporary Housing Units and Mobile Disaster Recovery Centers.
2. Logistics Plans and Exercises - Develops and provides cohesive and synchronized logistics plans and exercises to achieve both short and long term readiness requirements. Ensures deliberate planning efforts result in coordinated ConOps and Plans resulting in repeatable processes supporting optimized national logistics response and recovery operations supporting domestic emergencies and special events.
3. Distribution Management - Manages a comprehensive supply chain, warehouse and transportation operation using a Strategic Alliance to effectively and efficiently distribute supplies, equipment and services to support emergencies.
4. Property Management - Provides management oversight, internal control and technical reviews in the areas of property accountability, reutilization, and disposal of Disaster Operations equipment. FEMA is in the process of implementing an enterprise-wide property accounting and asset visibility system that is designed and implemented to ensure best value.

The strategic direction in LMD is focused on four key areas:

1. People: Develop a professional logistics workforce, including regional staff, through hiring, training, credentialing and professional development; foster an accountability and results based culture.
2. Customers: Develop collaborative relationships with key stakeholders; foster both horizontal and vertical coordination; develop bottom up requirement process.
3. Processes: Modernize and integrate the National Supply Chain Network; institute logistics planning to enhance response capability; develop and document key business policy and processes; perform analysis and take systematic approach to task/ issue resolution.
4. Systems: Modernize the logistics system network; upgrade and fully integrate our systems to achieve maximum capability effectiveness.

Management Directorate

The Management Directorate oversees Human Capital, Information Technology, Acquisition Management, Support Services and Facilities, the Disaster Reserve Workforce, Security, Records Management, Occupational Health, Safety and Environment; and Business Operations along seven strategic goals:

1. Hire, train, deploy, and retain a skilled workforce.
2. Provide a safe, secure, and productive work environment.
3. Provide information, resources, and support services.
4. Provide reliable, integrated, and secure communication and information systems.
5. Develop a results-oriented business approach that enhances FEMA's mission
6. Promote behavior focused on creating a customer service environment.
7. Among the ways to achieve this are through continuity of leadership and operations, unity of functions toward the accomplishment of FEMA's mission and priorities, and excellence in our delivery of services to all customers.[6]

Mitigation focuses on breaking the cycle of disaster damage, reconstruction, and repeated damage.

Mitigation Directorate

The Federal Insurance and Mitigation Administration (FIMA) manages the National Flood Insurance Program (NFIP) and a range of programs designed to reduce future losses to homes, businesses, schools, public buildings and critical facilities from floods, earthquakes, tornadoes and other natural disasters.

Mitigation focuses on breaking the cycle of disaster damage, reconstruction, and repeated damage. Mitigation efforts provide value to the American people by creating safer communities and reducing loss of life and property. Mitigation includes such activities as:

- Complying with or exceeding NFIP floodplain management regulations.
- Enforcing stringent building codes, flood-proofing requirements, seismic design standards and wind-bracing requirements for new construction or repairing existing buildings.
- Adopting zoning ordinances that steer development away from areas subject to flooding, storm surge or coastal erosion.
- Retrofitting public buildings to withstand hurricane-strength winds or ground shaking.
- Acquiring damaged homes or businesses in flood-prone areas, relocating the structures, and returning the property to open space, wetlands or recreational uses.
- Building community shelters and tornado safe rooms to help protect people in their homes, public buildings and schools in hurricane- and tornado-prone areas.

Mitigation's Value to Society

- Mitigation creates safer communities by reducing losses of life and property.
- Mitigation enables individuals and communities to recover more rapidly from disasters.
- Mitigation lessens the financial impact of disasters on individuals, the Treasury, state, local and tribal communities.
- Hazard Mitigation is sustained action taken to reduce or eliminate long-term risk to people and their property from hazards and their effects.

The Federal Insurance and Mitigation Administration was established on November 29, 1993. At that time, Mitigation became the cornerstone of emergency management, for the first time in the history of federal disaster assistance. The mission of the agency has shifted significantly since 1993, most notably through the creation of a separate and distinct group. FIMA's partners include a broad spectrum of stakeholders in federal, state, tribal and local government and the private sector. Partners also include professional associations and non-governmental groups involved in public policy and administration, insurance, higher education, the building sciences and urban planning.

Mitigation lessens the financial impact of disasters on individuals, the Treasury, state, local and tribal communities.

FIMA is comprised of three divisions: Risk Analysis, Risk Reduction and Risk Insurance. The primary functions of these divisions include:

- The Risk Analysis Division applies engineering and planning practices in conjunction with advanced technology tools to identify hazards, assess vulnerabilities, and develop strategies to manage the risks associated with natural hazards.
- The Risk Reduction Division works to reduce risk to life and property through the use of land use controls, building practices and other tools. These activities address risk in both the existing built environment and in future development, and they occur in both pre- and post-disaster environments.
- The Risk Insurance Division helps reduce flood losses by providing affordable flood insurance for property owners and by encouraging communities to adopt and enforce floodplain management regulations that mitigate the effects of flooding on new and improved structures.

FIMA's programs are significant components of the Nation's emergency management system. The statutorily authorized programs include:

- Risk Analysis Division
- Flood Map Modernization, including the Cooperating Technical Partners (CTP)
- National Dam Safety Program
- National Hurricane Program
- Mitigation Planning

- Risk Reduction Division
- Hazard Mitigation Grant Program (HMGP)
- Flood Mitigation Assistance Program (FMA)
- Pre-Disaster Mitigation (PDM)
- Severe Repetitive Loss (SRL)
- Repetitive Flood Claims (RFC)
- Community Rating System (CRS)
- National Earthquake Hazards Reduction Program (NEHRP)
- Building Science
- Risk Insurance Division
- National Flood Insurance Program (NFIP)

FEMA Offices

The Office of Environmental Planning & Historic Preservation provides management and oversight to all FEMA programs in their compliance with environmental planning and historic preservation laws, executive orders and regulations.

The goal is to minimize the disruption of essential operations in order to guarantee an Enduring Constitutional Government in response to a full threat spectrum of emergencies.

National Continuity Programs

It is the policy of the United States to maintain a comprehensive and effective continuity capability in order to ensure the preservation of our Constitutional form of government at all times. National Security Presidential Directive 51/ Homeland Security Presidential Directive 20, released in May 2007, establishes a comprehensive national policy on the continuity of Federal Government structures and operations. It also requires that continuity programs in the Federal Executive Branch (FEB) be incorporated into agency daily operations, and directs the coordination of Federal plans with State, local, territorial, tribal and private sector plans.

FEMA's National Continuity Programs Directorate is the Federal Executive Branch Lead Agent for continuity of national essential functions. The goal is to minimize the disruption of essential operations in order to guarantee an Enduring Constitutional Government in response to a full threat spectrum of emergencies. The scope of this mandate includes development and promulgation of Continuity of Operations (COOP) directives and guidance, education and training, and coordination between the Federal, State, local, territorial, tribal and private sectors. NCP also coordinates and participates in Federal, State and local COOP exercises.

NCP also manages the Integrated Public Alert and Warning System (IPAWS), the Nation's next generation alert and warning capability developed by NCP in partnership with multiple Federal Departments and Agencies. IPAWS meets the requirements of Executive Order 13407, signed by the President in 2006, which called for the development and implementation of an "effective, reliable, integrated, flexible, and comprehensive system to alert and warn the American people....and to ensure under all conditions the President can communicate with the American people."

National Preparedness

Established on April 1, 2007, FEMA's National Preparedness Directorate (NPD) is responsible for leading the Nation's efforts to enhance preparedness to prevent, protect from, respond to, and recover from disasters, natural and manmade. NPD strives to achieve a Nation prepared through a comprehensive cycle of planning, organizing and equipping, training, exercising, evaluating and improvement planning. The Divisions of the NPD are:

- Individual and Community Preparedness Division (ICPD)
- National Integration Center (NIC)
- National Training and Education
- National Training and Education Division (NTED)
- Center for Domestic Preparedness (CDP)
- Emergency Management Institute (EMI)
- National Exercise Division (NED)
- Technological Hazards Division (THD)
- National Preparedness Assessment Division (NPAD)

United States Fire Administration

As an entity of the Department of Homeland Security's Federal Emergency Management Agency, the mission of the USFA is to provide national leadership to foster a solid foundation for our fire and emergency services stakeholders in prevention, preparedness, and response.

Other FEMA Functions

Other functions under the auspices of FEMA Offices include:

- Center for Faith Based Initiatives and Neighborhood Partnerships
- Office of Chief Financial Officer
- Office of Disability Integration and Coordination
- Office of Equal Rights
- Office of the Executive Secretariat
- Office of External Affairs (includes Disaster Operations, Intergovernmental Affairs, International Affairs, Legislative Affairs, Private Sector Outreach, Public Affairs, Resource Management and Administration)
- Office of Chief Counsel
- Office of Federal Coordinating Officer Operations
- Office of National Capital Region Coordination
- Office of Policy and Programs Analysis
- Defense Production Act Program Division

FEMA Regional Operations

FEMA has 10 permanent regional offices, three permanent area offices, and various temporary disaster-related sites that carry out the agency's operations throughout the United States and its territories.

As FEMA is responsible to prescribe policy and develop systems to support national policy, personnel in the regions and the field are responsible for actually implementing policy and preparing for, responding to, recovering from and mitigating all hazards.

In addition to its headquarters in Washington, D.C., FEMA has 10 permanent regional offices, three permanent area offices, and various temporary disaster-related sites that carry out the agency's operations throughout the United States and its territories.

Among the delegated authorities of the regions are:

- The authority to issue mission assignments in excess of $10 million. Previously, regions could only approve up to $10 million without headquarters approval in the Enterprise Coordination and Approval Process (ECAP) systems.
- The authority to contract for aircraft to support requirements organic to that specific region. Previously, regions were required to rely on headquarters to find a contractor to fit the regional requirement. This was time consuming and inefficient.
- The restoration of regional authority to approve requisitions for non-disaster goods and services, thereby reducing previous delays incurred when the regions were required to seek headquarters approval.
- The authority to select and hire staff in senior regional positions. Previously, such hires had to be approved by FEMA headquarters.

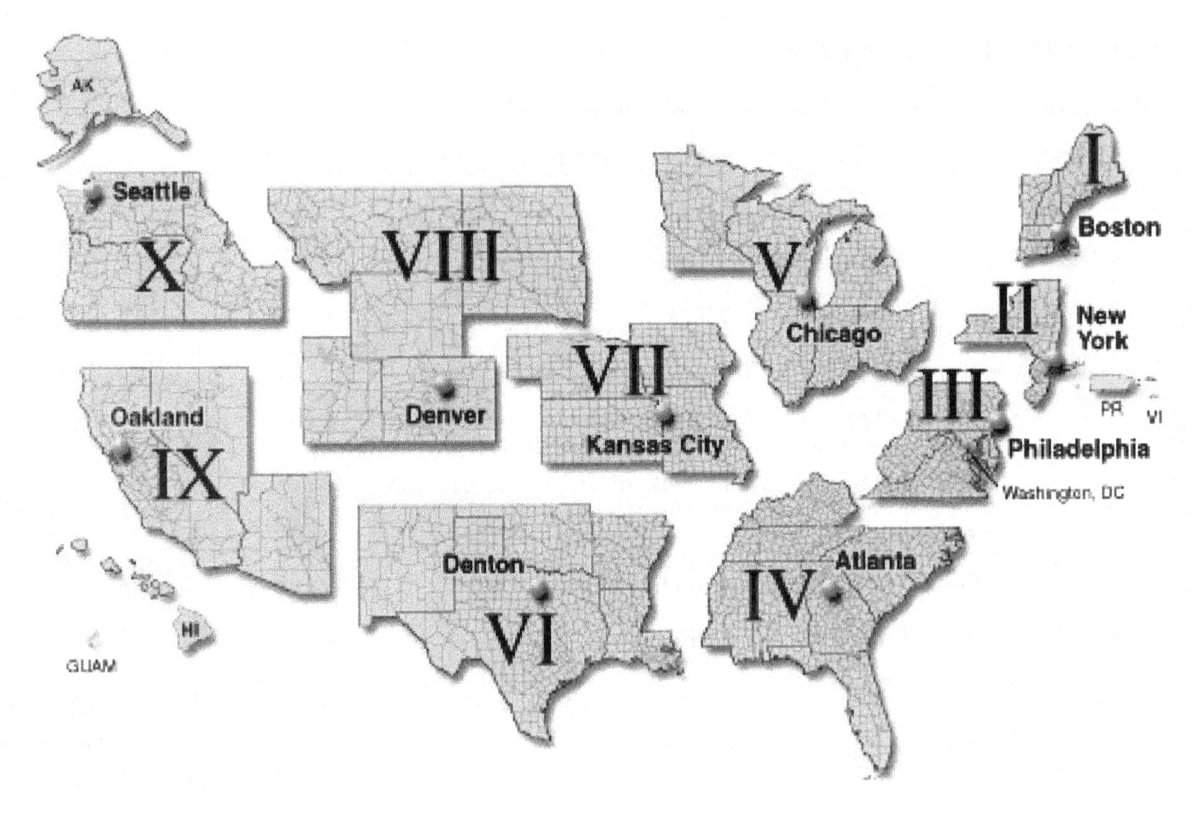

Figure 24.1: FEMA Regions

This ongoing regional delegation and empowerment effort reflects a fundamental institutional shift toward a more decentralized approach to disaster management, and serves to develop more robust regional offices.[7]

Emergency Response Teams

FEMA's emergency response is based on small, decentralized teams trained in such areas as the National Disaster Medical System (NDMS), Urban Search and Rescue (USAR), Disaster Mortuary Operations Response Team (DMORT), Disaster Medical Assistance Team (DMAT), and Mobile Emergency Resource Support (MERS).

National Disaster Medical System (NDMS)

The National Disaster Medical System (NDMS) is a federally coordinated system that augments the Nation's medical response capability. The overall purpose of the NDMS is to supplement an integrated National medical response capability for assisting State and local authorities in dealing with the medical impacts of major peacetime disasters and to provide support to the military and the Department of Veterans Affairs medical systems in caring for casualties evacuated back to the U.S. from overseas armed conventional conflicts.

The National Response Framework utilizes the National Disaster Medical System (NDMS), as part of the Department of Health and Human Services, Office of Preparedness and Response, under Emergency Support Function #8 (ESF #8), Health and Medical Services, to support Federal agencies in the management and coordination of the Federal medical response to major emergencies and federally declared disasters including:

- Natural Disasters
- Major Transportation Accidents
- Technological Disasters
- Acts of Terrorism including Weapons of Mass Destruction Events[8]

Urban Search and Rescue (US&R)

Urban search-and-rescue (US&R) involves the location, rescue (extrication), and initial medical stabilization of victims trapped in confined spaces. Structural collapse is most often the cause of victims being trapped, but victims may also be trapped in transportation accidents, mines and collapsed trenches.

Urban search-and-rescue is considered a "multi-hazard" discipline, as it may be needed for a variety of emergencies or disasters, including earthquakes, hurricanes, typhoons, storms and tornadoes, floods, dam failures, technological accidents, terrorist activities, and hazardous materials releases. The events may be slow in developing, as in the case of hurricanes, or sudden, as in the case of earthquakes.[9]

The National Disaster Medical System (NDMS) is a federally coordinated system that augments the Nation's medical response capability.

Mobile Emergency Response Support (MERS)

In response to Regional requests for support, FEMA provides mobile telecommunications, operational support, life support, and power generation assets for the on-site management of disaster and all-hazard activities. This support is managed by the Response and Recovery Directorate's Mobile Operations Division (RR-MO). These teams provide prompt and rapid multi-media communications, information processing, logistics, and operational support to Federal, State, and Local agencies during catastrophic emergencies and disasters for government response and recovery operations.[10]

Ready Program

Launched in February 2003, Ready is a national public service advertising campaign designed to educate and empower Americans to prepare for and respond to emergencies including natural disasters and potential terrorist attacks. The goal of the campaign is to get the public involved and ultimately to increase the level of basic preparedness across the nation. Are You Ready? is just one of many resources the Department of Homeland Security provides the citizens of this nation to help them be prepared against all types of hazards. The Department of Homeland Security's Ready Campaign seeks to help America be better prepared for even unlikely emergency scenarios.

Following a disaster, community members may be on their own for a period of time because of the size of the area affected, lost communications, and impassable roads. The Community Emergency Response Team (CERT) program supports local response capability by training volunteers to organize themselves and spontaneous volunteers at the disaster site, to provide immediate assistance to victims, and to collect disaster intelligence to support responders' efforts when they arrive.

Citizen Corps provides opportunities for people across the country to participate in a range of measures to make their families, their homes, and their communities safer from the threats of crime, terrorism, public health issues, and disasters of all kinds. Through public education, training opportunities, and volunteer programs, every American can do their part to be better prepared and better protected and to help their communities do the same.

Citizen Corps is managed at the local level by Citizen Corps Councils, which bring together leaders from law enforcement, fire, emergency medical and other emergency management, volunteer organizations, local elected officials, the private sector, and other community stakeholders. These Citizen Corps Councils organize public education on disaster mitigation and preparedness, citizen training, and volunteer programs to give people of all ages and backgrounds the opportunity to support their community's emergency services and to safeguard themselves and their property.[11]

Planning makes it possible to manage the entire life cycle of a potential crisis.

The Preparedness Cycle

The National Incident Management System (NIMS) defines preparedness as "a continuous cycle of planning, organizing, training, equipping, exercising, evaluating, and taking corrective action in an effort to ensure effective coordination during incident response." This 'preparedness cycle' is one element of a broader National Preparedness System to prevent, respond to, recover from, and mitigate against natural disasters, acts of terrorism, and other man-made disasters.

FEMA supports preparedness by developing policies, ensuring adequate plans are in place and are validated, defining necessary capabilities required to address threats, providing resources and technical assistance to jurisdictions, and integrating and synchronizing preparedness efforts throughout the Nation.[12]

Plan

Planning makes it possible to manage the entire life cycle of a potential crisis. Strategic and operational planning establishes priorities, identifies expected levels of performance and capability requirements, provides the standard for assessing capabilities, and helps stakeholders learn their roles. The planning elements identify what an organization's Standard Operating Procedures (SOP) or Emergency Operations Plans (EOP) should include for ensuring that contingencies are in place for delivering the capability during a large-scale disaster.

The National Response Framework presents the guiding principles that enable all response partners to prepare for and provide a unified national response to disasters and emergencies - from the smallest incident to the largest catastrophe. The Framework establishes a comprehensive, national, all-hazards approach to domestic incident response.

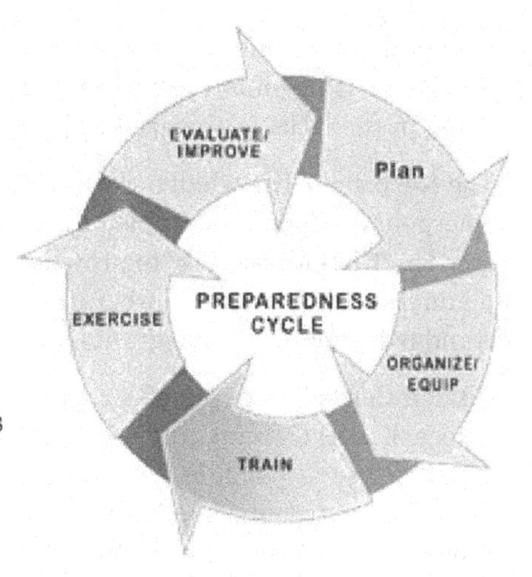

The Integrated Planning System (IPS) is being developed to coordinate and harmonize planning efforts across the Federal government as well as among Federal, State, local, tribal, and territorial partners.

Preparedness technical assistance (TA) services seek to build and sustain capabilities in support of the preparedness mission area. These services address the suite of priorities and capabilities outlined in the National Preparedness Guidelines. As capability gaps are identified within State and local jurisdictions, Preparedness TA services are designed, developed, and delivered to address those needs and build capabilities in the most critical areas.[13]

Organize and Equip

Organizing and equipping provide the human and technical capital stock necessary to build capabilities and address modernization and sustainability requirements.

Organizing and equipping provide the human and technical capital stock necessary to build capabilities and address modernization and sustainability requirements. Organizing and equipping include identifying what competencies and skill sets people delivering a capability should possess and ensuring an organization possesses the correct personnel. Additionally, it includes identifying and acquiring standard and/or surge equipment an organization may need to use when delivering a specific capability. This element of the Cycle is guided by stakeholder needs, national priorities identified in the National Preparedness Guidelines, capabilities-based planning described in the Target Capabilities List (TCL), and relevant legislation, policies, doctrine, and risk assessments.

Typing and Credentialing is the categorization and description of response resources that are commonly exchanged in disasters through mutual aid agreements. Resource typing definitions can give emergency responders the information they need to make sure they request and receive the appropriate resources during an emergency or disaster. Credentialing documents minimum professional qualifications, certifications, training and education requirements that define baseline criteria expected of emergency response professionals and volunteers for deployment as mutual aid to disasters.

System Assessment and Validation for Emergency Responders (SAVER) Program assists emergency responders in making procurement decisions. The SAVER Program conducts objective assessments and validations on commercial equipment and systems, and provides those results along with other relevant equipment information to the community in an operationally useful form. SAVER provides information on equipment that falls within the categories listed in the DHS Authorized Equipment List (AEL).

The Responder Knowledge Base (RKB) is a national information resource for emergency responders, funded by the FEMA National Preparedness Directorate. The RKB Mission is "to provide Emergency Responders, purchasers, and planners with a trusted, integrated, on-line source of information on products, standards, certifications, grants, and other equipment-related information."

Citizen Corps Partners and Programs provide resources for public education, outreach, and training and offer volunteer service opportunities for citizens to support first responders, disaster relief activities, and community safety efforts. These resources include the Community Emergency Response Team Program, which educates people about disaster preparedness for hazards that may impact their area and trains them in basic disaster response skills, such as fire safety, light search and rescue, team organization, and disaster medical operations.

The Emergency Management Assistance Compact (EMAC) is a national interstate mutual aid agreement that enables states to share resources during times of disaster. EMAC is administered by the National Emergency Management Agency (NEMA).[14]

Training provides first responders, homeland security officials, emergency management officials, private and non-governmental partners, and other personnel with the knowledge, skills, and abilities needed to perform key tasks required by specific capabilities.

Train

Training provides first responders, homeland security officials, emergency management officials, private and non-governmental partners, and other personnel with the knowledge, skills, and abilities needed to perform key tasks required by specific capabilities. Organizations should make training decisions based on information derived from the assessments, strategies, and plans developed in previous steps of the Preparedness Cycle. Regions, States and urban areas conduct Training and Exercise Planning Workshops (T&EPW) to review and establish priorities for training and exercises and develop Multi-Year Training and Exercise Plans to address the priorities.

The National Training Program (NTP) provides an organized approach to training for emergency managers and emergency response providers across the Nation that supports the National Preparedness Guidelines. The NTP provides policy, guidance, and tools that address training design, development, delivery, and evaluation, as appropriate. The NTP supports the development, promulgation, and regular updating, as necessary, of national voluntary consensus standards for training; and ensures that the training provided under the NTP is consistent with the standards.

FEMA offers a large number of training classes, either at its own centers, through programs at the state level, in cooperation with colleges and universities, or online. The Training and Education Division within FEMA's National Integration Center directly funds training for responders and provides guidance on training-related expenditures under FEMA's grant programs.[15]

The mission of the Center for Domestic Preparedness (CDP) is to train emergency response providers from state, local, and tribal governments, as well as the Federal government, foreign governments, and private entities, as available. The scope of training includes preparedness, protection, and response. CDP training for state, local, and tribal responders is fully funded by the U.S. Department of Homeland Security. International, Federal, and private sector responders may participate in CDP training on a space available, fee-for-service basis. Training partnerships at the Federal and state levels enable the CDP staff to take advantage of shared knowledge, to ensure the nation's responders receive the most up-to-date training. The CDP's interdisciplinary resident and non- resident training courses promote greater understanding among these diverse responder disciplines: Emergency Management, Emergency Medical Services, Fire Service, Governmental Administrative, Hazardous Materials, Healthcare, Law Enforcement, Public Health, Public Safety Communications, and Public Works.[16]

Exercise

Exercises assess and validate the speed, effectiveness and efficiency of capabilities, and test the adequacy of policies, plans, procedures, and protocols in a risk-free environment. Aside from actual events, they provide the best means of evaluating homeland security capabilities. Organizations should conduct exercises as scheduled in a Multi-Year Training and Exercise Schedule developed at the annual Training and Exercise Plan Workshop (T&EPW). By scheduling complementary training and exercise activities that gradually increase in complexity, the Multi-Year Training and Exercise Schedule systematically builds and enhances an organization's capabilities.

Exercises assess and validate the speed, effectiveness and efficiency of capabilities, and test the adequacy of policies, plans, procedures, and protocols in a risk-free environment.

The National Exercise Program (NEP) provides an organized approach to set priorities for exercises, reflect those priorities in a multi-year schedule of exercises that serves the strategic and policy goals of the U.S. Government, and address findings from those exercises through a disciplined interagency process. The NEP establishes the Homeland Security Exercise and Evaluation Program (HSEEP) as the exercise methodology and tools to support the NEP.

The Homeland Security Exercise and Evaluation Program (HSEEP) is a capabilities and performance-based exercise program that provides a standardized methodology and terminology for exercise design, development, conduct, evaluation, and improvement planning.

The National Exercise Simulation Center (NESC) is a Congressionally-mandated state-of-the-art training and exercise facility within FEMA Headquarters, and serves as a key element within the Federal Coordination Center (FCC). The FCC draws on the specialized capabilities of its FEMA elements, including the Disaster Operations Directorate, the National Preparedness Directorate, the Office of National Capital Region Coordination, and others as needed, to collaborate with and support deliberate planning, training, exercises and response operations coordination.

The Chemical Stockpile Emergency Preparedness Program (CSEPP) Exercises: Since 1988, FEMA and the U.S. Army have assisted communities surrounding the seven chemical stockpile sites to enhance their abilities to respond to the unlikely event of a chemical agent emergency. The US stockpile of chemical agents is safely stored at six sites across the country. These sites are located in Alabama, Arkansas, Colorado, Indiana/Illinois, Kentucky, Oregon/ Washington, and Utah. Sites comply with annual CSEPP exercise requirements.

FEMA established the Radiological Emergency Preparedness (REP) Program to (1) ensure the health and safety of citizens living around commercial nuclear power plants would be adequately protected in the event of a nuclear power plant accident; and (2) inform and educate the public about radiological emergency preparedness. REP Program responsibilities encompass only "offsite" activities, that is, State, tribal and local government emergency planning and preparedness activities, to including exercises that follow REP exercise methodology.[17]

Evaluate and Improve

The evaluation and improvement of mission and task performance is the final step of the Preparedness Cycle and crucial to informing risk assessments, managing vulnerabilities, allocating resources, and informing the other elements of the Cycle.

The evaluation and improvement of mission and task performance is the final step of the Preparedness Cycle and crucial to informing risk assessments, managing vulnerabilities, allocating resources, and informing the other elements of the Cycle. Organizations develop improvement plans and track corrective actions to address the capabilities identified in plans and tested in exercises or real events. In addition to corrective actions, assessment initiatives such as the State Preparedness Reports and FEMA-administered Gap Analysis tool provide the means to evaluate a States operational preparedness for key critical areas. Using this data to reassess and revise plans and protocols contributes to the beginning of the next Preparedness Cycle by ensuring that updated strategies and plans can be used to inform new preparedness-building activities.

The Corrective Action Program (CAP) provides a standard methodology for handling corrective actions and improvement plans. The CAP System is a web-based application that enables users to prioritize, track, and analyze improvement plans developed from exercises and real-world events.

Lessons Learned Information Sharing (LLIS) is the national network of Lessons Learned and Best Practices for emergency response providers and homeland security officials.

Emergency Management Accreditation Program (EMAP) is a standard-based voluntary assessment and accreditation process for state and local government programs responsible for coordinating prevention, mitigation, preparedness, response, and recovery activities for natural and human-caused disasters. [18]

Conclusion

FEMA manages and coordinates the Federal response to and recovery from major domestic disasters and emergencies of all types, in accordance with the Robert T. Stafford Disaster Relief and Emergency Assistance Act. The agency coordinates programs to improve the effectiveness of emergency response providers at all levels of government to respond to terrorist attacks, major disasters, and other emergencies. Through the Disaster Relief Fund, FEMA provides individual and public assistance to help families and communities impacted by declared disasters to rebuild and recover. FEMA is also responsible for helping to prepare state and local governments, through their state and local programs, to prevent or respond to threats or incidents of terrorism and other events. FEMA also administers hazard mitigation programs that reduce the risk to life and property from floods and other hazards. FEMA stands ready to provide rapid assistance and resources in emergency situations whenever state and local capabilities are overwhelmed or seriously threatened. At a disaster location, FEMA leads the Federal response and recovery effort by providing emergency management expertise and coordinating critical support resources from across the country. [19]

Questions

1. What is FEMA's role in preparing for and responding to disasters?
2. How is FEMA activated during disasters?
3. What benefits to society does mitigation provide?
4. How did Hurricane Katrina affect the organizational changes to FEMA?

Chapter 25

Science & Technology

Objectives

- Identify research interests of various S&T divisions.
- Explain the purpose of Integrated Product Teams.
- Know the different categories of research.
- Describe S&T's trend in R&D investment.

Introduction

The Directorate of Science and Technology (S&T) is the primary organization for research and development (R&D) in the Department of Homeland Security. With a budget of $932.6 million in FY2009, the directorate conducts R&D in several laboratories of its own and funds R&D conducted by other government agencies, the Department of Energy national laboratories, industry, and universities.

In the past, some Members of Congress have been highly critical of the directorate's performance. For example, in 2006, the House Appropriations Committee said it was "concerned about the ability of [the] S&T [Directorate] to advance the use of science and technology in battling terrorism and against other hazards related to homeland security," and the Senate Appropriations Committee called the directorate "a rudderless ship without a clear way to get back on course" and said it was "extremely disappointed with the manner in which [the] S&T [Directorate] is being managed."

More recently, management changes have considerably muted this criticism. For example, in 2007, the Senate Appropriations Committee stated that it was "pleased with the rapid progress S&T appears to be making toward resolving past difficulties. The new Under Secretary has restructured the directorate's programs, worked to obligate resources in a timely fashion, and instituted a capable budget office able to deliver timely, accurate, and comprehensible documents." Nevertheless, a number of fundamental issues remain.[1]

Mission

The Homeland Security Act of 2002 (P.L. 107-296), which established the Department of Homeland Security (DHS), created within DHS a Directorate of Science and Technology, headed by an Under Secretary for Science and Technology. The directorate was not given a concise statutory mission. Instead, the Homeland Security Act gave the Under Secretary a wide-ranging list of responsibilities and authorities. (For the complete list, see Appendix A.) In 2006, Under Secretary Jay M. Cohen summarized his interpretation of the S&T Directorate's multifaceted mission as follows: "The S&T Directorate's mission is to protect the homeland by providing Federal, State, local, and Tribal officials with state-of-the-art technology and resources." Some of the Under Secretary's responsibilities and authorities are primarily coordinative. These include

- planning and coordinating the federal civilian effort to develop countermeasures against terrorist threats;
- collaborating with the Secretary of Agriculture, the Attorney General, and the Secretary of Health and Human Services in the designation and regulation of biological select agents;
- coordinating with other appropriate executive agencies to reduce R&D duplication and identify unmet needs; and
- coordinating and integrating the department's activities in R&D, demonstration, testing, and evaluation.

All these tasks involve stakeholders who do not report to the Under Secretary, so the Under Secretary's ability to perform his duties relies on the cooperation of other agencies.

Another group of responsibilities and authorities are in support of other DHS organizations. These include

- advising the Secretary on R&D efforts and priorities;
- supporting the Under Secretary for National Protection and Programs (formerly the Under Secretary for Information Analysis and Infrastructure Protection) by assessing and testing vulnerabilities and threats; and
- overseeing department-wide guidelines for merit review of R&D.

Finally, some of the Under Secretary's responsibilities and authorities specify functions of the S&T Directorate itself. These include

- establishing and administering the primary R&D activities of the department; conducting basic and applied research, development, demonstration, testing, and evaluation;
- establishing a system for transferring technologies to federal, state, and local governments and the private sector; and
- generally supporting U.S. leadership in science and technology.[2]

The Chemical and Biological Division works to increase preparedness against agricultural, biological, and chemical threats through improved threat awareness, advanced surveillance and detection, and protective countermeasures

Organization

Under Secretary Cohen reorganized the management structure of the S&T Directorate soon after his confirmation in August 2006.

The directorate consists primarily of six research divisions: the Explosives; Chemical and Biological; Command, Control, and Interoperability; Borders and Maritime Security; Human Factors; and Infrastructure and Geophysical Divisions.6 These are the directorate's main performers and funders of R&D in their respective topical areas. The Offices of Research, Innovation, and Transition coordinate the activities of the divisions; they also conduct some activities of their own. Other functions are performed by the Offices of Test and Evaluation and Standards; Special Programs; and Agency and International Liaison. Each of these 12 divisions and offices is headed by a director who reports directly to the Under Secretary. The directors of the Offices of Research, Innovation, and Transition liaise with each of the six divisions.[3]

Chemical and Biological Division

The Chemical and Biological Division is the largest of the six research divisions. It works to increase preparedness against agricultural, biological, and chemical threats through improved threat awareness, advanced surveillance and detection, and protective countermeasures. The agriculture component develops veterinary vaccines and other animal disease countermeasures and models the spread of animal diseases. The biological countermeasures component includes programs in systems studies and decision support tools, threat awareness, surveillance and detection R&D, surveillance and detection operations, forensics, and response and restoration, but not R&D related to human medical countermeasures, which are the responsibility of the Department of Health and Human Services. The chemical countermeasures component includes chemical threat analysis, development of forensic tools, R&D on chemical detection technologies, and development of technologies for response and recovery.

Explosives Division

The Explosives Division develops technologies to detect, interdict, and lessen the impacts of nonnuclear explosives used in terrorist attacks against mass transit, civil aviation, and critical infrastructure. The bulk of its effort is devoted to explosives detection, largely through R&D programs that were transferred from the Transportation Security Administration in FY2006. It also includes R&D on protecting commercial aircraft against shoulder-fired, surface-to-air missiles (known as MANPADS, for man-portable air defense systems).

The Command, Control, and Interoperability Division is focused on communications for emergency responders, the security and integrity of the Internet, and other information-related topics.

Infrastructure and Geophysical Division

The Infrastructure and Geophysical Division carries out activities in two main areas: critical infrastructure protection and preparedness and response. The infrastructure protection component includes technology development for specific infrastructure sectors and geographical regions, modeling and simulation for decision support, and preparation of the National Plan for Research and Development in Support of Critical Infrastructure Protection. The preparedness and response component develops technologies such as protective equipment for first responders and information-management, decision-making, and training tools for incident commanders.

Command, Control, and Interoperability Division

The Command, Control, and Interoperability Division is focused on communications for emergency responders, the security and integrity of the Internet, and other information-related topics. Its conducts R&D on the interoperability and compatibility of communications equipment; cyber security; knowledge management tools; reconnaissance, surveillance, and investigative technologies; and threat assessment.

Borders and Maritime Security Division

The Borders and Maritime Security Division researches, develops, and transitions technologies to improve the security of U.S. borders and waterways. It has two focus areas, border protection and cargo security. The border protection component (known as Border Watch) develops tools for border security law enforcement officers and technologies for detection, identification, apprehension, and enforcement at land and maritime borders. The cargo security component develops sensor and communications technologies to improve the integrity of cargo container shipments.

Human Factors Division

The Human Factors Division focuses primarily on the social and behavioral sciences. Its R&D activities include developing biometric technologies for identifying known terrorists and criminals; understanding user acceptance and application of new technologies; improving the integration of human operators and technology for transportation security screening; understanding terrorist motivation, intent, and behavior; making risk communications more effective; and better identifying public needs during emergencies.

Research (Laboratory Facilities and University Programs)

The Office of Research includes the directorate's Laboratory Facilities and University Programs. Its director also liaises with the six research divisions as discussed above. Laboratory Facilities funds operation and construction of the S&T Directorate's own laboratories. The activities of the Laboratory Facilities program are executed by the Office of National Laboratories, one of a handful of organizational components of the S&T Directorate that were established by statute.140 University Programs manages the directorate's university centers and a program of scholarships and fellowships.

HSARPA has two main programs:

- *The Homeland Innovative Prototypical Solutions program is designed to demonstrate prototypes of high-payoff technologies in two to five years with moderate to high risk.*
- *The High Impact Technology Solutions program is designed to conduct high-risk basic research that provides proofs of concept for potential break-*

Innovation (HSARPA and SBIR)

The Office of Innovation includes the Homeland Security Advanced Research Projects Agency (HSARPA), another component that was established by statute. HSARPA has two main programs. The Homeland Innovative Prototypical Solutions program is designed to demonstrate prototypes of high-payoff technologies in two to five years with moderate to high risk. The High Impact Technology Solutions program is designed to conduct high-risk basic research that provides proofs of concept for potential breakthroughs. HSARPA also manages the S&T Directorate's program of Small Business Innovation Research (SBIR), which is funded through a mandated set-aside of DHS R&D budget, achieved by setting aside funds from each DHS R&D program. The director of the Office of Innovation also liaises with the six research divisions as discussed above.

Transition (SAFETY Act and Technology Clearinghouse)

The Office of Transition oversees interactions with DHS components outside the S&T Directorate to expedite technology transition. It also manages the Office of SAFETY Act Implementation, which evaluates and qualifies technologies for liability protection in accordance with the SAFETY Act,142 and the statutorily mandated Technology Clearinghouse. Its director also liaises with the six research divisions as discussed above.

Test and Evaluation and Standards

The Office of Test and Evaluation and Standards provides technical support and coordination to help emergency responders assess the safety, reliability, and effectiveness of equipment and procedures. It also aids in establishing test and evaluation methodology for the directorate and acts as the test and evaluation executive for the Department as a whole.

Special Programs

The Department of Homeland Security has original classification authority and funds some R&D projects that are classified (although Sec. 306(a) of the Homeland Security Act directs that "to the greatest extent practicable, research conducted or supported by the department shall be unclassified"). The Office of Special Programs oversees the directorate's classified projects.

Agency and International Liaison

The Office of Agency and International Liaison oversees the directorate's international outreach activities and interagency coordination responsibilities.

Historically, the focus of Environmental Measurements Laboratory was detection and monitoring of low-level radiation releases.

Management and Administration

Other activities of the directorate, including the Office of the Under Secretary, are funded by a separate appropriation for management and administration. This account also pays the salaries and expenses of all the directorate's federal employees.[4]

Laboratories and Other Assets

The S&T Directorate has a variety of R&D assets that support its activities. Some are laboratories that were transferred into the Department of Homeland Security when it was created in 2002. (The transfers became effective in early 2003.) Other assets have been established more recently under the authority of the Homeland Security Act.

Environmental Measurements Laboratory

The Environmental Measurements Laboratory (EML) in New York City was formerly in the Department of Energy. It was transferred to the S&T Directorate by Sec. 303 of the Homeland Security Act. Historically, the focus of EML was detection and monitoring of low-level radiation releases. The transfer of EML to the S&T Directorate required a realignment of EML's activities to meet homeland security goals. According to some experts, this realignment process was contentious. DHS officials reportedly debated whether EML is most appropriately positioned in the S&T Directorate or the Domestic Nuclear Detection Office (DNDO, discussed more below); whether EML should be closed; and whether EML should be reduced in size and the remaining capabilities relocated. In May 2007, Under Secretary Cohen testified that EML will remain in the S&T Directorate; that it will continue to operate, supporting both DNDO and other DHS organizations; and that it will remain in its current location but in smaller, "right sized" facilities. This realignment and scoping process is ongoing.

Plum Island Animal Disease Center

The Plum Island Animal Disease Center (PIADC), on Plum Island off the coast of Long Island, NY, was transferred from the Department of Agriculture to the S&T Directorate by Sec. 310 of the Homeland Security Act. The PIADC provides a federal facility where R&D can be performed on animal pathogens that might threaten livestock on a national level. Its research seeks to find quicker ways to diagnose animal diseases and to develop vaccines and other veterinary treatments for infected animals. The PIADC has been in service for over 50 years, and questions have been raised about the state of its laboratory infrastructure and the adequacy of that infrastructure to continue performing necessary R&D for DHS.

In January 2009, DHS announced that a new National Bio- and Agro-Defense Facility (NBAF) will be built on the campus of Kansas State University. The PIADC laboratories will be decommissioned once NBAF becomes fully operational. Some policymakers have expressed concern regarding the move of foot-and-mouth disease research from an island to the mainland, and the Government Accountability Office (GAO) has testified that more information and analysis should be performed to determine the magnitude of risks associated with moving such research from Plum Island to the mainland.

Congress has enacted a series of authorities relating to the proposed creation of the NBAF, transfer of PIADC research activities, and closure of PIADC. Through the 2008 farm bill, Congress addressed concerns regarding legal authority to perform live foot-and-mouth disease virus research on the mainland. The 2008 farm bill required the Secretary of Agriculture to issue a permit to DHS allowing research on live foot-and-mouth disease virus on the mainland at any successor facility to PIADC. Congress also responded to the perceived potential risks of performing such research on the mainland. Congress required DHS to complete a risk assessment of whether foot-and-mouth disease work can be done safely on the mainland and have this risk assessment reviewed by the GAO. Until this risk assessment and review is completed, funds appropriated in the Department of Homeland Security Appropriations Act, 2009 (P.L. 110-329, Division D) may not be used for construction of the NBAF.

DHS is evaluating options for the transition and future use of the PIADC facility. Possibilities that have been suggested include turning it into a government-run laboratory for alternative energy R&D, using the site for a wind farm, and selling the property for commercial development.14 Section 540 of the Department of Homeland Security Appropriations Act, 2009 (P.L. 110-329, Division D) directs DHS to "liquidate the Plum Island Asset" and makes the proceeds available to the S&T Directorate, subject to appropriations, to offset the cost of environmental remediation at the PIADC site and construction of the NBAF; any balance still remaining after that could be used for construction of a consolidated DHS headquarters. For more information on NBAF, see CRS Report RL34160, The National Bio- and Agro-Defense Facility: Issues for Congress.

Transportation Security Laboratory

The Transportation Security Laboratory (TSL) in Atlantic City, NJ, was formerly in the Transportation Security Administration (TSA) and before that in the Federal Aviation Administration. It became part of DHS along with the rest of TSA under Sec. 403 of the Homeland Security Act. It was transferred to the S&T Directorate in FY2006 as part of an effort to consolidate the department's R&D activities. The TSL performs research, development, and testing and evaluation activities, primarily in the area of detection and mitigation of explosives and conventional weapons threats.

National Biodefense Analysis and Countermeasures Center

The Homeland Security Act established a National Bio-Weapons Defense Analysis Center in the Department of Defense (Sec. 1708) and then transferred it, along with its funding, to the DHS S&T Directorate (Sec. 303). Subsequently renamed the National Biodefense Analysis and Countermeasures Center (NBACC), this center exists as both a program office and a laboratory facility. The facility, currently under construction in Ft. Detrick, MD, will include highbiocontainment laboratories that can perform homeland security biodefense research and bioforensics. When construction is complete, it will be operated by a contractor as a federally funded research and development center (FFRDC).

In March 2009, the S&T Directorate established the Homeland Security Studies and Analysis Institute (HSSAI) to provide mission-focused homeland security analysis and expertise focusing on program objectives, system requirements, and metrics.

Homeland Security Institute &

Homeland Security Studies and Analysis Institute

The Homeland Security Institute (HSI) was an FFRDC established under Sec. 312 of the Homeland Security Act and managed on the S&T Directorate's behalf by Analytic Services, Inc. The HSI assisted the directorate in addressing homeland security issues that require scientific, technical, and analytical expertise. Its main focus was systems analysis and evaluation. Most of its funds were received on a per-project basis from programs that request its assistance; in FY2008 and FY2009 it also received a separate appropriation of $5.0 million. Under a sunset provision in the Homeland Security Act as originally passed, the institute would have terminated in November 2005. The Department of Homeland Security Appropriations Act, 2005 (P.L. 108- 334) extended that termination date to April 25, 2009. That date was not extended further, so the statutory authority for the HSI has expired.

In March 2009, under Sec. 305 of the Homeland Security Act, which gives DHS general authority to establish FFRDCs, the S&T Directorate established the Homeland Security Studies and Analysis Institute (HSSAI). The functions of the HSSAI appear to be very similar to those of the HSI, and HSSAI is also managed by Analytic Services, Inc. The new institute will "provide mission-focused homeland security analysis and expertise focusing on program objectives, system requirements, and metrics." Its contract is for one year with up to four one-year extensions for total funding of up to $269 million.

Some Members of Congress have questioned HSI's ability to provide effective, independent analysis of DHS programs, because DHS provided its funding and because its contractor might wish to compete for a continuation of its management contract after the 2009 termination date (as indeed it did, successfully).19 On the other hand, Congress established the institute specifically to provide analysis to DHS, and there has been little congressional criticism of specific Homeland Security Institute reports. It remains to be seen how these concerns will carry over to the newly established HSSAI.

Homeland Security Systems Engineering and Development Institute

The Homeland Security Systems Engineering and Development Institute (HSSEDI) is another FFRDC, also established under Sec. 305 of the Homeland Security Act in March 2009. It will be managed on the S&T Directorate's behalf by the MITRE Corporation. The HSSEDI will provide the S&T Directorate with "advice on concept evolution, development integration, best practices in lifecycle systems engineering and management, and program-level technical and integration expertise across the homeland security enterprise." The HSSEDI contract is for one year with up to four one-year extensions for total funding of up to $443 million.

The Homeland Security Systems Engineering and Development Institute (HSSEDI), established in March 2009, will provide advice on concept evolution, development integration, and best practices in lifecycle systems engineering and management, and program-level technical and integration expertise across the homeland security enterprise.

University Centers

The Homeland Security Act requires the Under Secretary to establish at least one university based center for homeland security (Sec. 308).21 Twelve university centers of excellence have been established so far:

- the Center of Excellence for Command, Control and Interoperability, led by Rutgers University and Purdue University;22
- the Center for Border Security and Immigration (COE-BSI), led by the University of Arizona and the University of Texas at El Paso;
- the Center for Explosives Detection, Mitigation, and Response, led by Northeastern University and the University of Rhode Island;
- the Center for Maritime, Island and Port Security, led by the University of Hawaii and Stevens Institute of Technology;
- the Center for Natural Disasters, Coastal Infrastructure, and Emergency Management, led by the University of North Carolina at Chapel Hill and Jackson State University;
- the National Transportation Security Center of Excellence, led by Texas Southern University in Houston, Tougaloo College, and the University of Connecticut;

- the Center for Risk and Economic Analysis of Terrorism Events (CREATE), led by the University of Southern California;
- the National Center for Food Protection and Defense (NCFPD), led by the University of Minnesota;
- the National Center for Foreign Animal and Zoonotic Disease Defense (FAZD), led by Texas A&M University;
- the National Consortium for the Study of Terrorism and Responses to Terrorism (START), led by the University of Maryland;
- the National Center for the Study of Preparedness and Catastrophic Event Response (PACER), led by Johns Hopkins University; and
- the Center for Advancing Microbial Risk Assessment (CAMRA), led by Michigan State University (established jointly with the Environmental Protection Agency).

These centers are operated by consortia of universities. Some consortia include non-university partners. Although each consortium contains numerous members, funding and activities are typically concentrated at the lead institution and a small number of major partners. The centers are a mixture of entities established by statute and those established at the discretion of DHS. Funding for these centers is provided through the S&T Directorate's Office of University Programs. The research activities of the centers are not managed directly by DHS, but rather by administrative staff at each center. Each center's research strategy and plan is provided to DHS for review, however, and the centers attempt to align their work with the needs of the department. As part of the reorganization begun in 2006, the S&T Directorate plans to align the topics of the centers more closely with the research divisions. Over the next several years, where multiple centers currently align with a single division, some may be closed or merged, and new ones may be established.

In addition, several university-affiliated activities are sometimes considered additional centers of excellence:

- four University Affiliate Centers (UACs), led by Rutgers University, the University of Southern California, the University of Illinois at Urbana-Champaign, and the University of Pittsburgh, that work with the Institute for Discrete Sciences at Lawrence Livermore National Laboratory;
- five Regional Visualization and Analytics Centers (RVACs), led by Penn State University, Purdue University, Stanford University, the University of North Carolina at Charlotte, and the University of Washington, that collaborate with the National Visualization and Analytics Center at Pacific Northwest National Laboratory; and
- two centers funded by the Infrastructure and Geophysical Division (not University Programs): the Southeast Regional Research Initiative (SERRI) and the Kentucky Critical Infrastructure Protection Institute (KCI).

The UACs and RVACs support the Division of Command, Control, and Interoperability. DHS plans not to fund them after FY2008 and to transition their research activities to the new Center of Excellence for Command, Control, and Interoperability in FY2009.

The university centers of excellence and the university-affiliated activities provide the main connection between the S&T Directorate and the academic community. As such, the university centers of excellence are the primary mechanism for the S&T Directorate and the academic community to interact on R&D topics. The details of these centers have been an issue of congressional focus, with special interest given to how research at university centers of excellence relates to DHS R&D needs and S&T Directorate priorities. In 2007, Congress considered, but did not impose, limited terms for the university centers of excellence, and it has since established new university centers of excellence in specific research areas. Stakeholders resisted congressional efforts to curtail the duration of the university centers of excellence, but response to plans to realign the university centers of excellence has been more muted.

DOE National Laboratories

DHS has a special statutory relationship with the national laboratories of the Department of Energy (DOE):

> Notwithstanding any other law governing the administration, mission, use, or operations of any of the Department of Energy national laboratories and sites, such laboratories and sites are authorized to accept and perform work for the Secretary, consistent with resources provided, and perform such work on an equal basis to other missions at the laboratory and not on a noninterference basis with other missions of such laboratory or site.

DHS has a special statutory relationship with the national laboratories of the Department of Energy. The S&T Directorate can use this authority to engage the DOE national laboratories to perform research for DHS as if they were being tasked by DOE.

The S&T Directorate can use this authority to engage the DOE national laboratories to perform research for DHS as if they were being tasked by DOE. This authority reduces costs for DHS and gives its tasks equal priority with DOE tasks, unlike the tasks of other agencies that conduct R&D at the national laboratories under the status of "work for others." Early in its existence, the S&T Directorate identified a number of DOE national laboratories that perform R&D potentially relevant to homeland security, but it was criticized for having no strategy to use that capability. DOE and DHS have since entered into a memorandum of agreement regarding the use of DOE assets by DHS, and the S&T Directorate reported in May 2007 that it had aligned its use of the DOE national laboratories with its reorganized division structure. Eleven of the laboratories are included in this alignment; each division is aligned with between three and seven of them. The goal of the alignment process is to provide an enduring capability for basic research.[5]

Scope of R&D Role

The subject-matter boundaries of the directorate's R&D role within DHS have expanded and contracted since its establishment. As discussed above, it has absorbed programs from several other DHS organizations, but Congress rejected proposals that it take over certain Coast Guard activities, and the Domestic Nuclear Detection Office is now a separate organization with responsibility for radiological and nuclear countermeasures. Given that the S&T Directorate is not the only R&D operation within DHS, questions remain about what principles determine the types of R&D it should do, and when another organization should take on a particular R&D topic.

The scope of research undertaken by the S&T Directorate through its component entities also has been questioned. When DHS was established, Congress also created within the S&T Directorate the Homeland Security Advanced Research Projects Agency (HSARPA), which was to administer a newly established Acceleration Fund for Research and Development of Homeland Security Technologies.39 The scope of this agency has evolved since it was created. Initially, it was unclear how the S&T Directorate would implement HSARPA; given the similarity of its name to the Defense Advanced Research Projects Agency (DARPA), some experts in the scientific community believed that, like DARPA, it would fund high-risk, high-reward R&D. Instead, the S&T Directorate used HSARPA to conduct essentially all of its extramural activities, most of which were conventional R&D with only moderate risk.

As part of his reorganization of the S&T Directorate, Under Secretary Cohen redirected the work of HSARPA. The role of HSARPA is much reduced from past years, when it was responsible for nearly all of the directorate's extramural R&D. It is now focused on activities with high risk and high reward. Through its Homeland Innovative Prototypical Solutions (HIPS) and High Impact Technology Solutions (HITS) programs, HSARPA now performs research activities more in the DARPA model.

The best way to use HSARPA may continue to be a topic of congressional interest. Advocates of the DARPA model point out that while its risks are high, and only a small fraction of funded programs achieve their goals, the benefits from the successes can be great. On the other hand, because most programs do not achieve their goals, many will likely need to be funded before a success is realized. The high-risk, high-reward approach is therefore likely to require a sustained and significant financial commitment if it is to be successful.

Functions Other than R&D

Although the directorate's main role is R&D, its programs include a variety of other related functions. It is currently involved in standards development, technology testing and evaluation, and technology transfer. Until 2007, it conducted several operational programs, such as BioWatch, in which it deployed and operated equipment as well as developing it. It awards scholarships and fellowships, the purpose of which has sometimes been described as "capacity building" for future R&D—a topic in which some Members of Congress have been particularly interested. The Under Secretary also has several coordinative responsibilities involving other federal agencies. While the shift of operational programs to other organizations in 2007 suggests an attempt to focus on the main R&D role, the other activities and responsibilities remain. There has been no definitive explanation of the factors that determine which non-R&D functions are appropriate for the directorate and what determines their priority relative to R&D.

Prior to the establishment of DHS, no single agency had responsibility for homeland security, and homeland security was not generally considered to be an independent field of study. While academic R&D capability and educational programs in national security and defense existed, such capacity was lacking in the area of homeland security. As part of the S&T Directorate's efforts in "capacity building," the directorate funded scholarships and fellowships in addition to establishing university research centers. Some analysts have questioned the effectiveness of this program, as the scholars and fellows receiving financial assistance from DHS do not necessarily enter into homeland security employment or R&D.

The S&T Directorate has reduced the numbers of scholars and fellows and attempted to align scholarship and fellowship activities with those of the university centers of excellence. This may lead to greater synergies and effectiveness between the two programs but also may limit the scale of involvement of universities, students, and scientists interested in homeland security. Whether DHS, as an R&D funding entity, should continue to attempt to develop an academic homeland security infrastructure or instead focus on using more federal assets to perform R&D activities and provide experience and expertise in homeland security may continue to be a topic of interest to policymakers.

Prioritization and Strategic Planning

A long-standing congressional criticism of the S&T Directorate is that its planning and prioritization process is opaque. This perception of opacity has led to concerns about the accountability of the planning process and the quality of the decisions it produces. Directorate priorities can be somewhat inferred from the allocation of funding within the directorate, but no planning and prioritization documents were publicly available. In June 2007, for the first time, the directorate issued a strategic plan and a five-year R&D plan. In August 2008, the five year R&D plan was updated to reflect adjustments in funding and programmatic priorities. As described in these documents, a system of Integrated Product Teams (IPTs) now helps to provide end users with more input into the prioritization process.[6]

Integrated Product Teams (IPTs) are focused on a different topic and bring together decision-makers from DHS operational components and the S&T Directorate as well as select end-users.

Integrated Product Teams

The S&T Directorate has instituted procedures to solicit input from the operational components of DHS, to work with the components in identifying technology gaps and needs, and to develop mechanisms to meet those gaps and needs. The foundation of these new procedures is a set of Integrated Product Teams (IPTs). Each IPT is focused on a different topic and brings together decision-makers from DHS operational components and the S&T Directorate as well as select end-users. Each IPT consists of (1) customer representatives, whose role is to identify gaps in capability; (2) providers from the S&T Directorate, whose role is to provide technical solutions; (3) acquisition officials and/or financial officers, whose role is to validate and execute future acquisition plans; and (4) end user representatives, whose role is to provide the end users' perspectives. The intent is to help the operational units make informed decisions about technology investments, based on the S&T Directorate's understanding of technology and the state of applicable technology solutions. The specific goal is to identify technology solutions that can be developed and delivered to the acquisition programs of operational units within three years. Congress and other observers have generally taken a positive view of the IPT process compared with the directorate's previous priority-setting efforts.

One past criticism of the S&T Directorate has been that it has difficulty meeting the needs of end users. The IPT process explicitly recognizes the other DHS components as the consumers of the S&T Directorate's R&D efforts. It identifies requirements and capability gaps at the federal level. Although there can be input from the state and local level, the IPT structure does not encourage end users outside DHS, such as state and local first responders, to communicate their needs directly to the S&T Directorate. The expectation is that the DHS operational components that work with state and local agencies will understand their needs and represent their interests. To provide a direct route for first responders to communicate with S&T, the directorate has established the TechSolutions program. The goal of this program is to integrate first responder needs into the R&D pipeline and provide solutions through rapid prototyping or identification of existing technologies. It is unclear, however, how these needs are prioritized relative to each other or how TechSolutions interacts with the IPT process.[7]

Analysis of Threat Information

Like her predecessor, DHS Secretary Napolitano has stated that DHS should make decisions based on risk (in this context, the risk that different threats pose to homeland security).60 While risk methodologies are under exploration in the S&T Directorate, the extent to which they are incorporated into decision making is unclear. For example, a presidential directive tasks DHS with completing a biennial biological risk assessment. Although the content of that assessment has not been made public, many observers expect that it provides sufficient analysis and detail to identify priority areas for short-, medium-, and long-term R&D investments. For example, its results are being used by the Department of Health and Human Services to help prioritize biological countermeasure procurement through Project Bioshield. On the other hand, a committee of the National Academy of Sciences expressed fundamental concerns about this assessment and recommended that it not be used for prioritization until its flaws are rectified. Another presidential directive requires DHS to develop an integrated risk assessment for chemical, biological, radiological, and nuclear threats. The connection of these two risk assessments to the directorate's R&D budgeting process is not apparent, however, nor is it clear whether the directorate applies or plans to apply a similar risk assessment methodology to priority-setting in other threat areas or across all its activities. It should be noted that these risk assessments may contain information relating to national or homeland security vulnerabilities and, as such, might be incorporated into the directorate's planning processes through a nonpublic mechanism.

Interagency and intra-agency coordination plays an important role in ensuring that R&D plans and strategies are informed by threat information. The techniques used and considered by terrorists adapt and evolve. Technological countermeasures may be available that provide protection against these modified techniques, but they will be ineffective if they are not deployed prior to the techniques' use. Transfer of pertinent threat information from the intelligence community to DHS, and then to the S&T Directorate, may provide an advantage in developing counterterrorism technologies and enhancing preparedness.

Balance of R&D by Type and Performer

The scope of the S&T Directorate's activities is broad. Its R&D activities address the whole range of threats to homeland security (with the exception, since 2005, of most nuclear and radiological threats, which are addressed by the Domestic Nuclear Detection Office). It spans the spectrum from basic research to operational systems (though most operational functions have now been transferred to other DHS organizations). It conducts some activities directly in its own facilities and supports others indirectly through arrangements with the national laboratories, industry, universities, and other government agencies.

The directorate's stated goal is to devote 20% of its budget to basic research.

Basic Research, Applied Research, and Development

How the S&T Directorate allocates its resources between research and development is of interest to both policymakers and other stakeholders. The extent to which the S&T Directorate invests in basic research in particular is an issue of continuing congressional interest. Investment in basic research is generally believed to address long-term needs, provide a basis for future applied research and development, and lead to advances in knowledge across disciplines. Investment in development focuses more on the near term, with results that are typically narrower in scope but more immediately applicable. The directorate's R&D portfolio has been criticized as being skewed too much toward development, with not enough expenditure on basic research. As noted below, the directorate's stated goal is to devote 20% of its budget to basic research. According to DHS, the FY2009 budget request was the first to meet this goal.

In the Administration's annual budget documents, the Office of Management and Budget (OMB) provides an agency-by-agency analysis of federal R&D budget authority in four categories: basic research, applied research, development, and facilities and equipment. For this purpose, OMB defines the first three of these categories as follows:

- basic research: "systematic study directed toward a fuller knowledge or understanding of the fundamental aspects of phenomena and of observable facts without specific applications towards processes or products in mind."
- applied research: "systematic study to gain knowledge or understanding necessary to determine the means by which a recognized and specific need may be met."

- development: "systematic application of knowledge or understanding, directed toward the production of useful materials, devices, and systems or methods, including design, development, and improvement of prototypes and new processes to meet specific requirements."[8]

Independent analysis by the OMB and National Science Foundation (NSF) indicate 75% of DHS' R&D budget between 2003 and 2008 was evenly balanced between applied and developmental research. The 25% remaining funds were fairly split between basic research and facilities/equipment investments.

Intramural and Extramural Activities

Just as congressional policymakers are interested in the breakdown of the S&T Directorate's activities into basic research, applied research, and development, congressional policymakers are also interested in the balance between intramural and extramural activities. Former Under Secretary Cohen said that "we don't do S&T, we resource and we manage S&T." Nevertheless, the S&T Directorate funds both extramural R&D, through contracts, grants, and other arrangements with industry, academia, and others, and intramural R&D, conducted by government employees at DHS and other federal facilities. Before the 2006 reorganization, most extramural R&D was managed by HSARPA; that is no longer true.

When the S&T Directorate was established, its optimal investment strategy was unclear.

Operational Activities

Until 2007, the S&T Directorate contained several operational programs. The department's FY2008 budget request announced plans to transfer the BioWatch, Biological Warning and Incident Characterization, and Rapidly Deployable Chemical Detection System programs from the S&T Directorate's Chemical and Biological Division to the DHS Office of Health Affairs, and the SAFECOM program from the S&T Directorate's Command, Control, and Interoperability Division to the DHS Directorate of National Protection and Programs. In March 2007, Under Secretary Cohen noted that the four programs to be transferred "pre-date the IPT process" (discussed above) and "have reached technical maturity." The moves were also driven by the general reorganization of the S&T Directorate in 2006 and by the Department of Homeland Security Appropriations Act, 2007 (P.L. 109-295), which codified the position of DHS Chief Medical Officer (CMO), gave him primary responsibility for coordinating the department's biodefense activities, and led the department to create an Office of Health Affairs, headed by the CMO.[9]

Metrics and Goals for Directorate Output

When the S&T Directorate was established, its optimal investment strategy was unclear. The range of threats and vulnerabilities was broad, and the directorate initially placed a premium on identifying technologies in an advanced stage of development, transitioning them into deployable equipment, and providing this equipment to end users. One DHS official believed, "there's a lot of low-hanging fruit out there, capability that already exists, either commercially or in laboratory prototypes."

As the directorate matures and its R&D results are implemented and deployed, this focus on "low-hanging fruit" may need to evolve into a more diverse strategy that also includes more fundamental research and riskier investments. Fundamental or basic research is often identified as a key source of future technologies, and research with innately higher risk, but also higher reward, may have more potential for significant breakthroughs. Some experts advocate more S&T Directorate investment in these types of research:

> Failure to invest in longer-term research limits the prospects for future breakthroughs that could dramatically improve DHS's ability to fulfill its mission. As the S&T Directorate matures, so must its S&T portfolio—which means investing in a portfolio of both near-term and long-term research. I understand that the S&T Directorate's leadership now shares this view. I particularly welcome [the Under Secretary for Science and Technology's] plans to fund some high-risk but potentially very high payoff projects. A serious pathology that can overtake a technology development program is to become failure intolerant, forcing it to settle on safe bets that are less ambitious than its mission requires. Admiral Cohen will need your support if he hopes to avoid this—you will have to make sure he fails often enough, and to hold him accountable if he doesn't.

A key component of such a strategy is assessing the progress of funded research projects. Without effective assessment, it may be difficult to sustain investment in long-term research activities that appear to be progressing slowly, or conversely, it may be difficult to terminate projects that appear productive but are not leading toward an appropriate goal. Depending on the stage and purpose of the research activity, criteria for success (and thus for continued investment by the directorate) may vary. Substantial investments in planning may be needed to establish appropriate criteria and assess programs effectively.

The difficulty of establishing quantitative goals and metrics for R&D effectiveness is a well known challenge for the evaluation of R&D programs. The impact of longer-range research may not be evident for years after its completion. Even if success can be measured, success rates may vary widely between programs deemed as effective, depending on the character of the R&D undertaken. For example, the Defense Advanced Research Projects Agency (DARPA) funds high-risk, high-reward R&D. The likelihood of success for any individual DARPA activity is low, but that is expected. The success of the program overall is judged by the impact of the activities that are successful. In contrast, an R&D program engaged mainly in incremental end-stage development, where there is lower risk of failure, might be expected to have a higher project success rate but less impact for each particular result.

The Government Performance and Results Act of 1993 (GPRA, P.L. 103-62) attempted to address metrics and goals for federal agencies, creating greater efficiency, effectiveness, and accountability in federal spending, and requiring agencies to set goals and to use performance measures for management and, ultimately, for budgeting. Although the outcome of GPRA has been a foundation of performance-based planning for federal agencies, evaluation of strategic planning continues to be a weakness.

The Bush Administration also set a priority on performance measures as part of the budgetary process, establishing the program assessment rating tool (PART) as part of the performance assessment methodology used under the President's Management Agenda. Some of the S&T Directorate's research portfolios have undergone PART assessments, with a range of results. Some programs, such as the biological countermeasures program, were assessed as effective, while others, such as the chemical and explosive countermeasures program, were not. The PART assessment process highlights the series of factors that complicates assessment of the S&T Directorate programs. Existing programs transferred in whole or in part into the S&T Directorate may have lacked an initial homeland security focus, blunting their efficacy. New programs developed by the S&T Directorate with the necessary homeland security focus lack a history of operation and management, challenging the smooth and efficient implementation of the programs' stated goals.

Predicting and assessing the outcomes of basic research in particular is never easy

Measuring outcomes from programs with long time scales, where results are not expected to be seen for several years, may pose a challenge to the PART technique. As stated by the White House Office of Management and Budget, "the Administration is aware that predicting and assessing the outcomes of basic research in particular is never easy." At a minimum, the PART documentation for S&T Directorate programs aims to provide clearer information about program goals and performance, R&D management, and effective practices. To the extent that this is successful, this information helps to inform outside analysts of the directorate's plans.

Some observers had hoped that the directorate's strategic planning process would identify quantitative metrics and goals. This was not the case, however. The program work statements in the 2007 R&D plan mostly describe qualitative increases, improvements, and developments, rather than quantitative criteria.

Another, similar approach would be to use the Homeland Security Science and Technology Advisory Committee or an outside body, such as the National Academy of Sciences, to independently validate the directorate's strategic planning documents, with goals and metrics for the short, medium, and long terms. Statute has mandated comparable requirements in other S&T fields. While the S&T Directorate uses committees of the National Academies for advice on an ad hoc basis, it has not engaged the National Academies or any other organization to perform a rigorous, end-to-end assessment of the directorate's research activities.

Responsiveness to Stakeholders

The S&T Directorate's responsiveness to stakeholders has been a recurring issue since the department's creation. The S&T Directorate has continued to attempt to increase the quality and number of approaches available to stakeholders wishing to contact and do business with the department. In addition, it has attempted to improve relations with Members of Congress and congressional committees.

Industry

Companies with technologies potentially applicable to homeland security problems have sometimes had difficulty identifying appropriate contacts at the S&T Directorate. The S&T Directorate has taken several steps to improve its interactions with industry, including increasing its accessibility through the Internet, expanding stakeholder conference opportunities, and creating the position of a Chief Commercialization Officer. The directorate makes its Broad Agency Announcements (BAA) available on a website and via an e-mail mailing list, and it announces R&D solicitations targeted at small businesses on another website. All funding opportunities are also listed on the government-wide website FedBizOpps. The preferred mechanism for submission of unsolicited proposals is through the Office of Procurement Operations. Such submissions are sent to the Headquarters Office of Procurement Operations rather than directly to the S&T Directorate. The S&T Directorate itself maintains an email address for submissions of concepts and ideas. In May 2007, the directorate held a stakeholder conference for which Under Secretary Cohen at that time described the message as "we are open for business, and we know how to do business." Announcements of subsequent stakeholder conferences have listed goals such as "describ[ing] the business opportunities for private sector organizations and universities, ... demonstrating business partnership opportunities in S&T research, ... [and] explaining how to do business with the DHS S&T research enterprise." The directorate has held annual stakeholder meetings, one on each coast. These stakeholder meetings have been a mechanism to provide industry and other stakeholders with access to S&T Directorate personnel and provide for collaboration.

Companies with technologies potentially applicable to homeland security problems have sometimes had difficulty identifying appropriate contacts at the S&T Directorate.

In January 2009, the directorate released a "DHS S&T Long Range Broad Agency Announcement." This BAA was partly a response to concerns that entrepreneurs and researchers might be unable to bring their ideas to the directorate if there is no open request for proposals or BAA. The long-range BAA is open through December 31, 2009, and provides a vehicle for submission of a broad range of homeland security R&D ideas and proposals. It states, "Readers shall note that this is an announcement to declare S&T's broad role in competitive funding of meritorious research across a spectrum of science and engineering disciplines."

Former Under Secretary Cohen has also identified continued outreach efforts on the part of the directorate and the components of the directorate as efforts to encourage greater industry participation. The directorate has held or partnered with other groups to hold conferences in the United States and the

United Kingdom to engage stakeholders and provide attendees with access and contact. Emphasizing the importance of maintaining good contacts with industry and others, Former Under Secretary Cohen testified in 2008, "As I have often said, no one knows where good ideas may come from and for that reason I have been personally proactive in both seeking out and receiving technology briefs and opportunities from all sources. This is a culture I am working to instill throughout the DHS S&T Directorate."

The S&T Directorate established a Commercialization Office headed by a Chief Commercialization Officer. This office is responsible for developing and managing the S&T Directorate's outreach efforts with the private sector. Beyond these outreach efforts, the Commercialization Office also is engaged in developing detailed operational requirements documents that reflect the Departmental needs that might be met by private sector developmental activities. By combining these needs with estimates of the potential available market for a given product, the Commercialization Office attempts to induce the private sector to invest its own funds into developing solutions to departmental needs without the investment of federal R&D funds.

The results of these efforts have reportedly been positively received by industry. The S&T Directorate has been perceived as improving in the quality of interaction, speed of response, and provision of information to interested companies.[10]

Conclusion

The Directorate of Science and Technology (S&T) is the primary organization for research and development in the Department of Homeland Security. With a budget of $932.6 million in FY2009, the directorate conducts R&D in several laboratories of its own and funds R&D conducted by other government agencies, the Department of Energy national laboratories, industry, and universities. In the past, some Members of Congress have been highly critical of the directorate's performance. More recently, management changes have considerably muted this criticism. The new Under Secretary has restructured the directorate's programs, worked to obligate resources in a timely fashion, and instituted a capable budget office able to deliver timely, accurate, and comprehensible documents." Nevertheless, a number of fundamental issues remain.[11]

Questions

1. How is S&T structured to develop new homeland security technology?
2. What is the advantage of Integrated Product Teams?
3. What type of research is categorized as high-risk long-term payoff?
4. What type of research is categorized as low-risk near-term payoff?
5. How has S&T tended to invest R&D resources over the years?
6. Do you think the investments have been worthwhile?

Part V: Critical Partners

Chapter 26

Federal Partners

Objectives

- Explain the "homeland security enterprise".
- Identify federal homeland security responsibilities.
- Identify state and local homeland security responsibilities.
- Identify individual and community homeland security responsibilities.

Introduction

According to the Quadrenniel Homeland Security Review, homeland security is an "enterprise"—it requires the combined efforts of Federal, State, local, tribal, territorial, nongovernmental, and private-sector entities, as well as individuals, families, and communities who share a common national interest in the safety and security of America and the American population. The Department of Homeland Security (DHS) is one among many components of this national enterprise. In some areas, like securing our borders or managing our immigration system, the Department possesses unique capabilities and, hence, responsibilities. In other areas, such as critical infrastructure protection or emergency management, the Department's role is largely one of leadership and stewardship on behalf of those who have the capabilities to get the job done. In still other areas, such as counterterrorism, defense, and diplomacy, other Federal departments and agencies have critical roles and responsibilities, including the Departments of Justice, Defense, and State, the Federal Bureau of Investigation, and the National Counterterrorism Center. Homeland security will only be optimized when we fully leverage the distributed and decentralized nature of the entire enterprise in the pursuit of our common goals.[1]

The homeland security "enterprise" refers to the collective efforts and shared responsibilities of Federal, State, local, tribal, territorial, nongovernmental, and private-sector partners—as well as individuals, families, and communities—to maintain critical homeland security capabilities.

Roles & Responsibilities

The term "enterprise" refers to the collective efforts and shared responsibilities of Federal, State, local, tribal, territorial, nongovernmental, and private-sector partners—as well as individuals, families, and communities—to maintain critical homeland security capabilities. It connotes a broad-based community with a common interest in the public safety and well-being of America and American society and is composed of multiple partners and stakeholders whose roles and responsibilities are distributed and shared. Yet it is important to remember that these partners and stakeholders face diverse risks, needs, and priorities. The challenge for the enterprise, then, is to balance these diverse needs and priorities, while focusing on our shared interests and responsibilities to collectively secure the homeland.[2]

With the establishment of homeland security, and the linking of domestic security concerns to broader national security interests and institutions, there is a temptation to view homeland security so broadly as to encompass all national security and domestic policy activities. This is not the case. Homeland security is deeply rooted in the security and resilience of the Nation, and facilitating lawful interchange with the world. As such, it intersects with many other functions of government. Homeland security is built upon critical law enforcement functions, but is not about preventing all crimes or administering our Nation's judicial system. It is deeply embedded in trade activities, but is neither trade nor economic policy. It requires international engagement, but is not responsible for foreign affairs. Rather, homeland security is meant to connote a concerted, shared effort to ensure a homeland that is safe, secure, and resilient against terrorism and other hazards where American interests, aspirations, and way of life can thrive.[3]

Homeland security spans the authorities and responsibilities of Federal departments and agencies, State, local, tribal and territorial governments, the private sector, as well as private citizens and communities. For this reason, coordination and cooperation are essential to successfully carrying out and accomplishing the homeland security missions. Documents such as the National Infrastructure Protection Plan (NIPP) and National Response Framework (NRF), as well as documents produced by the National Counterterrorism Center, spell out roles and responsibilities for various aspects of homeland security. The following discussion highlights key current roles and responsibilities of the many actors across the homeland security enterprise. They are derived largely from statutes, Presidential directives, and other authorities, as well as from the NIPP and NRF.[4]

The President of the United States is the Commander in Chief and the leader of the Executive Branch of the Federal Government. The President, through the National Security and Homeland Security Councils and the National Security Staff, provides overall homeland security policy direction and coordination. As a result of Presidential Study Directive 1 (2009), which directed an examination of ways to reform the White House organization for counterterrorism and homeland security, the White House merged the staffs of the National Security Council and the Homeland Security Council into a single new integrated National Security Staff.

The Secretary of Homeland Security leads the Federal agency as defined by statute charged with homeland security: preventing terrorism and managing risks to critical infrastructure; securing and managing the border; enforcing and administering immigration laws; safeguarding and securing cyberspace; and ensuring resilience to disasters.

The Attorney General has lead responsibility for criminal investigations of terrorist acts or terrorist threats by individuals or groups inside the United States, or directed at United States citizens or institutions abroad, as well as for related intelligence collection activities within the United States. Following a terrorist threat or an actual incident that falls within the criminal jurisdiction of the United States, the Attorney General identifies the perpetrators and brings them to justice. The Attorney General leads the Department of Justice, which also includes the Federal Bureau of Investigation, Drug Enforcement Administration, and Bureau of Alcohol, Tobacco, Firearms, and Explosives, each of which has key homeland security responsibilities.

The Secretary of State has the responsibility to coordinate activities with foreign governments and international organizations related to the prevention, preparation, response, and recovery from a domestic incident, and for the protection of U.S. citizens and U.S. interests overseas. The Department of State also adjudicates and screens visa applications abroad.

The Secretary of Defense leads the Department of Defense (DoD), whose military services, defense agencies, and geographic and functional commands defend the United States from direct attack, deter potential adversaries, foster regional stability, secure and assure access to sea, air, space, and cyberspace, and build the security capacity of key partners. DoD also provides a wide range of support to civil authorities at the direction of the Secretary of Defense or the President when the capabilities of State and local authorities to respond effectively to an event are overwhelmed.

The Secretary of Health and Human Services leads the coordination of all functions relevant to Public Health Emergency Preparedness and Disaster Medical Response. Additionally, the Department of Health and Human Services (HHS) incorporates steady-state and incident-specific activities as described in the National Health Security Strategy. HHS is the coordinator and primary agency for Emergency Support Function (ESF) #8 – Public Health and Medical Services, providing the mechanism for coordinated Federal assistance to supplement State, local, tribal, and territorial resources in response to a public health and medical disaster, potential or actual incident requiring a coordinated Federal response, and/or during a developing potential health and medical emergency. HHS is also the Sector-Specific Agency for the Healthcare and Public Health Sector.

The Secretary of the Treasury works to safeguard the U.S. financial system, combat financial crimes, and cut off financial support to terrorists, WMD proliferators, drug traffickers, and other national security threats.

The Secretary of Agriculture provides leadership on food, agriculture, natural resources, rural development, and related issues based on sound public policy, the best available science, and efficient management. The Department of Agriculture (USDA) is the Sector-Specific Agency for the Food and Agriculture Sector, a responsibility shared with the Food and Drug Administration with respect to food safety and defense. In addition, USDA is the coordinator and primary agency for two Emergency Support Functions: ESF #4 – Firefighting and ESF #11 – Agriculture and Natural Resources. USDA, together with the Department of the Interior, also operates the National Interagency Fire Center.

The Director of National Intelligence serves as the head of the Intelligence Community (IC), acts as the principal advisor to the President and National Security Council for intelligence matters relating to national security, and oversees and directs implementation of the National Intelligence Program. The IC, composed of 16 elements across the U.S. Government, functions consistent with law, Executive order, regulations, and policy to support the national security-related missions of the U.S. Government. It provides a range of analytic products that assess threats to the homeland and inform planning, capability development, and operational activities of homeland security enterprise partners and stakeholders. In addition to IC elements with specific homeland security missions, the Office of the Director of National Intelligence maintains a number of mission and support centers that provide unique capabilities for homeland security partners, including the National Counterterrorism Center (NCTC), National Counterproliferation Center, and National Counterintelligence Executive. NCTC serves as the primary U.S. government organization for analyzing and integrating all intelligence pertaining to terrorism and counterterrorism, and conducts strategic operational planning for integrated counterterrorism activities.

The Secretary of Commerce, supportive of national economic security interests and responsive to Public Law and Executive direction, is responsible for promulgating Federal information technology and cybersecurity standards;

regulating export of security technologies; representing U.S. industry on international trade policy and commercial data flow matters; security and privacy policies that apply to the Internet's domain name system; protecting intellectual property; conducting cybersecurity research and development; and assuring timely availability of industrial products, materials, and services to meet homeland security requirements.

The Secretary of Education oversees discretionary grants and technical assistance to help schools plan for and respond to emergencies that disrupt teaching and learning. The Department of Education is a supporting Federal agency in the response and management of emergencies under the National Response Framework.

The Secretary of Energy maintains stewardship of vital national security capabilities, from nuclear weapons to leading edge research and development programs. The Department of Energy (DOE) is the designated Federal agency to provide a unifying structure for the integration of Federal critical infrastructure and key resources protection efforts specifically for the Energy Sector. It is also responsible for maintaining continuous and reliable energy supplies for the United States through preventive measures and restoration and recovery actions. DOE is the coordinator and primary agency for ESF #12 – Energy when incidents require a coordinated Federal response to facilitate the restoration of damaged energy systems and components.

The Administrator of the Environmental Protection Agency (EPA) leads the EPA, which is charged with protecting human health and the environment. For certain incidents, EPA is the coordinator and primary agency for ESF #10 – Oil and Hazardous Materials Response, in response to an actual or potential discharge and/or uncontrolled release of oil or hazardous materials. EPA is the Sector-Specific Agency for securing the Water Sector.

The Secretary of Housing and Urban Development is the coordinator and primary agency for ESF #14 – Long-Term Community Recovery, which provides a mechanism for coordinating Federal support to State, tribal, regional, and local governments, nongovernmental organizations (NGOs), and the private sector to enable community recovery from the long-term consequences of extraordinary disasters.

The Secretary of the Interior develops policies and procedures for all types of hazards and emergencies that impact Federal lands, facilities, infrastructure, and resources; tribal lands; and insular areas. The Department of the Interior (DOI) is also a primary agency for ESF #9 – Search and Rescue, providing specialized lifesaving assistance to State, tribal, and local authorities when activated for incidents or potential incidents requiring a coordinated Federal response. DOI, together with the Department of Agriculture, also operates the National Interagency Fire Center.

The Secretary of Transportation collaborates with DHS on all matters relating to transportation security and transportation infrastructure protection and in regulating the transportation of hazardous materials by all modes (including pipelines). The Secretary of Transportation is responsible for operating the national airspace system.

Other Federal Agencies are also part of the homeland security enterprise and contribute to the homeland security mission in a variety of ways. This includes agencies with responsibilities for regulating elements of the Nation's critical infrastructure to assure public health, safety, and the common defense, developing and implementing pertinent public policy, supporting efforts to assure a resilient homeland, and collaborating with those departments and agencies noted above in their efforts to secure the homeland.

Critical Infrastructure and Key Resource (CIKR) Owners and Operators develop protective programs and measures to ensure that systems and assets, whether physical or virtual, are secure from and resilient to cascading, disruptive impacts. Protection includes actions to mitigate the overall risk to CIKR assets, systems, networks, functions, or their interconnecting links, including actions to deter the threat, mitigate vulnerabilities, or minimize the consequences associated with a terrorist attack or other incident. CIKR owners and operators also prepare business continuity plans and ensure their own ability to sustain essential services and functions.

Major and Multinational Corporations operate in all sectors of trade and commerce that foster the American way of life and support the operation, security, and resilience of global movement systems. They take action to support risk management planning and investments in security as a necessary component of prudent business planning and operations. They contribute to developing the ideas, science, and technology that underlie innovation in homeland security. During times of disaster, they provide response resources (donated or compensated)—including specialized teams, essential service providers, equipment, and advanced technologies—through public-private emergency plans/partnerships or mutual aid and assistance agreements, or in response to requests from government and nongovernmental-volunteer initiatives.

Small Businesses contribute to all aspects of homeland security and employ more than half of all private-sector workers. They support response efforts by developing contingency plans and working with local planners to ensure that their plans are consistent with pertinent response procedures. When small businesses can survive and quickly recover from disasters, the Nation and economy are more secure and more resilient. They perform research and development, catalyze new thinking, and serve as engines of innovation for development of new solutions to key challenges in homeland security.

Governors are responsible for overseeing their State's threat prevention activities as well the State's response to any emergency or disaster, and take an active role in ensuring that other State officials and agencies address the range of homeland security threats, hazards, and challenges. During an emergency, Governors will play a number of roles, including the State's chief communicator Critical Infrastructure and Key Resource (CIKR) Owners and Operators develop protective programs and measures to ensure that systems and assets, whether physical or virtual, are secure from and resilient to cascading, disruptive impacts. Protection includes actions to mitigate the overall risk to CIKR assets, systems, networks, functions, or their interconnecting links, including actions to deter the threat, mitigate vulnerabilities, or minimize the consequences associated with a terrorist attack or other incident. CIKR owners and operators also prepare business continuity plans and ensure their own ability to sustain essential services and functions.

State and Territorial Governments coordinate the activity of cities, counties, and intrastate regions. States administer Federal homeland security grants to local and tribal (in certain grant programs) governments, allocating key resources to bolster their prevention and preparedness capabilities. State agencies conduct law enforcement and security activities, protect the Governor and other executive leadership, and administer State programs that address the range of homeland security threats, hazards, and challenges. States government officials lead statewide disaster and mitigation planning. During response, States coordinate resources and capabilities throughout the State and are responsible for requesting and obtaining resources and capabilities from surrounding States. States often mobilize these substantive resources and capabilities to supplement the local efforts before, during, and after incidents.

Tribal Leaders are responsible for the public safety and welfare of their membership. They can serve as both key decisionmakers and trusted sources of public information during incidents.

Tribal Governments, which have a special status under Federal laws and treaties, ensure the provision of essential services to members within their communities, and are responsible for developing emergency response and mitigation plans. Tribal governments may coordinate resources and capabilities with neighboring jurisdictions, and establish mutual aid agreements with other tribal governments, local jurisdictions, and State governments. Depending on location, land base, and resources, tribal governments provide law enforcement, fire, and emergency services as well as public safety to their members.

Mayors and other local elected and appointed officials (such as city managers) are responsible for ensuring the public safety and welfare of their residents, serving as their jurisdiction's chief communicator and a primary source of information for homeland security-related information, and ensuring their governments are able to carry out emergency response activities. They serve as both key decisionmakers and trusted sources of public information during incidents.

Local Governments provide front-line leadership for local law enforcement, fire, public safety, environmental response, public health, and emergency medical services for all manner of hazards and emergencies. Through the Urban Areas Security Initiative (UASI) program, cities (along with counties in many cases) address multijurisdictional planning and operations, equipment support and purchasing, and training and exercises in support of high-threat, high-density urban areas. UASI grants assist local governments in building and sustaining homeland security capabilities. Local governments coordinate resources and capabilities during disasters with neighboring jurisdictions, NGOs, the State, and the private sector.

County Leaders serve as chief operating officers of county governments, both rural and urban. This includes supporting and enabling the county governments to fulfill their responsibilities to constituents, including public safety and security. In some States, elected county officials such as sheriffs or judges also serve as emergency managers, search and rescue officials, and chief law enforcement officers.

County Governments provide front-line leadership for local law enforcement, fire, public safety, environmental response, public health, and emergency medical services for all manner of hazards and emergencies. In many cases, county government officials participate in UASIs with other urban jurisdictions to assist local governments in building and sustaining capabilities to prevent, protect against, respond to, and recover from threats or acts of terrorism. County governments coordinate resources and capabilities during disasters with neighboring jurisdictions, NGOs, the State, and the private sector.

The American Red Cross is a supporting agency to the mass care functions of ESF #6 – Mass Care, Emergency Assistance, Housing, and Human Services under the NRF. As the Nation's largest mass care service provider, the American Red Cross provides sheltering, feeding, bulk distribution of needed items, basic first aid, welfare information, and casework, among other services, at the local level as needed. In its role as a service provider, the American Red Cross works closely with local, tribal, and State governments to provide mass care services to victims of every disaster, large and small, in an affected area.

National Voluntary Organizations Active in Disaster (National VOAD) is a consortium of approximately 50 national organizations and 55 State and territory equivalents that typically send representatives to the Federal Emergency Management Agency's National Response Coordination Center to represent the voluntary organizations and assist in response coordination. Members of National VOAD form a coalition of nonprofit organizations that respond to disasters as part of their overall mission.

Nongovernmental Organizations (NGOs) provide sheltering, emergency food supplies, counseling services, and other vital support services to support response and promote the recovery of disaster victims. They often provide specialized services that help individuals with special needs, including those with disabilities, and provide resettlement assistance and services to arriving refugees. NGOs also play key roles in engaging communities to integrate lawful immigrants into American society and reduce the marginalization or radicalization of these groups.

Communities and community organizations foster the development of organizations and organizational capacity that act toward a common goal (such as Neighborhood Watch, Community Emergency Response Teams, or providing emergency food or shelter). These groups may possess the knowledge and understanding of the threats, local response capabilities, and special needs within their jurisdictions and have the capacity necessary to alert authorities of those threats, capabilities, or needs. Additionally, during an incident these groups may be critical in passing along vital incident communications to individuals and families, and to supporting critical response activities in the initial stages of a crisis.

Individuals and Families take the basic steps to prepare themselves for emergencies, including understanding the threats and hazards that they may face, reducing hazards in and around their homes, preparing an emergency supply kit and household emergency plans (that include care for pets and service animals), monitoring emergency communications carefully, volunteering with established organizations, mobilizing or helping to ensure community preparedness, enrolling in training courses, and practicing what to do in an emergency. These individual and family preparedness activities strengthen community resilience and mitigate the impact of disasters. In addition, individual vigilance and awareness can help communities remain safer and bolster prevention efforts.[5]

Conclusion

The path forward is clear—we must move with a sense of urgency and purpose to achieve our shared interest and common vision of a safer, more secure and resilient America. Each of us—government, business, and individual alike—has a role to play, contributing to the collective strength of this country. The message is clear: This Nation can protect itself. But we must all play a role—and in the commitment of each, we will secure the homeland for all.[6]

Questions

1. Who's responsible for U.S. homeland security?
2. Identify federal agencies and their homeland security responsibilities outside DHS.
3. How do state and local governments contribute to homeland security?
4. How do individuals and communities contribute to homeland security?

Chapter 27

Intelligence Community

Objectives

- Understand the organization and direction of the U.S. Intelligence Community.
- Know the relationship between intelligence and counterintelligence.
- Describe the roles and functions of the CIA and FBI.

Introduction

Intelligence is secret, state activity to understand or influence foreign entities. Intelligence collection and processing is conducted by the Intelligence Community, a federation of executive branch agencies and organizations that work separately and together to conduct intelligence activities necessary for the conduct of foreign relations and the protection of the national security of the United States. Intelligence has been a function of the Government since the founding of the Republic. While it has had various incarnations over time, intelligence has historically played a key role in providing support to U.S. military forces and in shaping the policies of the United States toward other countries.[1]

Intelligence Community

The Intelligence Community emerged over time in response to the intelligence needs of the United States. On July 27, 1947, President Truman signed into law the National Security Act of 1947, creating a postwar national security framework. A National Security Council (NSC) was created to coordinate national security policy. A Central Intelligence Agency (CIA) was established with the Director of Central Intelligence (DCI) at its head to "coordinate" national security intelligence. As a result of the attacks of September 11, 2001, the DCI was replaced by a new Director of National Intelligence (DNI).[2]

Intelligence is secret, state activity to understand or influence foreign entities.

On December 17, 2004, President George W. Bush signed into law the Intelligence Reform and Prevention of Terrorism Act of 2004, Public Law 108-458, creating the Office of Director of National Intelligence (ODNI) to lead a unified intelligence community and serve as the principal advisor to the President on intelligence matters. The DNI has authority to order the collection of new intelligence, to ensure the sharing of information among agencies and to establish common standards for the intelligence community's personnel. It is the DNI's responsibility to determine the annual budgets for all national intelligence agencies and offices and to direct how these funds are spent. These authorities vested in a single official who reports directly to the President were designed to make intelligence efforts better coordinated, more efficient, and more effective.[3]

The Intelligence Reform and Prevention of Terrorism Act of 2004 gave the Director of National Intelligence budgetary authority to direct the efforts of the Intelligence Community including the following:

1. The Central Intelligence Agency (CIA) has all-source analytical capabilities that cover the whole world outside U.S. borders. It produces a range of studies that cover virtually any topic of interest to national security policymakers. CIA also collects intelligence with human sources and, on occasion, undertakes covert actions at the direction of the President.

2. The National Security Agency (NSA), under the direction of the Department of Defense (DoD) is responsible for signals intelligence and has collection sites throughout the world.

3. The National Reconnaissance Office (NRO), also under the direction of the DoD, develops and operates reconnaissance satellites.
4. The National Geospatial-Intelligence Agency (NGA), another DoD agency, prepares the geospatial data—ranging from maps and charts to sophisticated computerized databases—necessary for targeting in an era dependent upon precision guided weapons.
5. The Defense Intelligence Agency (DIA) is responsible for defense attaches and for providing DoD with a variety of intelligence products.
6. The State Department's Bureau of Intelligence and Research (INR) is one of the smaller components of the Intelligence Community but is widely recognized for the high quality of its analyses.
7. The key intelligence functions of the FBI relate to counterterrorism and counterintelligence. The FBI has been reorganized in an attempt to ensure that intelligence functions are not subordinated to traditional law enforcement efforts. Most importantly, law enforcement information is now expected to be forwarded to other intelligence agencies for use in all-source products.
8. The intelligence organizations of the Army, Navy, Air Force, and Marines concentrate largely on concerns related to their specific missions. Their analytical products, along with those of DIA, supplement the work of CIA analysts and provide greater depth on key technical issues.
9. The Homeland Security Act (P.L. 107-296) provided the Department of Homeland Security (DHS) responsibilities for fusing law enforcement and intelligence information relating to terrorist threats to the homeland. The Office of Information Analysis in DHS participates in the inter-agency counterterrorism efforts and, along with the FBI, has focused on ensuring that state and local law enforcement officials receive information on terrorist threats from national-level intelligence agencies.
10. The Coast Guard, now part of DHS, deals with information relating to maritime security and homeland defense.
11. The Energy Department analyzes foreign nuclear weapons programs as well as nuclear non-proliferation and energy-security issues. It also has a robust counterintelligence effort.
12. The Treasury Department collects and processes information that may affect U.S. fiscal and monetary policies. Treasury also covers the terrorist financing issue.[4]

Intelligence Operations

Intelligence is a body of evidence and the conclusions drawn therefrom that is acquired and furnished in response to the known or perceived requirements of consumers. It is often derived from information that is concealed or not intended to be available for use by the acquirer. Intelligence comes in Raw and goes out Finished.

- Raw Intelligence is information that is collected from a single source and quickly evaluated. Reports may be produced from this intelligence and delivered to consumers if the information is time sensitive.
- Finished Intelligence is more fully analyzed and evaluated information. It is usually based upon raw intelligence collected from many (or all) sources and analyzed in this context.[5]

The process of creating reliable, accurate foreign intelligence, called the Intelligence Cycle, is dynamic and never ending. The intelligence process or cycle begins with questions—the answers to which inevitably lead to more questions.

1. Planning and Direction. The Intelligence Cycle begins by establishing the intelligence requirements of the policy makers—the President, the National Security Council, military commanders, and other officials in major departments and governmental agencies.[6]
2. Collection. Collection involves gathering raw data from which finished intelligence is produced.[7]
3. Processing and Exploitation converts large amounts of data to a form suitable for the production of finished intelligence; includes translations, decryption, and interpretation of information stored on film and magnetic media through the use of highly refined photographic and electronic processes.[8]
4. Analysis and Production. Analysis and Production involves the integration, evaluation, and analysis of all available data and the preparation of a variety of intelligence products, including timely, single-source, event-oriented reports and longer term, all source, finished intelligence studies.[9]
5. Dissemination. Dissemination is about delivering the products to consumers who request them.[10]

There are six basic intelligence sources, or collection disciplines:

- SIGINT. Signals intelligence is derived from signal intercepts comprising—however transmitted—either individually or in combination.
- IMINT. Imagery Intelligence includes representations of objects reproduced electronically or by optical means on film, electronic display devices, or other media.
- MASINT. Measurement and Signature Intelligence is technically derived intelligence data other than imagery and SIGINT.
- HUMINT. Human intelligence is derived from human sources.

- OSINT. Open-Source Intelligence is publicly available information appearing in print or electronic form including radio, television, newspapers, journals, the Internet, commercial databases, and videos, graphics, and drawings.
- GEOINT. Geospatial Intelligence is the analysis and visual representation of security related activities on the earth.[11]

Counterintelligence

An effective intelligence program requires an equally effective counterintelligence program. Counterintelligence safeguards U.S. intelligence capabilities while thwarting enemy intelligence efforts. The Intelligence Community is faced with the problem of identifying, understanding, prioritizing and counteracting the intelligence threats from foreign powers that are faced by the United States. According to Executive Order 12333, counterintelligence involves both "information gathered" and "activities conducted" in order to "to protect against espionage, other intelligence activities, sabotage or assassination conducted on behalf of foreign powers, organizations, or persons, or international terrorist activities but not including personnel, physical documents or communications security."[12]

Counterintelligence safeguards U.S. intelligence capabilities while thwarting enemy intelligence efforts.

The FBI

The Federal Bureau of Investigation (FBI) was founded in 1908 to serve as the primary investigative unit of the Department of Justice. Its missions include protecting the nation from foreign intelligence and terrorist threats, investigating serious federal crimes, providing leadership and assistance to law enforcement agencies, and being responsive to the public in the performance of these duties.[13]

In the wake of the September 2001 attacks, the FBI was strongly criticized for failing to focus on the terrorist threat, for failing to collect and strategically analyze intelligence, and for failing to share intelligence with other intelligence agencies (as well as among various FBI components). In response to criticisms of its role, the FBI introduced a series of reforms to transform the bureau from a largely reactive law enforcement agency focused on criminal investigations into a more mobile, agile, flexible, intelligence-driven agency to prevent acts of terrorism.[14]

Director Mueller committed to improving the FBI's intelligence program by consolidating and centralizing control over the Bureau's historically fragmented intelligence capabilities, both at FBI Headquarters and in the FBI's field offices by creating a new Directorate of Intelligence (DI) at Headquarters and establishing Field Intelligence Groups (FIGs) at each of the FBI's 56 field offices. The DI is responsible for implementing an integrated FBI-wide intelligence strategy, developing an intelligence analyst career path, and ensuring that intelligence is appropriately shared within the FBI as well as with other federal agencies. The Directorate also is charged with improving strategic analysis, implementing an intelligence requirements and collection regime, and ensuring that the FBI's intelligence policies are implemented. Finally, the office oversees the FBI's participation in the National Counterterrorism Center (NCTC).[15]

The 9/11 Commission essentially endorsed reforms the FBI initiated following the September 11 attacks. In its July 2004 report, the Commission recommended leaving the responsibility for counterterrorism intelligence collection with the FBI, but called for an integrated national security workforce within the Bureau consisting of agents, analysts, linguists, and surveillance specialists. Acting on the recommendations of the 9/11 Commission, and the endorsement of the WMD Commission, President Bush on June 29, 2005 directed the Attorney General to combine the mission, capabilities, and resources of the counterterrorism, counterintelligence, and intelligence elements of the FBI to create a new National Security Service to ensure the development of an institutional culture with a deep expertise in intelligence and national security within the FBI.[16]

The CIA

The FBI protects the nation from foreign intelligence and terrorist threats, investigating serious federal crimes, providing leadership and assistance to law enforcement agencies.

The Central Intelligence Agency was created in 1947 with the signing of the National Security Act by President Harry S. Truman. The act also created a Director of Central Intelligence (DCI) to serve as head of the United States intelligence community; act as the principal adviser to the President for intelligence matters related to the national security; and serve as head of the Central Intelligence Agency. The Intelligence Reform and Terrorism Prevention Act of 2004 amended the National Security Act to provide for a Director of National Intelligence who would assume some of the roles formerly fulfilled by the DCI, who was redesignated the Director of the Central Intelligence Agency (DCIA).[17]

The CIA remains the keystone of the Intelligence Community. It has all-source analytical capabilities that cover the whole world outside U.S. borders. CIA's main job is to keep top US officials aware of key intelligence issues. The DCIA serves as the head of the Central Intelligence Agency to:

- Collect intelligence through human sources and by other appropriate means;
- Correlate and evaluate intelligence related to the national security and provide appropriate dissemination of such intelligence;
- Provide overall direction for and coordination of the collection of national intelligence outside the United States through human sources; and
- Perform such other functions and duties related to intelligence affecting the national security as the President or the Director of National Intelligence may direct.

The CIA is the primary collector of HUMINT. HUMINT has been a systemic problem and contributed to the inability to gain prior knowledge of the 9/11 plots. In part, these criticisms reflect the changing nature of the international environment. During the Cold War, targets of U.S. HUMINT collection were government officials and military leaders. Intelligence agency officials working under cover as diplomats could approach potential contacts at receptions or in the context of routine embassy business. Today, however, the need is to seek information from clandestine terrorist groups or narcotics traffickers who do not appear at embassy social gatherings. HUMINT regarding such sources can be especially important as there may be little evidence of activities or intentions that can be gathered from imagery, and their communications may be carefully limited.[18]

National Counterterrorism Center

President Truman established the CIA in 1947 to prevent a future surprise attack against the United States similar to Pearl Harbor. In the aftermath of September 11, 2001, there was extensive public discussion of whether the attacks on the Pentagon and World Trade Center represented an "intelligence failure." Two authoritative reports concluded that the lack of adequate and timely coordination and communication within the Intelligence Community (IC) was one factor contributing to the inability of the IC to detect and prevent the terrorist attacks. In July 2004, the 9/11 Commission recommended the establishment of a National Counterterrorism Center (NCTC) to serve as a center for "... joint operational planning and joint intelligence, staffed by personnel from the various agencies...." On August 27, 2004, President George W. Bush signed Executive Order (EO) 13354 establishing a National Counterterrorism Center. Less than two months later, Congress passed the Intelligence Reform and Terrorism Prevention Act of 2004, P.L. 108-458, amending the National Security Act of 1947, to establish within the Office of the Director of National Intelligence, a National Counterterrorism Center.

The CIA remains the keystone of the Intelligence Community. It has all-source capabilities that cover the whole world outside U.S. borders. The CIA's main job is to keep top U.S. officials aware of key intelligence issues.

The first mission of the NCTC is to integrate and analyze all counterterrorism intelligence available to U.S. government departments and agencies and to serve as a knowledge bank on known and suspected terrorist and international terrorist groups.

The second function of the NCTC is to conduct strategic counterterrorism operational planning. Under Section 1021 of P.L. 108-458, the Director of the NCTC reports to the President on the planning and progress of joint military counterterrorism operations, a role traditionally reserved to components of the Department of Defense.[19]

Paramilitary Operations

At the direction of the President, the CIA may conduct covert and clandestine operations to influence political, economic, or military conditions abroad, where it is intended that the role of the United States Government will not be apparent or acknowledged publicly. Covert actions can include a wide range of clandestine efforts—from subsidizing foreign journals and political parties to participation in what are essentially military operations using paramilitary forces, forces or groups distinct from the regular armed forces of any country, but resembling them in organization, equipment, training or mission.

In the case of paramilitary operations, there is a clear potential for overlap with activities that can be carried out by DoD. In general, the CIA would be designated to conduct operations that are to be wholly covert or disavowable. In practice, responsibilities for paramilitary operations have been assigned by the National Security Council on a case-by-case basis. Historically, the CIA has worked closely alongside DoD personnel in military operations. On occasion it has also conducted clandestine military operations apart from the military. In the Afghan campaign and in Iraq, the CIA conducted paramilitary operations separate from or alongside Special Forces from the Defense Department. Some observers, and the 9/11 Commission have recommended that DoD assume responsibility for all such efforts to avoid duplication of effort. In addition, there had been media reports that CIA and DoD efforts in Afghanistan were not well coordinated. DCI Goss, testified in February 2005, however, that a joint review by CIA and DoD had reaffirmed the need for separate efforts. Observers note that CIA can hire paramilitary operators (in many instances retired military personnel) for specific missions of a limited duration; in addition, some missions may be more appropriate for non-uniformed personnel.[20]

Military Intelligence

Any information of possible foreign intelligence value that the Services may have obtained in a counterintelligence or domestic operation must be turned over to the FBI, which has the primary responsibility for domestic intelligence collection within the United States.

The US military has a limited role in collecting foreign intelligence in domestic operations. Collection of counterintelligence is allowed and required to protect US Government property and human resources. Any information of possible foreign intelligence value that the Services may have obtained in a counterintelligence or domestic operation must be turned over to the FBI, which has the primary responsibility for domestic intelligence collection within the United States. The Patriot Act eases some of the restrictions on foreign intelligence gathering within the United States, and affords the US intelligence community greater access to information gathered during criminal investigations. DoD intelligence activities are governed by the following references:[21]

- EO 12333, United States Intelligence Activities lays out the goals and direction of the national intelligence effort, and describes the roles, responsibilities and restrictions of the different elements of the US intelligence community;
- Deputy Secretary of Defense Memorandum, "Collecting, Reporting and Analysis of Terrorist Threat to DoD Within the United States," 2 May 2003;
- DoDDs 5240.1, DoD Intelligence Activities, and 5240.1-R, Procedures Governing the Activities of DoD Intelligence Components that Affect United States Persons implement the guidance contained in EO 12333 as it applies to DoD;
- Command, Control, Communications Intelligence Memorandum, "Authority to Collect Information on Domestic Terrorist and Other Groups Committing Illegal Acts that Pose a Threat to DoD," 27 January 1998, contains guidance for the collection of information on terrorists.
- SecDef Message dated 151147Z NOV 01, "Policy Guidance—Impact of

USA PATRIOT Act of 2001 on DoD Intelligence Activities and Intelligence Oversight," clarifies that the Act does not change the framework of DoD intelligence activities and does not change intelligence oversight guidance.

- DoDD 5200.27, Acquisition of Information Concerning Persons and Organizations not Affiliated with the Department of Defense, also pertains.[22]

Executive Order 12333

Issued under the Reagan Administration, EO 12333, "United States Intelligence Activities," authorizes DoD to collect national foreign intelligence, and conduct counterintelligence activities both inside and outside the United States, in coordination with the FBI and CIA respectively. EO 12333 allows collection efforts on US citizens as approved by the Attorney General under specific circumstances requiring probable cause. EO 12333 expressly prohibits human experimentation or assassination.[23]

DoDD 5240.1

DoD Directive 5240.1, "DoD Intelligence Activities," makes the following definitions:

- *Intelligence Activities* are the collection, production, and dissemination of foreign intelligence and counterintelligence by the DoD.
- *Foreign Intelligence* is information relating to the capabilities, intentions, and activities of foreign powers, organizations, or persons, but not including counterintelligence except for information on international terrorist activities.
- *Counterintelligence* is information gathered and activities conducted to protect against espionage, other intelligence activities, sabotage, or assassinations conducted for or on behalf of foreign powers, organizations, or persons, or international terrorist activities.

"DoD policy prohibits collecting, reporting, processing or storing information on individuals or organizations not affiliated with the Department of Defense"

- DoDD 5200.27

DoDD 5240.1 stipulates that "all DoD intelligence activities shall be carried out in strict conformity with the U.S. Constitution, applicable law, and EO 12333." The directive further states that "special emphasis [shall be] given to the protection of the constitutional rights and privacy of U.S. persons."[24]

DoDD 5200.27

DoDD 5200.27, "Acquisition of Information Concerning Persons and Organizations not Affiliated with the Department of Defense" further states that "DoD policy prohibits collecting, reporting, processing or storing information on individuals or organizations not affiliated with the Department of Defense," except under certain conditions including:

- Protection of DoD functions and property.
- Conducting security investigations on people requiring access to sensitive DoD material.

- Operations related to civil disturbance.

DoDD 5200.27 specifically prohibits the following activities:

- No information shall be acquired about a person or organization solely because of lawful advocacy of measures in opposition to Government policy.
- There shall be no physical or electronic surveillance of Federal, State, or local officials or of candidates for such offices.
- There shall be no electronic surveillance of any individual or organization, except as authorized by law.
- There shall be no covert or otherwise deceptive surveillance or penetration of civilian organizations unless specifically authorized by the Secretary of Defense, or his designee.
- No DoD personnel will be assigned to attend public or private meetings, demonstrations, or other similar activities for the purpose of acquiring information, the collection of which is authorized by this Directive without specific prior approval by the Secretary of Defense, or his designee. An exception to this policy may be made by the local commander concerned, or higher authority, when, in his judgment, the threat is direct and immediate and time precludes obtaining prior approval. In each such case a report will be made immediately to the Secretary of Defense, or his designee.[25]

SecDef Memo, November 1998

A Secretary of Defense memo issued November 18, 1998, provides policy guidance for disposition of sensitive data gathered on US citizens during the course of authorized DoD activities. If the DoD acquires information presenting a reasonable belief that somebody in the US poses a threat to DoD personnel, installations, information, or activities, the DoD must immediately alert the threatened entity and provide the information to the appropriate law enforcement authority. The DoD may retain the information for up to 90 days, unless specific authorization is granted to keep it longer.[26]

Under Secretary of Defense for Intelligence

The USD(I) is the principal staff assistant and advisor to the Secretary of Defense regarding intelligence, counterintelligence, security, sensitive activities, and other intelligence-related matters. In this capacity, the USD(I) exercises the Secretary of Defense's authority, direction, and control over the Defense Agencies and DoD Field Activities that are Defense intelligence, counterintelligence, or security components and exercises planning, policy, and strategic oversight over all DoD intelligence, counterintelligence, and security policy, plans, and programs.

As the senior DoD intelligence, counterintelligence, and security official below the Secretary and Deputy Secretary of Defense, the USD(I) exercises direction and control over:

- Defense Security Service
- DoD Counterintelligence Field Activity
- Defense Intelligence Agency
- National Geospatial-Intelligence Agency
- National Security Agency/Central Security Service
- National Reconnaissance Office

USD(I) also serves as the primary representative of the Secretary of Defense to the Office of the Director of National Intelligence (ODNI) and other members of the Intelligence Community.[27]

DoD Intel Support

Combat support agencies (CSAs), including intelligence organizations, provide direct support to the combatant commands performing homeland security during wartime or emergency situations and are subject to evaluation by the Chairman of the Joint Chiefs of Staff.

With respect to homeland security, DIA manages the DoD warning system that alerts DoD and the US Government of potential threats to the nation.

Defense Intelligence Agency

The DIA is responsible for satisfying military and military-related intelligence requirements for SecDef, CJCS, other Defense components, and, as appropriate, non-Defense agencies. With over 7,000 military and civilian employees worldwide, DIA is a major producer and manager of foreign military intelligence. It provides military intelligence to warfighters, defense policymakers and force planners in DoD and the intelligence community.

The Director of DIA serves as principal adviser to SecDef and to CJCS on matters of military intelligence. The Director also chairs the Military Intelligence Board that coordinates activities of the defense intelligence community. Moreover, the Director serves as the principal intelligence advisor to ASD(HD) and the military commands.

With respect to HS, DIA manages the DoD warning system that alerts DoD and the US Government of potential threats to the nation. DIA's Directorate for Intelligence Production, particularly the Defense Warning Office assesses the most likely developing threats and the high impact threats to military capabilities, and US national infrastructures upon which the military depends for stateside operations, training, and deployment.

DIA's Disruptive Technology Innovations Partnership (DTIP) program provides HD, and US infrastructure sectors with actionable information or time-sensitive intelligence assessments for correcting serious vulnerabilities. DTIP assessments prioritize vulnerabilities according to their national security impact were they to be exploited by state or non-state actors. DTIP assesses and warns of the impact of potential threats stemming from innovative applications of technologies against vulnerabilities.

DIA/J-2 has the ability to coordinate, establish, deploy, and operate a national intelligence support team (NIST) to Joint Task Force Civil Support (JTF-CS) in support of HS. The NIST can deploy within 72 hours and will provide JTF-CS with national-level intelligence support in the areas of terrorism, force protection, and WMD.[28]

National Security Agency

The resources of NSA are organized for the accomplishment of the following missions:

- The Information Assurance (IA) mission provides the solutions, products and services, and conducts defensive Information Operations (IO), to achieve IA for information infrastructures critical to US national security interests.
- The foreign signals intelligence or signals intelligence mission allows for an effective, unified organization and control of all the foreign signals collection and processing activities of the US. NSA is authorized to produce SIGINT in accordance with objectives, requirements and priorities established by the Director, CIA with the advice of the National Foreign Intelligence Board.
- NSA/Central Security Service executes SIGINT and information systems security activities and conducts related activities, as assigned by SecDef, including managing and providing operational control of the US SIGINT System.[29]

National Geospatial-Intelligence Agency

The NGA provides timely, relevant, and accurate geospatial intelligence (GEOINT) in support of national security objectives. GEOINT is the analysis and visual representation of security-related activities on the earth. NGA also:

- Supports customers in the defense, law enforcement, intelligence, federal and civil communities for HS mission areas with its analytic GEOINT capabilities.

- Supports defense missions for the common operating picture (COP), military operations assuredness, and force protection by building integrated datasets to support the HS COP and situational awareness. These datasets will provide a common frame of reference for federal decision makers and operational planners for critical infrastructure vulnerability analysis and for domestic crisis management (CrM) and consequence management (CM).
- In concert with other federal partners, serves as the imagery and geospatial data broker, integrator, and consolidator in building a single HS database to support domestic situational awareness, CrM and CM, and critical infrastructure protection.
- Provides integrated geospatial information in support of the planning and execution of HS exercises where there is federal, DoD, state and local government participation.
- Deploys fully equipped geospatial analytic teams to support military and civilian exercises as well as other crisis and NSSEs in real time.
- Provides direct, tailored geospatial information support.
- Provides personnel as part of NISTs to USNORTHCOM, USPACOM, and DHS. These NISTs provide day-to-day GEOINT support to the command with the capability to reach back to NGA for requirements that exceed the capacity or capability of the team at the command.[30]

Conclusion

Intelligence is secret, state activity to understand or influence foreign entities. Intelligence collection and processing is conducted by the Intelligence Community, a federation of executive branch agencies and organizations that work separately and together to conduct intelligence activities necessary for the conduct of foreign relations and the protection of the national security of the United States.

The US military has a limited role in collecting foreign intelligence in domestic operations. Collection of counterintelligence is allowed and required to protect US Government property and human resources. Any information of possible foreign intelligence value that the Services may have obtained in a counterintelligence or domestic operation must be turned over to the FBI, which has the primary responsibility for domestic intelligence collection within the United States. The Patriot Act eases some of the restrictions on foreign intelligence gathering within the United States, and affords the US intelligence community greater access to information gathered during criminal investigations.

Questions

1. What is intelligence?
2. What is counterintelligence?
3. Who directs the intelligence community and is the principal intelligence advisor to the President?
4. What agency plays a lead role in the intelligence community and is primarily responsible for HUMINT?
5. What are the intelligence responsibilities of the FBI?
6. What is the function of the National Counterterrorism Center (NCTC)?
7. Is the DoD allowed to spy on U.S. citizens?
8. What DoD agency manages DoD's warning system and alerts the government to potential threats?

Chapter 28

State, Local, & Tribal Partners

Objectives

- Understand the impetus driving "the need to share" intelligence information.
- Know the purpose and function of a State and Local Fusion Center (SLFC).
- Describe how DHS supports SLFCs.
- Identify risks associated with SLFCs.

Introduction

Improving intelligence gathering and information sharing at all levels of government has been a major concern and priority since the terrorist attacks of September 11, 2001. To promote greater information sharing and collaboration among federal, state, and local intelligence and law enforcement entities, state and local authorities established fusion centers throughout the country. These centers are a collaborative effort of two or more agencies that provide resources, expertise, and information to the center with the goal of maximizing its ability to detect, prevent, investigate, and respond to criminal and terrorist activity.

In June 2006, the Secretary of the Department of Homeland Security signed an implementation plan to support state and local fusion centers and designated the Office of Intelligence and Analysis as the executive agent for managing the department's role in the nationwide Fusion Center Initiative. The department's fusion center program is intended to provide information, people, technology, and other resources to fusion centers to create a web of interconnected information nodes across the country.[1]

Information sharing has become the primary means to detect, identify, and assess terrorist threats to and vulnerabilities of the homeland.

Fusion Centers

Improving intelligence gathering and information sharing at all levels of government has been a major concern and priority since the terrorist attacks of September 11, 2001. The Homeland Security Act of 2002 established the Department of Homeland Security (DHS) and charged it with coordinating activities and improving information sharing efforts among federal, state, local, and tribal government agencies and the private sector. Furthermore, the National Commission on Terrorist Attacks upon the United States, the 9/11 Commission, concluded that a lack of information sharing contributed to the inability to prevent the attacks. Moreover, in its 2004 final report, the 9/11 Commission promoted the value of state and local agencies in the information sharing process and recommended that DHS have the responsibility of coordinating these efforts.

Information sharing has become the primary means to detect, identify, and assess terrorist threats to and vulnerabilities of the homeland. To promote greater information sharing and collaboration among federal, state, and local intelligence and law enforcement entities, state and local authorities established fusion centers throughout the country.

Fusion centers are "a collaborative effort of two or more agencies that provide resources, expertise, and information to the center with the goal of maximizing their ability to detect, prevent, investigate, and respond to criminal and terrorist activity." They are joint multi-jurisdictional information centers that combine data from various sources and disciplines. The term fusion refers to the process of managing the flow of information and intelligence across all levels and sectors of government and private industry, and through analysis, provides meaningful intelligence.

To aid information sharing efforts further, Congress enacted the Intelligence Reform and Terrorism Prevention Act of 2004. This Act established the Information Sharing Environment within the Office of the Director of National Intelligence. The Information Sharing Environment is "an approach that facilitates the sharing of terrorism information." The Implementation Plan for the Information Sharing Environment envisions that the federal government will promote the establishment of a nationwide and integrated network of state and major urban area fusion centers to facilitate effective terrorism information sharing. This network of fusion centers would house federal, state, and local law enforcement and intelligence resources to provide useful sources of law enforcement and threat information, facilitate information sharing across jurisdictions and functions, and establish a conduit among federal, state, and local agencies.

Recognizing that state and local governments are vital partners in information sharing, federal agencies such as DHS, the Department of Justice, and the Office of the Director of National Intelligence have collaborated to assist in establishing and sustaining fusion centers.[2]

It has been argued that state, local, tribal law enforcement, first responders, and other public and private sector entities are uniquely positioned to collect information to identify emerging threats and assist in the development of a more comprehensive threat assessment. Former DHS Secretary Chertoff, speaking from his experience as a federal prosecutor and judge, noted that many organized crime cases were intelligence driven and that state and local police were best placed to discover anomalies in their communities that can lead to the prevention of violent acts. Although the fusion process goes beyond law enforcement or criminal intelligence, the counterterrorism role of state and local law enforcement has been outlined in numerous reports. Those who agree with Secretary Chertoff are apt to argue that the 800,000 plus law enforcement officers across the country know their communities most intimately and, therefore, are best placed to function as the "eyes and ears" of an extended national security community. They have the experience to recognize what constitutes anomalous behavior in their areas of responsibility and can either stop it at the point of discovery (a more traditional law enforcement approach) or follow the anomaly or criminal behavior, either unilaterally or jointly with the Federal Bureau of Investigation (FBI), to extract the maximum intelligence value from the activity (a more intelligence-based approach).[3]

State, local, tribal law enforcement, first responders, and other public and private sector entities are uniquely positioned to collect information to identify emerging threats and assist in the development of a more comprehensive threat assessment.

Information Sharing Requirements

On December 16, 2005, President Bush issued a memorandum prescribing the guidelines and requirements supporting the creation and implementation of the Information Sharing Environment. The President directed the heads of executive departments and agencies to work actively to create a culture of information sharing within their respective departments or agencies by assigning personnel and dedicating resources to terrorism-related information sharing. The President's guidelines recognized that state, local, and tribal authorities are critical to the nationwide efforts to prevent future terrorist attacks and are the first to respond when an attack occurs.

In August 2006, DHS and the Department of Justice published the Fusion Center Guidelines to help direct and provide assistance to developing fusion centers. These guidelines delineate 18 recommended elements for establishing and operating fusion centers. The guidelines are intended to improve consistency among the many different state and local fusion centers, enhance coordination, strengthen regional and national partnerships, and improve fusion center capabilities.

In October 2007, President Bush issued the first National Strategy for Information Sharing to prioritize and unify the Nation's efforts to advance terrorism-related information sharing. The strategy integrates Information Sharing Environment-related initiatives and sets forth a national plan to build on progress made in improving information sharing and establishing an integrated national information sharing capability. The National Strategy emphasizes that information on homeland security, terrorism, and law enforcement related to terrorism can come from multiple sources and all levels of government.

The National Strategy for Information Sharing prioritizes and unifies the Nation's efforts to advance terrorism-related information sharing.

The National Strategy designates fusion centers as vital assets critical to information sharing and antiterrorism efforts, and as the primary state and local focal points for receiving and sharing of terrorism-related information. As a part of the National Strategy, the federal government recommends that fusion centers achieve a baseline capability level and become interconnected with the federal government and each other. This collaboration is intended to create a nationwide, integrated network of fusion centers to enable the effective sharing of terrorism-related information.

Fusion centers vary in size, scope, jurisdiction, capability, and maturity. The missions of these centers also vary. For example, some fusion centers are focused specifically on terrorism-related threats, others deal with information sharing related to all crimes, while other centers focus on addressing all hazards.[4]

As of July 2009, there were 72 designated fusion centers around the country with 36 field representatives deployed.[5]

DHS Program Implementation

DHS uses the national intelligence and law enforcement communities to support state and local government requirements through its fusion center program. In June 2006, the Secretary signed the DHS Support Implementation Plan for State and Local Fusion Centers and designated the Office of Intelligence and Analysis (I&A) as its executive agent for managing the department's role in the nationwide Fusion Center Initiative. The implementation plan identified state and local governments among DHS' primary partners. It also explained DHS' role in supporting and developing state and local partnerships and highlighted domestic information gathering and analysis as DHS' "unique contribution to the national-level mission" to protect the Nation. Further, the Implementing Recommendations of the 9/11 Commission Act of 2007 codified the nationwide Fusion Center Initiative and DHS' role in it.

DHS' fusion center program is intended to provide information, people, technology, and other resources to fusion centers to create a nationwide web of interconnected information nodes. DHS views fusion centers as entities that provide critical sources of unique law enforcement and threat information, and facilitate sharing information across federal, state, and local jurisdictions and functions. DHS envisions creating partnerships with all state and local fusion centers to improve information flow between DHS and the fusion centers, and to improve the effectiveness of the centers in general. The goal is to enable DHS and the fusion center network to produce accurate, timely, relevant, and actionable intelligence products and services in support of securing the homeland.[6]

DHS Program Management

As the executive agent for managing DHS' fusion center program, Intelligence & Analysis is responsible for coordinating among its federal, state, local, tribal, and private sector partners to ensure the program's success. Each I&A division has a specific mission that in some way relates to the program. I&A is headed by an Under Secretary, who also serves as the department's Chief Intelligence Officer. The State and Local Program Office, which coordinates the fusion center program, is directed by a program manager. The State and Local Program Office contains three divisions:

1. State and Local Fusion Center Program Management Office;
2. Information Sharing Fellows Program; and
3. Law Enforcement Liaison Team.

The Program Management Office directs the day-to-day operations of DHS' fusion center program, including the management and coordination of deployed officers and Homeland Secure Data Network (HSDN) access. Through the Information Sharing Fellows Program, state or local representatives are detailed temporarily to I&A to familiarize state and local entities with DHS missions, capabilities, roles, and programs, and to promote information sharing among federal, state, and local entities. Law Enforcement Liaison Team representatives liaise with state and local law enforcement entities to advise them about DHS' role in the nationwide Fusion Center Initiative, promote state and local use of DHS systems and databases such as the Homeland Security Information Network, and improve information sharing.

As part of its support to fusion centers, DHS has provided more than $254 million, from FY 2004 to FY 2007, to state and local governments. DHS is also deploying personnel to fusion centers to facilitate state and local access to information, technology, and training. The Implementing Recommendations of the 9/11 Commission Act of 2007 specifies that DHS intelligence officers may be assigned from I&A, the Office of Infrastructure Protection, the Transportation Security Administration (TSA), U.S. Customs and Border Protection (CBP), U.S. Immigrations and Customs Enforcement (ICE), U.S. Coast Guard (USCG), and other DHS components as determined by the Secretary. I&A has deployed intelligence officers to work side by side with state and local authorities at fusion centers and to facilitate the two-way flow of timely, accurate, and actionable information on all types of threats. As of April 2008, I&A has deployed 22 intelligence officers, and the Under Secretary anticipates having 35 officers in major fusion centers nationwide by the end of FY 2008.[7]

DHS personnel assigned to fusion centers have operational and intelligence skills tailored to the unique needs of the locality to:

- help the classified and unclassified information flow,
- provide expertise,
- coordinate with local law enforcement and other agencies, and
- provide local awareness and access.

As of July 2009, there were 72 designated fusion centers around the country with 36 field representatives deployed. The Department has provided more than $254 million from FY 2004-2007 to state and local governments to support the centers.

The Homeland Security Data Network, which allows the federal government to move information and intelligence to the states at the Secret level, is deployed at 27 fusion centers. Through HSDN, fusion center staff can access the National Counterterrorism Center (NCTC), a classified portal of the most current terrorism-related information.[8]

Program Objectives

The State & Local Fusion Center (SLFC) program aims to enhance the lawful sharing of information consistent with DHS' statutory mission as defined by the Homeland Security Act of 2002. Success is dependent upon five essential elements: Communication, Collaboration, Understanding, Coordination, and Management Support.

DHS must ensure that communication with SLFCs is efficient and effective. The Department has created the Single Point of Service (SPS) for DHS information and intelligence support to State and local fusion centers to ensure that all inquires are responded to expeditiously by the appropriate elements within DHS. The SPS will not preclude the SLFCs from interacting with DHS components directly. The SPS is responsible for identifying the appropriate DHS resources to address requests, providing transparency across DHS entities, and tracking requests through to completion. DHS will continue to enhance its relationships with the SLFCs, by providing mechanisms to improve visibility to the appropriate stakeholders of DHS activities, such as analysts' conferences and regular DHS representative visits to the fusion centers. The Department will continue to develop other communications tools, including the Homeland Secure Data Network, the Homeland Security Information Network (HSIN) and the HSIN-Intelligence portal —to improve communications with fusion centers. DHS will develop Standing Operating Procedures (SOPs) to determine the specific organizations within DHS associated with specific types of SLFC interactions. These SOPs will address coordination of interactions across the Department in greater detail.

To enhance the partnership with SLFCs and deepen connections between DHS and SLFC analysts, DHS will expand existing collaborative analysis, assessment, and planning capabilities. DHS will continue to develop mechanisms to more effectively identify opportunities to collaborate to include the Fire Service, Public Health, and Emergency Management. DHS and SLFCs will expand the development of joint products and explore tools to improve the collaborative environment. The Department will also continue to support and develop collaborative bodies like the Homeland Security State and Local Intelligence Community of Interest (HS-SLIC). Operational components, in concert with the SLPO and other components, will conduct strategic planning, including resource projections, necessary to support field interactions with SLFCs.

As partnerships expand and are strengthened, DHS and the SLFCs will enhance their understanding of each other's capabilities and needs. DHS will enhance support to SLFCs on three critical dimensions of information support: 1) Response to the SLFCs' requests for information; 2) SLFC Priority Information Needs (PINS) that align with I&A analytic production to SLFC needs; and 3) Training and technical assistance tailored to the needs of the SLFC analytic cadre. The Department will expand its active engagement of SLFCs to understand their needs. SLFCs will better understand how information can be combined at the Federal level, and what types of DHS support are available and appropriate to meet their needs. Further, DHS will continue to work with the fusion centers to maintain an open dialogue about needs and capabilities and will educate the fusion centers on DHS headquarters and component capabilities. DHS will also provide SLFCs feedback on information received, and identify the types of information most useful for integration into DHS products.

DHS will continue to develop processes and tools to increase the transparency of activities and information exchanged with the fusion centers. All DHS components will be able to quickly view the recent and planned activities, such as conferences or site visits. The SPS will continue to facilitate coordination among the DHS components and ensure requests are responded to in a timely manner. The DHS Homeland Security Intelligence Council's Integrated Intelligence Board (HIIB), a body composed of the heads of intelligence functions from all DHS components and chaired by the Chief Intelligence Officer, will ensure mechanisms are in place to coordinate across DHS on analytic collaboration with SLFCs. Similar mechanisms will be implemented to provide visibility into products distributed to or available to the fusion centers, as well as training opportunities or assistance to increase awareness of what information and resources fusion centers have access to.

In an effort to establish a baseline level of capability in all fusion centers through the implementation of the Global Fusion Center Guidelines and the Office of the Director of National Intelligence – Information Sharing Environment Implementation Plan, DHS will continue to provide an integrated suite of support programs. DHS may revise the Homeland Security Grant Program Guidance as needed to enable the full implementation of the fusion process. In addition, the joint DHS/Department of Justice Fusion Process Technical Assistance Program will continue to support the establishment of baseline capabilities through the following activities:

- Fusion Process Technical Assistance Services;

- Fusion Center Exchange Program;
- Fusion Center Fellowship Program;
- Online Fusion Process Resource Center; and
- Other Specialized Fusion Process Support Services.[9]

Program Risks

There are several potential risks associated with fusion center development. Risks focus on factors that could ultimately diminish political and popular support for fusion centers, and ultimately result in their demise or marginalized contribution to the national homeland security mission.[10]

Civil Liberties Concerns or Violations.

Arguments against fusion centers often center around the idea that such centers are essentially pre-emptive law enforcement — that intelligence gathered in the absence of a criminal predicate is unlawfully gathered intelligence.

The essence of fusion is the integration and analysis of existing streams of information and intelligence for actionable public policy ends — be they counter-terrorism, broader counter-crime issues, or natural disaster response. Embedded in the fusion process is the assumption that the end product of the fusion process can lead to a more targeted collection of new intelligence, to include private sector data, which can help to prevent crime. It could be argued that through a more proactive and targeted intelligence process, one that has as its starting point an intelligence gap, or unknown about a particular threat, it is possible that sophisticated criminal groups could be undermined. However, the potential fusion center use of private sector data, the adoption of a more proactive approach, and the collection of intelligence by fusion center staff and partners has led to questions about possible civil liberties abuses. Director of National Intelligence, Mike McConnell, acknowledges the difficulty of balancing effective intelligence efforts with civil liberties concerns, stating:

> "The intelligence community has an obligation to better identify and counter threats to Americans while still safeguarding their privacy. But the task is [a] inherently a difficult one...[one] challenge is determining how and when it is appropriate to conduct surveillance on a group of Americans who are, say, influenced by al Qaeda's jihadist philosophy. On one level, they are U.S. citizens engaging in free speech and associating freely with one another. On another, they could be plotting terrorist attacks that could kill hundreds of people."

Arguments against fusion centers often center around the idea that such centers are essentially pre-emptive law enforcement — that intelligence gathered in the absence of a criminal predicate is unlawfully gathered intelligence. The argument is that the further law enforcement, public safety and private sector representatives get away from a criminal predicate, the greater the chances that civil liberties may be violated. Furthermore, it could be argued that one of the risks to the fusion center concept is that individuals who do not necessarily have the appropriate law enforcement or broader intelligence training will engage in intelligence collection that is not supported by law. The concern is to what extent, if at all, First Amendment protected activities may be jeopardized by fusion center activities. According to the American Civil Liberties Union (ACLU):

> "We're setting up essentially a domestic intelligence agency, and we're doing it without having a full debate about the risks to privacy and civil liberties." Furthermore, the ACLU is also concerned with having DHS perform a coordinating role at the federal level with respect to these centers. "We are granting extraordinary powers to one agency, without adequate transparency or safeguards, that hasn't shown Congress that it's ready for the job."

Most fusion center representatives appear to be aware of the need to be respectful of privacy and civil liberties as a result of 28 CFR Part 23, the Fusion Center Guidelines, the National Criminal Intelligence Sharing Plan (NCISP), DHS/Department of Justice-sponsored fusion center conferences, and DHS — provided Technical Assistance Training, as well as interactions with peer fusion centers. Several fusion centers had, or were in the process of creating, a governance board, to serve an oversight function, especially on civil liberty concerns. In one case, a fusion center cited concern for civil liberties as the reason it had specifically chosen a former judge to sit on its governing board. Many centers also claim to have privacy policies, a couple of which were reviewed by local ACLU or other civil liberties organization representatives.

"In a free country we punish men for the crimes they commit but never for the opinions they have."

- Harry S. Truman

However, few of the centers had aggressive outreach programs to explain to the public the type of intelligence activities their centers could and could not engage in. There are exceptions; for example, one state fusion center works closely with the most active civil liberties organization in the state, provides the center's standard operating procedures to the public, and has appointed a state attorney general office representative to the center's governing board in order to proactively address civil liberties issues. Another state center has brought in a nonprofit research and training organization to audit their operations, plans to invite civil liberties groups into the center to show its operations, and even stenciled the First Amendment and the following quote by Harry Truman on its walls:

> "In a free country we punish men for the crimes they commit but never for the opinions they have."

An official from a fusion center that advocated a proactive approach to civil liberties related outreach warned colleagues of the dangers of civil liberties abuses, saying, "even the perception of abuse associated with a single center, will be devastating for us all."

Those centers not engaged in a proactive civil liberties outreach effort cited the lack of need and/or the lack of funds as impediments for undertaking such an effort. Several fusion centers suggested they did not need such a proactive outreach program on civil liberties because there had been no local complaints about civil liberties abuses. In a few cases, fusion centers had done targeted outreach to assure specific communities that the fusion center and other law enforcement agencies were not out to target them, but these programs did not reach a large audience. Others suggested that other state/local agencies were responsible for such programs (although most of them were described as general homeland security-related, rather than specific to concerns related to the fusion center). In several cases, fusion centers suggested they wanted to do a public relations campaign, but they didn't have the necessary funds.

For purposes of criminal intelligence systems, most fusion centers operate under federal regulations, in addition to any applicable state policies, laws or regulations. At the federal level, the authorities which guide the FBI in collection of intelligence are the Attorney General's Guidelines for FBI National Security Investigations and Foreign Intelligence Collection. At the state and local levels, if there is any analogue to the Attorney General's guidelines for multijurisdictional criminal intelligence systems, it is 28 Code of Federal Regulations (CFR) -(Judicial Administration), Chapter 1 (Department of Justice), Part 23 (criminal intelligence systems operating policies). Many centers cite 28 CFR, Part 23 as the guiding legal mechanism for their criminal intelligence operations. By its terms, 28 CFR, Part 23, applies to "all criminal intelligence systems operating through support under the Omnibus Crime Control and Safe Streets Act of 1968, as amended." From the perspective of intelligence collection, the 28 CFR, Part 23 standard is reasonable suspicion. One of the operating principles of 28 CFR, Part 23 is that:

> "A project shall collect and maintain criminal intelligence information concerning an individual only if there is reasonable suspicion that the individual is involved in criminal conduct or activity and the information is relevant to that criminal conduct or activity."

Reasonable Suspicion or Criminal Predicate is established when information exists which established sufficient facts to give a trained law enforcement or criminal investigative agency officer, investigator, or employee a basis to believe that there is a reasonable possibility that an individuals or organization is involved in a definable criminal activity or enterprise.

The question of how to balance civil liberties with security remains an open issue the country often weighs. The balancing is, arguably, a moving target driven by the country's collective sense of security and safety. The nation cannot necessarily have absolute security, nor absolute liberty; a pendulum swings between relative amounts of each of these "public goods." The question, to which there is no definitive answer, raised here is how aggressive should fusion centers be in proactively collecting and analyzing intelligence that may go beyond that which may be entered into criminal intelligence systems that fall under federal law? Which entity at the federal level is auditing the activities of fusion centers to ensure civil liberties are not violated? Given that these centers are creations of state and local governments, should an entity of the federal government be the ultimate arbiter of civil liberties protection?

Time

Some homeland security observers suggest that the rush to establish and enhance state fusion centers is a post-9/11 reaction and that over time some of the centers may dissolve. It could be argued that in the absence of another terrorist attack or catastrophic natural disaster, over the course of the next 5 to 10 years, state and regional fusion centers may be eliminated and/or replaced by regional fusion organizations. The state fusion regional representation organizations may be an entity to facilitate future center consolidation efforts. Issues that may lead to state and regional fusion center consolidation into regional organizations include:

- Perceived lack of need by state leaders;
- State and federal financial constraints;
- Duplication of effort without showing tangible products and services within a given center; and
- Reduction of risks to a given geographic location.

Alternatively, if there are additional terrorist attacks or natural disasters in the near future and fusion centers can demonstrate their tangible value by serving as proactive, analytic and/or operational information/intelligence hubs, it is plausible that substantial additional federal, state, and local funds may flow to these centers.

Funding

Another potentially time-related risk is the threat diminished or eliminated federal and/or state funding poses to fusion center development. If the United States is not the target of a successful terrorist attack, homeland security funding, arguably, may decrease. If overall federal funding levels for homeland security decrease, it is possible that there will be some level of decrease in Homeland Security Grant Program (HSGP) funding. Such a decrease might force states to re-prioritize funds for those programs deemed the most critical to their jurisdiction. Specific federal programs that fund and/or support fusion centers (i.e. DHS and FBI detailee programs) could potentially also suffer under funding cuts. It is unclear how fusion centers would fare in such a situation. It is likely that the fate of fusion centers would differ drastically from state to state, depending on a range of factors, to include, their level of maturity, buy-in from other agency partners, their resource needs, and noted successes, balanced with other critical issues and programs within the jurisdiction.

One fusion center official stated that if federal funding went away, his fusion center would continue to operate, albeit with less staff and possibly with a more limited scope. It could be argued in some states that fusion centers would not be able to continue long after federal dollars and support ceases to exist. Others might disagree, believing it is quite possible that many fusion centers would survive despite dwindling federal support. It is even possible that many fusion centers would survive even after drastic decline in state and local funding because states and localities would be in a difficult position to officially dismantle these centers.[11]

Program Assessment

Coordination efforts with fusion centers continue to improve through the combined efforts of I&A and other federal, state, and local information sharing partners. Many state and local fusion center officials praised I&A's efforts on the nationwide Fusion Center Initiative. However, fusion center officials remain concerned that I&A has not developed an action plan to ensure that it understands and can meet the centers' evolving and unique needs. Such needs include:

- receiving adequate and timely information from DHS;
- assistance in navigating DHS' complex organization, and
- obtaining initial and ongoing training for state and local analysts.[12]

Fusion centers have experienced difficulty receiving adequate and timely information from DHS.

Fusion centers have experienced difficulty receiving adequate and timely information from DHS. Many fusion center officials said that they received irrelevant or outdated information in the past. In addition, center officials could not determine whether the information was adequately processed through all relevant systems or coordinated with other intelligence or law enforcement entities. However, according to I&A officials, I&A is striving to meet the needs of fusion centers. In an April 2008 speech, the Under Secretary for I&A recognized that state and local authorities have been analyzing and acting on information for years and the federal government must aggressively support these endeavors. As a result, I&A plans to increase its support to state and local partners in three main areas: standing information needs, Requests for Information, and use of open source information.[13]

Many fusion center officials reported frustrations when navigating DHS' complex organization, and are confused by the department's structure. As a result, state and local officials rely on their assigned I&A officer for fast, efficient, and adequate responses to their information needs. In response, I&A officials said that I&A continues to identify ways to improve the Request for Information process. For example, one I&A representative said that when there is an administrative request, such as a Request for Information about security clearances, the representative refers the request to I&A's State and Local Program Office, who could be immediately and appropriately tasked. In another example, should a request involve an analytical product, the representative refers the request to one of I&A's analytical branches for resolution. To discourage the practice of several fusion center officials contacting multiple DHS components directly for information, another I&A representative suggested creating a single email address to receive requests from fusion center officials and provide one "DHS answer." DHS is taking steps to facilitate efficient and coordinated communications between it and the fusion centers by enhancing I&A's Request for Information process and by requesting that each state that has multiple fusion centers designate one of its centers as the primary point of contact with DHS.[14]

Fusion center officials reported benefits from DHS communications, training, and outreach efforts, as these efforts enhance state and local officials' understanding of the federal intelligence community and their role within the community. However, fusion center officials expressed a need to obtain more structured and formalized analytical training to improve their ability to generate products for the intelligence community, and to facilitate coordination and communication between DHS and the fusion centers. Fusion center officials also reported that budget constraints limit their ability to send personnel to out-of-state training. One fusion center director said funds are not routinely available to send personnel to off-site training or conferences, and it can be difficult convincing state governments to fund such travel. A number of fusion center officials suggested that DHS conduct training outside of the Washington, DC, metropolitan area and explore the feasibility of online training modules to provide low- or no-cost training to state and local field personnel.[15]

Conclusion

Although elements of the information and intelligence fusion function were conducted prior to 9/11, often at state police criminal intelligence bureaus, the events of 9/11 provided the primary catalyst for the formal establishment of more the many state, local, and regional fusion centers across the country.

The value proposition for fusion centers is that by integrating various streams of information and intelligence, including that flowing from the federal government, state, local, and tribal governments, as well as the private sector, a more accurate picture of risks to people, economic infrastructure, and communities can be developed and translated into protective action. The ultimate goal of fusion is to prevent manmade (terrorist) attacks and to respond to natural disasters and manmade threats quickly and efficiently should they occur.[16]

Questions

1. Why is "the need to share" intelligence information an imperative for all levels of government?
2. How are State & Local Fusion Centers better positioned to prevent terrorism?
3. What kind of support does DHS provide SLFCs?
4. Why do some view SLFCs as threats to individual civil liberties?

Chapter 29

First Responders

Objectives

- Understand the critical role of first responders.
- Describe the NIMS framework.
- Understand the functions of the Incident Command System.
- Explain the responsibilities of the states to first responders.

"The United States will prepare to manage the consequences of any future terrorist attacks that may occur despite our best efforts at prevention. Therefore, homeland security seeks to improve the systems and prepare the individuals that will respond to acts of terror. The National Strategy for Homeland Security recognizes that after an attack occurs, our greatest chance to minimize loss of life and property lies with our local first responders—police officers, firefighters, emergency medical providers, public works personnel, and emergency management officials. Many of our efforts to minimize the damage focus on these brave and dedicated public servants."

— National Strategy for Homeland Security, July 2002

Introduction

First responders have traditionally been thought of as local fire, police, and emergency medical personnel who respond to events such as fires, floods, traffic or rail accidents, and hazardous materials spills. As a result of the increased concerns about bioterrorism and other potential terrorist attacks, the definition of first responders has been broadened. Section 2 of the Homeland Security Act defined emergency response providers as including "Federal, State, and local emergency public safety, law enforcement, emergency response, emergency medical (including hospital emergency facilities), and related personnel, agencies, and authorities."

America's first line of defense is the "first responder" community.

Homeland Security Presidential Directive 8 defined the term "first responder" as "individuals who in the early stages of an incident are responsible for the protection and preservation of life, property, evidence, and the environment, including emergency response providers as defined in section 2 of the Homeland Security Act of 2002, as well as emergency management, public health, clinical care, public works, and other skilled support personnel (such as equipment operators) that provide immediate support services during prevention, response, and recovery operations.

Considered the first to respond to natural disasters, domestic terrorism, and other emergencies, America's first line of defense is the "first responder" community. Properly trained and equipped first responders have the greatest potential to save lives, minimize injuries, and protect property.[1]

Effective emergency preparedness and response requires the coordinated planning and actions of multiple players from multiple first responder disciplines, jurisdictions, and levels of government as well as nongovernmental entities. Effective emergency preparedness and response requires putting aside parochialism and working together prior to and after an emergency event. As one participant in responding to Katrina put it, the aftermath of a major disaster is no time to be exchanging business cards. America's first line of defense is the "first responder" community.[2]

September 11, 2001 fundamentally changed the context of emergency management preparedness in the United States, including federal involvement in preparedness and response. The biggest challenge in emergency preparedness is getting effective cooperation in planning, exercises, and capability assessment and building across first responder disciplines and intergovernmental lines. DHS has developed several policy documents designed to define the federal government's role in supporting state and local first responders in emergencies, implement a uniform incident command structure across the nation, and identify performance standards that can be used in assessing state and local first responder capabilities.

National Incident Management System

The September 11, 2001, terrorist attacks and the 2004 and 2005 hurricane seasons highlighted the need to focus on improving emergency management, incident response capabilities, and coordination processes across the country. A comprehensive national approach, applicable at all jurisdictional levels and across functional disciplines, improves the effectiveness of emergency management/response personnel across the full spectrum of potential incidents and hazard scenarios (including but not limited to natural hazards, terrorist activities, and other manmade disasters). Such an approach improves coordination and cooperation between public and private agencies/organizations in a variety of emergency management and incident response activities. The National Incident Management System (NIMS) framework sets forth the comprehensive national approach

NIMS is based on the premise that utilization of a common incident management framework will give emergency management/ response personnel a flexible but standardized system for emergency management and incident response activities.

Incidents typically begin and end locally, and are managed on a daily basis at the lowest possible geographical, organizational, and jurisdictional level. However, there are instances in which successful incident management operations depend on the involvement of multiple jurisdictions, levels of government, functional agencies, and/or emergency responder disciplines. These instances require effective and efficient coordination across this broad spectrum of organizations and activities.

NIMS uses a systematic approach to integrate the best existing processes and methods into a unified national framework for incident management. Incident management refers to how incidents are managed across all homeland security activities, including prevention, protection, and response, mitigation, and recovery. This framework forms the basis for interoperability and compatibility that will, in turn, enable a diverse set of public and private organizations to conduct well-integrated and effective emergency management and incident response operations. Emergency management is the coordination and integration of all activities necessary to build, sustain, and improve the capability to prepare for, protect against, respond to, recover from, or mitigate against threatened or actual natural disasters, acts of terrorism, or other manmade disasters. It does this through a core set of concepts, principles, procedures, organizational processes, terminology, and standard requirements applicable to a broad community of NIMS users.

NIMS is based on the premise that utilization of a common incident management framework will give emergency management/response personnel a flexible but standardized system for emergency management and incident response activities. NIMS is flexible because the system components can be utilized to develop plans, processes, procedures, agreements, and roles for all types of incidents; it is applicable to any incident regardless of cause, size, location, or complexity. Additionally, NIMS provides an organized set of standardized operational structures, which is critical in allowing disparate organizations and agencies to work together in a predictable, coordinated manner.

1. Flexibility: The components of NIMS are adaptable to any situation, from routine, local incidents to incidents requiring the activation of interstate mutual aid to those requiring a coordinated Federal response, whether planned (e.g., major sporting or community events), notice (e.g., hurricane) or no-notice (e.g., earthquake). This flexibility is essential for NIMS to be applicable across the full spectrum of potential incidents, including those that require multiagency, multijurisdictional (such as incidents that occur along international borders), and/or multidisciplinary coordination. Flexibility in the NIMS framework facilitates scalability of emergency management and incident response activities. NIMS also provides the flexibility for unique implementation in specified areas around the Nation. The National Integration Center (NIC), as appropriate, will review and support implementation plans, which reflect these individual requirements and organizational structures, for consistency with NIMS concepts and principles.

NIMS integrates existing best practices into a consistent, nationwide, systematic approach to incident management that is applicable at all levels of government.

2. Standardization: Flexibility to manage incidents of any size requires coordination and standardization among emergency management/response personnel and their affiliated organizations. NIMS provides a set of standardized organizational structures that improve integration and connectivity among jurisdictions and disciplines, starting with a common foundation of preparedness and planning. Personnel and organizations that have adopted the common NIMS framework are able to work together, thereby fostering cohesion among the various organizations involved in all aspects of an incident. NIMS also provides and promotes common terminology, which fosters more effective communication among agencies and organizations responding together to an incident.

NIMS integrates existing best practices into a consistent, nationwide, systematic approach to incident management that is applicable at all levels of government, nongovernmental organizations (NGOs), and the private sector, and across functional disciplines in an all-hazards context. Five major components make up this systems approach: Preparedness, Communications and Information Management, Resource Management, Command and Management, and Ongoing Management and Maintenance.

NIMS Components

The components of NIMS were not designed to stand alone, but to work together in a flexible, systematic manner to provide the national framework for incident management.

1. Preparedness Effective emergency management and incident response activities begin with a host of preparedness activities conducted on an ongoing basis, in advance of any potential incident. Preparedness involves an integrated combination of assessment; planning; procedures and protocols; training and exercises; personnel qualifications, licensure, and certification; equipment certification; and evaluation and revision.
2. Communications and Information Management Emergency management and incident response activities rely on communications and information systems that provide a common operating picture to all command and coordination sites. NIMS describes the requirements necessary for a standardized framework for communications and emphasizes the need for a common operating picture. This component is based on the concepts of interoperability, reliability, scalability, and portability, as well as the resiliency and redundancy of communications and information systems.
3. Resource Management Resources (such as personnel, equipment, or supplies) are needed to support critical incident objectives. The flow of resources must be fluid and adaptable to the requirements of the incident. NIMS defines standardized mechanisms and establishes the resource management process to identify requirements, order and acquire, mobilize, track and report, recover and demobilize, reimburse, and inventory resources.
4. Command and Management The Command and Management component of NIMS is designed to enable effective and efficient incident management and coordination by providing a flexible, standardized incident management structure. The structure is based on three key organizational constructs: the Incident Command System, Multiagency Coordination Systems, and Public Information.

Ongoing Management and Maintenance Within the auspices of Ongoing Management and Maintenance, there are two components: the NIC and Supporting Technologies.

National Integration Center

Homeland Security Presidential Directive 5 required the Secretary of Homeland Security to establish a mechanism for ensuring the ongoing management and maintenance of NIMS, including regular consultation with other Federal departments and agencies; State, tribal, and local stakeholders; and NGOs and the private sector. The NIC provides strategic direction, oversight, and coordination of NIMS and supports both routine maintenance and the continuous refinement of NIMS and its components. The NIC oversees the program and coordinates with Federal, State, tribal, and local partners in the development of compliance criteria and implementation activities. It provides guidance and support to jurisdictions and emergency management/response personnel and their affiliated organizations as they adopt or, consistent with their status, are encouraged to adopt the system. The NIC also oversees and coordinates the publication of NIMS and its related products. This oversight includes the review and certification of training courses and exercise information.

Supporting Technologies

As NIMS and its related emergency management and incident response systems evolve, emergency management/response personnel will increasingly rely on technology and systems to implement and continuously refine NIMS. The NIC, in partnership with the Department of Homeland Security Science and Technology Directorate, oversees and coordinates the ongoing development of incident management-related technology, including strategic research and development.

NIMS & NRF

NIMS provides the template for the management of incidents, regardless of cause, size, location, or complexity... the NRF specifies Federal roles and structures for incidents in which Federal resources are involved.

NIMS provides the template for the management of incidents, regardless of cause, size, location, or complexity. This template establishes the structure, concepts, principles, processes, and language for the effective employment of capabilities nationally, whether those capabilities reside with Federal, State, tribal, or local jurisdictions or with the private sector or NGOs.

The National Response Framework (NRF), which superseded the National Response Plan, is an all-hazards framework that builds upon NIMS and describes additional specific Federal roles and structures for incidents in which Federal resources are involved.

The NRF provides the structure and mechanisms for national-level policy and operational direction for incident management to ensure timely and effective Federal support to State, tribal, and local related activities. The NRF is applicable to all Federal departments and agencies that participate in operations requiring a coordinated Federal response.

NIMS and the NRF are designed to improve the Nation's incident management capabilities and overall efficiency. During incidents requiring coordinated Federal support, the NRF provides the guidelines and procedures to integrate capabilities and resources into a cohesive, coordinated, and seamless national framework for incident management.

A basic premise of both NIMS and the NRF is that incidents typically be managed at the local level first. In the vast majority of incidents, local resources and local mutual aid agreements and assistance agreements will provide the first line of emergency management and incident response. If additional or specialized resources or capabilities are needed, Governors may request Federal assistance; however, NIMS is based on the concept that local jurisdictions retain command, control, and authority over response activities for their jurisdictional areas. Adhering to NIMS allows local agencies to better utilize incoming resources.

The fundamental role of preparedness in emergency management and incident response is a universal concept incorporated in both NIMS and the NRF. Though the specific elements of preparedness described within each document may vary slightly, the concepts remain complementary. The key elements found within the Preparedness component of NIMS and the NRF are described and organized in a fashion to best assist stakeholders in the development of efficient, effective emergency management and incident response capabilities.

Incident Command System

Most incidents are managed locally and are typically handled by local communications/ dispatch centers and emergency management/response personnel within a single jurisdiction. The majority of responses need go no further. In other instances, incidents that begin with a single response within a single jurisdiction rapidly expand to multidisciplinary, multijurisdictional levels requiring significant additional resources and operational support. The Incident Command System (ICS) provides a flexible core mechanism for coordinated and collaborative incident management, whether for incidents where additional resources are required or are provided from different organizations within a single jurisdiction or outside the jurisdiction, or for complex incidents with national implications (such as an emerging infectious disease or a bioterrorism attack). When a single incident covers a large geographical area, multiple local emergency management and incident response agencies may be required. The responding "agencies" are defined as the governmental agencies, though in certain circumstances nongovernmental organizations (NGOs) and private-sector organizations may be included. Effective cross-jurisdictional coordination using processes and systems is absolutely critical in this situation.

Most incidents are managed locally and are typically handled by local communications/ dispatch centers and emergency management/response personnel within a single jurisdiction.

ICS is used to organize on-scene operations for a broad spectrum of emergencies from small to complex incidents, both natural and manmade. The field response level is where emergency management/response personnel, under the command of an appropriate authority, carry out tactical decisions and activities in direct response to an incident or threat. Resources from the Federal, State, tribal, or local levels, when appropriately deployed, become part of the field ICS as prescribed by the local authority.

ICS is used by all levels of government—Federal, State, tribal, and local—as well as by many NGOs and the private sector. ICS is also applicable across disciplines. It is normally structured to facilitate activities in five major functional areas: Command, Operations, Planning, Logistics, and Finance/Administration. Intelligence/Investigations is an optional sixth functional area that is activated on a case-by-case basis.

ICS Management

ICS is based on 14 proven management characteristics, each of which contributes to the strength and efficiency of the overall system.

Common Terminology: ICS establishes common terminology that allows diverse incident management and support organizations to work together across a wide variety of incident management functions and hazard scenarios.

Modular Organization: The ICS organizational structure develops in a modular fashion based on the size and complexity of the incident, as well as the specifics of the hazard environment created by the incident. When needed, separate functional elements can be established, each of which may be further subdivided to enhance internal organizational management and external coordination. Responsibility for the establishment and expansion of the ICS modular organization ultimately rests with Incident Command, which bases the ICS organization on the requirements of the situation. As incident complexity increases, the organization expands from the top down as functional responsibilities are delegated. Concurrently with structural expansion, the number of management and supervisory positions expands to address the requirements of the incident adequately.

Every incident must have an action plan.

Management by Objectives: Management by objectives is communicated throughout the entire ICS organization and includes:

- Establishing incident objectives.
- Developing strategies based on incident objectives.
- Developing and issuing assignments, plans, procedures, and protocols.
- Establishing specific, measurable tactics or tasks for various incident management functional activities, and directing efforts to accomplish them, in support of defined strategies.
- Documenting results to measure performance and facilitate corrective actions.

Incident Action Planning: Centralized, coordinated incident action planning should guide all response activities. An Incident Action Plan (IAP) provides a concise, coherent means of capturing and communicating the overall incident priorities, objectives, strategies, and tactics in the context of both operational and support activities.

Every incident must have an action plan. However, not all incidents require written plans. The need for written plans and attachments is based on the requirements of the incident and the decision of the Incident Commander (IC) or Unified Command (UC). Most initial response operations are not captured with a formal IAP. However, if an incident is likely to extend beyond one operational period, become more complex, or involve multiple jurisdictions and/or agencies, preparing a written IAP will become increasingly important to maintain effective, efficient, and safe operations.

Manageable Span of Control: Span of control is key to effective and efficient incident management. Supervisors must be able to adequately supervise and control their subordinates, as well as communicate with and manage all resources under their supervision. The type of incident, nature of the task, hazards and safety factors, and distances between personnel and resources all influence span-of-control considerations.

Incident Facilities and Locations: Various types of operational support facilities are established in the vicinity of an incident, depending on its size and complexity, to accomplish a variety of purposes. The IC will direct the identification and location of facilities based on the requirements of the situation. Typically designated facilities include Incident Command Posts, Bases, Camps, Staging Areas, mass casualty triage areas, point-of-distribution sites, and others as required.

Comprehensive Resource Management: Maintaining an accurate and up-to-date picture of resource utilization is a critical component of incident management and emergency response. Resources to be identified in this way include personnel, teams, equipment, supplies, and facilities available or potentially available for assignment or allocation. Resource management is described in detail in Component III.

Integrated Communications: Incident communications are facilitated through the development and use of a common communications plan and interoperable communications processes and architectures. This integrated approach links the operational and support units of the various agencies involved and is necessary to maintain communications connectivity and discipline and to enable common situational awareness and interaction. Preparedness planning should address the equipment, systems, and protocols necessary to achieve integrated voice and data communications.

Establishment and Transfer of Command: The command function must be clearly established from the beginning of incident operations. The agency with primary jurisdictional authority over the incident designates the individual at the scene responsible for establishing command. When command is transferred, the process must include a briefing that captures all essential information for continuing safe and effective operations.

Chain of Command and Unity of Command: Chain of command refers to the orderly line of authority within the ranks of the incident management organization. Unity of command means that all individuals have a designated supervisor to whom they report at the scene of the incident. These principles clarify reporting relationships and eliminate the confusion caused by multiple, conflicting directives. Incident managers at all levels must be able to direct the actions of all personnel under their supervision.

Unified Command: In incidents involving multiple jurisdictions, a single jurisdiction with multiagency involvement, or multiple jurisdictions with multiagency involvement, Unified Command allows agencies with different legal, geographic, and functional authorities and responsibilities to work together effectively without affecting individual agency authority, responsibility, or accountability.

Accountability: Effective accountability of resources at all jurisdictional levels and within individual functional areas during incident operations is essential. To that end, Check-In/Check-Out, Incident Action Planning, Unity of Command, Personal Responsibility, Span of Control, and Resource Tracking are all principles of accountability.

Dispatch/Deployment: Resources should respond only when requested or when dispatched by an appropriate authority through established resource management systems. Resources not requested must refrain from spontaneous deployment to avoid overburdening the recipient and compounding accountability challenges.

Information and Intelligence Management: The incident management organization must establish a process for gathering, analyzing, assessing, sharing, and managing incident-related information and intelligence.

Incident Command Organization

Unified command is an important element in multijurisdictional or multiagency incident management.

The Incident Commander (IC) is responsible for overall management of an incident. Overall management includes Command Staff assignments required to support the command function. The Command and General Staffs are typically located at the Incident Command Post (ICP).

The command function may be conducted in one of two general ways:

1. Single Incident Commander: When an incident occurs within a single jurisdiction and there is no jurisdictional or functional agency overlap, a single IC should be designated with overall incident management responsibility by the appropriate jurisdictional authority. (In some cases where incident management crosses jurisdictional and/or functional agency boundaries, a single IC may be designated if agreed upon.) Jurisdictions should consider designating ICs for established Incident Management Teams (IMTs). The designated IC will develop the incident objectives on which subsequent incident action planning will be based. The IC will approve the IAP and all requests pertaining to ordering and releasing incident resources.
2. Unified Command: UC is an important element in multijurisdictional or multiagency incident management. It provides guidelines to enable agencies with different legal, geographic, and functional responsibilities to coordinate, plan, and interact effectively. As a team effort, UC allows all agencies with jurisdictional authority or functional responsibility for the incident to jointly provide management direction through a common set of incident objectives and strategies and a single IAP. Each participating agency maintains its own authority, responsibility, and accountability.

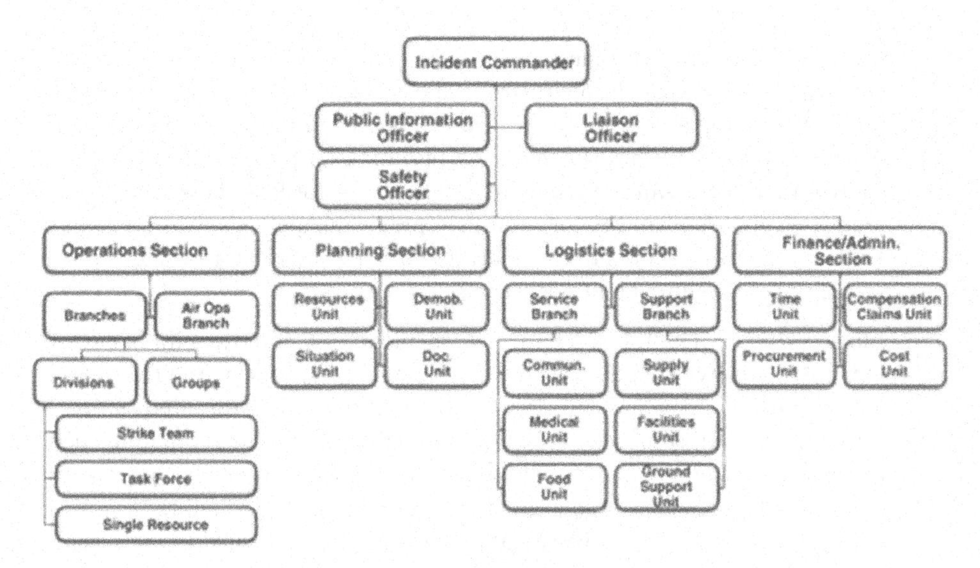

Figure 29.1: Incident Command Structure

Command Staff

In an incident command organization, the Command Staff typically includes a Public Information Officer, a Safety Officer, and a Liaison Officer, who report directly to the IC/UC and may have assistants as necessary. Additional positions may be required, depending on the nature, scope, complexity, and location(s) of the incident(s), or according to specific requirements established by the IC/UC.

1. Public Information Officer: The Public Information Officer is responsible for interfacing with the public and media and/or with other agencies with incident-related information requirements. The Public Information Officer gathers, verifies, coordinates, and disseminates accurate, accessible, and timely information on the incident's cause, size, and current situation; resources committed; and other matters of general interest for both internal and external audiences. The Public Information Officer may also perform a key public information-monitoring role. Whether the command structure is single or unified, only one Public Information Officer should be designated per incident. Assistants may be assigned from other involved agencies, departments, or organizations. The IC/UC must approve the release of all incident-related information. In large-scale incidents or where multiple command posts are established, the Public Information Officer should participate in or lead the Joint Information Center (JIC) in order to ensure consistency in the provision of information to the public.
2. Safety Officer: The Safety Officer monitors incident operations and advises the IC/UC on all matters relating to operational safety, including the health and safety of emergency responder personnel. The ultimate responsibility for the safe conduct of incident management operations rests with the IC/UC and supervisors at all levels of incident management. The Safety Officer is, in turn, responsible to the IC/UC for the systems and procedures necessary to ensure ongoing assessment of hazardous environments, including the incident Safety Plan, coordination of multiagency safety efforts, and implemen-

tation of measures to promote emergency responder safety as well as the general safety of incident operations. The Safety Officer has immediate authority to stop and/or prevent unsafe acts during incident operations. It is important to note that the agencies, organizations, or jurisdictions that contribute to joint safety management efforts do not lose their individual identities or responsibility for their own programs, policies, and personnel. Rather, each contributes to the overall effort to protect all responder personnel involved in incident operations.

3. Liaison Officer: The Liaison Officer is Incident Command's point of contact for representatives of other governmental agencies, NGOs, and the private sector (with no jurisdiction or legal authority) to provide input on their agency's policies, resource availability, and other incident-related matters. Under either a single-IC or a UC structure, representatives from assisting or cooperating agencies and organizations coordinate through the Liaison Officer. Agency and organizational representatives assigned to an incident must have the authority to speak for their parent agencies or organizations on all matters, following appropriate consultations with their agency leadership. Assistants and personnel from other agencies or organizations, public or private, involved in incident management activities may be assigned to the Liaison Officer to facilitate coordination.

4. Additional Command Staff: Additional Command Staff positions may also be necessary, depending on the nature and location(s) of the incident or specific requirements established by Incident Command. For example, a legal counsel might be assigned to the Planning Section as a technical specialist or directly to the Command Staff to advise Incident Command on legal matters, such as emergency proclamations, the legality of evacuation and quarantine orders, and legal rights and restrictions pertaining to media access. Similarly, a medical advisor might be designated to provide advice and recommendations to Incident Command about medical and mental health services, mass casualty, acute care, vector control, epidemiology, or mass prophylaxis considerations, particularly in response to a bioterrorism incident. In addition, a special needs advisor might be designated to provide expertise regarding communication, transportation, supervision, and essential services for diverse populations in the affected area.

General Staff

The General Staff is responsible for the functional aspects of the incident command structure. The General Staff typically consists of the Operations, Planning, Logistics, and Finance/Administration Section Chiefs. The Section Chiefs may have one or more deputies assigned, with the assignment of deputies from other agencies encouraged in the case of multijurisdictional incidents. The functional Sections are discussed more fully below.

Operations Section

This Section is responsible for all tactical activities focused on reducing the immediate hazard, saving lives and property, establishing situational control, and restoring normal operations. Lifesaving and responder safety will always be the highest priorities and the first objectives in the IAP.

1. Operations Section Chief: The Operations Section Chief is responsible to Incident Command for the direct management of all incident-related tactical activities. The Operations Section Chief will establish tactics for the assigned operational period. An Operations Section Chief should be designated for each operational period, and responsibilities include direct involvement in development of the IAP.
2. Branches: Branches may be functional, geographic, or both, depending on the circumstances of the incident. In general, Branches are established when the number of Divisions or Groups exceeds the recommended span of control. Branches are identified by the use of Roman numerals or by functional area.
3. Divisions and Groups: Divisions and/or Groups are established when the number of resources exceeds the manageable span of control of Incident Command and the Operations Section Chief. Divisions are established to divide an incident into physical or geographical areas of operation. Groups are established to divide the incident into functional areas of operation. For certain types of incidents, for example, Incident Command may assign evacuation or mass-care responsibilities to a functional Group in the Operations Section. Additional levels of supervision may also exist below the Division or Group level.
4. Resources: Resources may be organized and managed in three different ways, depending on the requirements of the incident.

The Operations Section is responsible for all tactical activities focused on reducing the immediate hazard, saving lives and property, establishing situational control, and restoring normal operations.

- Single Resources: Individual personnel or equipment and any associated operators.
- Task Forces: Any combination of resources assembled in support of a specific mission or operational need. All resource elements within a Task Force must have common communications and a designated leader.
- Strike Teams: A set number of resources of the same kind and type that have an established minimum number of personnel. All resource elements within a Strike Team must have common communications and a designated leader.

Planning Section

The Planning Section collects, evaluates, and disseminates incident situation information and intelligence to the IC/UC and incident management personnel. This Section then prepares status reports, displays situation information, maintains the status of resources assigned to the incident, and prepares and documents the IAP, based on Operations Section input and guidance from the IC/UC.

The Planning Section is comprised of four primary Units, as well as a number of technical specialists to assist in evaluating the situation, developing planning options, and forecasting requirements for additional resources. Within the Planning Section, the following primary Units fulfill functional requirements:

- Resources Unit: Responsible for recording the status of resources committed to the incident. This Unit also evaluates resources committed currently to the incident, the effects additional responding resources will have on the incident, and anticipated resource needs.
- Situation Unit: Responsible for the collection, organization, and analysis of incident status information, and for analysis of the situation as it progresses.
- Demobilization Unit: Responsible for ensuring orderly, safe, and efficient demobilization of incident resources.
- Documentation Unit: Responsible for collecting, recording, and safeguarding all documents relevant to the incident.
- Technical Specialist(s): Personnel with special skills that can be used anywhere within the ICS organization.

Logistics Section

The Logistics Section is responsible for all service support requirements needed to facilitate effective and efficient incident management, including ordering resources from off-incident locations. This Section also provides facilities, security (of the incident command facilities and personnel), transportation, supplies, equipment maintenance and fuel, food services, communications and information technology support, and emergency responder medical services, including inoculations, as required. Within the Logistics Section, six primary Units fulfill functional requirements:

- Supply Unit: Orders, receives, stores, and processes all incident-related resources, personnel, and supplies.
- Ground Support Unit: Provides all ground transportation during an incident. In conjunction with providing transportation, the Unit is also responsible for maintaining and supplying vehicles, keeping usage records, and developing incident Traffic Plans.
- Facilities Unit: Sets up, maintains, and demobilizes all facilities used in support of incident operations. The Unit also provides facility maintenance and security services required to support incident operations.
- Food Unit: Determines food and water requirements, plans menus, orders food, provides cooking facilities, cooks, serves, maintains food service areas, and manages food security and safety concerns.
- Communications Unit: Major responsibilities include effective communications planning as well as acquiring, setting up, maintaining, and accounting for communications equipment.
- Medical Unit: Responsible for the effective and efficient provision of medical services to incident personnel.

Finance/Administration Section

A Finance/Administration Section is established when the incident management activities require on-scene or incident-specific finance and other administrative support services. Some of the functions that fall within the scope of this Section are recording personnel time, maintaining vendor contracts, administering compensation and claims, and conducting an overall cost analysis for the incident. If a separate Section is established, close coordination with the Planning Section and Logistics Section is also essential so that operational records can be reconciled with financial documents.

The Finance/Administration Section is a critical part of ICS in large, complex incidents involving significant funding originating from multiple sources. In addition to monitoring multiple sources of funds, the Section Chief must track and report to Incident Command the accrued cost as the incident progresses. This allows the IC/UC to forecast the need for additional funds before operations are negatively affected. Figure 8 illustrates the basic organizational structure for a Finance/Administration Section. When such a Section is established, the depicted Units may be staffed as required. Within the Finance/Administration Section, four primary Units fulfill functional requirements:

- Compensation/Claims Unit: Responsible for financial concerns resulting from property damage, injuries, or fatalities at the incident.
- Cost Unit: Responsible for tracking costs, analyzing cost data, making estimates, and recommending cost savings measures.
- Procurement Unit: Responsible for financial matters concerning vendor contracts.
- Time Unit: Responsible for recording time for incident personnel and hired equipment.

Intelligence/Investigations Function

The collection, analysis, and sharing of incident-related intelligence are important elements of ICS. Normally, operational information and situational intelligence are management functions located in the Planning Section, with a focus on three incident intelligence areas: situation status, resource status, and anticipated incident status or escalation (e.g., weather forecasts and location of supplies). This information and intelligence is utilized for incident management decision making. In addition, technical specialists in the Planning Section may be utilized to provide specific information that supports tactical decisions.[3]

State Homeland Security Strategy

To implement a program that addresses State and local needs, States are required to conduct vulnerability, risk, and needs assessments and to develop a State Homeland Security Strategy. The assessment is prepared by the State's planning team; it outlines the State's goals for enhancing prevention, response, and recovery capabilities, and lists specific objectives and implementation steps for the use of planning, training, equipment, and exercise resources in attaining these objectives. Many States have adopted a regional approach to the distribution and sharing of resources. Numerous mutual aid agreements and emergency management assistance compacts have been executed, and coordination and cooperation have been enhanced among homeland security professionals at different levels of government and across disciplines. Strategy analysis has also provided DHS/ODP with a comprehensive picture of planning, equipment, training, exercise, and technical assistance needs across the Nation.[4]

Emergency Management Assistance Compacts

To implement a program that addresses State and local needs, States are required to conduct vulnerability, risk, and needs assessments and to develop a State Homeland Security Strategy.

The Emergency Management Assistance Compact (EMAC) is an agreement among member states to provide assistance after disasters overwhelm a state's capacity to manage consequences. The compact, initiated by the states and coordinated by the National Emergency Management Association, provides a structure for requesting emergency assistance from party states. EMAC also resolves some, but not all, potential legal and administrative obstacles that may hinder such assistance at the state level. EMAC also enhances state preparedness for terrorist attacks by ensuring the availability of resources for fast response and facilitating multi-state cooperation in training activities and preparedness exercises.[5]

Mutual Aid Agreements

Many State, Tribal, and local governments and private nonprofit organizations enter into mutual aid agreements to provide emergency assistance to each other in the event of disasters or emergencies. These agreements often are written, but occasionally are arranged verbally after a disaster or emergency occurs. Mutual aid agreements and assistance agreements are agreements between these agencies, organizations, and jurisdictions that provide a mechanism to quickly obtain emergency assistance in the form of personnel, equipment, materials, and other associated services. The primary objective is to facilitate rapid, short-term deployment of emergency support prior to, during, and after an incident.

Training and Exercises

Personnel with roles in emergency management and incident response at all levels of government—including persons with leadership positions, such as elected and appointed officials—should be appropriately trained to improve all-hazards capabilities nationwide. Additionally, nongovernmental organizations and private-sector entities with direct roles in response operations should be strongly encouraged to participate in NIMS training and exercises. Standardized NIMS training courses focused on the structure and operational coordination processes and systems, together with courses focused on discipline-specific and agency-specific expertise, help to ensure that emergency management/ response personnel can function together effectively during an incident. Training and exercises should be specifically tailored to the responsibilities of the personnel involved in incident management. Mentoring or shadowing opportunities, to allow less experienced personnel to observe those with more experience during an actual incident, should be incorporated to enhance training and exercising. Additionally, exercises should be designed to allow personnel to simulate multiple command, supervisory, or leadership roles whenever possible.

The Homeland Security Exercise and Evaluation Program (HSEEP) is a capabilities- and performance-based exercise program that provides a standardized policy, methodology, and language for designing, developing, conducting, and evaluating all exercises. HSEEP also facilitates the creation of self-sustaining, capabilities-based exercise programs by providing tools and resources such as policy and guidance, training, technology, and direct exercise support. This blended approach to HSEEP implementation promotes exercise expertise, while advancing a standardized means of assessing and improving preparedness across the Nation. HSEEP provides common processes, consistent terminology, tools, and policies that are practical and flexible for all exercise planners. The HSEEP volumes deliver exercise program guidelines that capture lessons learned and best practices of existing exercise approaches, while suggesting strategies that align exercise programs within a broader spectrum of preparedness activities, such as training, planning, and equipment purchases. The HSEEP approach can be adapted to a variety of scenarios and events.[6]

Community Emergency Response Teams (CERT)

The Community Emergency Response Team (CERT) Program educates people about disaster preparedness for hazards that may impact their area and trains them in basic disaster response skills, such as fire safety, light search and rescue, team organization, and disaster medical operations. Using the training learned in the classroom and during exercises, CERT members can assist others in their neighborhood or workplace following an event when professional responders are not immediately available to help. CERT members also are encouraged to support emergency response agencies by taking a more active role in emergency preparedness projects in their community.[7]

Conclusion

First responders need and deserve the best tools and practices available to help save lives and protect property. The Department of Homeland Security is committed to helping first responders nation-wide by ensuring that emergency response professionals are prepared, equipped and trained for any situation, and by bringing together information and resources to prepare for and respond to a terrorist attack, natural disaster or other large-scale emergency.[8]

Questions

1. What is the relationship between NIMS and ICS?
2. How does the ICS approach the "all hazards" emergency management model?
3. How do mutual aid and emergency management compacts assist first responders in their functions?
4. How do CERT efforts support First Responders?

Chapter 30

National Guard

Objectives

- Understand the dual-status of the National Guard.
- Know National Guard members are exempt from Posse Comitatus in Title 32 status.
- Explain the mechanism for sharing National Guard forces between States.

Introduction

Historically, the National Guard has served as a critical resource in emergencies and can be an effective force multiplier to civil authorities in responding to acts of terrorism at the state, local, and federal levels. In the wake of the September 11, 2001, terrorist attacks, the National Guard has expanded its traditional role in homeland defense and homeland security and readily supports local, territorial, state, and federal response agencies with needed equipment, facilities, and personnel. National Guard activities such as conducting vulnerability assessments; planning, training, and exercising with civilian emergency responders; and securing strategic facilities, such as airports, pharmaceutical labs, nuclear power plants, communications towers, and border crossings, have been a cornerstone in protecting our citizens from domestic acts of terrorism.

Governors command the National Guard of their respective states and territories, and the Guard is the only military force that the governor can call upon to respond to disasters and other emergencies. Thus, governors have an enormous stake in the ongoing effectiveness and efficiency of their National Guard.[1]

The National Guard is the oldest component of the Armed Forces of the United States.

Background

The National Guard is the oldest component of the Armed Forces of the United States and one of the nation's longest-enduring institutions. The National Guard traces its history back to the earliest English colonies in North America. Responsible for their own defense, the colonists drew on English military tradition and organized their able-bodied male citizens into militias.[2]

For most of its history, England had no full-time, professional Army. The English had relied on a militia of citizen-soldiers who had the obligation to assist in national defense. The first colonists in Virginia and Massachusetts knew that they had to rely on themselves for their own defense. America's citizen-soldiers who make up the National Guard of today have fought in every major American war since 1636.[3]

The colonial militias protected their fellow citizens from Indian attack, foreign invaders, and later helped to win the Revolutionary War. Following independence, the authors of the Constitution empowered Congress to "provide for organizing, arming, and disciplining the militia." However, recognizing the militia's state role, the Founding Fathers reserved the appointment of officers and training of the militia to the states. Today's National Guard still remains a dual state-Federal force.

Throughout the 19th century the size of the Regular Army was small, and the militia provided the bulk of the troops during the Mexican War, the early months of the Civil War, and the Spanish-American War. In 1903, important national defense legislation increased the role of the National Guard (as the militia was now called) as a Reserve force for the U.S. Army. In World War I, which the U.S. entered in 1917, the National Guard made up 40% of the U.S. combat divisions in France; in World War II, National Guard units were among the first to deploy overseas and the first to fight. Following World War II, National Guard aviation units, some of them dating back to World War I, became the Air National Guard, the nation's newest Reserve component. The Guard stood on the frontiers of freedom during the Cold War, sending soldiers and airmen to fight in Korea and to reinforce NATO during the Berlin crisis of 1961-1962. During the Vietnam war, almost 23,000 Army and Air Guardsmen were called up for a year of active duty; some 8,700 were deployed to Vietnam. Over 75,000 Army and Air Guardsmen were called upon to help bring a swift end to Desert Storm in 1991.

Since that time, the National Guard has seen the nature of its Federal mission change, with more frequent call ups in response to crises in Haiti, Bosnia, Kosovo, and the skies over Iraq. Most recently, following the attacks of September 11, 2001, more than 50,000 Guard members were called up by both their States and the Federal government to provide security at home and combat terrorism abroad. In the largest and swiftest response to a domestic disaster in history, the Guard deployed more than 50,000 troops in support of the Gulf States following Hurricane Katrina in 2005. Today, tens of thousands of Guard members are serving in Iraq and Afghanistan, as the National Guard continues its historic dual mission, providing to the states units trained and equipped to protect life and property, while providing to the nation units trained, equipped and ready to defend the United States and its interests, all over the globe.[4]

When National Guard units are not mobilized under federal control, they report to the Adjutant General of their state or territory.

Organization

When National Guard units are not mobilized under federal control, they report to the Adjutant General of their state or territory, or in the case of the District of Columbia, the Commanding General. Each Adjutant General is responsible to the Governor of his state (or in the case of the District of Columbia, the mayor.)

The Army National Guard and the Air National Guard are each led by their own director. The two directors are selected by the Secretary of the Army (for the Director of the Army National Guard) and the Secretary of the Air Force (for the Director of the Air National Guard.) Both directors report to the Chief of the NGB. Full-time staffs support the Chief of the NGB and the directors of the ARNG and the ANG.

National Guard Bureau

The National Guard Bureau (NGB) was formed to assist the states, territories and District of Columbia with procure funding for the Guard, administer policies and act as a liaison between the Departments of the Army and Air Force and the states.

The NGB is a joint bureau of the Departments of the Army and Air Force, and functions in both a staff and an operating capacity for each component. The NGB performs the federal functions of the Army National Guard (ARNG) and the Air National Guard (ANG). The senior leader at NGB is the Chief, National Guard Bureau, usually a Lieutenant General.[5]

Army National Guard

The Army National Guard exists in all 50 states, the Commonwealth of Puerto Rico, the territories of Guam and the Virgin Islands, and the District of Columbia. The structure of the Army National Guard allows for command and control of units by individual Governors or the President of the United States, depending upon the nature of the call to duty. When Army National Guard units are not mobilized or under federal control, they report to the Governors of their respective state or territory. The President serves as commander-in-chief for units mobilized for federal active duty.

Soldiers of the Army National Guard aiding their community during a flood will most likely be in a state active-duty status, reporting to their governor. Soldiers deployed overseas in support of a federal mission will be under the control of the President of the United States.[6]

The Posse Comitatus Act proscribes use of the Army or the Air Force to execute the law. It says nothing about the Navy, the Marine Corps, the Coast Guard, or the National Guard.[7] The courts have said that members of the National Guard when not in federal service are not covered by the Posse Comitatus Act. Similarly, Posse Comitatus is only applicable to members of the National Guard when they are in federal service.[8]

The Posse Comitatus Act proscribes use of the Army or the Air Force to execute the law... members of the National Guard when not in federal service are not covered by the Posse Comitatus Act.

The Army National Guard is structured across 50 states, three territories, and the District of Columbia. Each state governor serves as the commander in chief while the Adjutants' General are responsible for training and readiness. At the state level, the governors reserve the ability under the constitution to call up members of the Army National Guard in times of domestic emergency.[9]

The Army National Guard (ARNG) structures its forces to provide for a compatible and inter-operable force that is fully capable of accomplishing state, national, and international missions in war and peace. To meet these requirements, the ARNG maintains a balanced mix of combat, combat support (CS), and combat service support (CSS) units. These units are structured to integrate seamlessly with active component units as needed.

The ARNG is comprised of: 15 enhanced Separate Brigades, eight divisions, and three strategic brigades (31st SAB, 92nd SIB, and the 207th Scout Group). The ARNG also maintains two Special Forces groups (19th and 20th). The force composition of the ARNG is 52 percent combat, 17 percent CS, 22 percent CSS, and 9 percent table of distribution and allowances (TDA) units, typically state headquarters units.[10]

Following World War II, units of the Army National Guard were organized into the First and Fifth Continental United States Armies (CONUSA), formally responsible for the training of Army troops and the ground defense of the continental United States. In June 1971, Fifth Army moved to its current base at Fort Sam Houston, Texas. In January 2006, Fifth Army gave up its Reserve preparation obligations to First Army, and is now responsible for homeland defense and defense support to civil authority as U.S. Army North.[11]

Air National Guard

The Air National Guard is also administered by the National Guard Bureau, a joint bureau of the departments of the Army and Air Force, located in the Pentagon, Washington, D.C. It is one of the seven Reserve components of the United States armed forces that augments the active components in the performance of their missions.

The Air National Guard has both a federal and state mission. The dual mission, a provision of the U.S. Constitution, results in each guardsman holding membership in the National Guard of his or her state and in the National Guard of the United States.

The Air National Guard's federal mission is to maintain well-trained, well-equipped units available for prompt mobilization during war and provide assistance during national emergencies (such as natural disasters or civil disturbances). During peacetime, the combat-ready units and support units are assigned to most Air Force major commands to carry out missions compatible with training, mobilization readiness, humanitarian and contingency operations such as Operation Enduring Freedom in Afghanistan. Air National Guard units may be activated in a number of ways as prescribed by public law. Most of the laws may be found in Title 10 of the U.S. Code.

Each guardsman holds membership in the National Guard of his or her state and in the National Guard of the United States.

The Air National Guard provides almost half of the Air Force's tactical airlift support, combat communications functions, aeromedical evacuations and aerial refueling. In addition, the Air National Guard has total responsibility for air defense of the entire United States.

When Air National Guard units are not mobilized or under federal control, they report to the governor of their respective state, territory (Puerto Rico, Guam, Virgin Islands) or the commanding general of the District of Columbia National Guard. Each of the 54 National Guard organizations is supervised by the adjutant general of the state or territory. Under state law, the Air National Guard provides protection of life, property and preserves peace, order and public safety. These missions are accomplished through emergency relief support during natural disasters such as floods, earthquakes and forest fires; search and rescue operations; support to civil defense authorities; maintenance of vital public services and counterdrug operations.

The primary sources of full-time support for Air National Guard units are the dual-status military technician and guardsmen on active duty. These people perform day-to-day management, administration and maintenance. By law, dual-status military technicians are civil service employees of the federal government who must be military members of the unit that employs them. Technicians train with the unit and are mobilized with it when it's activated. Active-duty members serve under the command authority of their respective state or territorial governors until mobilized for federal duty. The Air National Guard has more than 106,000 officers and enlisted people who serve in 88 flying units and 579 mission support units.

The National Guard Bureau, both a staff and operating agency, administers the federal functions of the Army and the Air National Guard. As a staff agency, the National Guard Bureau participates with the Army and Air staffs in developing and coordinating programs that directly affect the National Guard. As an operating agency, the National Guard Bureau formulates and administers the programs for training, development and maintenance of the Army National Guard and Air National Guard and acts as the channel of communication between the Army, Air Force and the 54 states and territories where National Guard units are located.

Besides maintaining 94 percent of the U.S. alert sites for air defense, the Air National Guard provided 60 percent of intercept sorties flown in fiscal 2005 to protect U.S. air sovereignty while still performing many other Air Force-related roles and missions.

The Air National Guard provides tactical airlift, air refueling tankers, general purpose fighters, rescue and recovery capabilities, tactical air support, weather flights, strategic airlift, special operations capabilities and aeromedical evacuation units

Airlift squadrons fly C-130 Hercules, C-5 Galaxy, and C-17 Globemaster aircraft that transport people, equipment and supplies. Air refueling units, flying KC-135 Stratotankers, provide air-to-air refueling for strategic and tactical aircraft.

The Air National Guard has three rescue and recovery squadrons that fly HH-60 helicopters and HC-130 aircraft. These units provide important lifesaving capabilities and services to civilian and military agencies. Air support units that fly OA-10 Thunderbolt IIs provide forward air control support of close-air support missions. The general-purpose fighter force is equipped with F-15 Eagle, F-16 Fighting Falcon, A-10 and OA-10 aircraft.

Support units are essential to the Air Force mission. In the Air National Guard they include air traffic control units, combat communications squadrons, civil engineering and communication flights and squadrons. Support units also include weather flights, aircraft control and warning squadrons, a range control squadron and an electronic security unit.

Air National Guard weather flights provide weather support to Air Force and Army National Guard and Army Reserve divisions and brigades. During mobilization or federal call up, weather flight units are under the Air Combat Command, except for one, which falls under the Pacific Air Forces.

Civil engineering squadrons provide engineer and firefighter forces trained and equipped to deploy on short notice. Other civil engineering squadrons provide self-sufficient, deployable civil engineering teams to perform heavy repair and maintenance on air bases and remote sites.

Aerial port units provide trained people to support Air Mobility Command's two major theater war commitments. They deploy to 20 active-duty aerial port locations worldwide for annual tour training.

Medical units located with parent flying organizations provide day-to-day health care for flying and non-flying people during their two-week annual training period or during monthly two-day unit training assemblies.[12]

Homeland Security Role

Since the terrorist attacks of September 11, 2001, many have asserted that "homeland defense" and/or "homeland security" are natural, ideal, or logical missions for the reserve components of the armed forces, and that reserve missions and resources should be substantially reoriented so as to emphasize homeland security. Several rationales for this assumption have been advanced, including the following:

- As the focus of contingency planning expands to include attacks on U.S. territory, reserve forces, because of their members' long-term community ties, will be the most knowledgeable about local conditions, problems, and special circumstances.
- Reserve units are stationed at small armories and other facilities at thousands of locations, in major urban and suburban areas as well as rural ones, around the country. Active force units–particularly those of the Army and Marine Corps–tend to be concentrated at large bases, often in areas removed from major population centers (to provide enough space for training).
- The statutorily-defined, and constitutionally-derived, status of the National Guard as the organized militia of each state (10 USC 311), as well as a federal military reserve force (10 USC 10105-07, 10 USC 10111-13) enables the Guard to be used within the United States without posing questions of improper military intrusion into civil affairs.
- The reserves, by definition, exist only to augment the active forces in time of crisis, and the threat of a terrorist attack within the United States is an obvious example of such a crisis.[13]

During most of our nation's history our full-time, or "active" armed forces have been very small. Only since the end of World War II has the United States, in peacetime, maintained large military forces on active duty. Prior to 1945, the United States met its military needs with a very small full-time force augmented by ordinary citizens who were also part-time soldiers. These citizen-soldiers, called "militia," regularly gathered to practice military skills in case they were needed.

The basic advantage of citizen soldiers is economic. The Reserve Component includes approximately 1.2 million military personnel comprising about 45% of the military's Total Force, yet they cost only 8% of the entire DoD budget.

The Reserve Component is comprised of two distinct forces:

1. Federal Reserves
2. State National Guard

The Federal Reserves are similar to the Active Component in that they act at the direction of the President and are subject to Posse Comitatus under Title 10 of US Code. The State National Guard are different from the Active Component in that they act at the direction of the State Governor, and are exempt from Posse Comitatus under Title 32 of US Code. National Guard units lose their exemption when they are called on by the President to conduct federal missions under Title 10. All services, the Army, Navy, Marines, and Air Force, have a

Federal Reserve component. Only two services, the Army and Air Force, have a National Guard component.

Reserve members are required to train 2 days per month, plus two weeks per year, committing at least 39 days to military training per year. Independent of their training commitments, reservists may be "activated", or called to duty by the President, but only for specific periods under specific circumstances.

- If Congress declares war, the President may direct a Full Mobilization calling all reservists to duty for the duration of the war plus six months.
- If the President issues a Declaration of National Emergency, he may direct a Partial Mobilization calling up to 1 million reservists to duty for no more than 2 years.
- After issuing proper notification to Congress, the President may direct a Call-Up pulling as many as 200 thousand reservists into duty for up to 270 days.
- On their own, Service Secretaries may call reservists to duty for no more than 15 days, but there are no restrictions on reservists who volunteer for duty.[14]

Under the Uniformed Services Employment and Reemployment Act of 1994 (USERRA), if a military member leaves their civilian job for service in the uniformed services, they are entitled to return to their job, with accrued seniority.

Activated reserve forces receive the same pay and allowances as full-time active component personnel. The Uniformed Services Employment and Reemployment Rights Act of 1994 (USERRA), provides reemployment protection and other benefits for veterans and employees who perform military service. Under USERRA, if a military member leaves their civilian job for service in the uniformed services, they are entitled to return to their job, with accrued seniority, provided they meet the law's eligibility criteria. USERRA applies to voluntary as well as involuntary service.[15]

State Assets

The National Guard has established Joint Force Headquarters in each state to coordinate and integrate National Guard support to state and local civilian authorities, and receive and integrate the Guard forces dispatched by other governors under the Emergency Management Assistance Compact (EMAC) or other mutual aid agreements.

Every state National Guard also has developed rapid reaction forces that provide every state with a trained and ready combat arms force capable of quickly delivering company- and battalion-sized units. These reaction forces can help local and state law enforcement agencies by protecting key sites such as power plants and transportation hubs, establishing roadblocks, and securing Weapons of Mass Destruction incident sites.

The use of mutual assistance compacts and an increasingly strong nationwide resource-sharing alliance provides a robust, redundant, and resilient capability for the Guard to support any state in a Title 32 status. This capability falls within the Stafford Act and Chapter 15 of Title 10, which address the enforcement of laws to restore public order.

Unless and until activated for federal service, the National Guard is under the control of the governors as commanders-in-chief, in accordance with Article I, Section 8, clause 16 of the U.S. Constitution, which enables Congress:

> to provide for organizing, arming, and disciplining the militia, and for governing such part of them as may be employed in the service of the United States, reserving to the states respectively, the appointment of the officers, and the authority of training the militia according to the discipline prescribed by Congress . . . .

Title 32 of the United States Code (USC) affirms governors' command and control over the National Guard in peacetime, including use of the National Guard for domestic operations, without any restraints such as those pertaining to the Posse Comitatus Act. Title 10 of the USC is focused primarily on the use of active duty military forces to deal with war and other national defense crises. The Guard can be activated under Title 10 as a part of the forces under the command of the President of the United States. Governors believe that when National Guard members perform domestic missions they should do so in State Active Duty or Title 32 status rather than Title 10 status, unless and until the President has activated their unit under Title 10 for a federal mission requiring federal military forces, such as to repel an invasion.

Unless and until activated for federal service, the National Guard is under the control of the governors as commanders-in-chief.

As an alternative to granting a governor tactical control over Title 10 domestic military operations in the governor's state or territory, governors recognize that a Dual-Status National Guard commander can be appointed by the respective governor and the President pursuant to 32 USC Section 325. Pursuant to such appointment, the Dual Status National Guard commander would have command and control of all active, Guard, and reserve military personnel deployed to or within the state in support of or in response to the domestic event or emergency. Both federal reserve forces called to duty for an emergency, and follow-on, later arriving active duty forces should fall under the command and control of the dual-hatted commander.

If an emergency rises to a level of significance such that federal law or the Constitution permits the President or Congress to declare the event under federal control, the National Guard can be activated under Title 10 and would then serve directly under the President's command and control for the domestic event or emergency.[16]

Conclusion

The National Guard is considered a unique state-based military force (although primarily funded by the federal government and trained in accordance with federal standards) that is the "only military force shared by the states and the federal government." According to former National Guard Bureau Chief H. Steven Blum, the Guard's "unique ability to work in three legal statuses makes the Guard the most versatile DOD force available to the Federal Government for homeland security (HLS), homeland defense (HD), and military assistance to civil authorities (MACA)."[17]

Questions

1. Who commands National Guard forces?
2. When are National Guard forces exempt from Posse Comitatus.
3. Why is the National Guard "uniquely positioned" for homeland security missions?
4. What agreement allows Governors to share National Guard forces?

Part VI: Reflections

Chapter 31

Looking Back

Objectives

- Describe how DHS missions generally performed in the agency's first four years.
- Identify impediments that may have delayed or impaired DHS' progress.

Introduction

In 2007, as the Department of Homeland Security completed its fourth year of operation, six years after 9/11, the Government Accountability Office (GAO) conducted a review of the Department's performance. The GAO was asked to provide an assessment of DHS's progress and challenges during its first 4 years. The resulting report examined (1) What progress DHS made in implementing key mission and core management functions since its inception, and what challenges the department faced in its implementation efforts; and (2) What key themes affected DHS's implementation of its mission and management functions.[1]

Background

In July 2002, President Bush issued the National Strategy for Homeland Security. The strategy set forth overall objectives to prevent terrorist attacks within the United States, reduce America's vulnerability to terrorism, and minimize the damage and assist in the recovery from attacks that occur. The strategy set out a plan to improve homeland security through the cooperation and partnering of federal, state, local, and private sector organizations on an array of functions. The National Strategy for Homeland Security specified a number of federal departments, as well as nonfederal organizations, that have important roles in securing the homeland. In terms of federal departments, DHS was assigned a leading role in implementing established homeland security mission areas.

In November 2002, the Homeland Security Act of 2002 was enacted into law, creating DHS. This act defined the department's missions to include preventing terrorist attacks within the United States; reducing U.S. vulnerability to terrorism; and minimizing the damages, and assisting in the recovery from, attacks that occur within the United States. The act also specified major responsibilities for the department, including to analyze information and protect

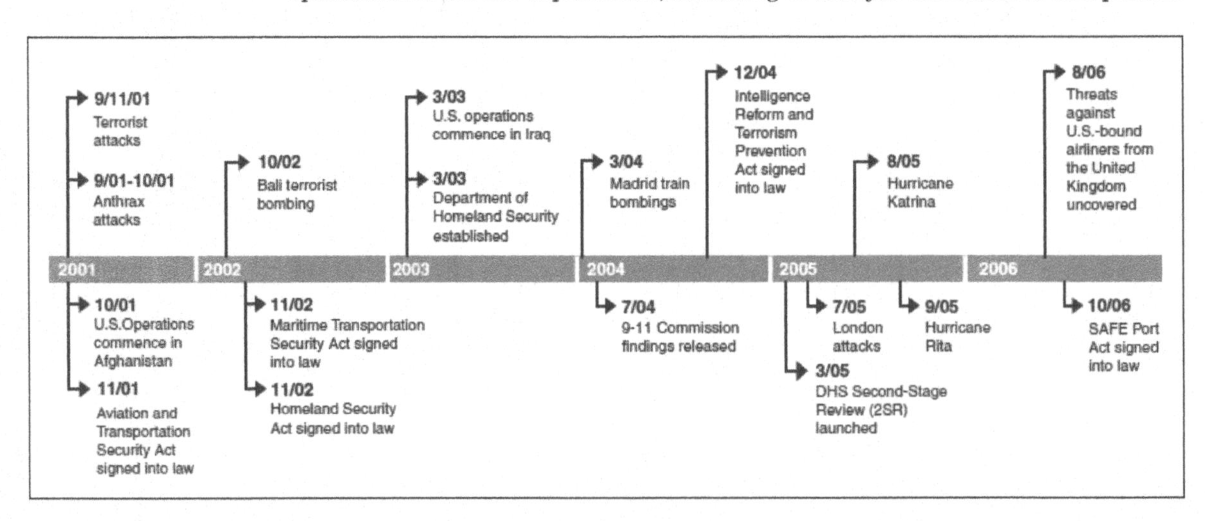

Figure 30.1: Selected Key Events That Have Affected Department of Homeland Security Implementation

infrastructure; develop countermeasures against chemical, biological, radiological, and nuclear, and other emerging terrorist threats; secure U.S. borders and transportation systems; and organize emergency preparedness and response efforts. DHS began operations in March 2003. Its establishment represented a fusion of 22 federal agencies to coordinate and centralize the leadership of many homeland security activities under a single department.

A variety of factors have affected DHS's efforts to implement its mission and management functions. These factors include both domestic and international events, such as Hurricanes Katrina and Rita, and major homeland security-related legislation. Figure 30.1 provides a timeline of key events that have affected DHS's implementation.[2]

GAO Review

In 2007, the Government Accountability Office conducted an assessments of DHS's progress across 14 mission and management areas identified in the National Strategy for Homeland Security, the goals and objectives set forth in the DHS strategic plan and homeland security presidential directives, past GAO reports, and studies conducted by the DHS Office of Inspector General (IG) and other organizations and groups, such as the 9/11 Commission and the Century Foundation.[3]

Mission Areas

1. Border Security
2. Immigration enforcement
3. Immigration services
4. Aviation security
5. Surface transportation security
6. Maritime security
7. Emergency preparedness and response
8. Critical infrastructure and key resources protection
9. Science and technology

Management Areas

1. Acquisition management
2. Financial management
3. Human capital management
4. Information technology management
5. Real property management

For each mission and management area, the GAO identified performance expectations and vetted them with DHS officials. These performance expectations are a composite of the responsibilities or functions—derived from legislation, homeland security presidential directives and executive orders, DHS planning documents, and other sources—that the department is to achieve. GAO analysts and subject matter experts reviewed prior work, DHS IG work, and evidence DHS provided between March and July 2007, including DHS officials' assertions when supported by documentation. On the basis of this analysis and experts' judgment, the GAO then assessed the extent to which DHS had achieved each of the expectations identified. Preliminary assessments were made for each performance expectation based solely on GAO and DHS IG work. In March through July, the GAO received additional information from DHS, which was used to inform the final assessments. In some cases the assessments remained the same as the preliminary ones, and in other cases they changed.

When review of prior work, the DHS IG's work, and DHS's documentation indicated that DHS had satisfied most of the key elements of a performance expectation, the GAO concluded that DHS had generally achieved it. When reviews showed that DHS had not yet satisfied most of the key elements of a performance expectation, the GAO concluded that DHS had generally not achieved it. More specifically, where prior work or that of the DHS IG indicated DHS had not achieved a performance expectation and DHS did not provide documentation to prove otherwise, the GAO concluded that DHS had generally not achieved it. For a small number of performance expectations the GAO could not make an assessment because the information available did not enable a clear assessment of DHS's progress.

The GAO used these performance expectation assessments to determine DHS's overall progress in each mission and management area. After making an assessment for each performance expectation, the GAO added up those rated as generally achieved, and divided this number by the total number of performance expectations for the mission or management area, excluding those performance expectations for which we could not make an assessment. If DHS generally achieved more than 75 percent of the identified performance expectations, the GAO identified its overall progress as substantial. When the number achieved was more than 50 percent but 75 percent or less, the GAO identified its overall progress as moderate. If DHS generally achieved more than 25 percent but 50 percent or less, the GAO identified its overall progress as modest. For mission and management areas in which DHS generally achieved 25 percent or less of the performance expectations, we identified overall progress as limited.[4]

Border Security

DHS's border security mission includes detecting and preventing terrorists and terrorist weapons from entering the United States; facilitating the orderly and efficient flow of legitimate trade and travel; interdicting illegal drugs and other contraband; apprehending individuals who are attempting to enter the United States illegally; inspecting inbound and outbound people, vehicles, and cargo; and enforcing laws of the United States at the border. As shown in table 30.1, the GAO identified 12 performance expectations for DHS in the area of border security and found that DHS has generally achieved 5 of them and has generally not achieved 7 others.

Performance expectation	Total
Generally achieved	5
Implement a biometric entry system to prevent unauthorized border crossers from entering the United States through ports of entry	
Develop a program to detect and identify illegal border crossings between ports of entry	
Develop a strategy to detect and interdict illegal flows of cargo, drugs, and other items into the United States	
Provide adequate training for all border-related employees	
Develop staffing plans for hiring and allocating human capital resources to fulfill the agency's border security mission	
Generally not achieved	7
Implement a biometric exit system to collect information on border crossers leaving the United States through ports of entry	
Implement a program to detect and identify illegal border crossings between ports of entry	
Implement a strategy to detect and interdict illegal flows of cargo, drugs, and other items into the United States	
Implement effective security measures in the visa issuance process	
Implement initiatives related to the security of certain documents used to enter the United States	
Ensure adequate infrastructure and facilities	
Leverage technology, personnel, and information to secure the border	
Overall assessment of progress	**Modest**

Table 30.1: Border Security Assessment

Immigration Enforcement

DHS's immigration enforcement mission includes apprehending, detaining, and removing criminal and illegal aliens; disrupting and dismantling organized smuggling of humans and contraband as well as human trafficking; investigating and prosecuting those who engage in benefit and document fraud; blocking and removing employers' access to undocumented workers; and enforcing compliance with programs to monitor visitors. As shown in table 30.2, the GAO identified 16 performance expectations for DHS in the area of immigration enforcement and found that DHS has generally achieved 8 of them and has generally not achieved 4 others. For 4 performance expectations, the GAO could not make an assessment.

Performance expectation	**Total**
Generally achieved	**8**
Develop a program to ensure the timely identification and removal of noncriminal aliens subject to removal from the United States	
Assess and prioritize the use of alien detention resources to prevent the release of aliens subject to removal	
Develop a program to allow for the secure alternative detention of noncriminal aliens	
Develop a prioritized worksite enforcement strategy to ensure that only authorized workers are employed	
Develop a comprehensive strategy to interdict and prevent trafficking and smuggling of aliens into the United States	
Develop a law enforcement strategy to combat criminal alien gangs in the United States and cross-border criminal activity	
Develop a program to screen and respond to local law enforcement and community complaints about aliens who many be subject to removal	
Develop staffing plans for hiring and allocating human capital resources to fulfill the agency's immigration enforcement mission	
Generally not achieved	**4**
Implement a program to ensure the timely identification and removal of noncriminal aliens subject to removal from the United States	
Ensure the removal of criminal aliens	
Implement a prioritized worksite enforcement strategy to ensure that only authorized workers are employed	
Implement a comprehensive strategy to interdict and prevent trafficking and smuggling of aliens into the United States	
No assessment made	4
Implement a program to allow for the secure alternative detention of noncriminal aliens	
Implement a law enforcement strategy to combat criminal alien gangs in the United States and cross-border criminal activity	
Disrupt and dismantle mechanisms for money laundering and financial crimes	
Provide training, including foreign language training, and equipment for all immigration enforcement personnel to fulfill the agency's mission	
Overall assessment of progress	**Moderate**

Table 30.2: Immigration Enforcement Assessment

Immigration Services

DHS's immigration services mission includes administering immigration benefits and working to reduce immigration benefit fraud. As shown in table 30.3, the GAO identified 14 performance expectations for DHS in the area of immigration services and found that DHS has generally achieved 5 of them and has generally not achieved 9 others.

Performance expectation	Total
Generally achieved	5
Institute process and staffing reforms to improve application processes	
Establish online access to status information about benefit applications	
Establish revised immigration application fees based on a comprehensive fee study	
Communicate immigration-related information to other relevant agencies	
Create an office to reduce immigration benefit fraud	
Generally not achieved	9
Eliminate the benefit application backlog and reduce application completion times to 6 months	
Establish a timetable for reviewing the program rules, business processes, and procedures for immigration benefit applications	
Institute a case management system to manage applications and provide management information	
Develop new programs to prevent future backlogs from developing	
Establish online filing for benefit applications	
Capture biometric information on all benefits applicants	
Implement an automated background check system to track and store all requests for applications	
Establish training programs to reduce fraud in the benefits process	
Implement a fraud assessment program to reduce benefit fraud	
Overall assessment of progress	Modest

Table 30.3: Immigration Services Assessment

Aviation Security

DHS's aviation security mission includes strengthening airport security; providing and training a screening workforce; prescreening passengers against terrorist watch lists; and screening passengers, baggage, and cargo. As shown in table 30.4, the GAO identified 24 performance expectations for DHS in the area of aviation security and found that DHS has generally achieved 17 of them and has generally not achieved 7 others.

Performance expectation	Total
Generally achieved	**17**
Implement a strategic approach for aviation security functions	
Ensure the screening of airport employees against terrorist watch lists	
Hire and deploy a federal screening workforce	
Develop standards for determining aviation security staffing at airports	
Establish standards for training and testing the performance of airport screener staff	
Establish a program and requirements to allow eligible airports to use a private screening workforce	
Train and deploy federal air marshals on high-risk flights	
Establish standards for training flight and cabin crews	
Establish a program to allow authorized flight deck officers to use firearms to defend against any terrorist or criminal acts	
Establish policies and procedures to ensure that individuals known to pose, or suspected of posing, a risk or threat to security are identified and subjected to appropriate action	
Develop and implement processes and procedures for physically screening passengers at airport checkpoints	
Develop and test checkpoint technologies to address vulnerabilities	
Deploy explosive detection systems (EDS) and explosive trace detection (ETD) systems to screen checked baggage for explosives	
Develop a plan to deploy in-line baggage screening equipment at airports	
Pursue the deployment and use of in-line baggage screening equipment at airports	
Develop a plan for air cargo security	
Develop and implement procedures to screen air cargo	
Generally not achieved	**7**
Establish standards and procedures for effective airport perimeter security	
Establish standards and procedures to effectively control access to airport secured areas	
Establish procedures for implementing biometric identifier systems for airport secured areas access control	
Develop and implement an advanced prescreening system to allow DHS to compare domestic passenger information to the Selectee List and No Fly List	
Develop and implement an international passenger prescreening process to compare passenger information to terrorist watch lists before aircraft departure	
Deploy checkpoint technologies to address vulnerabilities	
Develop and implement technologies to screen air cargo	
Overall assessment of progress	**Moderate**

Table 30.4: Aviation Security Assessment

Surface Transportation Security

DHS's surface transportation security mission includes establishing security standards and conducting assessments and inspections of surface transportation modes, which include passenger and freight rail; mass transit; highways, including commercial vehicles; and pipelines. As shown in table 30.5, the GAO identified 5 performance expectations for DHS in the area of surface transportation security and found that DHS has generally achieved 3 of them and has generally not achieved 2.

Performance expectation	Total
Generally achieved	**3**
Develop and adopt a strategic approach for implementing surface transportation security functions	
Conduct threat, criticality, and vulnerability assessments of surface transportation assets	
Administer grant programs for surface transportation security	
Generally not achieved	**2**
Issue standards for securing surface transportation modes	
Conduct compliance inspections for surface transportation systems	
Overall assessment of progress	**Moderate**

Table 30.5: Surface Transportation Assessment

Maritime Security

DHS's maritime security responsibilities include port and vessel security, maritime intelligence, and maritime supply chain security. As shown in table 30.6, the GAO identified 23 performance expectations for DHS in the area of maritime security and found that DHS has generally achieved 17 of them and has generally not achieved 4 others. For 2 performance expectations, we could not make an assessment.

Performance expectation	Total
Generally achieved	**17**
Develop national plans for maritime security	
Develop national plans for maritime response	
Develop national plans for maritime recovery	
Develop regional (port-specific) plans for security	
Develop regional (port-specific) plans for response	
Ensure port facilities have completed vulnerability assessments and developed security plans	
Ensure that vessels have completed vulnerability assessments and developed security plans	
Exercise security, response, and recovery plans with key maritime stakeholders to enhance security, response, and recovery efforts	
Implement a port security grant program to help facilities improve their security capabilities	
Establish operational centers to monitor threats and fuse intelligence and operations at the regional/port level	
Collect information on incoming ships to assess risks and threats	
Develop a vessel-tracking system to improve intelligence and maritime domain awareness on vessels in U.S. waters	
Collect information on arriving cargo for screening purposes	
Develop a system for screening and inspecting cargo for illegal contraband	
Develop a program to work with foreign governments to inspect suspicious cargo before it leaves for U.S. ports	
Develop a program to work with the private sector to improve and validate supply chain security	
Develop an international port security program to assess security at foreign ports	
Generally not achieved	**4**
Develop regional (port-specific) plans for recovery	
Implement a national facility access control system for port secured areas	
Develop a long-range vessel-tracking system to improve maritime domain awareness	
Develop a program to screen incoming cargo for radiation	
No assessment made	**2**
Develop a national plan to establish and improve maritime intelligence	
Develop standards for cargo containers to ensure their physical security	
Overall assessment of progress	**Substantial**

Table 30.6: Maritime Security Assessment

Emergency Preparedness & Response

DHS's emergency preparedness and response mission includes preparing to minimize the damage and recover from terrorist attacks and disasters; helping to plan, equip, train, and practice needed skills of first responders; and consolidating federal response plans and activities to build a national, coordinated system for incident management. As shown in table 30.7, the GAO identified 24 performance expectations for DHS in the area of emergency preparedness and response and found that DHS has generally achieved 5 of them and has generally not achieved 18 others. For 1 performance expectation, we could not make an assessment.

Performance expectation	Total
Generally achieved	**5**
Establish a program for conducting emergency preparedness exercises	
Develop a national incident management system	
Provide grant funding to first responders in developing and implementing interoperable communications capabilities	
Administer a program for providing grants and assistance to state and local governments and first responders	
Allocate grants based on assessment factors that account for population, critical infrastructure, and other risk factors	
Generally not achieved	**18**
Establish a comprehensive training program for national preparedness	
Conduct and support risk assessments and risk management capabilities for emergency preparedness	
Ensure the capacity and readiness of disaster response teams	
Coordinate implementation of a national incident management system	
Establish a single, all-hazards national response plan	
Coordinate implementation of a single, all-hazards response plan	
Develop a complete inventory of federal response capabilities	
Develop a national, all-hazards preparedness goal	
Develop plans and capabilities to strengthen nationwide recovery efforts	
Develop the capacity to provide needed emergency assistance and services in a timely manner	
Provide timely assistance and services to individuals and communities in response to emergency events	
Implement a program to improve interoperable communications among federal, state, and local agencies	
Implement procedures and capabilities for effective interoperable communications	
Increase the development and adoption of interoperability communications standards	
Develop performance goals and measures to assess progress in developing interoperability	
Provide guidance and technical assistance to first responders in developing and implementing interoperable communications capabilities	
Provide assistance to state and local governments to develop all-hazards plans and capabilities	
Develop a system for collecting and disseminating lessons learned and best practices to emergency responders	
No assessment made	**1**
Support citizen participation in national preparedness efforts	
Overall assessment of progress	**Limited**

Table 30.7: Emergency Preparedness & Response Assessment

CIKR Protection

DHS's critical infrastructure and key resources protection activities include developing and coordinating implementation of a comprehensive national plan for critical infrastructure protection, developing partnerships with stakeholders and information sharing and warning capabilities, and identifying and reducing threats and vulnerabilities. As shown in table 30.8, the GAO identified 7 performance expectations for DHS in the area of critical infrastructure and key resources protection and found that DHS has generally achieved 4 of them and has generally not achieved 3 others.

Performance expectation	Total
Generally achieved	**4**
Develop a comprehensive national plan for critical infrastructure protection	
Develop partnerships and coordinate with other federal agencies, state and local governments, and the private sector	
Identify and assess threats and vulnerabilities for critical infrastructure	
Support efforts to reduce threats and vulnerabilities for critical infrastructure	
Generally not achieved	**3**
Improve and enhance public/private information sharing involving attacks, threats, and vulnerabilities	
Develop and enhance national analysis and warning capabilities for critical infrastructure	
Provide and coordinate incident response and recovery planning efforts for critical infrastructure	
Overall assessment of progress	**Moderate**

Table 30.8: CIKR Protection Assessment

Science & Technology

DHS's science and technology efforts include coordinating the federal government's civilian efforts to identify and develop countermeasures to chemical, biological, radiological, nuclear, and other emerging terrorist threats. As shown in table 30.9, the GAO identified 6 performance expectations for DHS in the area of science and technology and found that DHS has generally achieved 1 of them and has generally not achieved 5 others.[5]

Performance expectation	Total
Generally achieved	1
Coordinate with and share homeland security technologies with federal, state, local, and private sector entities	
Generally not achieved	5
Develop a plan for departmental research, development, testing, and evaluation activities	
Assess emerging chemical, biological, radiological, and nuclear threats and homeland security vulnerabilities	
Coordinate research, development, and testing efforts to identify and develop countermeasures to address chemical, biological, radiological, nuclear, and other emerging terrorist threats	
Coordinate deployment of nuclear, biological, chemical, and radiological detection capabilities and other countermeasures	
Assess and evaluate nuclear, biological, chemical, and radiological detection capabilities and other countermeasures	
Overall assessment of progress	Limited

Table 30.9: Science & Technology Assessment

Conclusion

Over the past 4 years, DHS has made varying levels of progress in implementing its mission and management areas, as shown in the following table. In general, DHS has made more progress in its mission areas than in its management areas. Within its mission areas, DHS has made progress in developing plans and programs, but has faced challenges in its implementation efforts.

Key underlying themes have affected DHS's implementation efforts. These include strategies to achieve agency transformation, strategic planning and results management, risk management, information sharing, and partnerships and coordination. While DHS has made progress in transforming its component agencies into a fully functioning department, it has not yet addressed key elements of the transformation process, such as developing a comprehensive transformation strategy. In addition, transparency plays an important role in transformation efforts, but DHS's decision making has not always been transparent. DHS also has not yet fully adopted and applied a risk management approach in implementing its mission and management functions. Some DHS component agencies have taken steps to do so, but this approach is not yet used department wide. In addition, DHS has taken steps to share information and coordinate with homeland security partners, but has faced difficulties in these partnership efforts.

Given DHS's leading role in securing the homeland, it is critical that the department's mission and management programs operate as efficiently and effectively as possible. DHS has taken important actions to secure the border and transportation sectors and to prepare for and respond to disasters. DHS has had to undertake these missions while also working to transform itself into a fully functioning cabinet department—a difficult task for any organization. As DHS moves forward, it will be important for the department to continue to develop more measurable goals to guide implementation efforts and to enable better accountability. It will also be important for DHS to continually reassess its mission and management goals, measures, and milestones to evaluate progress made, identify past and emerging obstacles, and examine alternatives to effectively address those obstacles.[6]

Table: Summary of Assessments of DHS's Progress in Mission and Management Areas

Mission/ management area	Number of performance expectations	Number of expectations generally achieved	Number of expectations generally not achieved	Number of expectations not assessed	Overall assessment of progress
Border security	12	5	7	0	Modest
Immigration enforcement	16	8	4	4	Moderate
Immigration services	14	5	9	0	Modest
Aviation security	24	17	7	0	Moderate
Surface transportation security	5	3	2	0	Moderate
Maritime security	23	17	4	2	Substantial
Emergency preparedness and response	24	5	18	1	Limited
Critical infrastructure protection	7	4	3	0	Moderate
Science and technology	6	1	5	0	Limited
Acquisition management	3	1	2	0	Modest
Financial management	7	2	5	0	Modest
Human capital management	8	2	6	0	Limited
Information technology management	13	2	8	3	Limited
Real property management	9	6	3	0	Moderate
Total	**171**	**78**	**83**	**10**	

Source: GAO analysis.

Definitions:
Substantial progress: DHS has taken actions to generally achieve more than 75 percent of the identified performance expectations.
Moderate progress: DHS has taken actions to generally achieve more than 50 percent but 75 percent or less of the identified performance expectations.
Modest progress: DHS has taken actions to generally achieve more than 25 percent but 50 percent or less of the identified performance expectations.
Limited progress: DHS has taken actions to generally achieve 25 percent or less of the expectations.

Table 30.1: DHS Performance Summary

Questions

1. How would you assess DHS' first four year's performance?
2. Given all the obstacles, do you think this is a fair assessment?
3. Is the U.S. better off with our without DHS?

Chapter 32

Looking Ahead

Objectives

- Describe the purpose of the Quadrennial Homeland Security Review (QHSR).
- Identify the five DHS mission areas.

Introduction

Pursuant to the Implementing Recommendations of the 9/11 Commission Act of 2007, in 2009 the Department of Homeland Security undertook its first Quadrennial Homeland Security Review (QHSR).[1] The purpose of the QHSR is to outline the strategic framework to guide the activities of participants in homeland security toward a common end. A safe and secure homeland must mean more than preventing terrorist attacks from being carried out. It must also ensure that the liberties of all Americans are assured, privacy is protected, and the means by which the United States interchanges with the world—through travel, lawful immigration, trade, commerce, and exchange—are secured.

In addition, while the importance of preventing another terrorist attack in the United States remains undiminished, much has been learned since September 11, 2001, about the range of challenges the Nation faces. Hurricane Katrina, widespread international cyber attacks, the expansion of transnational criminal activities, and H1N1 influenza are examples of threats and hazards that are central to homeland security, requiring an equally wide variety of capabilities to address them.[2]

The purpose of QHSR is to elaborate upon this broader vision by outlining the strategic framework to guide the activities of participants in homeland security toward a common end. Thus, this QHSR will describe more comprehensively the Nation's homeland security interests, identify more clearly the critical homeland security missions, and define more completely a strategic approach to those missions by laying out the principal goals, essential objectives, and key strategic outcomes necessary for that strategic approach to succeed.[3]

Framing Homeland Security

Homeland security describes the intersection of evolving threats and hazards with traditional governmental and civic responsibilities for civil defense, emergency response, law enforcement, customs, border control, and immigration. In combining these responsibilities under one overarching concept, homeland security breaks down longstanding stovepipes of activity that have been and could still be exploited by those seeking to harm America. Homeland security also creates a greater emphasis on the need for joint actions and efforts across previously discrete elements of government and society.

Homeland security is a widely distributed and diverse—but unmistakable—national enterprise. The term "enterprise" refers to the collective efforts and shared responsibilities of Federal, State, local, tribal, territorial, nongovernmental, and private-sector partners—as well as individuals, families, and communities—to maintain critical homeland security capabilities. The use of the term connotes a broad-based community with a common interest in the public safety and well-being of America and American society that is composed of multiple actors and stakeholders whose roles and responsibilities are distributed and shared. As the Commander-in-Chief and the leader of the Executive Branch, the President of the United States is uniquely responsible for the safety, security, and resilience of the Nation. The White House leads overall homeland security policy direction and coordination. Individual Federal agencies, in turn, are empowered by law and policy to fulfill various aspects of the homeland security mission.

The Secretary of Homeland Security leads the Federal agency as defined by statute charged with homeland security: preventing terrorism and managing risks to critical infrastructure; securing and managing the border; enforcing and administering immigration laws; safeguarding and securing cyberspace; and ensuring resilience to disasters.

There are three key concepts that are essential to, and form the foundation for, a comprehensive approach to homeland security:

1. Security: Protect the United States and its people, vital interests, and way of life;
2. Resilience: Foster individual, community, and system robustness, adaptability, and capacity for rapid recovery; and
3. Customs and Exchange: Expedite and enforce lawful trade, travel, and immigration.

The QHSR outlines the Nation's homeland security missions, or broad areas of activity around which the homeland security enterprise is oriented. These missions are enterprise-wide, and not limited to the Department of Homeland Security. Hundreds of thousands of people from across the Federal Government, State, local, tribal, and territorial governments, the private sector, and other nongovernmental organizations are responsible for executing these missions. These homeland security professionals must have a clear sense of what it takes to achieve the overarching vision.

Thee keys to comprehensive homeland security:
1. Security
2. Resilience
3. Customs & Exchange

There are five homeland security missions. The missions and associated goals are as follows:

Mission 1: Preventing Terrorism and Enhancing Security

Goal 1.1: Prevent Terrorist Attacks

Goal 1.2: Prevent the Unauthorized Acquisition or Use of Chemical, Biological, Radiological, and Nuclear Materials and Capabilities

Goal 1.3: Manage Risks to Critical Infrastructure, Key Leadership, and Events

Mission 2: Securing and Managing Our Borders

Goal 2.1: Effectively Control U.S. Air, Land, and Sea Borders

Goal 2.2: Safeguard Lawful Trade and Travel

Goal 2.3: Disrupt and Dismantle Transnational Criminal Organizations

Mission 3: Enforcing and Administering Our Immigration Laws

Goal 3.1: Strengthen and Effectively Administer the Immigration System

Goal 3.2: Prevent Unlawful Immigration

Mission 4: Safeguarding and Securing Cyberspace

Goal 4.1: Create a Safe, Secure, and Resilient Cyber Environment

Goal 4.2: Promote Cybersecurity Knowledge and Innovation

Mission 5: Ensuring Resilience to Disasters

Goal 5.1: Mitigate Hazards

Goal 5.2: Enhance Preparedness

Goal 5.3: Ensure Effective Emergency Response

Goal 5.4: Rapidly Recover

By defining the homeland security missions and setting prioritized goals, objectives, and strategic outcome statements for each mission, we chart a course for action over the next 4 years.[4]

Preventing Terrorism & Enhancing Security

Preventing terrorism in the United States is the cornerstone of homeland security. Ensuring that malicious actors cannot conduct terrorist attacks within the United States, preventing the illicit or hostile use of chemical, biological, radiological, and nuclear (CBRN) materials or capabilities within the Unites States, and managing risks to our critical infrastructure and key resources helps us realize our vision of a secure and resilient Nation.

Key Strategic Outcomes

- Acts of terrorism against transportation systems are thwarted prior to successful execution.
- The manufacture, storage, or transfer of dangerous materials is protected by physical, personnel, and cybersecurity measures commensurate with the risks.
- Any release of high-consequence biological weapons is detected in time to protect populations at risk from the release.
- Critical infrastructure sectors adopt and sector partners meet accepted standards that measurably reduce the risk of disrupting public health and safety, critical government services, and essential economic activities.
- Governmental executive leadership is protected from hostile acts by terrorists and other malicious actors.

Goal 1.1: Prevent Terrorist Attacks. Malicious actors are unable to conduct terrorist attacks within the United States. Success in achieving this goal rests on our ability to strengthen public- and private-sector activities designed to counter terrorist efforts to plan and conduct attacks. Success also depends on strengthening our ability to investigate and arrest perpetrators of terrorist crimes and to collect intelligence that will help prevent future terrorist activities.

Objectives:

- Acquire, analyze, and appropriately share intelligence and other information on current and emerging threats.
- Deter, detect, and disrupt surveillance, rehearsals, and execution of operations by terrorists and other malicious actors.
- Protect potential targets against the capabilities of terrorists, malicious actors, and their support networks to plan and conduct operations.
- Prevent and deter violent extremism and radicalization that contributes to it.
- Increase community participation in efforts to deter terrorists and other malicious actors and mitigate radicalization toward violence.[5]

Goal 1.2: Prevent the Unauthorized Acquisition or Use of CBRN Materials and Capabilities. Malicious actors, including terrorists, are unable to acquire or move dangerous chemical, biological, radiological, and nuclear materials or capabilities within the United States. Although the Nation remains committed to preventing all attacks by terrorists and other malicious actors, certain chemical, biological, radiological, and nuclear attacks pose a far greater potential to cause catastrophic consequences. Consequently, particular attention must be paid to the security of dangerous chemical, biological, radiological, and nuclear materials and technologies.

"America's New Normalcy" proffers a view of the future—five years out—that the panel believes offers a reasonable, measurable, and attainable benchmark.

Objectives:

- Identify and understand potentially dangerous actors, technologies, and materials.
- Identify and understand potentially dangerous actors, technologies, and materials.
- Prevent the illicit movement of dangerous materials and technologies.
- Identify the presence of and effectively locate, disable, or prevent the hostile use of CBRN.[6]

Goal 1.3: Manage Risks to Critical Infrastructure, Key Leadership, and Events Key sectors actively work to reduce vulnerability to attack or disruption. The American way of life depends upon the effective functioning of the Nation's critical infrastructure and key resources, and the protection of key leadership and events. Although considerable advances have been made in identifying critical infrastructure assets and systems, and understanding the current, emerging, and future risks to those infrastructures, the breadth of the infrastructure, its increasing reliance on cyberspace, and its criticality necessitates continued diligence.

Objectives:

- Identify, attribute, and evaluate the most dangerous threats to critical infrastructure and those categories of critical infrastructure most at risk.

- Prevent high-consequence events by securing critical infrastructure assets, systems, networks, or functions—including linkages through cyberspace—from attacks or disruption.
- Enhance the ability of critical infrastructure systems, networks, and functions to withstand and rapidly recover from damage and disruption and adapt to changing conditions.
- Preserve continuity of government and ensure security at events of national significance.[7]

Securing & Managing Borders

A safe and secure homeland requires that we maintain effective control of our air, land, and sea borders; that we safeguard lawful trade and travel; and that we disrupt transnational organizations that engage in smuggling and trafficking across the U.S. border. This three-pronged approach to securing and managing our borders can only be achieved by working with partners from across the homeland security enterprise to establish secure and resilient global trading, transportation, and transactional systems that facilitate the flow of lawful travel and commerce. This approach also depends on partnerships with Federal, State, local, tribal, territorial, and international law enforcement agencies to share information and conduct coordinated and integrated operations. In working together, we can more effectively achieve our shared vision and preserve our freedoms and way of life.

Key Strategic Outcomes

- The entry or approach of all high-consequence WMD and related materials and technologies is prevented.
- Terrorists and other high-risk individuals are prevented from using commercial or noncommercial transportation destined for the United States.
- The identity of all individuals who are encountered at U.S. borders and in global movement systems entering the United States is verified.
- Individuals with known ties to terrorism or transnational criminal activities are not granted access to secure areas within the global movement system.
- No highly dangerous pathogens or organisms are introduced across U.S. borders.

Goal 2.1: Effectively Control U.S. Air, Land, and Sea Borders. Prevent the illegal flow of people and goods across U.S. air, land, and sea borders while expediting the safe flow of lawful travel and commerce. Key to achieving secure and well-managed borders are the broad legal authorities utilized by trained officers to conduct appropriate searches, seizures, arrests, and other key enforcement activities. These security and enforcement activities are balanced, however, by the need to facilitate the lawful transit of people and goods across our borders. Through the collection, analysis, and proper sharing of information, the use of screening and identification verification techniques, the employment of advanced detection and other technologies, the use of "trusted traveler" or "trusted shipper" approaches, and cooperation with our international partners and the private sector, we can achieve security at our borders, enforce the laws, and ensure our prosperity and freedom by speeding lawful travel and commerce.

Objectives:

- Prevent the illegal entry of people, weapons, dangerous goods, and contraband, and protect against cross-border threats to health, food, environment, and agriculture, while facilitating the safe flow of lawful travel and commerce.
- Prevent the illegal export of weapons, proceeds of crime, and other dangerous goods, and the exit of malicious actors.[8]

Goal 2.2: Safeguard Lawful Trade and Travel. Ensure security and resilience of global movement systems. The global economy is increasingly a seamless economic environment connected by systems and networks that transcend national boundaries. The United States is deeply linked to other countries through the flow of goods and services, capital and labor, and information and technology into and across our borders. As much as these global systems and networks are critical to the United States and our prosperity, their effectiveness and efficiency also make them attractive targets for exploitation by our adversaries, terrorists, and criminals. Thus, border security cannot begin simply at our borders. The earlier we can identify, understand, interdict, and disrupt plots and illegal operations, the safer we will be at home. In other words, our borders should not be our first line of defense against global threats. This premise demands a focus on using our national leverage to build partnerships to secure key nodes and conveyances in the global trading and transportation networks, as well as to manage the risks posed by people and goods in transit. Moreover, U.S. national interests—in a competitive U.S. economy and a stable global trading system—require us to work with international partners and the private sector to secure global movement systems. These same national interests are also served by ensuring the free, lawful movement of people and commerce through the global economy and across U.S. borders in a manner that does not impair economic vitality, while at the same time safeguarding privacy, civil rights, and civil liberties.

Objectives:

- Promote the security and resilience of key nodes of transaction and exchange within the global supply chain.
- Promote the security and resilience of conveyances in the key global trading and transportation networks.
- People seeking to come to the United States, as well as goods in transit, must be positively identified and determined not to pose a threat to this country or the larger global movement system as far in advance as possible.[9]

Goal 2.3: Disrupt and Dismantle Transnational Criminal Organizations. Disrupt and dismantle transnational organizations that engage in smuggling and trafficking across the U.S. border. We have also learned in the years since 9/11 that it is not enough to simply interdict trouble at the border or enhance the protection of global systems for trade and travel. Criminals, terrorist networks, and other malicious actors will seek to exploit the same interconnected systems and networks of the global economy for nefarious purposes, or create their own illicit pathways for smuggling and trafficking—of illegal drugs, illegal migrants, terrorists, or even highly dangerous weapons. When these organizations or actors are successful, they also may increase corruption and engage in a wide variety of other criminal activities such as money laundering, bulk cash smuggling, and intellectual property crime, which threaten the rule of law, potentially endanger lives, and generate wider destabilization. Thus, our border strategy must also focus on reducing the power and capability of these transnational criminal and terrorist organizations.

Objectives:

- Disrupt transnational criminal or terrorist organizations involved in cross-border smuggling, trafficking, or other cross-border crimes, dismantle their infrastructure, and apprehend their leaders.
- Identify, disrupt, and dismantle illicit pathways used by criminal and terrorist organizations.[10]

Enforcing and Administering Immigration Laws

A fair and effective immigration system must protect the public while also enriching American society and promoting economic prosperity. At the same time, it must also deter immigration violations, work to eliminate the conditions that foster illegal immigration, and improve the efficiency, fairness, and integrity of our immigration system.

Key Strategic Outcomes

- The identities of individuals seeking immigration services are verified at first contact and throughout the immigration process.
- All workers are verified as legally authorized to work in the United States.
- Real-time information, data, trends, and intelligence on terrorist or criminal organizations and individuals are accessible to all Federal immigration partners.
- Criminal organizations and individuals are prevented from transporting, housing, or harboring illegal aliens.
- All communities that are home to immigrant populations have programs that effectively integrate immigrants into American civic society.

Goal 3.1: Strengthen and Effectively Administer the Immigration System. Promote lawful immigration, expedite administration of immigration services, and promote the integration of lawful immigrants into American society. Effective administration of the immigration system depends on ensuring that immigration decisions are fair, lawful, and sound; that the immigration system is interactive and user friendly; that policy and procedural gaps are systematically identified and corrected; and that vulnerabilities that would allow persons to exploit the system are eliminated. In addition, effectively administering the immigration system includes efforts to integrate lawful immigrants into American society.

Objectives:

- Clearly communicate with the public about immigration services and procedures.
- Create a user-friendly system that ensures fair, consistent, and prompt decisions.
- Provide leadership, support, and opportunities to lawful immigrants to facilitate their integration into American society and foster community cohesion.[11]

Goal 3.2: Prevent Unlawful Immigration. Reduce conditions that encourage foreign nationals to illegally enter and remain in the United States, while identifying and removing those who violate our laws. To prevent illegal immigration, all agencies charged with immigration administration and enforcement activities must address conditions and factors that create incentives for those illegally entering and staying within the United States. This effort includes identifying the conditions and addressing gaps in current laws, policies, and procedures that foster illegal immigration. Enforcement efforts must prioritize the identification and removal of dangerous foreign nationals who threaten our national security or the safety of our communities and must include safe and humane detention conditions and respect for due process and civil rights as accorded by law.

Objectives:

- Eliminate the conditions that encourage illegal employment.
- Prevent fraud, abuse, and exploitation, and eliminate other systemic vulnerabilities that threaten the integrity of the immigration system.
- Prevent entry or admission of criminals, fugitives, other dangerous foreign nationals, and other unauthorized entrants.
- Arrest, detain, prosecute, and remove criminal, fugitive, dangerous, and other unauthorized foreign nationals consistent with due process and civil rights protections.[12]

Safeguarding & Securing Cyberspace

Our security and way of life depend upon a vast array of interdependent and critical networks, systems, services, and resources. To have an infrastructure that is secure and resilient, enables innovation and prosperity, and protects privacy and other civil liberties by design, we must secure cyberspace and manage other risks to its safe use.

Key Strategic Outcomes

- Critical information systems and information and communications services are secure, reliable, and readily available.
- Homeland security partners develop, update, and implement guidelines, regulations, and standards that ensure the confidentiality, integrity, and reliability of systems, networks, and data.
- Cyber disruptions or attacks are detected in real-time, consequences are mitigated, and services are restored rapidly.
- Academic institutions produce and homeland security partners sustain a cybersecurity workforce that meets national needs and enables competitiveness.
- Critical infrastructure sectors adopt and sector partners meet accepted standards that measurably reduce the risk of cyber disruption or exploitation.

Goal 4.1: Create a Safe, Secure, and Resilient Cyber Environment. Ensure malicious actors are unable to effectively exploit cyberspace, impair its safe and secure use, or attack the Nation's information infrastructure. Cyber infrastructure forms the backbone of the Nation's economy and connects every aspect of our way of life. While the cyber environment offers the potential for rapid technological advancement and economic growth, a range of malicious actors may seek to exploit cyberspace for dangerous or harmful purposes, cause mass disruption of communications or other services, and attack the Nation's infrastructure through cyber means. We must secure the system of networks and information upon which our prosperity relies while promoting economic growth, protecting privacy, and sustaining civil liberties. Both public- and private-sector efforts are required to achieve these aims. In addition, a robust law enforcement and counterintelligence capability is essential to the success of our cybersecurity efforts.

Objectives:

- Identify and evaluate the most dangerous threats to Federal civilian and private-sector networks and the Nation.
- Protect and make resilient information systems, networks, and personal and sensitive data.
- Disrupt the criminal organizations and other malicious actors engaged in high-consequence or wide-scale cyber crime.
- Manage cyber incidents from identification to resolution in a rapid and replicable manner with prompt and appropriate action.[13]

Goal 4.2: Promote Cybersecurity Knowledge and Innovation. Ensure that the Nation is prepared for the cyber threats and challenges of tomorrow. Cybersecurity is a dynamic field, and cyber threats and challenges evolve at breathtaking speed. Education, training, awareness, science, technology, and innovation must flourish in order to meet this challenge. While we must protect the Nation from cyber attacks that occur today, we must also prepare now to mitigate the most consequential cybersecurity risks that the United States and its people will face in 5, 10, and 20 years. We must make long-term investments that sustain a safe, secure, and reliable cyber environment, enable prosperity, further social and community uses of the Internet, and facilitate transactions and trade, while safeguarding privacy and civil liberties.

Objectives:

- Ensure that the public recognizes cybersecurity challenges and is empowered to address them.
- Develop the national knowledge base and human capital capabilities to enable success against current and future threats.
- Create and enhance science, technology, governance mechanisms, and other elements necessary to sustain a safe, secure, and resilient cyber environment.[14]

Ensuring Resilience to Disasters

The strategic aims and objectives for ensuring resilience to disasters are grounded in the four traditional elements of emergency management: hazard mitigation, enhanced preparedness, effective emergency response, and rapid recovery. Together, these elements will help create a Nation that understands the hazards and risks we face, is prepared for disasters, and can withstand and rapidly and effectively recover from the disruptions they cause.

Key Strategic Outcomes

- A standard for general community hazard mitigation is collaboratively developed and adopted by all communities.
- Individuals and families understand their responsibilities in the event of a community-disrupting event and have a plan to fulfill these responsibilities.
- Preparedness standards for life safety, law enforcement, mass evacuation and shelter-in-place, public health, mass care, and public works capabilities, including capacity levels for catastrophic incidents, have been developed and are used by all jurisdictions.
- Jurisdictions have agreements in place to participate in local, regional, and interstate mutual aid.
- All organizations with incident management responsibilities utilize the National Incident Management System, including the Incident Command System, on a routine basis and for all federally declared disasters and emergencies.

Goal 5.1: Mitigate Hazards. Strengthen capacity at all levels of society to withstand threats and hazards. Though the occurrence of some disasters is inevitable, it is possible to take steps to reduce the impact of damaging events that may occur. The Nation's ability to withstand threats and hazards requires an understanding of risks and robust efforts to reduce vulnerabilities. Mitigation provides a critical foundation to reduce loss of life and property by closing vulnerabilities and avoiding or lessening the impact of a disaster, thereby creating safer communities. Mitigation seeks to break out of the cycle of disaster damage, reconstruction, and repeated damage. Mitigating vulnerabilities reduces both the direct consequences and the response and recovery requirements of disasters.

Objectives:

- Improve individual and family capacity to reduce vulnerabilities and withstand disasters.
- Improve community capacity to withstand disasters by mitigating known and anticipated hazards.[15]

Goal 5.2: Enhance Preparedness. Engage all levels and segments of society in improving preparedness. Active participation by all segments of society in planning, training, organizing, and heightening awareness is an essential component of national preparedness. While efforts have traditionally focused on the preparedness of government and official first responders, individuals prepared to care for themselves and assist their neighbors in emergencies are important partners in community preparedness efforts. Because neighbor-to-neighbor assistance, when done safely, decreases the burden on first responders, individuals should be seen as force multipliers who may also offer specialized knowledge and skills.

Objectives:

- Ensure individual, family, and community planning, readiness, and capacity-building for disasters.
- Enhance and sustain nationwide disaster preparedness capabilities, to include life safety, law enforcement, mass evacuation and shelter-in-place, public health, mass care, and public works.[16]

Goal 5.3: Ensure Effective Emergency Response. Strengthen response capacity nationwide. Because it is impossible to eliminate all risks, a resilient Nation must have a robust capacity to respond when disaster strikes. Such response must be effective and efficient and grounded in the basic elements of incident management. When an incident occurs that is beyond local response capabilities, communities must be able to obtain assistance from neighboring jurisdictions and regional partners quickly, making a robust regional capacity vital to effective emergency response.

Objectives:

- Establish and strengthen pathways for clear, reliable, and current emergency information, including effective use of new media.
- Respond to disasters in an effective and unified manner.

- Improve governmental, nongovernmental, and private-sector delivery of disaster assistance.[17]

Goal 5.4: Rapidly Recover: Improve the Nation's ability to adapt and rapidly recover. Major disasters and catastrophic events produce changes in habitability, the environment, the economy, and even in geography that can often preclude a return to the way things were. We must anticipate such changes and develop appropriate tools, knowledge, and skills to adapt, improve sustainability, and maintain our way of life in the aftermath of disaster. Recent events have highlighted the challenges we face in dealing with disaster recovery. From sheltering and rehousing displaced survivors to reconstituting critical infrastructure and reestablishing the economic base of devastated areas, the challenges are profound. Individuals, businesses, nonprofit organizations, local, tribal, State, and Federal governments all have responsibilities in disaster recovery, underscoring the need to improve coordination and unity of effort.

Objectives:

- Establish and maintain nationwide capabilities for recovery from major disasters.
- Improve capabilities of families, communities, private-sector organizations, and all levels of government to sustain essential services and functions.[18]

Conclusion

The QHSR process (elaborated at Appendix B) and resulting report were designed to serve as a catalyst to spur the continued evolution and maturation of our Nation's homeland security enterprise—the diverse and distributed set of public and private actors from all corners of this Nation. Through this effort, we seek to foster a greater understanding of our shared responsibility and growing capability to protect ourselves from a range of threats and hazards.

In the years ahead, the world will be filled with breathtaking technological changes, social advances, and an accelerating flow of ideas, goods, and people around the world. These advancements and global interactions will enrich and improve our lives, but they may also be exploited by or may contribute to violent extremism, terrorist attacks, health threats, proliferation concerns, natural disasters, and cyber attacks—with many of these occurring, perhaps, at the same time.

The QHSR has set the stage for detailed analyses of homeland security capabilities and requirements across the homeland security enterprise. Stakeholders must now work to prioritize and identify the capabilities needed to achieve the goals, objectives, and outcomes identified in the QHSR, tie these requirements to resource allocation priorities, set performance criteria, and validate the allocation of roles and responsibilities.[19]

Questions

1. What is the purpose of the Quadrennial Homeland Security Review?
2. What is the most important mission area?
3. If DHS achieves all its goals and objectives, can the U.S. be declared "safe from terrorism"?
4. What are the hidden costs of pursuing this program?
5. What are the alternatives to this strategy?

Appendices

Appendix A

Glossary

AAR	After Action Report
ABA	American Banking Association
ACE	Automated Commercial Environment
ACTD	Advanced Concept Technology Demonstration
AEL	Authorized Equipment List
AES	Automated Export System
AFIS	Automated Fingerprint Identification System
APIS	Advance Passenger Information System
APR	Air Purifying Respirators
ASD(HD)	Assistant Secretary of Defense for Homeland Defense
ASU	Automated Scene Understanding
AT	Antiterrorism
ATC	Air Traffic Control Center
ATF	Bureau of Alcohol, Tobacco, and Firearms
ATM	Automatic Teller Machine
ATS	Automated Targeting System
ATSA	Aviation and Transportation Security Act
BTS	Border and Transportation Security
CA	Cooperative Agreement
CAPPS	Computer Assisted Passenger Prescreening System
CBIRF	Chemical-Biological Incident Response Force
CBP	U.S. Customs and Border Protection
CBRN	Chemical, Biological, Radiological, Nuclear, and Explosive
CB-RRT	Chemical and Biological Rapid Response Team
CBTB	Counter Measures Test Bed
CCTV	Closed Circuit Television
CDC	Centers for Disease Control and Prevention
CEC	Comprehensive Exercise Curriculum
CeCl	Cesium Chloride
CI/KR	Critical Infrastructure/Key Resources
CIA	Central Intelligence Agency
CII	Critical Infrastructure Information Act
COTS	Commercial-off-the-Shelf
CPX	Command Post Exercise

CREATE	Center for Risk and Economic Analysis of Terrorism Events
CSEPP	Chemical Stockpile Emergency Preparedness Program
CSG	Counterterrorism Security Group
CSI	Container Security Initiative
CSID	Centralized Scheduling and Information Desk
CSTARC	Cyber Security Tracking, Analysis, & Response Center
CT	Counterterrorism
CTC	Counterterrorist Center (CIA)
C-TPAT	Customs-Trade Partnership Against Terrorism
CWC	Chemical Weapons Convention
DC	Deputies Committee
DCI	Director of Central Intelligence
DFO	Disaster Field Office
DHHS	Department of Health and Human Services
DHS	Department of Homeland Security
DIA	Defense Intelligence Agency
DoD	Department of Defense
DoE	Department of Energy
DoI	Department of the Interior
DoJ	Department of Justice
DoS	Department of State
DoT	Department of Transportation
DPETAP	Domestic Preparedness Equipment Technical Assistance Program
DRO	Detention and Removal Operations
DSCA	Defense Support of Civil Authorities
EAS	Emergency Alert System
EBT	Electronic Benefits Transfer
ED	Education Department
EMP	Electromagnetic Pulse
EMS	Emergency Medical Service
EMT	Emergency Medical Team
EOC	Emergency Operations Center
EOP	Emergency Operating Procedure
EPA	Environmental Protection Agency

EPIC	Electronic Privacy Information Center
EPR	Emergency Preparedness and Response
EPW	Exercise Plan Workshop
ER	Emergency Room
ERT	Emergency Response Team
ERT-A	Emergency Response Team Advance Element
ESCAP	Electronic Crimes Special Agent Program
ESF	Emergency Support Function
ESFLG	Emergency Support Function Leaders Group
ESN	Electronic Serial Number
FAA	Federal Aviation Administration
FACA	Federal Advisory Committee Act
FAD	Foreign Animal Disease
FAMs	Federal Air Marshal Service
FAST	Free and Secure Trade
FBI	Federal Bureau of Investigation
FCD	Financial Crime Division (USSS)
FCO	Field Coordinating Officer
FDA	Food and Drug Administration
FE	Functional Exercise
FEMA	Federal Emergency Management Agency
FFRDC	Federally Funded Research and Development Center
FIF	Financial Institution Fraud
FISA	Foreign Intelligence Surveillance Act
FLETC	Federal Law Enforcement Training Center
FOC	FEMA Operations Center
FPS	Federal Protective Service
FRC	Federal Resource Coordinator
FSD	Forensic Services Division (USSS)
FSE	Full-Scale Exercise
FWPCA	Federal Water Pollution Control Act
FY	Fiscal Year
GAP	Grant Assistance Program
GIS	Geographic Information System

GSA	General Services Administration
HDER	Homeland Defense Equipment Reuse Program
HE	High Explosive
HEU	Highly Enriched Uranium
HR	House Resolution
HSARPA	Homeland Security Advanced Research Projects Agency
HSAS	Homeland Security Advisory System
HSC	Homeland Security Council
HSEEP	Homeland Security Exercise and Evaluation Program
HSGP	Homeland Security Grant Program
HSI	Homeland Security Institute
HSIN	Homeland Security Information Network
HSOC	Homeland Security Operations Center
HSPD	Homeland Security Presidential Directive
HSSTAC	Homeland Security Science and Technology Advisory Committee
HUD	Housing and Urban Development
IAB	Interagency Board
IAIP	Information Analysis and Infrastructure Protection
IBET	Integrated Border Enforcement Teams
ICE	U.S. Immigration and Customs Enforcement
ICP	Incident Command Post
ICS	Incident Command Structure
ICTAP	Interoperable Communication Technical Assistance Program
IDLH	Immediately Dangerous to Life or Health
IED	Improvised Explosive Device
IEEE	Institute of Electrical and Electronics Engineers
IEMS	Integrated Emergency Management System
IIMG	Interagency Incident Management Group
INA	Immigration and Nationality Act
IND	Improvised Nuclear Device
INS	Immigration and Naturalization Service
IOC	ICE Operations Center
IOM	Institute of Medicine
IP	Improvement Plan

ISIS	Integrated Surveillance Intelligence System
ISP	Internet Service Provider
JFO	Joint Field Office
JOC	Joint Operations Center
JTF	Joint Task Force
JTF-CS	Joint Task Force – Civil Support
JTTF	Joint Terrorism Task Force
LFA	Lead Federal Agent
LLIS	Lessons Learned Information Sharing
LNG	Liquefied Natural Gas
LVB	Large Vehicle Bomb
MACA	Military Assistance to Civil Authorities
MACC	Multiagency Command Center
MANPADS	Man-Portable Air Defense System
MEPP	Master Exercise Practitioner Program
MIN	Mobile Identification Number
MIPT	National Memorial Institute for Prevention of Terrorism
MMA	Major Metropolitan Area
MMRS	Metropolitan Medical Response System
MMS	Minerals Management Service (DOI)
MOU	Memorandum of Understanding
MSHA	Mine Safety & Health Administration
NAS	National Academy of Science
NATO	North Atlantic Treaty Organization
NAWAS	National Warning System
NCP	National Oil and Hazardous Substances Pollution Contingency Plan
NCSD	National Cyber Security Division
NDMS	National Disaster Medical System
NEADS	North East Air Defense Sector
NEP	National Exercise Program
NETC	National Emergency Training Center
NFOP	National Fugitive Operations Program
NFPA	National Fire Protection Association
NGA	National Geospatial-intelligence Agency

NGO Nongovernmental Organization

NHSA National Homeland Security Agency

NHSD National Homeland Security Department

NIC National Incident Commander

NII Non-Intrusive Inspection

NIJ National Institute of Justice

NIMS National Incident Management System

NIMS National Incident Management System

NIOSH National Institute for Occupational Safety and Health

NIST National Institute of Standards and Technology

NITSEEP National Intermodal Transportation Security Exercise and Evaluation Program

NJTTF National Joint Terrorism Task Force

NOA Notice of Arrival

NORAD North American Aerospace Defense Command

NORTHCOM Northern Command

NPSTC National Public Safety Telecommunications Council

NRC National Response Center

NRCC National Response Coordination Center

NRO National Reconnaissance Office

NRP National Response Plan

NSA National Security Agency

NSC National Security Council

NSDD National Security Decision Directive

NSSE National Special Security Event

NTC National Training Center

NYPO New York Project Office

OC Office of the Comptroller

ODP Office of Domestic Preparedness

OHS Office of Homeland Security

OIG Office of the Inspector General

OJP Office of Justice Program

OMB Office of Management and Budget

ONDCP Office of National Drug Control Policy

OPM Office of Personnel Management

ORD	Office of Research & Development
OSHA	Occupational Safety & Health Administration
OSLC	Office of State and Local Coordination
OSLGCP	Office of State and Local Government Coordination and Preparedness
OSTP	Office of Science and Technology Policy
PANYNJ	Port Authority of New York and New Jersey
PC	Principals Committee
PCB	Polychlorinated Biphenyl
PCC	Policy Coordinating Committee
PCII	Protected Critical Infrastructure Information
PDA	Preliminary Damage Assessment
PDD	Presidential Decision Directive
PEP	Propositioned Equipment Program
PFO	Principal Coordinating Officer
PIN	Personal Identification Number
PL	Public Law
PLO	Palestinian Liberation Organization
POC	Point of Contact
PPA	Performance Partnership Agreement
PPB	Programs, Plans, & Budgets
PPE	Personal Protective Equipment
PRD	Personal Radiation Detector
PREP	National Preparedness for Response Exercise (USCG)
QATT	Qualified Anti-Terrorism Technology
R&D	Research & Development
RADTEC	Radiation Detector Testing and Evaluation Center
RAMP	Remedial Action Management Program
RAT	Rapid Assistance Team
RDD	Radiological Dispersal Device
RDD	Radiological Dispersal Devices
RDT&E	Research, Development, Test, and Evaluation
REP	Radiological Emergency Preparedness
RICO	Racketeer Influenced and Corrupt Organizations Act
RISC	Regional Interagency Steering Committee

RPG	Rocket Propelled Grenade
RRCC	Regional Response Coordination Center
RSPA	Research and Special Programs Administration
RTI	Regional Technology Integration
RVSS	Remote Video Surveillance Systems (RVSS)
S&T	Science and Technology
SAA	State Administrative Agency
SAC	Special Agent-in-Charge
SAFETY	Support Anti-Terrorism by Fostering Effective Technologies Act
SAR	Suspicious Activity Report
SAR	Supplied Air Respirator
SB	Senate Bill
SBA	Small Business Administration
SBU	Sensitive-but-Unclassified
SCBA	Self-Contained Breathing Apparatus
SCIP	Statewide Communications Interoperability Planning
SCO	State Coordinating Officer
SCUBA	Self-Contained Underwater Breathing Apparatus
SDPP	State Domestic Preparedness Program
SEAL	Sea-Air-Land (Navy special forces)
SED	Systems Engineering and Development
SEL	Standard Equipment List
SENTRI	Secure Electronic Network for Travelers' Rapid Inspection
SEVIS	Student and Exchange Visitor System
SFLEO	Senior Federal Law Enforcement Official
SHSEEP	State Homeland Security Exercise and Evaluation Program
SHSGP	State Homeland Security Grant Programs
SIMCELL	Simulation Cell
SIOC	Strategic Information Operations Center (FBI)
SNS	Strategic National Stockpile
SOE	Senior Official Exercise
SONS	Spill of National Significance (USCG)
SOP	Standard Operating Procedure
SoR	Statement of Requirements

SPC	Special Processing Center
SUA	Special Unlawful Activities
TIC	Toxic Industrial Chemical
TOPOFF	Top Officials (exercise)
TRIA	Terrorism Risk Insurance Act
TSA	Transportation Security Administration
TSC	Terrorist Screening Center
TSWG	Technical Support Working Group
TTIC	Terrorist Threat Integration Center
TTX	Tabletop Exercise
UA	Universal Adversary
UASI	Urban Area Security Initiative
UAV	Unmanned Aerial Vehicle
UAWG	Urban Area Working Group
UC	Unified Command
UN	United Nations
USACE	United States Army Corps of Engineers
USC	United States Code
USCG	United States Coast Guard
USCIS	U.S. Citizenship and Immigration Services
USD(I)	Under Secretary of Defense for Intelligence
USDA	United States Department of Agriculture
USSS	United States Secret Service
US-VISIT	U.S. Visitor and Immigrant Status Indication Technology
WAWAS	Washington Area Warning System
WMD	Weapons of Mass Destruction

Appendix B

Bibliography

Chapter 1: 9-11 Survivors

1. Elsis, Mark R. (2005) "911 Timeline". Retrieved June 2, 2005 from http://www.911.timeline.net/.
2. Trevor, Greg. (2005) "A Race to Safety". Retrieved June 2, 2005 from http://www.coping.org/911/survivor/race.htm.
3. Mayblum, Adam. (2005) "The Price We Pay: A Survivor's Story". Retrieved June 2, 2005 from http://www.coping.org/911/survivor/price.htm.
4. Zoroya, Gregg. (2002) "The Griffiths". USATODAY.com. Retrieved June 2, 2005 from http://www.usatoday.com/lief/sept11/2002-09-10-survivor-griffiths_x.htm.
5. LaTorre, Cara. (2002) "Survivor: 'We didn't know what to do'". USATODAY.com. Retrieved June 2, 2005 from http://www.usatoday.com/news/sept11/2002-09-10-first-person-latorre_x.htm.
6. Barg, Jaede. (2002) "Survivor: 'The world has changed for us indeed'". USATODAY.com. Retrieved June 2, 2005 from http://www.usatoday.com/news/sept11/2002-09-09-first-person-barg_x.htm.
7. Borgo, Phyllis. (2002) "World Trade Center: First-person account". Retrieved June 2, 2005 from http://www.usatoday.com/news/sept11/2002-09-06-first-person-borgo_x.htm.
8. McLaughlin, Sean. (2002) "NY firefighters discuss 9/11 experience." *The Heights News*. September 10, 2002. Retrieved June 2, 2005 from http://www.bcheights.com/global_user_elements/printpage.cfm?storyid=268941.
9. Trevor, Greg. (2005) "A Race to Safety". Retrieved June 2, 2005 from http://www.coping.org/911/survivor/race.htm.
10. Mayblum, Adam. (2005) "The Price We Pay: A Survivor's Story". Retrieved June 2, 2005 from http://www.coping.org/911/survivor/price.htm.
11. Mayblum, Adam. (2005) "The Price We Pay: A Survivor's Story". Retrieved June 2, 2005 from http://www.coping.org/911/survivor/price.htm.
12. Trevor, Greg. (2005) "A Race to Safety". Retrieved June 2, 2005 from http://www.coping.org/911/survivor/race.htm.
13. Zoroya, Gregg. (2002) "The Griffiths". USATODAY.com. Retrieved June 2, 2005 from http://www.usatoday.com/lief/sept11/2002-09-10-survivor-griffiths_x.htm.
14. Borgo, Phyllis. (2002) "World Trade Center: First-person account". Retrieved June 2, 2005 from http://www.usatoday.com/news/sept11/2002-09-06-first-person-borgo_x.htm.
15. Barg, Jaede. (2002) "Survivor: 'The world has changed for us indeed'". USATODAY.com. Retrieved June 2, 2005 from http://www.usatoday.com/news/sept11/2002-09-09-first-person-barg_x.htm.
16. Barg, Jaede. (2002) "Survivor: 'The world has changed for us indeed'". USATODAY.com. Retrieved June 2, 2005 from http://www.usatoday.com/news/sept11/2002-09-09-first-person-barg_x.htm.
17. McLaughlin, Sean. (2002) "NY firefighters discuss 9/11 experience." *The Heights News*. September 10, 2002. Retrieved June 2, 2005 from http://www.bcheights.com/global_user_elements/printpage.cfm?storyid=268941.
18. Mayblum, Adam. (2005) "The Price We Pay: A Survivor's Story". Retrieved June 2, 2005 from http://www.coping.org/911/survivor/price.htm.
19. Barg, Jaede. (2002) "Survivor: 'The world has changed for us indeed'". USATODAY.com. Retrieved June 2, 2005 from http://www.usatoday.com/news/sept11/2002-09-09-first-person-barg_x.htm.
20. McLaughlin, Sean. (2002) "NY firefighters discuss 9/11 experience." *The Heights News*. September 10, 2002. Retrieved June 2, 2005 from http://www.bcheights.com/global_user_elements/printpage.cfm?storyid=268941.
21. Elsis, Mark R. (2005) "911 Timeline". Retrieved June 2, 2005 from http://www.911.timeline.net/.
22. LaTorre, Cara. (2002) "Survivor: 'We didn't know what to do'". USATODAY.com. Retrieved June 2, 2005 from http://www.usatoday.com/news/sept11/2002-09-10-first-person-latorre_x.htm.
23. Borgo, Phyllis. (2002) "World Trade Center: First-person account". Retrieved June 2, 2005 from http://www.usatoday.com/news/sept11/2002-09-06-first-person-borgo_x.htm.
24. Barg, Jaede. (2002) "Survivor: 'The world has changed for us indeed'". USATODAY.com. Retrieved June 2, 2005 from http://www.usatoday.com/news/sept11/2002-09-09-first-person-barg_x.htm.
25. LaTorre, Cara. (2002) "Survivor: 'We didn't know what to do'". USATODAY.com. Retrieved June 2, 2005 from http://www.usatoday.com/news/sept11/2002-09-10-first-person-latorre_x.htm.
26. McLaughlin, Sean. (2002) "NY firefighters discuss 9/11 experience." *The Heights News*. September 10, 2002. Retrieved June 2, 2005 from http://www.bcheights.com/global_user_elements/printpage.cfm?storyid=268941.
27. Trevor, Greg. (2005) "A Race to Safety". Retrieved June 2, 2005 from http://www.coping.org/911/survivor/race.htm.

28. Mayblum, Adam. (2005) "The Price We Pay: A Survivor's Story". Retrieved June 2, 2005 from http://www.coping.org/911/survivor/price.htm.

29. Borgo, Phyllis. (2002) "World Trade Center: First-person account". Retrieved June 2, 2005 from http://www.usatoday.com/news/sept11/2002-09-06-first-person-borgo_x.htm.

30. Elsis, Mark R. (2005) "911 Timeline". Retrieved June 2, 2005 from http://www.911.timeline.net/.

31. Morin, Terry. (2001) "Eyewitness Account of Pentagon Attack." Retrieved June 2, 2005 from http://www.coping.org/911/survivor/pentagon.htm.

32. LaTorre, Cara. (2002) "Survivor: 'We didn't know what to do'". USATODAY.com. Retrieved June 2, 2005 from http://www.usatoday.com/news/sept11/2002-09-10-first-person-latorre_x.htm.

33. Barg, Jaede. (2002) "Survivor: 'The world has changed for us indeed'". USATODAY.com. Retrieved June 2, 2005 from http://www.usatoday.com/news/sept11/2002-09-09-first-person-barg_x.htm.

34. Ibid

35. Ibid

36. Elsis, Mark R. (2005) "911 Timeline". Retrieved June 2, 2005 from http://www.911.timeline.net/.

37. McLaughlin, Sean. (2002) "NY firefighters discuss 9/11 experience." *The Heights News*. September 10, 2002. Retrieved June 2, 2005 from http://www.bcheights.com/global_user_elements/printpage.cfm?storyid=268941.

38. Borgo, Phyllis. (2002) "World Trade Center: First-person account". Retrieved June 2, 2005 from http://www.usatoday.com/news/sept11/2002-09-06-first-person-borgo_x.htm.

39. Trevor, Greg. (2005) "A Race to Safety". Retrieved June 2, 2005 from http://www.coping.org/911/survivor/race.htm.

40. Ibid

41. Mayblum, Adam. (2005) "The Price We Pay: A Survivor's Story". Retrieved June 2, 2005 from http://www.coping.org/911/survivor/price.htm.

42. Ibid

43. McLaughlin, Sean. (2002) "NY firefighters discuss 9/11 experience." *The Heights News*. September 10, 2002. Retrieved June 2, 2005 from http://www.bcheights.com/global_user_elements/printpage.cfm?storyid=268941.

44. Ibid

45. Ibid

46. Ibid

47. Zoroya, Gregg. (2002) "The Griffiths". USATODAY.com. Retrieved June 2, 2005 from http://www.usatoday.com/lief/sept11/2002-09-10-survivor-griffiths_x.htm.

48. Overberg, Paul. (2002) "Final Sept. 11 death toll remains elusive". USATODAY.com. Retrieved June 2, 2005 from http://www.usatoday.com/news/sept11/2002-08-22-death-toll_x.htm.

Chapter 2: 9-11 Attacks

1. The National Commission on Terrorist Attacks Upon the United States (2004) "The 9/11 Commission Report", pp 1-14. July 22, 2004.

2. The National Commission on Terrorist Attacks Upon the United States (2004) "The 9/11 Commission Report", pp 2. July 22, 2004.

Chapter 3: 9-11 Analysis

1. The 9/11 Commission Report. (2004) "Executive Summary", pp 1-16.

Chapter 4: Terrorist Threat

1. Wikipedia.Org. (2004) "United States Department of Homeland Security". Retrieved October 23, 2004 from http://en.wikipedia.org/wiki/Department_of_Homeland_Security.

2. TerrorismFiles.Org. (2004) "Definition of Terrorism". Retrieved October 18, 2004, from http://www.terrorismfiles.org/encyclopedia/terrorism.html.

3. Roberts, Adam (2004) "The Changing Face of Terrorism". Retrieved October 29, 2004, from http://www.bbc.co.uk/history.

4. Federal Bureau of Investigation (1998) "Terrorism in the United States." 1998.

5. Roberts, Adam (2004) "The Changing Face of Terrorism". Retrieved October 29, 2004, from http://www.bbc.co.uk/history.

6. Brake, Jeffrey D. (2001) "Terrorism and the Military's Role in Domestic Crisis Management: Background and Issues for Congress". April 19, 2001.

7. United States Congress (1995) "Testimony of Acting DCI William O. Studeman, Omnibus Counterterrorism Act of 1995". April 6, 1995.

8. Federal Bureau of Investigation (1998) "Terrorism in the United States." 1998.

9. Wikipedia.Org. (2004) "Oklahoma City Bombing". Retrieved October 23, 2004 from http://en.wikipedia.org/wiki/Oklahoma_City_bombing.

10. Brake, Jeffrey D. (2001) "Terrorism and the Military's Role in Domestic Crisis Management: Background and Issues for Congress". April 19, 2001.

11. The National Commission on Terrorist Attacks Upon the United States (2004) "The 9/11 Commission Report". July 22, 2004.

12. Brake, Jeffrey D. (2001) "Terrorism and the Military's Role in Domestic Crisis Management: Background and Issues for Congress". April 19, 2001.

13. Brake, Jeffrey D. (2001) "Terrorism and the Military's Role in Domestic Crisis Management: Background and Issues for Congress". April 19, 2001.

14. Bhatt and Silber (2007) "Radicalization in the West: The Homegrown Threat", NYPD Intelligence Division, pg. 2.

15. Bhatt and Silber (2007) "Radicalization in the West: The Homegrown Threat", NYPD Intelligence Division, pg. 16.

16. Bhatt and Silber (2007) "Radicalization in the West: The Homegrown Threat", NYPD Intelligence Division, pg. 2.

17. Bhatt and Silber (2007) "Radicalization in the West: The Homegrown Threat", NYPD Intelligence Division, pg. 5.

18. Brake, Jeffrey D. (2001) "Terrorism and the Military's Role in Domestic Crisis Management: Background and Issues for Congress". April 19, 2001.

Chapter 5: Islamic Extremism

1. The National Commission on Terrorist Attacks Upon the United States (2004) "The 9/11 Commission Report", pp 47-54. July 22, 2004.

Chapter 6: Catastrophic Terrorism

1. Advisory Panel to Assess Domestic Response Capabilities For Terrorism Involving Weapons of Mass Destruction (1999) "Assessing the Threat". December 15, 1999.

2. Wikipedia.Org (2004) "Weapons of Mass Destruction". Retrieved November 6, 2004 from http://en.wikipedia.org/wiki/Weapons_of_mass_destruction.

3. NTI.Org (2004) "Definitions of WMD". Retrieved November 6, 2004 from http://www.nti.org/f_wmd411/flal.html.

4. Advisory Panel to Assess Domestic Response Capabilities For Terrorism Involving Weapons of Mass Destruction (1999) "Assessing the Threat". December 15, 1999.

5. Siegrist, David W. (2004) "The Threat of Biological Attack: Why Concern Now?". Retrieved November 6, 2004 from http://www.cdc.gov/ncidod/EID/vol5no4/siegrist.htm.

6. Porteus, Liza (2003) "Weapons of Mass Destruction Handbook". July 8, 2003.

7. Siegrist, David W. (2004) "The Threat of Biological Attack: Why Concern Now?". Retrieved November 6, 2004 from http://www.cdc.gov/ncidod/EID/vol5no4/siegrist.htm.

8. Wikipedia.Org (2004) "Chemical Warfare". Retrieved November 6, 2004 from http://en.wikipedia.org/wiki/Chemical_warfare.

9. Porteus, Liza (2003) "Weapons of Mass Destruction Handbook". July 8, 2003.

10. Porteus, Liza (2003) "Weapons of Mass Destruction Handbook". July 8, 2003.

11. Wikipedia.Org (2004) "Sarin Gas Attack on the Tokyo Subway". Retrieved November 7, 2004 from http://en.wikipedia.org/wiki/Sarin_gas_attack_on_the_Tokyo_subway.

12. Porteus, Liza (2003) "Weapons of Mass Destruction Handbook". July 8, 2003.

13. Carson Mark, Theodore Taylor, Eugene Eyster, William Maraman, Jacob Weschler (2004) "Can Terrorists Build Nuclear Weapons?". Retrieved November 1, 2004 from http://www.nci.org/k-m/makeab.htm.

14. Matthew Bunn, George Bunn (2001) "Reducing the Threat of Nuclear Theft and Sabotage", Conference Proceedings, Symposium on International Safeguards: Verification and Nuclear Material Security, Vienna, Austria, October 29—November 2, 2001.

15. Porteus, Liza (2003) "Weapons of Mass Destruction Handbook". July 8, 2003.

16. Senate Committee on Foreign Relations (2002) "Testimony of Dr. Henry Kelly, President of Federation of American Scientists". March 6, 2002.

17. Capricorn.Org (2004) "The Terrorist's Handbook". Retrieved November 8, 2004 from http://www.capricorn.org/~akira/home/terror.html.

18. International Society of Explosives Engineers (2003) "Securing Explosives, A Prime Responsibility of Industry". September 16, 2003.

19. Capricorn.Org (2004) "The Terrorist's Handbook". Retrieved November 8, 2004 from http://www.capricorn.org/~akira/home/terror.html.

20. Wikipedia.Org. (2004) "Oklahoma City Bombing". Retrieved October 23, 2004 from http://en.wikipedia.org/wiki/Oklahoma_City_bombing.

21. Bush, George W. (2002) "National Strategy for Homeland Security". July 2002.

Chapter 7: Natural Disasters

1. United States Senate (2006) "Hurricane Katrina: A Nation Still Unprepared." Report of the Senate Committee on Homeland Security and Governmental Affairs." May 2006. pg. 2.
2. Ibid. pp. 3-4.
3. Ibid. pp. 4-5.
4. Ibid. pp. 5-8.
5. Ibid. pp. 8-18.
6. Ibid. pg. 2.

Chapter 8: U.S. National Security

1. Chairman of the Joint Chiefs of Staff (2000). *Joint Publication 1, Joint Warfare of the Armed Forces of the United States*. November 14, 2000, p. I-1.
2. Kaiser, Frederick M. (2003). "American National Government: An Overview." Library of Congress Congressional Research Service Report for Congress, updated May 20, 2003, p. CRS-1.
3. Ibid., CRS-2.
4. Ibid., CRS-2.
5. Chairman of the Joint Chiefs of Staff (2001). *Joint Publication 0-2, Unified Action Armed Forces (UNAAF).* July 10, 2001, p. I-1.
6. Chairman of the Joint Chiefs of Staff (2001). *Joint Publication 0-2, Unified Action Armed Forces (UNAAF).* July 10, 2001, pp. I-2 – I-3.
7. White, Richard L. (2005). "Framework for Military Power," Chapter 3 in *United States Military Power*. FastPlanet Technologies, 2005, p. 19.
8. Chairman of the Joint Chiefs of Staff (2000). *Joint Publication 1: Joint Warfare of the Armed Forces of the United States*. November 14, 2000, pp. I-6 – I-7.
9. Chairman of the Joint Chiefs of Staff (2001). *Joint Publication 0-2, Unified Action Armed Forces (UNAAF).* July 10, 2001, p. II-1.
10. Chairman of the Joint Chiefs of Staff (2000). *Joint Publication 1: Joint Warfare of the Armed Forces of the United States*. November 14, 2000, pp. I-7.
11. Ibid., I-7.
12. White, Richard L. (2005). "Framework for Military Power," Chapter 3 in *United States Military Power*. FastPlanet Technologies, 2005, p. 19.
13. US Department of State (1997). "History of the National Security Council, 1947 – 1997." Office of the Historian Bureau of Public Affairs, August 1997.
14. Elsea, Jennifer K. (2006). "Declarations of War and Authorizations for the Use of Military Force: Historical Background and Legal Implications." Library of Congress Congressional Research Service Report for Congress, updated August 11, 2006, p. CRS-1.
15. Ibid., CRS-1 – CRS-4.
16. Ibid., CRS-6.
17. Ibid., CRS-22 – CRS-28.
18. Ibid., CRS-16 – CRS-18.
19. Perl, Raphael (2006). "Terrorism and National Security: Issues and Trends." Library of Congress Congressional Research Service Report for Congress, updated February 2, 2006, pp. CRS-5 – CRS-6.
20. Elsea, Jennifer (2001). "Terrorism and the Law of War: Trying Terrorists as War Criminals before Military Commissions." Library of Congress Congressional Research Service Report for Congress, updated December 11, 2001, pp. CRS-10 – CRS-11.
21. Ibid., CRS-1 – CRS-2.
22. Ibid., CRS-1 – CRS-2.
23. Ibid., CRS-10.

Chapter 9: Combating Terrorism

1. The National Commission on Terrorist Attacks Upon the United States (2004) "The 9/11 Commission Report", July 22, 2004.
2. Perl, Raphael F. (2001) "Terrorism, the Future, and U.S. Foreign Policy", CRS Issue Brief for Congress, Congressional Research Service, The Library of Congress. September 13, 2001.
3. Brake, Jeffrey D. (2001) "Terrorism and the Military's Role in Domestic Crisis Management: Background and Issues for Congress". April 19, 2001.
4. The United States Congress (2002) "The Homeland Security Act of 2002". November 25, 2002.
5. Perl, Raphael F. (2001) "Terrorism, the Future, and U.S. Foreign Policy", CRS Issue Brief for Congress, Congressional Research Service, The Library of Congress. September 13, 2001.
6. The White House (2001) Executive Order 13228 "Establishing the Office of Homeland Security and the Homeland Security Council". October 8, 2001.
7. Perro, Catherine M., Lt. Col., USAF (2004) "The Homeland Security Council—The Best Structure for the President?". National Defense University, National War College. 2004.
8. The White House (2001) Executive Order 13228 "Establishing the Office of Homeland Security and the Homeland Security Council". October 8, 2001.
9. Bush, George W. (2003) "National Strategy for Combating Terrorism". February 2003.
10. National Strategy for Combating Terrorism, September 2006. pg. 1.
11. Ibid., pg. 23.

12. Bush, George W. (2003) "National Strategy for Combating Terrorism". February 2003.

Chapter 10: DHS Origins

1. Wikipedia.Org. (2004) "United States Department of Homeland Security". Retrieved October 23, 2004 from http://en.wikipedia.org/wiki/Department_of_Homeland_Security.
2. United States General Accounting Office (2001) "Combating Terrorism, Selected Challenges and Related Recommendations". September 20, 2001.
3. The White House (1982) "Managing Terrorist Incidents", National Security Decision Directive 30. April 10, 1982.
4. Brake, Jeffrey D. (2001) "Terrorism and the Military's Role in Domestic Crisis Management: Background and Issues for Congress". April 19, 2001.
5. United States General Accounting Office (2001) "Combating Terrorism, Selected Challenges and Related Recommendations". September 20, 2001.
6. National Commission on Terrorism (2000) "Countering the Changing Threat of International Terrorism". June 7, 2000.
7. Panel to Assess Domestic Response Capabilities for Terrorism Involving Weapons of Mass Destruction (2000) "II. Toward a National Strategy for Combating Terrorism". December 15, 2000.
8. The United States Commission on National Security/21st Century (2001) Phase III Report "Road Map for National Security: Imperative for Change". February 15, 2001.
9. United States General Accounting Office (2001) "Combating Terrorism, Selected Challenges and Related Recommendations". September 20, 2001.
10. Scardaville, Michael (2002) "Principles for Creating an Effective U.S. Department of Homeland Security", The Heritage Foundation Backgrounder. June 12, 2002.
11. Kirk, Robert S. (2002) "Department of Homeland Security: Should the Transportation Security Administration be Included?" Congressional Research Staff Report to Congress. July 24, 2002.
12. Thomas.Loc.Gov (2004) "Bill Summary and Status", H.R. 5005. Retrieved December 4, 2004 from http://Thomas.loc.gov/cgi-bin/bdquery/z?d107:HR05005.
13. Wikipedia.Org. (2004) "United States Department of Homeland Security". Retrieved October 23, 2004 from http://en.wikipedia.org/wiki/Department_of_Homeland_Security.
14. ArmsControlCenter.Org (2004) "DoHS Countdown: Play-by-Play Archive". Retrieved December 4, 2004 from http://www.armscontrolcenter.org/terrorism/playbyplay/archive.html.

Ch. 11: National Strategy for Homeland Security

1. Bush, George W. (2002) "National Strategy for Homeland Security". July 2002.
2. Homeland Security Council (2007) "National Strategy for Homeland Security", October 2007. pp. 5-7.
3. Homeland Security Council (2007) "National Strategy for Homeland Security", October 2007. pg. 1.

Chapter 12: DHS Organization

1. Department of Homeland Security (2004). "Performance and Accountability Report, Fiscal Year 2003."
2. Department of Homeland Security (2010). Retrieved from http://www.dhs.gov/xabout/responsibilities.shtm/ on June 7, 2010.
3. Department of Homeland Security (2008). Brief Documentary History of the Department of Homeland Security 2001-2008.
4. Best, Richard (2009) "The National Security Council: An Organizational Assessment." Congressional Research Service Report for Congress. June 8, 2009. pp. 23-24.
5. Department of Homeland Security (2008). Brief Documentary History of the Department of Homeland Security 2001-2008..
6. Halchin, L. Elaine (2004). Location of Federal Government Offices, Congressional Research Staff Report to Congress, July 14, 2004.
7. Department of Homeland Security (2004). Performance an Accountability Report, Fiscal Year 2003.
8. Hogue, Henry B. (2006) "Federal Emergency Management and Homeland Security Organization: Historical Developments and Legislative Options." Congressional Research Service Report for Congress. Upated June 1, 2006. pg. CRS-1.
9. Ibid. pp. CRS-20 - CRS-21.
10. Ibid. pp. CRS-22 - CRS-25.
11. Department of Homeland Security (2008). Brief Documentary History of the Department of Homeland Security 2001-2008.
12. Department of Homeland Security (2010). Retrieved from http://www.dhs.gov/xabout/structure/ on June 7, 2010.

13. Department of Homeland Security Subcomponents and Agencies. Retrieved from http://www.dhs.gov/xabout/structure/, June 7, 2010.

14. Office of the Press Secretary (2002). President to Propose Department of Homeland Security. June 6, 2002.

Chapter 13: Intelligence & Warning

1. Best, Richard A., Jr. (2003) "Homeland Security: Intelligence Support", Congressional Research Staff Report for Congress. May 14, 2003.

2. Randol, Mark A. (2009) "The Department of Homeland Security Intelligence Enterprise: Operational Overview and Oversight Challenges for Congress", Congressional Research Staff Report for Congress. May 27, 2009. pp. 1-3.

3. Ibid. pp. 7-9.

4. Ibid. pp. 4-5.

5. Ibid. pp. 5-6.

6. Ibid. pp. 9-11.

7. Ibid. pp. 11-12.

8. Reese, Shawn (2008) "Homeland Security Advisory System: Possible Issues for Congressional Oversight. Congressional Research Service Report to Congress. January 29, 2008. Summary.

9. The White House (2002). "Gov. Ridge Announces Homeland Security Advisory System", White House Press Release. March 12, 2002.

10. Reese, Shawn (2008) "Homeland Security Advisory System: Possible Issues for Congressional Oversight. Congressional Research Service Report to Congress. January 29, 2008. pg. CRS-1.

11. Ibid. Summary.

12. Ibid. pg. CRS-5.

13. Ibid. pg. CRS-7.

14. Ibid. pg. CRS-9.

15. Ibid. pp. CRS-10 - CRS-11.

16. Ibid. pg. CRS-13.

17. Homeland Security Advisory Council (2009) "Homeland Security Advisory System Task Force Report and Recommendations". September 2009. pg. 1.

18. Ibid. pg. 2.

19. Best, Richard A. Jr. (2010) "The National Counterterrorism Center (NCTC) - Responsibilities and Potential Congressional Concerns". Congressional Research Service Report for Congress. January 15, 2010. pp. 2-4.

20. Ibid. pp. 6-7.

21. Ibid. pp. 7-9.

22. James D. Torr. "Introduction." At Issue: Homeland Security. Ed. James D. Torr. San Diego: Greenhaven Press, 2003. August 2004. 6 June 2010. <http://www.enotes.com/homeland-security-article/39554>.

23. Best, Richard A., Jr. (2003) "Homeland Security: Intelligence Support", Congressional Research Staff Report for Congress. May 14, 2003.

Ch. 14: Border & Transportation Security

1. Haddal, C.C. (2010). CRS R41237: People Crossing Borders: An Analysis of U.S. Border Protection Policies. May 13, 2010, p 1.

2. Department of Homeland Security (2010). Quadrennial Homeland Security Review Report: A Strategic Framework for a Secure Nation. February, 2010, p 24.

3. Lake, J. E., Robinson, W. H., & Seghetti, L. M. (2005). CRS Report RL32839: Border and Transportation Security: The Complexity of the Challenge. March 29, 2005, p 1.

4. Department of Homeland Security (2005). Securing Our Borders. Retrieved April 20, 2005 from http://www.dhs.gov/dhspublic/display?theme=50&content=875&print=true.

5. Department of Homeland Security Subcomponents and Agencies. Retrieved June 7, 2010 from http://www.dhs.gov/xabout/structure/.

6. Haddal, C. C. (2010). CRS Report RS21899, Border Security: Key Agencies and Their Missions. January 26, 2010.

7. Ibid.

8. Randol, M. (2010). CRS R40602. The Department of Homeland Security Intelligence Enterprise: Operational Overview and Oversight Challenges for Congress. March 19, 2010

9. Department of Homeland Security (2009). Budget in Brief, Fiscal Year 2009, pp41.

10. U.S. Immigrations and Customs Enforcement Fact Sheet, FY 2010, Retrieved June 12, 2010 from http://www.ice.gov/pi/news/factsheets/index.htm.

11. U.S. Immigrations and Customs Enforcement, Border Security and Immigration Enforcement Fact Sheet, at http://www.ice.gov/graphics/news/factsheets/061704det_FS.htm.

12. U.S. Immigrations and Customs Enforcement, Office of Investigations Fact Sheet, http://www.ice.gov/graphics/news/factsheets/investigation_FS.htm.

13. U.S. Immigrations and Customs Enforcement Organization, at http://www.ice.gov/graphics/about/organization/index.htm.

14. U.S. Immigrations and Customs Enforcement, Office of Intelligence Organization, at http://www.ice.gov/graphics/about/organization/org_intell.htm.

15. U.S. Immigration and Customs Enforcement, at http://www.ice.gov/about/index.htm

16. Haddal, C. C. (2010). CRS Report RS21899, Border Security: Key Agencies and Their Missions. January 26, 2010.

17. Lake, J. E. (2010). CRS IS40280: Issue Statement on Border Security. January 12, 2010.

18. Haddal, C. C. (2010). CRS R41237: People Crossing Borders: An Analysis of U.S. Border Protection Policies. May 13, 2010.

19. Department of Homeland Security (2010). Quadrennial Homeland Security Review Report: A Strategic Framework for a Secure Homeland. February, 2010, p 24.

Chapter 15: Domestic Counterterrorism

1. The National Commission on Terrorist Attacks Upon the United States (2004) "The 9/11 Commission Report", July 22, 2004. pp 153-272.

2. Bush, George W. (2002) "National Strategy for Homeland Security". July 2002. pp. 26-27.

3. Cumming, Alfred (2004) "FBI Intelligence Reform Since September 11, 2001: Issues and Options for Congress." Congressional Research Service Report for Congress, August 4, 2004. Summary.

4. Doyle Charles (2002) "The USA PATRIOT Act: A Sketch", Congressional Research Staff Report for Congress. April 15, 2002.

5. Cumming, Alfred (2004) "FBI Intelligence Reform Since September 11, 2001: Issues and Options for Congress." Congressional Research Service Report for Congress, August 4, 2004. pg. CRS-46.

Chapter 16: Critical Infrastructure Protection

1. United States Government Accountability Office (2010) "Critical Infrastructure Protection: Update to National Infrastructure Protection Plan Includes Increased Emphasis on Risk Management and Resilience." March 2010. pg. 1.

2. Bush, George W. (2002) "National Strategy for Homeland security". July 2002. pp. 29-30.

3. Department of Homeland Security (2009) "National Infrastructure Protection Plan: Partnering to enhance protection and resiliency." pg. 110.

4. United States Government Accountability Office (2010) "Critical Infrastructure Protection: Update to National Infrastructure Protection Plan Includes Increased Emphasis on Risk Management and Resilience." March 2010. pp. 1-4.

5. Ibid. pg. 7.

6. Department of Homeland Security (2009) "National Infrastructure Protection Plan: Partnering to enhance protection and resiliency." pg. 2.

7. United States Government Accountability Office (2010) "Critical Infrastructure Protection: Update to National Infrastructure Protection Plan Includes Increased Emphasis on Risk Management and Resilience." March 2010. pg. 7.

8. Ibid. pg. 7.

9. Department of Homeland Security (2009) "National Infrastructure Protection Plan: Partnering to enhance protection and resiliency." pp. 3-4.

10. Ibid. pg. 33.

11. United States Government Accountability Office (2009) "The Department of Homeland Security's (DHS) Critical Infrastructure Protection cost-Benefit Report." June 26, 2009. pg. 2.

12. Department of Homeland Security (2009) "National Infrastructure Protection Plan: Partnering to enhance protection and resiliency." pg. 4.

13. Ibid. pg. 1.

14. Ibid. pg. 4.

15. Ibid. pg. 4.

16. United States Government Accountability Office (2010) "Critical Infrastructure Protection: Update to National Infrastructure Protection Plan Includes Increased Emphasis on Risk Management and Resilience." March 2010. pg. 4.

17. Ibid. Assessment.

18. Bush, George W. (2003) "The National Strategy to Secure Cyberspace". February 2003.

19. Department of Homeland Security (2003) "Press Release: Ridge Creates New Division to Combat Cyber Threats". June 6, 2003.

20. Bush, George W. (2002) "National Strategy for Homeland Security". July 2002.

Ch.17: Defending Against Catastrophic Threats

1. Busch, George W. (2002) "National Strategy for Homeland Security". July 2002. pg. 37.

2. Shea, Dana A. (2004) "Terrorism: Background on Chemical, Biological, and toxin Weapons and Options for Lessening Their Impact." Congressional Research Service Report for Congress. December 1, 2004. pgs. CRS-1.

3. Ibid. CRS-8.

4. Gottron & Shea (2010) "Federal Efforts to Address Bioterrorism: Selected Issues for Congress." Congressional Research Service Report for Congress. March 18, 2010. pp. 8-9.

5. Ibid. pg. 1.

6. Ibid. pp. 4-5.

7. Ibid. pp. 2-3.

8. United States Government Accountability Office (2009) "BIOSURVEILLANCE: Developing a Collaboration Strategy Is Essential to Fostering Interagency Data and Resource Sharing." December 2009. pp. 5.

9. Ibid. pp. 8-9.

10. Ibid. pp. 8-9.

11. DHS Office of Inspector General (2007) "DHS' Management of BioWatch Program." January 2007. pg. 2.

12. Ibid. pg. 4.

13. Brodsky, Benjamin (2007) "The Next Generation of Sensor Technology for the BioWatch Program." Monterey Institute for International Studies, James Martin Center for Nonproliferation Studies. September 2007.

14. DHS Office of Inspector General (2007) "Better Management Needed for the National Bio-Surveillance Integration System Program." July 2007. pp. 2-3.

15. United States Government Accountability Office (2009) "BIOSURVEILLANCE: Developing a Collaboration Strategy Is Essential to Fostering Interagency Data and Resource Sharing." December 2009. pp. 5-6.

16. Ibid. pp. 5-6.

17. www.dhs.gov (2010) "Weapons of Mass Destruction and Biodenfese Office", retrieved 13 Jun 10 from http://www.dhs.gov/xabout/structure/gc_1205180907841.shtm.

18. United States Government Accountability Office (2009) "BIOSURVEILLANCE: Developing a Collaboration Strategy Is Essential to Fostering Interagency Data and Resource Sharing." December 2009. pp. 5-6.

19. www.dhs.gov (2010) "Weapons of Mass Destruction and Biodenfese Office", retrieved 13 Jun 10 from http://www.dhs.gov/xabout/structure/gc_1205180907841.shtm.

20. www.dhs.gov (2010) "National Biodefense Analysis and Countermeasures Center." Retrieved 13 Jun 10 from http://www.dhs.gov/files/labs/gc_1166211221830.shtm.

21. Monke, Jim (2007) "Agroterrorism: Threats and Preparedness." Congressional Research Service Report for Congress. March 12, 2007. pg. Summary.

22. Ibid. pg. CRS-5.

23. Ibid. pg. CRS-6.

24. Ibid. March 12, 2007. pg. CRS-8.

25. Ibid. pg. CRS-9.

26. Ibid. pg. CRS-13 - CRS-14.

27. Ibid. pg. CRS-13 - CRS-19.

28. Ibid. pg. CRS-15 - CRS-16.

29. Ibid. pg. CRS-16.

30. Ibid. pg. CRS-26 - CRS-27.

31. Ibid. pg. CRS-26.

32. Gottron, Monke, Shea (2009) "The National Bio- and Agro-Defense Facility: Issues for Congress." Congressional Research Service Report for Congress. December 14, 2009. Pg. Summary.

33. Monke, Jim (2007) "Agroterrorism: Threats and Preparedness." Congressional Research Service Report for Congress. March 12, 2007. pg. CRS-21 - CRS-22.

34. Ibid. pg. CRS-23 - CRS-24.

35. Shea, Dana A. (2004) "Terrorism: Background on Chemical, Biological, and toxin Weapons and Options for Lessening Their Impact." Congressional Research Service Report for Congress. December 1, 2004. pg. CRS-2.

36. Ibid. pp. CRS-3 - CRS-4.

37. Ibid. pg. CRS-4.

38. Ibid. pg. CRS-5.

39. Ibid. pp. CRS-6 - CRS-7.

40. Ibid. pg. CRS-7 - CRS-8.

41. United States General Accounting Office (2003) "BIOTERRORISM: Preparedness Varied across State and Local Jurisdictions." April 2003. pg. 6.

42. Canada, Ben (2002) "State and Local Preparedness for Terrorism: Policy Issues and Options." Congressional Research Service Report for Congress. February 5, 2002. pg. CRS-1.

43. Ibid. Executive Summary.

44. FEMA (2010) "Fiscal Year (FY) 2010 Homeland Security Grant Program (HSGP) Frequently Asked Questions (FAQs)." Retrieved 13 Jun 10 from http://www.fema.gov/pdf/government/grant/2010/fy10_hsgp_faq.pdf.

45. www.dhs.gov (2010) "FY 2010 Homeland Security Grant Program (HSGP)." Retrieved 13 Jun 10 from http://www.fema.gov/government/grant/hsgp/index.shtm.

46. Shea, Dana A. (2009) "The Global Nuclear Detection Architecture: Issues for Congress." Congressional Research Service Report for Congress. March 25, 2009. pg. 1.

47. Ibid. pg. 2.

48. Ibid. Summary.

49. www.dhs.gov (2010) "Domestic Nuclear Detectino Office." Retrieved 11 Jun 10 from http://www.dhs.gov/xabout/structure/editorial_0766.shtm.

50. Shea, Dana A. (2009) "The Global Nuclear Detection Architecture: Issues for Congress." Congressional Research Service Report for Congress. March 25, 2009. pp. 1-2.

51. Ibid. pp. 2-3.

52. Ibid. pp. 6-7.

53. Commission on the Prevention of Weapons of Mass Destruction Proliferation and Terrorism (2010) "Prevention of WMD Proliferation and Terrorism Report Card: An Assessment of the U.S. Government's Progress in Protecting the United States from weapons of Mass Destruction Proliferation and Terrorism." January 2010. Opening Letter.

54. Ibid. pp. 1-5.

55. Bush, George W. (2002) "National Strategy for Homeland Security." July 2002. pg. ix.

Chapter 18: Emergency Preparedness & Response

1. Bush, George W. (2002) "National Strategy for Homeland Security." July, 2002. pp. 41-42.

2. Ibid. pg. 42.

3. Lindsay, Bruce R. (2008) "The National Response Framework: Overview and Possible Issues for Congress." November 20, 2008. pg. CRS-3.

4. Ibid. pg. CRS-3 - CRS-4.

5. Ibid. pp. CRS-1 - CRS-2.

6. Ibid. pg. CRS-4.

7. Department of Homeland Security (2008) "National Response Framework." January 2008. pg. 1.

8. Ibid. pg. 13.

9. Ibid. pg. 21.

10. Ibid. pg. 24.

11. Ibid. pp. 41-42.

12. Ibid. pg. 40.

13. Ibid. pp. 41-42.

14. Ibid. pg. 42.

15. Ibid. pg. 40.

16. Ibid. pg. 33.

17. Ibid. pg. 34.

18. Ibid. pg. 34.

19. Ibid. pg. 36.

20. Ibid. pg. 44.

21. Ibid. pg. 57.

22. Ibid. pg. 57.

23. Lindsay, Bruce R. (2008) "The National Response Framework: Overview and Possible Issues for Congress." November 20, 2008. pg. CRS-8.

24. Department of Homeland Security (2008) "National Response Framework." January 2008. pg. 4.

25. Ibid. pg. 48.

26. Ibid. pg. 49.

27. Ibid. pg. 50.

28. Ibid. pg. 51.

29. Ibid. pg. 52.

30. Ibid. pp. 61-62.

31. Ibid. pg. 63.

32. Ibid. pg. 67.

33. Ibid. pg. 68.

34. Ibid. pg. 69.

35. Kapp, Lieu, Peterman, & Petersen (2008) "Homeland Emergency Preparedness and the National Exercise Program: Background, Policy Implications, and Issues for Congress." Congressional Research Service Report for Congress. November 10, 2008. pg. CRS-6.

36. Ibid. pg. CRS-7.

37. Ibid. pg. CRS-9.

38. Ibid. pp. CRS-9 - CRS-10.

39. Ibid. CRS-10.

40. Ibid. pp. CRS-10 - CRS-11.

41. Ibid. CRS-11.

42. Ibid. pg. CRS-11.

43. Ibid. pp. CRS-11 - CRS-12.

44. Ibid. pg. CRS-12.

45. Ibid. pg. CRS-13.

46. Ibid. pp. CRS-13 - CRS-14.

47. Ibid. pp. CRS-34 - CRS-35.

48. Department of Homeland Security (2007) "National Preparedness Guidelines." September 2007. pg. iii.

49. Department of Homeland Security (2008) "National Response Framework." January 2008. pg. 9.

50. Ibid. pg. 3.

51. Ibid. pg. 29.

52. Ibid. pg. 49.

Chapter 19: U.S. Secret Service

1. United States Secret Service (2005). Protection. Retrieved June 24, 2005 from http://www.ustreas.gov/usss/protection.shtml

2. United States Secret Service (2005). Investigative Mission. Retrieved June 24, 2005 from http://www.ustreas.gov/usss/Investigations.shtml

3. United States Secret Service (2005). Counterfeit Division. Retrieved June 24, 2005 from http://www.ustreas.gov/usss/counterfeit.shtml

4. United States Secret Service (2005). Financial Crimes Division. Retrieved June 24, 2005 from http://www.ustreas.gov/usss/financial_crimes.shtml

5. United States Secret Service (2005). Forensic Services Division. Retrieved June 24, 2005 from http://www.ustreas.gov/usss/forensics.shtml

6. United States Secret Service (2005). Frequently Asked Questions. Retrieved June 24, 2005 from http://www.ustreas.gov/usss/faq.shtml

7. United States Secret Service (2010). Secret Service History: Today. Retrieved June 26, 2010 from http://www.secretservice.gov/history.shtml#TODAY

8. U.S. Secret Service (2010). National Threat Assessment Center. Retrieved June 26, 2010 from http://www.secretservice.gov/ntac.shtml

9. USSS Strategic Plan (2008)

Chapter 20: U.S. Coast Guard

1. O'Rourke, Ronald (2006) "Homeland Security: Coast Guard Operations - Background and Issues for Congress." Congressional Research Service Report for Congress. October 25, 2006. Summary.

2. U.S. Coast Guard (2009) "U.S. Coast Guard: America's Maritime Guardian." U.S. Coast Guard Publication 1. May 2009. pp. 3-15.

3. Ibid. pp. 18-23.

4. Ibid. pg. 15.

Chapter 21: Border Patrol

1. Department of Homeland Security (2005). Securing Our Borders. Retrieved April 20, 2005 from http://www.dhs.gov/dhspublic/display?theme=50&content=875&print=true.

2. Department of Homeland Security (2010). Who We Are and What We Do. Retrieved June 13, 2010 from http://www.cbp.gov/xp/cgov/border_security/border_patrol/who_we_are.xml.

3. Department of Homeland Security (2010). 85 Years of Protected By. Retrieved June 13, 2010 from http://www.cbp.gov/xp/cgov/border_security/border_patrol/85th_anniversary.xml.

4. Department of Homeland Security, Bureau of Customs and Border Protection, "National Border Patrol Strategy," September, 2004. Hereafter referred to as BP National Strategy.

5. BP National Strategy. P 6-7. September, 2004.

6. Department of Homeland Security (2010). Who We Are and What We Do. Retrieved June 13, 2010 from http://www.cbp.gov/xp/cgov/border_security/border_patrol/who_we_are.xml.

7. Nunez-Neto, B (2008). CRS RL32562. Border Security: The Role of the U.S. Border Patrol. November 20, 2008.

8. CBP.gov (2010). Border Patrol Sectors. Retrieved June 21, 2010 from http://www.cbp.gov/xp/cgov/border_security/border_patrol/border_patrol_sectors/.

9. U.S. Customs and Border Protection Fact Sheet (2010). Retrieved June 14, 2010 from http://www.customs.gov/linkhandler/cgov/newsroom/fact_sheets/border/border_patrol/bp_sog.ctt/bp_sog.pdf.

10. Nunez-Neto, B (2008). CRS RL32562. Border Security: The Role of the U.S. Border Patrol. November 20, 2008.

11. BP National Strategy. P 4. September, 2004.

12. CBP (2010). Secure Border Initiative (SBI). Retrieved 14 June 2010 from http://www.cbp.gov/xp/cgov/border_security/sbi/

13. CBP (2010). Secure Border Initiative (SBI). Retrieved 14 June 2010 from http://www.cbp.gov/xp/cgov/border_security/sbi/sbi_net/

14. CBP (2010). Tactical Infrastructure/Border Fence. Retrieved 14 June 2010 from http://www.cbp.gov/xp/cgov/border_security/ti/about_ti/ti_history.xml

15. USCBP (2009). SBI Northern Border Project Fact Sheet. December, 2009.

16. World Customs Organization (2005). Framework of Standards to Facilitate Global Trade. June, 2005.

17. CBP.gov (2010). Customs Mutual Assistance Agreements (CMAA) by Country. Retrieved June 21, 2010 from http://www.cbp.gov/xp/cgov/border_security/international_operations/international_agreements/cmaa.xml.

18. CBP.gov (2010). International Visitor Program (IVP). Retrieved June 21, 2010 from http://www.cbp.gov/xp/cgov/border_security/international_operations/international_agreements/ivp.xml.

19. U.S. Customs and Border Patrol (2010). C-TPAT Overview. Retrieved June 14, 2010 from http://www.cbp.gov/xp/cgov/trade/cargo_security/ctpat/what_ctpat/ctpat_overview.xml.

20. CBP.gov (2010). Security Filing 10+2. Retrieved June 14, 2010 from http://www.cbp.gov/xp/cgov/trade/cargo_security/carriers/security_filing/

21. Department of Homeland Security (2005). Immigration and Customs Enforcement (ICE) Fact Sheet. Retrieved April 20, 2005 from http://www.customs.gov/xp/cgov/PrintMe.xml?xml=$/content/enforcement/amo/newsroom.

22. Department of Homeland Security (2005). Immigration and Customs Enforcement (ICE) Fact Sheet. Retrieved April 20, 2005 from http://www.customs.gov/xp/cgov/PrintMe.xml?xml=$/content/enforcement/amo/newsroom.

23. Department of Homeland Security (2010). US VISIT. Retrieved June 21, 2010 from http://www.dhs.gov/files/programs/usv.shtm .

24. CBP.gov (2010). Border Patrol History. Retrieved June 21, 2010 from http://www.cbp.gov/xp/cgov/border_security/border_patrol/border_patrol_ohs/history.xml.

Ch. 22: Transportation Security Administration

1. TSA.gov (2010). What is TSA? Retrieved June 16, 2010 from http://www.tsa.gov/who_we_are/what_is_tsa.shtm.

2. TSA.gov (2010). Who We Are. Retrieved June 17, 2010 from http://www.tsa.gov/who_we_are/index.shtm

3. Transportation and Security Administration (2005). Aviation and Transportation Security Act (ATSA), Public Law 107-71. Retrieved April 21, 2005 from htgtp://www.tsa/gov/public/display?theme=38&content=0900051980003581&print=yes.

4. Department of Homeland Security Office of the Inspector General (2005). Review of the Transportation Security Administration's Role in the Use and Dissemination of Airline Passenger Data (Redacted). March, 2005.

5. Government Accountability Report (2008). GAO-08-456T: Transportation Security Administration Has Strengthened Planning to Guide Investments in Key Aviation Security Programs, but More Work Remains, February 2008, p. 18.

6. Ibid, p. 11

7. Department of Homeland Security Office of the Inspector General (2008). HS-OIG-08-66: TSA's Administration and Coordination of Mass Transit Security Programs, June 2008, p. 4.

8. Government Accountability Report (2008). GAO-08-933R: TSA's Explosives Detection Canine Program: Status of Increasing Number of Canine Teams, July 2008, p. 15

9. Department of Homeland Security (2009). Budget in Brief FY2009, p. 41-42.

10. United States Congress (2001). Public Law 107-71, Aviation and Transportation Security Act. November 19, 2001.

11. Department of Homeland Security (2009). Budget in Brief FY2009, p. 42

12. Ibid, p. 42

13. TSA.gov (2010). Layers of Security. Retrieved June 17, 2010 from http://www.tsa.gov/what_we_do/layers/index.shtm.

14. TSA.gov (2010). Secure Flight Program. Retrieved June 17, 2010 from http://www.tsa.gov/what_we_do/layers/secureflight/index.shtm

15. TSA.gov (2010). Myth vs Fact: TSA Flight School retrieved June 17, 2010 from http://www.tsa.gov/approach/mythbusters/flight_school.shtm

16. TSA.gov (2010). Layers of Security. Retrieved June 17, 2010 from http://www.tsa.gov/what_we_do/layers/index.shtm.

17. Government Accountability Report (2008). GAO 08-456T: Transportation Security Administration Has Strengthened Planning to Guide Investments in Key Aviation Security Programs, but More Work Remains, February 28, 2008.

18. Peterman, D. R. (2006) CRS IB10135: Transportation Security: Issues for the 109th Congress, June 23, 2006.

19. Rossides, G. D. (2009). Statement before the Subcommittee on Transportation Security and Infrastructure Protection Committee on Homeland Security, United States House of Representatives. June 10, 2009.

20. TSA.gov (2010). Black Diamond Self Select Lanes. Retrieved June 17, 2010 from http://www.tsa.gov/approach/black_diamond.shtm.

Chapter 23: Immigration & Customs

1. U.S. Office of Management and Budget (2008). Budget of the United States, FY2008. Retrieved June 26, 2010 from http://www.whitehouse.gov/omb/rewrite/budget/fy2008/homeland.html

2. Department of Homeland Security (2010). Department Responsibilities, Enforcing Our Immigration Laws. Retrieved June 26, 2010 from http://www.dhs.gov/xabout/gc_1240610592951.shtm

3. U.S. Immigration and Customs Enforcement (2007). ICE 2007 Annual Report: Protecting National Security and Upholding Public Safety. www.ice.gov.

4. Department of Homeland Security (2010). Moving to the United States. Retrieved June 26, 2010 from http://www.dhs.gov/files/programs/moving-to-the-usa.shtm

5. Wasem, Ruth E. (2010). CRS-RS22111: Alien Legalization and Adjustment of Status: A Primer. February 2, 2010.

6. Wikipedia (2010). U.S. Immigrations and Customs Enforcement. Retrieved June 25, 2010 from http://en.wikipedia.org/wiki/U.S._Immigration_and_Customs_Enforcement

7. U.S. Citizenship and Immigration Service (2010). What We Do. Retrieved June 26, 2010 from http://www.uscis.gov/portal/site/uscis/menuitem.eb1d4c2a3e5b9ac89243c6a7543f6d1a/?vgnexoid=fb89520b9f9a3210VgnVCM100000b92ca60aRCRD&vgnextchannel=fb89520b9f9a3210VgnVCM100000b92ca60aRCRD

8. Wasem, Ruth E. (2010). CRS R40501: Immigration Reform Issues in the 111th Congress. February 2, 2010.

9. Department of Homeland Security (2010). Budget in Brief, FY2011.

10. United States National Security Strategy (2010). May, 2010.

Chapter 24: FEMA

1. FEMA website (history)

2. CRS Report (2006). RL33369.

3. FEMA website (History)

4. CRS Report (2009). RL34146

5. FEMA disaster ops fact sheet

6. FEMA MGMT FACT SHEET

7. Garratt, D. & Russell, T. (2010). Ensuring Strong FEMA Regional Offices: An Examination of Resources and Responsibilities. Statement made before the House of Representatives Committee on Homeland Security and the Subcommittee on Emergency Communications, Preparedness and Response. March 16, 2010.

8. U.S. Department of Health and Human services (2010). National Disaster Medical System (NDMS). Retrieved June 22, 2010 from http://www.hhs.gov/aspr/opeo/ndms/index.html

9. FEMA.gov (2010). Urban Search and Rescue (US&R). Retrieved June 22, 2010 from http://www.fema.gov/emergency/usr/

10. FEMA.gov (2010). Mobile Operations Capability Guide for Emergency Managers and Planners. Retrieved June 22, 2010 from http://www.fema.gov/emergency/mers/index.shtm

11. FEMA (2004). Are You Ready? An In-depth Guide to Citizen Preparedness.

12. FEMA.gov (2010). Preparedness. Retrieved June 22, 2010 from http://www.fema.gov/prepared/

13. FEMA.gov (2010). Plan. Retrieved June 22, 2010 from http://www.fema.gov/prepared/plan.shtm

14. FEMA.gov (2010). Organize and Equip. Retrieved June 22, 2010 from http://www.fema.gov/prepared/org.shtm

15. FEMA.gov (2010). Training. Retrieved June 22, 2010 from http://www.fema.gov/prepared/org.shtm

16. Center for Domestic Preparedness (2010). CDP Fact Sheet. Retrieved June 21, 2010 from https://cdp.dhs.gov/

17. FEMA.gov (2010). Exercise. Retrieved June 22, 2010 from http://www.fema.gov/prepared/exercise.shtm

18. FEMA.gov (2010). Evaluate and Improve. Retrieved June 22, 2010 from http://www.fema.gov/prepared/eval.shtm

19. Department of Homeland Security (2010). Budget in Brief, FY2011.

Chapter 25: Science & Technology

1. Morgan & Shea (2009) "The DHS Directorate of Science and Technology: Key Issues for Congress." Congressional Research Service Report for Congress. June 22, 2009. pg. 1.
2. Ibid. pp. 1-3.
3. Ibid. pp. 3-4.
4. Ibid. pp. 48-52.
5. Ibid. pp. 5-12.
6. Ibid. pp. 13-15.
7. Ibid. pp. 17-18.
8. Ibid. pp. 19-21.
9. Ibid. pp. 25-26.
10. Ibid. pp. 36-40.
11. Ibid. pg. 1.

Chapter 26: Federal Partners

1. Department of Homeland Security (2010) "Quadrennial Homeland Security Review Report: A Strategic Framework of a Secure Homeland." February 2010. pg. iii.
2. Ibid. pg. 12.
3. Ibid. pg. 13.
4. Ibid. pg. A-1.
5. Ibid. pp. A-1 - A-8.
6. Ibid. pg. 78.

Chapter 27: Intelligence Community

1. Warner, Michael (2005). "Understanding Our Craft; Wanted: A Definition of Intelligence." Retrieved November 17, 2005 from file://C:\DOCUME~1 \CWP\LOCALS~1\Temp\CJLSLA7O.htm.
2. Government Printing Office (2005). "The Evolution of the U.S. Intelligence Community–An Historical Overview." Retrieved November 17, 2005 from http://www.access.gpo.gov/intelligence/int/ int022.html.
3. White House (2004). "President Signs Intelligence Reform and Terrorism Prevention Act." December 17, 2004. Retrieved November 17, 2005 from http:// www.whitehouse.gov/news/releases/2004/12/ print/20041217-1.html.
4. Intelligence.gov (2005). "United States Intelligence Community: Members of the Intelligence Community." Retrieved November 17, 2005 from http:// www.intelligence.gov/1-members.shtml.
5. Intelligence.gov (2005). "United States Intelligence Community: The Character of Intelligence." Retrieved November 21, 2005 from http:// www.intelligence.gov/2-character.shtml.
6. Intelligence.gov (2005). "United States Intelligence Community: Planning and Direction." Retrieved November 21, 2005 from http:// www.intelligence.gov/2-business_cycle1.shtml.
7. Intelligence.gov (2005). "United States Intelligence Community: Collection." Retrieved November 21, 2005 from http://www.intelligence.gov/2- business_cycle2.shtml.
8. Intelligence.gov (2005). "United States Intelligence Community: Processing and Exploitation." Retrieved November 21, 2005 from http:// www.intelligence.gov/2-business_cycle3.shtml.
9. Intelligence.gov (2005). "United States Intelligence Community: Analysis and Production." Retrieved November 21, 2005 from http:// www.intelligence.gov/2-business_cycle4.shtml.
10. Intelligence.gov (2005). "United States Intelligence Community: Dissemination." Retrieved November 21, 2005 from http://www.intelligence.gov/2- business_cycle5.shtml.
11. Intelligence.gov (2005). "United States Intelligence Community: Collection." Retrieved November 21, 2005 from http://www.intelligence.gov/2- business_cycle2.shtml.
12. Intelligence.gov (2005). "United States Intelligence Community: Counterintelligence." Retrieved November 21, 2005 from http://www.intelligence.gov/2- counterint.shtml.
13. Federal Bureau of Investigation (2005). "FBI History." Retrieved December 8, 2005 from file:// C:\DOCUME~1\CWP\LOCALS~1 \Temp\E95ZAESJ.htm.
14. Cumming, Alfred (2005). "Intelligence Reform Implementation at the Federal Bureau of Investigation: Issues and Options for Congress." Congressional Research Service Report for Congress, August 16, 2005.
15. Ibid.
16. Ibid.
17. Central Intelligence Agency (2005). "History of the CIA." Retrieved November 17, 2005 from http:// www.cia.gov/cia/publications/cia_today/ ciatoday_02.shtml.
18. Best, Richard A. (2005). "Intelligence Issues for Congress." Congressional Research Service Issue Brief for Congress, updated June 3, 2005.
19. Masse, Todd M. (2005). "The National Counterterrorism Center: Implementation Challenges and Issues for Congress." Congressional Research Service Report for Congress, updated March 24, 2005.

20. Best and Feickert (2005). "Special Operations forces (SOF) and CIA Paramilitary Operations: Issues for Congress." Congressional Research Service Report for Congress, January 4, 2005.
21. United States Joint Chiefs of Staff (2006). *Joint Publication 3-26, Homeland Security*. August 2, 2005. p. I-15.
22. Ibid., I-15 – I-16.
23. The White House (1981). "United States Intelligence Activities." Executive Order 12333, December 4, 1981.
24. Department of Defense (1988). "DoD Intelligence Activities." Department of Defense Directive 5240.1, April 25, 1988.
25. Department of Defense (1980). "Acquisition of Information Concerning Persons and Organizations Not Affiliated with the Department of Defense." Department of Defense Directive 5200.27, January 7, 1980.
26. Office of the Secretary of Defense (1998). "Policy Guidance for Intelligence Support to Force Protection." November 18, 1998.
27. Department of Defense (2005). "Under Secretary of Defense for Intelligence (USD(I))." Department of Defense Directive 5143.01, November 23, 2005.
28. United States Joint Chiefs of Staff (2006). *Joint Publication 3-26, Homeland Security*. August 2, 2005, p. B-2.
29. Ibid., B-3.
30. Ibid., B-4..

Chapter 28: State, Local, & Tribal Partners

1. DHS Office of Inspector General (2008) "DHS' Role in State and Local Fusion Centers is Evolving." December 2008. pg. 1.
2. Ibid. pp. 2-3.
3. Rollins, John (2008) "Fusion Centers: Issues and Options for Congress." Congressional Research Service Report for Congress. January 18, 2008. pg. CRS-7.
4. DHS Office of Inspector General (2008) "DHS' Role in State and Local Fusion Centers is Evolving." December 2008. pp. 4-5.
5. www.dhs.gov (2010) "State and Local Fusion Centers." Retrieved 19 Jun 10 from http://www.dhs.gov/files/programs/gc_1156877184684.shtm.
6. DHS Office of Inspector General (2008) "DHS' Role in State and Local Fusion Centers is Evolving." December 2008. pp. 5-6.
7. Ibid. pp. 6-8.
8. www.dhs.gov (2010) "State and Local Fusion Centers." Retrieved 19 Jun 10 from http://www.dhs.gov/files/programs/gc_1156877184684.shtm.
9. Department of Homeland Security (2008) "Department of Homeland Security Interaction with State and Local Fusion Centers: Concept of Operations." December 2008. pp. 9-11.
10. Rollins, John (2008) "Fusion Centers: Issues and Options for Congress." Congressional Research Service Report for Congress. January 18, 2008. pg. CRS-9.
11. Ibid. pp CRS-10 - CRS-15.
12. DHS Office of Inspector General (2008) "DHS' Role in State and Local Fusion Centers is Evolving." December 2008. pg. 8.
13. Ibid. pg. 9.
14. Ibid. pp. 12-13.
15. Ibid. pg. 13.
16. Rollins, John (2008) "Fusion Centers: Issues and Options for Congress." Congressional Research Service Report for Congress. January 18, 2008. Summary..

Chapter 29: First Responders

1. Department of Homeland Security (2005). About First Responders. Retrieved April 28, 2005 from http://www.dhs.gov/dhspublic/display?theme=63&content=237&print=true
2. Jenkins, W.O. (2006). GAO-06-467T: Emergency Preparedness and Response, Some Issues and Challenges with Major Emergency Incidents, February 23, 2006.
3. Department of Homeland Security (2008). National Incident Management System. December, 2008.
4. Department of Homeland Security Office for Domestic Preparedness (2004). Homeland Security Exercise and Evaluation Program, Volume 1: Overview and Doctrine. May, 2004.
5. Lindsey, Bruce R. (2008). CRS RL34585: The Emergency Management Assistance Compact (EMAC): An Overview. July 21, 2008.
6. FEMA.gov (2010). NIMS Resource Center: Preparedness. Retrieved June 25, 2010 from http://www.fema.gov/emergency/nims/Preparedness.shtm#item2
7. Citizencorps.gov (2010). Citizens Emergency Response Teams (CERT). Retrieved June 25, 2010 from http://www.citizencorps.gov/cert/
8. DHS.gov (2010). First Responders. Retrieved June 25, 2010 from http://www.dhs.gov/xfrstresp/.

Chapter 30: National Guard

1. National Governors Association (2009) "Policy Position HHS-03: Army and Air National Guard." Retrieved 27 Jun 10 from http://www.nga.org/portal/site/nga/menuitem.8358ec82f5b198d18a278110501010a0/?vgnextoid=24ca9e2f1b091010VgnVCM1000001a01010aRCRD.
2. National Guard Bureau (2006) "About the National Guard", retrieved December 11, 2006 from http://www.ngb.army.mil/About/default.aspx.
3. Department of Defense (2004) "Introduction to the Office of the Assistant Secretary of Defense for Reserve Affairs", September 9, 2004.
4. National Guard Bureau (2006) "About the National Guard", retrieved December 11, 2006 from http://www.ngb.army.mil/About/default.aspx.
5. Army National Guard (2006) "Organization" retrieved December 11, 2006 from http://www.arng.army.mil/organization.aspx.
6. Army National Guard (2006) "Command Structure", retrieved December 11, 2006 from http://www.arng.army.mil/org_command.aspx.
7. Doyle, Charles (2000) "The Posse Comitatus Act & Related Matters: The Use of the Military to Execute Civilian Law", Congressional Research Staff Report to Congress, June 1, 2000, pp CRS-39.
8. Ibid. pp CRS-42 – CRS-43.
9. Army National Guard (2006) "Command Structure", retrieved December 11, 2006 from http://www.arng.army.mil/org_command.aspx.
10. Army National Guard (2006) "Force Structure", retrieved December 11, 2006 from http://www.arng.army.mil/org_force.aspx.
11. Wikipedia.Org (2006) "U.S. Fifth Army", retrieved December 11, 2006 from http://en.wikipedia.org/wiki/US_Fifth_Army.
12. Air Force Link (2006) "U.S. Air Force Fact Sheet: Air National Guard", retrieved December 11, 2006 from http://www.af.mil/factsheets/factsheet_print.asp?fsID=160&page=1 10/19/2006.
13. Goldrich, Robert L. (2002) "Homeland Security and the Reserves: Threat, Mission, and Force Structure Issues", Congressional Research Service Report for Congress, September 10, 2002, retrieved December 11, 2006 from http://www.au.af.mil/au/awc/awcgate/crs/rl31564.pdf., pp CRS-1 – CRS-2.
14. Department of Defense (2004) "Introduction to the Office of the Assistant Secretary of Defense for Reserve Affairs", September 9, 2004.
15. Army Judge Advocate General Office (2006) "Uniformed Services Employment & Reemployment Rights Act of 1994 (USERRA)", retrieved October 19, 2006 from http://www.jagcnet.army.mil/JAGCNETInternet/Homepages/AC/Legal%20Assistance%.
16. National Governors Association (2009) "Policy Position HHS-03: Army and Air National Guard." Retrieved 27 Jun 10 from http://www.nga.org/portal/site/nga/menuitem.8358ec82f5b198d18a278110501010a0/?vgnextoid=24ca9e2f1b091010VgnVCM1000001a01010aRCRD.
17. Cuchalter, Alice R. (2007) "Military Support to Civil Authorities: The Role of the Department of Defense in Support of Homeland Defense." A Report Prepared by the Federal Research Division, Library of Congress, under an interagency Agreement with the commission on the National Guard and Reserves. February 2007. pg. 2.

Chapter 31: Looking Back

1. Government Accountability Office (2007) "Department of Homeland Security: Progress Report on Implementation of Mission and Management Functions." August 17, 2007. pg. 4.
2. Government Accountability Office (2007) "Department of Homeland Security: Progress Report on Implementation of Mission and Management Functions." September 18, 2007. pp. 6-7.
3. Ibid. pg. 8.
4. Ibid. pp. 8-10.
5. Ibid. pp. 12-20.
6. Ibid. Summary.

Chapter 32: Looking Ahead

1. Department of Homeland Security (2010) "Quadrennial Homeland Security Review Report: A Strategic Framework for a Secure Homeland." February 2010. pg. iii.
2. Ibid. pg. vii.
3. Ibid. pg. 3.
4. Ibid. pp. viii-xi.
5. Ibid. pp. 38-39.
6. Ibid. pp. 40-41.
7. Ibid. pp. 41-42.
8. Ibid. pp. 44-46.

9. Ibid. pp. 46-48.
10. Ibid. pp. 48-49.
11. Ibid. pp. 50-51.
12. Ibid. pp. 52-53.
13. Ibid. pp. 54-56.
14. Ibid. pp. 56-58.
15. Ibid. pp. 59-60.
16. Ibid. pp. 60-61.
17. Ibid. pp. 62-63.
18. Ibid. pp. 63-64.
19. Ibid. pg. 77.